# MACROECONOMICS

## FOURTH EDITION

## MICHAEL PARKIN

UNIVERSITY OF WESTERN ONTARIO

▲ ADDISON-WESLEY

AN IMPRINT OF ADDISON WESLEY LONGMAN, INC.

READING, MASSACHUSETTS • MENLO PARK, CALIFORNIA • NEW YORK • HARLOW, ENGLAND
DON MILLS, ONTARIO • SYDNEY • MEXICO CITY • MADRID • AMSTERDAM

Library of Congress Cataloging-in-Publication Data

Parkin, Michael, 1939–
    Macroeconomics/Michael Parkin.—4th ed.
        p.      cm.
    Includes bibliographical references and index.
    ISBN 0-201-31691-9 (softcover)
    1. Macroeconomics.       I.   Title.
    HB172.5.P36   1997
    339—dc21                              97–11786
                                              CIP

Printed in the United States of America.

1 2 3 4 5 6 7 8 9 – RNT – 0100999897

| | |
|---|---|
| Senior Editor: | Denise J. Clinton |
| Project Editor: | Lena Buonanno |
| Editorial Assistant: | Jennifer Vito |
| Senior Development Manager: | Sylvia Mallory |
| Supplements Editor: | Joan Twining |
| Development Assistant: | Rebecca Ferris |
| Managing Editor: | James Rigney |
| Senior Production Supervisor: | Nancy H. Fenton |
| Art and Design Director: | Karen Rappaport |
| Senior Design Supervisor: | Barbara T. Atkinson |
| Technical Illustrator: | Richard Parkin, RWP Graphics |
| Photo Researchers: | Billie Porter and Sandy Schneider |
| Prepress Buying Manager: | Sarah McCracken |
| Electronic Production Administrator: | Sally Simpson |
| Copyeditor: | Barbara Willette |
| Production Services: | Sarah Hallet Corey |
| Permissions Editor: | Mary Dyer |
| Indexer: | Alexandra Nickerson |
| Senior Manufacturing Manager: | Roy Logan |
| Manufacturing Supervisor: | Hugh Crawford |
| Executive Marketing Manager: | Beth Toland |
| Marketing Manager: | Quinn Perkson |
| Marketing Coordinator: | Lois Carter |
| Printer: | World Color |

# About **Michael Parkin**

**Michael Parkin received** his training as an economist at the Universities of Leicester and Essex in England. Currently in the Department of Economics at the University of Western Ontario, Canada, Professor Parkin has held faculty appointments at Brown University, the University of Manchester, the University of Essex, and Bond University. He has served on the editorial boards of the *American Economic Review* and the *Journal of Monetary Economics* and as managing editor of the *Canadian Journal of Economics*. Professor Parkin's research on macroeconomics, monetary economics, and international economics has resulted in over 160 publications in journals and edited volumes, including the *American Economic Review*, the *Journal of Political Economy*, the *Review of Economic Studies*, the *Journal of Monetary Economics*, and the *Journal of Money, Credit and Banking*. It became most visible to the public with his work on inflation that discredited the use of wage and price controls. Michael Parkin also spearheaded the movement toward European monetary union. Professor Parkin is an experienced and dedicated teacher of introductory economics.

# Preface

To change the way students see the world—this is my purpose in teaching economics and my goal in preparing the fourth edition of this text. There is no greater satisfaction for a teacher than to share the joy of students who have begun to understand the powerful lessons of the economic approach. But these lessons are hard to learn. Every day in my classroom, I relive the challenges of gaining the insights that we call the economist's way of thinking and recall my own early struggles with this discipline. In preparing this edition, I have been privileged to draw on the experiences not only of my own students but also of the many teachers and students who have used the previous editions.

The principles of economics course is constantly evolving, and the past few years have seen some major shifts of emphasis, especially in macroeconomics. Today's principles course springs from today's concerns about productivity growth, the information revolution, the emerging market economies of Central Europe and Asia, and the expansion of global trade and investment. Increasingly, we recognize the value of teaching long-run fundamentals as a basis for understanding these issues and as a springboard to understanding short-run economic fluctuations. With a tradition established in my third edition, this book allows you to place an early emphasis on long-run fundamentals and to teach the theory of long-run economic growth using nothing more than the tools of supply and demand.

# The Fourth Edition Approach

THIS BOOK HAS BEEN CRAFTED TO ACHIEVE five overriding goals:

- Focus on the core ideas.
- Explain the issues and problems of our time.
- Create a flexible teaching and learning tool.
- Make modern economics accessible.
- Make efficient use of new information technologies.

## Focus on Core Ideas

A flood of new concepts and a new way of thinking can overwhelm students. Our goal as teachers is to help students cut through to the core concepts that a student needs to think like an economist, both during and beyond the principles course. Consistent with this goal, I focus on a few central ideas: choice, tradeoff, opportunity cost, choosing at the margin, incentives, the gains from voluntary exchange, the power of markets, and the role of government. For the economy as a whole, the value of production equals total expenditure and total income. Living standards improve when production per person increases. Prices rise when the quantity of money increases faster than production. Unemployment can result from market failure but can be productive.

The core tool of demand and supply is thoroughly explained and repeatedly used throughout both the micro and macro chapters.

## Explain the Issues and Problems of Our Time

The core ideas and tools are used repeatedly to help students understand the issues that confront them in today's world. These issues include the environment, immigration, widening income gaps, the productivity growth slowdown, budget deficits, restraining inflation, watching for the next recession, avoiding protectionism, and the long-term growth of output and incomes.

## Create a Flexible Teaching and Learning Tool

We teachers of economics hold strong views about what to teach and how to teach, yet we do not all hold the *same* view. This diversity of opinion poses a special challenge to textbook authors, especially in macroeconomics. This book is carefully organized to be useful in a wide range of situations and to appeal to a diversity of teachers. The book's flexibility is demonstrated in the "Flexibility Chart" and "Alternative Sequences" table that appear on pp. XVI and XVII. This book can be used to teach all the traditional macro sequences, which place the main emphasis on short-term fluctuations in output, prices, and unemployment. It can support a course with a Keynesian emphasis or one with a monetarist emphasis. This book can also be used to teach a course that places an early emphasis on the long-term growth of output and incomes.

## Make Modern Economics Accessible

This book presents economics as a serious, lively, and evolving science that tries to explain the economic world around us. It presents new ideas, such as dynamic comparative advantage, game theory and its applications, the modern theory of the firm, information, public choice, new growth theory, and real business cycle theory. But it presents these new topics by using the familiar core ideas and tools.

In some areas, economics is relatively settled. In other areas, controversy persists. Where matters are settled, I present what is known; where controversy persists, I present the alternative viewpoints. This positive approach to economics is vital for students who will enter a world in which simple ideologies have become irrelevant and the economic landscape is changing at a rapid pace.

Always recalling my own early struggles with economics, I place the student at center stage and write for the student. I am conscious that many students find economics hard. Consequently, my goal has been to make the material as accessible as possible. I use language that makes for an easy read and that doesn't intimidate.

Each chapter opens with a clear statement of learning objectives, a real-world, student-friendly vignette that grabs attention, and a brief chapter preview. Once in the chapter, I do not reduce economics to a set of recipes to be memorized. Instead, I encourage the student to try to understand each concept. To accomplish this goal, I illustrate every principle with examples that have been selected both to hold the student's interest and to bring the subject to life. And to foster an enthusiasm and confidence in the student, when I present a new principle, I put it to work right away and use it to illuminate a current real-world problem or issue.

## Make Efficient Use of New Information Technologies

The supplements that accompany this text, and the text itself, make carefully thought-out and efficient use of the new information age technologies. We have worked hard to avoid the hype that often surrounds software and Web-based supplements and create true value for students and teachers. Our *Economics in Action* tutorial and quizzing software has been thoroughly redesigned and revised in the light of the lessons we've learned from its earlier versions. And new to this edition, we have created a World Wide Web site that provides features and content that is timely and constantly updated. The text has extensive links both to *Economics in Action* and the Internet.

## Key Revisions in the Fourth Edition

ECONOMICS, FOURTH EDITION, HAS BEEN CAREfully revised on the basis of extensive reviews to:

■ Place stronger emphasis on core economic principles
■ Reflect the most modern and recent economic developments
■ Shorten and make the material even more accessible, and
■ Strengthen the pedagogical features.

To achieve these goals, I have added a new chapter and topics, reorganized and streamlined existing chapters, and created three new pedagogical features.

### New Chapter

Chapter 1, "What is Economics?" uses a photo essay approach to lay out the key questions and big ideas of economics. The photos were carefully selected to motivate students and show them that economics is truly a part of their lives.

### New Coverage

Chapter 6, "Measuring GDP, Inflation, and Economic Growth," presents the chain-weighted measure of real output. Chapter 12, "Fiscal Policy," includes a new section on the supply-side effects of fiscal policy.

### New Organization

"Aggregate Supply and Aggregate Demand," now appears as Chapter 7 and is used as the overview model for both long-run and short-run macro issues. A flexible modular structure is maintained that allows the teacher to cover the *AS-AD* setup and then move to either Part IV, "Aggregate Supply and Economic Growth," or Part V, "Aggregate Demand and Inflation," depending on preferences.

### More Accessible

Chapter 9, "Capital, Investment, and Saving," has been extensively revised. Consumption coverage has been removed from this chapter, and the chapter focus has been placed on investment and saving. This chapter now covers long-run aspects of fiscal policy.

Chapter 11, "Expenditure Multipliers," includes a clearer and more accessible discussion of the multiplier. Chapter 12, "Fiscal Policy," includes a revised, simplified, presentation of fiscal policy multipliers.

Chapter 19, "The Balance of Payments and the Dollar," is extensively revised to make the theory of the exchange rate a more standard application of demand and supply.

### Streamlined

Using new technology to deliver information, I have removed Chapter 20, "Emerging Economies," and made it available in electronic form over the Internet. You can access this material at the Parkin Web site.

### Updated

The text, graphics, and examples have been updated to reflect the most current available data.

### Three New Pedagogical Features

The three new pedagogical features are:

■ Reading Between the Lines with Policy Watch
■ Web and Critical Thinking Exercises
■ Part Openers

**Policy Watch** I have added an element to many of the *Reading Between the Lines* features that asks the student to think about the policy issues raised by a news article and to participate in the public policy debate through "You're the Voter" questions. All the old Reading Between the Lines features have been replaced by new articles from *The Wall Street Journal, The Economist, The New York Times,* and from many regional newspapers.

**Web and Critical Thinking Exercises**    The pedagogy of the fourth edition has been carefully developed to encourage students to learn more about economics and to use technology as a means of researching and analyzing current events.

New to the fourth edition are end-of-chapter Internet-based exercises that ask students to access real-world data from Web sites such as those of the Bureau of Labor Statistics, the Federal Reserve Board, and the Penn World Table. An icon in the margin ⊕ identifies these questions.

Also new to this edition are a set of Critical Thinking exercises that further test and build students' analytical skills.

Selected end-of-chapter questions are linked to *Economics in Action* Version 3.0 and coverage will expand with subsequent releases of the software.

**Part Openers**    Economic Legends Past & Present is a new part opener that traces the evolution of economic thought and connects the ideas of economics with the events that shaped those ideas. This new feature unites the past and the present with interviews with key economists of today including Nobel Prize winner Robert E. Lucas, Jr., growth theorist Paul Romer, and First Deputy Managing Director of the International Monetary Fund, Stanley Fischer.

# Features that Enhance the Learning Process

THIS FOURTH EDITION, LIKE ITS PREDECESSORS, is packed with special features designed to enhance the learning process.

## The Art Program: Showing the Economic Action

Earlier editions of this book set new standards with their highly successful and innovative art programs. My goal has always been to show "where the economic action is." The figures and diagrams in this book continue to generate an enormously positive response, confirming my view that graphical analysis is the most important tool for teaching and learning economics. But it is a tool that gives many students much difficulty. Because many students find graphs hard to work with, the art has been designed to communicate economic principles unambiguously and clearly. The data-based art clearly reveals the data and trends. In addition, diagrams that illustrate economic processes consistently distinguish among key economic players (firms, households, governments, and markets).

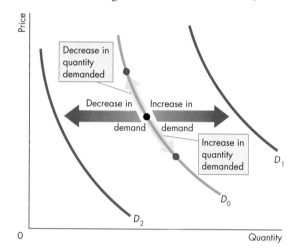

A consistent protocol in style, notation, and use of color, includes:

- Highlighting shifted curves, points of equilibrium, and the most important features in red
- Using arrows in conjunction with color to lend directional movement to what are usually static presentations
- Pairing graphs with data tables from which the curves have been plotted
- Using color consistently to underscore the content and referring to such use of color in the text and captions
- Labeling key pieces of information in graphs with boxed notes

The entire art program has been developed with the study and review needs of the student in mind. It has the following features:

- Marking the most important figures and tables with a red icon and listing them at the end of the chapter under the head "Key Figures and Tables"
- Using complete, informative captions that encapsulate major points in the graph so that students

can preview or review the chapter by skimming through the art

## Learning Aids: Pedagogy that Leads to Active Learning

The careful pedagogical plan has been refined to ensure that this book complements and reinforces classroom learning. Each chapter contains the following pedagogical elements:

**Objectives**   A list of learning objectives that enable students to see exactly where the chapter is going and to set their goals before they begin the chapter. The goals are linked directly to the chapter's major heads.

**Chapter Openers**   Intriguing puzzles, paradoxes, or metaphors frame questions that are unraveled and resolved as the chapter progresses.

**Highlighted In-Text Reviews**   Frequent, succinct summaries in list format are included for review.

**Key Terms**   Highlighted terms within the text form the first part of a three-tiered review of vocabulary. These terms are repeated with page references in the chapter summary and in the end-of-book glossary.

**Key Figures and Tables**   The most important figures and tables are identified with the ◆ and listed in the summary at the end of each chapter.

**End-of-Chapter Study Material**   Chapters close with a summary that includes lists of key terms, figures and tables (with page references); and questions, problems, and critical thinking exercises.

New to this edition, the end-of-chapter summaries are in a concise list form.

End-of-chapter problems have been revised to include many new problems and many that use diagrams. Problems identified by an icon 🖥 are linked to my *Economics in Action* software package or the Parkin Web site. New to this edition, each chapter has a set of *critical thinking* questions based on *Reading Between the Lines* and on current policy topics. In many problems and critical thinking questions, identified by an icon ⊕, I send the student to *Internet sites* such as the Bureau of Labor Statistics, the Department of Commerce, and the Fed and the Parkin Web site. My hope is to encourage the student to stay up to date and gain confidence using the Internet to access information.

## The Learning and Teaching Package

ADDISON-WESLEY'S EDITORS, THE SUPPLEMENTS authors, and I have worked closely together to ensure that our integrated text and supplements package provides students and teachers with a seamless learning and teaching experience.* The authors of the supplements are outstanding economists and teachers who have brought their own human capital (and that of their students) to the job of ensuring that the supplements are of the highest quality and value. The package contains three broad components:

■ Tools to enhance learning
■ Tools to enhance teaching
■ Tools for the electronic classroom

### Tools to Enhance Learning

**Study Guide**   Available in microeconomics and macroeconomics split versions, the fourth edition Study Guide was prepared by Mark Rush of the University of Florida. Carefully coordinated with the main text, and the Test Bank, each chapter of the Study Guide contains:

■ Key concepts
■ Helpful hints
■ True/false/uncertain questions that ask students to explain their answers
■ Multiple-choice questions
■ Short-answer questions
■ You're the Teacher, which lets the student explain common questions or misconceptions.
■ New to this edition, end-of-chapter quizzes and practice final exams

Several elements of the Study Guide are geared to building critical thinking skills: True/false/uncertain questions; multiple-choice answers that include explanations of why the answer is correct; *You're the Teacher* sections; and *Reading Between the Lines* exercises. Other elements are geared to make studying economics a bit easier. The key concepts are a study

*Some supplement items might not be available to adopters outside the United States.

aid. The helpful hints focus on ways to better understand the principles or to avoid common pitfalls.
The multiple-choice questions are plentiful and their
answers contain detailed explanations; the part
overview midterm examination allow the student to
simulate an exam.

The study guide includes an essay, "Should the
Study of Economics Be Part of Your Future?," written
by Robert Whaples of Wake Forest University. This
essay describes the value of studying economics for
both majors and non-majors. It includes information
on career options for those with an economics degree,
what the study of economics entails, what graduate
school is like, and references for further reading.

### Economics in Action Interactive Software

Students across the nation and around the world have
used the path-breaking *Economics in Action*, a widely
acclaimed computer learning tool, to increase their
success in the principles course.

With *Economics in Action* Release 3.0, which
accompanies the fourth edition, students will have
fun working the tutorials, answering questions that
give instant explanations, and testing themselves
ahead of their mid-term exams. One of my students
told me that using *EIA* is like having a private professor in your dorm room! The new release of the software has the following features:

- Step-by-step, graph-based tutorials
- A graph-making tool with data for the United
  States, Canada, twelve European countries, Japan,
  and Australia
- A quiz tool that generates drag-and-drop,
  true/false, multiple-choice, and numeric questions
- A self-testing tool that simulates tests and gathers
  results
- A problem-solving tool that allows students to
  solve homework problems from the text
- A figure gallery that builds text figures and cap-
  tions.

**The Parkin Web Site**   The Parkin Web site provides a rich array of learning tools that are carefully
integrated with the text and other components of the
package. A weekly electronic *Reading Between the
Lines* provides an effective way of motivating students
and keeping them up to date on economics in the
news. A periodic electronic *Point-Counterpoint* feature encourages students to participate in the con-
temporary policy debate. A weekly quiz that uses

completely new questions (not found in the study
guide, test banks, or *Economics in Action*) provides
students with frequent review and testing material.
On-line office hours enable students to consult me
directly with their learning problems. And carefully
selected links provide students with a guide to economic resources on the Internet.

The Parkin Web site will become a must-visit site
for all teachers and students of the principles of economics. Whether you are a teacher or a student, you
can reach all my Internet services at
http://hepg.awl.com/parkin/econ100.

### Tools to Enhance Teaching

**Test Bank**   Revised test items in **Volume I** were prepared by Robert Whaples of Wake Forest University
and Carol Dole of the University of North Carolina
to thoroughly reflect the content and terminology of
the fourth edition. The file includes 5,000 multiple-
choice questions, of which about one third are new to
this edition. Each chapter includes a section of questions that parallel questions in the study guide.

New to the fourth edition, **Volume II** Test Bank
contains 5,000 new questions comprising multiple-
choice, true/false, and short answers. These test items
were prepared by Carol Dole of the University of
North Carolina and James Giordano and Peter
Zaleski of Villanova University.

**Computerized Test Bank**   Testing software is
available for DOS, Windows, and Macintosh. It
includes all questions in the printed test banks. This
software gives instructors the ability to view graphs
on the screen, add questions, edit questions, scramble
question order and answer options, and more. An on-
line quiz component is also provided with the
Computerized Test Bank.

**Instructor's Manual**   A revised instructor's manual
has been prepared by Mark Rush of the University of
Florida. The instructor's manual is designed to integrate the teaching and learning package, serving as a
guide to all supplements. Each chapter includes a
chapter outline, changes in the fourth edition, teaching suggestions, the big picture (how the chapter
relates to what has come before and what comes
later), cross-references to the acetates, software units,
additional discussion questions, answers to the review
questions, and answers to the problems.

An introductory section written by Byron Brown of Michigan State University and Dennis Hoffman of Arizona State University presents technology ideas for professors who are just getting started with electronic teaching tools. This section talks about teaching in a multimedia classroom, how to use electronic tools in the lecture, and how to integrate *Economics in Action* into the course.

**Acetates and Overlays**   Key figures from the text are rendered in full color on the acetates. Several figures include overlays that make it easy to walk through the figure as you lecture. The acetates are enlarged and simplified to be more legible in large classrooms. They are available to qualified adopters of the textbook (contact your Addison-Wesley sales representative).

## Tools for the Electronic Classroom

**PowerPoint Electronic Lectures**   A complete lecture framework in Microsoft PowerPoint is available for Macintosh and Windows. Prepared by Jeffrey Caldwell of Rose State College, this presentation support system breaks chapters down into lecture-size bites and includes key figures from the text, animated graphs, and speaking notes.

**Economics in Action Software**   Instructors can use *Economics in Action* interactive software in the classroom. Its full-screen display option makes it possible to use its many analytical graphs as "electronic transparencies" and to do live graph manipulation and curve-shifting in lectures. Its figure gallery of animated slides from the text provides high quality graphics for the classroom. Its real-world data sets and graphing utility enable time-series graphs and scatter diagrams to be made and displayed in the classroom. Additionally, *Economics in Action* is a helpful review tool for instructors to use with their students or assign to their students to help reinforce economic principles before tests or exams.

**Parkin on the World Wide Web**   Instructors can use the Parkin Web site in a suitably equipped classroom. The weekly electronic *Reading Between the Lines* provides an effective way of motivating and organizing a lecture. And the electronic *Point-Counterpoint* feature provides a handy way of organizing a classroom debate. The weekly quiz can also be used for in-class review.

**The Parkin Internet Exchange**   This medium of on-line support includes mailing list discussion groups, access to information through ftp, and a World Wide Web home page. You can share teaching tips and ideas for using the book and supplements and discuss current economic events. To subscribe to the Parkin mailing list, send an e-mail to majordomo@aw.com and write Subscribe ParkinPr in the body of the message. An internet discussion group is also available for students. They can talk with other students about the course, the book, and economics. To subscribe to the Parkin student mailing list, send a e-mail to majordomo@aw.com and write Subscribe ParkinSt in the body of the message.

## Acknowledgments

WHILE THE EXTENT OF MY DEBTS CANNOT BE fully acknowledged, it is a joy to record my gratitude to the many people who have helped me to produce this book, some without realizing just how helpful they were.

I thank those of my current and former colleagues at the University of Western Ontario who have taught me a great deal that can be found in these pages: Jim Davies, Jeremy Greenwood, Ig Horstmann, Peter Howitt, Greg Huffman, David Laidler, Phil Reny, Chris Robinson, John Whalley, and Ron Wonnacott. I also thank Doug McTaggart of Bond University and Christopher Findlay of the University of Adelaide, co-authors of the Australian edition. Their suggestions arising from their adaptation of earlier editions have been extremely helpful in preparing this edition.

It is a special pleasure to acknowledge my debt and express my thanks to the several thousand students whom I have been privileged to teach. The instant response that comes from the look of puzzlement or enlightenment has taught me, more than anything else, how to teach economics.

My sponsoring editor, Denise Clinton, has been a constant source of inspiration and encouragement. I want to place on record her crucial role in developing our new approach to macroeconomics. I could not have undertaken the transformation of macro without her clear-headed vision and tough empirical approach. I am enormously impressed by and grateful to her.

It has been a pleasure to work day by day with Lena Buonanno, my development editor. Lena even went so far as to enrol in a principles of economics course (using a competing text!) in order to be well prepared for her task. She organized conference calls focus groups, and reviewers. She also took care of the interviews and helped the interviewees and me to make our conversations accessible to our student readers. Lena has brought a personal and professional commitment to this project that is rare and impressive. I am deeply grateful to her.

Joan Twining, Supplements Editor, has planned, organized, and managed the task of creating a large and high-quality supplements package. All of the supplements authors and I thank Joan for her extroadinary editorial and personal skills and for the energy and commitment she has given us.

Our Senior Development Manager, Sylvia Mallory, has been a steady source of support and it is she who proposed that we revise Chapter 1 as a photo essay. I am excited about the way this suggestion evolved, and I thank Sylvia for her inspiring idea. I thank Marjorie Singer Anderson for her development support on the macro chapters. Billie Porter and Sandy Schneider did the photo research. Nancy Fenton has been my levelheaded, no-nonsense, I-can do-anything, senior production editor for two editions and I renew my thanks to her for directing the design and production effort. Barbara Willette has again been copyeditor and I thank her for continuing to coax yet better English from my keyboard. I also thank Ed Moura, Vice President and General Manager of Addison-Wesley's Higher Education Publishing Group, for his support of this project and for ensuring that it is directed by the most talented editors in the business.

I thank the supplements authors: Mark Rush, Jeffrey Caldwell, Carol Dole, Robert Whaples, James Giordano, Peter Zaleski, Byron Brown, and Dennis Hoffman. Mark has played a crucial role in the creation of this edition and has been a constant source of good advice and good humor. Robert Whaples is another extraordinary helper who went well beyond the call of duty or the scope of the checkbook in his manuscript, accuracy, and study guide reviews; his participation in conference call; and his writing of an essay for the study guide. I am deeply grateful to him. I also thank Carol Dole and Robert Whaples for their accuracy reviews of page proof. Byron Brown and Dennis Hoffman have written excellent essays for the instructor's manual. Others who helped shape my

ideas for the new macro sequence are Robert Gillette, Dennis Hoffman, Manfred Keil, Robert Rossana, Scott Simkins, and Larry Wimmer.

I thank my research assistants. Jeannie Gillmore helped me to find good news articles and wrote useful outlines and first drafts of each *Reading Between the Lines* feature. She also provided other general research assistance, along with Christine Bies, Jane McAndrew, and Tom Adam.

I thank Richard Parkin, who created the electronic art manuscript and final art files and has contributed many ideas that have improved the figures in this book.

As with the previous editions, this one owes an enormous debt to Robin Bade. I dedicate this book to her and again thank her for her work. She has read every word that I have written, commented in detail on every draft, created many of the end-of-chapter review questions and problems, inspired me when I have been flagging, and managed the entire project from its initial conception through its three editions and through seven editions published in other countries. I could not have written this book without the unselfish help she has given me. My thanks to her are unbounded.

The empirical test of this book's value continues to be made in the classroom. I would appreciate hearing from instructors and students about how I can continue to improve it in future editions.

Michael Parkin
Department of Economics
University of Western Ontario
London, Ontario, N6A 5C2
Parkin@sscl.uwo.ca

# Reviewers

Tajudeen Adenekan, Bronx Community College
Milton Alderfer, Miami-Dade Community College
William Aldridge, Shelton State Community College
Stuart Allen, University of North Carolina—
    Greensboro
Sam Allgood, University of Nebraska—Lincoln
Neil Alper, Northeastern University
Alan Anderson, Fordham University
Jeff Ankrom, Wittenberg University

Fatma Antar, Manchester Community Technical College

Kofi Apraku, University of North Carolina—Asheville

Moshen Bahmani-Oskooee, University of Wisconsin—Milwaukee

Donald Balch, University of South Carolina

Mehmet Balcilar, Wayne State University

A. Paul Ballantyne, University of Colorado

Sue Bartlett, University of South Florida

Valerie R. Bencivenga, University of Texas—Austin

Ben Bernanke, Princeton University

Margot Biery, Tarrant County Community College South

John Bittorowitz, Ball State University

Sunne Brandmeyer, University of South Florida

Baird Brock, Central Missouri State University

Byron Brown, Michigan State University

Jeffrey Buser, Columbus State Community College

Alison Butler, Florida International University

Tania Carbiener, Southern Methodist University

Kevin Carey, University of Miami

Kathleen A. Carroll, University of Maryland—Baltimore County

Michael Carter, University of Massachusetts—Lowell

Adhip Chaudhuri, Georgetown University

Gopal Chengalath, Texas Tech University

Daniel Christiansen, Albion College

John J. Clark, Community College of Allegheny County—Allegheny Campus

Meredith Clement, Dartmouth College

Michael B. Cohn, U.S. Merchant Marine Academy

Robert Collinge, University of Texas—San Antonio

Doug Conway, Mesa Community College

Larry Cook, University of Toledo

Bobby Corcoran, Middle Tennesee State University

Kevin Cotter, Wayne State University

James Peery Cover, University of Alabama—Tuscaloosa

Eleanor D. Craig, University of Delaware

Jim Craven, Clark College

Stephen Cullenberg, University of California—Riverside

David Culp, Slippery Rock University

Norman V. Cure, Macomb Community College

Dan Dabney, University of Texas—Austin

Andrew Dane, Angelo State University

Joseph Daniels, Marquette University

David Denslow, University of Florida

Mark Dickie, University of Georgia

James Dietz, California State University—Fullerton

Carol Dole, University of North Carolina—Charlotte

Ronald Dorf, Inver Hills Community College

John Dorsey, University of Maryland—College Park

Amrik Singh Dua, Mt. San Antonio College

Thomas Duchesneau, University of Maine—Orono

Lucia Dunn, Ohio State University

Donald Dutkowsky, Syracuse University

John Edgren, Eastern Michigan University

David J. Eger, Alpena Community College

Ibrahim Elsaify, State University of New York—Albany

Kenneth G. Elzinga, University of Virginia

M. Fazeli, Hofstra University

Philip Fincher, Louisiana Tech University

F. Firoozi, University of Texas—San Antonio

David Franck, University of North Carolina—Charlotte

Alwyn Fraser, Atlantic Union College

Eugene Gentzel, Pensacola Junior College

Andrew Gill, California State University—Fullerton

Robert Giller, Virginia Polytechnic Institute and Sate University

Robert Gillette, University of Kentucky

James N. Giordano, Villanova University

Maria Giuili, Diablo College

Richard Gosselin, Houston Community College

John Graham, Rutgers University

John Griffen, Worcester Polytechnic Institute

Robert Guell, Indiana State University

Jamie Haag, University of Oregon

Daniel Hagen, Western Washington University

David R. Hakes, University of Northern Iowa

Craig Hakkio, Federal Reserve Bank, Kansas City

Ann Hansen, Westminster College

Jonathan Haughton, Northeastern University

Randall Haydon, Wichita State University

Jolien A. Helsel, Kent State University

John Herrmann, Rutgers University

John M. Hill, Delgado Community College

Lewis Hill, Texas Tech University

Tom Hoerger, Vanderbilt University

Calvin Hoerneman, Delta College

Dennis L. Hoffman, Arizona Sate University

Paul Hohenberg, Rensselaer Polytechnic Institute

Jim H. Holcomb, University of Texas—El Paso

Harry Holzer, Michigan State University

Djehane Hosni, University of Central Florida

Harold Hotelling, Jr., Lawrence Technical University

Calvin Hoy, County College of Morris

Julie Hunsaker, Wayne State University

Beth Ingram, University of Iowa
Michael Jacobs, Lehman College
Dennis Jansen, Texas A & M University
Frederick Jungman, Northwestern Oklahoma Sate University
Paul Junk, University of Minnesota—Duluth
Leo Kahane, California State University—Hayward
E. Kang, St. Cloud State University
Arthur Kartman, San Diego State University
Manfred W. Keil, Claremont McKenna College
Rose Kilburn, Modesto Junior College
Robert Kirk, Indiana University—Purdue University—Indianapolis
Norman Kleinberg, City University of New York, Baruch College
Robert Kleinhenz, California Sate University—Fullerton
Joseph Kreitzer, University of St. Thomas
David Lages, Southwest Missouri State University
Leonard Lardaro, University of Rhode Island
Kathryn Larson, Elon College
Luther D. Lawson, University of North Carolina—Wilmington
Elroy M. Leach, Chicago State University
Jay Levin, Wayne State University
Tony Lima California State University—Hayward
William Lord, University of Maryland—Baltimore County
K.T. Magnusson, Salt Lake City Community College
Mark Maier, Glendale Community College
Beth Maloan, University of Tennessee—Martin
Jean Mangan, California State University—Sacramento
Michael Marlow, California Polytechnic State University
Akbar Marvasti, University of Houston
Wolfgang Mayer, University of Cincinnati
John McArthur, Wofford College
Amy McCormick, College of William and Mary
Gerald McDougall, Wichita State University
Russel McCullough, Iowa State University
Stephen McGary, Ricks College
Richard D. McGrath, College of William and Mary
Richard McIntyre, University of Rhode Island
John McLeod, Georgia Institute of Technology
Charles Meyer, Iowa Sate University
Peter Mieszkowski, Rice University
John Mijares, University of North Carolina—Asheville
Judith W. Mills, Southern Connecticut State University

Glen Mitchell, Nassau Community College
Jeannette C. Mitchell, Rochester Institute of Technology
Khan Mohabbat, Northern Illinois University
W. Douglas Morgan, University of California—Santa Barbara
William Morgan, University of Wyoming
Joanne Moss, San Francisco State University
Edward Murphy, Southwest Texas State University
Kathryn Nantz, Fairfield University
William S. Neilson, Texas A & M University
Bart C. Nemmers, University of Nebraska—Lincoln
Anthony O'Brien, Lehigh University
Mary Olson, Washington University
Jim B. O'Niell, University of Delaware
Farley Ordovensky, University of the Pacific
Z. Edward O'Relley, North Dakota State University
Jan Palmer, Ohio University
Michael Palumbo, University of Houston
G. Hossein Parandvash, Western Oregon State College
Randall Parker, East Carolina University
Robert Parks, Washington University
David Pate, St. John Fisher College
Donald Pearson, Eastern Michigan University
Mary Anne Pettit, Southern Illinois University—Edwardsville
Kathy Phares, University of Missouri—St. Louis
William A. Phillips, University of Southern Maine
Dennis Placone, Clemson University
Charles Plot, California Institute of Technology—Pasadena
Mannie Poen, Houston Community College
Kathleen Possai, Wayne State University
Ulrika Praski-Stahlgren, University College in Gavle-Sandviken, Sweden
K.A. Quartey, Talladega College
Herman Quirmbach, Iowa State University
Peter Rangazas, Indiana University—Purdue
Vaman Rao, Western Illinois University
Laura Razzolini, University of Mississippi
J. David Reed, Bowling Green State University
Robert H. Renshaw, Northern Illinois University
W. Gregory Rhodus, Bentley College
John Robertson, Paducah Community College
Malcolm Robinson, University of North Carolina—Greensboro
Richard Roehl, University of Michigan—Dearborn
Thomas Romans, State University of New York—Buffalo

David R. Ross, Bryn Mawr College
Thomas Ross, St. Louis University
Robert J. Rossana, Wayne State University
Rochelle Ruffer, Ithaca College
Mark Rush, University of Florida
Gary Santoni, Ball State University
John Saussy, Harrisburg Area Community College
David Schlow, Pennsylvania State University
Paul Schmitt, St. Clair County Community College
Martin Sefton, Indianapolis University
Rod Shadbegian, University of Massachusetts—
 Dartmouth
Gerald Shilling, Eastfield College
Dorothy R. Siden, Salem State College
Scott Simkins, North Carolina Agricultural and
 Technical State University
Chuck Skoro, Boise State University
Phil Smith, DeKalb College
William Doyle Smith, University of Texas—El Paso
Frank Steindl, Oklahoma Sate University
Jeffrey Stewart, New York University
Allan Stone, Southwest Missouri State University

Courtenay Stone, Ball State University
Mark Strazicich, Ohio State University—Newark
Robert Stuart, Rutgers University
Gilbert Suzawa, University of Rhode Island
David Swaine, Andrews University
Kay Unger, University of Montana
Anthony Uremovic, Joliet Junior College
David Vaughn, City University, Washington
Francis Wambalaba, Portland State University
Rob Wassmer, Wayne State University
Paul A. Weinstein, University of Maryland—
 College Park
Lee Weissert, St. Vincent College
Robert Whaples, Wake Forest University
Larry Wimmer, Brigham Young University
Mark Witte, Northwestern University
Willard E. Witte, Indiana University
Cheonsik Woo, Clemson University
Douglas Wooley, Radford University
Ann Al Yasiri, University of Wisconsin—Platteville
John T. Young, Riverside Community College
Michael Youngblood, Rock Valley College

# Macroeconomics Flexibility

| **Core** | **Policy** | **Optional** |
|---|---|---|
| **1.** What is Economics? | | **2.** Making and Using Graphs |
| **3.** The Economic Problem | | Good chapter for student's with fear of graphs. |
| **4.** Demand and Supply | | |
| **5.** A First Look at Macroeconomics | | |
| **6.** Measuring GDP, Inflation and Economic Growth | | |
| Chapter 8, Employment, Wages, and Unemployment may be studied immediately following Chapter 6. | | |
| **7.** Aggregate Supply and Aggregate Demand | | |
| Chapter 7 may de delayed and studied after Chapter11 | | |
| **8.** Employment, Wages, and Unemployment | If you wish to emphasize short-term fluctuations, you may delay coverage of this block of chapters on aggregate supply and long-term growth. | |
| **9.** Investment, Capital, and Interest | | |
| Includes a section on long-run aspects on fiscal policy | | |
| **10.** Economic Growth | | |
| The section on growth theory is optional | | |
| **11.** Expenditure Multipliers | **12.** Fiscal Policy | If you wish to emphasize short-term fluctuations, you may cover this block of chapters before those on aggregate supply and long-term growth. |
| **13.** Money | **14.** Monetary Policy | |
| **15.** Inflation | | **16.** The Business Cycle |
| | **17.** Macroeconomic Policy Challenge | |
| | | **18.** Trading with the World |
| | | **19.** The Balance of Payments and the Dollar |

# Four Alternative Sequences for a Macro Principles Course

| Early Long-Term Growth | Late Long-Term Growth | Keynesian Perspective | Monetarist Perspective |
|---|---|---|---|
| 5 A First Look at Macroeconomics | 5 A First Look at Macroeconomics | 5 A First Look at Macroeconomics | 5 A First Look at Macroeconomics |
| 6 Measuring GDP, Inflation, and Economic Growth | 6 Measuring GDP, Inflation, and Economic Growth | 6 Measuring GDP, Inflation, and Economic Growth | 6 Measuring GDP, Inflation, and Economic Growth |
| 8 Employment and Unemployment | 8 Employment and Unemployment | 8 Employment and Unemployment | 8 Employment and Unemployment |
| 9 Capital, Investment, and Saving | 7 Aggregate Supply and Aggregate Demand | 11 Expenditure Multipliers | 7 Aggregate Supply and Aggregate Demand |
| 10 Economic Growth | 11 Expenditure Multipliers | 7 Aggregate Supply and Aggregate Demand | 13 Money |
| 7 Aggregate Supply and Aggregate Demand | 12 Fiscal Policy | 12 Fiscal Policy | 14 Monetary Policy |
| 11 Expenditure Multipliers | 13 Money | 13 Money | 15 Inflation |
| 12 Fiscal Policy | 14 Monetary Policy | 14 Monetary Policy | 11 Expenditure Multipliers |
| 13 Money | 15 Inflation | 15 Inflation | 12 Fiscal Policy |
| 14 Monetary Policy | 9 Capital, Investment, and Saving | 9 Capital, Investment, and Saving | 9 Capital, Investment, and Saving |
| 15 Inflation | 10 Economic Growth | 10 Economic Growth | 10 Economic Growth |
| 16 The Business Cycle | 16 The Business Cycle | 16 The Business Cycle | 16 The Business Cycle |
| 17 Macroeconomic Policy Challenges | 17 Macroeconomic Policy Challenges | 17 Macroeconomic Policy Challenges | 17 Macroeconomic Policy Challenges |
| 19 The Balance of Payments and the Dollar (optional) | 19 The Balance of Payments and the Dollar (optional) | 19 The Balance of Payments and the Dollar (optional) | 19 The Balance of Payments and the Dollar (optional) |

## Credits

(continuation from p. II)

**Part 1:** Adam Smith (p. 2), Corbis-Bettmann. Pin factory (p. 3), Culver Pictures. Woman holding silicon wafer (p. 3), Tony Stone Images. Mancur Olson, Jr. (pp. 4, 6), Michael Kress.

**Chapter 1:** P. 8 top: Kindra Clineff/The Picture Cube; p. 8 bottom: David Frazier Photolibrary; p. 9: Owen Franken/Tony Stone Images; p. 9 inset: George Rose/Gamma Liaison; p. 10 top left: Larry Prosor/SuperStock; p. 10 top right: Charles Gupton/The Stock Market; p. 10 bottom left: Chip Henderson/Tony Stone Images; p. 10 bottom right: Paul Conklin/PhotoEdit; p. 11 top: Bruce Ayres/Tony Stone Images; p. 11 bottom right: David Joel/Tony Stone Images; p. 12 top: Roger Allyn Lee/Tony Stone Images; p. 12 bottom: David Young-Wolff/PhotoEdit; p. 13: Ed Bock/The Stock Market; p. 14 top: David Young-Wolff/PhotoEdit; p. 14 bottom: David Young-Wolff/PhotoEdit; p. 15 top: Cameramann International, Ltd.; p. 15 bottom: Christian Bossu-Pica/Tony Stone Images; p. 16 top left: Karl Cummels/SuperStock; p. 16 top right: Ron McMillan/Gamma-Liaison; p. 16 bottom left: James D'Addio/The Stock Market; p. 16 bottom right: David Young-Wolff/PhotoEdit; p. 17 top left: Tony Freeman/PhotoEdit; p. 17 right: Rob Crandal/The Image Works; p. 17 bottom left: Steven Wernberg/Tony Stone Images; p. 18 left: Scott Foresman - Addison Wesley Longman; p. 18 center: David Young-Wolff/PhotoEdit; p. 18 right: Focus on Sports; p. 19 top left: Terry Vine/Tony Stone Images; p. 19 bottom left: Reinstein/The Image Works; p. 19 right: Benjamin Rondel/The Stock Market; p. 20: Alan Thornton/Tony Stone Images; p. 21 top right: Chuck Savage/The Stock Market; p. 21 bottom left: David R. Frazier Photolibrary; p. 21 bottom right: Ariel Skelley/The Stock Market; p. 22: Dennis Black/Black Star; p. 24: Jeff Greenberg/PhotoEdit.

**Part 2:** Alfred Marshall (p. 62), Stock Montage. Scene along the railroad route (p. 63), Corbis-Bettmann. Newark Airport (p. 63), Steve Proehl/The Image Bank. Paul R. Milgrom (pp. 64, 66), Jenny Thomas. The data (p. 87) are from the World Wide Web site of the FAO (Food and Agricultural Organization of the United Nations) in Rome.

**Part 3:** John Maynard Keynes (p. 92), Stock Montage. Worker destroying spinning jenny in England (p. 93), The Bettmann Archive. AT&T network Center (p. 93), Hank Morgan. Robert E. Lucas (pp. 94, 96), Loren Santow.

**Part 4:** Joseph Schumpeter (p. 164), Corbis-Bettmann. McCormick's first reaping machine, ca. 1834 (p. 165), The Granger Collection. Fiber optics (p. 165), © The Stock Market/Jon Feingersh. Paul Romer (p. 166), © Christopher Irion.

**Part 5:** Milton Friedman (p. 236), Marshall Henrichs/Addison-Wesley. German housewife burning Reichmarks in 1923 (p. 237), UPI/Corbis-Bettmann. Brazilians stocking up on foor before price increase (p. 237), © Carlos Humberto TDC/Contact Press Images. Bennett T. McCallum (p. 238), David Smith.

**Part 6:** Irving Fisher (p. 362), Yale University Archives, Manuscripts and Archives, Yale Library. Depositors outside door of closed bank (p. 363), Corbis-Bettmann. Boarded-up shop (p. 363), © Susan van Etten. Frederic S. Mishkin (pp. 364, 366), Peter Murphy.

**Part 7:** David Ricardo (p. 420), Corbis-Bettmann. Poster advertising ships sailing for California (p. 421), Corbis-Bettmann. Container ship (p. 421), M. Fife/SuperStock. Stanley Fischer (p. 422), John Skowronski.

# Brief Contents

# part 1 Introduction

## Chapter 1

### What Is Economics?   7

Summary (Key Points, Key Figures and Tables, and Key Terms), Questions, Problems, and Critical Thinking Exercises appear at the end of each chapter.

# Contents

# part 2 How Markets Work

# part 3 Macroeconomic Overview

# part 4 Aggregate Supply and Economic Growth

**part 5** Aggregate Demand and Inflation

# Your Economics Course

You are living at a time that future historians will call the *Information Revolution*. We reserve the word "Revolution" for big events that influence all future generations. ◆ During the *Agricultural Revolution*, which occurred 10,000 years ago, people learned to domesticate animals and plant crops. They stopped roaming in search of food and settled in villages and eventually towns and cities, where they developed markets in which to exchange their products. ◆ During the *Industrial Revolution*, which began 240 years ago, people used science to create new technologies. This revolution brought extraordinary wealth for most, but created conditions in which some were left behind. It brought social and political tensions that we still face today. ◆ During today's *Information Revolution*, people who have the ability and opportunity to embrace the new technologies are prospering on an unimagined scale. But the incomes and living standards of the less educated are falling behind, and social and political tensions are increasing. Today's revolution has a global dimension. Some of the winners live in previously poor countries in Asia, and some of the losers live in the United States. ◆ So you are studying economics at an interesting time. Whatever *your* motivation is for studying economics, *my* objective is to help you do well in your course, to enjoy it, and to develop a deeper understanding of the economic world around you. ◆ There are three reasons why I hope that we both succeed. First, a decent understanding of economics will help you become a full participant in the Information Revolution. Second, an understanding of economics will help you play a more effective role as a citizen and voter and enable you to add your voice to those who are looking for solutions to our social and political problems. Third, you will enjoy the sheer fun of *understanding* the forces at play and how they are shaping our world. ◆ If you do find economics interesting, think seriously about majoring in the subject. A degree in economics gives the best training available in problem solving, offers lots of opportunities to develop conceptual skills, and opens doors to a wide range of graduate courses, including the MBA, and to a wide range of jobs. You can read more about the benefits of an economics degree in Robert Whaples's essay in your *Study Guide*. ◆ Economics was born during the Industrial Revolution. We'll look at its birth and meet its founder, Adam Smith. Then we'll talk with one of today's creative economic thinkers, Professor Mancur Olson of the University of Maryland. ◆ In the next three chapters, we'll begin to study the science that Adam Smith began. You will encounter the questions, methods, and ideas of economics in Chapter 1. And in Chapter 3, you will learn about Adam Smith's key insight: specialization and exchange bring economic wealth. In optional Chapter 2, you have an opportunity to learn about the graph tools that we use in economics. But first, let's meet Adam Smith.

# Understanding the Sources of Economic Wealth

## The Father of Economics: Adam Smith

Adam Smith was a giant of a scholar who contributed to ethics and jurisprudence as well as economics. Born in 1723 in Kirkcaldy, a small fishing town near Edinburgh, Scotland, Smith was the only child of the town's customs officer (who died before Adam was born).

His first academic appointment, at age 28, was as Professor of Logic at the University of Glasgow. He subsequently became tutor to a wealthy Scottish duke, whom he accompanied on a two-year grand European tour, following which he received a pension of £300 a year—ten times the average income at that time.

With the financial security of his pension, Smith devoted ten years to writing *An Inquiry into the Nature and Causes of the Wealth of Nations*, which was published in 1776. Many people had written on economic issues before Adam Smith, but he made economics a science. Smith's account was so broad and authoritative that no subsequent writer on economics could advance ideas without tracing their connections to those of Adam Smith.

> *"It is not from the benevolence of the butcher, the brewer, or the baker that we expect our dinner, but from their regard to their own interest."*
>
> ADAM SMITH
>
> THE WEALTH OF NATIONS

## The Issues and Ideas

Why are some nations wealthy while others are poor? This question lies at the heart of economics. And it leads directly to a second question: What can poor nations do to become wealthy?

Adam Smith, who is regarded by many scholars as the founder of economics, attempted to answer these questions in his book *The Wealth of Nations*, published in 1776. Smith was pondering these questions at the height of the Industrial Revolution. During these years, new technologies were invented and applied to the manufacture of cotton and wool cloth, iron, transportation, and agriculture.

Smith wanted to understand the sources of economic wealth, and he brought his acute powers of observation and abstraction to bear on the question. His answer:

- The division of labor
- Free markets

The division of labor—breaking tasks down into simple tasks and becoming skilled in those tasks—is the source of "the greatest improvement in the productive powers of labor," said Smith. The division of labor became even more productive when it was applied to creating new technologies. Scientists and engineers, trained in extremely narrow fields, became specialists at inventing. Their powerful skills accelerated the advance of technology, so by the 1820s, machines could make consumer goods faster and more accurately than any craftsman could. And by the 1850s, machines could make other machines that labor alone could never have made.

But, said Smith, the fruits of the division of labor are limited by the extent of the market. To make the market as large as possible, there must be no impediments to free trade both within a country and among countries. Smith argued that when each person makes the best possible economic choice, that choice leads as if by "an invisible hand" to the best outcome for society as a whole. The butcher, the brewer, and the baker each pursue their own interests but, in doing so, also serve the interests of everyone else.

## THEN...

Adam Smith speculated that one person, working hard, using the hand tools available in the 1770s, might possibly make 20 pins a day. Yet, he observed, by using those same hand tools but breaking the process into a number of individually small operations in which people specialize—by the division of labor—ten people could make a staggering 48,000 pins a day. One draws out the wire, another straightens it, a third cuts it, a fourth points it, a fifth grinds it. Three specialists make the head, and a fourth attaches it. Finally, the pin is polished and packaged. But a large market is needed to support the division of labor: One factory employing ten workers would need to sell more than 15 million pins a year to stay in business.

## ...AND NOW

If Adam Smith were here today, he would be fascinated by the computer chip. He would see it as an extraordinary example of the productivity of the division of labor and of the use of machines to make machines that make other machines. From a design of a chip's intricate circuits, cameras transfer an image to glass plates that work like stencils. Workers prepare silicon wafers on which the circuits are printed. Some slice the wafers, others polish them, others bake them, and yet others coat them with a light-sensitive chemical. Machines transfer a copy of the circuit onto

the wafer. Chemicals then etch the design onto the wafer. Further processes deposit atom-sized transistors and aluminum connectors. Finally, a laser separates the hundreds of chips on the wafer. Every stage in the process of creating a computer chip uses other computer chips. And like the pin of the 1770s, the computer chip of the 1990s benefits from a large market—a global market—to buy chips in the huge quantities in which they are produced efficiently.

Many economists have worked on the big themes that Adam Smith began. One of these economists is Mancur Olson, of the University of Maryland, whom you can meet on the following pages.

**Mancur Olson, Jr., is**
Distinguished University Professor
of Economics at the University of
Maryland, a position he has held
since 1978. Professor Olson was
born in Grand Forks, North
Dakota, in 1932. He was an under-
graduate at North Dakota State
University, a Rhodes Scholar at
Oxford University (M.A. 1960),
and a graduate student at Harvard
University (Ph.D. 1963).

Professor Olson's research covers
a wide area, and his major work is
on the problems that lead to and
are caused by collective choices
by groups such as businesses, labor
unions, or governments. He has
studied the effects of collective
choices on economic growth and
on the transition from Communism
to a market economy.

Michael Parkin talked with
Professor Olson about his work,
how it connects with the origins of
economics and the work of Adam
Smith, and the insights it offers us
in facing today's problems.

**What attracted you to economics?**
I became enchanted with the first
economics book that I read, *Defense
Without Inflation* by Albert Gaylord
Hart. I had never before come upon
anything that used logical deduction
from basic assumptions to derive general principles about how the world
worked. The fun and relevance of economics captivated me and made me
want to be an economist. When economics writing and teaching are really
good, they make clear what a wonderful
and fascinating subject economics is.

**Can you describe the connection
between this set of ideas and your own
and the earlier ideas of Adam Smith?**
I'm enormously indebted to Adam
Smith and to the other great economists who have written over the last
two and a quarter centuries. Long ago
the great physicist Isaac Newton said
that if he was able to see farther, it was
because he stood on the shoulders of
giants. Not only do economists of
today have the legacy of Adam Smith,
but also other giants such as Ricardo,
Malthus, Mill, and Marshall. Thus the
economist today stands on the shoulders of giants standing on shoulders of
giants—on a great pyramid of genius.

**Adam Smith thought that he under-
stood the major reason for differences
in the wealth of nations, and he attrib-
uted this mainly to the extent to which
people exploited the advantages of the
division of labor and specialization on
the one hand and then coordinated
their individual activities by allowing
self-interest to rule in the marketplace.
Was Smith right?**
Adam Smith put forth one of the most
important truths ever told, but it's still
not the whole truth. What he neglected
to point out is that, to achieve prosperity, societies need what I call "market-
augmenting government." Many suppose that governments only repress or
interfere with markets, but the richest
societies have governments that, on

balance, increase the number of markets. In an anarchy, people are fighting instead of trading. The government that replaces the anarchy is already augmenting markets because a peaceful order increases the incentive to produce and to trade.

Many people think that once there is peace, all the needed markets arise spontaneously, but this is true of only one of the two types of markets. One kind of market does arise simply because the gains from trade are often very large and the parties can reap these gains without any outside help. When people trade goods and cash on the spot, these trades are self-enforcing. When trades are self-enforcing, markets spring up by themselves, and if governments make them illegal, they may even exist as black markets.

The other kind of market exists only when there is third-party enforcement of contracts. Consider long-term loans. A lender has to give up the money at the outset, so the lender is a fool to lend unless he or she can be reasonably confident that the money will be paid back with interest. Thus lenders lend and borrowers can borrow only if an impartial third party, such as the government's legal system, will enforce the loan contract, often by seizing the assets purchased with the loan in the interest of the lender. The gains from trade in capital markets, insurance markets, and many other markets can be realized only if there is a contract-enforcing and thus market-augmenting government. The richest (or First World) countries have such governments and thus have not only self-enforcing markets but also a huge range of markets that depend upon third-party enforcement. By contrast, the countries of the Third World and those that are in transition from Communism (the Second World) do not have mar-ket-augmenting governments, and they usually have little more than self-enforcing markets.

While most goods and services are provided most efficiently through the market, there are some goods and services that the market cannot provide. Firms can make money producing the kinds of goods that we find in the stores because they can keep us from getting the goods unless we pay the going price. But there are other kinds of goods that are collective or public goods—goods that, if available to anyone, are automatically available to everyone in some category or country, whether or not a person contributed anything toward the cost of providing the good. A population cannot obtain such goods through voluntary or market behavior. Virtually everyone prefers clean air to polluted air, but that does not mean that the people in a metropolitan area will voluntarily spend a few hundred extra dollars to have their cars equipped with pollution abatement technology. If there were, say, a million individuals in a metropolitan area, a typical individual would get only about one millionth of the benefit from the increment in clean air that resulted because that individual paid for pollution abatement technology. But that individual would pay the whole cost of any pollution abatement technology that the individual purchased. A person would also obtain the benefit of any pollution abatement by others, whether or not that person had done anything to reduce pollution or not.

This means that, even if absolutely everyone agreed that clean air was worth more than it cost and everyone would vote in favor of making the pollution abatement technology compulsory, no one individual would gain from voluntarily contributing to or "buying" this good. Voluntary or market mechanisms therefore cannot provide any substantial population with pollution abatement or any other collective good. This is the paradoxical logic of collective action: Rational individual behavior leads to a collectively irrational outcome. It is because of the logic of collective action that certain goods and services, such as law and order and national defense, have to be funded through compulsory taxation. It is because of this logic that we need government.

This logic also helps to explain the behavior of some types of non-governmental organizations. Consider, for example, the benefits that a lobby provides to an industry. If a lobby gets a tariff for an

*A key idea is that the incentive structures of societies overwhelmingly determine how well their economies perform.*

industry, the price rises for all of the producers in that industry. Every producer in the industry gets the benefit of the tariff, whether that producer paid any of the costs of the lobbying or not. Therefore lobbying organizations provide a benefit that is a collective good to their constituents. Similarly, by restricting output and raising prices, cartels also provide a collective good to those who sell the product that benefits from the monopoly price.

**What are the key ideas and insights that continually inform you and constitute the foundations of your work?**

A key idea is that the incentive structures of societies overwhelmingly determine how well their economies perform. One important determinant of this is the power of the special interest organizations that I mentioned in response to your last question. As time goes on in stable democracies, more organizations representing the firms or workers in an industry or occupation develop the selective incentives that enable them to overcome the difficulties of collective action. Each individual industry is small in relation to the economy as a whole. Suppose, for the sake of easy arithmetic, that the firms or workers in a special interest organization earn exactly 1 percent of the nation's income. Then they gain from using their lobbying or cartel power to change the distribution of income in their favor. They seek such things as tariff protection, tax loopholes, and higher prices or wages. This makes the economy less productive. The members of the special interest organization will, when they earn 1 percent of income, bear on the average only about 1 percent of the total loss arising from the redistribution to themselves, but they receive everything that is redistributed to them. Thus they gain from their lobbying or cartel power until the nation's income falls by a hundred times as much as they obtain! So an economy with a dense network of special interest organizations is like a china shop filled with wrestlers battling over its contents—and breaking much more than they carry away.

Another important determinant of the structure of incentives is the quality of the legal system's enforcement of contracts and com-

pany law and its protection of property rights. This mainly determines whether a society can mobilize the capital—and the modern technologies that are normally embodied in capital goods—needed for either capital-intensive or large scale production. Most of the countries in the First World have the rule of law with respect to property and contract as to other things. Most countries in the Second and Third Worlds do not have the rule of law and thus also lack good property and contract rights. This is, I believe, the single most important reason why the First World

---

*Economic development requires ... governments so strong that they're expected to last indefinitely but so inhibited that they never abridge individual rights.*

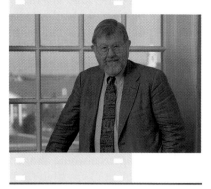

---

countries are rich and the countries of the Second and the Third Worlds are mostly still poor.

The structure of incentives that a society needs to prosper does not spring up spontaneously

but is a result of social accumulation and governmental design. There is no private property, for example, without government; there may be possessions, in the sense that a dog possesses a bone, but no socially sanctioned property right. Just as governments are indispensable for private property, so they are often the greatest threat to private property. Governments have the power to seize whatever property they want. In much of the world, private property is insecure because governments often expropriate it or because governments are so unstable or weak that individuals cannot be sure the government will be able to protect private property indefinitely. Economic development requires something that's rather rare: governments so strong that they're expected to last indefinitely but so inhibited that they never abridge individual rights.

**Is an economics degree a sensible place to begin preparing for a twenty-first century career?**

Economics, far more than any other social science, has a body of powerful ideas that illuminate the problems that individuals and societies face. Economics ideas will be indispensable in the next century as in the present one. The problem is to make their value apparent to the student. Some economics instruction sets out the logic of models without relating them frequently to observation. It's said, "The glory of opera is that it is words and music," and the glory of economics is that it is both logic and observation. Only when the two go together—only when the teacher of economics makes it clear how the logic of economic theory illuminates what we observe around us—does the great practical value of economics become apparent.

# What is Economics?

From the moment you wake up each morning to the moment you fall asleep again each night, your life is filled with *choices*. Your first choice is when to get up. Will you start running the moment the alarm goes off, or will you linger for a few minutes and listen to the radio? What will you wear today? You check the weather forecast and make that decision. Then, what will you have for breakfast? Will you drive to school or take the bus? Which classes will you attend? Which assignments will you complete? What will you do for lunch? Will you play tennis, swim, run, or skate today? How will you spend your evening? Will you study, relax at home with a video, or go to the movies? ◆ You face decisions like these every day. But on some days, you face choices that can change the entire direction of your life. What will you study? Will you major in economics, business, law, or film? ◆

## A Day in Your Life

While you are making your own decisions, other people are making theirs. And some of the decisions that other people make will have an impact on your own subsequent decisions. Your school decides its course offerings for next year. Stephen Spielberg decides what his next movie will be. General Motors decides what new models to introduce and how many of this year's models to produce. A team of eye doctors decides on a new experiment that will lead them to a cure for nearsightedness. The U.S. Congress decides to cut defense spending and to lower taxes. The Federal Reserve Board decides to raise interest rates. ◆ All these choices and the decisions made by you and everyone else are examples of economics in your life. ◆ This chapter takes a first look at the subject you are about to study. It defines economics. Then it expands on that definition with five big questions that economists try to answer and eight big ideas that define the economic way of thinking. These questions and ideas are the foundation on which your course is built. The chapter concludes with a description of how economists go about their work, the scientific method they use, and the pitfalls they try to avoid. When you have completed your study of this chapter, you will have a good sense of what economics is about and you'll be ready to start learning economics and using it to gain a new view of the world.

## After studying this chapter, you will be able to:

- Define economics

- Explain the five big questions that economists seek to answer

- Explain eight ideas that define the economic way of thinking

- Describe how economists go about their work

# Big Economic Questions

## A Definition of Economics

All economic questions and problems arise from **scarcity**—they arise because our wants exceed the resources available to satisfy them.

We want good health and long life, material comfort, security, physical and mental recreation, and knowledge. None of these wants is completely satisfied for everyone, and everyone has some unsatisfied wants. While many people have all the material comfort they want, many others do not. And no one feels entirely satisfied with her or his state of health and expected length of life. No one feels entirely secure, even in the post-Cold War era, and no one has enough time for sport, travel, vacations, movies, theater, reading, and other leisure pursuits.

The poor and the rich alike face scarcity. A child wants a 75¢ can of soft drink and a 50¢ pack of gum but has only $1.00 in her pocket. She experiences scarcity. A student wants to go to a party on Saturday night but also wants to spend that same night catching up on late assignments. He experiences scarcity. A millionaire wants to spend the weekend playing golf *and* attending a business strategy meeting and cannot do both. She experiences scarcity. Even parrots face scarcity—there just aren't enough crackers to go around!

*Not only do I want a cracker—we all want a cracker!*

Drawing by Modell; ©1985 The New Yorker Magazine, Inc.

Faced with scarcity, we must *choose* among the available alternatives.

**Economics** is the *science of choice*—the science that explains the choices we make and how those choices change as we cope with scarcity.

All economic choices can be summarized in five big questions about the goods and services we produce. These questions are: What? How? When? Where? Who?

## 1 **What** goods and services are produced and in **what** quantities?

**Goods and services** are all the things that we value and are willing to pay for. We produce a dazzling array of goods and services that range from necessities such as houses to leisure items such as camping vehicles and equipment. We build more than a million new homes every year. And these homes are more spacious and better equipped than they were 20 years ago. We make several million new leisure vehicles, tents, portable microwaves, refrigerators, telephones, television sets, and VCRs, all of which make outdoor living and vacations more attractive and more comfortable.

What determines whether we build more homes or make more camping gear and develop more campsites? How do these choices change over time? And how are they affected by the ongoing changes in technology that make an ever-widening array of goods and services available to us?

## 2 **How** are goods and services produced?

In a vineyard in France, basket-carrying workers pick the annual grape crop by hand. In a vineyard in California, a huge machine and a few workers do the same job that a hundred French grape harvesters do. Look around you and you will see many examples of this phenomenon—the same job being done in different ways. In some supermarkets, checkout clerks key

in prices. In others, they use a laser scanner. One farmer keeps track of livestock feeding schedules and inventories by using paper and pencil records, while another uses a personal computer. GM hires workers to weld auto bodies in some of its plants and uses robots to do the job in others.

Why do we use machines in some cases and people in others? Do mechanization and technological change destroy more jobs than they create? Do they make us better off or worse off?

## 3 When are goods and services produced?

On a building site, there is a surge of production activity and people must work overtime to keep production flowing fast enough. An auto factory closes for the summer, temporarily laying off its workers, and its production dries up.

Sometimes, economy-wide production slackens off and even shrinks in what is called a *recession*. At other times, economy-wide production expands rapidly. We call these ebbs and flows of production the *business cycle*. When production falls, jobs are lost and unemployment climbs. Once, during the Great Depression of the 1930s, production fell so much that one quarter of the work force was jobless.

During the past few years, production has decreased in Russia and its Central and Eastern Europe neighbors as these countries try to change the way they organize their economies.

What makes production rise and fall? When will production fall again in the United States? Can the government prevent production from falling?

## 4 Where are goods and services produced?

The Kellogg Company, of Battle Creek, Michigan, makes breakfast cereals in 20 countries and sells them in 160 countries. Kellogg's business in Japan is so huge that it has a Web site in Japanese to promote its products! Honda, the Japanese auto producer, makes cars and motorcycles on most continents.

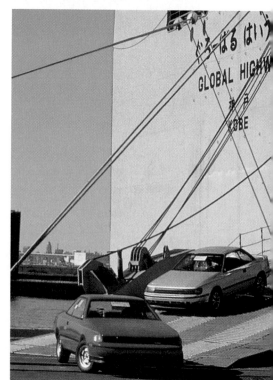

"Globalization through localization" is its slogan. But it produces some cars in one country and ships them for sale in another. We in the United States even import some cars from Japan.

In today's global economy, people who are separated by thousands of miles cooperate to produce many goods and services. Software engineers in Silicon Valley work via the Internet with programmers in India. American Express card charge slips are processed in Barbados. But there is a lot of local concentration of production as well. Most American carpets are made in Dalton, Georgia. And most of our movies are made in Los Angeles.

What determines where goods and services are produced? And how are changing patterns of production location changing the jobs we do and the wages we earn?

## 5 Who consumes the goods and services that are produced?

Who consumes the goods and services produced depends on the incomes that people earn. Doctors earn much higher incomes than nurses and medical assistants. So doctors get more of the goods and services produced than nurses and medical assistants do.

You probably know about many other persistent differences in incomes. Men, on the average, earn more than women. Whites, on the average, earn more than minorities. College graduates, on the average, earn more than high school graduates. Americans, on the average, earn more than Europeans, who in turn earn more, on the average, than Asians and Africans. But there are some significant exceptions. The people of Japan and Hong Kong now earn an amount similar to that of Americans. And there is a lot of income inequality throughout the world.

What determines the incomes we earn? Why do doctors earn larger incomes than nurses? Why do women and minorities earn less than white males?

These five big economic questions give you a sense of what economics is *about*. They tell you about the *scope of economics*. But they don't tell you what economics *is*. They don't tell you how economists *think* about these questions and seek answers to them. Let's find out how economists approach economic questions by looking at some big ideas that define the *economic way of thinking*.

# Big Ideas of Economics

**1** A choice is a **trade-off**— we give up something to get something else—and the highest-valued alternative we give up is the **opportunity cost** of the activity chosen.

Whatever we choose to do, we could have done something else instead. We trade off one thing for another. "There ain't no such thing as a free lunch" is not just a clever throwaway line. It expresses the central idea of economics— that every choice involves a cost.

We use the term **opportunity cost** to emphasize that when we make a choice in the face of scarcity, we give up an opportunity to do something else. The opportunity cost of any action is the highest-valued alternative forgone. The action that you choose not to do—the highest-valued alternative forgone—is the cost of the action that you choose to do.

You can quit school right now, or you can remain in school. If you quit and take a job at McDonald's, you might earn enough to buy some CDs, go to the movies, and spend lots of free time with your friends. If you remain in school, you can't afford these things. You will be able to buy these things later, and that is one of the payoffs from being in school. But for now, when you've bought your books, you have nothing left for CDs and movies. And doing assignments means that you've got less time for

hanging around with your friends. The opportunity cost of being in school is the alternative things that you would have done if you had quit school.

Opportunity cost is the highest-valued alternative forgone. It is not *all* the possible alternatives forgone. For example, your economics lecture is at 8:30 on a Monday morning. You contemplate two alternatives to attending the lecture: staying in bed for an hour or jogging for an hour. You can't stay

in bed and jog for that same hour. The opportunity cost of attending the lecture is not the cost of an hour in bed and the cost of jogging for an hour. If these are the only alternatives you contemplate, then you have to decide which one you would do if you did not go to the lecture. The opportunity cost of attending a lecture for a jogger is a forgone hour of exercise; the opportunity cost of attending a lecture for a late sleeper is a forgone hour in bed.

## 2  We make choices in small steps, or at the **margin**, and choices are influenced by **incentives**.

Everything that we do involves a decision to do a little bit more or a little bit less of an activity. You can allocate the next hour between studying and e-mailing your friends. But the choice is not "all-or-nothing." You must decide how many minutes to allocate to each activity. To make this decision, you compare the benefit of a little bit more study time with its cost.

The mother of a young child must decide how to allocate her time between being with her child and working for an income. Like your decision about study time, this decision too involves comparing the benefit of a little bit more income with the cost of a little bit less time with her child.

The benefit that arises from an increase in an activity is called **marginal benefit.** For example, suppose that a mother is working 2 days a week and is thinking about increasing her work to 3 days. Her marginal benefit is the benefit she will get from the additional day of work. It is *not* the benefit she gets from all 3 days. The reason is that she already has the benefit from 2 days work, so she doesn't count this benefit as resulting from the decision she is now making.

The cost of an increase in an activity is called **marginal cost.** For the mother of the young child, the marginal cost of increasing her work to 3 days a week is the cost of the additional day not

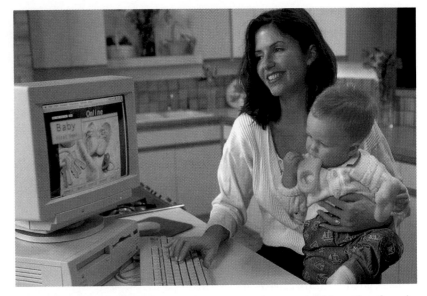

spent with her child. It does not include the cost of the two days she is already working.

To make her decision, the mother compares the marginal benefit from an extra day of work with its marginal cost. If the marginal benefit exceeds the marginal cost, she works the extra day. If the marginal cost exceeds the marginal benefit, she does not work the extra day.

By evaluating marginal benefits and marginal costs and choosing only those actions that bring greater benefit than cost, we use our scarce resources in the way that makes us as well off as possible.

Our choices respond to incentives. An **incentive** is an inducement to take a particular action. The inducement can be a benefit—a carrot—or a cost—a stick. A change in opportunity cost—in marginal cost—and a change in marginal benefit changes the incentives that we face and leads to changes in our actions.

For example, suppose the daily wage rate rises and nothing else changes. With a higher daily wage

rate, the marginal benefit of working increases. For the young mother, the opportunity cost of spending a day with her child has increased. She now has a bigger incentive to work an extra day a week. Whether or not she does so depends on how she evaluates the marginal benefit of the additional income and marginal cost of spending less time with her child.

Similarly, suppose the cost of day care rises and nothing else changes. The higher cost of day care increases the marginal cost of working. For the young mother, the opportunity cost of spending a day with her child has decreased. She now has a smaller incentive to work an extra day a week. Again, whether or not she changes her actions in response to a change in incentives depends on how she evaluates the marginal benefit and marginal cost.

The central idea of economics is that by looking for changes in marginal cost and marginal benefit, we can predict the way choices will change in response to changes in incentives.

# 3 Voluntary exchange makes *both* buyers and sellers better off, and **markets** are an **efficient** way to organize exchange.

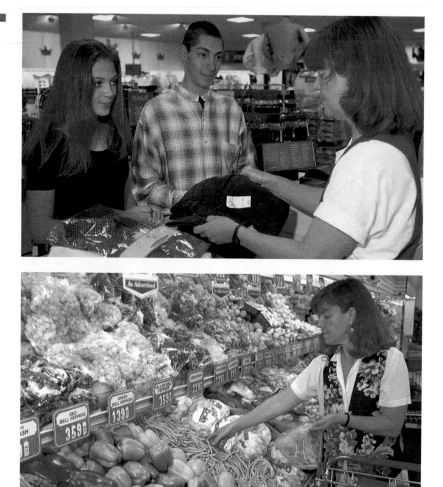

When you shop for food, you give up some money in exchange for a basket of vegetables. But the food is worth the price you have to pay. You are better off having exchanged some of your money for the vegetables. The food store receives a payment that makes its operator happy too. Both you and the food store operator gain from your purchase.

Similarly, when you work at a summer job, you receive a wage that you've decided is sufficient to compensate you for the leisure time you must give up. But the value of your work to the firm that hires you is at least as great as the wage it pays you. So again, both you and your employer gain from a **voluntary exchange.**

You are better off when you buy your food. And you are better off when you sell your labor during the summer vacation. Whether you are a buyer or a seller, you gain from voluntary exchange with others.

What is true for you is true for everyone else. Everyone gains from voluntary exchange.

In our organized economy, exchanges take place in **markets** and for money. We sell our labor in exchange for an income in the labor market. And we buy the goods and services we've chosen to consume in a wide variety of markets—markets for vegetables, cof-

fee, movies, videos, muffins, haircuts, and so on. At the other side of these transactions, firms buy our labor and sell us the hundreds of different consumer goods and services we buy.

Markets are **efficient** in the sense that they send resources to the place where they are valued most highly. For example, a frost kills Florida's orange crop and sends the price of orange juice through the roof. This increase in price, with all other prices remaining unchanged, increases the opportunity cost of drinking orange juice. The people who place the highest value on orange

juice are the ones who keep drinking it. People who place a lower value on orange juice now have an incentive to substitute other fruit juices.

Markets are not the only way to organize the economy. An alternative is called a command system. In a **command system,** some people give orders (commands) and other people obey those orders. A command system is used in the military and in many firms. And it was used in the former Soviet Union to organize the entire economy. But the market is a superior method of organizing an entire economy.

**4** The market does not always work efficiently and sometimes, government action is necessary to overcome **market failure** and lead to a more efficient use of resources.

**Market failure** is a state in which the market does not use resources efficiently.

If you pay attention to the news media, you might get the impression that the market almost never does a good job. It makes credit card interest rates too high. It makes the wages of fast food workers too low. It causes the price of coffee to go through the ceiling every time Brazil has a serious frost. It increases the world price of oil when political instability threatens the Middle East. These examples are not cases of market failure. They are examples of the market doing its job of helping us to allocate our scarce resources and ensure that they are used in the activities in which they are most highly valued.

Buyers never like it when prices rise. But sellers love it. And sellers never like it when prices fall. But buyers are happy. Rising and falling prices make news because they bring changes in fortunes. Some people win and some lose. Everyone gains from voluntary exchange, as you've just seen, but other things remaining the same, the higher the price, the more the seller gains and the less the buyer gains.

Because a high price brings a bigger gain to the seller, there is

an incentive for sellers to try to control a market. When a single producer controls an entire market, the producer can restrict production and raise the price. This action brings market failure. The quantity of the good available is too small. Some people believe that Intel restricts the quantity of computer chips when it introduces a new design in order to get a high price for it. Eventually, the price falls, but at first, Intel sells its new design for a high price and makes a bigger profit.

Market failure can also arise when producers don't take into account the costs they impose on other people. For example, electricity utilities create pollution such as acid rain that destroys plants and forests and lowers farm production. If these costs were taken into account, we would produce less electricity.

Market failure can also arise because some goods, such as the air traffic control system, must be consumed by everyone equally. None of us has an incentive voluntarily to pay our share of the cost of such a service. Instead, we try to free ride on everyone else. But if everyone tries to free ride, no one gets a ride!

To overcome market failure, governments regulate markets with antitrust laws and environmental protection laws. And the government discourages the production and consumption of some goods and services (tobacco and alcohol for example) by taxing them and encourages the production and consumption of some other items (health care and schooling for example) by subsidizing them.

## 5 For the economy as a whole, **expenditure** *equals* **income** *equals* the **value of production.**

When you buy a coffee milkshake, you spend $2. But what happens to that money? The server gets some of it in wages, the owner of the building gets some of it as rent, and the owner of the milk bar gets some of it as profit. The suppliers of the milk, ice cream, and coffee also get some of your $2. But these suppliers spend part of what they receive on wages and rent. And they keep part of it as profit. Your $2 of expenditure creates exactly $2 of incomes for all the people who have contributed to making the milkshake, going all the way back to the farmer in Brazil who grew the coffee beans.

Your expenditure generates incomes of an equal amount. The same is true for everyone else's expenditure. So for the economy as a whole, total expenditure on goods and services equals total income.

One way to value the things you buy is to use the prices you pay for them. So the value of all the goods and services bought equals total expenditure. Another way to value the items you buy is to use the cost of production. This cost is the total amount paid to the people who produced the items—the total income generated by your expenditure. But we've just seen that total expenditure and total income are equal, so they also equal the value of production.

## 6 Living standards improve when **productivity** increases.

By automating a car production line, one worker can produce a greater output. But if one worker can produce more cars, then more people can enjoy owning a car. The same is true for all goods and services. By increasing output per person, we enjoy a higher standard of living and buy more goods and services.

The dollar value of production can increase for any of three reasons: because prices rise, because production per person—**productivity**—increases or because the population increases.

But only an increase in productivity brings an improvement in living standards. A rise in prices brings higher incomes, but only in dollars. The extra income is just enough to pay the higher prices, not enough to buy more goods and services. An increase in population brings an increase in *total* production but not an increase in production per person.

# 7 Inflation occurs when the quantity of money increases faster than production.

Prices rise in a process called **inflation** when the quantity of money in circulation increases faster than production. This leads to a situation of "too much money chasing too few goods." As people bring more money to market, sellers see that they can raise their prices. But when these sellers go to buy their supplies, they find that the prices they face increase. With too much money around, money starts to lose value.

In some countries, inflation has been rapid. One such country is Poland. Since 1990, prices in Poland have risen more than sevenfold. In the United States, we have moderate inflation of about 3 percent a year.

Some people say that by increasing the quantity of money, we can create jobs. The idea is that if more money is put into the economy, when it is spent, businesses sell more and so hire more labor to produce more goods.

Initially, an increase in money might increase production and create jobs. But eventually, it only increases prices and leaves production and jobs unchanged.

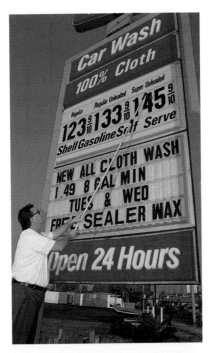

# 8 Unemployment can result from market failure but some unemployment is productive.

Unemployment is ever present. Sometimes its rate is low and sometimes it is high. Also, unemployment fluctuates over the business cycle.

Some unemployment is normal and efficient. We choose to take our time finding a suitable job rather than rushing to accept the first one that comes along. Similarly, businesses take their time in filling vacancies. The unemployment that results from these careful searches for jobs and workers improves productivity because it helps to assign people to their most productive jobs.

Some unemployment results from fluctuations in expenditure and can be wasteful.

These eight ideas lie at the heart of economics, and you will repeatedly return to them at every point in your study of the subject. To complete your introduction to economics, we next describe how economists go about their work. We're going to describe what economists do.

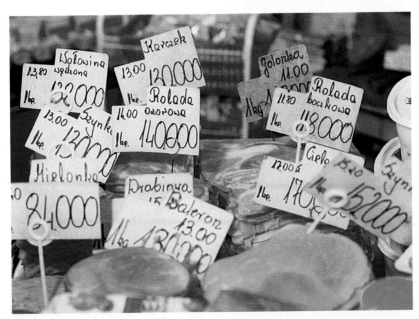

# What Economists Do

Economists work on the wide array of problems that arise from the five big questions that you reviewed at the start of this chapter. And they use the big ideas that you've just studied to search for answers. How do they go about their work? What special problems and pitfalls do they encounter? Let's look at these questions.

## Microeconomics and Macroeconomics

You can take either a micro or a macro view of the spectacular display of national flags in a Korean sports stadium. The micro view is of a single participant and the actions he or she is taking. The macro view is the patterns formed by the joint actions of all the individuals participating in the entire display.

You can look at the economy with either a micro or a macro view. These two views define the two major branches of the subject: microeconomics and macroeconomics.

**Microeconomics** is the study of the decisions of individual people and businesses and the interaction of those decisions in markets. It seeks to explain the prices and quantities of individual goods and services. Microeconomics also studies the effects of government regulation and taxes on the prices and quantities of individual goods and services. For example, microeconomics studies the forces that determine the prices of cars and the quantities of cars produced and sold. It also studies the effects of regulations and taxes on the prices and quantities of cars.

**Macroeconomics** is the study of the national economy and the global economy as a whole. It seeks to explain *average* prices and the *total* employment, income, and production. Macroeconomics also studies the effects of taxes, government spending, and the government budget deficit on total jobs and incomes. It also studies the effects of money and interest rates.

## Economic Science

Economics is a social science (along with political science, psychology, and sociology). A major task of economists is to discover how the economic world works. In pursuit of this goal, economists (like all scientists) distinguish between two types of statements:

- What *is*
- What *ought* to be

Statements about what *is* are called *positive* statements. They say what is currently believed about the way the world operates. A positive statement might be right or wrong. And a positive statement can be tested by checking it against the facts. When a chemist does an experiment in her laboratory, she is attempting to check a positive statement against the facts.

Statements about what *ought* to be are called *normative* statements. These statements depend on values and cannot be tested. When Congress debates a motion, it is ultimately trying to decide what ought to be. It is making a normative statement.

To see the distinction between positive and normative statements, consider the controversy over global warming. Some scientists believe that centuries of the burning of coal and oil are increasing the carbon dioxide content of the earth's atmosphere and leading to higher temperatures that eventually will have devastating consequences for life on this planet. "Our planet is warming because of an increased carbon dioxide buildup in the atmosphere" is a positive statement. It can (in principle and with sufficient data) be tested. "We ought to cut back on our use of carbon-based fuels such as coal and oil" is

a normative statement. You may agree with or disagree with this statement, but you can't test it. It is based on values. Health-care reform provides an economic example of the distinction. "Universal health care will cut the amount of work time lost to illness" is a positive statement. "Every American should have equal access to health care" is a normative statement.

The task of economic science is to discover and catalog positive statements that are consistent with what we observe in the world and that enable us to understand how the economic world works. This task is a large one that can be broken into three steps:

- Observation and measurement
- Model building
- Testing models

## Observation and Measurement

First, economists keep track of the amounts and locations of natural and human resources, of wages and

work hours, of the prices and quantities of the different goods and services produced, of taxes and government spending, and of the quantities of goods and services bought from and sold to other countries. This list gives a flavor of the array of things that economists can observe and measure.

## Model Building

The second step toward understanding how the economic world works is to build a model. An **economic model** is a description of some aspect of the economic world that includes only those features of the world that are needed for the purpose at hand. A model is simpler than the reality it describes. What a model includes and what it leaves out result from *assumptions* about what is essential and what are inessential details.

You can see how ignoring details is useful—even essential—to our understanding by thinking about a model that you see every day: the TV weather map. The weather map is a model that helps to predict the temperature, wind speed and direction, and precipitation over a future period.

The weather map shows lines called isobars—lines of equal barometric pressure. It doesn't show the interstate highways. The reason is that our theory of the weather tells us that the pattern of air pressure, not the location of the highways, determines the weather.

An economic model is similar to a weather map. It tells us how a number of variables are determined by a number of other variables. For example, an economic model of the 1994 Los Angeles earthquake might tell us the effects of the earthquake and the government's relief efforts on the number of houses and apartments, rents and prices, jobs, and commuting times.

## Testing

The third step is testing the model. A model's predictions may correspond to or be in conflict with the facts. By comparing the model's predictions with the facts, we are able to test a model and develop an economic theory. An **economic theory** is a generalization that summarizes what we think

we understand about the economic choices that people make and the performance of industries and entire economies. It is a bridge between an economic model and the real economy.

A theory is created by a process of building and testing models. For example, meteorologists have a theory that if the isobars form a particular pattern at a particular time of the year (a model), then it will snow (reality). They have developed this theory by repeated observation and by carefully recording the weather that follows specific pressure patterns.

Economics is a young science. It was born in 1776 with the publication of Adam Smith's *The Wealth of Nations* (see pp. 2-3). Over the past 220 years, economics has discovered many useful theories. But in many areas, economists are still looking for answers. The gradual accumulation of economic knowledge gives most economists some faith that their methods will, eventually, provide usable answers to the big economic questions.

But progress in economics comes slowly. Let's look at some

of the obstacles to progress in economics.

## Obstacles and Pitfalls in Economics

We cannot easily do economic experiments. And most economic behavior has many simultaneous causes. For these two reasons, it is difficult in economics to unscramble cause and effect.

### Unscrambling Cause and Effect

By changing one factor at a time and holding all the other relevant factors constant, we isolate the factor of interest and are able to investigate its effects in the clearest possible way. This logical device, that all scientists use to identify cause and effect, is called *ceteris paribus*. **Ceteris paribus** is a Latin term that means "other things being equal" or "if all other relevant things remain the same." Ensuring that other things are equal is crucial in many activities, including athletic events, and all successful attempts to make scientific progress use this device.

Economic models (like the models in all other sciences) enable the influence of one factor at a time to be isolated in the imaginary world of the model. When we use a model, we are able to imagine what would happen if only one factor changed. But *ceteris paribus* can be a problem in economics when we try to test a model.

Laboratory scientists, such as chemists and physicists, perform experiments by actually holding all the relevant factors constant except for the one under investigation. In the nonexperimental sciences, such as economics (and astronomy), we usually observe the outcomes of the *simultaneous* operation of many factors. Consequently, it is hard to sort out the effects of each individual factor and to compare the effects with what a model predicts. To cope with this problem, economists take three complementary approaches.

First, they look for pairs of events in which other things were equal (or similar). An example might be to study the effects of unemployment insurance on the unemployment rate by comparing the United States with Canada on the presumption that the people in the two economies are sufficiently similar. Second, economists use statistical tools—called *econometrics.* And third, when they can, they perform experiments. This relatively new approach puts real subjects (usually students) in a decision-making situation and varies their incentives in some way to discover how they respond to one factor at a time.

Economists try to avoid *fallacies*—errors of reasoning that lead to a wrong conclusion. But two fallacies are common, and you need to be on your guard to avoid them. They are the:

■ Fallacy of composition

■ *Post hoc* fallacy

### Fallacy of Composition

The fallacy of composition is the (false) statement that what is true of the parts is true of the whole or that what is true of the whole is true of the parts. Think of the true statement "Speed kills" and its implication that going more slowly saves lives. If an entire freeway moves at a lower speed, everyone on the highway has a safer ride.

But suppose that only one driver slows down and all the other drivers try to maintain their original speed. In this situation, there will probably be more accidents because more cars will change lanes to overtake the slower vehicle. In this example, what is true for the whole is not true for a part.

The fallacy of composition arises mainly in macroeconomics, and it stems from the fact that the parts interact with each other to produce an outcome for the whole that might differ from the intent of the parts. For example, a firm lays off some workers to cut costs and improve its profits. If all firms take similar actions, incomes fall and so does spending. The firm sells less, and its profits don't improve.

### Post Hoc Fallacy

Another Latin phrase—*post hoc ergo propter hoc*—means "after this, therefore because of this." The *post hoc* fallacy is the error of reasoning that a first event *causes* a second event because the first occurred before the second. Suppose you are a visitor from a far-off world. You observe lots of people shopping in early December, and then you see them opening gifts and partying on

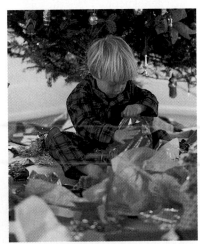

Christmas day. Does the shopping cause Christmas, you wonder. After a deeper study, you discover that Christmas causes the shopping. A later event causes an earlier event.

Unraveling cause and effect is difficult in economics. And just looking at the timing of events often doesn't help. For example, the stock market booms, and some months later the economy expands—jobs and incomes grow. Did the stock market boom cause the economy to expand? Possibly, but perhaps businesses started to plan the expansion of production because a new technology that lowered costs had become available. As knowledge of the plans spread, the stock market reacted to *anticipate* the economic expansion. To disentangle cause and effect, economists use economic models and data and, to the extent that they can, perform experiments.

Economics is a challenging science. Does the difficulty of getting answers in economics mean that anything goes and that economists disagree on most questions? Perhaps you've heard the joke: "If you laid all the economists in the world end to end, they still wouldn't reach agreement." Does the joke make a valid point?

## Agreement and Disagreement

Economists agree on a remarkably wide range of questions. And surprisingly, the agreed view of economists often disagrees with the popular and sometimes politically correct view. When Fed Chairman Alan Greenspan testifies before the Senate Banking Committee, his words are rarely controversial among economists, even when they generate endless debate in the press and Congress.

Here are 12 propositions[1] with which at least 7 out of every 10 economists broadly agree:

- Tariffs and import restrictions make most people worse off.

- A large federal budget deficit has an adverse effect on the economy.

- Cash payments to welfare recipients make them better off than do transfers-in-kind of equal cash value.

- A minimum wage increases unemployment among young workers and low-skilled workers.

- A tax cut can help to lower unemployment when the unemployment rate is high.

- The distribution of income in the United States should be more equal.

- Inflation is primarily caused by a rapid rate of money creation.

- The government should restructure welfare along the lines of a "negative income tax."

- Rent ceilings cut the availability of housing.

- Pollution taxes are more effective than pollution limits.

- The redistribution of income is a legitimate role for the U.S. government.

- The federal budget should be balanced on the average over the business cycle, but not every year.

Which are positive and which are normative? Notice that economists are willing to offer their opinions on normative issues as well as their professional views on positive questions. Be on the lookout for normative propositions dressed up as positive propositions.

You are now ready to start *doing* economics. As you get into the subject, you will see that we rely heavily on graphs. You must be comfortable with this method of reasoning. If you need some help with it, take your time in working carefully through Chapter 2. If you are already comfortable with graphs, then you are ready to jump right into Chapter 3.

---

[1] These are propositions generally supported or supported with provisos by more than 7 out of 10 economists according to a survey by Richard M. Alston, J.R. Kearl, and Michael B. Vaughan, "Is There a Consensus Among Economists," *American Economic Review*, 82 (May 1992), pp. 203-209. I have simplified the language in some cases and you should check the original for the exact propositions and percentages agreeing.

# SUMMARY

## Key Points

### A Definition of Economics (p. 8)

■ Economics is the *science of choice*—the science that explains the choices that we make to cope with scarcity.

### Big Economic Questions (pp. 8–11)

■ Economists try to answer five big questions about goods and services:
  1. What?
  2. How?
  3. When?
  4. Where?
  5. Who?
  *What* are the goods and services produced, *how, when*, and *where* are they produced, and *who* consumes them?

■ These questions interact to determine the standards of living and the distribution of well-being in the United States and around the world.

### Big Ideas of Economics (pp. 12–17)

■ A choice is a tradeoff, and the highest-value alternative forgone is the opportunity cost of what is chosen.

■ Choices are made at the margin and are influenced by incentives.

■ Markets enable both buyers and sellers to gain from voluntary exchange.

■ Sometimes government actions are needed to overcome market failure.

■ For the economy as a whole, expenditure equals income and equals the value of production.

■ Living standards rise when production per person increases.

■ Prices rise when the quantity of money increases faster than production.

■ Unemployment can result from market failure but can also be productive.

### What Economists Do (pp. 18-22)

■ Microeconomics is the study of individual decisions, and macroeconomics is the study of the economy as a whole.

■ Positive statements are about what *is* and normative statements are about what *ought* to be.

■ To explain the economic world, economists build and test economic models.

■ Economists use the *ceteris paribus* assumption to try to disentangle cause and effect, and they are careful to avoid the fallacy of composition and the *post hoc* fallacy.

■ Economists agree on a wide range of questions about how the economy works.

### Key Terms

*Ceteris paribus,* 20
Command system, 14
Economic model, 19
Economic theory, 20
Economics, 8
Efficient, 14
Expenditure, 16
Goods and services, 8
Incentive, 13
Income, 16
Inflation, 17
Macroeconomics, 18
Margin, 13

Marginal benefit, 13
Marginal cost, 13
Market, 14
Market failure, 15
Microeconomics, 18
Opportunity cost, 12
Productivity, 16
Scarcity, 8
Tradeoff, 12
Unemployment, 17
Value of production, 16
Voluntary exchange, 14

# QUESTIONS

1. Give a definition of economics.
2. What is scarcity? Give some examples of rich people and poor people facing scarcity.
3. Why does scarcity force us to make choices?
4. Give some examples, different from those in the chapter, of each of the five big economic questions.
5. Why do you care about *what* goods and services are produced? Give some examples of goods that you value highly and goods on which you place a low value.
6. Why do you care about *how* goods and services are produced? [Hint: Think about cost.]
7. Why do you care about *when* or *where* goods and services are produced?

8. Why do you care about *who* gets the goods and services that are produced?

9. What do we mean by the related ideas of *tradeoff* and *opportunity cost?* Give some examples of tradeoffs that you have made today and of opportunity costs that you have incurred.

10. What is *marginal* cost and *marginal* benefit and why are they relevant for making a decision? Give some examples.

11. What is a market and why does it enable both buyers and sellers to gain from exchange?

12. Give some examples for market failure.

13. Explain why for the economy as a whole, expenditure equals income and the value of production.

14. What makes living standards rise?

15. What makes prices rise?

16. Why does unemployment occur? Is all unemployment a problem?

## P R O B L E M S

1. You plan to go to school this summer. If you do, you won't be able to take your usual job that pays $6,000 for the summer and you won't be able to live at home for free. The cost of your tuition will be $2,000, textbooks $200, and living expenses $1,400. What is the opportunity cost of going to summer school?

2. On Valentine's Day, Bernie and Catherine exchanged gifts: Bernie sent Catherine red roses and Catherine bought Bernie a box of chocolates. Each spent $15. They also spent $50 on dinner and split the cost evenly. Did either Bernie or Catherine incur any opportunity costs? If so, what were they? Explain your answer.

3. The local mall has free parking, but the mall is always very busy and it usually takes 30 minutes to find a parking space. Today when you found a vacant spot, Harry also wanted it. Is parking really free at this mall? If not, what did it cost you to park today? When you parked your car today, did you impose any costs on Harry? Explain your answers.

## C R I T I C A L    T H I N K I N G

1. This man is homeless and you can see all his possessions in the photograph.

Use the five big questions and the eight big ideas of economics to organize a short essay about the economic life of the man in the photograph. Does he face scarcity? Does he make choices? Can you interpret his choices as being in his own best interest? Can either his own choices or the choices of others make this man better off? If so, how?

# 2

# Making and Using Graphs

British Prime Minister Benjamin Disraeli is reputed to have said that "There are three kinds of lies: lies, damned lies, and statistics." One of the most powerful ways of conveying statistical information is in the form of a graph. And like statistics, graphs can lie. But the right graph does not lie. It reveals a relationship that would otherwise be obscure. ◆ Graphs are a modern invention. They first appeared in the late eighteenth century, long after the discovery of logarithms and calculus. But today, in the age of the personal computer and video display, graphs have become as important as words and numbers. How do economists use graphs? What types of graphs do they use? What do graphs reveal and what can they hide? ◆ The big questions that economics tries to answer—questions that you studied in

## Three Kinds of Lies

Chapter 1—are difficult ones. They involve relationships among a large number of variables. Almost nothing in economics has a single cause. Instead, a large number of variables interact with each other. It is often said that in economics, everything depends on everything else. Changes in the quantity of ice cream consumed are caused by changes in the price of ice cream, the temperature, and many other factors. How can we make and interpret graphs of relationships among several variables? ◆ In this chapter, you are going to look at the kinds of graphs that economists use. You are going to learn how to make them and read them. You are also going to learn how to determine the magnitude of the influence of one variable on another by calculating the slope of a line and of a curve. ◆ There are no graphs or techniques used in this book that are more complicated than those explained and described in this chapter. If you are already familiar with graphs, you may want to skip (or skim) this chapter. Whether you study this chapter thoroughly or give it a quick pass, you can use it as a handy reference, returning to it whenever you need extra help in understanding the graphs that you encounter in your study of economics.

## After studying this chapter, you will be able to:

■ Make and interpret a time-series graph, a scatter diagram, and a cross-section graph

■ Distinguish between linear and nonlinear relationships and between relationships that have a maximum and a minimum

■ Define and calculate the slope of a line

■ Graph relationships among more than two variables

## Graphing Data

GRAPHS REPRESENT A QUANTITY AS A DISTANCE ON a line. Figure 2.1 gives two examples. A distance on the horizontal line represents temperature, measured in degrees Fahrenheit. A movement from left to right shows an increase in temperature. A movement from right to left shows a decrease in temperature. The point marked 0 represents zero degrees Fahrenheit. To the right of 0, the temperatures are positive. To the left of 0, the temperatures are negative (as indicated by the minus sign in front of the numbers).

A distance on the vertical line represents altitude or height, measured in thousands of feet above sea level. The point marked 0 represents sea level. Points above 0 represent feet above sea level. Points below 0 (indicated by a minus sign) represent feet below sea level.

There are no rigid rules about the scale for a graph. The scale is determined by the range of the variables being graphed.

The main point of a graph is to enable us to visualize the relationship between two variables. And to accomplish this, we set two scales perpendicular to each other, like those in Fig. 2.1.

The two scale lines are called *axes*. The vertical line is called the *y*-axis, and the horizontal line is called the *x*-axis. The letters *x* and *y* appear on the axes of Fig. 2.1. Each axis has a zero point, which is shared by the two axes. This zero point, common to both axes, is called the *origin*.

To show something in a two-variable graph, we need two pieces of information. We need the value of the variable *x* and the value of the variable *y*. For example, off the coast of Alaska on a winter's day, the temperature is 32 degrees, which we will call the value of *x*. A fishing boat is located at 0 feet above sea level, which we'll call the value of *y*. These two bits of information appear as point *a* in Fig. 2.1. A climber at the top of Mount McKinley on a very cold day is 20,320 feet above sea level and the temperature is 0 degrees. These two pieces of information appear as point *b*. The position of the climber on a warmer day might be at the point marked *c*. This point represents the peak of Mt. McKinley when the temperature is 32 degrees.

Two lines, called coordinates, can be drawn from point *c* in the graph. One of these lines runs from *c* to the horizontal axis. This line is called the *y*-coordinate. Its length is the same as the value marked off on

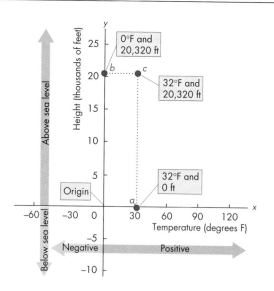

### FIGURE 2.1
## Making a Graph

All graphs have axes that measure quantities as distances. Here, the horizontal axis (*x*-axis) measures temperature. A rightward movement shows an increase in temperature. The vertical axis (*y*-axis) measures height. An upward movement shows an increase in height. Point *a* represents a fishing boat at sea level (0 on the *y*-axis) on a day when the temperature is 32° (32° on the *x*-axis). Point *b* represents a climber at the top of Mt. McKinley (20,320 feet above sea level on the *y*-axis) on a day when the temperature on Mt. McKinley is 0° (0° on the *x*-axis). Point *c* represents a climber at the top of Mt. McKinley, 20,320 feet above sea level (on the *y*-axis) on a day when the temperature on Mt. McKinley is 32° (on the *x*-axis).

the *y*-axis. The other of these lines runs from *c* to the vertical axis. This line is called the *x*-coordinate. Its length is the same as the value marked off on the *x*-axis. To describe a point in a graph, we simply use the values of its *x*- and *y*-coordinates.

Graphs like that in Fig. 2.1 can be used to show any type of quantitative data about two variables. Economists use graphs similar to the one in Fig. 2.1 to reveal and describe the relationships among economic variables. To do so, they use three main types of graphs, which we'll now study. They are:

- Scatter diagrams
- Time-series graphs
- Cross-section graphs

## Scatter Diagrams

A **scatter diagram** plots the value of one economic variable against the value of another variable. Such a graph is used to reveal whether a relationship exists between two economic variables. It is also used to describe a relationship.

**Consumption and Income** Figure 2.2(a) shows a scatter diagram of the relationship between consumption and income. The x-axis measures average income, and the y-axis measures average consumption. Each point shows consumption per person (on the average) and income per person in the United States in a given year from 1986 to 1995. The points for the ten years are "scattered" within the graph. Each point is labeled with a two-digit number that shows us its year. For example, the point marked 92 shows us that in 1992, income per person was $18,000 and consumption per person was $16,500.

The dots in this graph form a pattern, which reveals a positive relationship between these two variables. That is, when income increases, consumption also increases.

**Phone Calls and Price** Figure 2.2(b) shows a scatter diagram of the relationship between the number of international phone calls made from the United States and the average price per minute.

The dots in this graph reveal that as the price per minute falls, the number of calls increases.

**Unemployment and Inflation** Figure 2.2(c) shows a scatter diagram of inflation and unemployment in the United States. The dots in this graph form a pattern that shows us there is no clear relationship between these two variables. By its lack of a distinct pattern, the graph shows us that there is no simple relationship between inflation and unemployment in the United States.

**Correlation and Causation** A scatter diagram that shows a clear relationship between two variables, such as Fig. 2.2(a) or Fig. 2.2(b), tells us that the two variables have a high correlation. When a high correlation is present, we can predict the value of one variable from the value of the other variable. But correlation does not imply causation. Sometimes a high correlation is just a coincidence, but sometimes it does

### FIGURE 2.2

## Scatter Diagrams

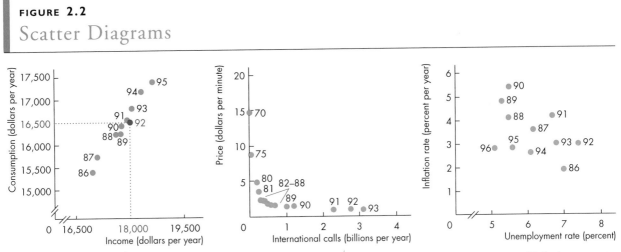

**(a) Consumption and income**

**(b) International phone calls and prices**

**(c) Unemployment and inflation**

A scatter diagram reveals the relationship between two variables. Part (a) shows the relationship between consumption and income between 1986 and 1995. Each point shows the values of the two variables in a specific year. For example, in 1992, average income was $18,000 and average consumption was $16,500. The pattern formed by the points shows that as income increases, so does consumption. Part (b) shows the relationship between the price of an international phone call and the number of phone calls made per year between 1970 and 1993. This graph shows that as the price of a phone call has fallen, the number of calls made has increased. Part (c) shows the inflation rate and unemployment rate in the United States between 1986 and 1996. This graph shows that inflation and unemployment are not closely related.

arise from a causal relationship. It is likely, for example, that increasing income causes increasing consumption (Fig. 2.2a) and that falling phone call prices cause more calls to be made (Fig. 2.2b).

**Breaks in the Axes**   Two of the graphs you've just looked at, Fig. 2.2(a) and Fig. 2.2(c), have breaks in their axes, as shown by the small gaps. The breaks indicate that there are jumps from the origin, 0, to the first values recorded.

In Fig. 2.2(a), the breaks are used because the lowest value of consumption exceeds $15,000 and the lowest value of income exceeds $16,500. With no breaks in the axes of this graph, there would be a lot of empty space, all the points would be crowded into the top right corner, and we would not be able to see whether a relationship exists between these two variables. By breaking the axes, we are able to bring the relationship into view.

Putting a break in the axes is like using a zoom lens to bring the relationship into the center of the graph and magnify it so that it fills the graph.

**Misleading Graphs**   Breaks can be used to highlight a relationship. But they can also be used to mislead and create a wrong impression—to make a graph that lies. The most common way of making a graph lie is to use axis breaks and to also either stretch or compress a scale. The most effective way to see the power of this kind of lie is to make some graphs that use this technique. For example, redraw Fig. 2.2(a) but make the $y$-axis that measures consumption run from zero to $45,000 and keep the $x$-axis the same as the one shown. The graph will now create the impression that despite huge income growth, consumption has barely changed.

To avoid being misled, it is a good idea to get into the habit of always looking closely at the values and the labels on the axes of a graph before you start to interpret it.

## Time-Series Graphs

A **time-series graph** measures time (for example, months or years) on the $x$-axis and the variable or variables in which we are interested on the $y$-axis. Figure 2.3 shows an example of a time-series graph. In this graph, time (on the $x$-axis) is measured in years, which run from 1966 to 1996. The variable that we are interested in is the price of coffee, and it is measured on the $y$-axis.

A time-series graph conveys an enormous amount of information quickly and easily, as this example illustrates. It shows:

- The *level* of the price of coffee—when it is *high* and *low*. When the line is a long way from the $x$-axis, the price is high. When the line is close to the $x$-axis, the price is low.

- How the price *changes*—whether it *rises* or *falls*. When the line slopes upward, as in 1976, the price is rising. When the line slopes downward, as in 1978, the price is falling.

- The *speed* with which the price changes—whether it rises or falls *quickly* or *slowly*. If the line is very steep, then the price rises or falls quickly. If the line is not steep, the price rises or falls slowly. For example, the price rose very quickly in 1976 and 1977. The price went up again in 1993 but slowly. Similarly, when the price was falling in 1978, it

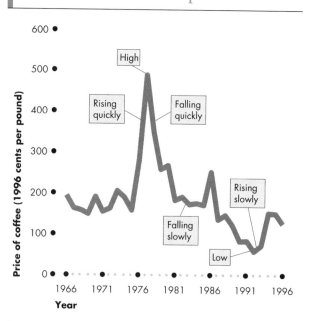

FIGURE 2.3

A Time-Series Graph

A time-series graph plots the level of a variable on the $y$-axis against time (day, week, month, or year) on the $x$-axis. This graph shows the price of coffee (in 1996 cents per pound) each year from 1966 to 1996. It shows us when the price of coffee was *high* and when it was *low*, when the price *increased* and when it *decreased*, and when it changed *quickly* and when it changed *slowly*.

fell quickly, but during the early 1980s, it fell more slowly.

A time-series graph also reveals whether there is a trend. A **trend** is a general tendency for a variable to rise or fall. You can see that the price of coffee had a general tendency to fall from the mid-1970s to the early 1990s. That is, although there were ups and downs in the price, there was a general tendency for it to fall.

A time-series graph also lets us compare different periods quickly. Figure 2.3 shows that the 1980s were different from the 1970s. The price of coffee fluctuated more violently in the 1970s than it did in the 1980s. This graph conveys a wealth of information, and it does so in much less space than we have used to describe only some of its features.

**Comparing Two Time-Series**  Sometimes we want to use a time-series graph to compare two different variables. For example, suppose you want to know whether the balance of the government's budget fluctuates with the unemployment rate. You can examine the government's budget balance and the unemployment rate by drawing a graph of each of them on the same time scale. But we can measure the government's budget balance either as a surplus or as a deficit. Figure 2.4(a) plots the budget surplus. The scale of the unemployment rate is on the left side of the figure, and the scale of the government's budget surplus is on the right. The orange line shows unemployment, and the blue line shows the budget surplus. This figure shows that the unemployment rate and the government's budget surplus move in opposite directions.

Figure 2.4(b) uses a scale for the government's budget balance measured as a deficit. That is, we flip the right-side scale over. This figure shows that the unemployment rate and the government's budget deficit move in the same direction.

**Scatter Diagram for Comparing Two Time Series**
We can compare two time series in a graph like Fig. 2.4 or in a scatter diagram like Fig. 2.2. Which is better? There is no right answer to this question. If the purpose of the graph is to show *both* the way two variables have changed over time and how they are related to each other, then the time-series graph does the better job. But if the purpose of the graph is to check the strength of the relationship between two variables, then a scatter diagram does a better job. A relationship that looks strong in a time-series graph often looks weak in a scatter diagram.

FIGURE **2.4**

Time-Series Relationships

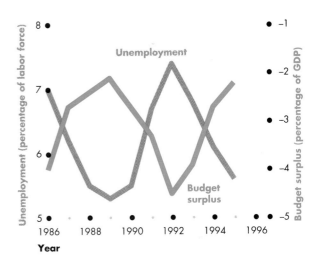

**(a) Unemployment and budget surplus**

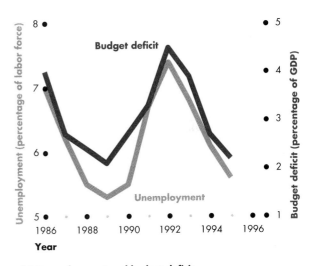

**(b) Unemployment and budget deficit**

These two graphs show the unemployment rate and the balance of the government's budget. The unemployment line is identical in the two parts. Part (a) shows the budget surplus—*taxes minus spending*—on the right scale. It is hard to see a relationship between the budget surplus and unemployment. Part (b) shows the budget as a deficit—*spending minus taxes*. It inverts the scale of part (a). With the scale for the budget balance inverted, the graph reveals a tendency for unemployment and the budget deficit to move together.

## Cross-Section Graphs

A **cross-section graph** shows the values of an economic variable for different groups in a population at a point in time. Figure 2.5 is an example of a cross-section graph. It shows average income per person in the ten largest metropolitan areas in the United States in 1995. This graph uses bars rather than dots and lines, and the length of each bar indicates average income per person. Figure 2.5 enables you to compare the average incomes per person in these ten cities. And you can do so much more quickly and clearly than by looking at a list of numbers.

The cross-section graph in Fig. 2.5 is also an example of a *bar chart*. We often use bars rather than lines in cross-section graphs, but there are no fixed rules about whether to use lines, dots, or bars. It is a matter of taste.

You've now seen how we can use graphs in economics to show economic data and to reveal relationships between variables. Next, we're going to learn how to use graphs in a more abstract way. We'll learn how economists use graphs to construct and display economic models.

### FIGURE 2.5

## A Cross-Section Graph

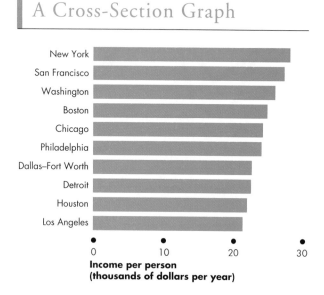

A cross-section graph shows the level of a variable across the members of a population. This graph shows the average income per person in each of the ten largest metropolitan areas in the United States in 1995.

## Graphs Used in Economic Models

THE GRAPHS USED IN ECONOMICS ARE NOT always designed to show real-world data. Often they are used to show general relationships among the variables in an economic model.

An **economic model** is a stripped down, simplified description of an economy or of a component of an economy such as a business or a household. It consists of statements about economic behavior that can be expressed as equations or as curves in a graph. Economists use models to explore the effects of different policies or other influences on the economy in ways that are similar to the use of model airplanes in wind tunnels and models of the climate.

You will encounter many different kinds of graphs in economic models, but there are some repeating patterns. Once you've learned to recognize these patterns, you will instantly understand the meaning of a graph. Here, we'll look at the different types of curves that are used in economic models, and we'll see some everyday examples of each type of curve. The patterns to look for in graphs are the four cases in which:

- Variables move in the same direction
- Variables move in opposite directions
- Variables have a maximum or a minimum
- Variables are unrelated

Let's look at these four cases.

### Variables That Move in the Same Direction

Figure 2.6 shows graphs of the relationships between two variables that move up and down together. A relationship between two variables that move in the same direction is called a **positive relationship** or a **direct relationship**. Such a relationship is shown by a line that slopes upward.

Figure 2.6 shows three types of relationships, one that has a straight line and two that have curved lines. But all the lines in these three graphs are called curves. Any line on a graph—no matter whether it is straight or curved—is called a *curve*.

A relationship shown by a straight line is called a **linear relationship.** Figure 2.6(a) shows a linear

**FIGURE 2.6**

Positive (Direct) Relationships

**(a) Positive linear relationship**   **(b) Positive becoming steeper**   **(c) Positive becoming less steep**

Each part of this figure shows a positive (direct) relationship between two variables. That is, as the value of the variable measured on the *x*-axis increases, so does the value of the variable measured on the *y*-axis. Part (a) shows a linear relationship—as the two variables increase together, we move along a straight line. Part (b) shows a positive relationship such that as the two variables increase together, we move along a curve that becomes steeper. Part (c) shows a positive relationship such that as the two variables increase together, we move along a curve that becomes flatter.

relationship between the number of miles traveled in 5 hours and speed. For example, point *a* shows us that we will travel 200 miles in 5 hours if our speed is 40 miles an hour. If we double our speed to 80 miles an hour, we will travel 400 miles in 5 hours.

Part (b) shows the relationship between distance sprinted and recovery time (the time it takes the heart rate to return to its normal resting rate). This relationship is an upward-sloping one shown by a curved line that starts out fairly flat but then becomes steeper as we move along the curve away from the origin. The reason this curve slopes upward and becomes steeper is because the additional recovery time needed from sprinting an additional 100 yards increases. It takes less than 5 minutes to recover from 100 yards but more than 10 minutes to recover from the third 100 yards.

Part (c) shows the relationship between the number of problems worked by a student and the amount of study time. This relationship is shown by an upward-sloping curved line that starts out fairly steep and becomes flatter as we move away from the origin. Study time becomes less productive as you study for more hours and become more tired.

## Variables That Move in Opposite Directions

Figure 2.7 shows relationships between things that move in opposite directions. A relationship between variables that move in opposite directions is called a **negative relationship** or an **inverse relationship**.

Part (a) shows the relationship between the number of hours available for playing squash and the number of hours for playing tennis. One extra hour spent playing tennis means one hour less playing squash and vice versa. This relationship is negative and linear.

Part (b) shows the relationship between the cost per mile traveled and the length of a journey. The longer the journey, the lower is the cost per mile. But as the journey length increases, the cost per mile decreases, and the fall in the cost is smaller, the longer the journey. This feature of the relationship is shown by the fact that the curve slopes downward, starting out steep at a short journey length and then becoming flatter as the journey length increases. This relationship arises because some of the costs are fixed,

**FIGURE 2.7**

Negative (Inverse) Relationships

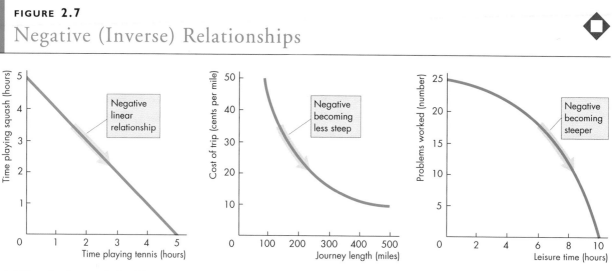

**(a) Negative linear relationship**    **(b) Negative becoming less steep**    **(c) Negative becoming steeper**

Each part of this figure shows a negative (inverse) relationship between two variables. Part (a) shows a linear relationship—as one variable increases and the other variable decreases, we move along a straight line. Part (b) shows a negative relationship such that as the journey length increases, the curve becomes less steep. Part (c) shows a negative relationship such that as leisure time increases, the curve becomes steeper.

such as auto insurance, and the fixed costs are spread over a longer journey.

Part (c) shows the relationship between the amount of leisure time and the number of problems worked by a student. Increasing leisure time produces an increasingly large reduction in the number of problems worked. This relationship is a negative one that starts out with a gentle slope at a small number of leisure hours and becomes steeper as the number of leisure hours increases. This relationship is a different view of the idea shown in Fig. 2.6(c).

## Variables That Have a Maximum or a Minimum

Many relationships in economic models have a maximum or a minimum. For example, firms try to make the maximum possible profit and to produce at the lowest possible cost. Figure 2.8 shows relationships that have a maximum or a minimum.

Part (a) shows the relationship between rainfall and wheat yield. When there is no rainfall, wheat will

not grow, so the yield is zero. As the rainfall increases up to 10 days a month, the wheat yield also increases. With 10 rainy days each month, the wheat yield reaches its maximum at 40 bushels an acre (point *a*). Rain in excess of 10 days a month starts to lower the yield of wheat. If every day is rainy, the wheat suffers from a lack of sunshine and the yield falls back to zero. This relationship is one that starts out sloping upward, reaches a maximum, and then slopes downward.

Part (b) shows the reverse case—a relationship that begins sloping downward, falls to a minimum, and then slopes upward. An example of such a relationship is the gasoline cost per mile as the speed of travel increases. At low speeds, the car is creeping along in a traffic snarl-up. The number of miles per gallon is low, so the gasoline cost per mile is high. At very high speeds, the car is traveling faster than its most efficient speed, and again the number of miles per gallon is low and the gasoline cost per mile is high. At a speed of 55 miles an hour, the gasoline cost per mile traveled is at its minimum (point *b*). This relationship is one that starts out sloping downward, reaches a minimum, and then slopes upward.

**FIGURE 2.8**
## Maximum and Minimum Points

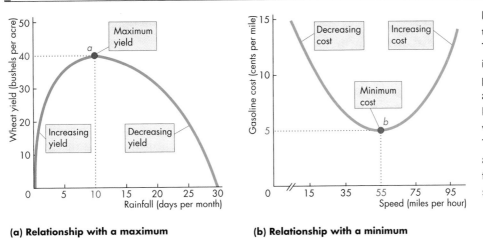

Part (a) shows a relationship that has a maximum point, *a*. The curve slopes upward as it rises to its maximum point, is flat at its maximum, and then slopes downward. Part (b) shows a relationship with a minimum point, *b*. The curve slopes downward as it falls to its minimum, is flat at its minimum, and then slopes upward.

**(a) Relationship with a maximum**   **(b) Relationship with a minimum**

### Variables That Are Unrelated

There are many situations in which no matter what happens to the value of one variable, the other variable remains constant. Sometimes we want to show the independence between two variables in a graph, and Fig. 2.9 shows two ways of achieving this.

In describing the graphs in Fig. 2.6 through 2.9, we have talked about the slopes of curves. Let's look more closely at the concept of slope.

**FIGURE 2.9**
## Variables That Are Unrelated

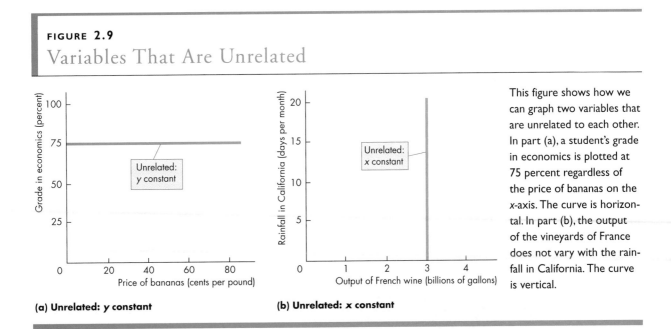

This figure shows how we can graph two variables that are unrelated to each other. In part (a), a student's grade in economics is plotted at 75 percent regardless of the price of bananas on the *x*-axis. The curve is horizontal. In part (b), the output of the vineyards of France does not vary with the rainfall in California. The curve is vertical.

**(a) Unrelated: *y* constant**   **(b) Unrelated: *x* constant**

# The Slope of a Relationship

WE CAN MEASURE THE INFLUENCE OF ONE variable on another by the slope of the relationship. The **slope** of a relationship is the change in the value of the variable measured on the $y$-axis divided by the change in the value of the variable measured on the $x$-axis. We use the Greek letter $\Delta$ (*delta*) to represent "change in." Thus $\Delta y$ means the change in the value of the variable measured on the $y$-axis, and $\Delta x$ means the change in the value of the variable measured on the $x$-axis. Therefore the slope of the relationship is

$$\Delta y \, / \, \Delta x.$$

If a large change in the variable measured on the $y$-axis ($\Delta y$) is associated with a small change in the variable measured on the $x$-axis ($\Delta x$), the slope is large and the curve is steep. If a small change in the variable measured on the $y$-axis ($\Delta y$) is associated with a large change in the variable measured on the $x$-axis ($\Delta x$), the slope is small and the curve is flat.

We can make the idea of slope sharper by doing some calculations.

## The Slope of a Straight Line

The slope of a straight line is the same regardless of where on the line you calculate it. Thus the slope of a straight line is constant. Let's calculate the slopes of the lines in Fig. 2.10. In part (a), when $x$ increases from 2 to 6, $y$ increases from 3 to 6. The change in $x$ is +4—that is, $\Delta x$ is 4. The change in $y$ is +3—that

**FIGURE 2.10**

## The Slope of a Straight Line

**(a) Positive slope**

**(b) Negative slope**

To calculate the slope of a straight line, we divide the change in the value of the variable measured on the y-axis ($\Delta y$) by the change in the value of the variable measured on the x-axis ($\Delta x$) as we move along the curve. Part (a) shows the calculation of a positive slope. When $x$ increases from 2 to 6, $\Delta x$ equals 4.

That change in $x$ brings about an increase in $y$ from 3 to 6, so $\Delta y$ equals 3. The slope ($\Delta y/\Delta x$) equals $3/4$. Part (b) shows the calculation of a negative slope. When $x$ increases from 2 to 6, $\Delta x$ equals 4. That increase in $x$ brings about a decrease in $y$ from 6 to 3, so $\Delta y$ equals $-3$. The slope ($\Delta y/\Delta x$) equals $-3/4$.

is, $\Delta y$ is 3. The slope of that line is

$$\frac{\Delta y}{\Delta x} = \frac{3}{4}.$$

In part (b), when $x$ increases from 2 to 6, $y$ decreases from 6 to 3. The change in $y$ is *minus* 3—that is, $\Delta y$ is –3. The change in $x$ is *plus* 4—that is, $\Delta x$ is 4. The slope of the curve is

$$\frac{\Delta y}{\Delta x} = \frac{-3}{4}.$$

Notice that the two slopes have the same magnitude (3/4), but the slope of the line in part (a) is positive (+3/+4 = 3/4), while that in part (b) is negative (–3/+4 = –3/4). The slope of a positive relationship is positive; the slope of a negative relationship is negative.

### The Slope of a Curved Line

The slope of a curved line is trickier. The slope of a curved line is not constant. Its slope depends on where on the line we calculate it. There are two ways to calculate the slope of a curved line: You can calculate the slope at a point, or you can calculate the slope across an arc of the line. Let's look at the two alternatives.

**Slope at a Point**    To calculate the slope at a point on a curve, you need to construct a straight line that has the same slope as the curve at the point in question. Figure 2.11 shows how this is done. Suppose you want to calculate the slope of the curve at point *a*. Place a ruler on the graph so that it touches point *a* and no other point on the curve, then draw a straight line along the edge of the ruler. The straight red line is this line, and it is the tangent to the curve at point *a*. If the ruler touches the curve only at point *a*, then the slope of the curve at point *a* must be the same as the slope of the edge of the ruler. If the curve and the ruler do not have the same slope, the line along the edge of the ruler will cut the curve instead of just touching it.

Now that you have found a straight line with the same slope as the curve at point *a*, you can calculate the slope of the curve at point *a* by calculating the slope of the straight line. Along the straight line, as $x$ increases from 0 to 4 ($\Delta x = 4$), $y$ increases from 2 to 5

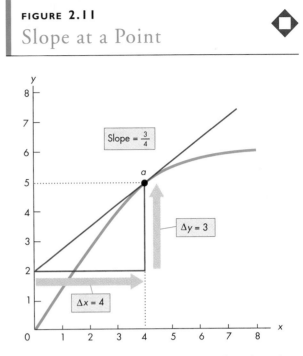

**FIGURE 2.11**

## Slope at a Point

To calculate the slope of the curve at point *a*, draw the red line that just touches the curve at *a*—the tangent. The slope of this straight line is calculated by dividing the change in *y* by the change in *x* along the line. When *x* increases from 0 to 4, $\Delta x$ equals 4. That change in *x* is associated with an increase in *y* from 2 to 5, so $\Delta y$ equals 3. The slope of the red line is 3/4. So the slope of the curve at point *a* is 3/4.

($\Delta y = 3$). Therefore the slope of the line is

$$\frac{\Delta y}{\Delta x} = \frac{3}{4}.$$

Thus the slope of the curve at point *a* is 3/4.

**Slope Across an Arc**    An arc of a curve is a piece of a curve. In Fig. 2.12, you are looking at the same curve as in Fig. 2.11. But instead of calculating the slope at point *a*, we are going to calculate the slope across the arc from *b* to *c*. You can see that the slope at *b* is greater than the slope at *c*. When we calculate the slope across an arc, we are calculating the average slope between two points. As we move along the arc from *b* to *c*, *x* increases from 3 to 5 and *y* increases from 4 to 5.5. The change in *x* is 2 ($\Delta x = 2$), and the

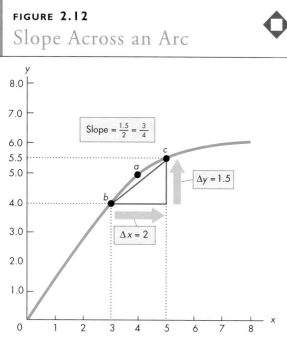

FIGURE 2.12
Slope Across an Arc

$$\text{Slope} = \frac{1.5}{2} = \frac{3}{4}$$

$\Delta y = 1.5$

$\Delta x = 2$

To calculate the average slope of the curve along the arc *bc*, draw a straight line from *b* to *c*. The slope of the line *bc* is calculated by dividing the change in *y* by the change in *x*. In moving from *b* to *c*, $\Delta x$ equals 2 and $\Delta y$ equals 1.5. The slope of the line *bc* is 1.5 divided by 2, or ¾. So the slope of the curve across the arc *bc* is ¾.

change in *y* is 1.5 ($\Delta y = 1.5$). Therefore the slope of the line is

$$\frac{\Delta y}{\Delta x} = \frac{15}{2} = \frac{3}{4}.$$

Thus the slope of the curve across the arc *bc* is ¾.

This calculation gives us the slope of the curve between points *b* and *c*. The actual slope calculated is the slope of the straight line from *b* to *c*. This slope approximates the average slope of the curve along the arc *bc*. In this particular example, the slope across the arc *bc* is identical to the slope of the curve at point *a*. But the calculation of the slope of a curve does not always work out so neatly. You might have some fun constructing counterexamples.

You now know how to make and interpret a graph. But so far, we've limited our attention to graphs of two variables. We're now going to learn how to graph more than two variables.

## Graphing Relationships Among More Than Two Variables

WE HAVE SEEN THAT WE CAN GRAPH THE relationship between two variables as a point formed by the *x*- and *y*-coordinates in a two-dimensional graph. You may be thinking that although a two-dimensional graph is informative, most of the things in which you are likely to be interested involve relationships among many variables, not just two. For example, the amount of ice cream consumed depends on the price of ice cream and the temperature. If ice cream is expensive and the temperature is low, people eat much less ice cream than when ice cream is inexpensive and the temperature is high. For any given price of ice cream, the quantity consumed varies with the temperature, and for any given temperature, the quantity of ice cream consumed varies with its price.

Figure 2.13 shows a relationship among three variables. The table shows the number of gallons of ice cream consumed each day at various temperatures and ice cream prices. How can we graph these numbers?

To graph a relationship that involves more than two variables, we use the *ceteris paribus* assumption.

**Ceteris Paribus**   The Latin phrase **ceteris paribus**, means "other things remaining the same." Every laboratory experiment is an attempt to create *ceteris paribus* and isolate the relationship of interest. We use the same method to make a graph.

Figure 2.13(a) shows an example. There, you can see what happens to the quantity of ice cream consumed when the price of ice cream varies while the temperature is held constant. The line labeled 70°F shows the relationship between ice cream consumption and the price of ice cream if the temperature is 70°F. The numbers used to plot that line are those in the third column of the table in Fig. 2.13. For example, if the temperature is 70°F, 10 gallons are consumed when the price is 60¢ a scoop, and 18 gallons are consumed when the price is 30¢ a scoop. The curve labeled 90°F shows consumption as the price varies if the temperature is 90°F.

We can also show the relationship between ice cream consumption and temperature while the price of ice cream remains constant, as shown in Fig. 2.13(b). The curve labeled 60¢ shows how the consumption

**FIGURE 2.13**

Graphing a Relationship Among Three Variables

**(a) Price and consumption at a given temperature**

**(b) Temperature and consumption at a given price**

**(c) Temperature and price at a given consumption**

The quantity of ice cream consumed depends on its price and the temperature. The table gives some hypothetical numbers that tell us how many gallons of ice cream are consumed each day at different prices and different temperatures. For example, if the price is 60¢ a scoop and the temperature is 70°F, 10 gallons of ice cream are consumed. This set of values is highlighted in the table and each part of the figure. To graph a relationship among three variables, the value of one variable is held constant. Part (a) shows the relationship between price and consumption when temperature is held constant. One curve holds temperature at 90°F and the other at 70°F. Part (b) shows the relationship between temperature and consumption when the price is held constant. One curve holds the price at 60¢ a scoop and the other at 15¢ a scoop. Part (c) shows the relationship between temperature and price when consumption is held constant. One curve holds consumption at 10 gallons and the other at 7 gallons.

| Price (cents per scoop) | Ice cream consumption (gallons per day) | | | |
|---|---|---|---|---|
| | **30°F** | **50°F** | **70°F** | **90°F** |
| 15 | 12 | 18 | 25 | 50 |
| 30 | 10 | 12 | 18 | 37 |
| 45 | 7 | 10 | 13 | 27 |
| **60** | 5 | 7 | **10** | 20 |
| 75 | 3 | 5 | 7 | 14 |
| 90 | 2 | 3 | 5 | 10 |
| 105 | 1 | 2 | 3 | 6 |

of ice cream varies with the temperature when ice cream costs 60¢ a scoop, and a second curve shows the relationship when ice cream costs 15¢ a scoop. For example, at 60¢ a scoop, 10 gallons are consumed when the temperature is 70°F and 20 gallons when the temperature is 90°F.

Figure 2.13(c) shows the combinations of temperature and price that result in a constant consumption of ice cream. One curve shows the combination that results in 10 gallons a day being consumed, and the other shows the combination that results

in 7 gallons a day being consumed. A high price and a high temperature lead to the same consumption as a lower price and a lower temperature. For example, 10 gallons of ice cream are consumed at 90°F and 90¢ a scoop, at 70°F and 60¢ a scoop, and at 50°F and 45¢ a scoop.

◆ With what you have learned about graphs, you can move forward with your study of economics. There are no graphs in this book that are more complicated than those that have been explained here.

## SUMMARY

## Key Points

### Graphing Data (pp. 26–30)

- Time-series graphs show trends, cycles, and other fluctuations in economic data.
- Scatter diagrams show the relationship between two variables. They show whether two variables are positively related, negatively related, or unrelated.
- Cross-section graphs show how variables change across the members of a population.

### Graphs Used in Economic Models (pp. 30–33)

- Graphs are used to show relationships among variables in economic models.
- Relationships can be positive (an upward-sloping curve), negative (a downward-sloping curve), positive and then negative (have a maximum point), negative and then positive (have a minimum point), or unrelated (a horizontal or vertical curve).

### The Slope of a Relationship (pp. 34–36)

- The slope of a relationship is calculated as the change in the value of the variable measured on the $y$-axis divided by the change in the value of the variable measured on the $x$-axis—that is, $\Delta y/\Delta x$.
- A straight line has a constant slope.
- A curved line has a varying slope. To calculate the slope of a curved line, we calculate the slope at a point or across an arc.

### Graphing Relationships Among More Than Two Variables (pp. 36–37)

- To graph a relationship among more than two variables, we hold constant the values of all the variables except two.
- We then plot the value of one of the variables against the value of another.

## Key Figures

## Key Terms

## QUESTIONS

1. What are the three types of graphs used to show economic data?
2. Give an example of a time-series graph.
3. List three things that a time-series graph shows quickly and easily.
4. Give three examples, different from those in the chapter, of scatter diagrams that show a positive relationship, a negative relationship, and no relationship.
5. Draw some graphs to show the relationships between two variables:
   a.   That move in the same direction.
   b.   That move in opposite directions.
   c.   That have a maximum.
   d.   That have a minimum.
6. Which of the relationships in question 5 is a positive relationship and which a negative relationship?
7. What are the two ways of calculating the slope of a curved line?
8. How do we graph a relationship among more than two variables?

## PROBLEMS

🖥 1. The official inflation rate in the United States and the interest rate on U.S. Treasury bills between 1976 and 1996 were as follows:

| Year | Inflation rate | Interest rate |
| --- | --- | --- |
| | (percent per year) | |
| 1976 | 5.8 | 5.0 |
| 1977 | 6.5 | 5.3 |
| 1978 | 7.6 | 7.2 |
| 1979 | 11.3 | 10.0 |
| 1980 | 13.5 | 11.5 |
| 1981 | 10.3 | 14.0 |
| 1982 | 6.2 | 10.7 |
| 1983 | 3.2 | 8.6 |
| 1984 | 4.3 | 9.6 |
| 1985 | 3.6 | 7.5 |
| 1986 | 1.9 | 6.0 |
| 1987 | 3.6 | 5.8 |
| 1988 | 4.1 | 6.7 |
| 1989 | 4.8 | 8.1 |
| 1990 | 5.4 | 7.5 |
| 1991 | 4.2 | 5.4 |
| 1992 | 3.0 | 3.4 |
| 1993 | 3.0 | 3.0 |
| 1994 | 2.6 | 4.3 |
| 1995 | 2.5 | 5.5 |
| 1996 | 3.3 | 5.0 |

a. Draw a time-series graph of the inflation rate and use your graph to determine (i) the year in which inflation was highest, (ii) the year in which it was lowest, (iii) the years in which it increased, (iv) the years in which it decreased, (v) the year in which it increased most, and (vi) the year in which it decreased most.

b. What have been the main trends in U.S. inflation?

🖥 2. Use the data in problem 1.

a. Draw a time-series graph of the interest rate and use your graph to determine (i) the year in which the interest rate was highest, (ii) the year in which it was lowest, (iii) the years in which it increased, (iv) the years in which it decreased, (v) the year in which it increased most, and (vi) the year in which it decreased most.

b. What have been the main trends in the interest rate?

🖥 3. Use the data in problem 1.

a. Draw a scatter diagram to show the relationship between the inflation rate and the interest rate.

b. Describe the relationship, if one exists, between the inflation rate and the interest rate.

🖥 4. Use the information in the following table to draw a graph that shows the relationship between two variables x and y.

| x | y |
| --- | --- |
| 0 | 0 |
| 1 | 1 |
| 2 | 4 |
| 3 | 9 |
| 4 | 16 |
| 5 | 25 |
| 6 | 36 |
| 7 | 49 |
| 8 | 64 |

a. Is the relationship between x and y positive or negative?

b. Does the slope of the relationship increase or decrease as the value of x increases?

c. Try to think of some possible economic relationships that might be similar to this one.

🖥 5. Use the information in the following table to draw a graph that shows the relationship between two variables x and y.

| x | y |
| --- | --- |
| 0 | 50 |
| 1 | 48 |
| 2 | 44 |
| 3 | 32 |
| 4 | 16 |
| 5 | 0 |

a. Is the relationship between x and y positive or negative?

b. Does the slope of the relationship increase or decrease as the value of x increases?

c.  Try to think of some possible economic relationships that might be similar to this one.

6.  Use the data in problem 5 to:
a.  Calculate the slope of the relationship between $x$ and $y$ when $x$ equals 4.
b.  Calculate the slope of the arc when $x$ increases from 3 to 4.
c.  Calculate the slope of the arc when $x$ increases from 4 to 5.
d.  Calculate the slope of the arc when $x$ increases from 3 to 5.
e.  What do you notice that is interesting about your answers to (b), (c), and (d) compared with your answer to (a)?

7.  Use the information in the following figure to calculate the slope of the relationship shown at point $a$.

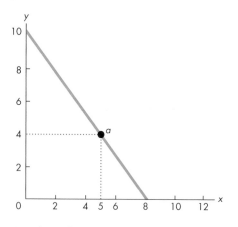

8.  Use the information in the following figure to calculate:
a.  The slope of the relationship shown at point $a$.
b.  The slope of the relationship shown at point $b$.
c.  The slope of the relationship across the arc $ab$.
d.  Can you find a point between $a$ and $b$ that has the same slope of the arc $ab$? Approximately, what are the values of $x$ and $y$ for this point?

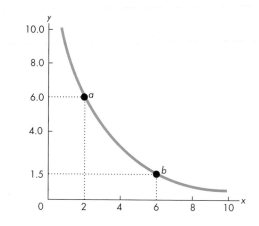

9.  The following table gives data on the price of a balloon ride, the temperature, and the number of rides taken per day.

| Price | Balloon rides (number per day) | | |
| (dollars per ride) | 50°C | 70°C | 90°C |
|---|---|---|---|
| 5.00 | 32 | 40 | 50 |
| 10.00 | 27 | 32 | 40 |
| 15.00 | 18 | 27 | 32 |
| 20.00 | 10 | 18 | 27 |

Draw graphs that show the relationship among:
a.  The price and the number of rides taken, holding the temperature constant.
b.  The number of rides taken and temperature, holding the price constant.
c.  The temperature and price, holding the number of rides taken constant.

10. Visit the Parkin Home Page on the World Wide Web (at http://hepg.awl.com/parkin/econ100).
a.  Use the link provided to find data for the latest twelve months on the Consumer Price Index (CPI).
b.  Make some graphs to show whether the CPI is rising or falling and whether its rate of rise or fall is increasing or decreasing.
c.  Write a brief description of the data and draw some conclusions about what your findings mean for you and your family.

# 3

# The Economic Problem

We live in a style that surprises our grandparents and would have astonished our great-grandparents. Most of us live in more spacious homes than they did. We eat more, grow taller, and are even born larger than they were. Video games, cellular phones, gene splices, and personal computers did not exist even 20 years ago. But today it is hard to imagine life without these things. Economic growth has made us richer than our grandparents. And we are not alone in experiencing an expansion in the goods and services that we consume. Many nations around the world are not only sharing our experience: They are setting the pace. Hong Kong, Taiwan, Singapore, Korea, and China are expanding at unheard of rates. But economic growth does not liberate us from scarcity. Why not? Why, despite our immense wealth, must we still make choices and face costs? Why are there no "free lunches"? ◆ We see an incredible amount of specialization and trade in the world. Each one of us specializes in a particular job—as a lawyer, a car maker, a home maker. We have become so specialized that one farm worker can feed 100 people. Less than one sixth of the U.S. work force is employed in manufacturing. More than half of the work force is employed in wholesale and retail trade, banking and finance, government, and other services. Why do we specialize? How do we benefit from specialization and trade? ◆ Over many centuries, institutions and social arrangements have evolved that we take for granted. One of them is property rights and the political and legal system that protects them. Another is markets. Why have these social arrangements evolved? How do they increase production? ◆ These are the questions that we study in this chapter. We begin with the core economic problem: scarcity and choice and the concept of the production possibility frontier. We then learn about the central idea of economics—efficiency. We also discover how we can expand production by accumulating capital and by specializing and trading. ◆ What you will learn in this chapter is the foundation on which all economics is built. You will receive big dividends from a careful study of this material.

## Making the Most of It

## After studying this chapter, you will be able to:

- Explain the fundamental economic problem

- Define the production possibility frontier

- Define and calculate opportunity cost

- Explain the conditions in which resources are used efficiently

- Explain how economic growth expands production possibilities

- Explain how specialization and trade expand production possibilities

## Resources and Wants

TWO FACTS DOMINATE OUR LIVES:

- We have limited resources.
- We have unlimited wants.

These two facts define **scarcity**, a condition in which the resources available are insufficient to satisfy people's wants.

Scarcity is a universal fact of life. It confronts each one of us individually, and it confronts our families, local communities, and nations.

The fundamental economic problem is to use our limited resources to produce the items that we value most highly. **Economics** is the study of the *choices* people make to cope with *scarcity*. It is the study of how we each individually try to get the most out of our own limited resources and of how in that endeavor, we interact with each other. Let's look a bit more closely at our limited resources and unlimited wants.

### Limited Resources

The resources that can be used to produce goods and services are grouped into four categories:

- Labor
- Land
- Capital
- Entrepreneurship

**Labor** is the time and effort that we devote to producing goods and services. It includes the physical and mental work of people who make cars and cola, gum and glue, wallpaper and watering cans.

**Land** is the gifts of nature that we use to produce goods and services. It includes the air, the water, and the land surface as well as the minerals that lie beneath the surface of the earth.

**Capital** is the goods that we have produced and that we can now use to produce other goods and services. It includes interstate highways, buildings, dams and power projects, airports and jumbo jets, car production lines, shirt factories, and cookie shops.

Capital also includes **human capital**, which is the knowledge and skill that people obtain from education and on-the-job training. You are building human capital right now as you work on your economics course and other subjects. And your human capital will continue to grow when you get a full-time job and become better at it. Human capital improves the *quality* of labor.

**Entrepreneurship** is the resource that organizes labor, land, and capital. Entrepreneurs come up with new ideas about what, how, when, and where to produce, make business decisions, and bear the risks that arise from these decisions.

Our limited resources are converted into goods and services by using the technologies available. These technologies are limited by our knowledge—our human capital—and by our other resources.

### Unlimited Wants

Our wants are limited only by our imaginations and are effectively unlimited. We want food and drink, clothing, housing, education, and health care. We want some of these things so badly that we call them *necessities*. But we also want many other things. We want cars and airplanes, movie theaters and videos, popcorn and soda, Walkmans and tapes, books and magazines, restaurant meals, vacations at the beach and in the mountains, music and poetry, and instant telecommunication across the globe.

Some of these wants are less pressing than others, but they are all wants. We even want things that are technologically impossible today but about which we fantasize. We want to live longer and healthier lives. Some of us want to hitchhike the galaxy and be beamed around the universe.

Because our wants exceed our resources, we must make choices. We must rank our wants and decide which wants to satisfy and which to leave unsatisfied. We try to get the most out of our resources.

### R E V I E W

- Economics is the study of the choices that people make to cope with scarcity.
- Our limited resources are labor, land, capital, and entrepreneurship.
- Our unlimited wants must be ranked, and we must choose which wants to satisfy.
- In making choices, we try to get the most out of our resources.

We'll begin our study of the choices people make by looking at the limits to production and at a fundamental implication of choice—opportunity cost.

# Resources, Production Possibilities, and Opportunity Cost

EVERY WORKING DAY, IN MINES, FACTORIES, shops, and offices and on farms and construction sites across the United States, 125 million people produce a vast variety of goods and services valued at around $27 billion. The quantities of goods and services that can be produced are limited by our available resources and by technology. That limit is described by the production possibility frontier.

The **production possibility frontier** (*PPF*) is the boundary between those combinations of goods and services that can be produced and those that cannot.

To illustrate the production possibility frontier in a graph, we focus our attention on two goods at a time. In focusing on two goods, we hold the quantities produced of all the other goods and services constant—a device called the *ceteris paribus* assumption. That is, we look at a *model* of the economy in which everything remains the same except for the production of the two goods we are currently considering.

Let's look at the production possibility frontier for two goods that most students buy: bottles of soda and blank audio tapes.

## Production Possibility Frontier

The *production possibility frontier* for soda and tapes shows the limits to the production of these two goods, given the total resources available to produce them. Figure 3.1 shows this production possibility frontier. The table lists some combinations of the quantities of tapes and soda that can be produced given the resources available, and the figure graphs these combinations. The quantity of tapes produced is shown on the *x*-axis, and the quantity of soda produced is shown on the *y*-axis. (The numbers are hypothetical.)

Because the *PPF* shows the *limits* to production, we cannot attain the points outside the frontier. They are points that describe wants that cannot be satisfied. We can produce at all the points *inside* the *PPF* and *on* the *PPF*. They are attainable points.

Suppose that in a typical month, 4 million tapes and 5 million bottles of soda are produced. Figure 3.1 shows this combination as point *e* and as possibility *e* in the table. Figure 3.1 also shows other production possibilities. For example, we might stop

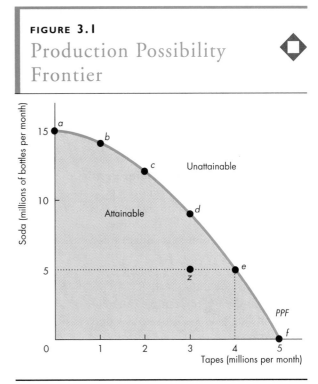

**FIGURE 3.1**

## Production Possibility Frontier

| Possibility | Tapes (millions per month) | | Soda (millions of bottles per month) |
| --- | --- | --- | --- |
| a | 0 | and | 15 |
| b | 1 | and | 14 |
| c | 2 | and | 12 |
| d | 3 | and | 9 |
| e | 4 | and | 5 |
| f | 5 | and | 0 |

The table lists six points on the production possibility frontier for tapes and soda. Row *a* tells us that if we produce no tapes, the maximum quantity of soda we can produce is 15 million bottles a month. The rows of the table are graphed as points *a, b, c, d, e,* and *f* in the figure. The line passing through these points is the production possibility frontier (*PPF*). It separates the attainable from the unattainable. We can produce at any point inside the orange area or on the frontier. Points outside the frontier are unattainable. Points inside the frontier such as point z are inefficient because it is possible to use the available resources to produce more of either or both goods.

producing tapes and move all the people who produce them into bottling soda. This case is shown as point *a* in the figure and possibility *a* in the table.

The quantity of soda produced increases to 15 million bottles a month, and tape production dries up. Alternatively, we might close down the bottling plants and switch all the resources into producing tapes. In this situation, we produce 5 million tapes a month. This case is shown as point *f* in the figure and possibility *f* in the table.

## Production Efficiency

We achieve **production efficiency** if we cannot produce more of one good without producing less of some other good. When production is efficient, we are at a point *on* the *PPF*. If we are at a point *inside* the *PPF*, such as point *z*, production is *inefficient* because we have some *unused* resources or we have some *misallocated* resources or both.

Resources are unused when they are idle but could be working. For example, we might leave some of the bottling plants idle or some workers might be unemployed.

Resources are *misallocated* when they are assigned to tasks for which they are not the best match. For example, we might assign skilled bottling machine operators to work in a tape factory and skilled tape makers to work in a bottling plant. We could get more tapes *and* more bottles of soda from these same workers if we reassigned them to the tasks that more closely match their skills.

If we produce at a point inside the *PPF* such as *z*, we can use our resources more efficiently to produce more tapes, more soda, or more of *both* tapes and soda. But if we produce at a point *on* the *PPF*, we are using our resources efficiently and we can produce more of one good only if we produce less of the other. We face a *tradeoff*.

## Tradeoff

On the production possibility frontier, every choice involves a **tradeoff**—we must give up something to get something else. On the *PPF* in Fig. 3.1, we must give up some soda to get more tapes (or give up some tapes to get more soda).

Tradeoffs arise in every imaginable real-world situation. At any given point in time, we have a fixed amount of labor, land, capital, and entrepreneurship. By using our available technologies, we can employ these resources to produce goods and services. But we are limited in what we can produce. This limit defines a boundary between what we can attain and what we

cannot attain. This boundary is the real-world's production possibility frontier, and it defines the tradeoffs that we must make. On our real-world *PPF*, we can produce more of any one good or service only if we produce less of some other goods or services.

When doctors say we must spend more on AIDS and cancer research, they are suggesting a tradeoff: more medical research for less of some other things. When Bill Clinton says he wants to spend more on education and health care, he is suggesting a tradeoff: more education and health care for less national defense or less private spending (because of higher taxes). When your parents say that you should study more, they are suggesting a tradeoff: more study time for less leisure or less sleep. When an environmental group argues for less logging, it is suggesting a tradeoff: greater conservation of endangered wildlife for less paper.

All tradeoffs involve a cost—an opportunity cost.

## Opportunity Cost

The **opportunity cost** of an action is the highest-valued alternative forgone. We can make the concept of opportunity cost more precise by using the production possibility frontier. Along the frontier, there are only two goods, so there is only one alternative forgone—some quantity of the other good. Given our current resources and technology, we can produce more tapes only if we produce fewer bottles of soda. The opportunity cost of producing an additional tape is the number of bottles of soda we must forgo. Similarly, the opportunity cost of producing an additional bottle of soda is the quantity of tapes we must forgo.

For example, at point *c* in Fig. 3.1, we produce fewer tapes and more bottles of soda than we do at point *d*. If we choose point *d* over point *c*, the additional 1 million tapes *cost* 3 million bottles of soda. One tape costs 3 bottles of soda.

We can also work out the opportunity cost of choosing point *c* over point *d* in Fig. 3.1. If we move from point *d* to point *c*, the quantity of soda produced increases by 3 million bottles and the quantity of tapes produced decreases by 1 million. So if we choose point *c* over point *d*, the additional 3 million bottles of soda *cost* 1 million tapes. One bottle of soda costs $1/3$ of a tape.

**Opportunity Cost Is a Ratio**  Opportunity cost is a ratio. It is the decrease in the quantity produced of one good divided by the increase in the quantity produced of another good as we move along the production possibility frontier.

Because opportunity cost is a ratio, the opportunity cost of producing soda is equal to the *inverse* of the opportunity cost of producing tapes. Check this proposition by returning to the calculations we've just worked through. When we move along the *PPF* from *c* to *d*, the opportunity cost of a tape is 3 bottles of soda. The inverse of 3 is $1/3$, so if we decrease the production of tapes and increase the production of soda by moving from *d* to *c*, the opportunity cost of a bottle of soda must be $1/3$ of a tape. You can check that this number is correct. If we move from *d* to *c*, we produce 3 million more bottles of soda and 1 million fewer tapes. Because 3 million bottles cost 1 million tapes, the opportunity cost of 1 bottle of soda is $1/3$ of a tape.

**Increasing Opportunity Cost** The opportunity cost of a tape increases as the quantity of tapes produced increases. Also, the opportunity cost of soda increases as the quantity of soda produced increases. This phenomenon of increasing opportunity cost is reflected in the *shape* of the *PPF*—it is bowed outward.

When a large quantity of soda and a small quantity of tapes are produced—between points *a* and *b* in Fig. 3.1—the frontier has a gentle slope. A given increase in the quantity of tapes *costs* a small decrease in the quantity of soda, so the opportunity cost of a tape is a small amount of soda.

When a large quantity of tapes and a small quantity of soda are produced—between points *e* and *f* in Fig. 3.1—the frontier is steep. A given increase in the quantity of tapes *costs* a large decrease in the quantity of soda, so the opportunity cost of a tape is a large amount of soda.

The production possibility frontier is bowed outward because resources are not all equally productive in all activities. Production workers with many years of experience working for PepsiCo are very good at producing soda but not very good at making tapes. So if we move these people from PepsiCo to 3M, we get a small increase in the quantity of tapes but a large decrease in the quantity of soda.

Similarly, plastics engineers and production workers who have spent many years working for 3M are good at producing tapes but not so good at bottling soda. So if we move these people from 3M to PepsiCo, we get a small increase in the quantity of soda but a large decrease in the quantity of tapes.

The more we try to produce of either good, the less productive are the additional resources we use to produce that good and the larger is the opportunity cost of a unit of that good.

**Increasing Opportunity Costs Are Everywhere** Just about every activity that you can think of is one with an *increasing* opportunity cost. Two examples are the production of food and the production of health-care services. We allocate the most skillful farmers and the most fertile land to the production of food. And we allocate the best doctors and least fertile land to the production of health-care services. If we shift fertile land and tractors away from farming to hospitals and ambulances and ask farmers to become hospital porters, the production of food drops drastically and the increase in the production of health-care services is small. The opportunity cost of a unit of health-care services rises. Similarly, if we shift our resources away from health care toward farming, we must use more doctors and nurses as farmers and more hospitals as hydroponic tomato factories. The decrease in the production of health-care services is large, but the increase in food production is small. The opportunity cost of a unit of food rises.

This example is extreme and unlikely, but these same considerations apply to any pair of goods that you can imagine: housing and diamonds, wheelchairs and golf carts, pet food and breakfast cereals.

---

## R E V I E W

- The production possibility frontier (*PPF*) is the boundary between production levels we can attain and cannot attain.

- When we produce at a point on the *PPF*, production is efficient.

- In choosing among points on the *PPF*, we face a tradeoff of one good for another.

- Every tradeoff involves an opportunity cost—the highest-valued alternative forgone.

- As we move along the *PPF* and produce more of one good, the opportunity cost of a unit of that good increases.

We've seen that production possibilities are limited by the production possibility frontier. And we've seen that production on the *PPF* is efficient. But there are many possible quantities we can produce on the *PPF*. How do we choose among them? How do we know which point on the frontier is the best one?

## Using Resources Efficiently

How do we decide whether to spend more on AIDS and cancer research? Whether to vote for an education and health-care package or a tax cut? Whether to join an environmental group and press for a greater conservation of endangered wildlife?

These are big questions that have enormous consequences. But the essence of the answer can be seen by thinking about the simpler question: How do we decide how many tapes and how many bottles of soda to produce?

We decide by calculating and comparing two numbers:

■ Marginal cost
■ Marginal benefit

### Marginal Cost

**Marginal cost** is the opportunity cost of producing *one more unit* of a good or service. You've seen how we can calculate opportunity cost as we move along the production possibility frontier. The marginal cost of a tape is the opportunity cost of *one* tape—the quantity of soda that must be given up to get one more tape—as we move along the *PPF*.

Figure 3.2 illustrates the marginal cost of a tape. If all the available resources are used to produce soda, 15 million bottles of soda and no tapes are produced. If we now decide to produce 1 million tapes, how much soda do we have to give up? You can see the answer in Fig. 3.2(a). To produce 1 million more tapes, we move from *a* to *b* and the quantity of soda decreases by 1 million bottles to 14 million a month. So the opportunity cost of the first 1 million tapes is 1 million bottles of soda.

If we decide to increase the production of tapes to 2 million, how much soda must we give up? This time, we move from *b* to *c* and the quantity of soda decreases by 2 million bottles. So the second million tapes costs 2 million bottles of soda.

You can repeat this calculation for an increase in the quantity of tapes produced from 2 million to 3 million, then to 4 million, and finally to 5 million. Figure 3.2(a) shows these opportunity costs as a series of steps. Each additional million tapes costs more bottles of soda than the preceding million did.

We've just calculated the opportunity cost of tapes in blocks of 1 million at a time and generated

FIGURE **3.2**

## Opportunity Cost and Marginal Cost

Increasing opportunity cost of tapes ...

**(a) *PPF* and opportunity cost**

... means increasing marginal cost of tapes

**(b) Marginal cost**

Opportunity cost is measured along the *PPF* in part (a). If the production of tapes increases from zero to 1 million, the opportunity cost of the first 1 million tapes is 1 million bottles of soda. If the production of tapes increases from 1 million to 2 million, the opportunity cost of the second 1 million tapes is 2 million bottles of soda. The opportunity cost of tapes increases as the production of tapes increases. Marginal cost is the opportunity cost of producing one more unit. Part (b) shows the marginal cost of a tape as the *MC* curve.

the steps in Fig. 3.2(a). If we now calculate the opportunity cost of tapes one at a time, we obtain the *marginal cost* of a tape. In Fig. 3.2(b), the line labeled *MC* shows the marginal cost of a tape. The marginal cost of each additional tape in terms of forgone soda increases, so the marginal cost curve slopes upward.

To use our resources efficiently, we must compare the marginal cost of a tape with its marginal benefit. Let's now look at marginal benefit.

## Marginal Benefit

The **marginal benefit** is the benefit that a person receives from consuming one more unit of a good or service. The marginal benefit from a good or service is measured as the maximum amount that a person is willing to pay for one more unit of it. It is a general principle that the more we have of any good or service, the smaller is our marginal benefit from it—the principle of *decreasing marginal benefit*.

To understand the principle of decreasing marginal benefit, think about your own marginal benefit from tapes. If tapes are very hard to come by and you can buy only one or two a year, you might be willing to pay a high price to get one more tape. But if tapes are readily available and you have as many as you can use, you are willing to pay almost nothing for yet one more tape.

In everyday life, we think of prices as money—as dollars per tape. But you have just been thinking about cost as opportunity cost, which is not a dollar cost but a cost in terms of a forgone alternative. You can also think about prices in the same terms. The price you pay for something is not the number of dollars you give up, but the goods and services that you would have bought with those dollars.

To see this idea more clearly, let's continue with the example we used to study the *PPF* and opportunity cost: tapes and soda. The marginal benefit from a tape can be expressed as the number of bottles of soda that a person is willing to forgo to get a tape. This amount decreases as the quantity of tapes available increases. Figure 3.3 illustrates the marginal benefit from tapes. (Again, the numbers are hypothetical.)

In row *a*, 0.5 million tapes a month are available and at that quantity, people are willing to pay 5 bottles of soda for a tape. As the quantity of tapes available increases, the amount that people are willing to pay for a tape falls. When 4.5 million tapes a month are available, people are willing to pay only 1 bottle of soda for a tape.

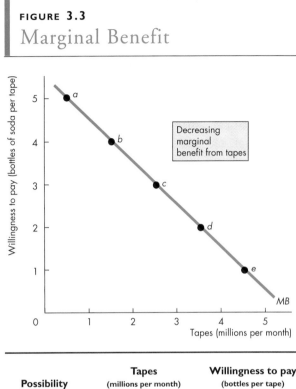

**FIGURE 3.3**

## Marginal Benefit

| Possibility | Tapes (millions per month) | Willingness to pay (bottles per tape) |
|---|---|---|
| a | 0.5 | 5 |
| b | 1.5 | 4 |
| c | 2.5 | 3 |
| d | 3.5 | 2 |
| e | 4.5 | 1 |

The fewer the number of tapes available, the more soda people are willing to give up to get an additional tape. If only 0.5 million tapes a month are available, people are willing to pay 5 bottles of soda for a tape. But if 4.5 million tapes a month are available, people will pay only 1 bottle of soda for a tape. Decreasing marginal benefit is a universal feature of people's preferences.

The marginal benefit from a tape and the opportunity cost of a tape are both measured in bottles of soda. But they are not the same concept. The *opportunity cost* of a tape is the amount of soda that people *must forgo* to get another tape. The *marginal benefit* from a tape is the amount of soda that people *are willing to forgo* to get another tape.

You now know how to calculate marginal cost and marginal benefit. Let's use these concepts to discover the efficient quantity of tapes to produce.

## Efficient Use of Resources

Resource use is **efficient** when we produce the goods and services that we value most highly. That is, when we are using our resources efficiently, we cannot produce more of any good without giving up something that we value even more highly.

We always choose *at the margin*. We compare marginal cost and marginal benefit. If the marginal benefit from a good exceeds the marginal cost of the good, we increase production of that good. If marginal cost exceeds marginal benefit, we decrease production of the good. And if marginal benefit equals marginal cost, we stick with the current production.

This principle is just like the decisions you make when you go shopping. You have $10 to spend and are thinking about buying a CD or a box of floppy disks. You figure that you will get more value from the CD than from the floppy disks, so you spend your $10 on the CD. You have allocated scarce resources to their highest-value use. The marginal benefit from a CD is greater than (or equal to) its marginal cost, the box of floppy disks. The marginal benefit from a box of floppy disks is less than its marginal cost. No matter what the good or service, if you can afford it and you think it is worth the price, you buy it. If you think it not worth its price, you pass it up.

We can illustrate an efficient use of resources by continuing to use the example of soda and tapes. Figure 3.4 shows the marginal cost and marginal benefit of tapes. Suppose we produce 1.5 million tapes a month. The marginal cost of a tape is 2 bottles of soda. But the marginal benefit from a tape is 4 bottles of soda. Because someone values an additional tape more highly than it costs to produce, we can get more value from our resources by moving some of them out of soda production and into tape production.

Now suppose we produce 3.5 million tapes a month. The marginal cost of a tape is now 4 bottles of soda. But the marginal benefit from a tape is only 2 bottles of soda. Because an additional tape costs more to produce than anyone thinks it is worth, we can get more value from our resources by moving some of them away from tape production and into soda production.

But suppose we produce 2.5 million tapes a month. Marginal cost and marginal benefit are now equal at 3 bottles of soda. This allocation of resources between tapes and soda is efficient. If more tapes are produced, the forgone soda is worth more than the additional tapes. If fewer tapes are produced, the forgone tapes are worth more than the additional soda.

### FIGURE 3.4
## Efficient Use of Resources

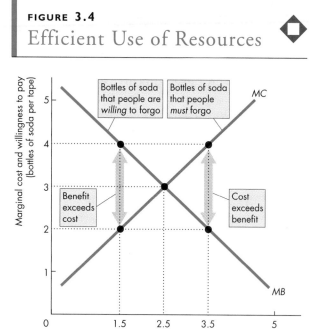

The greater the quantity of tapes produced, the smaller is the marginal benefit (*MB*) from a tape—the fewer bottles of soda people are willing to give up to get an additional tape. But the greater the quantity of tapes produced, the greater is the marginal cost (*MC*) of a tape—the more bottles of soda people must give up to get an additional tape. When marginal benefit equals marginal cost, resources are being used efficiently.

### R E V I E W

■ The marginal cost of a good or service is the opportunity cost of increasing its production by one unit.

■ The marginal benefit from a good or service is the maximum amount that someone is willing to pay for an additional unit.

■ Resources are used efficiently when they cannot be reallocated to increase the value of production.

■ When marginal benefit equals marginal cost, resources are used efficiently.

You now understand the limits to production and the conditions under which resources are used efficiently. Your next task is to study the expansion of production possibilities.

# Economic Growth

DURING THE PAST 30 YEARS, PRODUCTION IN THE United States has expanded by 80 percent. Such an expansion of production is called **economic growth**. Can economic growth enable us to overcome scarcity and avoid opportunity cost? You are going to see that economic growth does not overcome scarcity and avoid opportunity cost. You are also going to see that the faster we make production grow, the greater is the opportunity cost of economic growth.

## The Cost of Economic Growth

Two key factors influence economic growth: technological change and capital accumulation. **Technological change** is the development of new goods and of better ways of producing goods and services. **Capital accumulation** is the growth of capital resources.

As a consequence of technological change and capital accumulation, we have an enormous quantity of cars that enable us to produce more transportation than when we had only horses and carriages; we have satellites that make global communications possible on a scale that is much larger than that produced by the earlier cable technology. But new technologies and new capital have an opportunity cost. In order to use resources in research and development and to produce new capital, we must decrease our production of consumption goods and services. Let's look at this opportunity cost.

Instead of studying the *PPF* of tapes and soda, we'll hold the quantity of soda produced constant and examine the *PPF* for tapes and tape-making machines. Figure 3.5 shows this *PPF* as the blue curve *abc*. If we devote no resources to producing tape-making machines, we produce at point *a*. If we produce 3 million tapes a month, we can produce 6 tape-making machines at point *b*. If we produce no tapes, we can produce 10 tape-making machines a month at point *c*.

The amount by which our production possibilities expand depends on the resources we devote to technological change and capital accumulation. If we devote no resources to this activity (point *a*), the frontier remains at *abc*—the blue curve in Fig. 3.5. If we cut the current production of tapes and produce 6 machines a month (point *b*), then in the future, we'll have more capital and our *PPF* rotates outward to the

## FIGURE 3.5

## Economic Growth

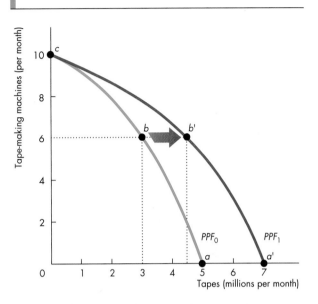

$PPF_0$ shows the limits to the production of tapes and tape-making equipment, with the production of all other goods and services remaining constant. If we devote no resources to producing tape-making machines and produce 5 million tapes a month, we remain stuck at point *a*. But if we decrease tape production to 3 million a month and produce 6 tape-making machines a month, at point *b*, our production possibilities will expand. After a year, the production possibility frontier shifts outward to $PPF_1$ and we can produce at point *b'*, a point outside the original *PPF*. We can shift the *PPF* outward, but we cannot avoid opportunity cost. The opportunity cost of producing more tapes in the future is fewer tapes today.

position shown by the red curve. The fewer resources we devote to producing tapes and the more resources we devote to producing machines, the greater is the expansion of our production possibilities.

Economic growth is not free. To make it happen, we devote resources to producing new machines and less to producing tapes. In Fig. 3.5, we move from *a* to *b*. There is no free lunch. The opportunity cost of more tapes in the future is fewer tapes today. Also, economic growth is no magic formula for abolishing scarcity. On the new production possibility frontier, we continue to face opportunity costs.

The ideas about economic growth that we have explored in the setting of the audio tape industry also apply to nations. Let's look at two examples.

## Economic Growth in the United States and Hong Kong

If as a nation we devote all our resources to producing consumer goods and none to research and capital accumulation, our production possibilities in the future will be the same as they are today. To expand our production possibilities in the future, we must devote fewer resources to producing consumption goods and some resources to accumulating capital and developing technologies so we can produce more consumption goods in the future. The decrease in today's consumption is the opportunity cost of an increase in future consumption.

The experiences of the United States and Hong Kong make a striking example of the effects of our choices on the rate of economic growth. In 1960, the production possibilities per person in the United States were more than four times those in Hong Kong (see Fig. 3.6). The United States devoted one fifth of its resources to accumulating capital and the other four fifths to consumption. In 1960, the United States was at point *a* on its *PPF*. Hong Kong devoted one third of its resources to accumulating capital and two thirds to consumption. In 1960, Hong Kong was at point *a* on its *PPF*.

Since 1960, both countries have experienced economic growth, but growth in Hong Kong has been more rapid than growth in the United States. Because Hong Kong devoted a bigger fraction of its resources to accumulating capital, its production possibilities expanded more quickly.

In 1997, the *PPF* per person in the United States and Hong Kong were similar. If Hong Kong continues to devote a similar proportion of its resources to accumulating capital (at point *b* on the 1997 *PPF*), it will continue to grow more rapidly than the United States and its frontier will move out beyond our own. But if Hong Kong increases its consumption and decreases its capital accumulation (moving to point *c* on its 1997 production possibility frontier), then its rate of economic growth will slow.

The United States is typical of the rich industrial countries, which include Western Europe, Japan, and Canada. Hong Kong is typical of the fast-growing Asian economies, which include Taiwan, Thailand, South Korea, and China. These countries have grown at between 5 percent a year and almost 10 percent a year, which is much faster than the growth rate of the United States. If the current differences in growth rates persist, these other countries will eventually close the gap on the United States as Hong Kong has done.

---

### FIGURE 3.6

## Economic Growth in the United States and Hong Kong

In 1960, the production possibilities per person in the United States were much larger than those in Hong Kong. But Hong Kong devoted more of its resources to accumulating capital than did the United States, so its production possibility frontier has shifted out more quickly than has that of the United States. In 1997, the two production possibilities per person were similar.

---

### R E V I E W

- Economic growth results from technological change and capital accumulation.
- The opportunity cost of economic growth is a decrease in current consumption.
- By decreasing current consumption, we can devote more resources to developing new technologies and accumulating capital and can speed up the rate of economic growth.

Next, we're going to study another way we expand our production possibilities—the amazing fact that buyers and sellers gain from specialization and trade.

# Gains from Trade

PEOPLE CAN PRODUCE FOR THEMSELVES ALL THE goods that they consume, or they can concentrate on producing one good (or perhaps a few goods) and then trade with others—exchange some of their own goods for those of others. Concentrating on the production of only one good or a few goods is called *specialization*. We are going to discover how people gain by specializing in the production of the good in which they have a *comparative advantage* and trading with each other.

## Comparative Advantage

A person has a **comparative advantage** in an activity if that person can perform the activity at a lower opportunity cost than anyone else. Differences in opportunity costs arise from differences in individual abilities and from differences in the characteristics of other resources.

No one excels at everything. One person is an outstanding pitcher but a poor catcher; another person is a brilliant lawyer but a poor teacher. In almost all human endeavors, what one person does easily, someone else finds difficult. The same applies to land and capital. One plot of land is fertile but has no mineral deposits; another plot of land has outstanding views but is infertile. One machine has great precision but is difficult to operate; another machine is fast but often breaks down.

Although no one excels at everything, some people excel and can outperform others in many activities. But such a person does not have a *comparative* advantage in every activity. For example, John Grisham is a better lawyer than most people. But he is an even better writer of fast-paced thrillers. His *comparative* advantage is in writing.

Because people's abilities and the quality of their resources differ, they have different opportunity costs of producing various goods. Such differences give rise to comparative advantage. Let's explore the idea of comparative advantage by looking at two audio cassette factories, one operated by Tom and the other operated by Nancy.

**Tom's Factory**  To simplify the story quite a lot, suppose that audio cassettes have just two components: a length of tape and a plastic case. Tom has two production lines, one for tape and one for cases.

FIGURE 3.7

## Production Possibilities in Tom's Factory

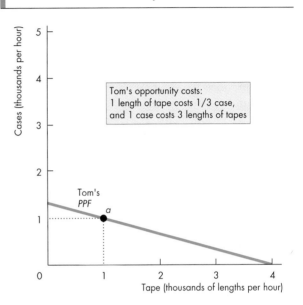

Tom's opportunity costs:
1 length of tape costs 1/3 case, and 1 case costs 3 lengths of tapes

Tom can produce tape and cassette cases along the production possibility frontier *PPF*. For Tom, the opportunity cost of 1 length of tape is $\frac{1}{3}$ of a case and the opportunity cost of 1 case is 3 lengths of tape. If Tom produces at point *a*, he can produce 1,000 cassette cases and 1,000 lengths of tape an hour.

Figure 3.7 shows Tom's production possibility frontier for tape and cases. It tells us that if Tom uses all his resources to make tape, he can produce 4,000 lengths of tape an hour. The *PPF* in Fig. 3.7 also tells us that if Tom uses all his resources to make cases, he can produce 1,333 cases an hour. But to produce cases, Tom must decrease his production of tape. For each 1 case produced, he must decrease his production of tape by 3 lengths.

Tom's opportunity cost of producing 1 case is 3 lengths of tape.

Similarly, if Tom wants to increase his production of tape, he must decrease his production of cases. For each 1,000 lengths of tape produced, he must decrease his production of cases by 333. So

Tom's opportunity cost of producing 1 length of tape is 0.333 case.

**Nancy's Factory**   The other factory, operated by Nancy, can also produce cases and tape. But Nancy's factory has machines that are custom made for case production, so they are more suitable for producing cases than tape. Also, Nancy's work force is more skilled in making cases.

This difference between the two factories means that Nancy's production possibility frontier—shown along with Tom's *PPF* in Fig. 3.8—is different from Tom's. If Nancy uses all her resources to make tape, she can produce 1,333 lengths an hour. If she uses all her resources to make cases, she can produce 4,000 an hour. To produce tape, Nancy must decrease her production of cases. For each 1,000 additional lengths of tape produced, she must decrease her production of cases by 3,000.

Nancy's opportunity cost of producing 1 length of tape is 3 cases.

Similarly, if Nancy wants to increase her production of cases, she must decrease her production of tape. For each 1,000 additional cases produced, she must decrease her production of tape by 333 lengths. So

Nancy's opportunity cost of producing 1 case is 0.333 length of tape.

Suppose that Tom and Nancy produce both tapes and cases and that each produces 1,000 lengths of tape and 1,000 cases—1,000 cassettes—an hour. That is, each produces at point *a* on their production possibility frontiers. Total production is 2,000 cassettes an hour.

In which of the two goods does Nancy have a comparative advantage? Recall that comparative advantage is a situation in which one person's opportunity cost of producing a good is lower than another person's opportunity cost of producing that same good. Nancy has a comparative advantage in producing cases. Nancy's opportunity cost of a case is 0.333 length of tape, whereas Tom's is 3 lengths of tape.

You can see her comparative advantage by looking at the production possibility frontiers for Nancy and Tom in Fig. 3.8. Nancy's production possibility frontier is steeper than Tom's. To produce one more case, Nancy gives up less tape than Tom. Hence Nancy's opportunity cost of a case is less than Tom's. This means that Nancy has a comparative advantage in producing cases.

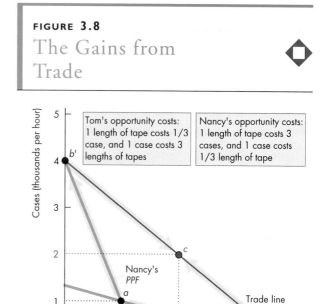

**FIGURE 3.8**

## The Gains from Trade

Tom's opportunity costs:
1 length of tape costs 1/3 case, and 1 case costs 3 lengths of tapes

Nancy's opportunity costs:
1 length of tape costs 3 cases, and 1 case costs 1/3 length of tape

Tom and Nancy each produce at point *a* on their respective *PPFs*. Nancy has a comparative advantage in cases, and Tom has a comparative advantage in tape. If Nancy specializes in cases, she produces at point *b'* on her *PPF*. If Tom specializes in tape, he produces at point *b* on his *PPF*. They then exchange cases for tape along the red "Trade line." Nancy buys tape from Tom for less than her opportunity cost of producing it, and Tom buys cases from Nancy for less than his opportunity cost of producing them. Each goes to point *c*—a point outside his or her *PPF*—where each has 2,000 cassettes an hour. Tom and Nancy double their rate of production with no change in resources.

Tom's comparative advantage is in producing tape. His production possibility frontier is less steep than Nancy's. This means that Tom gives up fewer cases to produce one more length of tape than Nancy does. Tom's opportunity cost of producing a length of tape is 0.333 case, which is less than Nancy's 3 cases. So Tom has a comparative advantage in producing tape.

Because Nancy has a comparative advantage in cases and Tom in tape, they can both gain from specialization and exchange.

## Achieving the Gains from Trade

If Tom, who has a comparative advantage in tape production, puts all his resources into that activity, he can produce 4,000 lengths of tape an hour—point *b* on his *PPF*. If Nancy, who has a comparative advantage in producing cases, puts all her resources into that activity, she can produce 4,000 cases an hour—point *b* on her *PPF*. By specializing, Tom and Nancy together can produce 4,000 cases and 4,000 lengths of tape an hour, double their total production without specialization. By specialization and exchange, Tom and Nancy can get *outside* their production possibility frontiers.

To achieve the gains from specialization, Tom and Nancy must trade with each other. Suppose they agree to the following deal: Each hour, Nancy produces 4,000 cases, Tom produces 4,000 lengths of tape, and Nancy supplies Tom with 2,000 cases in exchange for 2,000 lengths of tape. With this deal in place, Tom and Nancy move along the red "Trade line" to point *c*. At this point, each produces 2,000 cassettes an hour—double their previous production rate. These are the gains from specialization and trade.

Both parties to the trade share the gains. Nancy, who can produce tape at an opportunity cost of 3 cases per length of tape, can buy tape from Tom for a price of 1 case per length. Tom, who can produce cases at an opportunity cost of 3 lengths of tape per case, can buy cases from Nancy at a price of 1 length per case. Nancy gets her tape more cheaply, and Tom gets his cases more cheaply.

## Absolute Advantage

Suppose that Nancy invents and patents a production process that makes her *four* times as productive as she was before in the production of both cases and tape. With her new technology, Nancy can produce 16,000 cases an hour (4 times the original 4,000) if she puts all her resources into that activity. Alternatively, she can produce 5,332 lengths of tape (4 times the original 1,333) if she puts all her resources into that activity. Nancy now has an **absolute advantage** in producing *both* goods—using the same quantity of resources as Tom, she can produce more of both goods than Tom can produce.

But Nancy does not have a *comparative* advantage in both goods. She can produce four times as much of *both* goods as before, but her *opportunity cost* of 1

length of tape is still 3 cases. And this opportunity cost is higher than Tom's. So Nancy can still get tape at a lower cost by exchanging cases for tape with Tom.

A key point to recognize is that it is *not* possible for *anyone* to have a comparative advantage in everything. So gains from specialization and trade are always available when opportunity costs diverge.

## Dynamic Comparative Advantage

At any given point in time, the available resources and technologies determine the comparative advantages that individuals and nations have. But just by repeatedly producing a particular good or service, people become more productive in that activity, a phenomenon called **learning-by-doing**. Learning-by-doing is the basis of *dynamic* comparative advantage. **Dynamic comparative advantage** is a comparative advantage that a person (or country) possesses as a result of having specialized in a particular activity and, as a result of learning-by-doing, having become the producer with the lowest opportunity cost.

Hong Kong, South Korea, and Taiwan are examples of countries that have pursued dynamic comparative advantage vigorously. They have developed industries in which initially they did not have a comparative advantage but, through learning-by-doing, became low opportunity cost producers in those industries. An example is the decision to develop a genetic engineering industry in Singapore. Singapore probably did not have a comparative advantage in genetic engineering initially. But it might develop one as its scientists and production workers become more skilled in this activity.

## R E V I E W

- A person has a comparative advantage in producing a good if that person's opportunity cost of producing the good is lower than everyone else's.
- Production increases if people specialize in the activity in which they have a comparative advantage.
- By specializing in the activities in which they have a comparative advantage and trading, everyone can gain.
- Dynamic comparative advantage can result from learning-by-doing.

# The Market Economy

INDIVIDUALS AND COUNTRIES GAIN BY SPECIALIZ-
ing in the production of those goods and services in
which they have a comparative advantage and trading
with each other. This source of economic wealth was
identified by Adam Smith in his *Wealth of Nations,*
published in 1776—see pp. 2–3.

But for billions of people who specialize in producing millions of different goods and services to be
able to reap these gains, trade must be organized. But
trade need not be *planned* or *managed* by a central
authority. In fact, when such an arrangement has
been tried, as it was for 60 years in Russia, the result
has been less than dazzling.

Trade is organized by using social institutions.
The two key ones are:

- Property rights
- Markets

## Property Rights

**Property rights** are social arrangements that govern the ownership, use, and disposal of resources,
goods, and services. *Real property* includes land and
buildings—the things we call property in ordinary
speech—and durable goods such as plant and equipment. *Financial property* includes stocks and bonds
and money in the bank. *Intellectual property* is the
intangible product of creative effort. This type of
property includes books, music, computer programs,
and inventions of all kinds and is protected by copy-
rights and patents.

If property rights are not enforced, the incentive
to specialize and produce the goods in which each
person has a comparative advantage is weakened, and
some of the potential gains from specialization and
trade are lost. If people can easily steal the production
of others, then time, energy, and resources are devoted
not to production, but to protecting possessions.

Establishing property rights is one of the greatest
challenges facing Russia and other Eastern European
nations as they seek to develop market economies.
Even in countries where property rights are well
established, such as the United States, protecting
intellectual property is proving to be a challenge in
the face of modern technologies that make it relatively easy to copy audio and video material, computer programs, and books.

## Markets

In ordinary speech, the word *market* means a place
where people buy and sell goods such as fish, meat,
fruits, and vegetables. In economics, a *market* has a
more general meaning. A **market** is any arrangement that enables buyers and sellers to get information and to do business with each other. An example
is the market in which oil is bought and sold—the
world oil market. The world oil market is not a place.
It is the network of oil producers, oil users, whole-
salers, and brokers who buy and sell. In the world oil
market, decision makers do not meet physically. They
make deals throughout the world by telephone, fax,
and direct computer link.

In the example we've just studied, Nancy and
Tom get together and do a deal. They agree to
exchange cassette cases for lengths of tape. But in a
market economy, Nancy sells cassette cases to a dealer
in plastic products and buys lengths of tape from a
dealer in electronic recording media. Similarly, Tom
buys cassette cases and sells lengths of tape in these
same two markets. Tom can use Nancy's cases and
Nancy can use Tom's lengths of tape and yet be
unaware of each other's existence.

## Circular Flows in the Market Economy

Figure 3.9 identifies two types of markets: goods
markets and resource markets. *Goods markets* are
those in which goods and services are bought and
sold. *Resource markets* are those in which productive
resources are bought and sold.

Households decide how much of their labor,
land, capital, and entrepreneurship to sell or rent in
resource markets. They receive incomes in the form
of wages, rent, interest, and profit. Households also
decide how to spend their incomes on goods and services produced by firms. Firms decide the quantities
of resources to hire, how to use them to produce
goods and services, what goods and services to
produce, and in what quantities.

Figure 3.9 shows the flows that result from these
decisions by households and firms. The red flows
are the resources that go from households through
resource markets to firms and the goods and services
that go from firms through goods markets to households. The green flows in the opposite direction are
the payments made in exchange for these items.

How do markets coordinate all these decisions?

**FIGURE 3.9**

Circular Flows in the Market Economy

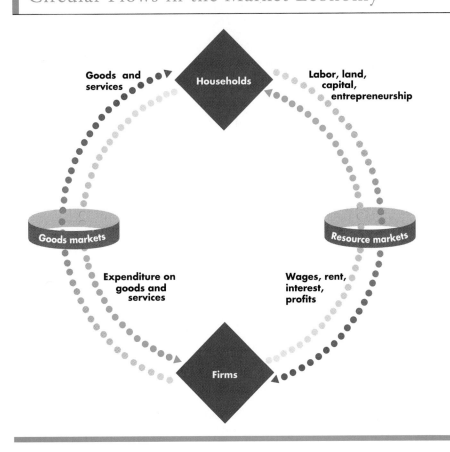

Goods and services

Households

Labor, land, capital, entrepreneurship

Goods markets

Resource markets

Expenditure on goods and services

Wages, rent, interest, profits

Firms

Households and firms make economic choices. Households choose the quantities of labor, land, capital, and entrepreneurship to sell or rent to firms in exchange for wages, rent, interest, and profits. Households also choose how to spend their incomes on the various types of goods and services available. Firms choose the quantities of resources to hire and the quantities of the various goods and services to produce. Goods markets and resource markets coordinate these choices of households and firms. Resources and goods flow clockwise (red), and money payments flow counterclockwise (green).

## Coordinating Decisions

Markets coordinate individual decisions through price adjustments. To see how, think about your local market for hamburgers. Suppose that some people who want to buy hamburgers are not able to do so. To make the choices of buyers and sellers compatible, buyers must scale down their appetites or more hamburgers must be offered for sale (or both must happen). A rise in the price of hamburgers produces this outcome. A higher price encourages producers to offer more hamburgers for sale. It also curbs the appetite for hamburgers and changes some lunch plans. Fewer people buy hamburgers, and more buy hot dogs. More hamburgers (and more hot dogs) are offered for sale.

Alternatively suppose that more hamburgers are available than people want to buy. In this case, to make the choices of buyers and sellers compatible, more hamburgers must be bought or fewer hamburgers must be offered for sale (or both). A fall in the price of ham-

burgers achieves this outcome. A lower price encourages firms to produce a smaller quantity of hamburgers. It also encourages people to buy more hamburgers.

◆ You have now begun to see how economists approach economic questions. Scarcity, choice, and divergent opportunity costs explain why we specialize and trade and why property rights and markets have developed. You can see the lessons you've learned in this chapter all around you. *Reading Between the Lines* on pp. 56–57 gives an example. It explores the *PPF* that you face as you make your decisions about whether to remain in school or quit school and take a job.

In Chapter 4, you are going to learn how markets work and see why prices adjust to coordinate buying plans and selling plans. You are then going to study macroeconomics. You will discover how *aggregate* demand and *aggregate* supply determine the average level of prices and the quantity of goods and services produced in the economy as a whole.

# Policy WATCH

## Opportunity Cost: The Cost and Benefit of a College Degree

**Essence** of **THE STORY**

PORTLAND PRESS HERALD, MAY 2, 1996

# High Cost Blocks Education

Robin McAlister of South Portland has fallen into a disheartening routine: Sit down at the kitchen table, scan the classifieds, apply for a job, get turned down.

"I need computer experience," said McAlister, a 39-year-old single mother, who lost her clerical job at a physician's office in January. "Because of the lack of computer training, I don't qualify for general office positions." ...

Like thousands of other Mainers, McAlister has learned a fundamental truth: People who don't have the skills needed in today's high-tech, highly competitive environment rarely find good jobs. ...

A five-month investigation by The Portland Newspapers found that education increasingly separates successful workers who earn good pay from those who are struggling to find a job that pays a livable wage. Yet the cost of getting the skills needed for a decent job is spiraling out of reach for many Mainers. ...

Jobs that pay a livable wage increasingly demand computer-literate, college-educated workers. A college degree doesn't guarantee a good-paying job, but it gives workers a better chance at getting one. An estimated 78 percent of the jobs in Maine that pay $15 an hour or more generally require a college degree. ...

Although a college degree doesn't guarantee a job, the economy is creating work for highly educated people. A computer analysis by The Portland Newspapers found the number of jobs in Maine for people with advanced degrees and technical training is rapidly increasing.

Since 1989, the number of jobs for people with a master's degree has jumped an estimated 21 percent; jobs demanding associate degrees from technical colleges have grown by 16 percent; work for people with a doctorate increased about 11 percent; and jobs that generally require a bachelor's degree have increased about 5 percent.

By comparison, jobs that generally don't require a college education have declined an estimated 1 percent.

There's a huge gap in pay between the two groups. In Maine, the average hourly wage for jobs that generally require a college degree is twice that for occupations that don't, about $18 an hour vs. $9 an hour, according to an analysis by The Portland Newspapers of state and federal databases. ...

Mainers must strive to increase their skills and continue their education after high school to succeed in today's intensely competitive global market. ...

Reprinted with permission.

■ People who lack high-tech skills rarely find good jobs in today's competitive environment.

■ Education is a factor in wage determination. The average hourly wage for jobs requiring a college degree is twice as much as that for jobs requiring less than a completed college education.

■ Although a college degree does not guarantee a job, the economy is creating more jobs for college graduates than for non–college graduates.

# Economic

## A N A L Y S I S

■ The opportunity cost of a college degree is forgone consumption. The payoff is an increase in lifetime production possibilities.

■ Figure 1 shows the choices facing a high school graduate. This person can consume education goods and services such as tuition, books and other supplies, and study time, measured on the *y*-axis, or other goods and services, measured on the *x*-axis.

■ The person can consume at any point along the blue *PPF*. By going to college, the student chooses point *a*. She increases her use of educational goods and services to *A* and decreases her consumption of other goods and services.

■ With a college degree, consumption possibilities expand to the red *PPF* in Fig. 1.

■ A college graduate can choose to spend even more on education to get a professional degree.

■ Figure 2 shows the choices facing a college graduate. To get a professional degree, a college graduate selects point *c* on the blue *PPF*, forgoes consumption and increases

the use of educational goods and services to *B*.

■ The red *PPF* in Fig. 2 shows the expanded possibilities with a professional degree. It is now possible for this person to consume at point *d* or at another point along the red *PPF*.

■ The greater the resources devoted to education, the greater are the future consumption possibilities. For people who have the required ability, the future benefits from education exceed the costs by a significant amount.

■ The news article says that a college graduate earns twice the income of a non–college graduate. Other data suggest that the difference is about 60 percent. Either way, the difference is large.

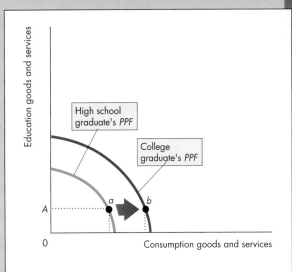

Figure 1  **High school graduate's choices**

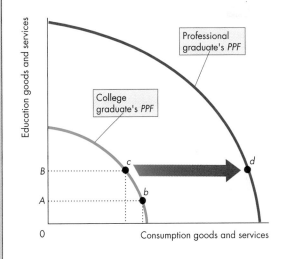

Figure 2  **College graduate's choices**

## You're

### THE VOTER

■ In his 1997 State of the Union address, President Clinton said that he wants every American to have a college education.

■ Why do you think the President needs to worry about college education?

■ With such huge returns from education, why don't more people remain in school for longer?

■ What is the opportunity cost of President Clinton's plan?

■ Would you vote for or against a tax increase to enable everyone to attend college? Why or why not?

# SUMMARY

## Key Points

### Resources and Wants (p. 42)

- Economic activity arises from scarcity—resources are insufficient to satisfy people's wants.
- Resources are labor, land, capital (including human capital), and entrepreneurship.
- We choose how to use our resources and try to get the most out of them.

### Resources, Production Possibilities, and Opportunity Cost (pp. 43–45)

- The production possibility frontier, *PPF*, is the boundary between production levels that are attainable and those that are not attainable when all the available resources are used to their limit.
- Production efficiency occurs at points on the *PPF*.
- Along the *PPF*, the opportunity cost of producing more of one good is the amount of the other good that must be given up.
- The opportunity cost of a good increases as the production of the good increases.

### Using Resources Efficiently (pp. 46–48)

- The marginal cost of a good is the opportunity cost of producing one more unit.
- The marginal benefit from a good is the maximum amount of another good that a person is willing to forgo to obtain more of the first good.
- The marginal benefit of a good decreases as the amount available increases.
- Resources are used efficiently when the marginal cost of each good is equal to its marginal benefit.

### Economic Growth (pp. 49–50)

- Economic growth, which is the expansion of production possibilities, results from capital accumulation and technological change.
- The opportunity cost of economic growth is forgone current consumption.

### Gains from Trade (pp. 51–53)

- A person has a comparative advantage in producing a good if that person can produce the good at a lower opportunity cost than everyone else can.
- People gain by specializing in the activity in which they have a comparative advantage and trading with others.
- Dynamic comparative advantage arises from learning-by-doing.

### The Market Economy (pp. 54–55)

- Property rights and markets enable people to gain from specialization and trade.
- Markets coordinate decisions and help to allocate resources to *higher* value uses.

## Key Figures

Figure 3.1    Production Possibility Frontier, 43
Figure 3.4    Efficient Use of Resources, 48
Figure 3.8    The Gains from Trade, 52
Figure 3.9    Circular Flows in the Market Economy, 55

## Key Terms

Absolute advantage, 53
Capital, 42
Capital accumulation, 49
Comparative advantage, 51
Dynamic comparative advantage, 53
Economic growth, 49
Economics, 42
Efficient, 48
Entrepreneurship, 42
Human capital, 42
Labor, 42
Land, 42
Learning-by-doing, 53
Marginal benefit, 47
Marginal cost, 46
Market, 54
Opportunity cost, 44
Production efficiency, 44
Production possibility frontier, 43
Property rights, 54
Scarcity, 42
Technological change, 49
Tradeoff, 44

## QUESTIONS

1. What is the fundamental economic problem?
2. What are the resources used to produce goods and services?
3. How does the production possibility frontier illustrate scarcity?
4. How does the production possibility frontier illustrate the fact that every choice involves a tradeoff?
5. How does the production possibility frontier illustrate production efficiency?
6. How does the production possibility frontier illustrate opportunity cost?
7. Why is opportunity cost a ratio?
8. Why does the production possibility frontier for most goods bow outward?
9. Why does opportunity cost generally increase as the quantity produced of a good increases?
10. What is marginal cost and how is it measured?
11. How do we measure the marginal benefit from a good?
12. How does the marginal benefit from a good change as the quantity of that good increases?
13. What is production efficiency and how does it relate to the production possibility frontier?
14. Under what conditions are resources used efficiently?
15. What shifts the production possibility frontier outward?
16. How do choices influence the pace of economic growth?
17. What is the opportunity cost of economic growth?
18. Why do people specialize and trade?
19. How do people gain from specialization and trade?
20. Is production still efficient when people specialize? Explain why or why not.
21. What are the gains from specialization and trade?
22. Distinguish between comparative advantage and absolute advantage.
23. What is dynamic comparative advantage and how does it arise?
24. Why are social arrangements such as markets and property rights necessary?
25. What are the main functions of markets?

## PROBLEMS

1. Wendell enjoys playing tennis, but the more time he spends on tennis, the lower is his grade in economics. The figure shows the tradeoff he faces.

Calculate Wendell's opportunity cost of two hours of tennis if he increases the time he plays tennis from:
a.  4 to 6 hours a week.
b.  6 to 8 hours a week.

2. In problem 1, describe the relationship between the time Wendell spends playing tennis and the opportunity cost of an hour of tennis.

3. If Wendell's opportunity cost of increasing his grade were constant regardless of how much time he spent playing tennis, what would be the shape of his *PPF*? Which shape seems more likely, the one in the figure above or the one that answers this question?

4. Suppose that Leisureland produces only two goods: food and sunscreen. The table gives its production possibilities.

| Food (pounds per month) | | Sunscreen (gallons per month) |
|---|---|---|
| 300 | and | 0 |
| 200 | and | 50 |
| 100 | and | 100 |
| 0 | and | 150 |

a.  Draw a graph of Leisureland's production possibility frontier.
b.  What are the opportunity costs of producing food and sunscreen in Leisureland? List them at each output given in the table.

c. Why are these opportunity costs the same at each output level?

5. Suppose that the people in Leisureland are willing to give up 5 pounds of food per gallon of sunscreen if they have 25 gallons of sunscreen, 2 pounds of food per gallon of sunscreen if they have 75 gallons of sunscreen, and 1 pound of food per gallon of sunscreen if they have 125 gallons of sunscreen.
  a. Draw a graph of Leisureland's marginal benefit from sunscreen.
  b. On the same graph, plot the opportunity cost of producing sunscreen.
  c. What is Leisureland's efficient use of sunscreen?
  d. What is the efficient production of food?

6. Busyland produces only food and sunscreen, and its production possibilities are as follows:

| Food (pounds per month) | | Sunscreen (gallons per month) |
|---|---|---|
| 150 | and | 0 |
| 100 | and | 100 |
| 50 | and | 200 |
| 0 | and | 300 |

  a. Draw a graph of Busyland's production possibility frontier.
  b. What are the opportunity costs of producing food and sunscreen in Busyland? List them at each output given in the table.

7. Suppose that in problems 4 and 6, Leisureland and Busyland do not specialize and trade with each other. Leisureland produces and consumes 50 pounds of food and 125 gallons of sunscreen per month. Busyland produces and consumes 150 pounds of food per month and no sunscreen. Now the countries begin to trade with each other.
  a. What good does Leisureland sell to Busyland and what good does it buy from Busyland?
  b. What are the maximum quantities of food and sunscreen that the two countries can produce if each country specializes in the activity at which it has a comparative advantage?

8. Wendell in problem 1 has the marginal benefit curve shown in the figure.

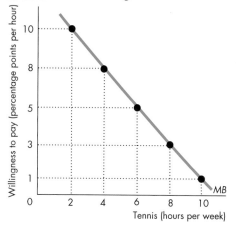

  a. If Wendell uses his time efficiently, what grade will he get?
  b. Why would Wendell be worse off getting a higher grade?

## CRITICAL THINKING

1. After you have studied *Reading Between the Lines* on pp. 56–57, answer the following questions:
  a. Draw a graph that shows the opportunity cost of education. Does the opportunity cost of education increase as the quantity of education increases?
  b. If all colleges and universities were private institutions that charged full-cost tuition, would the opportunity cost of a college education increase, decrease, or remain unchanged? Explain your answer.
  c. Most colleges and universities operate a school year of around 30 weeks. So for 22 weeks each year, classrooms are empty and professors do no teaching. Is this arrangement inefficient or efficient? Explain your answer.
  d. What do you think are the main benefits from education? Do all the benefits accrue to the people who receive education? Do other people benefit as well?

# Part 2

# How Markets Work

## The Amazing Market

The market is an amazing instrument. It enables people who have never met and who know nothing about each other to interact and do business. It also enables us to allocate our scarce resources to the uses that we value most highly. Markets can be very simple or highly organized. ◆ A simple market is one that the American historian Daniel J. Boorstin describes in *The Discoverers* (p. 161). In the late fourteenth century,

> The Muslim caravans that went southward from Morocco across the Atlas Mountains arrived after twenty days at the shores of the Senegal River. There the Moroccan traders laid out separate piles of salt, of beads from Ceutan coral, and cheap manufactured goods. Then they retreated out of sight. The local tribesmen, who lived in the strip mines where they dug their gold, came to the shore and put a heap of gold beside each pile of Moroccan goods. Then they, in turn, went out of view, leaving the Moroccan traders either to take the gold offered for a particular pile or to reduce the pile of their merchandise to suit the offered price in gold. Once again the Moroccan traders withdrew, and the process went on. By this system of commercial etiquette, the Moroccans collected their gold.

An organized market is the New York Stock Exchange that trades many millions of stocks each day. Another is an auction at which the U.S. government sells rights to broadcasters and cellular telephone companies for the use of the air waves. ◆ All of these markets determine the prices at which exchanges take place and enable both buyers and sellers to benefit. ◆ Everything and anything that can be exchanged is traded in markets. There are markets for goods and services; for resources such as labor, capital, and raw materials; for dollars, pounds, and yen; for goods to be delivered now; and for goods to be delivered in the future. Only the imagination places limits on what can be traded in markets. ◆ The following chapter explains how markets work. It begins by explaining a crucial distinction between money price and relative price. This distinction runs right through the macroeconomics that you will meet in the rest of the book. The chapter then explains the laws of demand and supply. You will discover the forces that determine buying plans and selling plans and you'll see how prices adjust to coordinate these plans. You will also learn how to use the laws of demand and supply to explain why some prices rise, some fall, and others rise and fall like a roller coaster ride. ◆ What you learn about supply and demand is fundamental to your entire study of economics. It will help to understand price movements in the world around you. And it will help you in your study of macroeconomics. ◆ Before you begin Chapter 4, spend a few minutes with the economists who discovered the laws of demand and supply. Also, look at the interview with Paul Milgrom of Stanford University, who is one of today's most influential economists who studies and even helps to create auction markets.

# Discovering the Laws of Demand and Supply

## The Economist: Alfred Marshall

**Alfred Marshall (1842–1924) grew up in an England that was being transformed by the railroad and by the expansion of manufacturing. Mary Paley Marshall was one of Marshall's students at Cambridge, and when Alfred and Mary married, in 1877, celibacy rules barred Marshall from continuing to teach at Cambridge. By 1884, with more liberal rules, the Marshalls returned to Cambridge, where Alfred became Professor of Political Economy.**

**Many others had a hand in refining the theory of demand and supply, but the first thorough and complete statement of the theory as we know it today was set out by Alfred Marshall, with the acknowledged help of Mary. Published in 1890, the monumental treatise *Principles of Economics*, became the textbook on economics on both sides of the Atlantic for almost half a century. Marshall was an outstanding mathematician, but he kept mathematics and even diagrams in the background. His supply and demand diagram appears only in a footnote.**

*"The forces to be dealt with are ... so numerous, that it is best to take a few at a time. ... Thus we begin by isolating the primary relations of supply, demand, and price."*

ALFRED MARSHALL

THE PRINCIPLES OF ECONOMICS

## The Issues and Ideas

The laws of demand and supply that you will study in the following chapter were discovered during the 1830s by Antoine-Augustin Cournot (1801–1877), a professor of mathematics at the University of Lyon, France. Although Cournot was the first to use demand and supply, it was the development and expansion of the railroads during the 1850s that gave the newly emerging theory its first practical applications. Railroads then were at the cutting edge of technology just as airlines are today. And as in the airline industry today, competition among the railroads was fierce.

Dionysius Lardner (1793–1859), an Irish professor of philosophy at the University of London, used demand and supply to show railroad companies how they could increase their profits by cutting rates on long-distance business on which competition was fiercest and by raising rates on short-haul business on which they had less to fear from other transportation suppliers. Today, economists use the principles that Lardner worked out during the 1850s to calculate the freight rates and passenger fares that will give airlines the largest possible profit. And the rates calculated have a lot in common with the railroad rates of the nineteenth century. On local routes on which there is little competition, fares per mile are highest, and on long-distance routes on which the airlines compete fiercely, fares per mile are lowest.

Known satirically among scientists of the day as "Dionysius Diddler," Lardner worked on an amazing range of problems from astronomy to railway engineering to economics. A colorful character, he would have been a regular guest of David Letterman if late-night talk shows had been around in the 1850s. Lardner visited the École des Ponts et Chaussées (School of Bridges and Roads) in Paris and must have learned a great deal from Jules Dupuit.

In France, Jules Dupuit (1804–1866), a French engineer/economist, used demand to calculate the benefits from building a bridge and, once the bridge was built, for calculating the toll to charge for its use. His work was the forerunner of what is today called *cost-benefit analysis*. Working with the principles invented by Dupuit, economists today calculate the costs and benefits of highways and airports, dams, and power stations.

## THEN...

Dupuit used the law of demand to determine whether a bridge or canal would be valued enough by its users to justify the cost of building it. Lardner first worked out the relationship between the cost of production and supply and used demand and supply theory to explain the costs, prices, and profits of railroad operations. He also used the theory to discover ways of increasing revenue by raising rates on short-haul business and lowering them on long-distance freight.

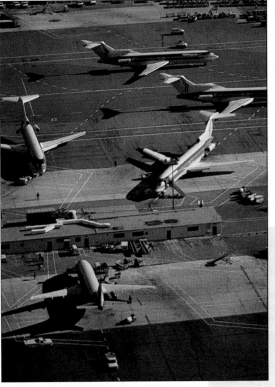

## ...AND NOW

Today, using the same principles devised by Dupuit, economists calculate whether the benefits of expanding airports and air-traffic control facilities are sufficient to cover their costs, and airline companies use the principles developed by Lardner to set their prices and to decide when to offer "seat sales." Like the railroads before them, the airlines charge a high price per mile on short flights, for which they face little competition, and a low price per mile on long flights, for which competition is fierce.

**Markets do an amazing job. And the laws of demand and supply help us to understand how markets work. But in some situations, a market must be designed and institutions must be created to enable the market to operate. In recent years, economists have begun to use their tools to design and create markets. And one of the chief architects of new style markets is Paul Milgrom of Stanford University, whom you can meet on the following pages.**

# Talking with

**Paul R. Milgrom** is Professor of Economics at Stanford University and an Associate Editor of the *American Economic Review*, the leading journal that publishes economic research. He is founder and president of Market Design, Inc., a young company that designs new auction and market rules for businesses and governments. Born in Detroit, Michigan, in 1948, Professor Milgrom was an undergraduate at the University of Michigan and a graduate student at Stanford University (Ph.D. 1979). He taught at Northwestern University and Yale University before returning to Stanford in 1987.

Professor Milgrom is an economic theorist, which means that he uses mathematical techniques to study economic behavior. His work on auctions has been especially influential and has found practical applications in auctioning items ranging from radio spectrum (used in paging and cellular telephones) to mining rights.

Michael Parkin talked with Professor Milgrom about his work, how it connects with the theory of demand and supply developed by Cournot and Marshall.

**Professor Milgrom, how did you become an economist?**

I came into the house of economics through an unmarked side door, not knowing where I was until I was well inside. The main entrance is through a graduate degree in economics, but I have no university degree in economics at any level. My undergraduate studies were in mathematics and statistics, and my graduate studies were in business. It was in graduate school that I stumbled across a brilliant study of auction theory by William Vickrey—work for which he was awarded the Nobel Prize 21 years later, in 1996. Vickrey's work surprised me and convinced me that mathematical analysis could help me to understand auctions and could even point the way to new, improved types of auctions.

**Auctions, like all market arrangements, bring buyers and sellers together. Doesn't the supply and demand model explain how auctions work?**

The supply and demand model is the economist's workhorse for day-to-day market analysis. It provides a wonderful way to summarize some of the main factors affecting prices and quantities and to explain how prices guide important choices.

But the model is silent about how the rules that govern trade are set or how they affect economic outcomes. Also, it is not very helpful for thinking about technology decisions that can have a huge impact on economic outcomes. For example, the way standards are set for cellular telephone systems determines whether the same phone will work on different systems in different parts of the nation and the world. In Europe, a single standard allows a consumer to go from country to country and still have a working telephone. In the United States, where no single standard exists, a consumer may find that her telephone fails to operate even with the system in the next town.

Obviously, that failure depresses the sales of cellular phone service, although it has nothing to do with the consumer preferences for communications or with the cost or availability of the cellular telephone technology.

So institutions influence prices and quantities and the kinds of plans that people make. And sometimes, institutions such as standards-setting bodies can solve problems that a market guided only by prices can't deal with effectively.

**Let's return to auctions. What is auction theory? How does it relate to supply and demand?**
Auctions are institutions that determine the prices and other terms at which buyers and sellers will trade. Auction theory explains how the rules of an auction affect its outcome.

Sellers want auctions that generate the highest price. Buyers want auctions that generate the lowest price. Auction houses want auctions that balance the interests of buyers and sellers and ensure a continuing flow of customers for future auctions.

In the U.S. auctions of radio spectrum, the government's main objective was to assign spectrum efficiently.

The supply and demand model does not include a place for auction rules. It supposes that buyers and sellers know all the relevant prices when they make their decisions. In reality, that is not always true.

Often in an auction, bidders must make a choice without knowing all the relevant prices.

**What are the main types of auctions and why are there so many different types? Why isn't one type best?**
An auction may be either sealed or open. In a sealed auction, the bids are written and the best bids win. In open auctions, there is usually a sequence of bids with each bidder getting an opportunity to respond to the bids of others. Within these two auction types, there is great variety.

The sealed bid has two advantages over the open auction. First, the bidders don't have to be gathered together physically at one time to conduct the auction. In bidding at a used car warehouse, for example, the bidders (usually used car dealers) examine the cars at times that are convenient for themselves and leave behind a sealed envelope with their bids. There is a deadline for bids. When the deadline passes, the bids are opened and the bidders are notified of the results.

Second, it is harder for bidders to collude and depress the price received by the seller. With sealed bids, a member of a ring of buyers who agree to keep prices low might be tempted to submit a slightly higher bid and take advantage of the low bids by other ring members. The temptation to cheat in an open auction is much less, because the other ring members can punish the cheater by driving up the price when the member violates the agreement.

Open auctions have advantages, too. When a single item is being sold and price is the key factor, an open auction eliminates the guesswork of sealed bids. The bidder with the highest value can outbid the competitors. Also, when a large number of items are to be sold and the bidders are present for an open auction, the items can be sold quickly in sequence.

**What advances have we made in auction theory?**
Since Vickrey initiated auction theory some 35 years ago, we have improved our ability to predict how different types of auctions perform. And we've learned how to design auctions with particular objectives in mind. We even have developed mathematical descriptions of "optimal auctions," which are theoretically the best auction designs for achieving particular objectives.

We still haven't implemented an optimal auction in a real situation, but a small group of economists have used auction theory to design significant new auctions. Recently, I was among a group that proposed a brand-new auction design called a "simultaneous ascending auction." This type of auction is an open auction of many different items, all of which can be bid for simultaneously.

The U.S. Federal Communications Commission used such an auction to sell licenses to use radio spectrum for telecommunications services. The auction was the largest in history and generated gross revenues of $24 billion.

More important to me, the new auction design performed as predicted and led to much more efficient license assignments than other kinds of auctions could have achieved.

The radio spectrum auctions have shaped competition in wireless communications and have determined which firms will operate businesses in which parts of the country.

**Why did selling the frequency spectrum need a simultaneous ascending bid auction? And how does such an auction work?**

Bidders want to acquire licenses to provide a wireless communications service covering certain geographic areas. A bidder might want to use one of two available bands of spectrum to provide services in, say, Los Angeles County. If either spectrum band will do and the bidder needs just one, then the licenses to use these bands are economic substitutes.

But a bidder might also be willing to pay more to acquire a license covering southern California if he or she could also acquire a license covering northern California. These licenses are complements. One reason why licenses might be complements is that the two areas can share some facilities and lower costs. Another reason is that an owner of both licenses might be able to provide a more valuable service to consumers and so charge a higher price for it.

The simultaneous ascending bid auction handles both situations well. In such an auction, the bidding for the northern and southern California licenses, and in fact *all* the licenses, goes on at the same time, and bidding remains open on all the individual licenses until bidding for all licenses is complete. In an auction like this, a bidder who is interested in the California licenses can bid for both and can cease bidding when the combination price gets too high. This is a far from perfect solution, but it is much better

than any of the traditional alternatives and seems to have performed well in the sale of spectrum licenses in the United States.

**What differences are today's information technologies making to the problems of auction design?**

Without modern information technology, the simultaneous ascending auction of radio spectrum licenses couldn't have been conducted. In a large version of the auction, both the auctioneer and the bidders need to keep track of bids on hundreds or even thousands of licenses simultaneously. Software programs have been created to facilitate submitting bids and tracking the auction results.

**How do you advise today's undergraduate to prepare for a career in economics? What besides economics should he or she study?**

The best economists are technically able, curious about the world, concerned about human welfare, flexible in their perspectives, and dedicated to clear, analytical thinking. Courses can help with some of these things. Students can certainly learn mathematical and statistical concepts as undergraduates.

To enjoy a career as an economist, you have to go beyond the academic abstractions and incorporate elements that excite you. Many students study economics because of their specific social concerns, for example, wanting to understand the sources of poverty in their home countries and to discern the paths out of poverty. For those students, I recommend reading widely and studying other social sciences to learn about the culture and politics of poverty and the kinds of barriers they create to good economic policies. There are so many ways to incorporate one's pleasures in an economics career! I have friends and colleagues who've studied the economics of sports, of wine prices, of the performing arts, and of the Internet. By weaving their personal and professional interests together, they eliminate the sharp divide between their career and their leisure. These are the folks I hold up as role models.

> *The best economists are technically able, curious about the world, concerned about human welfare, flexible in their perspectives, and dedicated to clear, analytical thinking.*

# Chapter 4

# Demand and Supply

Slide, rocket, and roller coaster—Disneyland rides? No. Commonly used descriptions of prices changes. ◆ CD players have taken a price slide from around $1,100 (in today's money) in 1983 to less than $100 today. And during these years, the quantity of CD players bought has increased steadily. What caused this price slide? Why didn't brisk buying keep the price high? ◆ The price of health care has rocketed. Yet despite rocketing prices, people buy more health services every year. Why did people buy ever larger amounts of health care during the 1980s and early 1990s when its price rocketed? ◆ The prices of bananas, coffee, and other agricultural commodities follow a roller coaster. Why does the price of bananas roller-coaster even when people's tastes for bananas barely change? ◆ The prices of many things we buy are remarkably steady. For example, the price of an audio cassette tape has not changed much. But despite its steady price, the number of tapes people buy increases each year. Why do people buy more tapes even though their price is no lower than it was a decade ago? And why do firms sell more tapes even though they can't get higher prices for them? ◆ Economics is about the choices people make to cope with scarcity. These choices are guided by costs and benefits and are co-ordinated through markets. ◆ The tool that explains how markets work is demand and supply. It is central to the whole of economics. It is used to study issues as diverse as wages and jobs, rents and housing, pollution, crime, consumer protection, education, welfare, health care, the value of money, and interest rates. ◆ Your careful study of this topic will bring big rewards both in your further study of economics and in your everyday life. Once you understand demand and supply, you will view the world through new eyes. When you have completed your study of demand and supply, you will be able to explain how prices are determined and make predictions about price slides, rockets, and roller coasters. But first, we're going to take a closer look at the idea of price. Just what is a price?

## Slide, Rocket, and Roller Coaster

---

**After studying this chapter, you will be able to:**

- ■ Distinguish between a money price and a relative price

- ■ Explain the main influences on demand

- ■ Explain the main influences on supply

- ■ Explain how prices and quantities bought and sold are determined by demand and supply

- ■ Explain why some prices fall, some rise, and some fluctuate

- ■ Use demand and supply to make predictions about price changes

## Price and Opportunity Cost

ECONOMIC ACTIONS ARISE FROM SCARCITY— wants exceed the resources available to satisfy them. Faced with *scarcity,* people must make choices. And to make choices, they compare *costs* and *benefits.* Choices are influenced by opportunity costs. If the opportunity cost of a good or service increases, consumers look for less costly substitutes and decrease their purchases of the more costly item.

We are going to build on this fundamental idea and study both the way people respond to *prices* and the forces that determine prices. But to pursue these tasks, we need to understand the relationship between price and opportunity cost.

In everyday life, the *price* of an object is the number of dollars that must be given up in exchange for it. Economists refer to this price as the *money price.*

The *opportunity cost* of an action is the highest-valued alternative forgone. If, when you buy a cup of coffee, the highest-valued thing you forgo is some gum, then the opportunity cost of buying a coffee is the *quantity* of gum forgone. We can calculate this quantity from the money prices of coffee and gum.

If the money price of coffee is $1 a cup and the money price of gum is 50¢ a pack, then the opportunity cost of one cup of coffee is two packs of gum. To calculate this opportunity cost, we divide the price of a cup of coffee by the price of a pack of gum and find the *ratio* of one price to the other. The ratio of one price to another is called a **relative price**, and a *relative price is an opportunity cost.* It is the price of good *X* divided by the price of good *Y,* and it tells us how many units of good *Y* must be given up to get one more unit of good *X.*

There are many relative prices—coffee to gum, coffee to Coke, coffee to everything else, gum to Coke, gum to everything else, Coke to everything else—and we need a convenient way of expressing relative prices.

The normal way of expressing a relative price is in terms of what a "basket" of all goods and services cost in a particular year. To calculate this relative price, we divide the money price of a good by the money price of a "basket" of all goods (called a *price index*). The resulting relative price tells us the opportunity cost of an item in terms of how much of the "basket" of all goods must be given up to buy it.

Figure 4.1 illustrates the distinction between a money price and a relative price. The green curve shows the money price of wheat and tells us that the

### FIGURE 4.1
## The Price of Wheat

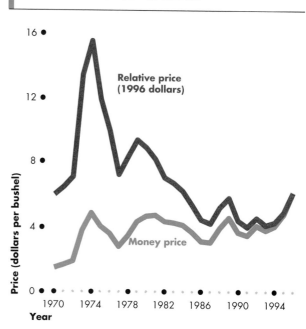

The money price of wheat—the number of dollars that must be given up for a bushel of wheat—has fluctuated between $1.50 and $6.20. But the *relative* price or *opportunity cost* of wheat, expressed in 1996 dollars, has fluctuated between $4.00 and $15.60 and has tended to fall. The fall in the relative price of wheat is obscured by the behavior of the money price.

*Sources:* Price of wheat, *International Financial Statistics,* International Monetary Fund, Washington, D.C., 1997; Consumer Price Index, *Economic Report of the President,* U.S. Government Printing Office, Washington, D.C., 1997.

money price has fluctuated but has tended to rise. The red curve shows the relative price of wheat—the price relative to that of a basket of goods and services in 1996. This curve tells us about the opportunity cost of wheat. It shows what the price would have been each year if the price of the basket had been the same as it was in 1996. The relative price of wheat peaked in 1974 and has tended to fall since that year.

The theory of demand and supply that we are about to study determines *relative prices,* and the word "price" means *relative* price. When we predict that a price will fall, we do not mean that its *money* price will fall—although it might. We mean that its *relative* price will fall. That is, its price will fall *relative* to the average price of other goods and services.

Let's now begin our study of demand and supply, starting with demand.

# Demand

IF YOU DEMAND SOMETHING, THEN YOU

- Want it,
- Can afford it, and
- Have made a definite plan to buy it.

*Wants* are the unlimited desires or wishes that people have for goods and services. How many times have you thought that you would like something "if only you could afford it" or "if it weren't so expensive"? Scarcity guarantees that many—perhaps most—of our wants will never be satisfied. Demand reflects a decision about which wants to satisfy.

The **quantity demanded** of a good or service is the amount that consumers plan to buy during a given time period at a particular price. The quantity demanded is not necessarily the same amount as the quantity actually bought. Sometimes the quantity demanded is greater than the amount of goods available, so the quantity bought is less than the quantity demanded.

The quantity demanded is measured as an amount per unit of time. For example, suppose that you consume one cup of coffee a day. The quantity of coffee that you demand can be expressed as 1 cup a day or 7 cups a week or 365 cups a year. Without a time dimension, we cannot tell whether a particular quantity demanded is large or small.

## What Determines Buying Plans?

The amount of any particular good or service that consumers plan to buy depends on many factors. The main ones are:

- The price of the good
- The prices of related goods
- Income
- Population
- Preferences
- Expected future prices

We first look at the relationship between the quantity demanded and the price of a good. To study this relationship, we hold constant all other influences on consumers' planned purchases and ask: How does the quantity demanded of the good vary as its price varies, other things remaining the same?

## The Law of Demand

The law of demand states:

Other things remaining the same, the higher the price of a good, the smaller is the quantity demanded.

Why does a higher price reduce the quantity demanded? For two reasons:

1. Substitution effect
2. Income effect

**Substitution Effect**   When the price of a good rises, other things remaining the same, its *relative* price—its opportunity cost—rises. Although each good is unique, it has *substitutes*—other goods that can be used in its place. As the opportunity cost of a good rises, people buy less of that good and more of its substitutes.

**Income Effect**   When a price changes and all other influences on buying plans remain unchanged, the price rises *relative* to people's incomes. So faced with a higher price and an unchanged income, people cannot afford to buy all the things they previously bought. The quantities demanded of at least some goods and services must be decreased. Normally, the good whose price has increased is one of those bought in a smaller quantity.

To see the substitution effect and the income effect at work, think about the effects of changes in the price of blank audio cassette tapes. Many different goods provide a service similar to that provided by a tape. For example, a compact disc, a prerecorded tape, a radio or television broadcast, and a live concert all provide similar services to a tape. Suppose that tapes initially sell for $3 each and then the price doubles to $6. People now substitute compact discs and prerecorded tapes for blank tapes—the substitution effect. And faced with a tighter budget, they buy fewer tapes as well as less of other goods and services—the income effect. The quantity of tapes demanded decreases for these two reasons.

Now suppose the price of a tape falls to $1. People now substitute blank tapes for compact discs and prerecorded tapes—the substitution effect. And with a budget that now has some slack from the lower price of tapes, people buy more tapes as well as more of other goods and services—the income effect. The quantity of tapes demanded increases for these two reasons.

## Demand Curve and Demand Schedule

You are now about to study one of the two most used curves in economics, the demand curve. And you are going to encounter one of the most critical distinctions: the distinction between *demand* and *quantity demanded*.

The term **demand** refers to the entire relationship between the quantity demanded and the price of a good, and it is illustrated by the demand curve and the demand schedule. The term *quantity demanded* refers to a point on a demand curve—the quantity demanded at a particular price.

Figure 4.2 shows the demand curve for tapes. A **demand curve** shows the relationship between the quantity demanded of a good and its price when all other influences on consumers' planned purchases remain the same.

The table in Fig. 4.2 is the demand schedule for tapes. A *demand schedule* lists the quantities demanded at each different price when all the other influences on consumers' planned purchases—such as income, population, preferences, and future prices—remain the same. For example, if the price of a tape is $1, the quantity demanded is 9 million tapes a week. If the price of a tape is $5, the quantity demanded is 2 million tapes a week. The other rows of the table show the quantities demanded at prices of $2, $3, and $4.

We graph the demand schedule as a demand curve with the quantity demanded on the horizontal axis and the price on the vertical axis. The points on the demand curve labeled *a* through *e* represent the rows of the demand schedule. For example, point *a* on the graph represents a quantity demanded of 9 million tapes a week at a price of $1 a tape.

**Willingness and Ability to Pay**  Another way of looking at the demand curve is as a willingness-and-ability-to-pay curve. And the willingness-and-ability-to-pay is a measure of *marginal benefit*.

If a small quantity is available, the highest price that someone is willing and able to pay for one more unit is high. But as the quantity available increases, the marginal benefit of each additional unit falls and the highest price that someone is willing and able to pay for it also falls along the demand curve.

In Fig. 4.2, if 2 million tapes are available each week, the highest price that someone is willing to pay for the 2 millionth tape is $5. But if 9 million tapes are available each week, someone is willing to pay only $1 for the last tape bought.

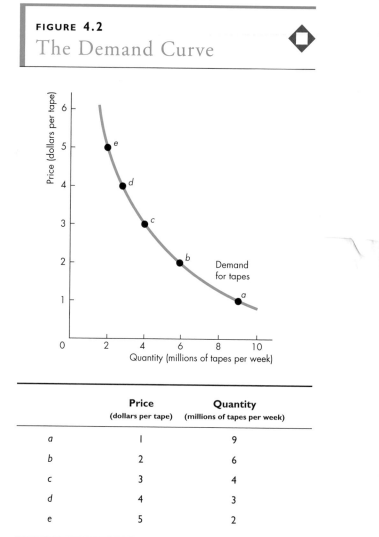

**FIGURE 4.2**

## The Demand Curve

|   | Price (dollars per tape) | Quantity (millions of tapes per week) |
|---|---|---|
| a | 1 | 9 |
| b | 2 | 6 |
| c | 3 | 4 |
| d | 4 | 3 |
| e | 5 | 2 |

The table shows a demand schedule listing the quantity of tapes demanded at each price if all other influences on buyers' plans remain the same. At a price of $1 a tape, 9 million tapes a week are demanded; at a price of $3 a tape, 4 million tapes a week are demanded. The demand curve shows the relationship between quantity demanded and price, everything else remaining the same.

The demand curve slopes downward: As price decreases, the quantity demanded increases. The demand curve can be read in two ways. For a given price, it tells us the quantity that people plan to buy. For example, at a price of $3 a tape, the quantity demanded is 4 million tapes a week. For a given quantity, the demand curve tells us the maximum price that consumers are willing and able to pay for the last tape available. For example, the maximum price that consumers will pay for the 6 millionth tape is $2.

## A Change in Demand

When any factor that influences buying plans other than the price of the good changes, there is a **change in demand**. Figure 4.3 illustrates an increase in demand. When demand increases, the demand curve shifts rightward and the quantity demanded is greater at each and every price. For example, at a price of $5, on the original (blue) demand curve, the quantity demanded is 2 million tapes a week. On the new (red) demand curve, the quantity demanded is 6 million tapes a week. Look closely at the numbers in the table in Fig. 4.3 and check that the quantity demanded is higher at each price.

Let's look at the factors that bring a change in demand. There are five key factors to consider.

**I. Prices of Related Goods** The quantity of tapes that consumers plan to buy depends in part on the prices of substitutes for tapes. A **substitute** is a good that can be used in place of another good. For example, a bus ride is a substitute for a train ride; a hamburger is a substitute for a hot dog, and a compact disc is a substitute for a tape. If the price of a substitute for a tape increases, people buy less of the substitute and more tapes. For example, if the price of a CD rises, people buy fewer CDs and more tapes. The demand for tapes increases.

The quantity of tapes that people plan to buy also depends on the prices of complements of tapes. A **complement** is a good that is used in conjunction with another good. Hamburgers and fries are complements. So are spaghetti and meat sauce, and so are tapes and Walkmans. If the price of a Walkman falls, people buy more Walkmans *and more tapes*. It is a fall in the price of a Walkman that increases the demand for tapes in Fig. 4.3.

**2. Income** Another influence on demand is consumer income. When income increases, consumers buy more of most goods, and when income decreases, they buy less of most goods. Although an increase in income leads to an increase in the demand for *most* goods, it does not lead to an increase in the demand for *all* goods. A **normal good** is one for which demand increases as income increases. An **inferior good** is one for which demand decreases as income increases. Long-distance transportation has examples of both normal goods and inferior goods. As incomes increase, the demand for air travel (a normal good) increases and the demand for long-distance bus trips (an inferior good) decreases.

**FIGURE 4.3**

# An Increase in Demand

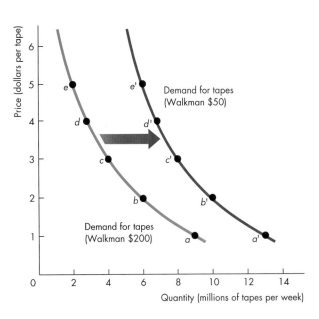

| Original demand schedule | | | New demand schedule | | |
|---|---|---|---|---|---|
| Walkman $200 | | | Walkman $50 | | |
| | **Price** (dollars per tape) | **Quantity** (millions of tapes per week) | | **Price** (dollars per tape) | **Quantity** (millions of tapes per week) |
| a | 1 | 9 | a' | 1 | 13 |
| b | 2 | 6 | b' | 2 | 10 |
| c | 3 | 4 | c' | 3 | 8 |
| d | 4 | 3 | d' | 4 | 7 |
| e | 5 | 2 | e' | 5 | 6 |

A change in any influence on buyers' plans other than the price of the good itself results in a new demand schedule and a shift of the demand curve. A change in the price of a Walkman changes the demand for tapes. At a price of $3 a tape (row c of the table), 4 million tapes a week are demanded when the Walkman costs $200 and 8 million tapes a week are demanded when the Walkman costs only $50. A *fall* in the price of a Walkman *increases* the demand for tapes because the Walkman is a complement of tapes. When demand *increases*, the demand curve shifts *rightward*, as shown by the shift arrow and the resulting red curve.

**3. Population**    Demand also depends on the size and the age structure of the population. The larger the population, the greater is the demand for all goods and services. And the smaller the population, the smaller is the demand for all goods and services.

For example, the demand for car parking spaces or movies or tapes or just about anything you can imagine is much greater in New York City (population 7.5 million) than it is in Boise City, Idaho (population 150,000).

Also, the larger the proportion of the population in a given age group, the greater is the demand for the types of goods and services used by that age group.

For example, in 1995, there were about 3.3 million 19-year-olds in the United States compared with almost 4 million in 1990. As a result, the demand for college places decreased during the 1990s. During these same years, the number of people living in the United States aged 85 years and over increased from 3 million in 1990 to 3.7 million. As a result, the demand for nursing home services increased.

**4. Preferences**    Demand depends on preferences. *Preferences* are an individual's attitudes toward goods and services. For example, a rock music fanatic has a much greater taste for tapes than does a tone-deaf workaholic. As a consequence, even if they have the same incomes, their demands for tapes will be very different.

**5. Expected Future Prices**    If the price of a good is expected to rise in the future and if the good can be stored, the opportunity cost of obtaining the good for future use is lower now than it will be when the price has increased. So people retime their purchase—they substitute over time. They buy more of the good now before its price is expected to rise (and less after), so the current demand for the good increases.

For example, suppose that Florida is hit by a severe frost that damages the season's orange crop. You expect the price of orange juice to soar. So, anticipating the higher price, you fill your freezer with enough frozen juice to get you through the next six months. Your current demand for frozen orange juice has increased (and your future demand has decreased).

Similarly, if the price of a good is expected to fall in the future, the opportunity cost of buying the good in the present is high relative to what it is expected to be in the future. So again, people retime their purchases. They buy less of the good now before its price is expected to fall (and more after), so the current demand for the good decreases.

---

> **TABLE 4.1**
> # The Demand for Tapes
>
> **THE LAW OF DEMAND**
>
> The quantity of tapes demanded
>
> | *Decreases if:* | *Increases if:* |
> |---|---|
> | ■ The price of a tape rises | ■ The price of a tape falls |
>
> **CHANGES IN DEMAND**
>
> The demand for tapes
>
> | *Decreases if:* | *Increases if:* |
> |---|---|
> | ■ The price of a substitute falls | ■ The price of a substitute rises |
> | ■ The price of a complement rises | ■ The price of a complement falls |
> | ■ Income falls* | ■ Income rises* |
> | ■ The population decreases | ■ The population increases |
> | ■ The price of a tape is expected to fall in the future | ■ The price of a tape is expected to rise in the future |
>
> *A tape is a normal good.

Computer prices are constantly falling, and this fact poses a dilemma. Will you buy a new computer now, in time for the start of the school year, or will you wait until the price has fallen some more? Because people expect computer prices to keep falling, the current demand for computers is less (the future demand is greater) than it otherwise would be.

Table 4.1 summarizes the influences on demand and the direction of those influences.

## A Change in the Quantity Demanded Versus a Change in Demand

Changes in the factors that influence buyers' plans cause either a change in the quantity demanded or a change in demand. Equivalently, they cause either a movement along the demand curve or a shift of the demand curve.

The distinction between a change in the quantity demanded and a change in demand is the same as that between a movement along the demand curve and a shift of the demand curve.

A point on the demand curve shows the quantity demanded at a given price. So a movement along the demand curve shows a **change in the quantity demanded**. The entire demand curve shows demand. So a shift of the demand curve shows a **change in demand**. Figure 4.4 illustrates and summarizes these distinctions.

**Movement Along the Demand Curve**   If the price of a good changes but everything else remains the same, there is a movement along the demand curve. The negative slope of the demand curve reveals that a decrease in the price of a good or service increases the quantity demanded—the law of demand.

In Fig. 4.4, if the price of a good falls when everything else remains the same, the quantity demanded of that good increases and there is a movement down the demand curve $D_0$. If the price rises when everything else remains the same, the quantity demanded decreases and there is a movement up the demand curve $D_0$.

**A Shift of the Demand Curve**   If the price of a good remains constant but some other influence on buyers' plans changes, there is a change in demand for that good. We illustrate a change in demand as a shift of the demand curve. For example, a fall in the price of the Walkman—a complement of tapes—increases the demand for tapes. We illustrate this increase in the demand for tapes with a new demand schedule and a new demand curve. If the price of the Walkman falls, consumers buy more tapes regardless of whether the price of a tape is high or low. That is what a rightward shift of the demand curve shows—that more tapes are bought at each and every price.

In Fig. 4.4, when any influence on buyers' planned purchases changes, other than the price of the good, the demand curve shifts and there is a *change* (an increase or a decrease) *in demand*. A rise in income (for a normal good), in population, in the price of a substitute, or in the expected future price of the good or a fall in the price of a complement shifts the demand curve rightward (to the red demand curve $D_1$). This represents an *increase in demand*. A fall in income (for a normal good), in population, in the price of a substitute, or in the expected future price of the good or a rise in the price of a complement shifts the demand curve leftward (to the red demand curve $D_2$). This represents a *decrease in demand*. (For an inferior good, the effects of changes in income are in the direction opposite to those described above.)

**FIGURE 4.4**

A Change in the Quantity Demanded Versus a Change in Demand

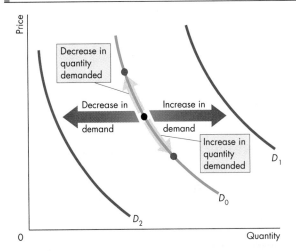

When the price of the good changes, there is a movement along the demand curve and a *change in the quantity demanded*, shown by the blue arrows on demand curve $D_0$. When any other influence on buying plans changes, there is a shift of the demand curve and a *change in demand*. An increase in demand shifts the demand curve rightward (from $D_0$ to $D_1$). A decrease in demand shifts the demand curve leftward (from $D_0$ to $D_2$).

**R E V I E W**

- The quantity demanded is the amount of a good that consumers plan to buy during a given period of time at a particular price. Other things remaining the same, the quantity demanded increases as price decreases.
- Demand is the relationship between quantity demanded and price, other things remaining the same.
- When the price of the good changes and all other influences on buying plans remain the same, there is a change in the quantity demanded and a movement along the demand curve.
- When any influence on buying plans other than the price of the good changes, there is a change in demand and a shift of the demand curve.

# Supply

IF A FIRM SUPPLIES A GOOD OR SERVICE, THE FIRM

- Has the resources and technology to produce it,
- Can profit from producing it, and
- Has made a definite plan to produce it and sell it.

A supply is more that just having the *resources* and the *technology* to produce something. *Resources and technology* are the constraints that limit what is possible.

Many useful things can be produced, but they are not produced unless it is profitable to do so. Supply reflects a decision about which technologically feasible items to produce.

The **quantity supplied** of a good or service is the amount that producers plan to sell during a given time period at a particular price. The quantity supplied is not necessarily the same amount as the quantity actually sold. Sometimes the quantity supplied is greater than the quantity demanded, so the quantity bought is less than the quantity supplied.

Like the quantity demanded, the quantity supplied is measured as an amount per unit of time. For example, suppose that GM produces 1,000 cars a day. The quantity of cars supplied by GM can be expressed as 1,000 a day or 7,000 a week or 365,000 a year. Without the time dimension, we cannot tell whether a particular number is large or small.

## What Determines Selling Plans?

The amount of any particular good or service that producers plan to sell depends on many factors. The main ones are:

- The price of the good
- The prices of resources used to produce the good
- Technology
- The number of suppliers
- The prices of related goods produced
- Expected future prices

Let's first look at the relationship between the price of a good and the quantity supplied. To study this relationship, we hold constant all the other influences on the quantity supplied. We ask: How does the quantity supplied of a good vary as its price varies?

## The Law of Supply

The law of supply states:

Other things remaining the same, the higher the price of a good, the greater is the quantity supplied.

Why does a higher price increase the quantity supplied? It is because of *increasing marginal cost*. As the quantity produced of any good increases, the marginal cost of producing the good increases. (You can refresh your memory of increasing marginal cost in Chapter 3, p. 46.)

It is never worth producing a good if the price received for it does not at least cover marginal cost. So when the price of a good rises, other things remaining the same, producers are willing to incur the higher marginal cost and increase production. The higher price brings forth an increase in the quantity supplied.

Let's now illustrate the law of supply with a supply curve and a supply schedule.

## Supply Curve and Supply Schedule

You are now going to study the second of the two most used curves in economics, the supply curve. And you're going to learn about the critical distinction between *supply* and *quantity supplied*.

The term **supply** refers to the entire relationship between the quantity supplied and the price of a good, and it is illustrated by the supply curve and the supply schedule. The term *quantity supplied* refers to a point on a supply curve—the quantity supplied at a particular price.

Figure 4.5 shows the supply curve of tapes. A **supply curve** shows the relationship between the quantity supplied of a good and its price when all other influences on producers' planned sales remain the same. It is a graph of a supply schedule.

The table in Fig. 4.5 sets out the supply schedule for tapes. A *supply schedule* lists the quantities supplied at each different price when all the other influences on producers' planned sales remain the same. For example, if the price of a tape is $1, the quantity supplied is zero—on row *a* of the table. If the price of a tape is $2, the quantity supplied is 3 million tapes a week—on row *b*. The other rows of the table show the quantities supplied at prices of $3, $4, and $5.

**FIGURE 4.5**

## The Supply Curve

The table shows the supply schedule of tapes. For example, at $2 a tape, 3 million tapes a week are supplied; at $5 a tape, 6 million tapes a week are supplied. The supply curve shows the relationship between the quantity supplied and price, everything else remaining the same. The supply curve usually slopes upward: As the price of a good increases, so does the quantity supplied.

A supply curve can be read in two ways. For a given price, its tells us the quantity that producers plan to sell. And for a given quantity, it tells us the minimum price that producers are willing to accept for that quantity.

|  | Price (dollars per tape) | Quantity (millions of tapes per week) |
|---|---|---|
| a | 1 | 0 |
| b | 2 | 3 |
| c | 3 | 4 |
| d | 4 | 5 |
| e | 5 | 6 |

To make a supply curve, we graph the quantity supplied on the horizontal axis and the price on the vertical axis, just as in the case of the demand curve. The points on the supply curve labeled *a* through *e* represent the rows of the supply schedule. For example, point *a* on the graph represents a quantity supplied of zero at a price of $1 a tape.

**Minimum Supply Price**   Just as the demand curve has two interpretations, so too does the supply curve. The demand curve can be interpreted as a willingness-and-ability-to-pay curve. The supply curve can be interpreted as a minimum-supply-price curve. It tells us the lowest price at which someone can profitably sell another unit.

If a small quantity is produced, the lowest price at which someone can profitably sell one more unit is low. But if a large quantity is produced, the lowest price at which someone can profitably sell one more unit is high.

In Fig. 4.5, if 6 million tapes are produced each week, the lowest price that a producer is willing to accept for the 6 millionth tape is $5. But if only 4 million tapes are produced each week, the lowest price that a producer is willing to accept for the 4 millionth tape is $3.

## A Change in Supply

When any factor that influences selling plans other than the price of the good changes, there is a **change in supply**. Let's look at the five key factors that change supply.

**1. Prices of Productive Resources**   The prices of productive resources influence supply. The easiest way to see this influence is to think about the supply curve as a minimum-supply-price curve. If the prices of productive resources rise, the lowest price a producer is willing to accept rises so supply decreases. For example, during 1996, the price of jet fuel increased and the supply of air transportation decreased. Similarly, a rise in the minimum wage decreased the supply of hamburgers. If the wages of tape producers rise, the supply of tapes decreases.

**2. Technology**   Advances in technology are the single biggest influence on supply. New technologies create new products and lower the costs of producing existing products. As a result, they change supply. For example, the development of a new technology for tape production by Sony and Minnesota Mining and Manufacturing (3M) has lowered the cost of producing tapes and increased the supply of tapes.

**3. The Number of Suppliers**   Supply also depends on the number of suppliers. The larger the number of firms that produce a good, the greater is the supply of the good. As firms enter an industry, the supply in that industry increases. As firms leave an industry, the supply in that industry decreases. For example, over the past two years, there has been a huge increase in the number of firms that produce and manage World Wide Web sites. As a result, the supply of Internet and World Wide Web services has increased enormously.

**4. Prices of Related Goods Produced**   The prices of related goods and services that firms produce influence supply. For example, if the price of prerecorded tapes rises, the supply of blank tapes decreases. Blank tapes and prerecorded tapes are *substitutes in production*—goods that can be produced by using the same resources. If the price of beef rises, the supply of cowhide increases. Beef and cowhide are *complements in production*—goods that must be produced together.

**5. Expected Future Prices**   If the price of a good is expected to rise, the return from selling the good in the future is higher than it is in the present. So the current supply decreases.

Figure 4.6 illustrates an increase in supply. When supply increases, the supply curve shifts rightward and the quantity supplied is larger at each and every price. For example, at a price of $2, on the original (blue) supply curve, the quantity supplied is 3 million tapes a week. On the new (red) supply curve, the quantity supplied is 6 million tapes a week. Look closely at the numbers in the table in Fig. 4.6 and check that the quantity supplied is larger at each price.

Table 4.2 summarizes the influences on supply and the directions of those influences.

## A Change in the Quantity Supplied Versus a Change in Supply

Changes in the factors that influence producers' planned sales cause either a change in the quantity supplied or a change in supply. Equivalently, they cause either a movement along the supply curve or a shift of the supply curve.

A point on the supply curve shows the quantity supplied at a given price. So a movement along the

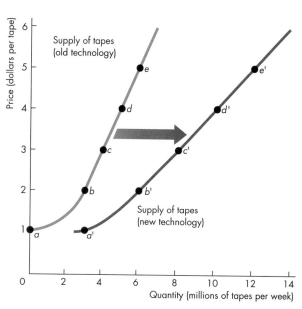

**FIGURE 4.6**

## An Increase in Supply

| Original supply schedule<br>Old technology | | New supply schedule<br>New technology | |
|---|---|---|---|
| **Price**<br>(dollars<br>per tape) | **Quantity**<br>(millions of tapes<br>per week) | **Price**<br>(dollars<br>per tape) | **Quantity**<br>(millions of tapes<br>per week) |
| a    1 | 0 | a'    1 | 3 |
| b    2 | 3 | b'    2 | 6 |
| c    3 | 4 | c'    3 | 8 |
| d    4 | 5 | d'    4 | 10 |
| e    5 | 6 | e'    5 | 12 |

A change in any influence on sellers' plans other than the price of the good itself results in a new supply schedule and a shift of the supply curve. For example, if Sony and 3M invent a new, cost-saving technology for producing tapes, the supply of tapes changes.

At a price of $3 a tape, 4 million tapes a week are supplied when producers use the old technology (row c of the table) and 8 million tapes a week are supplied when producers use the new technology. An advance in technology *increases* the supply of tapes and shifts the supply curve *rightward*, as shown by the shift arrow and the resulting red curve.

supply curve shows a **change in the quantity supplied**. The entire supply curve shows supply. So a shift of the supply curve shows a **change in supply**.

Figure 4.7 illustrates and summarizes these distinctions. If the price of a good falls and everything else remains the same, the quantity supplied of that good decreases and there is a movement down the supply curve $S_0$. If the price of a good rises and everything else remains the same, the quantity supplied increases and there is a movement up the supply curve $S_0$. When any other influence on selling plans changes, the supply curve shifts and there is a change in supply. If the supply curve is $S_0$ and if production costs fall supply increases and the supply curve shifts to the red supply curve $S_1$. If production costs rise, supply decreases and the supply curve shifts to the red supply curve $S_2$.

---

### TABLE 4.2

## The Supply of Tapes

**THE LAW OF SUPPLY**

The quantity of tapes supplied

| *Decreases if:* | *Increases if:* |
|---|---|
| ■ The price of a tape falls | ■ The price of a tape rises |

**CHANGES IN SUPPLY**

The supply of tapes

| *Decreases if:* | *Increases if:* |
|---|---|
| ■ The price of a resource used to produce tapes rises | ■ The price of a resource used to produce tapes falls |
| | ■ More efficient technologies for producing tapes are discovered |
| ■ The number of tape producers decreases | ■ The number of tape producers increases |
| ■ The price of a substitute in production rises | ■ The price of a substitute in production falls |
| ■ The price of a complement in production falls | ■ The price of a complement in production rises |
| ■ The price of a tape is expected to rise in the future | ■ The price of a tape is expected to fall in the future |

---

### FIGURE 4.7

## A Change in the Quantity Supplied Versus a Change in Supply

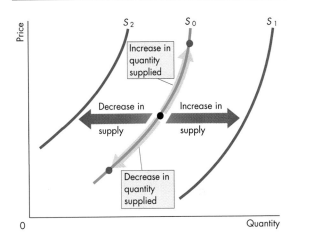

When the price of the good changes, there is a movement along the supply curve and a *change in the quantity supplied*, shown by the blue arrows on supply curve $S_0$. When any other influence on selling plans changes, there is a shift of the supply curve and a *change in supply*. An increase in supply shifts the supply curve rightward (from $S_0$ to $S_1$). A decrease in supply shifts the supply curve shifts leftward (from $S_0$ to $S_2$).

---

### R E V I E W

■ The quantity supplied is the amount of a good that producers plan to sell during a given period at a given price. Other things remaining the same, the quantity supplied increases as price increases.

■ Supply is the relationship between quantity supplied and price, other things remaining the same.

■ When the price of the good changes, other things remaining the same, there is a change in the quantity supplied and a movement along the supply curve.

■ Changes in other influences on selling plans change supply and shift the supply curve.

Let's now bring demand and supply together and see how prices and quantities are determined.

## Market Equilibrium

WE HAVE SEEN THAT WHEN THE PRICE OF A good rises, the quantity demanded *decreases* and the quantity supplied *increases*. We are now going to see how prices coordinate the plans of buyers and sellers and achieve an equilibrium.

An *equilibrium* is a situation in which opposing forces balance each other. Equilibrium in a market occurs when the price balances the plans of buyers and sellers. The **equilibrium price** is the price at which the quantity demanded equals the quantity supplied. The **equilibrium quantity** is the quantity bought and sold at the equilibrium price. A market moves toward its equilibrium because:

■ Price regulates buying and selling plans
■ Price adjusts when plans don't match

### Price as a Regulator

The price of a good regulates the quantities demanded and supplied. If the price is too high, the quantity supplied exceeds the quantity demanded. If the price is too low, the quantity demanded exceeds the quantity supplied. There is one price at which the quantity demanded equals the quantity supplied. Let's work out what that price is.

Figure 4.8 shows the market for tapes. The table shows the demand schedule (from Fig. 4.2) and the supply schedule (from Fig. 4.5). If the price of a tape is $1, the quantity demanded is 9 million tapes a week, but no tapes are supplied. The quantity demanded exceeds the quantity supplied by 9 million tapes a week. In other words, at a price of $1 a tape, there is a shortage of 9 million tapes a week. This shortage is shown in the final column of the table. At a price of $2 a tape, there is still a shortage, but only of 3 million tapes a week. If the price of a tape is $5, the quantity supplied exceeds the quantity demanded. The quantity supplied is 6 million tapes a week, but the quantity demanded is only 2 million. There is a surplus of 4 million tapes a week. The one price at which there is neither a shortage nor a surplus is $3 a tape. At that price, the quantity demanded is equal to the quantity supplied: 4 million tapes a week. The equilibrium price is $3 a tape, and the equilibrium quantity is 4 million tapes a week.

Figure 4.8 shows that the demand curve and supply curve intersect at the equilibrium price of $3 a

### FIGURE 4.8
## Equilibrium

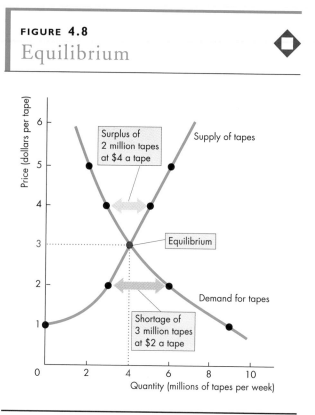

| Price (dollars per tape) | Quantity demanded | Quantity supplied | Shortage (–) or surplus (+) |
|---|---|---|---|
| | (millions of tapes per week) | | |
| 1 | 9 | 0 | –9 |
| 2 | 6 | 3 | –3 |
| 3 | 4 | 4 | 0 |
| 4 | 3 | 5 | +2 |
| 5 | 2 | 6 | +4 |

The table lists the quantities demanded and quantities supplied as well as the shortage or surplus of tapes at each price. If the price is $2 a tape, 6 million tapes a week are demanded and 3 million are supplied. There is a shortage of 3 million tapes a week, and the price rises. If the price is $4 a tape, 3 million tapes a week are demanded and 5 million are supplied. There is a surplus of 2 million tapes a week, and the price falls. If the price is $3 a tape, 4 million tapes a week are demanded and 4 million are supplied. There is neither a shortage nor a surplus. Neither buyers nor sellers have any incentive to change the price. The price at which the quantity demanded equals the quantity supplied is the equilibrium price.

tape. At each price *above* $3 a tape, there is a surplus of tapes. For example, at $4 a tape, the surplus is 2 million tapes a week, as shown by the blue arrow. At each price *below* $3 a tape, there is a shortage of tapes. For example, at $2 a tape, the shortage is 3 million tapes a week, as shown by the red arrow.

## Price Adjustments

You've seen that if the price is below equilibrium there is shortage and if the price is above equilibrium there is a surplus. But can we count on the price to change and eliminate a shortage or surplus? We can, because such price changes are mutually beneficial to both buyers and sellers. Let's see why the price changes when there is a shortage or a surplus.

**A Shortage Forces the Price Up**  Suppose the price of a tape is $2. Consumers plan to buy 6 million tapes a week, and producers plan to sell 3 million tapes a week. Consumers can't force producers to sell more than they plan, so the quantity actually offered for sale is 3 million tapes a week. In this situation, powerful forces operate to increase the price and move it toward the equilibrium price. Some producers, noticing lines of unsatisfied consumers, move their prices up. Some producers increase their output. As producers push their prices up, the price rises toward its equilibrium. The rising price reduces the shortage because it decreases the quantity demanded and increases the quantity supplied. When the price has increased to the point at which there is no longer a shortage, the forces moving the price stop operating and the price comes to rest at its equilibrium.

**A Surplus Forces the Price Down**  Suppose the price of a tape is $4. Producers plan to sell 5 million tapes a week, and consumers plan to buy 3 million tapes a week. Producers cannot force consumers to buy more than they plan, so the quantity that is actually bought is 3 million tapes a week. In this situation, powerful forces operate to lower the price and move it toward the equilibrium price. Some producers, unable to sell the quantities of tapes they planned to sell, cut their prices. In addition, some producers scale back production. As producers cut prices, the price falls toward its equilibrium. The falling price decreases the surplus because it increases the quantity demanded and decreases the quantity supplied. When the price has fallen to the point at which there is no longer a surplus, the forces moving the price

stop operating, and the price comes to rest at its equilibrium.

**The Best Deal Available for Buyers and Sellers**
When the price is below equilibrium, it is forced upward toward the equilibrium. Why don't buyers resist the increase and refuse to buy at the higher price? Because they value the good more highly than the current price and they cannot satisfy all their demands at the current price. In some markets— an example is the market for rental accommodation in Atlanta during the 1996 Olympic Games—the buyers might even be the ones who force the price upward by offering higher prices to divert the limited quantities away from other buyers.

When the price is above equilibrium, it is bid downward toward the equilibrium. Why don't sellers resist this decrease and refuse to sell at the lower price? Because their minimum supply price is below the current price and they cannot sell all they would like to at the current price. Normally, it is the sellers who force the price downward by offering lower prices to gain market share from their competitors.

At the price at which the quantity demanded and the quantity supplied are equal, neither buyers nor sellers can do business at a better price. Buyers pay the highest price they are willing to pay for the last unit bought, and sellers receive the lowest price at which they are willing to supply the last unit sold.

When people freely make offers to buy and sell, and when demanders try to buy at the lowest possible price and suppliers try to sell at the highest possible price, the price at which trade takes place is the equilibrium price—the price at which the quantity demanded equals the quantity supplied. The price coordinates the plans of buyers and sellers.

---

### R E V I E W

■ The equilibrium price is the price at which buyers' and sellers' plans match each other—the price at which the quantity demanded equals the quantity supplied.

■ At prices below the equilibrium price, there is a shortage and the price rises.

■ At prices above the equilibrium price, there is a surplus and the price falls.

■ Only at the equilibrium price are there no forces acting on the price to make it change.

## Predicting Changes in Price and Quantity

THE DEMAND AND SUPPLY THEORY WE HAVE JUST studied provides us with a powerful way of analyzing influences on prices and the quantities bought and sold. According to the theory, a change in price stems from either a change in demand or a change in supply or a change in both. Let's look first at the effects of a change in demand.

### A Change in Demand

What happens to the price and quantity of tapes if the demand for tapes increases? We can answer this question with a specific example. Suppose the price of a Walkman falls from $200 to $50. Because the Walkman and tapes are complements, the demand for tapes increases, as is shown in the table in Fig. 4.9. The original demand schedule and the new one are set out in the first three columns of the table. The table also shows the supply schedule for tapes.

The original equilibrium price is $3 a tape. At that price, 4 million tapes a week are demanded and supplied. When demand increases, the price that makes the quantity demanded equal the quantity supplied is $5 a tape. At this price, 6 million tapes are bought and sold each week. When demand increases, both the price and the quantity increase.

Figure 4.9 shows these changes. The figure shows the original demand for and supply of tapes. The original equilibrium price is $3 a tape, and the quantity is 4 million tapes a week. When demand increases, the demand curve shifts rightward. The equilibrium price rises to $5 a tape, and the quantity supplied increases to 6 million tapes a week, as highlighted in the figure. There is an *increase in the quantity supplied* but *no change in supply*—a movement along, but no shift of, the supply curve.

We can reverse the exercise that we've just conducted. We can work out what happens if we start at a price of $5 a tape with 6 million tapes a week being bought and sold and then demand decreases to its original level. Such a decrease in demand might arise from a fall in the price of CDs or CD players (both substitutes for tapes). The decrease in demand shifts the demand curve leftward. The equilibrium price falls to $3 a tape, and the equilibrium quantity decreases to 4 million tapes a week.

FIGURE 4.9

## The Effects of a Change in Demand

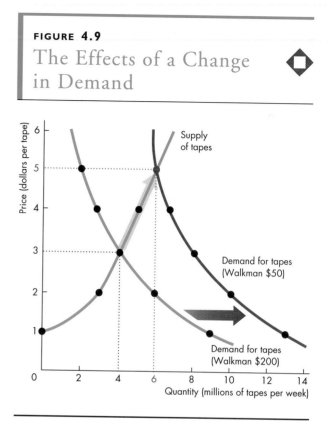

| Price | Quantity demanded | | Quantity supplied |
|---|---|---|---|
| (dollars per tape) | (millions of tapes per week) | | (millions of tapes per week) |
| | Walkman $200 | Walkman $50 | |
| 1 | 9 | 13 | 0 |
| 2 | 6 | 10 | 3 |
| 3 | 4 | 8 | 4 |
| 4 | 3 | 7 | 5 |
| 5 | 2 | 6 | 6 |

With the price of a Walkman at $200, the demand for tapes is the blue curve. The equilibrium price is $3 a tape, and the equilibrium quantity is 4 million tapes a week. When the price of a Walkman falls from $200 to $50, the demand for tapes increases and the demand curve shifts rightward to become the red curve.

At $3 a tape, there is now a shortage of 4 million tapes a week. The price of a tape rises to a new equilibrium of $5 a tape. As the price rises to $5, the quantity supplied increases—shown by the blue arrow on the supply curve—to the new equilibrium quantity of 6 million tapes a week. Following an increase in demand, the quantity supplied increases but supply does not change—the supply curve does not shift.

We can now make our first two predictions:

■ When demand increases, both the price and the quantity increase.

■ When demand decreases, both the price and the quantity decrease.

## A Change in Supply

Suppose that Sony and 3M introduce a new cost-saving technology in their tape production plants. The new technology increases the supply of tapes. The new supply schedule (the same one that was shown in Fig. 4.6) is presented in the table in Fig. 4.10. What are the new equilibrium price and quantity? The answer is highlighted in the table: The price falls to $2 a tape, and the quantity increases to 6 million a week. You can see why by looking at the quantities demanded and supplied at the old price of $3 a tape. The quantity supplied at that price is 8 million tapes a week, and there is a surplus of tapes. The price falls. Only when the price is $2 a tape does the quantity supplied equal the quantity demanded.

Figure 4.10 illustrates the effect of an increase in supply. It shows the demand curve for tapes and the original and new supply curves. The initial equilibrium price is $3 a tape and the quantity is 4 million tapes a week. When the supply increases, the supply curve shifts rightward. The equilibrium price falls to $2 a tape, and the quantity demanded increases to 6 million tapes a week, highlighted in the figure. There is an *increase in the quantity demanded* but *no change in demand*—a movement along, but no shift of, the demand curve.

The exercise that we've just conducted can be reversed. If we start out at a price of $2 a tape with 6 million tapes a week being bought and sold, we can work out what happens if supply decreases to its original level. Such a decrease in supply might arise from an increase in the cost of labor or raw materials. The decrease in supply shifts the supply curve leftward. The equilibrium price rises to $3 a tape, and the equilibrium quantity decreases to 4 million tapes a week.

We can now make two more predictions:

■ When supply increases, the quantity increases and the price falls.

■ When supply decreases, the quantity decreases and the price rises.

**FIGURE 4.10**

# The Effects of a Change in Supply

| Price | Quantity demanded | Quantity supplied (millions of tapes per week) | |
|---|---|---|---|
| (dollars per tape) | (millions of tapes per week) | old technology | new technology |
| 1 | 9 | 0 | 3 |
| 2 | 6 | 3 | 6 |
| 3 | 4 | 4 | 8 |
| 4 | 3 | 5 | 10 |
| 5 | 2 | 6 | 12 |

With the old technology, the supply of tapes is shown by the blue supply curve. The equilibrium price is $3 a tape, and the equilibrium quantity is 4 million tapes a week. When the new technology is adopted, the supply of tapes increases and the supply curve shifts rightward to become the red curve.

At $3 a tape, there is now a surplus of 4 million tapes a week. The price of a tape falls to a new equilibrium of $2 a tape. As the price falls to $2, the quantity demanded increases—shown by the blue arrow on the demand curve—to the new equilibrium quantity of 6 million tapes a week. Following an increase in supply, the quantity demanded increases but demand does not change—the demand curve does not shift.

## A Change in Both Demand and Supply

You can now predict the effects of a change in either demand or supply on the price and the quantity. But what happens if *both* demand and supply change together? To answer this question, we look first at the case in which demand and supply move in the same direction—either both increase or both decrease. Then we look at the case in which they move in opposite directions—demand decreases and supply increases or demand increases and supply decreases.

**Demand and Supply Change in the Same Direction**  We've seen that an increase in the demand for tapes increases the price of tapes and increases the quantity bought and sold. And we've seen that an increase in the supply of tapes lowers the price of tapes and increases the quantity bought and sold. Let's now examine what happens when both of these changes occur together.

The table in Fig. 4.11 brings together the numbers that describe the original quantities demanded and supplied and the new quantities demanded and supplied after the fall in the price of the Walkman and the improved tape production technology. These same numbers are illustrated in the graph. The original (blue) demand and supply curves intersect at a price of $3 a tape and a quantity of 4 million tapes a week. The new (red) supply and demand curves also intersect at a price of $3 a tape but at a quantity of 8 million tapes a week.

An increase in either demand or supply increases the quantity. So when both demand and supply increase, so does quantity.

An increase in demand raises the price, and an increase in supply lowers the price, so we can't say whether the price will rise or fall when demand and supply increase together. In this example, the price does not change. But notice that if demand increases by slightly more than the amount shown in the figure, the price will rise. And if supply increases by slightly more than the amount shown in the figure, the price will fall.

We can now make two more predictions:

- When *both* demand and supply increase, the quantity increases and the price increases, decreases, or remains constant.

- When *both* demand and supply decrease, the quantity decreases and the price increases, decreases, or remains constant.

### FIGURE 4.11

## The Effects of an Increase in Both Demand and Supply

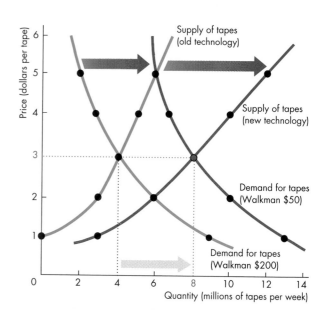

| Price (dollars per tape) | Original quantities (millions of tapes per week) | | New quantities (millions of tapes per week) | |
|---|---|---|---|---|
| | Quantity demanded Walkman $200 | Quantity supplied old technology | Quantity demanded Walkman $50 | Quantity supplied new technology |
| 1 | 9 | 0 | 13 | 3 |
| 2 | 6 | 3 | 10 | 6 |
| 3 | 4 | 4 | 8 | 8 |
| 4 | 3 | 5 | 7 | 10 |
| 5 | 2 | 6 | 6 | 12 |

When a Walkman costs $200 and the old technology is used to produce tapes, the price of a tape is $3 and the quantity is 4 million tapes a week. A fall in the price of a Walkman increases the demand for tapes, and improved technology increases the supply of tapes. The new supply curve intersects the new demand curve at $3 a tape, the same price as before, but the quantity increases to 8 million tapes a week. These increases in demand and supply increase the quantity but leave the price unchanged.

**Demand and Supply Change in Opposite Directions** Let's now see what happens when demand and supply change together but move in *opposite* directions. An improved production technology increases the supply of tapes as before. But now the price of CD players falls. A CD player is a *substitute* for tapes. With less costly CD players, more people buy them and switch from buying tapes to buying discs, and the demand for tapes decreases.

The table in Fig. 4.12 describes the original and new demand and supply schedules. These schedules are shown as the original (blue) and new (red) demand and supply curves in the graph. The original demand and supply curves intersect at a price of $5 a tape and a quantity of 6 million tapes a week. The new supply and demand curves intersect at a price of $2 a tape and at the original quantity of 6 million tapes a week.

A decrease in demand or an increase in supply lowers the price. So when a decrease in demand and an increase in supply occur together, the price falls.

A decrease in demand decreases the quantity, and an increase in supply increases the quantity, so we can't say for sure which way the quantity will change when demand decreases and supply increases at the same time. In this example, the decrease in demand and the increase in supply are such that the increase in quantity brought about by an increase in supply is offset by the decrease in quantity brought about by a decrease in demand—so the quantity does not change. But notice that if demand had decreased slightly more than shown in the figure, the quantity would have decreased. And if supply had increased by slightly more than shown in the figure, the quantity would have increased.

We can now make two more predictions:

- When demand decreases and supply increases, the price falls and the quantity increases, decreases, or remains constant.
- When demand increases and supply decreases, the price rises and the quantity increases, decreases, or remains constant.

**Make Your Own Summary Figure** You've now seen the eight combinations of changes in demand and supply, each on its own and both together. Problem 6 on p. 90 invites you to review the predictions for each case. Don't skip this problem. And make your own summary figure for each case. There is no good substitute for drawing your own figures and becoming thoroughly familiar with these eight predictions.

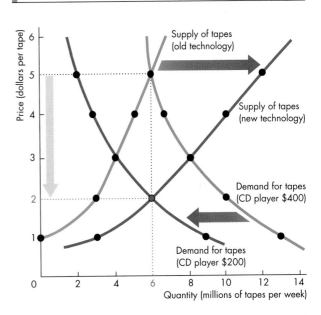

FIGURE 4.12

The Effects of a Decrease in Demand and an Increase in Supply

| Price (dollars per tape) | Original quantities (millions of tapes per week) | | New quantities (millions of tapes per week) | |
|---|---|---|---|---|
| | Quantity demanded CD player $400 | Quantity supplied old technology | Quantity demanded CD player $200 | Quantity supplied new technology |
| 1 | 13 | 0 | 9 | 3 |
| 2 | 10 | 3 | 6 | 6 |
| 3 | 8 | 4 | 4 | 8 |
| 4 | 7 | 5 | 3 | 10 |
| 5 | 6 | 6 | 2 | 12 |

When a CD player costs $400 and the old technology is used to produce tapes, the price of a tape is $5 and the quantity is 6 million tapes a week. A fall in the price of a CD player decreases the demand for tapes, and improved technology increases the supply of tapes. The new supply curve intersects the new demand curve at $2 a tape, a lower price, but in this case the quantity remains constant at 6 million tapes a week. The decrease in demand and increase in supply lower the price but leave the quantity unchanged.

## CD Players, Health Care, and Bananas

Earlier in this chapter, we looked at some facts about prices and quantities of CD players, health care, and bananas. Let's use the theory of demand and supply that we have just studied to explain the movements in the prices and quantities of those goods.

**A Price Slide: CD Players**    Figure 4.13(a) shows the market for CD players. In 1983, when CD players were first manufactured, very few producers made them and the supply was small. The supply curve was $S_0$. In 1983, there weren't many titles on CDs and the demand for CD players was small. The demand curve was $D_0$. The quantities supplied and demanded in 1983 were equal at $Q_0$, and the price was $1,100 (1994 dollars). As the technology for making CD players improved and as more and more factories began to produce CD players, the supply increased by a large amount and the supply curve shifted rightward from $S_0$ to $S_1$. At the same time, increases in incomes, a decrease in the price of CDs, and an increase in the number of titles on CDs increased the demand for CD players. But the increase in demand was much smaller than the increase in supply. The demand curve shifted rightward from $D_0$ to $D_1$. With the new demand curve $D_1$ and the new supply curve $S_1$, the equilibrium price fell to $170 in 1994 and the quantity increased to $Q_1$. The large increase in supply combined with a smaller increase in demand resulted in an increase in the quantity of CD players and a dramatic fall in the price. Figure 4.13(a) shows the CD player price slide.

**A Price Rocket: Health Care**    Figure 4.13(b) shows the market for health-care services. In 1980, the supply curve for health-care services was $S_0$. Advances in medical technology have greatly increased the range and complexity of conditions that can be treated and have increased the supply of health-care services. But large increases in doctors' compensation and costs have escalated the cost of providing health care and have decreased supply. The net change in supply resulting from these two opposing forces has been an increase. The supply curve has shifted rightward from $S_0$ to $S_1$. At the same time that supply increased by a relatively modest amount, the demand for health care increased enormously. Some of the increase resulted from higher incomes, some from an aging population, and some from a demand for newly available treatments. The combination of these influences on demand resulted in the demand curve shifting from $D_0$ to $D_1$. The combined effect of a large increase in demand and a small increase in supply was an increase in the quantity from $Q_0$ to $Q_1$ and an increase in price from 100 (an index number) in 1980 to 160 in 1995. Figure 4.13(b) shows the health-care price rocket.

**A Price Roller Coaster: Bananas**    Figure 4.13(c) shows the market for bananas. The demand for bananas—curve $D$—does not change much over the years. But the supply of bananas, which depends mainly on the weather, fluctuates between $S_0$ and $S_1$. With good growing conditions, the supply curve is $S_1$. With bad growing conditions, supply decreases and the supply curve is $S_0$. As a consequence of fluctuations in supply, the quantity fluctuates between $Q_0$ and $Q_1$. The price of bananas fluctuates between 33 cents per pound (1995 cents), the maximum price, and 20 cents per pound, the minimum price. Figure 4.13(c) shows the banana price roller coaster.

**The Invisible Hand**    Adam Smith said that each buyer and seller in a market "is led by an invisible hand to promote an end which was no part of his intention." What did he mean? He meant that when each one of us makes decisions to buy or sell to achieve the best outcome for ourselves and when our decisions are coordinated in free markets, we end up achieving the best outcome for everyone.

Although markets are amazing instruments, it turns out that they do not always work quite as perfectly as Adam Smith imagined. If you go on to study *micro*economics, you will discover the conditions under which markets are efficient and why they sometimes fail to achieve the best possible outcome for everyone. If you go on to study *macro*economics, you will discover the reasons why the market economy produces fluctuations in output and employment and sometimes creates persistent unemployment.

◆ You now know the basic theory of demand and supply. By using this theory, you can explain past fluctuations in prices and quantities and also make predictions about future fluctuations. *Reading Between the Lines* on pp. 86-87 shows you the theory in action in the world price of wheat and in the U.S. price of bread in 1996. You will see lots of news articles about this type of issue. Watch for stories on frosts in Brazil and the price of coffee or frost in Florida and the price of orange juice.

FIGURE 4.13

# Price Slide, Rocket, and Roller Coaster

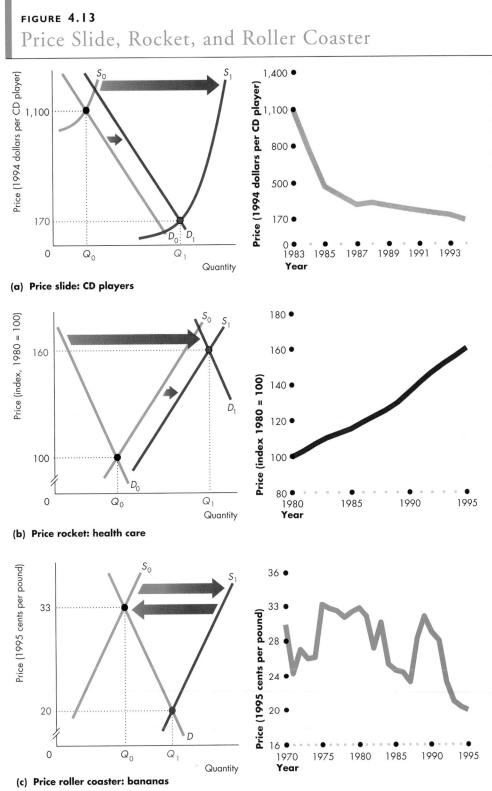

(a) Price slide: CD players

(b) Price rocket: health care

(c) Price roller coaster: bananas

A large increase in the supply of CD players, from $S_0$ to $S_1$ combined with a small increase in demand, from $D_0$ to $D_1$, resulted in an increase in the quantity of CD players bought and sold from $Q_0$ to $Q_1$. The average price of CD players fell from $1,100 in 1983 to $170 in 1994—a price slide.

*Source: U.S. Bureau of the Census, Statistical Abstract of the United States: 1994 (114th edition.) Washington, D.C., 1994.*

A large increase in demand for health care, from $D_0$ to $D_1$, combined with a small increase in the supply, from $S_0$ to $S_1$, has resulted in an increase in the quantity of health care, from $Q_0$ to $Q_1$ and a rise in the price of health care from 100 in 1980 to 160 in 1995—a price rocket.

*Source: Economic Report of the President, 1996.*

The demand for bananas remains constant at $D$. But supply fluctuates between $S_0$ and $S_1$. As a result, the price of bananas has fluctuated between 20 cents per pound and 33 cents per pound—a price roller coaster.

*Source: International Financial Statistics Yearbook, International Monetary Fund, Washington, D.C., 1996.*

# Demand and Supply: The Price of Bread

RALEIGH NEWS OBSERVER, JUNE 28, 1996

## It Takes a Lot of Bread to Buy a Loaf

BY DUDLEY PRICE

... Record wheat prices this spring are finding their way to grocery stores, where shoppers are paying more for bread than almost anyone can remember. ...

Bob Dirkes, senior vice president for marketing for Interstate Brands Corp. of Kansas City, Mo., says it's the biggest increase in 15 years. "The increase in the cost of flour is primarily what's causing that."

Bakers and grocery chains say they tried to keep prices down despite rising wheat and flour costs during the past two years. But now, they are passing along those costs to the consumers.

Nationally, bread prices in May were 8 percent higher than they were a year ago, Dirkes said. ...

A loaf of Sunbeam bread, for example, now costs $1.63, up 42 percent from $1.19 a year ago, said David Colling, a company route salesman in Raleigh. ... Bakery owners and agriculture experts say further declines predicted for this year's wheat harvest probably will lead to even higher prices. ...

Bob Murphy, chief statistician for the state Department of Agriculture, said farmers in the nation's largest wheat-producing states—Kansas, Texas and Oklahoma—weren't spared by droughts that cut the nation's other grain crops. ...

Wheat farmers have seen production decline every year since 1994, when 1.66 billion bushels were harvested, Murphy said.

This year's harvest is expected to be 1.37 billion bushels, a 17 percent decline in just two years.

As a result, wheat and flour prices have increased. A bushel of wheat that Wednesday sold for $5.93 on the Kansas City exchange cost $5.06 just a year ago.

Although the higher cost of wheat is the primary reason bread prices have risen, Dirkes said, high prices at the gas pumps also play a role in higher food costs. ... "Thirty-five percent of the cost of a loaf of bread is the cost of getting it from the bakery to the grocery store."

Reprinted with permission.

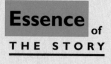

## Essence of THE STORY

- Between mid-1995 and mid-1996, the price of bread increased from $1.19 to $1.63 a loaf and the price of wheat increased from $5.06 to $5.93 a bushel.

- Droughts decreased U.S. wheat production from 1.66 billion bushels in 1994 to an estimated 1.37 billion bushels in 1996.

- The rise in the price of wheat was the primary cause of the rise in the price of bread.

- But a rise in gasoline prices also contributed to the rise in the price of bread.

# Economic

## A N A L Y S I S

■ U.S. wheat production is about 12 percent of the world total, and U.S. wheat consumption is about 6 percent of the world total (see the table).

■ Because wheat is easy to transport, its price is determined by supply and demand in a *world* market, which is shown in Fig. 1.

■ In 1995, demand was $D_{95}$ and supply was $S_{95}$. The price was $5 a bushel, and the quantity consumed was 20.6 billion bushels.

■ In 1996, the price of wheat increased to $6 a bushel but the quantity of wheat consumed remained constant at 20.6 billion bushels.

■ This outcome occurred because supply decreased to $S_{96}$ and demand increased to $D_{96}$. With a decrease in supply and an increase in demand, the price increased. But the decrease in supply and increase in demand left the quantity unchanged.

■ The news article says that supply decreased in 1996 because of a drought in the United States. The U.S. drought contributed to the decrease in world supply.

■ But another factor that decreased world supply was the expected *future* price of wheat. The table shows that traders held on to more inventories. Traders hold wheat to sell later when they expect a higher price in the future.

■ The news article identifies the rise in the price of wheat as a main cause of the rise in the price of bread.

■ Figure 2 shows the market for Sunbeam bread. The demand is $D$. In 1995, supply was $S_{95}$ and the price was $1.19 a loaf.

■ The rise in the price of wheat increased the cost of producing bread and decreased the supply of bread. The supply curve shifted leftward from $S_{95}$ to $S'$. Other factors, such as higher fuel costs, also decreased supply and the supply curve shifted farther leftward to $S_{96}$.

■ The price increased to $1.63 a loaf.

■ The rise in the price of bread brought a decrease in the quantity of bread demanded, which is shown by a movement along the demand curve for bread.

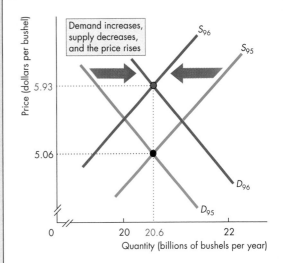

**Figure 1  The world market for wheat**

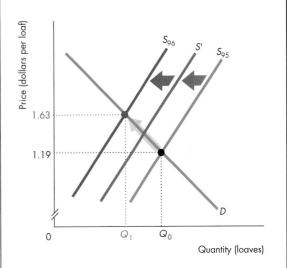

**Figure 2  The market for Sunbeam bread**

| World Wheat Consumption | 1994–95 | 1995–96 |
|---|---|---|
| (billions of bushels) | | |
| United States | 1.3 | 1.2 |
| Rest of world | 19.3 | 19.4 |
| World | 20.6 | 20.6 |
| **World Wheat Production** | **1994–95** | **1995–96** |
| United States | 2.4 | 2.2 |
| Rest of world | 17.3 | 18.2 |
| World | 19.7 | 20.4 |
| Change in wheat inventory | −1.0 | −0.2 |

# SUMMARY

## Key Points

### Price and Opportunity Cost (p. 68)

- Opportunity cost is a relative price. We measure relative price by dividing the price of one good by the price (index) of a basket of all goods.
- Demand and supply determines relative prices.

### Demand (pp. 69–73)

- Demand is the relationship between the quantity demanded of a good and its price when all other influences on buying plans remain the same.
- The higher the price of a good, other things remaining the same, the smaller is the quantity demanded.
- Demand depends on the price of the good, the prices of substitutes and complements, income, population, preferences, and expected future prices.

### Supply (pp. 74–77)

- Supply is the relationship between the quantity supplied of a good and its price when all other influences on selling plans remain the same.
- The higher the price of a good, other things remaining the same, the greater is the quantity supplied.
- Supply depends on the price of the good, the prices of resources used to produce it, technology, the number of producers, the prices of related goods produced, and expected future prices.

### Market Equilibrium (pp. 78–79)

- At the equilibrium price, the quantity demanded equals the quantity supplied.
- At prices above equilibrium, there is a surplus and the price falls.
- At prices below equilibrium, there is a shortage and the price rises.

### Predicting Changes in Price and Quantity (pp. 80–85)

- An increase in demand brings a rise in price and an increase in the quantity supplied. (A decrease in demand brings a fall in price and a decrease in the quantity supplied.)
- An increase in supply brings a fall in price and an increase in the quantity demanded. (A decrease in supply brings a rise in price and a decrease in the quantity demanded.)
- An increase in demand and an increase in supply bring an increased quantity but an ambiguous price change. An increase in demand and a decrease in supply raise the price and bring an ambiguous quantity change.
- Fill in the table in problem 6 (p. 90) for a complete summary of the predictions.

## Key Figures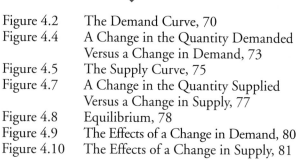

## Key Terms

# QUESTIONS

1. Distinguish between a money price and a relative price. Which is an opportunity cost and why?
2. Define the quantity demanded of a good or service.
3. Define the quantity supplied of a good or service.
4. List the main factors that influence the amount that consumers plan to buy and say whether an increase in each factor increases or decreases consumers' planned purchases.
5. List the main factors that influence the quantity that producers plan to sell and say whether an increase in each factor increases or decreases firms' planned sales.
6. State the law of demand and the law of supply.
7. If a fixed amount of a good is available, what does the demand curve tell us about the price that consumers are willing to pay for that fixed quantity?
8. If consumers are willing to buy only a certain fixed quantity, what does the supply curve tell us about the price at which firms will supply that quantity?
9. Distinguish between:
   a. A change in demand and a change in the quantity demanded.
   b. A change in supply and a change in the quantity supplied.
10. Why is the price at which the quantity demanded equals the quantity supplied the equilibrium price?
11. What are the forces that operate in a market if:
    a. The price is below the equilibrium price?
    b. The price is above the equilibrium price?
12. What is the effect on the price of a tape and the quantity of tapes sold if:
    a. The price of a CD increases?
    b. The price of a Walkman increases?
    c. The supply of CD players increases?
    d. Consumers' incomes increase and firms that produce tapes switch to new cost-saving technology?
    e. The prices of the resources used to make tapes increase?
13. What is the effect on the price of a tape and the quantity of tapes sold in question 12 if:
    a. Events (a) and (e) occur simultaneously?
    b. Events (b) and (e) occur simultaneously?

# PROBLEMS

1. Suppose that one of the following events occurs:
   a. The price of gasoline rises.
   b. The price of gasoline falls.
   c. All speed limits on highways are abolished.
   d. An engine that runs on cheap alcohol is invented.
   e. Robot production plants lower the cost of producing cars.
   f. The rates for auto insurance double.
   g. A massive and high-grade oil supply is discovered in Mexico.
   h. The price of cars rises.
   i. The price of cars falls.
   j. The summer temperature is 10 degrees lower than normal.

   State which of the above events produces the following effects. (Each event might have more than one effect.)
   (i)    An increase in the demand for gasoline
   (ii)   A decrease in the demand for gasoline
   (iii)  An increase in the supply of gasoline
   (iv)   A decrease in the supply of gasoline
   (v)    An increase in the quantity of gasoline demanded
   (vi)   An increase in the quantity of gasoline supplied
   (vii)  A decrease in the quantity of gasoline demanded
   (viii) A decrease in the quantity of gasoline supplied

2. The demand and supply curves for pizza are as follows:

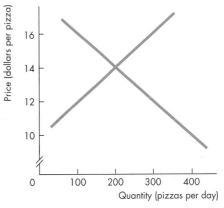

   a. What is the equilibrium price of pizza?
   b. What is the equilibrium quantity of pizza?

3. The demand and supply schedules for gum are as follows:

| Price (cents per pack) | Quantity demanded | Quantity supplied |
|---|---|---|
| | (millions of packs a week) | |
| 20 | 180 | 30 |
| 30 | 160 | 60 |
| 40 | 140 | 90 |
| 50 | 120 | 120 |
| 60 | 100 | 140 |
| 70 | 80 | 160 |
| 80 | 60 | 180 |

a. What is the equilibrium price of gum?
b. What is the equilibrium quantity of gum?

Suppose that a huge fire destroys one half of the gum-producing factories. The supply of gum decreases to one half of the amount shown in the above supply schedule.

c. What is the new equilibrium price of gum?
d. What is the new equilibrium quantity of gum?
e. Has there been a shift in or a movement along the supply curve of gum?
f. Has there been a shift in or a movement along the demand curve for gum?
g. As the gum factories destroyed by fire are rebuilt and gradually resume gum production, what will happen to:
   (i) The price of gum?
   (ii) The quantity of gum bought?
   (iii) The demand for gum?
   (iv) The supply curve of gum?

4. Suppose the demand and supply schedules for gum are those in problem 3. An increase in the teenage population increases the demand for gum by 40 million packs per week.
   a. Write out the new demand schedule for gum.
   b. What is the new equilibrium quantity of gum?
   c. What is the new equilibrium price of gum?
   d. Has there been a shift in or a movement along the demand curve for gum?
   e. Has there been a shift in or a movement along the supply curve of gum?

5. Suppose the demand and supply schedules for gum are those in problem 3. An increase in the teenage population increases the demand for gum by 40 million packs per week, and

simultaneously the fire described in problem 2 occurs, wiping out one half of the gum-producing factories.
   a. Draw a graph of the original and new demand and supply curves.
   b. What is the new equilibrium quantity of gum?
   c. What is the new equilibrium price of gum?

6. Complete the table by inserting in each column an up arrow (↑) for increase, a down arrow (↓) for decrease and a question mark (?) for indeterminate (can increase or decrease depending on the size of the change in demand and supply). To fill in this table, draw a separate demand and supply diagram for each of the eight cases.

| | Increase in demand | No change in demand | Decrease in demand |
|---|---|---|---|
| **Increase in supply** | P  Q | P  Q | P  Q |
| **No change in supply** | P  Q | P — Q — | P  Q |
| **Decrease in supply** | P  Q | P  Q | P  Q |

## CRITICAL THINKING

1. Study the story about the price of bread and the price of wheat in *Reading Between the Lines,* pp. 86–87 and then:
   a. Describe the changes in the price of wheat in the United States and the rest of the world.
   b. Explain what happened to the quantity of wheat demanded by consumers in the United States and show the change in the quantity demanded in the figure.
   c. Explain why the price of wheat is determined in a world market but the price of bread is determined in local markets.

2. Visit the World Wide Web site of the FAO (the Food and Agricultural Organization of the United Nations) in Rome. (You will find a link to it at the Parkin home page.) Gather data on world and U.S. production and consumption of wheat for the most recent period available and update the table on p. 87. Then draw a new version of Fig. 1 on p. 87 to explain what has happened to the world economy since 1996.

# Part 3

# Macroeconomic Overview

## The Big Picture

Macroeconomics is a large and controversial subject. It is interlaced with political ideological disputes. And it is a field in which charlatans as well as serious thinkers have much to say. This page is a map that will guide you through this challenging but interesting terrain of macroeconomics and help you to keep the big picture in view. ◆ There is no better place to begin than with the core questions of macroeconomics, which are what causes:

- Economic growth
- Business cycles
- Unemployment
- Inflation

The three chapters in this part provide a first take on these questions. ◆ In Chapter 5, you will learn some facts about economic growth, business cycles, unemployment, and inflation in the United States and around the world. ◆ In Chapter 6, you will learn how we measure the economy's output and prices. These measures are used to calculate the rate of economic growth, business cycle fluctuations, and inflation. You'll discover that making these measurements is not straightforward and that small measurement errors can have a big effect on our perceptions about how we are doing. ◆ In Chapter 7, you will study the macroeconomic version of supply and demand—*aggregate supply* and *aggregate demand*. The aggregate supply–aggregate demand model is the big picture model. It explains both the long-term trends in economic growth and inflation and the short-term business cycle fluctuations in production, jobs, and inflation. ◆ The chapters that follow look behind aggregate supply and aggregate demand. First, in Chapters 8 through 10, you will study long-run aggregate supply and long-term growth. This material is so central to the oldest question in macroeconomics that some professors like students to jump into it right away *before* studying aggregate supply and aggregate demand. Second, in Chapters 11 through 15, you will study aggregate demand and the sources of fluctuations in production and prices and long-term trends in inflation. This material is central to the macroeconomics that Keynes developed, and some people like to study it before aggregate supply and long-term growth. Third, in Chapters 16 and 17, you will study the alternative theories of the business cycle and the problems of stabilizing the economy and achieving faster growth. ◆ Before beginning your study of macroeconomics, let's spend a few minutes with the leading economists who developed the subject. We'll talk with one of today's macroeconomic revolutionaries, Robert E. Lucas, Jr., of the University of Chicago.

# Macroeconomic Revolutions

## The Economist: John Maynard Keynes

John Maynard Keynes, born in England in 1883, was one of the outstanding minds of the twentieth century. He wrote on probability as well as economics, represented Britain at the Versailles peace conference at the end of World War I, was a master speculator on international financial markets (an activity he conducted from bed every morning and which made and lost him several fortunes), and played a prominent role in creating the International Monetary Fund. He was a member of the Bloomsbury Group, a circle of outstanding artists and writers that included E. M. Forster, Bertrand Russell, and Virginia Woolf. Keynes was a controversial and quick-witted figure. A critic once complained that Keynes had changed his opinion on some matter, to which Keynes retorted, "When I discover I am wrong, I change my mind. What do you do?"

> "... The ideas of economists and political philosophers, both when they are right and when they are wrong, are more powerful than is commonly understood. Indeed the world is ruled by little else."
>
> JOHN MAYNARD KEYNES
>
> *THE GENERAL THEORY OF EMPLOYMENT, INTEREST, AND MONEY*

## The Issues and Ideas

During the Industrial Revolution, as technological change created new jobs and destroyed old ones, people began to wonder whether the economy could create enough jobs and sufficient demand to buy all the things that the new industrial economy could produce.

Jean-Baptiste Say argued that production creates incomes that are sufficient to buy everything that is produced—supply creates its own demand—an idea that came to be called *Say's Law*.

Say and Keynes would have had a lot to disagree about. Jean-Baptiste Say, born in Lyon, France, in 1767 (he was 9 years old when Adam Smith's *The Wealth of Nations* was published), suffered the wrath of Napoleon for his views on government and the economy. In today's America, Say would be leading the Republican charge for a smaller and leaner government. Say was the most famous economist of his era on both sides of the Atlantic. His book, *Traité d'économie politique* (*A Treatise on Political Economy*), published in 1803, became a best selling university economics textbook in both Europe and America.

As the Great Depression of the 1930s became more severe and more prolonged, Say's Law looked less and less relevant. John Maynard Keynes revolutionized macroeconomic thinking by turning Say's Law on its head, arguing that production does not depend on supply. Instead, it depends on what people are willing to buy—on demand. Or as Keynes put it, production depends on *effective demand*. It is possible, argued Keynes, for people to refuse to spend all of their incomes. If businesses fail to spend on new capital the amount that people plan to save, demand might be less than supply. In this situation, resources might go unemployed and remain unemployed indefinitely.

The influence of Keynes persists even today, more than 60 years after the publication of his main work. But during the past 20 years, Nobel Laureate Robert E. Lucas, Jr., with significant contributions from a list of outstanding macroeconomists too long to name, has further revolutionized macroeconomics. Today, we know a lot about economic growth, unemployment, inflation, and business cycles. And we know how to use fiscal policy and monetary policy to improve macroeconomic performance. But we don't yet have all the answers. Macroeconomics remains a field of lively controversy and exciting research.

## Then...

In 1776, James Hargreaves, an English weaver and carpenter, developed a simple hand-operated machine called a spinning jenny (pictured here). Using this machine, a person could spin 80 threads at once. Thousands of hand-wheel spinners, operators of machines that could spin only one thread, lost their jobs. They protested by wrecking spinning jennies. In the long run, the displaced hand-wheel spinners found work, often in factories that manufactured the machines that had

destroyed their previous jobs. From the earliest days of the Industrial Revolution to the present day, people have lost their jobs as new technologies have automated what human effort had previously been needed to accomplish.

## ...And Now

Advances in computer technology have made it possible for us to dial our own telephone calls to any part of the world and get connected in a flash. A task that was once performed by telephone operators, who made connections along copper wires, is now performed faster and more reliably by computers along fiber-optic cables. Just as the Industrial Revolution transformed the textile industry, so today's Information Revolution is transforming the telecommunications industry. In the process, the mix of jobs is changing. There are fewer jobs for telephone operators but more jobs for telephone systems designers, builders, managers, and marketers. In the long run, as people spend the income they earn in their changing jobs, supply creates its own demand, just as Say predicted. But does supply create its own demand in the short run, when displaced workers are unemployed?

Keynes and Robert E. Lucas, Jr., would have had plenty of disagreements too. Lucas, of the University of Chicago, has lead a revolution in macroeconomics that has enabled economists to build model (artificial) economies that display properties similar to those of the actual economy and to use these models to study the effects of alternative policies on macroeconomic performance. A cornerstone of the new macroeconomics is the idea of "rational expectations": People use all the available information to make economic forecasts. This information includes economists' theories about how the economy works. Lucas, like Say, believes that it is easier for government intervention to do harm than good. Said Lucas, "I don't want to manage the U.S. economy. And I don't think anybody else should take the job either." You can meet Professor Lucas on the following pages.

# Talking with

**Robert E. Lucas, Jr.,** is a professor of economics at the University of Chicago, a position he has held since 1975. Professor Lucas was born in Yakima, Washington, in 1937. He earned his B.A. and his Ph.D. from the University of Chicago in 1959 and 1963, respectively.

In 1995, Professor Lucas received the Nobel Prize for Economic Science for his work on developing the theory of rational expectations. Challenging the Keynesian theories of economic fluctuations, this new macroeconomic theory is based on the hypothesis that people and businesses make rational decisions based on rational expectations and markets reconcile individual decisions by balancing supply and demand, even in a recession.

Michael Parkin spoke with Professor Lucas about rational expectations macroeconomics, his views of economic policy, and the legacy of Keynes.

**Why are you an economist?**
I grew up in a family where everyone talked about politics and economics every night at dinner. So I've been concerned with social questions as long as I can remember. My experience as an undergraduate history major confirmed my belief in the importance of economic forces.

**You applied the idea of rational expectations to macroeconomics and to expectations about inflation. How has that hypothesis changed the way we think about things?**
It ties down a loose end that shouldn't have been there. Any important economic decision depends on what you think about the future. Rational expectations is a way of dealing with that.

**What do you see as the chief criticism of the rational expectations hypothesis?**
Here's the genuine difficulty people have with the idea. You would never discover the idea of rational expectations by introspection. Rational expectations describes something that has to be true of the outcome of a much more complicated underlying process. But it doesn't describe the actual thought process people use in trying to figure out the future. Our behavior is adaptive. We try some mode of behavior. If it's successful, we do it again. If not, we try something else. Rational expectations describes the situation when you've got it right.

**Can you give an example?**
In economics, we're mostly concerned about repetitive events and decisions of some consequence. Our capitalist economy has been operating under pretty much the same laws for 200 years now. People aren't reacting to every monetary contraction as if it's the first time it ever happened: That is just inconceivable. I think people have developed certain ways of living with regular events as best they can.

> *People aren't reacting to every monetary contraction as if it's the first time it ever happened.*

**One of the most significant developments in macroeconomics in recent years has been real business cycle theory. How do you evaluate this approach?**

Real business cycle theory asks what the time path of the economy's GDP or employment would be under the best possible macroeconomic policy. The early authors of this approach asked themselves what fraction of the actual variation in GDP you could account for if you restricted yourself to the fluctuations in the rate of technological change. Their initial answer was: All of it, that there is nothing left over for traditional macroeconomic theory to account for. I don't think that can be right.

For example, you can't account for something like the events of 1929 to 1933, when real output fell by a quarter in four years, as if it resulted from the changes in the rate at which technology was decaying. The Depression didn't occur because production techniques got worse. But real business cycle theory has shown us that real forces are much more important than we had thought and that the questions addressed by traditional macroeconomics are not as important as we once thought. That's the important message.

**How can we introduce monetary forces into a macroeconomic model that at the same time pays serious attention to real forces, one that shows fluctuations in price as well as in output?**

This question is the subject of my Nobel Lecture, "Monetary Neutrality." I think it is the central question of macroeconomics, but it remains unresolved today, as it did when David Hume first addressed it in the eighteenth century.

**Your early work focused primarily on short-term macroeconomic problems. For the past 10 years, you've increasingly devoted your life to thinking about long-term growth. Why has your work changed in that direction?**

When I began taking economics courses in the early 1960s, the Great Depression of the 1930s was a key topic of discussion for all my professors. The study of macroeconomics was, at that time, the study of how to prevent depressions and how to get out of them. The United States has not had a serious depression since the 1930s, and we should not be surprised that macroeconomic study has switched from a depression focus to a growth focus. If you ask what determines our income today relative to what it was in the 1960s, 99 percent of the answer is economic growth.

> *If you ask what determines our income today relative to what it was in the 1960s, 99 percent of the answer is economic growth.*

**What can we bring to the study of growth today that Smith couldn't bring to it when he tried to figure out what caused the wealth of nations.**

When Adam Smith wrote about the wealth of nations, he was thinking about a world in which no country had ever experienced sustained growth in living standards. Some countries had higher *levels* of income than others, and Smith was interested in understanding why those differences existed. But Smith never observed or imagined a country where production could grow at 3 percent per year for a century and more. Smith also lacked good data, by modern standards. We now have tremendous data sets on income and the growth of income for the richest and poorest countries. During the past 10 years, growth theory has evolved from being the study of the United States, the United Kingdom, and a few other very wealthy economies to being the comparative study of rich and poor economies. The hope is that the same general theoretical principles will apply to both.

**There's about a 25 to 1 difference between the United States and India in per capita production. How do you explain that difference?**

Only a small fraction can be explained by the differences in physical capital. U.S. workers have better equipment than Indian workers, and that's certainly a factor in making them more productive, but a much more important factor is human capital. The level of education and training of the U.S. worker is much higher than the typical Indian worker. Once human capital is introduced—and placed at the center of growth theory—a lot of things start falling into place and it becomes much easier to understand the enormous differences in incomes.

How do you explain the astonishing growth rates of per capita incomes in East Asia compared with the 1 to 2 percent growth rates of North America?

The countries of East Asia are catching up with those of Europe and North America. The Industrial Revolution has opened them up to trade with the more advanced countries of the world. East Asia is experiencing annual growth rates of 6 to 8 percent. Nothing like that ever occurred in the United States or the United Kingdom, the countries that were leaders from the start of the Industrial Revolution. East Asian countries are rapidly learning technology that took decades to produce.

You were a student of Milton Friedman, the architect of the movement called monetarism. How do you distinguish this approach from the kind of macroeconomics that you are responsible for creating?

I'm not that big on the distinction. I think of myself as a monetarist. But the term does refer to several different things. One aspect of what people call monetarism is just an emphasis on the quantity of some money as a determinant of prices and of economic activity. In some ways, I think that revolution has been so successful that it doesn't seem like a revolution any more. In this day and age, no one talks about the price level, exchange rates, or interest rates without talking about the quantity of money. In that sense, we're all monetarists. The second aspect of monetarism is a hostility toward

the government's continual management of the economy. The role of government, in a monetarist perspective, is to make its own behavior on fiscal or monetary policy simple and predictable and then just to let the system operate without fine tuning. That view, I think, is absolutely right.

*Economics is a great major. ... economics is a good pre–almost anything major.*

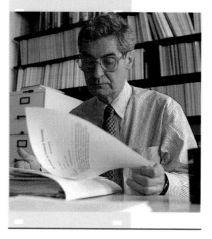

In recent years, we've experienced the biggest peacetime government budget deficit ever. How have you viewed the deficit over the years?

I was a deficit alarmist in the early years of the Reagan administration because I thought the deficits would be inflationary. Well, that just hasn't happened. I've become more sympathetic to people like Larry Kotlikoff, who argued that

the deficit just doesn't measure anything we care about, since things like future social security liabilities are arbitrarily excluded.

What for you is the legacy of Keynes?

Keynes' influence was almost entirely political. He wrote *The General Theory* in the 1930s at a time when many of the major countries were in the process of moving away from liberal democracy and capitalism toward fascism in Germany and Italy and toward Communism in Russia. These countries appeared to deal better with the depression of the 1930s than countries like ours that stayed with liberal institutions. Keynes' message in *The General Theory* is that we can deal with depressions within the framework of a basically capitalistic economy and liberal democratic institutions. This is an important message to get across.

The intellectual forefathers of modern macroeconomics are, for me, the classical economists, Smith and Ricardo, the neoclassical work of Marshall, and the generation of our teachers, Arrow, Friedman, and Samuelson.

Would you advise undergraduates to major in economics?

Economics is a great major. I feel economics is a good pre–almost anything major. Most of the economics majors at the University of Chicago will go to law school, professional school, or work for a while. Our students have a lot of electives to choose from; they have a broad, liberal arts education.

# 5

# A First Look at Macroeconomics

During the past 100 years, the quantity of goods and services produced in the nation's farms, factories, shops, and offices has expanded more than twentyfold. As a result, we have a much higher living standard than our grandparents had. Will production always expand? Will your world be more prosperous than today's? ◆ For most of us, a high standard of living means finding a good job. What kind of job will you find when you graduate? Will you have lots of choice, or will you face a labor market with a high unemployment rate in which jobs are hard to find? ◆ A high standard of living means being able to afford to buy life's necessities and some fun. If prices rise too quickly, some people get left behind and must trim what they buy. Prices have increased slowly over the past few years. But can we count on them

## What Will Your World Be Like?

rising slowly in the future? What will the dollar buy next year? What will it buy in 10 years when you are paying off your student loan? And what will it buy in 50 years when you are spending your life's savings in retirement? ◆ Every year since 1970, the government has spent more than it has raised in taxes. And most years, we have imported more goods and services from the rest of the world than we have exported to it. We have experienced large and persistent government and international deficits. How will these deficits affect your future? ◆ To keep production expanding and prevent an economic slowdown, the federal government and the Federal Reserve Board—the nation's financial managers—take policy actions. What kinds of actions do they take? How do their actions influence production, jobs, prices, and the ability of Americans to compete in the global marketplace? ◆ These are the questions of macroeconomics. The macroeconomic events through which we are now living are tumultuous and exciting. With what you learn in these chapters, you will be able to understand these events, the policy challenges they bring, and the political debate they stir. You will be able to prepare yourself better for your world, the economic world that you will enter when you graduate and in which you will earn your living.

## After studying this chapter, you will be able to:

■ Describe the origins of macroeconomics and the problems it deals with

■ Describe the long-term trends and short-term fluctuations in economic growth, unemployment, inflation, and government and international deficits

■ Explain why economic growth, unemployment, inflation, and deficits matter

■ Identify the macroeconomic policy challenges and describe the tools available for meeting them

## Origins and Issues of Macroeconomics

ECONOMISTS BEGAN TO STUDY LONG-TERM economic growth, inflation, and international payments as long ago as the 1750s, and this work was the origin of macroeconomics. But modern macroeconomics did not emerge until the **Great Depression**, a decade (1929–1939) of high unemployment and stagnant production throughout the world economy. In the Depression's worst year, 1933, the production of U.S. farms, factories, shops, and offices was only 70 percent of its 1929 level and 25 percent of the labor force was unemployed. These were years of human misery on a scale that is hard to imagine today. They were also years of extreme pessimism about the ability of the market economy to work properly. Many people believed that private ownership, free markets, and democratic political institutions could not survive.

The science of economics had no solutions to the Great Depression. The major alternative system of central planning and socialism seemed increasingly attractive. It was in this climate of economic depression and political and intellectual turmoil that modern macroeconomics emerged with the publication in 1936 of John Maynard Keynes' *The General Theory of Employment, Interest, and Money* (see p. 92).

### Short-Term Versus Long-Term Goals

Keynes' theory was that depression and high unemployment result from insufficient private spending and that to cure these problems, the government must increase its spending. Keynes' focused primarily on the *short term*. He wanted to cure an immediate problem almost regardless of the *long-term* consequences of the cure. "In the long run," said Keynes, "we're all dead."

But Keynes believed that after his cure for depression had restored the economy to a normal condition, the long-term problems of inflation and slow economic growth would return. And he suspected that his cure for depression, increased government spending, might trigger inflation and might lower the long-term growth rate of production. With a lower long-term growth rate, the economy would create fewer jobs. If this outcome did occur, a policy aimed at lowering unemployment in the short run might end up increasing it in the long run.

By the late 1960s and through the 1970s, Keynes' predictions became a reality. Inflation increased, economic growth slowed down, and in some countries, unemployment became persistently high. The causes of these developments are complex. But they point to an inescapable conclusion: The long-term problems of inflation, slow growth, and persistent unemployment and the short-term problems of depression and economic fluctuations intertwine and are most usefully studied together. So although macroeconomics was reborn during the Great Depression, it has now returned to its older tradition. Today, macroeconomics studies long-term economic growth and inflation as well as short-term business fluctuations and unemployment.

### The Road Ahead

There is no unique way to study macroeconomics. Because its rebirth was a product of depression, the common practice for many years was to pay most attention to short-term output fluctuations and unemployment but to never completely lose sight of the long-term issues. When a rapid inflation emerged during the 1970s, this topic returned to prominence. During the 1980s, when long-term growth slowed in the United States and other rich industrial countries but exploded in East Asia, economists redirected their energy toward economic growth. During the 1990s, as information technologies continue to shrink the globe, the international dimension of macroeconomics has become more prominent. The result of these developments is that modern macroeconomics is a broad subject that studies all the issues we've just identified: long-term economic growth, unemployment, and inflation. It also studies two new problems: the government budget and international deficits.

Over the past 40 years, economists have developed a clearer understanding of the forces that determine macroeconomic performance and have devised policies that they hope will improve this performance. Your main goal is to become familiar with the theories of macroeconomics and the policies they make possible. To set you on your path toward this goal, we're going to take a first look at economic growth, unemployment, inflation, and deficits and learn why these macroeconomic phenomena merit our attention.

# Economic Growth

YOUR PARENTS ARE RICHER THAN YOUR GRAND-parents were when they were young. But are you going to be richer than your parents? And are your children going to be richer than you? The answers depend on the rate of economic growth.

**Economic growth** is the expansion of the economy's production possibilities. It can be pictured as an outward shift of the production possibility frontier (*PPF*)—see Chapter 3, pp. 49–50.

We measure economic growth by the increase in real gross domestic product. **Real gross domestic product** (also called **real GDP**) is the value of the total production of all the nation's farms, factories, shops, and offices linked back to the prices of a single year. Real GDP in the United States is currently linked back to the prices of 1992 (called 1992 dollars). We link back to the dollar prices of a single year to eliminate the influence of *inflation*—the increase in prices—and determine how much production has grown from one year to another. (Real GDP is explained more fully in Chapter 6 on pp. 128–129.)

Real GDP is not a perfect measure of total production because it does not include everything that is produced. It excludes the things we produce for ourselves at home (preparing meals, doing laundry, house painting, gardening, and so on). It also excludes production that people hide to avoid taxes or because it is illegal—the underground economy. But despite its shortcomings, real GDP is the best measure of total production available. Let's see what it tells us about economic growth in the United States.

## Economic Growth in the United States

Figure 5.1 shows real GDP in the United States since 1960 and highlights two features of economic growth:

- The growth of potential GDP
- Fluctuations of real GDP around potential GDP

**The Growth of Potential GDP** When all the economy's resources are fully employed, the value of production is called **potential GDP**. Real GDP fluctuates around potential GDP, and the rate of long-term economic growth is measured by the growth rate of potential GDP. It is shown by the steepness of the potential GDP line (the black line) in Fig. 5.1.

During the 1960s, real GDP grew at an unusually rapid rate of 4.4 percent a year. But the growth rate of output per person slowed during the 1970s, a phenomenon called the **productivity growth slowdown**. Faster growth might have returned during the late 1980s and 1990s, but it is too soon to be certain about this possibility.

Why did the productivity growth slowdown occur? This question is controversial. One possible cause is a sharp rise in the relative price of energy. How this factor might have slowed productivity growth is explored in Chapter 10 on pp. 221–222. Whatever its cause, the productivity growth slowdown means that we all have smaller incomes today than we would have had if the economy had continued to grow at its 1960s rate.

Let's now look at GDP fluctuations.

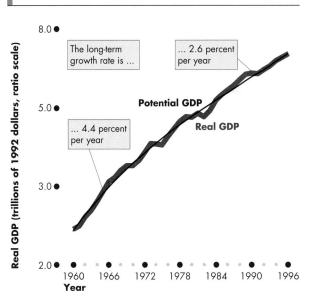

**FIGURE 5.1**

## Economic Growth in the United States

The long-term economic growth rate, measured by the growth of potential GDP, was 4.4 percent a year during the 1960s but slowed to 2.6 percent a year during the mid-1970s. Growth has remained slower into the 1990s. Real GDP fluctuates around potential GDP.

*Source:* U.S. Department of Commerce, *National Income and Product Accounts of the United States.*

**Fluctuations Around Potential GDP**   Real GDP fluctuates around potential GDP in a business cycle. A **business cycle** is the periodic but irregular up-and-down movement in production. It is measured by fluctuations in real GDP around potential GDP. When real GDP is less than potential GDP, some resources are underused. For example, some labor is unemployed and capital is underutilized. When real GDP is greater than potential GDP, resources are being *over*used. Many people work longer hours than they are willing to put up with in the long run, capital is worked so intensively that it is not maintained in prime working order, delivery times lengthen, bottlenecks occur, and backorders increase.

Business cycles are not regular, predictable, or repeating cycles like the phases of the moon. Their timing changes unpredictably. But cycles do have some things in common. Every business cycle has two phases:

1. A recession
2. An expansion

and two turning points:

1. A peak
2. A trough

Figure 5.2 shows these features of the most recent business cycle in the United States. A **recession** is a period during which real GDP decreases—the growth rate of real GDP is negative—for at least two successive quarters. The most recent recession, which is highlighted in the figure, began in the third quarter of 1990 and ended in the first quarter of 1991. This recession lasted for three quarters. An **expansion** is a period during which real GDP increases. The most recent expansion began in the second quarter of 1991 and was still in progress during 1997. An earlier expansion ended with the onset of recession in the third quarter of 1990.

When a business cycle expansion ends and a recession begins, the turning point is called a *peak*. The most recent peak occurred in the second quarter of 1990. When a business cycle recession ends and a recovery begins, the turning point is called a *trough*. The most recent trough occurred in the first quarter of 1991.

---

**FIGURE 5.2**
The Most Recent U.S. Business Cycle

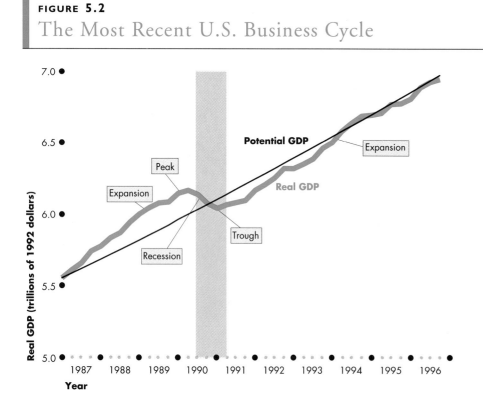

A business cycle has two phases: recession and expansion. The most recent recession (highlighted) ran from the third quarter of 1990 through the first quarter of 1991. Then a new expansion began in the second quarter of 1991. A business cycle has two turning points, a peak and a trough. In the most recent business cycle, the peak occurred in the second quarter of 1990 and the trough occurred in the first quarter of 1991.

**The Recent Recession in Historical Perspective**

The recession of 1990–1991 seemed severe while we were passing through it, but compared with earlier recessions, it was mild. You can see how mild it was by looking at Fig. 5.3, which shows a longer history of U.S. economic growth. The biggest decrease in real GDP occurred during the Great Depression of the 1930s. A large decrease also occurred in 1946 and 1947, immediately after World War II. In more recent times, severe recessions occurred during the mid-1970s, following oil price hikes by the Organization of Petroleum Exporting Countries (OPEC), and during the early 1980s.

Each of these economic downturns was more severe than that in 1990–1991. But you can see that the Great Depression was much more severe than anything that followed it. This episode was so extreme that we don't call it a recession. We call it a *depression*.

This last truly great depression occurred before governments started taking policy actions to stabilize the economy. It also occurred before the birth of modern macroeconomics. Is the absence of another great depression a sign that macroeconomics has contributed to economic stability? Some people believe it is. Others doubt it. We'll evaluate these opinions on a number of occasions in this book.

We've looked at real GDP growth and fluctuations in the United States. But is the U.S. experience typical? Do other countries share our experience? Let's see whether they do.

## Economic Growth Around the World

A country might have a rapid growth rate of real GDP, but it might also have a rapid population growth rate. To compare growth rates over time and across countries, we use the growth rate of real GDP *per person*. Real GDP per person is real GDP divided by the population. For example, U.S. real GDP in 1996 was $6,903 billion (1992 dollars), and the population of the United States was 265.5 million. So U.S. real GDP per person was $6,903 billion divided by 265.5 million, which equals $26,000.

Figure 5.4 shows real GDP per person between 1960 and 1996 for three of the world's largest economies: the United States, Japan, and Germany.

---

**FIGURE 5.3**

## Long-Term Economic Growth in the United States

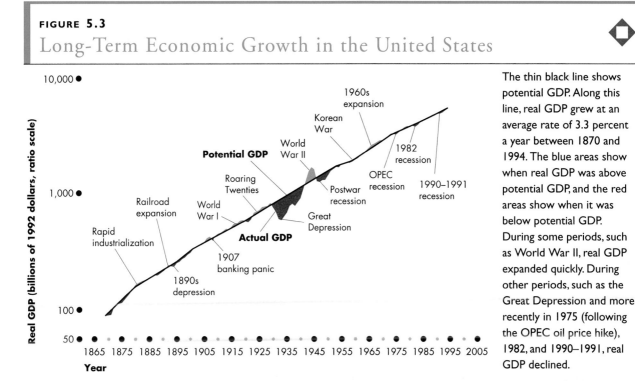

The thin black line shows potential GDP. Along this line, real GDP grew at an average rate of 3.3 percent a year between 1870 and 1994. The blue areas show when real GDP was above potential GDP, and the red areas show when it was below potential GDP. During some periods, such as World War II, real GDP expanded quickly. During other periods, such as the Great Depression and more recently in 1975 (following the OPEC oil price hike), 1982, and 1990–1991, real GDP declined.

*Sources:* 1869–1928, Christina D. Romer, "The Prewar Business Cycle Reconsidered: New Estimates of Gross National Product, 1869–1908," *Journal of Political Economy* 97, (1989) 1–37. 1929–1996, U.S. Department of Commerce, *National Income and Product Accounts of the United States*.

In these countries, three features of the paths of real GDP per person stand out:

- Similar productivity growth slowdowns
- Similar business cycles
- Different long-term trends in potential GDP

**Similar Productivity Growth Slowdowns**    U.S. real GDP per person grew at a rate of 2.9 percent a year during the 1960s but slowed to 1.3 percent a year during the 1970s and 1980s and 0.9 percent a year during the 1990s. In Germany, the growth of real GDP per person slowed from 3.5 percent a year during the 1960s to 2 percent a year during the 1970s and 1980s and 1 percent a year during the 1990s. In Japan, the slowdown was more spectacular, from 8.5 percent a year during the 1960s to 3.1 percent a year during the 1970s and 1980s and 1.5 percent a year during the 1990s.

The slowdown experienced by the United States, Japan, and Germany was experienced by most other industrial countries. Exceptions were the major oil-producing nations.

**Similar Business Cycles**    The three big economies have also experienced similar business cycles. Each economy had an expansion running from the early or mid-1960s through 1973, a recession from 1973 to 1975, an expansion through 1979, another recession in the early 1980s, and a long expansion through the rest of the 1980s.

Like the common productivity growth slowdown, this common business cycle is also shared by most economies around the world.

**Different Long-Term Trends in Potential GDP**
Perhaps the most striking feature of Fig. 5.4 is the variation in the long-term growth rates of the three big economies. In 1960, real GDP per person was $9,900 in the United States, $6,600 in Germany, and $3,000 in Japan. So in round numbers, in 1960, Germany produced twice as much per person as Japan, and the United States produced three times as much per person as Japan.

But during the 1960s, Japan's production streaked upward like a rocket leaving Cape Canaveral. When U.S. long-term growth of real GDP per person was

---

**FIGURE 5.4**

## Economic Growth in Three Large Economies

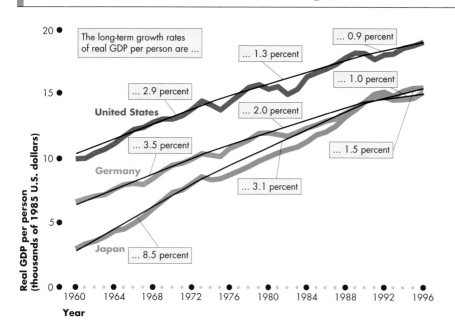

Economic growth in three large economies, the United States, Germany, and Japan, has followed a similar pattern. The growth rate in all three countries slowed during the 1970s, and each country has had similar business cycles. But Japan has grown fastest, and Germany too has grown faster than the United States.

*Sources:* The data for 1960 through 1992 are from "The Penn World Table," *Quarterly Journal of Economics,* May 1991, pp. 327–368. New computer disk supplement (Mark 5.6a). The data use comparable international relative prices converted to 1985 U.S. dollars. The data for 1993-1996 are from *International Financial Statistics* (Washington, D.C.: International Monetary Fund, 1997).

2.9 percent a year, Germany achieved a rate of 3.5 percent a year, and Japan achieved an astonishing 8.5 percent a year. These differences in the long-term growth trend survived the productivity growth slowdown. After the slowdown, even though Japan's growth rate more than halved, its growth of real GDP per person still exceeded the U.S. rate before the slowdown.

Because it has achieved such a high growth rate, Japan has narrowed the gap between its own level of real GDP per person and that of the United States and has overtaken Germany.

Figure 5.5 compares the growth of the U.S. economy with that of several other countries and regions since 1978. Among the industrial countries (the red bars), Japan has grown the fastest and the European Union has grown the slowest. The U.S. growth rate has been toward the low end of the range for industrial countries. The developing countries and the countries in transition to a market economy (the green bars) have experienced a wide range of growth rates. The most rapid growth has occurred in Asia, where the average growth rate has exceeded 7 percent a year—three times the U.S. growth rate. The slowest growth has been in Russia and the other countries of Central and Eastern Europe, where production has shrunk. Africa has also grown slowly. With the exception of these regions, growth rates in the developing countries have exceeded that of the United States.

## Benefits and Costs of Economic Growth

What are the benefits and costs of economic growth? Does it matter whether the long-term growth rate slows as it did during the 1970s?

The main benefit of long-term economic growth is expanded consumption possibilities, including more health care for the poor and elderly, more cancer and AIDS research, more space research and exploration, better roads, and more and better housing. We can even have cleaner lakes, more trees, and cleaner air by devoting more resources to environmental problems.

When the long-term growth rate slows, some of these benefits are lost, and the loss can be large. For example, if long-term growth had not slowed in the United States during the 1970s, real GDP in 1996 would have been $8,650 billion, or $32,600 per

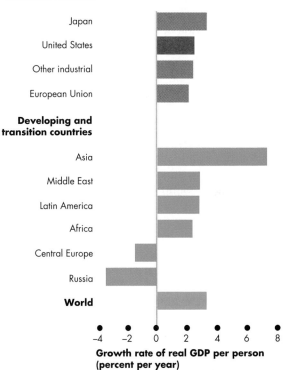

**FIGURE 5.5**

Growth Rates Around the World

Between 1978 and 1996, the growth rate of real GDP has been lower in the United States than in some other industrial countries. The developing countries of Asia have had the most rapid growth rates and those of Africa, Central and Eastern Europe, and Russia have had the slowest growth.

Source: *World Economic Outlook* (Washington D.C.: International Monetary Fund, October 1996), pp. 167, 173–176.

person. Instead, it was $6,903 billion, or $26,000 per person. So if the long-term trend of the 1960s had persisted, as a nation we would have had $1,750 billion more to spend. Each person (on the average) would have had $6,600 more. If the government had taken one third of this extra income, it could have provided more health care, education, day-care services, highways, space stations, and a super-collider with no decrease in its provision of other goods and services, and its budget would be in a huge surplus. At the same time, you might have had another $4,400 a year to spend on whatever pleased you.

The main cost of economic growth is forgone consumption. To sustain a high growth rate, resources must be devoted to advancing technology and accumulating capital rather than to producing goods and services for current consumption. This cost cannot be avoided. But it brings the benefit of greater consumption in the future.

Two other possible costs of faster growth are a more rapid depletion of exhaustible natural resources such as oil and natural gas and increased pollution of the air, rivers, and oceans. But neither of these two costs is inevitable. The technological advances that bring economic growth help us to economize on natural resources and to clean up the environment. For example, more efficient auto engines cut the gasoline use and tailpipe emissions.

A fourth possible cost of faster growth is more frequent job changes and more frequent moves from one region of the country to another. For example, during the 1990s, the South (Sun Belt) expanded and people migrated there from the Northeast and Midwest (the Rust Belt).

The pace of economic growth is determined by the choices that people make to balance the benefits and costs of economic growth. You'll study these choices and their consequences in Chapters 9 and 10.

## R E V I E W

▣ Economic growth is the expansion of production possibilities. The long-term trend in economic growth is measured by the growth rate of potential GDP.

▣ Long-term growth in the United States and other countries slowed during the 1970s and 1980s.

▣ Real GDP growth fluctuates in a business cycle. An *expansion* to a *peak* is followed by a *recession*, *trough,* and a new *expansion*.

▣ The main benefit of economic growth is expanded consumption possibilities. The main costs are less *current* consumption, possibly resource depletion and environmental pollution, and rapid changes in jobs and locations.

We've seen that real GDP grows and that it fluctuates over the business cycle. The business cycle brings fluctuations in the number of jobs available and in unemployment. Let's now examine these core macroeconomic problems.

# Jobs and Unemployment

W̲HAT KIND OF LABOR MARKET WILL YOU ENTER when you graduate? Will there be plenty of good jobs to choose from, or will there be so much unemployment that you will be forced to take a low-paying job that doesn't use your education? The answer depends, to a large degree, on the total number of jobs available and on the unemployment rate.

## Jobs

The U.S. economy is an incredible job-creating machine. In 1996, 127 million people had jobs. That number is 20 million more than in 1985 and 23 million more than in 1975. Every year, on the average, the U.S. economy creates an *additional* 1.8 million jobs.

When President Clinton took office in 1993, he predicted that 8 million jobs would be created during his four-year term. In an average four-year period, the economy creates 7.2 million jobs, so President Clinton was ambitious. As it turns out, the businesses of the United States created 8.2 million jobs during these four years.

The pace of job creation and destruction fluctuates over the business cycle. More jobs are destroyed than created during a recession, so the number of jobs decreases. But more jobs are created than destroyed during an expansion, so the number of jobs increases. For example, during the recession of 1990–1991, the number of jobs fell by more than 1 million, but through the expansion that followed, 2 million jobs were created each year. During the expansion of the 1980s, jobs were created at an even faster pace of 2.5 million jobs each year.

## Unemployment

Not everyone who wants a job can find one. On any one day in a normal or average year, seven million people are unemployed, and during a recession or depression, unemployment rises above this level. For example, in the recession of 1991, almost nine million people were looking for jobs.

A person is defined as being **unemployed** if he or she does not have a job but is available for work, is willing to work, and has made some effort to find work within the previous four weeks. The sum of the people who are unemployed and the people who are employed is called the **labor force**. The **unemployment rate** is the percentage of the people in the labor force who are unemployed. (The concepts of the labor force and unemployment are explained more fully in Chapter 8 on pp. 170–171.)

The unemployment rate is not a perfect measure of the underutilization of labor for two main reasons. First, it excludes discouraged workers. A **discouraged worker** is a person who does not have a job, is available for work, and is willing to work but who has given up the effort to find work. Many people switch between the unemployment and discouraged worker categories in both directions every month. Second, the unemployment rate measures unemployed people rather than unemployed labor hours. As a result, the unemployment rate excludes part-time workers who want full-time jobs.

Despite these two limitations, the unemployment rate is the best available measure of underused labor resources. Let's look at some facts about unemployment.

## Unemployment in the United States

Figure 5.6 shows the unemployment rate in the United States from 1929 through 1996. Three features stand out. First, during the Great Depression of the 1930s, the unemployment rate climbed to an all-time high of 25 percent in 1933 and remained high throughout the 1930s. After 1934, the official rate probably overstates unemployment because it counts as unemployed the people who had make-work jobs created by governments.

Second, although in recent years we have not experienced anything as devastating as the Great Depression, we have seen some high unemployment rates during recessions. Figure 5.6 highlights three of them—the OPEC recession of the mid-1970s, the 1982 recession, and the 1990–1991 recession.

Third, unemployment never falls to zero. In the period since the Great Depression, the average unemployment rate has been close to 6 percent.

How does U.S. unemployment compare with unemployment in other countries?

---

**FIGURE 5.6**

## Unemployment in the United States

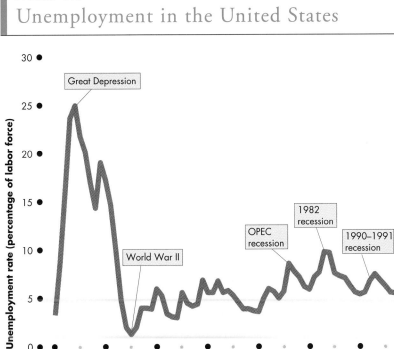

Unemployment is a persistent feature of economic life, but its rate varies. At its worst—during the Great Depression—25 percent of the labor force was unemployed. Even in recent recessions, the unemployment rate climbed toward 10 percent. Between the late 1960s and 1982, there was a general tendency for the unemployment rate to increase. The unemployment rate has remained below its peak during the 1982 recession and has fallen during the 1990s.

*Source: Economic Report of the President, 1997.*

## Unemployment Around the World

Figure 5.7 shows the unemployment rate in Canada, Western Europe, and Japan and compares those unemployment rates with that of the United States. Over the period shown in this figure, U.S. unemployment averaged 7 percent, much higher than Japanese unemployment, which averaged 2.5 percent, but lower than Canadian unemployment, which averaged 9.6 percent, and European unemployment, which averaged 8.1 percent.

U.S. unemployment fluctuates over the business cycle. It increases during a recession and decreases during an expansion. Like U.S. unemployment, Canadian and European unemployment increase during recessions and decrease during expansions. The cycles in Canadian unemployment are similar to those in U.S. unemployment, but the European cycle is out of phase with the U.S. cycle. Also, European unemployment was on a rising trend through the 1980s. In contrast with the other countries, Japanese unemployment has remained remarkably stable.

We've looked at some facts about unemployment in the United States and in other countries. Let's now look at some of the consequences of unemployment that make it the serious problem that it is.

## Why Unemployment Is a Problem

Unemployment is a serious economic, social, and personal problem for two main reasons:

■ Lost production and incomes
■ Lost human capital

**Lost Production and Incomes**    The loss of a job brings an immediate loss of income and production. These losses are devastating for the people who bear them and make unemployment a frightening prospect for everyone. Unemployment insurance creates a safety net, but it does not provide the same living standard as having a job provides.

**Lost Human Capital**    Prolonged unemployment can permanently damage a person's job prospects. For example, a manager loses his job when his employer downsizes. Short of income, he becomes a taxi driver. After a year in this work, he discovers that he can't compete with new MBA graduates. He eventually gets hired as a manager but in a small firm and at a low wage. He has lost some of his human capital.

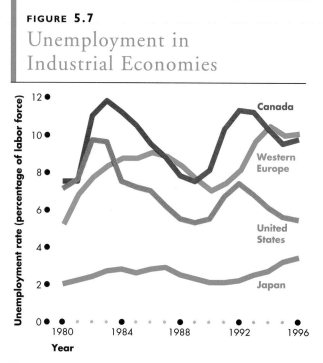

**FIGURE 5.7**

## Unemployment in Industrial Economies

The unemployment rate in the United States has been lower than that in Canada and Western Europe but higher than that in Japan. The cycles in Canadian unemployment are similar to those in the United States. Western European unemployment has a cycle that is out of phase with the U.S. unemployment cycle. Unemployment in Japan has drifted upward in recent years.

*Source: Economic Report of the President, 1997.*

The costs of unemployment are spread unequally, which makes unemployment a highly charged political problem, as well as a serious economic problem.

## R E V I E W

■ On the average, the U.S. economy creates 1.8 million additional jobs a year.
■ The unemployment rate fluctuates over the business cycle and never disappears.
■ Unemployment brings a loss of income, production, and human capital. The costs fall unevenly and make unemployment a social and political problem.

Let's now turn to the third major problem: inflation.

## Inflation

PRICES ON THE AVERAGE CAN BE RISING, FALLING, or stable. **Inflation** is a process of rising prices. We measure the *inflation rate* as the percentage change in the *average* level of prices or the **price level**. A common measure of the price level is the *Consumer Price Index* (CPI). The CPI tells us how the average price of all the goods and services bought by a typical urban household changes from month to month. (The CPI is explained in Chapter 6, p. 127).

So that you can see in a concrete way how the inflation rate is measured, let's do a calculation. In December 1996, the CPI was 158.6, and in December 1995, it was 153.5, so the inflation rate during 1996 was

$$\text{Inflation} = \frac{158.6 - 153.5}{153.5} \times 100$$

$$= 3.3\%.$$

### Inflation in the United States

Figure 5.8 shows the U.S. inflation rate from 1960 through 1996. You can see from this figure that during the early 1960s, the inflation rate was between 1 and 2 percent a year. Inflation began to increase in the late 1960s at the time of the Vietnam War. But the largest increases occurred in 1974 and 1980, years in which the actions of the Organization of Petroleum Exporting Countries (OPEC) resulted in exceptionally large increases in the price of oil. Inflation was brought under control in the early 1980s when Federal Reserve chairman Paul Volcker pushed interest rates up and people cut back on their spending. Since 1983, inflation has been relatively mild, and during the 1990s, its rate has fallen yet further.

The inflation rate rises and falls over the years, but it rarely becomes negative. If the inflation rate is negative, the price *level* is falling and we have **deflation**. Since the 1930s, the price level has generally risen—the inflation rate has been positive. Thus even when the inflation rate is low, as it was in 1961 and 1986, the price level is rising.

**FIGURE 5.8**

## Inflation in the United States

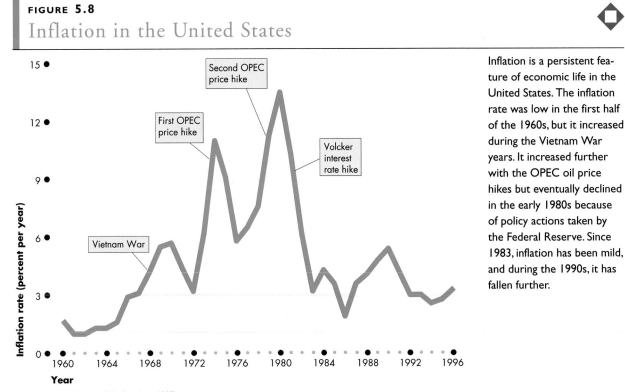

Inflation is a persistent feature of economic life in the United States. The inflation rate was low in the first half of the 1960s, but it increased during the Vietnam War years. It increased further with the OPEC oil price hikes but eventually declined in the early 1980s because of policy actions taken by the Federal Reserve. Since 1983, inflation has been mild, and during the 1990s, it has fallen further.

*Source: Economic Report of the President, 1997.*

## Inflation Around the World

Figure 5.9 shows inflation around the world since 1970. It also shows the U.S. inflation rate in a broader perspective. Part (a) shows that the U.S. inflation rate has been similar to that of other industrial countries. You can also see that all the industrial countries shared the burst of double-digit inflation during the 1970s and the fall in inflation during the 1980s. Part (b) shows that the average inflation rate of industrial countries has been very low compared with that of the developing counties. Among the developing countries, the most extreme inflation in recent times has occurred in the former Yugoslavia, where its rate has exceeded 6,000 percent per year.

## Is Inflation a Problem?

If inflation were predictable, it would not be much of a problem. But inflation is not predictable. Unpredictable inflation makes the economy behave a bit like a casino in which some people gain and some lose and no one can predict where the gains and losses will fall. Gains and losses occur because of unpredictable changes in the value of money. Money is used as a measuring rod of value in the transactions that we undertake. Borrowers and lenders, workers and employers, all make contracts in terms of money. If the value of money varies unpredictably over time, then the amounts *really* paid and received—the quantity of goods that the money will buy—also fluctuate unpredictably. Measuring value with a measuring rod whose units vary is a bit like trying to measure a piece of cloth with an elastic ruler. The size of the cloth depends on how tightly the ruler is stretched.

In a period of rapid, unpredictable inflation, resources get diverted from productive activities to forecasting inflation. It becomes more profitable to forecast the inflation rate correctly than to invent a new product. Doctors, lawyers, accountants, farmers—just about everyone—can make themselves better off, not by specializing in the profession for which they have been trained but by spending more of their time dabbling as amateur economists and inflation forecasters and managing their investment portfolios.

From a social perspective, this diversion of talent resulting from inflation is like throwing scarce resources onto the garbage heap. This waste of resources is a cost of inflation.

**FIGURE 5.9**

## Inflation Around the World

**(a) The United States and other industrial countries**

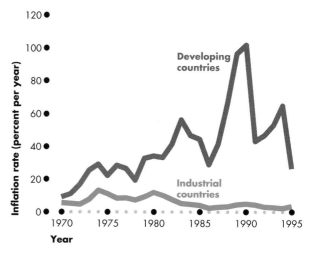

**(b) Industrial countries and developing countries**

Inflation in the United States is similar to that in the other industrial countries. Compared with the developing countries, inflation in the United States and the other industrial countries is low.

*Source: International Financial Statistics Yearbook 1996*, (Washington, D.C.: International Monetary Fund, 1996).

The most serious type of inflation is called *hyperinflation*—an inflation rate that exceeds 50 percent a month. At the height of a hyperinflation, workers are often paid twice a day because money loses its value so quickly. As soon as workers are paid, they rush out to spend their wages before they lose too much value.

Hyperinflation is rare but there have been some spectacular examples of it. Several European countries experienced hyperinflation during the 1920s after World War I and again during the 1940s after World War II. But hyperinflation is more than just a historical curiosity. It occurs in today's world. In 1994, the African nation of Zaire had a hyperinflation that peaked at a *monthly* inflation rate of 76 percent. Also in 1994, Brazil almost reached the hyperinflation stratosphere with a monthly inflation rate of 40 percent. A cup of coffee that cost 15 cruzeiros in 1980 cost 22 *billion* cruzeiros in 1994.

Inflation imposes costs, but getting rid of inflation is also costly. Policies that lower the inflation rate increase the unemployment rate. Most economists think the increase in the unemployment rate that accompanies a fall in the inflation rate is temporary. But some economists say that higher unemployment is a permanent cost of low inflation. The cost of lowering inflation must be evaluated when an anti-inflation policy is pursued. You will learn more about inflation and the costs of curing it in Chapter 15.

## R E V I E W

- Inflation is a process of rising prices and a falling value of money.
- Inflation is a serious problem because its rate is usually unpredictable.
- Unpredictable inflation brings unpredictable gains and losses to borrowers and lenders, workers and employers, and it diverts resources from producing goods and services to forecasting inflation.
- Anti-inflation polices bring a temporary but costly increase in unemployment.

Now that we've studied economic growth and fluctuations, unemployment, and inflation, let's turn to the fourth macroeconomic problem: deficits. What happens when a government spends more than it collects in taxes? And what happens when a nation buys more from other countries that it sells to them? Do governments and nations face the problem that you and I would face if we spent more than we earned? Do they run out of funds? Let's look at these questions.

# Deficits

DEFICITS GENERATE A LOT OF ANXIETY AND MEDIA discussion. Two deficits in particular are never far from the headlines. They are:

- Government budget deficit
- International deficit

## Government Budget Deficit

If the federal government spends more than it collects in taxes, it has a deficit—a **government budget deficit**. In the United States, the federal government has had a deficit every year since 1970. How big is the government budget deficit? Is it getting bigger, or is it being brought under control?

Figure 5.10(a) answers these questions. It shows the federal government budget deficit since 1960. So that we can compare the deficit in one year with that in another year, we measure it as a percentage of GDP. The concept of GDP (which is explained more fully in Chapter 6, pp. 118-126) equals total income in the economy. So you can think of the deficit as a percentage of GDP as the number of cents of deficit per dollar of income earned by an average person.

You can see that every year since 1970, the government has had a deficit. That deficit swelled to almost 5 percent of GDP in 1975 and again in 1983 and 1992. Throughout the 1980s and 1990s, the deficit had never been less than 2 percent of GDP until 1996, when it fell to 1.7 percent of GDP. Since 1992, the government budget deficit has been shrinking. But it has shrunk before. Has the deficit now finally been brought under control, or will it swell again as it has done before? In Chapter 12, we'll study the policies that have lowered the deficit in recent years.

## International Deficit

When we import goods and services from the rest of the world, we make payments to foreigners. When we export goods and services to the rest of the world, we receive payments from foreigners. If our imports exceed our exports, we have an international deficit.

Figure 5.10(b) shows the history of the international deficit of the United States since 1960. The figure shows the balance on the **current account**, which includes our exports minus our imports but

FIGURE 5.10

## Government Budget and International Deficits

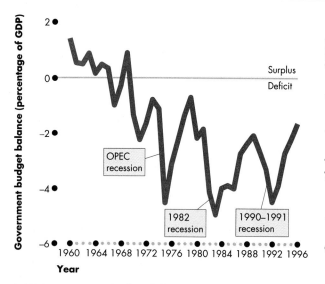

**(a) U.S. government budget deficit**

**(b) U.S. international deficit**

In part (a), the federal government's deficit increased as a percentage of GDP before 1982 and shrank after 1982. In part (b), the U.S. international deficit (measured by the current account) was generally in surplus until the 1980s. During the expansion of the 1980s, a large international deficit emerged. The deficit almost disappeared during the 1990–1991 recession, but it reappeared during the 1990s expansion.

*Sources:* The government budget balance is the U.S. federal government's budget deficit, *Economic Report of the President,* 1997. The international balance is the current account balance, *Survey of Current Business,* U.S. Department of Commerce, March 1997.

also takes interest payments paid to and received from the rest of the world into account. To compare one year with another, the figure shows the current account as a percentage of GDP. The U.S. current account deficit has fluctuated, and since 1980, it has ranged from close to zero to almost 4 percent of GDP. Our imports have usually exceeded our exports.

### Do Deficits Matter?

Why do deficits cause anxiety? What happens when a government cannot cover its spending with taxes or when a country buys more from other countries than it sells to them?

If you spend more than you earn, you have a deficit. And to cover your deficit, you have to borrow. But when you borrow, you must pay interest on your debt. Just like you, if a government or a nation has a deficit, it must borrow. And like you, the government and the nation must pay interest on their debts.

Whether borrowing and paying out huge amounts of interest are a good idea depends on what the borrowed funds are used for. If you borrow to finance a vacation, you must eventually tighten your belt, cut spending, and repay your debt as well as pay interest on the debt. But if you borrow to invest in a business that earns a large profit, you might be able to repay your debt and pay the interest on it while continuing to increase your spending. It is the same with a government and a nation. A government or a nation that borrows to increase its consumption might be heading for trouble later. But a government or a nation that borrows to buy assets that earn a profit might be making a sound investment.

You will learn more about government budget deficits in Chapter 12 and about the international current account deficit in Chapter 19.

◼ When government spending exceeds tax receipts, a government has a budget deficit.

◼ The U.S. government has had a persistent deficit since 1970.

◼ When imports exceed exports, a nation has an international deficit.

◼ The United States has had a fluctuating international deficit during the 1980s and 1990s.

## Macroeconomic Policy Challenges and Tools

FROM THE TIME OF ADAM SMITH's *THE WEALTH of Nations* in 1776 until the publication of Keynes' *General Theory of Employment, Interest, and Money* in 1936, it was widely believed that the only economic role for government was to enforce property rights. The economy behaves best, it was believed, if the government leaves people free to pursue their own best interests. The macroeconomics of Keynes challenged this view. Keynes' central point was that the economy will not fix itself and that government actions are needed to achieve and maintain full employment. The U.S. government declared full employment as a policy goal soon after World War II ended.

### Policy Challenges and Tools

Today, the five widely agreed challenges for macroeconomic policy are to:

1. Boost economic growth
2. Stabilize the business cycle
3. Reduce unemployment
4. Keep inflation low
5. Reduce the government and international deficits

But how can we do all these things? What are the tools available to pursue the macroeconomic policy challenges? Macroeconomic policy tools are divided into two broad categories:

◼ Fiscal policy
◼ Monetary policy

**Fiscal Policy**   Making changes in taxes and government spending is called **fiscal policy**. This range of policy actions is under the control of the federal government. Fiscal policy can be used to try to boost long-term growth by creating incentives that encourage saving, investment and technological change. Fiscal policy can also be used to try to smooth out the business cycle. When the economy is in a recession, the government might cut taxes or increase its spending. Conversely, when the economy is in a rapid expansion, the government might increase taxes or cut its spending in an attempt to slow real GDP growth and prevent inflation from increasing. Fiscal policy is discussed in Chapter 12.

**Montary Policy**   Changing interest rates and the amount of money in the economy is called **monetary policy**. These actions are under the control of the Federal Reserve (the Fed). The principal aim of monetary policy is to keep inflation in check. To achieve this objective, the Fed prevents money from expanding too rapidly. Monetary policy can also be used to smooth the business cycle. When the economy is in recession, the Fed might lower interest rates and inject money into the economy. And when the economy is in a rapid expansion, the Fed might increase interest rates in an attempt to slow real GDP growth and prevent the inflation from increasing. Monetary policy is discussed in Chapters 13 and 14.

◼ The macroeconomic policy challenges are to boost economic growth, stabilize the business cycle, reduce unemployment, keep inflation low, and reduce the government and international deficits.

◼ To meet these challenges, the government uses fiscal policy (taxes and government spending) and the Fed uses monetary policy (interest rates and money supply).

◆ In your study of macroeconomics, you will learn what is currently known about the causes of economic growth, business cycles, unemployment, inflation, and government and international deficits and about the policy choices and challenges that the government and the Fed face. *Reading Between the Lines* on pp. 112–113 looks at the state of the U.S. macroeconomy in 1996 and examines the long expansion, falling unemployment, and low inflation of the 1990s.

# Economy Watching

THE RECORD, HACKENSACK, NJ, DECEMBER 29, 1996

## Count on Economists to Coo Over the Nation's Numbers

BY MARTIN CRUTSINGER
THE ASSOCIATED PRESS

Washington—Economists, normally staid practitioners of what is called "the dismal science," are sounding downright giddy these days. The object of their delight, the good old U.S. economy.

No less an authority than Alan Greenspan, the Federal Reserve chairman, described the economy as fundamentally the best he has seen in three decades.

Searching for their own superlatives, some private economists have taken to calling this the "nirvana economy," a state of perfect economic bliss.

And as they prepare their outlooks for the new year, they're predicting the good times will continue to roll in 1997, with no threat of recession to disrupt an economic expansion that is already the third longest in U.S. history. ...

Finishing up its sixth year of uninterrupted growth, the current recovery's growth rates have not been stellar. But its slow, steady growth has avoided past boom-bust cycles in which overly rapid growth created inflation and forced the Federal Reserve to raise interest rates, triggering a recession. ...

While President Clinton cited his stewardship of the economy as a principal reason for his reelection, economists generally give most of the credit to Greenspan and his colleagues at the Fed.

In 1995, the central bank raised interest rates, trying to dampen growth to keep inflation from veering out of control. The effort succeeded and produced the so-called soft landing in which growth slowed enough to keep inflation in check but without a recession.

Economists believe 1997 will in many ways be a replay of 1996: moderate growth will keep inflation levels low and let the Fed stay on the sidelines for another year. ...

The last downturn ended in March 1991 and economists believe the current expansion should continue for some time to come. If it lasts until the end of 1998, it will surpass the long expansion of the 1980s. Some economists think 2000 could be the danger point for a downturn, noting that the country has been in recession in the last four years ending in a zero, 1960, 1970, 1980, and 1990.

## Essence of THE STORY

■ Alan Greenspan, chairman of the Federal Reserve, describes the economy as the best he has experienced in three decades.

■ By 1997, the economy had expanded for six years—the third longest expansion in U.S. history.

■ If the 1990s expansion lasts until the end of 1998, it will surpass the long expansion of the 1980s.

■ Some people say that 2000 could be the danger point for a downturn, because the U.S. economy has been in recession in the last four years ending in a zero—1960, 1970, 1980, and 1990.

# Economic

## A N A L Y S I S

■ Figure 1 shows the expansions in real GDP since 1921. The longest expansion lasted for almost 10 years during the 1960s. The second longest lasted for almost 8 years during the 1980s. The 1990s expansion is the third longest since World War II.

■ Figure 2 shows the 1990s expansion. Real GDP started out below potential GDP in the recession of 1990-1991. Real GDP expanded and, by mid-1994, was close to potential GDP. Both real GDP and potential GDP have grown at a similar rate since 1994.

■ Figure 3 shows the unemployment rate during the 1990s expansion. Unemployment peaked in 1992 and fell quickly through 1994. It has been steady at around 5.5 since 1995.

■ Figure 4 shows the inflation rate during the 1990s expansion. Beginning at almost 5 percent a year, the inflation rate has fallen to around 2 percent a year, its lowest level since the 1960s.

■ Expansions that last as long as the 1990s expansion are rare, and the current expansion will at some time come to an end.

■ The news article says that some people expect the next recession to occur in 2000 because "the country has been in recession in the last four years ending in a zero, 1960, 1970, 1980, and 1990."

■ There is nothing in the causes of recessions to think that timing of these four earlier recessions were anything other than coincidences.

■ The next recession will begin when some *currently unforeseeable* event brings a cut in spending and a surge in layoffs. In the past, such events have occurred on the average every 4 years but with a range that runs from 1 year to 10 years.

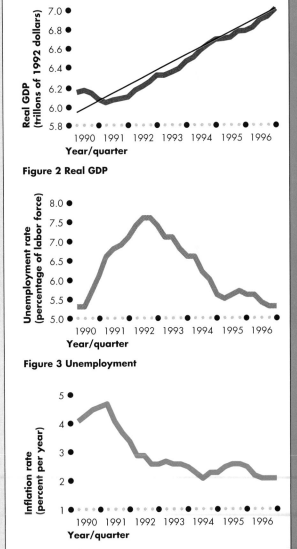

Figure 1 Expansion since 1921

Figure 2 Real GDP

Figure 3 Unemployment

Figure 4 Inflation

# SUMMARY

## Key Points

### Origins and Issues of Macroeconomics (p. 98)

- Macroeconomics studies economic growth and fluctuations, unemployment, inflation, and deficits.

### Economic Growth (pp. 99–104)

- Economic growth is the expansion of potential GDP. Real GDP fluctuates around potential GDP in a business cycle.
- Countries have similar productivity growth slow-downs and business cycles but different long-term trends in potential GDP.
- The main benefit of long-term economic growth is higher future consumption, and the main cost is lower current consumption.

### Jobs and Unemployment (pp. 104–106)

- The U.S. economy creates 1.8 million jobs a year, but unemployment persists.
- Unemployment increases during a recession and decreases during an expansion. The U.S. unemployment rate is lower than that in Canada and Western Europe but higher than that in Japan.
- Unemployment can permanently damage a person's job prospects.

### Inflation (pp. 107–109)

- Inflation, a process of rising prices, is measured by the percentage change in the CPI.
- Inflation is a problem because it lowers the value of money and makes money less useful as a measuring rod of value.

### Deficits (pp. 109–111)

- When government spending exceeds tax receipts, the government has a budget deficit.

- When imports exceed exports, a nation has an international deficit.
- Deficits are financed by borrowing.

### Macroeconomic Policy Challenges and Tools (p. 112)

- The macroeconomic policy challenge is to use fiscal policy and monetary policy to boost long-term growth, stabilize the business cycle, lower unemployment, tame inflation, and prevent large deficits.

## Key Figures ◆

## Key Terms

## QUESTIONS

1. What is economic growth and how is the long-term economic growth rate measured?
2. Is real GDP an ideal measure of total production? Explain why or why not.
3. Distinguish between actual real GDP and potential GDP.
4. Describe the productivity growth slowdown that occurred in the United States and other countries during the 1970s.
5. What is a business cycle? Describe its phases.
6. In what phase of the business cycle was the U.S. economy during 1975? 1980? 1985? 1995?
7. What are the benefits of long-term economic growth?
8. What are the costs of long-term economic growth?
9. What is unemployment?
10. Describe the main features of unemployment in the United States since 1930.
11. What does the unemployment rate tell us about the underutilization of labor? Explain your answer.
12. What are the main costs of unemployment?
13. Why is unemployment a serious problem?
14. Compare the unemployment rate in the United States since 1980 with that in Canada.
15. What is inflation? How is it measured?
16. What are some of the costs of inflation?
17. Compare inflation in the United States since 1970 with inflation in other industrial countries.
18. Why is inflation a problem?
19. What determines a government's budget deficit? How has the federal government's budget deficit evolved since 1970?
20. What is a country's international deficit? How has the U.S. international deficit changed since 1970?
21. What are the main challenges and tools of macroeconomic policy?
22. Distinguish between fiscal policy and monetary policy.

## PROBLEMS

1. Obtain data on the growth rates of real GDP for the United States, Canada, Japan, the European Union, and the developing countries of Africa, Asia, the Middle East and Europe, and the Western Hemisphere since 1977. You will find the data in the most recent issue of the *Economic Report of the President* or by using the Parkin Web Link. Use what you have discovered to answer the following questions:
   a. Which region of the world has grown fastest during the past 20 years?
   b. In which regions is production shrinking rather than growing?
   c. Describe the growth of Japan in recent years and compare it with that in the United States.
   d. Compare the growth rates of the four big economies in the European Union (France, Germany, Italy, and the United Kingdom). Which has the fastest growth rate over the 1990s?

2. Study the figure, which shows real GDP in Mexico, and then answer the following questions:
   a. How many recessions did Mexico experience during this period?
   b. In which quarters, if any, did Mexico experience a business cycle peak?

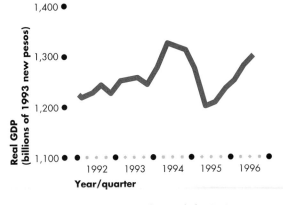

   c. In which quarters, if any, did Mexico experience a business cycle trough?
   d. In which quarters, if any, did Mexico experience an expansion?

⊕ http://hepg.awl.com/parkin/econ100

e. In which years was economic growth in Mexico positive?

f. In which years was economic growth in Mexico negative?

3. Obtain data on unemployment rates in the United States and other major industrial countries. You can find the data in the *Monthly Labor Review* or from the Parkin Web Link.

a. Compare the behavior of unemployment in the United States with that in the other countries.

b. Which country had the lowest and which the highest unemployment rate in 1995?

c. Which country had the lowest and which the highest teenage unemployment rate in 1995?

d. Draw a graph and determine whether the unemployment rates move up and down together. Which country or countries stand out as having an especially low unemployment rate.

4. Use the data in the Variable Graphing tool in the *Economics in Action* tutorial software to answer the following questions:

a. Which country had the highest real GDP growth rate: the United States, Canada, France, or Japan?

b. Which country had the highest unemployment rate: the United States, Canada, Sweden, or Japan?

c. Which country had the lowest inflation rate: the United States, Canada, France, or Japan?

d. Which country had the largest government budget deficit: the United States, Australia, Ireland, or Japan?

e. Which countries, if any, that feature in the *Economics in Action* macroeconomics data set did not have a recession during the 1990s?

5. Obtain data on the Consumer Price Index in your home city (or the nearest city for which you can get the data). You can find the data in the *CPI Detailed Report* (monthly) or from the Parkin Web Link. Then answer the following questions:

a. Has your local CPI been higher or lower than the U.S. average CPI?

b. Has your local inflation rate been higher or lower than the U.S. average inflation rate?

c. Can you think of an explanation for what you've discovered?

6. Obtain data on the federal government budget deficit as a percentage of GDP since the Great Depression. You can find the data in the *Economic Report of the President* (annual) or from the Parkin Web Link. Then answer the following questions:

a. In how many years since 1934 has the federal government had a budget surplus?

b. In which years were government budget deficits at their highest levels?

c. Can you detect a trend in the deficit since World War II?

d. Can you find periods in which the deficit was decreasing?

e. In which earlier period did the deficit behave in a way similar to its behavior during the 1990s?

7. Obtain data on the United States current account deficit and the current account deficits or surpluses of Japan and Canada. You can find these data from the Parkin Web Link:

a. Do Japan and Canada have deficits or surpluses during the 1990s?

b. When the U.S. deficit increases, what happens to the deficit or surplus in Canada and Japan?

c. Can you think of reasons for the relationships you describe in your answer to b?

# CRITICAL THINKING

1. Study *Reading Between the Lines* on pp. 112–113 and then answer the following questions:

a. When did the most recent expansion begin?

b. How long has the most recent expansion lasted? Is it an unusually long expansion? Compare its length with that of other expansions since World War II and before World War II?

c. Can you think of convincing reasons why the 1990s expansion has been a long one?

d. Alan Greenspan was pleased with the economy in 1996. What actions do you think he should be considering taking to keep the economy expanding with low inflation?

# 6

# Measuring GDP, Inflation, and Economic Growth

When Motorola contemplates spending $1 billion developing a wireless communications system in China, it pays close attention to forecasts of China's real GDP. When AT&T plans to expand its fiber-optics network, it uses forecasts of long-term growth in the U.S. economy. The outcomes of many business decisions turn on the quality of forecasts of economic conditions. ◆ A key input for making economic forecasts is gross domestic product, or GDP, which is like a barometer of a nation's economy. Economists pore over the numbers, looking at past trends and seeking patterns that might give a glimpse of the future. How do economic statisticians add up all the production of the country to arrive at the number called GDP? What exactly *is* GDP? ◆ Most of the time, our economy grows, but sometimes it shrinks. To reveal the rate of growth (or shrinkage), we must remove the effects of inflation on GDP and assess how *real* GDP is changing. How do we remove the inflation component of GDP to reveal real GDP? ◆ From economists to home makers, all types of people pay close attention to another economic barometer, the Consumer Price Index, or CPI. The Department of Labor publishes new figures each month, and analysts in newspapers and on TV quickly leap to conclusions about the causes of recent changes in prices and the prospects for future changes. How does the government determine the CPI? How well does it measure a consumer's living costs and the inflation rate? ◆ Some countries are rich, while others are poor and only now are in the process of developing their industries and reaching their productive potential. How do we compare incomes in one country with incomes in another? How can we make international comparisons of GDP? ◆ In this chapter, you are going to find out how economic statisticians measure real GDP and the price level. You are also going to learn how they use these measures to assess the economic growth rate and the inflation rate and to compare macroeconomic performance across countries.

## Economic Barometers

**After studying this chapter, you will be able to:**

■ Explain why aggregate income, expenditure, and product are equal

■ Explain how GDP is measured

■ Explain how the Consumer Price Index (CPI) and the GDP deflator are measured

■ Explain the shortcomings of the CPI and the GDP deflator as measures of inflation

■ Explain how *real* GDP is measured

■ Explain the shortcomings of real GDP growth as a measure of improvements in living standards

## Gross Domestic Product

WHAT EXACTLY IS GDP, HOW IS IT CALCULATED, what does it mean, and why do we care about it? You are going to discover the answers to these questions in this chapter. First, what *is* GDP? **GDP**, or **gross domestic product**, is the value of the *aggregate* production of goods and services in a country during a given time period—usually a year. The GDP of the United States, which measures the value of aggregate production in the United States during a year, was $7,576 billion in 1996.

How is GDP calculated? In a nutshell, GDP is calculated by valuing everything that is produced and adding all the values together. But precisely *what* is valued and *how* it is valued? To answer these questions, you need to understand two fundamental principles of economic accounting:

■ The distinction between flows and stocks
■ The equality of income, expenditure, and the value of production

### Flows and Stocks

To keep track of our personal economic transactions and the economic transactions of a country, we distinguish between flows and stocks. A **flow** is a quantity per unit of time. The water that is running from an open faucet into a bathtub is a flow. So are the number of CDs that you buy during a month and the amount of income that you earn during a month. GDP is a flow. It is the value of the goods and services produced in a country *during a given time period*.

A **stock** is a quantity that exists at a point in time. The water in a bathtub is a stock. So are the number of CDs that you own and the amount of money in your savings account.

**Capital and Investment** The key macroeconomic stock is capital. **Capital** is the plant, equipment, buildings, and inventories of raw materials and semifinished goods that are used to produce other goods and services. The amount of capital in the economy exerts a big influence on GDP. Two flows change the stock of capital: investment and depreciation. Investment is the purchase of new capital. It increases the stock of capital. (Investment includes additions to inventories.) **Depreciation** is the decrease in the stock of capital that results from wear and tear and obsolescence.

Another name for depreciation is *capital consumption*. The total amount spent on adding to the stock of capital and on replacing depreciated capital is called **gross investment**. The amount spent on adding to the stock of capital is called **net investment**. Net investment equals gross investment minus depreciation.

Figure 6.1 illustrates these concepts. On January 1, 1997, Tom's Tapes, Inc. had 3 machines. This quantity was its initial capital. During 1997, Tom's scrapped an older machine. This quantity is its depreciation. After depreciation, Tom's stock of capital was down to 2 machines. But also during 1997, Tom's bought 2 new machines. This amount is its gross investment. By December 31, 1997, Tom's Tapes had 4 machines, so its capital had increased by 1 machine. This amount is Tom's net investment. Tom's net investment equals its gross investment (the

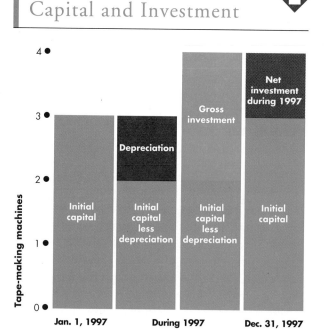

**FIGURE 6.1**

Capital and Investment

Tom's Tapes has a capital stock at the end of 1997 that equals its capital stock at the beginning of the year plus its net investment. Net investment is equal to gross investment less depreciation. Tom's gross investment is the 2 new machines bought during the year, and its depreciation is the 1 machine that Tom's scrapped during the year.

purchase of 2 new machines) minus its depreciation (1 machine scrapped).

The example of Tom's Tapes factory can be applied to the economy as a whole. The nation's capital stock decreases because capital depreciates and increases because of gross investment. The change in the nation's capital stock from one year to the next equals its net investment.

**Wealth and Saving**   Another macroeconomic stock is **wealth**, which is the value of all the things that people own. What people *own*, a stock, is related to what they *earn*, a flow. People *earn* an *income*, which is the amount they receive during a given time period from supplying the services of resources. Income can be either consumed or saved. **Consumption expenditure** is the amount spent on consumption goods and services. **Saving** is the amount of income remaining after meeting consumption expenditures. Saving adds to wealth, and dissaving (negative saving) decreases wealth.

For example, suppose that at the end of the school year, you have $250 in a savings account and some textbooks that are worth $300. That's all you own. Your wealth is $550. Suppose that you take a summer job and earn an income of $5,000. You are extremely careful and spend only $1,000 through the summer on consumption goods and services. At the end of the summer, when school starts again, you have $4,250 in your savings account. Your wealth is now $4,550. Your wealth has increased by $4,000, which equals your saving of $4,000. Your saving of $4,000 equals your income of $5,000 minus your consumption expenditure of $1,000.

National wealth and national saving work just like this personal example. The wealth of a nation at the start of a year equals its wealth at the start of the previous year plus its saving during the year. Its saving equals its income minus its consumption expenditure.

We'll make the idea of the nation's income and consumption expenditure more precise a bit later in this chapter. Before doing so, let's see what the stocks and flows that we've just learned about imply for the recurring theme of macroeconomics: short-term fluctuations in actual real GDP and long-term growth in potential GDP.

**The Short Term Meets the Long Term**   You saw in Chapter 22 that potential GDP grows incessantly, year after year. You also saw that actual real GDP grows and fluctuates around potential GDP. The stocks and flows that you've just studied influence *both* the long-term growth in potential GDP and the short-term fluctuations in actual GDP. One of the reasons why potential GDP grows is that the capital stock grows. One of the reasons that real GDP fluctuates is that investment fluctuates. So capital and investment as well as wealth and saving are part of the key to understanding the growth of potential GDP and the fluctuations of real GDP.

The flows of investment and saving together with the flows of income and consumption expenditure interact in a circular flow of income and expenditure. In this circular flow, income equals expenditure, which also equals the value of production. This amazing equality is the foundation on which a nation's economic accounts are built and from which its GDP is measured.

## Income, Expenditure, and the Value of Production

To see that for the economy as a whole, income equals expenditure and also equals the value of production, we study the circular flow of income and expenditure.

Figure 6.2 illustrates the circular flow of income and expenditure. In the figure, the economy consists of four sectors: households, firms, governments, and the rest of the world (the purple diamonds). It has three types of markets: resource markets, goods (and services) markets, and financial markets. Focus first on households and firms.

**Households and Firms**   Households sell and firms buy the services of labor, capital, land, and entrepreneurship in resource markets. For these resource services, firms pay income to households: wages for labor services, interest for the use of capital, rent for the use of land, and profits for entrepreneurship. Firms' retained earnings—profits that are not distributed to households—are also part of the household sector's income. You can think of retained earnings as being income that households save and lend back to firms. Figure 6.2 shows the *aggregate income* received by all households in payment for the services of resources by the blue dots labeled $Y$.

Firms sell and households buy consumer goods and services—such as popcorn and soda, movies and chocolate bars, microwave ovens and inline skates, dental and dry cleaning services—in the markets for goods and services. The total payment that households make for these goods and services is *consumption*

## FIGURE 6.2

# The Circular Flow of Income and Expenditure

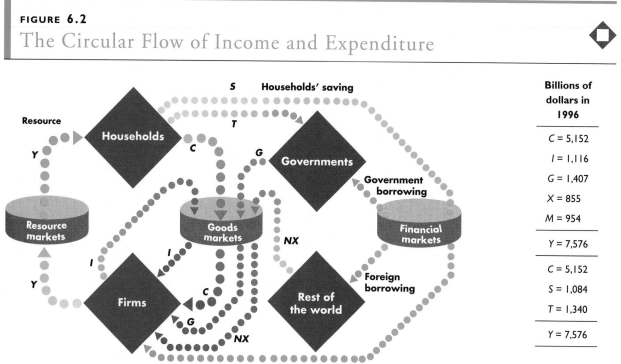

| Billions of dollars in 1996 |
| --- |
| C = 5,152 |
| I = 1,116 |
| G = 1,407 |
| X = 855 |
| M = 954 |
| Y = 7,576 |
| C = 5,152 |
| S = 1,084 |
| T = 1,340 |
| Y = 7,576 |

In the circular flow of income and expenditure, households receive incomes (Y) from firms (blue flow) and make consumption expenditures (C); firms make investment expenditures (I); governments purchase goods and services (G); the rest of the world purchases net exports (NX)—(red flows). Aggregate income (blue flow) equals aggregate expenditure (red flows). Households' saving (S) and net taxes (T) leak from the circular flow. Firms borrow to finance their investment expenditures, and governments and the rest of the world borrow to finance their deficits or lend their surpluses (green flows). The table gives the values for the flows in 1996. Net exports (NX) is exports (X) minus imports (M).

Source: U.S. Department of Commerce, *Survey of Current Business* (March 1997).

*expenditure.* Figure 6.2 shows consumption expenditure by the red dots labeled *C*.

Firms buy and sell new capital equipment in the goods market. For example, IBM sells 1,000 PCs to General Motors, or Boeing sells an airplane to United Airlines. Some of what firms produce might not be sold at all and is added to inventory. For example, if GM produces 1,000 cars and sells 950 of them, the other 50 cars remain unsold and GM's inventory of cars increases by 50. When a firm adds unsold output to inventory, we can think of the firm as buying goods from itself. The purchase of new plant, equipment, and buildings and the additions to inventories are *investment.*

Figure 6.2 shows investment by the red dots labeled *I.* Notice that in the figure, investment flows from firms through the goods markets and back to firms. Some firms produce capital goods, and other

firms buy them (and firms "buy" inventories from themselves).

Firms finance their investment by borrowing from households in financial markets. Households' saving flows into financial markets, and firms' borrowing flows out of financial markets. Figure 6.2 shows these flows by the green dots labeled "Households' saving" or *S* and "Firms' borrowing." These flows are neither income nor expenditure. Income is a payment for the services of a resource, and expenditure is a payment for goods or services.

**Governments**   Governments buy goods and services, called **government purchases**, from firms. In Fig. 6.2 these government purchases are shown as the red flow *G.* Governments use taxes to pay for their purchases. Figure 6.2 shows taxes as net taxes by the green dots labeled *T.* **Net taxes** are equal to taxes paid to governments minus transfer payments received from governments and minus interest payments from the government on its debt. *Transfer payments* are cash transfers from governments to households and firms such as social security benefits, unemployment compensation, and subsidies.

When government purchases (*G*) exceed net taxes (*T*), the government has a budget deficit, which it finances by borrowing in financial markets (shown by the green dots labeled "Government borrowing.")

**Rest of World Sector**    Firms export goods and services to the rest of the world and import goods and services from the rest of the world. The value of exports minus the value of imports is called **net exports**. Figure 6.2 shows net exports by the red flow *NX*.

If the value of exports exceeds the value of imports, net exports are positive and flow from the rest of the world to firms. But if the value of exports is less than the value of imports, net exports are negative and flow from firms to the rest of the world.

If net exports are positive, the rest of the world is in deficit and we are in surplus. To finance its deficit, the rest of the world borrows from the domestic economy or sells domestic assets that it owns. For example, Korean Airlines can borrow in New York to finance the purchase of new airplanes from Boeing. These transactions take place in financial markets, and they are shown by the green flow labeled "Foreign borrowing."

If net exports are negative, we are in deficit and the rest of the world is in surplus. To finance our deficit, we borrow from the rest of the world or we sell foreign assets that we own. For example, a California winemaker might borrow in Frankfurt, Germany, to finance the purchase of a German-made grape-picking machine. Again, these transactions take place in financial markets. To illustrate this case in Fig. 6.2, we would reverse the directions of the flows of net exports and foreign borrowing.

To help you keep track of the different types of flows that make up the circular flow of income and expenditure, the flows are color-coded in Fig. 6.2. The red flows are expenditures on goods and services, the blue flow is income, and the green flows are financial transfers. The expenditure flows (red flows) are consumption expenditure, investment, government purchases, and net exports. The income flow (blue flow) is aggregate income. The financial transfers (green flows) are saving, net taxes, govern-

ment borrowing, foreign borrowing, and firms' borrowing.

**Gross Domestic Product**    Gross domestic product is the value of *aggregate production* in a country during a year. Production can be valued in two ways:

1. By what buyers pay for it
2. By what it costs producers to make it

From the viewpoint of buyers, goods are worth the prices paid for them. From the viewpoint of producers, goods are worth what it costs to make them. Fortunately, the value of production is the same regardless of which viewpoint we take. Let's see why.

**Expenditure Equals Income**    The total amount that buyers pay for the goods and services produced is *aggregate expenditure*. Let's focus on aggregate expenditure in Fig. 6.2. The expenditures on goods and services are shown by the red flows. Firms' revenues from the sale of goods and services equal consumption expenditure (*C*) plus investment (*I*) plus government purchases of goods and services (*G*) plus net exports (*NX*). The sum of these four flows is equal to aggregate expenditure on goods and services.

The total amount it costs producers to make goods and services is equal to the incomes paid for resource services. This amount is shown by the blue flow in Fig. 6.2.

The sum of the red flows equals the blue flow. The reason is that everything a firm receives from the sale of its output is paid out as incomes to the owners of the resources that it employs. That is,

$$Y = C + I + G + NX,$$

or aggregate income (*Y*) equals aggregate expenditure (*C* + *I* + *G* + *NX*).

The buyers of aggregate production pay an amount equal to aggregate expenditure, and the sellers of aggregate production pay an amount equal to aggregate income. Because aggregate expenditure equals aggregate income, these two methods of valuing aggregate production give the same answer. So

Aggregate production, or GDP, equals aggregate expenditure and equals aggregate income.

The circular flow of income and expenditure is the foundation on which the national economic accounts are built. It is used to provide the two approaches to measuring GDP. And it is used to create other accounts that help us to keep track of the flows of saving and investment, the government's budget, and the balance of our exports and imports.

Let's look next at how the circular flows you've just studied enable us to keep track of how investment is financed.

## How Investment Is Financed

Investment, which adds to the stock of capital, is one of the determinants of the rate at which production grows. Investment is financed by:

- National saving
- Borrowing from the rest of the world

**National Saving**    The amount of saving by households and businesses plus government saving is called **national saving**. Saving by households and businesses, $S$, equals income minus taxes minus consumption expenditure. Government saving equals net taxes minus government purchases of goods and services, $(T - G)$. If the government has a budget surplus, $(T - G)$ is positive and this surplus is a source of finance for investment. But if the government has a budget deficit, $(T - G)$ is negative and part of saving is used to finance the government deficit. So

$$\text{National saving} = S + (T - G).$$

**Borrowing from the Rest of the World**    If we spend more on foreign goods and services than the rest of the world spends on ours, we must borrow from the rest of the world to pay the difference. That is, if the value of our imports $(M)$ exceeds the value of our exports $(X)$, we must borrow from the rest of the world an amount equal to $(M - X)$. In this case, part of the rest of the world's saving finances our negative net exports and frees up an equal amount of national saving to finance investment in the United States. Conversely, if foreigners spend more on U.S.-made goods and services than we spend on theirs, foreigners must borrow from us to pay the difference. That is, part of U.S. national saving flows to the rest of the world and is not available to finance U.S. investment.

In 1996, U.S. investment was $1,116 billion. This investment was financed by $1,017 billion of national saving and $99 billion of funds borrowed from the rest of the world.

## REVIEW

- Production, income, and expenditure are flows. Capital and wealth are stocks. The flow of investment adds to the stock of capital, and the flow of saving adds to the stock of wealth.
- Aggregate expenditure equals consumption expenditure plus investment plus government purchases plus exports minus imports.
- Aggregate expenditure equals aggregate income equals GDP.
- Investment is financed by national saving plus borrowing from the rest of the world.

Let's now see how the Department of Commerce uses the circular flows to measure GDP.

## Measuring U.S. GDP

To measure GDP, the Department of Commerce uses two approaches:

- Expenditure approach
- Income approach

### The Expenditure Approach

The *expenditure approach* measures GDP by using data on consumption expenditure, investment, government purchases, and net exports. Table 6.1 shows this approach. The first column gives the terms used in the *National Income and Product Accounts of the United States* (published by the Department of Commerce). The next column gives the symbol we've used in our GDP equations. GDP using the expenditure approach is the sum of personal consumption expenditures $(C)$, gross private domestic investment $(I)$, government purchases of goods and services $(G)$, and net exports of goods and services $(NX)$.

*Personal consumption expenditures* are the expenditures by households on goods and services produced in the United States and in the rest of the world. They include goods such as CDs and books and services such as banking and legal advice. They do *not* include the purchase of new homes, which is counted as part of investment.

## TABLE 6.1
## GDP: The Expenditure Approach

◆

| Item | Symbol | Amount in 1996 (billions of dollars) | Percentage of GDP |
|---|---|---|---|
| Personal consumption expenditures | C | 5,152 | 68.0 |
| Gross private domestic investment | I | 1,116 | 14.7 |
| Government purchases of goods and services | G | 1,407 | 18.6 |
| Net exports of goods and services | NX | −99 | −1.3 |
| **Gross domestic product** | Y | 7,576 | 100.0 |

The expenditure approach measures GDP by adding personal consumption expenditures (C), gross private domestic investment (I), government purchases of goods and services (G), and net exports (NX). In 1996, GDP measured by the expenditure approach was $7,576 billion. Two thirds of aggregate expenditure is on personal consumption goods and services.

Source: U.S. Department of Commerce, Survey of Current Business (March 1997).

*Gross private domestic investment* is expenditure on capital equipment and buildings by firms and expenditure on new homes by households. It also includes the change in business inventories.

*Government purchases of goods and services* are the purchases of goods and services by all levels of government. This item includes expenditures on national defense and garbage collection. But it does *not* include *transfer payments*. These payments, such as medical aid and social security benefits, are not purchases of goods and services. They are transfers of funds from government to households.

*Net exports of goods and services* are the value of exports minus the value of imports. This item includes computers that IBM sells to Volkswagen, the German car producer, (a U.S. export) and Mazda RX7s that your local dealer buys from Japan (a U.S. import).

Table 6.1 shows the relative importance of the four items of aggregate expenditure. The largest component is personal consumption expenditures, and the smallest is net exports (negative in 1996).

**Expenditures Not in GDP** Aggregate expenditure, which equals GDP, does not include all the things that people and businesses buy. To distinguish total expenditure on GDP from other items of spending, we call the expenditure included in GDP *final expenditure.* Spending that is not part of final expenditure and not part of GDP include the purchase of:

- Intermediate goods and services
- Used goods
- Financial assets

**Intermediate goods and services** are the goods and services that firms buy from each other and use as inputs in the goods and services that they eventually sell to final users. When Dell Corp. buys computer chips from Intel Corp., it buys an intermediate good. A Dell computer is a final good, but an Intel chip is an intermediate good. To count the expenditure on intermediate goods and services as well as the expenditure on the final good involves counting the same thing twice—called *double counting.*

A good can sometimes be an intermediate good and sometimes a final good. For example, the ice cream that you buy on a hot summer day is a final good, but the ice cream that a diner buys and uses to make sundaes is an intermediate good. Whether a good is intermediate or final depends on what it is used for, not on what it is.

Expenditure on *used goods* is not part of GDP because these goods were counted as part of GDP in the period in which they were produced and in which they were new goods. For example, a 1990 automobile was part of GDP in 1990. If the car is traded on the used car market in 1997, the amount paid for the car is not part of GDP in 1997.

Firms often sell *financial assets* such as bonds and stocks to finance purchases of newly produced capital goods. The expenditure on newly produced capital goods is part of GDP, but the expenditure on financial securities is not. GDP includes the amount spent on new capital, not the amount spent on pieces of paper.

Let's look at the second way of measuring GDP, the income approach.

## The Income Approach

The *income approach* measures GDP by summing the incomes that firms pay households for the resources they hire—wages for labor, interest for capital, rent for land, and profits for entrepreneurship. Let's see how the income approach works.

The *National Income and Product Accounts* divide incomes into five categories:

1. Compensation of employees
2. Net interest
3. Rental income
4. Corporate profits
5. Proprietors' income

*Compensation of employees* is the payment for labor services. It includes net wages and salaries (called "take-home pay") that workers receive plus taxes withheld on earnings plus fringe benefits such as social security and pension fund contributions.

*Net interest* is the interest households receive on loans they make minus the interest households pay on their own borrowing.

*Rental income* is the payment for the use of land and other rented inputs. It includes payments for rented housing and imputed rent for owner-occupied housing. (Imputed rent is an estimate of what home-owners would pay to rent the housing they own and use themselves. By including this item in the national income accounts, we measure the total value of housing services, whether they are owned or rented.)

*Corporate profits* are the profits of corporations. Some of these profits are paid to households in the form of dividends, and some are retained by corporations as undistributed profits. They are all income.

*Proprietors' income* is a mixture of the previous four items. It is difficult to split the income earned by the owner-operator of a business into compensation for labor, payment for the use of capital, and profit, so the national income accounts lump all these items into a single category.

Table 6.2 shows these five incomes and their relative magnitudes. Compensation of employees is the largest income category.

The sum of these five categories of incomes is called *net domestic income at factor cost*. The term *factor cost* is used because *factor of production* is another name for a productive resource. But *net domestic income at factor cost* is not GDP. We must make two further adjustments to get to GDP, one from *factor cost* to *market prices* and another from *net* product to *gross* product.

**Factor Cost to Market Prices**    When we add up all the final expenditures on goods and services, we arrive at a total called domestic product at *market prices*. These expenditures are valued at the market prices that people pay for the various goods and services. Another way of valuing goods and services is at factor cost. *Factor cost* is the value of a good or service measured by adding together the costs of all the resources used to produce it. If the only economic transaction were between households and firms—if there were no government taxes or subsidies—the market price and factor cost values would be the same. But the presence of indirect taxes and subsidies makes these two methods of valuation differ.

An *indirect tax* is a tax paid by consumers when they buy goods and services. (In contrast, a *direct tax* is a tax on income.) State sales taxes and taxes on alcohol, gasoline, and tobacco products are indirect

**TABLE 6.2**

## GDP: The Income Approach

| Item | Amount in 1996 (billions of dollars) | Percentage of GDP |
|---|---|---|
| Compensation of employees | 4,449 | 58.7 |
| Net interest | 405 | 5.4 |
| Rental income | 127 | 1.7 |
| Corporate profits | 650 | 8.6 |
| Proprietors' income | 518 | 6.8 |
| Indirect taxes *less* Subsidies | 569 | 7.5 |
| Capital consumption (depreciation) | 858 | 11.3 |
| **Gross domestic product** | 7,576 | 100.0 |

The sum of all incomes plus indirect taxes less subsidies equals net domestic income. GDP equals net domestic income plus capital consumption (depreciation). In 1996, GDP measured by the income approach was $7,576 billion.

*Source:* U.S. Department of Commerce, *Survey of Current Business* (March 1997).

taxes. Because of indirect taxes, consumers pay more for some goods and services than producers receive. Market price exceeds factor cost. For example, if the sales tax is 7 percent, when you buy a $1 chocolate bar you pay $1.07. The factor cost of the chocolate bar including profit is $1. The market price is $1.07.

A *subsidy* is a payment by the government to a producer. Payments made to grain growers and dairy farmers are subsidies. Because of subsidies, consumers pay less for some goods and services than producers receive. Factor cost exceeds market price.

To get from factor cost to market price, we add indirect taxes and subtract subsidies. Making this adjustment brings us one step closer to GDP, but it does not quite get us there. We must make one further adjustment.

**Net Domestic Product to Gross Domestic Product** What do the words *gross* and *net* mean? *Gross* means *before* subtracting *depreciation*—the decrease in the value of the capital stock that results from wear and tear and obsolescence. *Net* means *after* subtracting depreciation.

*Gross investment* is a component of aggregate expenditure. So total expenditure includes depreciation and is a gross measure. The *net profit* of businesses—profit *after* subtracting depreciation—is a component of aggregate incomes. So total income excludes depreciation and is a net measure.

To get *gross* domestic product from the income approach, we must add depreciation to aggregate income.

Table 6.2 summarizes these calculations and shows how the income approach leads to the same estimate of GDP as the expenditure approach after the adjustments that we've just described have been made.

## Valuing the Output of Industries

The methods used to measure GDP can also be used to measure the contribution that an industry makes to GDP. But to measure the value of production of an individual industry, we count only the value added by that industry. **Value added** is the value of a firm's production minus the value of the *intermediate goods* that the firm buys from other firms. Equivalently, it is the sum of the incomes (including profits) paid to the resources used by the firm.

Figure 6.3 illustrates value added by looking at the brief life of a loaf of bread. It starts with the

farmer, who grows the wheat. The farmer hires labor, capital, and land and pays wages, interest, and rent for these resources. The farmer also earns a profit. The entire value of the wheat produced is the farmer's value added. The miller buys wheat from the farmer and turns it into flour. The miller hires labor and capital, pays wages and interest, and earns a profit. The miller has now added value to the wheat bought from the farmer. The baker buys flour from the miller. The price of the flour includes the value added by both the farmer and the miller. The baker adds more value by turning the flour into bread. The grocer buys the bread from the baker. The price paid by the grocer includes the value added by the farmer, the miller, and the baker. At this stage, the value of the loaf is its *wholesale* value. The grocer adds further value by

**FIGURE 6.3**

## Value Added and Final Expenditure

A consumer's expenditure on bread (the green bar) is equal to the sum of the value added at each stage in its production (the red bars). The blue bars illustrate intermediate expenditure. Intermediate expenditure, for example the amount paid by the baker for the purchase of flour from the miller, equals the value added by the farmer and the miller. So to include intermediate expenditure and final expenditure double counts some value added.

making the loaf available in a convenient place and time. The consumer buys the bread for a price—its *market price*—that includes the value added by the farmer, the miller, the baker, and the grocer.

**Final Goods and Intermediate Goods** To value output, we count only *value added* because the sum of the value added at each stage of production equals expenditure on the *final good*. By using value added, we avoid double counting. In the above example, the only thing that has been produced and consumed is a loaf of bread—shown by the green bar in Fig. 6.3. The value added at each stage is shown by the red bars, and the sum of the red bars equals the green bar. The transactions involving intermediate goods, shown by the blue bars, are not part of value added and are not counted as part of the value of output or of GDP.

**Aggregate Expenditure, Income, and GDP**
You've seen that aggregate expenditure equals aggregate income. And you've seen that the Department of Commerce uses both aggregate expenditure and aggregate income to measure GDP. Why does it use two approaches when they are supposed to be the same? The answer is that although the two concepts of the value of aggregate production are identical, the actual measurements, which are based on samples of information, give slightly different answers. The expenditure approach uses data from surveys of retail stores, house building, and business investment, the accounts of the federal, state, and local government, customs records, and many other sources. The income approach uses data supplied by the Internal Revenue Service. None of these sources gives a complete coverage of all the items that make up aggregate expenditure and aggregate income. So by using the two approaches, the Department of Commerce can check one aggregate against the other. The small discrepancy between the approaches is used to adjust both approaches to make them equal.

Figure 6.4 shows this equality between the approaches to measuring GDP and summarizes the expenditure, income, and product concepts.

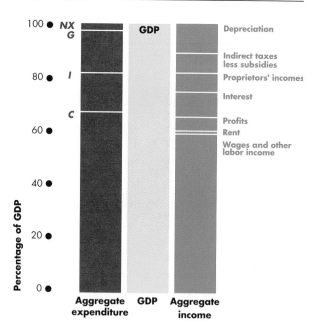

**FIGURE 6.4**

## Aggregate Expenditure, Output, and Income

The red bar illustrates the components of aggregate expenditure as well as their relative magnitudes. Net exports, the smallest component, is shown here as a positive quantity, but in some years it is negative. The green bar illustrates the components of aggregate income and their relative magnitudes. The figure illustrates the equality between aggregate expenditure, aggregate income, and GDP (the yellow bar).

---

R E V I E W

- The *expenditure approach* to measuring GDP sums consumption expenditure, investment, government purchases, and net exports.
- The *income approach* to measuring GDP sums wages, interest, rent, and profits.
- To value the production of an industry, we calculate the value added of that industry.

So far, in our study of GDP and its measurement, we've been concerned with the dollar value of GDP and its components. But the dollar value of GDP can change either because prices change or because there is a change in the volume of goods and services produced—a change in *real* GDP. Let's now see how we measure the price level and distinguish between the dollar value and the real value of GDP.

# The Price Level and Inflation

THE PRICE LEVEL IS THE AVERAGE LEVEL OF PRICES measured by a *price index*. The **inflation rate** is the percentage change in the price level from one year to the next. The two main price indexes that are used in the United States today are:

- The Consumer Price Index
- The GDP deflator

Let's see how the two price indexes are calculated.

## The Consumer Price Index

The **Consumer Price Index (CPI)** measures the average level of prices of the goods and services that a typical urban family buys. The Bureau of Labor Statistics (BLS) publishes the CPI every month. To construct the CPI, the BLS first selects a base period (currently the three-year period 1982–1984) and surveys consumer spending patterns to determine the "basket" of goods and services that people bought in the base period. That basket contains around 400 different goods and services.

Then, every month, the BLS sends a team of observers to more than 50 urban centers in the United States to record the prices of the 400 items. The CPI

is calculated by valuing the basket at the current month's prices and expressing its value as a percentage of the value of the same basket in the base period.

Table 6.3 shows an example of the CPI calculation. The basket contains 5 pounds of oranges, 6 haircuts, and 100 bus rides. The table shows the prices in the base period and total expenditure. A typical consumer buys 5 pounds of oranges at $0.80 a pound and spends $4 on oranges. Expenditure on haircuts and bus rides is worked out in the same way. Total expenditure is the sum of expenditures on the three goods, which is $210.

To calculate the CPI for the current period, we need only discover the prices of the goods in the current period. We do not need to know the quantities bought. Suppose that the prices are those shown in Table 6.3 under "Current period." We can now calculate the current period's value of the basket. For example, the current price of oranges is $1.20 per pound, so the current period's value of the oranges in the basket (5 pounds) is 5 multiplied by $1.20, which is $6. The quantities of haircuts and bus rides are valued at this period's prices in a similar way. The total value of the basket in the current period is $231.

The CPI is the ratio of the current period's value of the basket to the base period's value, multiplied by 100. In Table 6.3, the CPI is 110 in the current period. The current period's price of the basket is 10 percent higher than it was in the base period.

---

**TABLE 6.3**
## The CPI: A Simplified Calculation

| Base-period basket | Base period | | Current period | |
|---|---|---|---|---|
| | Price | Expenditure | Price | Expenditure |
| 5 pounds of oranges | $ 0.80/pound | $ 4 | $ 1.20/pound | $ 6 |
| 6 haircuts | $ 11.00 each | $ 66 | $ 12.50 each | $ 75 |
| 100 bus rides | $ 1.40 each | $ 140 | $ 1.50 each | $ 150 |
| Total expenditure | | $210 | | $231 |
| **CPI** | $\frac{\$210.00}{\$210.00} \times 100 = 100$ | | $\frac{\$231.00}{\$210.00} \times 100 = 110$ | |

A fixed basket of goods—5 pounds of oranges, 6 haircuts, and 100 bus rides—is valued in the base period at $210. Prices change, and that same basket is valued at $231 in the current period. The CPI is equal to the current-period value of the basket divided by the base-period value of the basket, multiplied by 100. In the base period the CPI is 100, and in the current period the CPI is 110.

## The GDP Deflator

The **GDP deflator** measures the average level of prices of all the goods and services that are included in GDP.

To calculate the GDP deflator, we use the formula

$$\text{GDP deflator} = \frac{\text{Nominal GDP}}{\text{Real GDP}} \times 100.$$

In this formula, **nominal GDP** is GDP valued in the current year's prices. It is the dollar value of GDP. **Real GDP** is GDP in a base year (currently 1992) scaled up by the growth rate of real GDP since the base year. But how do we calculate real GDP growth? Let's find out.

## Real GDP Growth: A Chain-Weighted Measure

The **chain-weighted output index** is an index number that measures the growth rate of real GDP. To learn how to calculate such an index, let's study an imaginary economy that produces only oranges and video games. Table 6.4 lists the quantities produced and prices of these goods in 1992 and 1993.

Our goal is to calculate a chain-weighted output index that compares the 50 oranges and 5 video games produced in 1992 with the 45 oranges and 7 video games produced in 1993. To make a comparison, we must value the items using prices. But we have two sets of price: 1992 and 1993 prices. The chain-weighted output index uses *both* sets of prices.

---

**TABLE 6.4**

## Calculating a Chain-Weighted Output Index

| Item | 1992 quantities | 1992 prices | 1992 quantities valued at 1992 prices | 1993 prices | 1992 quantities valued at 1993 prices |
|---|---|---|---|---|---|
| Oranges | 50 | $1.00 | $50 | $2.00 | $100 |
| Video games | 5 | $10.00 | $50 | $8.00 | $40 |
| Totals | | | A = $100 | | D = $140 |

| Item | 1993 quantities | 1992 prices | 1993 quantities valued at 1992 prices | 1993 prices | 1993 quantities valued at 1993 prices |
|---|---|---|---|---|---|
| Oranges | 45 | $1.00 | $45 | $2.00 | $90 |
| Video games | 7 | $10.00 | $70 | $8.00 | $56 |
| Totals | | | B = $115 | | E = $146 |

**Output index**          $C = B \div A = 1.150$          $F = E \div D = 1.043$

**Chain-weighted output index** (geometric mean of C and F = $\sqrt{1.150 \times 1.043}$ ) = 1.095

**Growth rate** in 1993 using chain-weighted output index          9.5 percent

---

In 1992, an imaginary economy produces 50 oranges at $1 each and 5 video games at $10 each and in 1993, the economy produces 45 oranges at $2 each and 7 video games at $8 each. Nominal GDP in 1992 is $100 (A in the table). The value of the 1993 quantities in the 1992 prices is $115 (B in the table). Output valued in 1992 prices has grown by 15 percent (B is 15 percent larger than A).

Nominal GDP in 1993 is $146 (E in the table). The value of 1992 quantities in the 1993 prices is $140 (D in the table). Output valued in 1993 prices has grown by 4.3 percent (E is 4.3 percent larger than D). The chain-weighted output index is the geometric mean of the two indexes C and F and is 1.095. Real GDP in 1993 is equal to real GDP in 1992 multiplied by 1.095. The growth rate in 1993 is 9.5 percent.

The calculations needed are the following:

■ Nominal GDP in 1992 (total expenditure on oranges and video games during 1992), which is $100 (*A* in the table).

■ The value of output in 1993 using the 1992 prices, which is $115 (*B*).

■ An output index for 1993, which equals the value of output in 1993 using 1992 prices divided by nominal GDP in 1992. That index is 1.150 (*C*).

■ Nominal GDP in 1993, which is $146 (*E*).

■ The value of output in 1992 using the 1993 prices, which is $140 (*D*).

■ A second output index for 1993, which equals nominal GDP in 1993 divided by the value of output in 1992 using 1993 prices. That index is 1.043 (*F*).

■ The chain-weighted index for 1993, which is the *geometric means* of the two output indexes for 1993. (A geometric mean is a special kind of average that is used for calculating average growth rates. For two numbers it is the square root of their product.) In the table, this index is 1.095, which means that the growth rate of real GDP in 1993 is 9.5 percent.

The calculation is repeated every year and always uses data for the current year and the previous year. Real GDP is calculated by applying the current year's growth rate to the previous year's real GDP. Each year is chained to the base year by a series of "links," each of which uses information from only the year in question and the previous year. So unlike the CPI, the weights for the GDP deflator are constantly changing.

**Back to the GDP Deflator**  With an estimate of real GDP, we can now calculate the GDP deflator. Let's use the numbers we've calculated in Table 6.4 in the formula for the GDP deflator. Nominal GDP is $146 and real GDP is $109.5, so the GDP deflator is

$$\text{GDP deflator} = \frac{\$146}{\$109.5} \times 100 = 133.3.$$

A GDP deflator of 133.3 tells us that the price level in the current year is 33.3 percent higher than the price level in the base year. In the base year, nominal GDP equals real GDP and the GDP deflator is 100.

You can think of nominal GDP as a balloon that is blown up by growing production and rising prices. In Fig. 6.5, the GDP deflator lets the inflation air out of the nominal GDP balloon—the contribution of

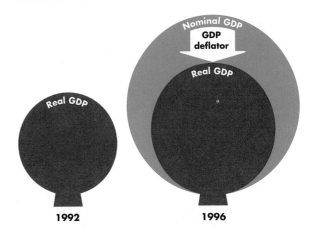

**FIGURE 6.5**

# The U.S. GDP Balloon

Part of the rise in GDP comes from inflation and part from increased production—an increase in real GDP. The GDP deflator lets some air out of the GDP balloon so that we can see the extent to which production has grown.

*Source: Economic Report of the President, 1997.*

rising prices—so that we can see what has happened to *real* GDP. The red balloon for 1992 shows real GDP in that year. The green balloon shows *nominal* GDP in 1996. The red balloon for 1996 shows real GDP for that year. To see real GDP in 1996, we *deflate* nominal GDP using the GDP deflator.

## R E V I E W

■ We measure the price level by using the CPI and the GDP deflator.

■ The CPI measures the average price of a fixed basket of goods and services that a typical family buys.

■ The GDP deflator measures the average price of the changing basket of goods and services that make up GDP.

■ The GDP deflator is calculated as nominal GDP divided by real GDP (multiplied by 100). Real GDP is measured by using a chain-linked output index that uses the prices of the current year and the previous year.

## The Biased CPI

A MAJOR PURPOSE OF THE CPI IS TO MEASURE inflation, and the measure is put to practical use. For example, it is used to determine cost of living adjustments to Social Security payments and changes in tax brackets—the income ranges over which different income tax rates apply. The data generated by the CPI survey are also used, along with other information, in the calculations of real GDP, nominal GDP, and the GDP deflator.

Measuring the inflation rate accurately is of crucial importance. A 1 percent upward bias in the estimated inflation rate translates into a 1 percent downward bias in the estimated growth rate of real GDP.

How good a measure of inflation is the CPI? Does a 2.7 percent increase in the CPI mean that the cost of living has increased by 2.7 percent? Does a 3 percent increase in the GDP deflator mean that the prices of the goods and services that make up real GDP have increased by 3 percent?

Despite the importance of getting the numbers right, the CPI and the GDP deflator give different views of the inflation rate, and neither index is a perfect measure. Figure 6.6 shows the difference in the two measures. The average inflation rate over the period shown is 4.9 percent a year for the CPI and 4.8 percent a year for the GDP deflator, but the CPI fluctuates more than the GDP deflator. Worse, *both* measures of inflation probably overstate the inflation rate.

### The Sources of Bias

The main sources of bias in the CPI are:

- New goods bias
- Quality change bias
- Commodity substitution bias
- Outlet substitution bias

**New Goods Bias**    New goods keep replacing old goods. For example, PCs have replaced typewriters. If you want to compare the price level in 1997 with that in 1977, you somehow have to compare the price of a computer today with that of a typewriter in 1977. Because PCs are more expensive than typewriters, the arrival of these new goods puts an upward bias into the estimate of the price level.

### FIGURE 6.6
## Two Measures of Inflation

The CPI and the GDP deflator have similar averages over the period shown here—4.9 percent a year for the CPI and 4.8 percent a year for the GDP deflator—but the CPI fluctuates more than the GDP deflator, and both measures probably overstate the inflation rate.

*Source: Economic Report of the President, 1997.*

**Quality Change Bias**    Most goods undergo constant quality improvement. Cars, VCRs, TVs, computers, CD players, and even textbooks get better year after year. Improvements in quality sometimes bring higher prices. But such price increases are not inflation. For example, suppose that a 1997 car is 5 percent better and costs 5 percent more than a 1995 car. Adjusted for the quality change, the price of the car has been constant. But in calculating the CPI, the price of the car will be counted as having increased by 5 percent.

**Commodity Substitution Bias**    A change in the CPI measures the percentage change in the price of a *fixed* basket of goods and services. But changes in relative prices lead consumers to seek less costly items and to substitute such items in place of items whose prices have increased. For example, if the price of beef rises but the price of chicken remains constant, consumers substitute chicken for beef—they increase their consumption of chicken and decrease their consumption of beef. They might consume the same number of calories and the same amount of protein and get the same (or very similar) enjoyment from their food. The cost of the protein that people are actually buying has not changed, but the CPI records that it has increased because it does not take such a substitution into account.

**Outlet Substitution Bias**    People do not only change the items they buy when relative prices change. They also change their shopping patterns. With higher prices, people use discount stores more frequently and convenience stores less frequently. This phenomenon is called *outlet substitution*. By being careful to find the least-cost outlets, consumers can cut the prices they pay. And when prices rise, the incentive to seek lower-cost outlets increases. The CPI surveys do not monitor the outlet substitutions that people make.

Because of the four sources of bias, the Consumer Price Index, which is based on a fixed basket, overstates the effects of a given price change on the price level and therefore on the inflation rate.

To reduce the bias problems, the Bureau of Labor Statistics revises the basket used for calculating the CPI about every 10 years. The current plan is to revise the CPI in 1998 by using a basket of goods and services based on spending patterns in 1993–1995. The BLS also uses some sophisticated statistical techniques to reduce the biases.

## The Magnitude of the Bias

How big is the bias in the measurement of the CPI? This question was tackled in 1996 by a Congressional Advisory Commission on the Consumer Price Index chaired by Michael Boskin, an economics professor at Stanford University. This commission said that the CPI overstates inflation by 1.1 percentage points a year. That is, if the CPI reports that inflation is 3.1 percent a year, most likely inflation is actually 2 percent a year.

## Is the GDP Deflator Biased?

The GDP deflator is calculated from nominal GDP and the chain-linked estimate of real GDP growth. In principle, real GDP includes new goods and quality improvements. It is also based on people's actual expenditures and so reflects substitutions of both commodities and retail outlets. So in principle, the GDP deflator is not subject to the biases of the CPI. But in practice, the GDP deflator suffers from some of the CPI's problems. To arrive at its estimate of real GDP, the Commerce Department does not directly measure the physical quantities produced. Instead, it estimates quantities by dividing expenditures by price indexes. And one of these price indexes is the CPI. So the biased CPI injects a bias into the GDP deflator.

## Some Consequences of the Bias

The bias in the CPI has three main consequences. It:

- Distorts private contracts
- Increases government outlays
- Biases estimates of real earnings

Many private agreements, such as wage contracts, are linked to the CPI. For example, a firm and its workers might agree to a three-year wage deal that increases the wage rate by 2 percent a year *plus* the percentage increase in the CPI. Such a deal ends up giving the workers more real income than the firm intended.

Close to a third of federal government outlays are linked directly to the CPI. And while a bias of 1 percent a year seems small, accumulated over a decade, it adds up to almost a trillion dollars of additional expenditures.

According to official government statistics, since 1973, real hourly earnings in manufacturing industries have *fallen* by 13 percent. If the CPI is adjusted for the bias estimated by the Boskin Commission, this picture is transformed into one in which real earnings have *increased* by 13 percent!

## R E V I E W

- The arrival of new goods, quality changes, commodity substitution, and outlet substitution make the CPI a biased measure of the price level.
- It is estimated that the CPI overstates the inflation rate by 1.1 percentage points per year.
- The CPI is an input into the calculation of the GDP deflator, so it too is biased.

You now know some limitations of the price level. Let's next look at the limitations of the real GDP data.

# The Limitations of Real GDP

ESTIMATES OF REAL GDP AND THE REAL GDP growth rate are used for three main purposes:

- Economic welfare comparisons
- International comparisons of GDP
- Business cycle assessment and forecasting

Although real GDP is used for these three purposes, it is not a perfect measure for any of them. We'll look at how real GDP is used and its limitations in each of the three cases.

## Economic Welfare

**Economic welfare** is a comprehensive measure of the general state of economic well-being. Real GDP growth is one indicator of an improvement in economic welfare. Today, with a real GDP per person in the United States of about $25,000, we are much better off than we were in 1960, when real GDP per person was $12,500. But are we twice as well off? Does real GDP give us a full and accurate measure of economic welfare? It does not. The reason is that economic welfare depends on many other factors that are not measured by real GDP (or that are not measured accurately by real GDP). Some of these factors are:

- Overadjustment for inflation
- Household production
- Underground economic activity
- Health and life expectancy
- Leisure time
- Environment quality
- Political freedom and social justice

**Overadjustment for Inflation**   You've seen that the price indexes used to measure inflation give an upward-biased estimate of true inflation. They give a downward-biased estimate of the growth rate of real GDP. When car prices rise because cars have gotten better (safer, more fuel efficient, more comfortable), the CPI and the GDP deflator count the price increase as inflation. So what is really an increase in production is counted as an increase in price rather than an increase in real GDP. It is deflated away by the wrongly measured higher price level. The magnitude of this bias is less than the bias in the CPI (less than 1.1 percentage points a year), but its exact magnitude is not known.

**Household Production**   An enormous amount of production takes place every day in our homes. Changing a light bulb, cutting the grass, washing the car, growing vegetables, and teaching a child to catch a ball are all examples of productive activities that do not involve market transactions and are not counted as part of GDP.

Household production has become much more capital intensive over the years. As a result, less labor is used in household production than in earlier periods. For example, a microwave meal that takes just a few minutes to prepare uses a great deal of capital and almost no labor. Because we use less labor and more capital in household production, it is not easy to work out whether household production has increased or decreased over time. But it is likely that market production counted in GDP has increasingly replaced household production. Two trends point in this direction. One is the trend in the number of people who hold jobs, which has increased from 60 percent in 1970 to 67 percent in 1996. The other is the trend in the purchase of traditionally home-produced goods and services in the market. For example, more and more families now eat in fast food restaurants—one of the fastest-growing industries in the United States—and use day-care services. This trend means that an increasing proportion of food preparation and child care that used to be part of household production is now measured as part of GDP.

**Underground Economic Activity**   The *underground economy* is the part of the economy that is purposely hidden from the view of the government so as to avoid taxes and regulations or because the goods and services being produced are illegal. Because underground economic activity is unreported, it is omitted from GDP.

The underground economy is easy to describe, even if it is hard to measure. It includes the production and distribution of illegal drugs, production that uses illegal labor that is paid less than the minimum wage, and jobs done for cash to avoid paying income taxes. This last category might be quite large and includes tips earned by cab drivers, hairdressers, and hotel and restaurant workers.

Estimates of the scale of the underground economy range between 9 and 30 percent of GDP ($630 billion to $2,100 billion) in the United States and much more in some countries. It is particularly large in some Eastern European countries that are making a transition from Communist economic planning to a market economy.

Provided that the underground economy is a reasonably stable proportion of the total economy, the growth rate of real GDP still gives a useful estimate of changes in economic welfare. But sometimes production shifts from the underground to the rest of the economy, and sometimes it shifts the other way. The underground economy expands relative to the rest of the economy if taxes become especially high or if regulations become especially restrictive. And the underground economy shrinks relative to the rest of the economy if the burdens of taxes and regulations are eased. During the 1980s, when tax rates were cut, there was an increase in the reporting of previously hidden income, and tax revenues increased. So some part (but probably a very small part) of the expansion of real GDP during the 1980s represented a shift from the underground economy rather than an increase in production.

**Health and Life Expectancy**   Good health and a long life—the hopes of everyone—do not show up in real GDP, at least not directly. A higher real GDP does enable us to spend more on medical research, health care, a good diet, and exercise equipment. And as real GDP has increased, our life expectancy has lengthened—from 70 years at the end of World War II to approaching 80 years today. Infant deaths and death in childbirth, two fearful scourges of the nineteenth century, have almost been eliminated.

But we face new health and life expectancy problems every year. AIDS, drug abuse, and violence are taking young lives at a rate that causes serious concern. When we take these negative influences into account, we see that real GDP growth overstates the improvements in economic welfare.

**Leisure Time**   Leisure time is an economic good that adds to our economic welfare. Other things being equal, the more leisure we have, the better off we are. Our time spent working is valued as part of GDP, but our leisure time is not. Yet from the point of view of economic welfare, that leisure time must be at least as valuable to us as the wage that we earn on the last hour worked. If it were not, we would work instead of taking the leisure. Over the years, leisure time has steadily increased. The workweek has become shorter, more people take early retirement, and the number of vacation days has increased.

These improvements in economic well-being are not reflected in GDP.

**Environment Quality**   The quality of the environment is directly affected by economic activity. The burning of hydrocarbon fuels is the most visible activity that damages our environment. But it is not the only example. The depletion of exhaustible resources, the mass clearing of forests, and the pollution of lakes and rivers are other major environmental consequences of industrial production.

Resources that are used to protect the environment are valued as part of GDP. For example, the value of catalytic converters that help to protect the atmosphere from automobile emissions are part of GDP. But if we did not use such pieces of equipment and instead polluted the atmosphere, we would not count the deteriorating air that we were breathing as a negative part of GDP.

An industrial society possibly produces more atmospheric pollution than an agricultural society does. But such pollution does not always increase as we become wealthier. One of the things that wealthy people value is a clean environment, and they devote resources to protecting it. Compare the pollution that was discovered in East Germany in the late 1980s with pollution in the United States. East Germany, a relatively poor country, polluted its rivers, lakes, and atmosphere in a way that is unimaginable in the United States or in wealthy West Germany.

**Political Freedom and Social Justice**   Most people value political freedoms such as those provided by the U.S. Constitution. And they value social justice or fairness—equality of opportunity and of access to social security safety nets that protect people from the extremes of misfortune.

A country might have a very large real GDP per person but have limited political freedom and equity. For example, a small elite might enjoy political liberty and extreme wealth while the vast majority are effectively enslaved and live in abject poverty. Such an economy would generally be regarded as having less economic welfare than one that had the same amount of real GDP but in which political freedoms were enjoyed by everyone. Today, China has rapid real GDP growth but limited political freedoms, while Russia has a decreasing real GDP and an emerging democratic political system. Economists have no easy way to determine which of these countries is better off.

**The Bottom Line** Do we get the wrong message about changes (or differences) in economic welfare by looking at changes (or differences) in real GDP? The influences omitted from real GDP are probably important and could be large. Developing countries have a larger underground economy and a larger amount of household production than do developed countries. So as an economy develops and grows, part of the apparent growth might reflect a switch from underground to regular production and from home production to market production. This measurement error overstates the rate of economic growth and the improvement in economic welfare.

Other influences on living standards include the amount of leisure time available, the quality of the environment, the security of jobs and homes, the safety of city streets, and so on. It is possible to construct broader measures that combine the many influences that contribute to human happiness. Real GDP will be one element in those broader measures, but it will by no means be the whole of them.

## International Comparisons of GDP

All the problems we've just reviewed affect economic welfare of every country, so to make international comparisons of economic welfare, factors additional to real GDP must be used. But real GDP comparisons are a major component of international welfare comparisons, and two special problems arise in making these comparisons. First, the real GDP of one country must be converted into the same currency units as the real GDP of the other country. Second, the same prices must be used to value the goods and services in the countries being compared. Let's look at these two problems by using a striking example, a comparison of the United States and China.

In 1992 (the most recent year for which we can make this comparison), real GDP per person in the United States was $24,408. The official Chinese statistics published by the International Monetary Fund (IMF) say that real GDP per person in China in 1992 was 2,028 yuan. (The yuan is the currency of China.) On the average, during 1992, $1 U.S. was worth 5.762 yuan. If we use this exchange rate to convert Chinese yuan into U.S. dollars, we get a value of $352.

The official comparison of China and the United States makes China look extremely poor. In 1992, real GDP per person in the United States was 69 times that in China.

### FIGURE 6.7
## Two Views of Real GDP in China

According to the official statistics of the International Monetary Fund (IMF) and the World Bank, China is a poor developing country. But according to an alternative view, Penn World Table (PWT), which is based on purchasing power prices, China has a real GDP more than 6 times the official view and has the world's third largest total production.

*Sources: International Financial Statistics Yearbook* 1994, (Washington, D.C.: International Monetary Fund, *World Development Report, 1994,* (Washington, D.C.; World Bank, 1994); "The Penn World Table: An Expanded Set of International Comparisons, 1950–1988," *Quarterly Journal of Economics,* May 1991, pp. 327–368; new computer diskette, Mark 5.6a, January 15, 1995; and the author's calculations.

Figure 6.7 shows the official story of real GDP in China between 1968 and 1992. But Fig. 6.7 also shows another story. It shows an estimate of real GDP per person in China that is much larger than the official measure. Let's see how this alternative measurement is made.

GDP in the United States is measured by using prices that prevail in the United States. China's GDP is measured by using prices that prevail in China. But the relative prices in the two countries are very different. Some goods that are expensive in the United States cost very little in China. These items get a small weight in China's real GDP. If, instead of using China's prices, all the goods and services produced in China are valued at the prices prevailing in the United States, then a more valid comparison can be made of GDP in the two countries. Such a comparison uses prices called *purchasing power parity prices.*

Robert Summers and Alan Heston, economists in the Center for International Comparisons at the University of Pennsylvania, have used purchasing power parity prices to construct real GDP data for more than 100 countries. These data, which are published in the Penn World Table (PWT), tell a remarkable story about China. The PWT data use 1985 as the base year, so they are measured in 1985 dollars. According to the Penn World Table, in 1992, real GDP per person in the United States was 12 times that of China, not the 69 times shown in the official data.

Figure 6.7 shows the PWT view of China and compares it with the official view. The difference in the two views arises from the prices used. The official statistics use Chinese prices, while the PWT data use purchasing power parity prices.

Despite large differences in estimates of the *level* of China's real GDP, there is much less doubt about its growth rate. The economy of China is expanding at an extraordinary rate, and it is for this reason that most businesses are paying a great deal of attention to the prospects of expanding their activities in China and the other Asian economies.

U.S. real GDP is measured quite reliably. But China's is not. The alternative measures of China's real GDP are somewhat unreliable, and the truth about GDP in China is not known.

## Business Cycle Assessment and Forecasting

When the Fed decides to raise interest rates to slow an expansion that it believes is too strong, it looks at the latest estimates of real GDP and inflation. But we've seen that the inflation rate is biased. Does this bias hamper our ability to isolate the phases of the business cycle? It does not. The reason is that the bias in the CPI does not change over the business cycle. The CPI is inaccurate by a similar amount every year. So while inflation mismeasurement leads to wrong estimates of long-term real GDP growth, it does not cause a wrong assessment of the phase of the business cycle.

The fluctuations in economic activity measured by real GDP tell a reasonably accurate story about the phase of the business cycle that the economy is in. When real GDP grows, the economy is in a business cycle expansion, and when real GDP shrinks (for two quarters), the economy is in a recession. Also, as real GDP fluctuates, so do employment and unemployment.

But real GDP fluctuations probably exaggerate or overstate the fluctuations in total production and economic welfare. The reason is that when business activity slows down in a recession, household production increases and so does leisure time. When business activity speeds up in an expansion, household production and leisure time decrease. Because household production and leisure time increase in a recession and decrease in an expansion, real GDP fluctuations tend to overstate the fluctuations in total production and in economic welfare. But the directions of change of real GDP, total production, and economic welfare are probably the same.

## R E V I E W

■ Real GDP is not an accurate measure of economic welfare because it undervalues quality improvements, omits some production, and ignores indicators of economic welfare such as health and life expectancy, leisure time, the environment, and political freedom.

■ To make international comparisons of real GDP, we must use purchasing power parity prices.

■ Real GDP understates the long-term growth rate and overstates business cycle fluctuations.

◆ In Chapter 5 we studied the macroeconomic performance of the United States in recent years—the growth and fluctuations in real GDP, unemployment, inflation, and deficits. We've now studied the methods used to measure some of these indicators of macroeconomic performance. We've seen how real GDP and the price level are measured, and we've seen what these measures mean.

In Chapter 7, we study *aggregate* demand and *aggregate* supply. This aggregate model parallels the demand and supply model of a single market. And it serves as an overview and backdrop against which to place your study of economic growth, unemployment, and inflation. An understanding of this model will help you to find your way through what can sometimes seem like a macroeconomic maze.

Before you embark on this next topic, spend a few minutes with *Reading Between the Lines* on pp. 136–137, which explores the consequences of the bias in the CPI for the measurement of real GDP and real hourly earnings. You'll be surprised by the numbers.

# Policy
## WATCH

 Correcting the CPI Bias

*THE NEW YORK TIMES, DECEMBER 1, 1996*

# Sorry, Wrong Numbers So Maybe It Wasn't the Economy

**By FLOYD NORRIS**

Economic statistics are thrust into the news every day, with a portentous exactitude that can send Wall Street soaring or reeling, influence Government policy, even sway elections. Did consumer prices rise one-tenth of a percent more than was expected? Was economic growth a half percentage point less than people had been hoping?

But what if the statistics are wrong? And what if they are consistently wrong in the same direction? Over time, that can produce a very distorted picture of the economy, with unfortunate effects brought about not by the economy but by our perceptions of it and with those perceptions having effects of their own. ...

This week a commission headed by Michael Boskin, the Stanford economist and former adviser to President Bush, will report to the Senate Finance Committee that inflation, as measured by the Consumer Price Index, has been rising at a far slower pace than we had thought. Economists who have studied the issue now generally agree that inflation has been overstated, although some argue that the error is relatively small and may not make a significant difference.

The commission was appointed last year because of serious doubts about how changes in benefits and tax brackets, which have a major effect on the deficit, are calculated. A conclusion that the Consumer Price Index [CPI] has been overstated could lead to efforts to reduce the automatic increases in certain benefits, notably Social Security. That's sure to provoke a fight.

But perhaps even more important are changes that may be necessary in our view of the economy for the last two decades. For much of that time, even as America came roaring back into a preeminent position in technological leadership and the stock market zoomed, economists have been looking at statistics that showed a weak economy. And politicians have been trying to address public angst over economic decline. ...

Leonard Nakamura, an economist with the Federal Reserve Bank of Philadelphia, is known for his work on inflation. ... His estimates of the overstatement are among the largest ... at about 1.25 percent annually in the mid-1970s, rising to about 2.75 percent now. ...

- Economic statistics can influence stock markets and government policy and, if inaccurate, economic statistics can produce a distorted picture of the economy.

- In December 1996, a commission headed by Michael Boskin reported to the Senate Finance Committee that the CPI overstates the inflation rate.

- Economists generally agree that the CPI overstates the inflation rate but are uncertain about the magnitude of the overstatement.

- For the last 20 years, technology has advanced and the stock prices have increased, but economic statistics have shown slow economic growth.

- Leonard Nakamura, an economist at the Federal Reserve Bank of Philadelphia, says the economic statistics are wrong and that inflation has been overstated—by 1.25 percent a year during the mid-1970s to 2.75 percent a year in 1996.

# Economic

## A N A L Y S I S

■ Leonard Nakamura, a research economist at the Federal Reserve Bank of Philadelphia, believes that inflation has been overstated for at least 20 years. He says that the overstatement was approximately 1.25 percent annually during the mid-1970s, rising to approximately 2.75 percent annually by the mid-1990s.

■ Figure 1 shows Mr. Nakamura's estimate of the Consumer Price Index. His index equals 100 in 1975. According to Mr. Nakamura, the price level doubled between 1975 and 1996, not tripled as has been reported in the official data.

■ If we accept Mr. Nakamura's revised price level, we must change other economic indicators that are expressed in constant dollars.

■ Figure 2 shows the implications of Mr. Nakamura's assumptions for real GDP. Using his new inflation figures, real GDP has increased by twice as much as reported in the official data.

■ Figure 3 shows the impact of the new view of prices on real hourly earnings. The official view is that since 1975, real hourly earnings have *decreased* by 9 percent. The new view is that real hourly earnings have *increased* by 35 percent!

■ Mr. Nakamura's views are toward the upper end of the range of what economists believe, but they are not outrageous. He could be correct. If he is correct, the U.S. economy is in even better shape than Alan Greenspan, President Clinton, and many other leading public commentators dared to believe.

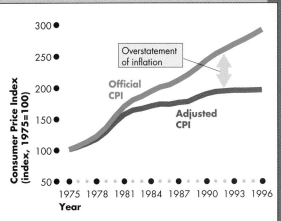

**Figure 1   Consumer Price Index**

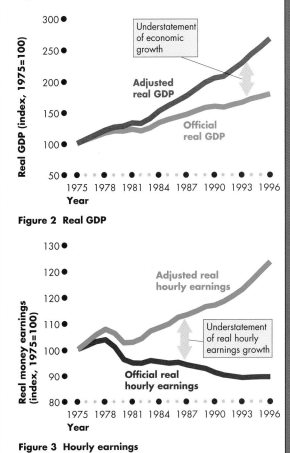

**Figure 2   Real GDP**

**Figure 3   Hourly earnings**

## You're

### THE VOTER

■ As a taxpayer and voter, do you care whether the government's economic statistics are accurate?

■ Try to think of reasons why is matters *to you* that the official statistics are accurate?

■ Would you be willing to see government funds diverted from some existing use and spent on data gathering and processing to get better measures of prices, real GDP, and real earnings?

# SUMMARY

## Key Points

### Gross Domestic Product (pp. 118–122)

- Gross domestic product (GDP) is the value of total production in a country during a given period.
- GDP is calculated by using the circular flow of income and expenditure.
- Aggregate expenditure on goods and services equals aggregate income and GDP.

### Measuring U.S. GDP (pp. 122–126)

- Because aggregate expenditure, aggregate income, and the value of aggregate production are equal, we can measure GDP by using the expenditure approach or the income approach.
- The expenditure approach sums consumption expenditure, investment, government purchases of goods and services, and net exports.
- The income approach sums wages, interest, rent, and profit.

### The Price Level and Inflation (pp. 127–129)

- Inflation is measured by the rate of change of the CPI or the GDP deflator.
- The price level is measured by the Consumer Price Index (CPI) and the GDP deflator.
- The CPI measures the average price of goods and services typically consumed by American families.
- The GDP deflator measures the average price of all goods and services that make up GDP.

### The Biased CPI (pp. 130–131)

- The CPI gives an upward-biased measure of inflation because some goods disappear and new goods become available, and the quality of many goods and services improves over time.
- The CPI is further biased because it ignores the fact that as relative prices change, consumers substitute less expensive items for more expensive items.
- The size of the bias might be large.

### The Limitations of Real GDP (pp. 132–135)

- Real GDP is not a perfect measure of aggregate production or economic welfare because it excludes quality improvements, household production, the underground economic activity, health and life expectancy, leisure time, environmental quality, and political freedom and social justice.
- The growth rate of real GDP gives a good indication of the phases of the business cycle.

## Key Figures and Tables

## Key Terms

## QUESTIONS

1. Distinguish between a stock and a flow.
2. What are the main macroeconomic stocks? What are the flows that change them?
3. List the components of aggregate expenditure.
4. What are the components of aggregate income?
5. Why does aggregate income equal aggregate expenditure and the value of output (GDP)?
6. Distinguish between government purchases of goods and services and transfer payments.
7. Explain the expenditure approach to measuring GDP.
8. Explain the income approach to measuring GDP.
9. Explain how real GDP and the growth rate of real GDP are calculated.
10. Distinguish between expenditure on final goods and expenditure on intermediate goods?
11. What is value added? How is it calculated?
12. What are the two main price indexes used to measure the price level?
13. How is the Consumer Price Index calculated?
14. How is the GDP deflator calculated?
15. How is real GDP calculated?
16. How is the growth rate of real GDP calculated?
17. Is the CPI biased? If so, how?
18. Is real GDP a good measure of economic welfare? If not, why not?
19. Is the growth of real GDP a good measure of the growth of real economic activity?
20. Compare the fluctuations of real GDP with the phases of the business cycle.

## PROBLEMS

1. The figure at the bottom of the page shows the flows of income and expenditure on Lotus Island during 1996. The amounts are thousands of dollars.

   Calculate Lotus Island's
   a. Aggregate expenditure.
   b. Aggregate income.
   c. GDP.
   d. Government budget deficit.
   e. Household saving.
   f. Government saving.
   g. Foreign borrowing.
   h. National saving.

2. Use the figure at the bottom of the page to calculate:
   a. Firms' borrowing.
   b. Government borrowing.
   c. Rest of the world's borrowing.

3. Cindy, the owner of The Great Cookie, spends $100 on eggs, $50 on flour, $45 on milk, $10 on utilities, and $60 on wages to produce 200 great cookies. Cindy sells her cookies for $1.50

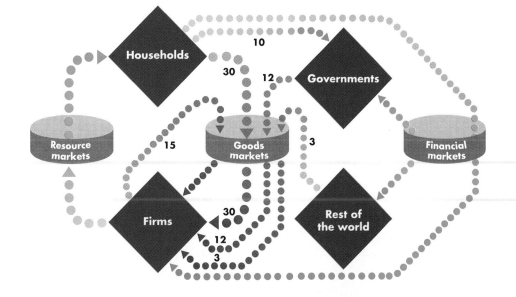

each. Calculate the value added per cookie at The Great Cookie.

4. Bananaland produces only two goods: bananas and sunscreen. The quantities of these goods produced and their prices in 1996 and 1997 are:

| Good | 1996 quantity | 1997 quantity |
|------|---------------|---------------|
| Bananas | 1,000 pounds | 1,100 pounds |
| Sunscreen | 500 gallons | 525 gallons |

| Good | 1996 price | 1997 price |
|------|------------|------------|
| Bananas | $2 per pound | $3 per pound |
| Sunscreen | $10 per gallon | $8 per gallon |

Calculate

a.  Bananaland's GDP in 1996 and 1997.
b.  The chain-weighted output index in 1997.
c.  The growth rate of real GDP in 1997.
d.  Real GDP in 1997 in 1996 dollars.
e.  The GDP deflator in 1997.
f.  The inflation rate in 1997.

5. A typical family living on Sandy Island consumes only apple juice, bananas, and cloth. In the base year the typical family spent $40 on apple juice, $45 on bananas, and $25 on cloth. Prices in the base year were $4 a gallon for apple juice, $3 a pound for bananas, and $5 a yard for cloth. In the current year, apple juice costs $3 a gallon, bananas cost $4 a pound, and cloth costs $7 a yard. Calculate:

a.  The basket used in the CPI.
b.  The Consumer Price Index in the current year.
c.  The inflation rate between the base year and the current year.

---

# CRITICAL THINKING

1. Study *Reading Between the Lines* on pp. 136–137 and then answer the following questions:
   a.  How large does Mr. Nakamura believe the bias in the CPI to be?
   b.  How does Mr. Nakamura's estimate of the CPI bias compare with that of the Boskin commission?
   c.  Write a brief description of the U.S. economy since 1975 based on the view of the official statistics and based on the view of Mr. Nakamura.
   d.  If Mr. Nakamura's view of the economy is correct, how different does economic growth look during the terms of Presidents Carter, Reagan, Bush, and Clinton compared with each other and compared with the official data?
   e.  Should social security benefits be linked to the measured CPI or to an estimate of the true CPI?
   f.  What difference, if any, do you think there would be in the distribution of income between workers and business owners if the bias in the CPI had been discovered 10 years ago?

2. Use the link on the Parkin Web site to visit the Federal Reserve Economic Data (FRED) Web site at the Federal Reserve Bank of St. Louis. There you can obtain the latest data on real GDP, nominal GDP, and the GDP deflator as well as the data for the previous year.
   a.  What was the GDP deflator in the most recent year?
   b.  What was the GDP deflator in the previous year?
   c.  What is the inflation rate as measured by the GDP deflator between these two years?
   d.  What was real GDP in the most recent year?
   e.  What was real GDP in the previous year?
   f.  What is the real GDP growth rate between these two years?
   g.  Check that, for the data you have obtained, nominal GDP divided by real GDP equals the deflator.

http://hepg.awl.com/parkin/econ100

# 7

# Aggregate Supply and Aggregate Demand

During the past 30 years, U.S. real GDP has more than doubled. In fact, a doubling of real GDP every 30 years has been routine. What forces drive our economy to grow? ◆ At the same time that real GDP has grown, we've experienced first a rise and then a fall in inflation. In 1967, U.S. prices were rising at a rate of 3 percent a year. In 1981, the peak inflation year, prices increased by 10 percent. Today, the inflation rate stands at about 2.5 percent a year. The result of all this inflation is that you need $400 today to buy what $100 bought in 1967. What causes inflation? And why did its rate explode during the 1970s? ◆ Our economy does not expand at a constant pace. Instead, it ebbs and flows over the business cycle. For example, we had a recession during 1990

## What Makes Our Garden Grow?

and early 1991. For half a year, real GDP decreased. Then began a long period of expansion that was still in progress in mid-1997. What makes real GDP grow at an uneven pace? Why does growth sometimes speed up, and why does real GDP sometimes shrink? ◆ When economic growth speeds up in Asia and Europe, we benefit because we sell more goods and services abroad. And when economic growth slows in the rest of the world, we suffer because the demand for our goods and services decreases. But some influences on our economy are home made and stem from the actions of the government and the Federal Reserve Board (the Fed) in Washington. How do events in the rest of the world and the policy actions of the government and the Fed affect production and prices? ◆ To answer these questions, we need a *model* of real GDP and the price level. Our main task in this chapter is to study such a model: the *aggregate supply–aggregate demand model*. Our second task is to use the aggregate supply–aggregate demand (or *AS-AD*) model to answer the questions we've just posed. You'll discover that this model enables us to understand the forces that make our economy expand, that bring inflation, and that cause business cycle fluctuations. You will also find that this model is a useful tool with which to organize your entire study of macroeconomics.

## After studying this chapter, you will be able to:

■ Explain what determines aggregate supply

■ Explain what determines aggregate demand

■ Explain macroeconomic equilibrium

■ Explain the effects of changes in aggregate supply and aggregate demand on economic growth, inflation, and business cycles

■ Explain U.S. economic growth, inflation, and business cycles by using the *AS-AD* model.

# Aggregate Supply

THE AGGREGATE SUPPLY–AGGREGATE DEMAND model enables us to understand three features of macroeconomic performance:

- Growth of potential GDP
- Inflation
- Business cycle fluctuations

The model uses the concepts of *aggregate* supply and *aggregate* demand to determine *real GDP* and the *price level* (the *GDP deflator*). We begin by looking at the fundamental limits to production that influence aggregate supply.

## Aggregate Supply Fundamentals

The *quantity of real GDP supplied* ($Y$) depends on just three factors:

- The quantity of labor ($N$)
- The quantity of capital ($K$)
- The state of technology ($T$)

The influence of these three factors on the quantity of real GDP supplied is described by the **aggregate production function**, which is written as the equation:

$$Y = F(N, K, T).$$

In words, the quantity of real GDP supplied is determined by (is a function $F$ of) the quantities of labor and capital and of the state of technology. The larger $N$, $K$, or $T$, the greater is $Y$.

At any given time, the quantity of capital and the state of technology are fixed. They depend on decisions that were made in the past. The population is also fixed. But the quantity of labor is not fixed. It depends on decisions made by people and firms about the supply of and demand for labor.

Firms demand labor only if it is profitable to do so. And the lower the wage rate, which is the cost of labor, the greater is the quantity of labor demanded. People supply labor only if doing so is the most valuable use of their time. And the higher the wage rate, which is the return to labor, the greater is the quantity of labor supplied. The wage rate that makes the quantity of labor demanded equal to the quantity of labor supplied is the equilibrium wage rate. At this wage rate, there is **full employment.**

Even at full employment, there are always some people looking for jobs and some firms looking for people to hire. The reason is that there is constant turnover in the labor market. Every day, some jobs are destroyed as businesses reorganize or fail. Some jobs are created as new businesses start up or existing ones expand. Some workers decide, for any of a thousand personal reasons, to quit their jobs. And other people decide to start looking for a job. This constant churning in the labor market prevents unemployment from ever disappearing. At full employment, the unemployment rate is called the **natural rate of unemployment**. In 1997, the natural rate of unemployment is about 5.5 percent.

The quantity of real GDP supplied when unemployment is at its natural rate and there is full employment is **potential GDP**. Potential GDP depends on the full-employment quantity of labor, the quantity of capital, and the state of technology.

Over the business cycle, employment fluctuates around full employment and real GDP fluctuates around potential GDP. You saw these fluctuations in Chapter 5 (Figs. 5.2 and 5.3 on pp. 100–101).

To study the economy at full employment and over the business cycle, we distinguish two time frames for aggregate supply:

- Long-run aggregate supply
- Short-run aggregate supply

## Long-Run Aggregate Supply

The economy is constantly bombarded by events that move real GDP away from potential GDP and, equivalently, that move the unemployment rate away from full employment. Following such an event, forces operate to take real GDP back toward potential GDP and restore full employment. The **macroeconomic long run** is a time frame that is sufficiently long for these forces to have done their work so that real GDP equals potential GDP and full employment prevails.

The **long-run aggregate supply curve** is the relationship between the quantity of real GDP supplied and the price level in the long run when real GDP equals potential GDP. Figure 7.1 shows this relationship as the vertical line labeled *LAS*. Along the long-run aggregate supply curve, as the price level changes, real GDP remains at potential GDP, which in Fig. 7.1 is $7 trillion. The long-run aggregate

**FIGURE 7.1**

# Long-Run Aggregate Supply

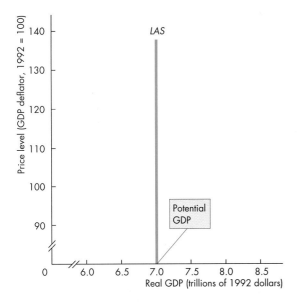

The long-run aggregate supply (*LAS*) curve shows the relationship between potential GDP and the price level. Potential GDP is independent of the price level, so the *LAS* curve is vertical at potential GDP.

supply curve is always vertical and is located at potential GDP.

The long-run aggregate supply curve is vertical because potential GDP is independent of the price level. The reason for this independence is that a movement along the *LAS* curve is accompanied by a change in *two* sets of prices: the prices of goods and services—the price level—and the prices of productive resources. A 10 percent increase in the prices of goods and services is matched by a 10 percent increase in wage rates and other resource prices. That is, the price level, wage rate, and other resource prices all change by the same percentage, and *relative prices* and the *real wage rate* remain constant. When the price level changes but relative prices and the real wage rate remain constant, real GDP also remains constant.

**Production at a Pepsi Plant** You can see why real GDP remains constant when all prices change by the same percentage by thinking about production

decisions at a Pepsi bottling plant. The plant is producing the quantity of Pepsi that maximizes profit. The plant can increase production, but only by incurring a higher *marginal cost* (see Chapter 3, pp. 42–43). So the firm has no incentive to change production.

## Short-Run Aggregate Supply

The **macroeconomic short run** is a period during which real GDP has fallen below or risen above potential GDP. At the same time, the unemployment rate has risen above or fallen below the natural rate.

The **short-run aggregate supply curve** is the relationship between the quantity of real GDP supplied and the price level in the short run when the money wage rate, other resource prices, and potential GDP remain constant. Figure 7.2 shows a short-run aggregate supply curve as the upward-sloping curve labeled *SAS*. This curve is based on the short-run aggregate supply schedule, and each point on the aggregate supply curve corresponds to a row of the aggregate supply schedule. For example, point *a* on the short-run aggregate supply curve and row *a* of the schedule tell us that if the price level is 100, the quantity of real GDP supplied is $6 trillion.

At point *c*, the price level is 110 and the quantity of real GDP supplied is $7 trillion, which equals potential GDP. If the price level is higher than 110, real GDP exceeds potential GDP; if the price level is below 110, real GDP is less than potential GDP.

**Back at the Pepsi Plant** You can see why the short-run aggregate supply curve slopes upward by returning to the Pepsi bottling plant. The plant produces the quantity that maximizes profit. If the price of Pepsi rises and wage rates and other costs don't change, the *relative price* of Pepsi rises and the firm has an incentive to increase its production. The higher relative price of Pepsi covers the higher marginal cost of producing more Pepsi, so the firm increases production.

Similarly, if the price of Pepsi falls and wage rates and other costs don't change, the lower relative price is not sufficient to covers the marginal cost of Pepsi, so the firm decreases production.

Again, what's true for Pepsi bottlers is true for the producers of all goods and services. So when the price level rises and the money wage rate and other resource prices remain constant, the quantity of real GDP supplied increases.

FIGURE **7.2**
## Short-Run Aggregate Supply

| | Price Level (GDP deflator) | Real GDP (trillions of 1992 dollars) |
|---|---|---|
| a | 100 | 6.0 |
| b | 105 | 6.5 |
| c | 110 | 7.0 |
| d | 115 | 7.5 |
| e | 120 | 8.0 |

The short-run aggregate supply (*SAS*) curve shows the relationship between the quantity of real GDP supplied and the price level when the money wage rate, other resource prices, and potential GDP are constant. The short-run aggregate supply curve *SAS* is based on the schedule in the table. The short-run aggregate supply curve is upward-sloping because firms' costs increase as the rate of output increases, so a higher price is needed, relative to the prices of productive resources, and bring forth an increase in the quantity produced. On the *SAS* curve, when the price level is 110, real GDP equals potential GDP. If the price level is greater than 110, real GDP exceeds potential GDP; if the price level is below 110, real GDP is less than potential GDP.

## Movements Along the *LAS* and *SAS* Curves

Figure 7.3 summarizes what you've just learned about the *LAS* and *SAS* curves. When the price level, the money wage rate, and other resource prices rise by the same percentage, relative prices remain constant and real GDP remains at potential GDP. There is a *movement along* the *LAS* curve.

When the price level rises but the money wage rate and other resource prices remain constant, the quantity of real GDP supplied increases and there is a *movement along* the *SAS* curve.

Let's next study the influences that bring changes in aggregate supply.

## Changes in Aggregate Supply

You've just seen that a change in the price level brings a movement along the aggregate supply curves but it does not change aggregate supply. Aggregate supply changes when influences on production plans other than the price level change. Let's begin by looking at factors that change potential GDP.

**Changes in Potential GDP**   When potential GDP changes, both long-run aggregate supply and short-run aggregate supply change. Potential GDP changes for three reasons:

1. Change in the full-employment quantity of labor
2. Change in the quantity of capital
3. Advance in technology.

***Change in the Full-Employment Quantity of Labor***   A Pepsi bottling plants that employs 100 workers bottles more Pepsi than an otherwise identical plant that employs 10 workers. The same is true for the economy as a whole. The larger the quantity of labor employed, the greater is GDP.

Over time, potential GDP increases because the labor force increases. But (with constant capital and technology) *potential* GDP increases only if the full-employment quantity of labor increases. Fluctuations in employment over the business cycle bring fluctuations in real GDP. But these changes in real GDP are fluctuations around potential GDP. They are not changes in potential GDP and long-run aggregate supply.

## FIGURE 7.3

## Movements Along the Aggregate Supply Curves

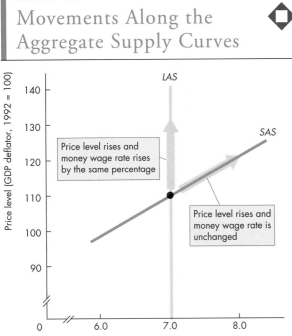

A rise in the price level with no change in the money wage rate and other resource prices brings an increase in the quantity of real GDP supplied and a movement along the short-run aggregate supply curve. A rise in the price level with equal percentage rises in the money wage rate and other resource prices keeps the quantity of real GDP supplied constant and brings a movement along the long-run aggregate supply curve.

***Change in the Quantity of Capital*** A Pepsi plant with two production lines bottles more Pepsi than does an otherwise identical plant that has only one production line. For the economy as a whole, the larger the quantity of capital, the more productive is the labor force and the greater is its potential GDP. Potential GDP per person in the capital-rich United States is vastly greater than that in capital-poor China and Russia.

Capital includes *human capital*. One Pepsi plant is managed by an economics major with an MBA and has a labor force with an average of 10 years experience. This plant produces a much larger output than an otherwise identical plant that is managed by someone with no business training or experience and that has a young labor force that is new to bottling.

The first plant has a greater amount of human capital than the second. For the economy as a whole, the larger the quantity of *human capital*—the skills that people have acquired in school and through on-the-job training—the greater is potential GDP.

***Advance in Technology*** A Pepsi plant that has pre–computer age machines produces less than one that uses the latest robot technology. Technological change enables firms to produce more from any given amount of inputs. So even with fixed quantities of labor and capital, improvements in technology increase potential GDP.

Technological advances are by far the most important source of increased production over the past two centuries. Because of technological advances, one farmer in the United States today can feed 100 people, and one auto worker can produce almost 14 cars and trucks in a year.

Figure 7.4 shows the effect of a change in potential GDP. Initially, the long-run aggregate supply curve is $LAS_0$ and the short-run aggregate supply curve is $SAS_0$. If an increase in the quantity of capital or a technological advance increases potential GDP to $8 trillion, long-run aggregate supply increases and the long-run aggregate supply curve shifts rightward to $LAS_1$. Short-run aggregate supply also increases, and the short-run aggregate supply curve shifts rightward to $SAS_1$.

You've seen how a change in potential GDP changes aggregate supply. Let's now look at the effects of changes in money wages and other resource prices.

**Changes in Money Wages and Other Resource Prices** A change in the money wage rate or in the money prices of any other resources, such as the price of oil, changes short-run aggregate supply but does not change long-run aggregate supply.

Money wages and resource prices affect short-run aggregate supply through their influence on firms' costs. The higher the money wage rate and other resource prices, the higher are firms' costs and the smaller is the quantity that firms are willing to supply at each price level. Thus an increase in the money wage rate and other resource prices decreases short-run aggregate supply.

Changes in the money wage rate and other resource prices do not change long-run aggregate supply. The reason is that along the long-run aggregate supply curve, any change in the money wage rate or other resource price is accompanied by an equal percentage change in the price level. With no change

**FIGURE 7.4**

## A Change in Potential GDP

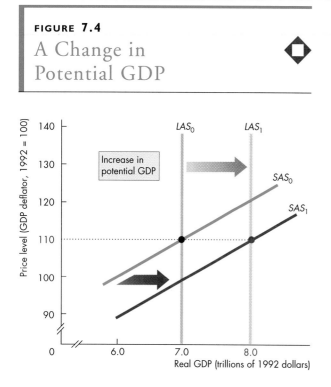

An increase in potential GDP increases both long-run aggregate supply and short-run aggregate supply and shifts both aggregate supply curves rightward, from $LAS_0$ to $LAS_1$ and from $SAS_0$ to $SAS_1$.

**FIGURE 7.5**

## A Change in the Money Wage Rate

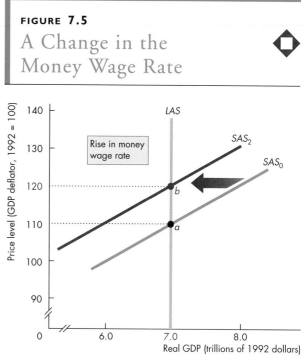

A rise in the money wage rate decreases short-run aggregate supply and shifts the short-run aggregate supply curve left-ward from $SAS_0$ to $SAS_2$. A rise in the money wage rate does not change potential GDP, so the long-run aggregate supply curve does not shift.

in *relative* prices, firms have no incentive to change production and potential GDP remains constant.

Figure 7.5 shows the effect on aggregate supply of an increase in the money wage rate (or an increase in the money price of other resources). Initially, the short-run aggregate supply curve is $SAS_0$. A rise in the money wage rate *decreases* short-run aggregate supply and shifts the short-run aggregate supply curve leftward to $SAS_2$.

The vertical distance between the original *SAS* curve and the new *SAS* curve is determined by the percentage change in the money wage rate. That is, the percentage increase in the price level between point *a* and point *b* equals the percentage increase in the money wage rate.

Because potential GDP does not change when the money wage rate changes, long-run aggregate supply does not change. The long-run aggregate supply curve remains at *LAS*.

## REVIEW

▪ A change in the price level that is accompanied by an equal percentage change in the money wage rate keeps real GDP at potential GDP and brings a movement along the *LAS* curve.

▪ An increase in the price level with no change in the money wage rate brings an increase in the quantity of real GDP supplied and a movement along the *SAS* curve.

▪ An increase in potential GDP increases both long-run aggregate supply and short-run aggregate supply and shifts the *LAS* curve and the *SAS* curve rightward.

▪ An increase in the money wage rate decreases short-run aggregate supply but leaves long-run aggregate supply unchanged. The *SAS* curve shifts leftward.

# Aggregate Demand

THE QUANTITY OF REAL GDP DEMANDED IS THE sum of the real consumption expenditure ($C$), investment ($I$), government purchases ($G$), and exports ($X$) minus imports ($M$). That is,

$$Y = C + I + G + X - M.$$

The *quantity of real GDP demanded* is the total amount of final goods and services produced in the United States that people, businesses, governments, and foreigners plan to buy. What determines these buying plans?

Buying plans depend on many factors. Some of the main ones are:

- The price level
- Expectations
- Fiscal policy and monetary policy
- The world economy

We first focus on the relationship between the quantity of real GDP demanded and the price level, and to study this relationship, we hold constant all other influences on buying plans. We then ask: How does the quantity of real GDP demanded vary as the price level varies?

## The Aggregate Demand Curve

Other things remaining the same, the higher the price level, the smaller is the quantity of real GDP demanded. This relationship between the quantity of real GDP demanded and the price level is called **aggregate demand**. Aggregate demand is described by an *aggregate demand schedule* and an *aggregate demand curve*.

Figure 7.6 shows an aggregate demand curve (*AD*) and an aggregate demand schedule. Each point on the *AD* curve corresponds to a row of the schedule. For example, point $c'$ on the *AD* curve and row $c'$ of the schedule tell us that if the price level is 110, the quantity of real GDP demanded is $7 trillion.

The aggregate demand curve slopes downward for two reasons:

- Wealth effect
- Substitution effects

**FIGURE 7.6**

## Aggregate Demand

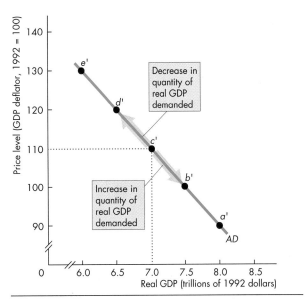

| | **Price Level**<br>(GDP deflator) | **Real GDP**<br>(trillions of 1992 dollars) |
|---|---|---|
| $a'$ | 90 | 8.0 |
| $b'$ | 100 | 7.5 |
| $c'$ | 110 | 7.0 |
| $d'$ | 120 | 6.5 |
| $e'$ | 130 | 6.0 |

The aggregate demand curve (*AD*) shows the relationship between the quantity of real GDP demanded and the price level. The aggregate demand curve is based on the schedule in the table. Each point $a'$ through $e'$ on the curve corresponds to the row in the table identified by the same letter. Thus when the price level is 110, the quantity of real GDP demanded is $7.0 trillion, shown by point $c'$ in the figure.

**Wealth Effect** When the price level rises but other things remain the same, *real* wealth decreases. Real wealth is the amount of money in the bank, bonds, stocks, and other assets that people own, measured not in dollars but in terms of the goods and services that this money, bonds, and stock will buy.

People save and hold money, bonds, and stocks for many reasons. One reason is to build up funds for college expenses. Another reason is to build up enough funds to meet possible medical or other big bills. But the biggest reason is to build up enough funds to provide a retirement income.

If the price level rises, real wealth decreases. People then try to restore their wealth. To do so, they must increase saving and, equivalently, decrease consumption. Such a decrease in consumption is a decrease in aggregate demand.

**Maria's Wealth Effect**   You can see how the wealth effect works by thinking about Maria's buying plans. Maria lives in Belgrade, Serbia. She has worked hard all summer and saved 20,000 dinars (the dinar is the currency of Serbia), which she plans to spend attending graduate school when she's finished her economics degree. So Maria's wealth is 20,000 dinars. Maria has a part-time job, and her income from this job pays her current expenses. The price level in Serbia rises by 100 percent, and now Maria needs 40,000 dinars to buy what 20,000 once bought. To try to make up some of the fall in value of her savings, Maria saves even more and cuts her current spending to the bare minimum.

**Substitution Effects**   When the price level rises and other things remain the same, interest rates rise. The full reason why is explained in Chapter 15 on pp. 354–355. But the basic reason is easy to see. A rise in the price level decreases the real value of the money in people's pockets and bank accounts. With a smaller amount of real money around, banks and other lenders can get a higher interest rate on loans. But faced with higher interest rates, people and businesses delay plans to buy new capital and consumer durable goods and cut back on spending.

This substitution effect involves substituting goods in the future for goods in the present and is called an *intertemporal* substitution effect—a substitution across time. Saving increases to increase future consumption.

To see this intertemporal substitution effect more clearly, think about your own plan to buy a new computer. At an interest rate of 5 percent a year, you might borrow $2,000 and buy the new machine you've been researching. But at an interest rate of 10 percent a year, you might decide the payments would be too high. You don't abandon your plan to buy the computer, but you decide to delay your purchase.

A second substitution effect works through international prices. When the U.S. price level rises and other things remain the same, some of those other things are the prices in other countries. So a rise in the U.S. price level makes U.S.-made goods and services more expensive relative to foreign-made goods and services. This change in relative prices encourages people to spend less on U.S.-made items and more on foreign-made items. For example, if the U.S. price level rises relative to the Canadian price level, Canadians buy fewer U.S.-made cars (U.S. exports decrease) and Americans buy more Canadian-made cars (U.S. imports increase).

**Maria's Substitution Effects**   In Belgrade, Serbia, Maria makes some substitutions. She was planning on trading in her old motor scooter and getting a new one. But with a higher price level, and faced with higher interest rates, she decides to make her old scooter last one more year. Also, with the prices of Serbian goods sharply increasing, Maria substitutes a low cost dress made in Malaysia for the Serbian-made dress she had originally planned to buy.

**Changes in the Quantity of Real GDP Demanded**
When the price level changes and other things remain the same, the quantity of real GDP demanded changes. Such a change is shown by a movement along the aggregate demand curve. The arrows in Fig. 7.6 illustrate changes in the quantity of real GDP demanded.

We've now seen how the quantity of real GDP demanded changes when the price level changes. How do other influences on buying plans affect aggregate demand?

## Changes in Aggregate Demand

A change in any factor that influences buying plans other than the price level brings a change in aggregate demand. The main factors are:

- Expectations
- Fiscal policy and monetary policy
- The world economy

**Expectations**   Expectations about future incomes, inflation, and profits influence buying plans today. An increase in expected future income increases the amount of consumption goods (especially big-ticket items like cars) that people plan to buy today and increases aggregate demand.

An increase in the expected future inflation rate increases aggregate demand because people decide to buy more goods and services at today's relatively lower prices. An increase in expected future profit increases the investment that firms plan to undertake today and increases aggregate demand.

**Fiscal Policy and Monetary Policy**  The government's attempt to influence the economy by setting and changing taxes, transfer payments, and government purchases is called **fiscal policy**. A decrease in taxes or an increase in transfer payments—unemployment benefits, social security benefits, and welfare payments—with no change in government purchases increases aggregate demand. Both of these influences operate by increasing households' *disposable* income. **Disposable income** is aggregate income minus taxes plus transfer payments. The greater the disposable income, the greater is the quantity of consumption goods and services that households plan to buy and the greater is aggregate demand.

Government purchases of goods and services are one component of aggregate demand. So if taxes and transfer payments don't change but the government plans to buy more spy satellites and highways, aggregate demand increases.

**Monetary policy** consists of changes in interest rates and in the quantity of money in the economy. The quantity of money is determined by the Fed and by the banks (in a process described in Chapters 13 and 14). An increase in the quantity of money in the economy increases aggregate demand. To see why money affects aggregate demand, imagine that the Fed borrows the army's helicopters, loads them with millions of new $10 bills, and sprinkles them like confetti across the nation. People gather the newly available money and plan to spend some of it. So the quantity of goods and services demanded increases. But people don't plan to spend all the new money. They plan to save some of it and lend it to others through the banks. Interest rates fall, and with lower interest rates, people plan to buy more consumer durables and firms plan to increase their investment.

**The World Economy**  Two main world economy influences on aggregate demand are the foreign exchange rate and foreign income. The *foreign exchange rate* is the amount of a foreign currency that you can buy with a U.S. dollar. Other things

**FIGURE 7.7**

Changes in Aggregate Demand

Aggregate demand

*Decreases if*
- Expected future incomes, inflation, or profits decrease
- Fiscal policy decreases government purchases, increases taxes, or decreases transfer payments
- Monetary policy decreases the quantity of money and increases interest rates
- The exchange rate increases or foreign income decreases

*Increases if*
- Expected future incomes, inflation, or profits increase
- Fiscal policy increases government purchases, decreases taxes, or increases transfer payments
- Monetary policy increases the quantity of money and decreases interest rates
- The exchange rate decreases or foreign income increases

remaining the same, a rise in the foreign exchange rate decreases aggregate demand. To see how the foreign exchange rate influences aggregate demand, suppose that $1 exchanges for 100 Japanese yen. A Fujitsu phone (made in Japan) costs 12,500 yen, and an equivalent Motorola phone (made in the United States) costs $110. In U.S. dollars, the Fujitsu phone costs $125, so people around the world buy the cheaper U.S. phone. Now suppose the exchange rate rises to 125 yen. At 125 yen per dollar, the Fujitsu phone costs $100 and is now cheaper than the Motorola phone. People will switch from the U.S. phone to the Japanese phone. U.S. exports will decrease and U.S. imports will increase, so U.S. aggregate demand will decrease.

An increase in foreign income increases U.S. exports and increases U.S. aggregate demand. For example, an increase in income in Japan and Germany increases the purchases of U.S.-made goods and services that Japanese and German consumers and producers plan to make.

**Shifts of the Aggregate Demand Curve**   When aggregate demand changes, the aggregate demand curve shifts. Figure 7.7 shows two changes in aggregate demand and summarizes the factors bringing about such changes.

The aggregate demand curve shifts rightward, from $AD_0$ to $AD_1$, when expected future incomes, inflation, or profits increase, government purchases on goods and services increase, taxes are cut, transfer payments increase, the quantity of money increases and interest rates fall, the foreign exchange rate falls, or foreign income increases. The aggregate demand curve shifts leftward, from $AD_0$ to $AD_2$, when expected future incomes, inflation, or profits decrease, government purchases of goods and services decrease, taxes increase, transfer payments decrease, the quantity of money decreases and interest rates rise, the foreign exchange rate rises, or foreign income decreases.

## R E V I E W

- The aggregate demand curve shows the relationship between the price level and the quantity of real GDP demanded, other things remaining the same.
- When the price level rises, the quantity of real GDP demanded decreases because real wealth decreases, interest rates rise, and the prices of domestic goods and services increase relative to those of foreign goods and services.
- Changes in expectations, fiscal policy, monetary policy, and the world economy change aggregate demand and shift the aggregate demand curve.

# Macroeconomic Equilibrium

THE PURPOSE OF THE AGGREGATE SUPPLY– aggregate demand model is to explain changes in real GDP and the price level. To achieve this purpose, we combine aggregate supply and aggregate demand and determine macroeconomic equilibrium. There is a macroeconomic equilibrium for each of the time frames for aggregate supply: a long-run equilibrium and a short-run equilibrium. Long-run equilibrium is the state toward which the economy is heading. Short-run equilibrium is the normal state of the economy as it fluctuates around potential GDP.

We'll begin our study of macroeconomic equilibrium by looking first at the short run.

### Short-Run Macroeconomic Equilibrium

The aggregate demand curve tells us the quantity of real GDP demanded at each price level, and the short-run aggregate supply curve tells us the quantity of real GDP supplied at each price level. **Short-run macroeconomic equilibrium** occurs when the quantity of real GDP demanded equals the quantity of real GDP supplied. That is, short-run equilibrium occurs at the point of intersection of the *AD* curve and the *SAS* curve. Figure 7.8 shows such an equilibrium at a price level of 110 and real GDP of $7 trillion (points *c* and *c'*).

To see why this position is the equilibrium, think about what happens if the price level is something other than 110. Suppose, for example, that the price level is 120 and that real GDP is $8 trillion (at point *e*) on the *SAS* curve. The quantity of real GDP demanded is less than $8 trillion, so firms are unable to sell all their output. Unwanted inventories pile up, and firms cut both production and prices. Production and prices are cut until firms can sell all their output. This situation occurs only when real GDP is $7 trillion and the price level is 110.

Now suppose the price level is 100 and real GDP is $6 trillion (at point *a*) on the *SAS* curve. The quantity of real GDP demanded exceeds $6 trillion, so firms are unable to meet the demand for their output. Inventories decrease, and customers clamor for goods and services. So firms increase production and raise prices. Production and prices increase until firms can

## FIGURE 7.8
### Short-Run Equilibrium

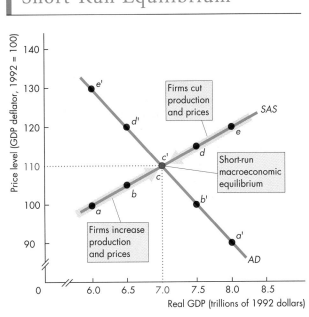

Short-run macroeconomic equilibrium occurs when real GDP demanded equals real GDP supplied—at the intersection of the aggregate demand curve (*AD*) and the short-run aggregate supply curve (*SAS*). Here, such an equilibrium occurs at points *c* and *c'*, where the price level is 110 and real GDP is $7 trillion. If the price level is 120 and real GDP is $8 trillion (point *e*), firms will not be able to sell all their output. They will decrease production and cut prices. If the price level is 100 and real GDP is $6 trillion (point *a*), people will not be able to buy all the goods and services they demand. Firms will increase production and raise their prices. Only when the price level is 110 and real GDP is $7 trillion can firms sell all that they produce and people buy all that they demand. This is the short-run macroeconomic equilibrium.

meet demand. This situation occurs only when real GDP is $7 trillion and the price level is 110.

In short-run equilibrium, the money wage rate is fixed. It does not adjust to bring full employment. So in the short run, real GDP can be greater than or less than potential GDP. But in the long run, the money wage rate does adjust and real GDP moves toward potential GDP. We are going to study this adjustment process. But first, let's look at the economy in long-run equilibrium.

## Long-Run Macroeconomic Equilibrium

**Long-run macroeconomic equilibrium** occurs when real GDP equals potential GDP—equivalently, when the economy is on its *long-run* aggregate supply curve. Figure 7.9 shows long-run equilibrium, which occurs at the intersection of the aggregate demand curve and the long-run aggregate supply curve (the blue curves). Long-run equilibrium comes about because the money wage rate adjusts. Potential GDP and aggregate demand determine the price level, and the price level influences the money wage rate. In long-run equilibrium, the money wage rate has adjusted to put the (green) short-run aggregate supply through the long-run equilibrium point.

We'll look at this adjustment process later in this chapter. But first, let's use the *AS-AD* model to study economic growth and inflation.

## FIGURE 7.9
### Long-Run Equilibrium

In long-run macroeconomic equilibrium, real GDP equals potential GDP. So long-run equilibrium occurs where the aggregate demand curve intersects the long-run aggregate demand curve. In the long run, aggregate demand determines the price level and has no effect on real GDP. The money wage rate adjusts in the long run so that the *SAS* curve intersects the *LAS* curve at the long-run equilibrium price level.

## Economic Growth and Inflation

Economic growth occurs because, over time, the quantity of labor grows, capital is accumulated, and technology advances. These changes increase potential GDP and shift the long-run aggregate supply curve rightward. Figure 7.10 shows such a shift. The growth rate of potential GDP is determined by the pace at which labor grows, capital is accumulated, and technology advances.

Inflation occurs when, over time, aggregate demand increases by more than long-run aggregate supply. That is, inflation occurs if the aggregate demand curve shifts rightward by more than the rightward shift in the long-run aggregate supply curve. Figure 7.10 shows such shifts.

If aggregate demand increased at the same pace as long-run aggregate supply, we would experience real GDP growth with no inflation.

In the long run, the main influence on aggregate demand is the growth rate of the quantity of money. At times when the quantity of money increases rapidly, aggregate demand increases quickly and the inflation rate is high. When the growth rate of the quantity of money slows, other things remaining the same, the inflation rate eventually decreases.

Our economy experiences growth and inflation, like that shown in Fig. 7.10. But it does not experience *steady* growth and *steady* inflation. Real GDP fluctuates around potential GDP in a business cycle, and inflation also fluctuates. When we study the business cycle, we ignore economic growth. By doing so, we can see the business cycle more clearly.

## Business Cycles

The business cycle occurs because aggregate demand and short-run aggregate supply fluctuate but the money wage rate does not adjust quickly enough to keep real GDP at potential GDP. Figure 7.11 shows three types of short-run equilibrium.

In part (a) there is a below full-employment equilibrium. A **below full-employment equilibrium** is a macroeconomic equilibrium in which potential GDP exceeds real GDP. The amount by which potential GDP exceeds real GDP is called a **recessionary gap**. This name reminds us that a gap has opened up between potential GDP and real GDP either because the economy has experienced a recession or because real GDP, while growing, has grown more slowly than potential GDP.

The below full-employment equilibrium shown in Fig. 7.11(a) occurs where the aggregate demand curve $AD_0$ intersects short-run aggregate supply curve $SAS_0$ at a real GDP of $6.8 trillion and a price level of 110. The recessionary gap is $0.2 trillion. The U.S. economy was in a situation similar to that shown in Fig. 7.11(a) in the early 1980s and again in the early 1990s. In those years, real GDP was less than potential GDP.

Figure 7.11(b) is an example of *long-run equilibrium* in which real GDP equals potential GDP. In this example, the equilibrium occurs where the aggregate demand curve $AD_1$ intersects the short-run aggregate supply curve $SAS_1$ at an actual and potential GDP of $7 trillion. The U.S. economy was in a situation such as that shown in Fig. 7.11(b) in mid-1996.

Figure 7.11(c) shows an above full-employment equilibrium. An **above full-employment equilibrium** is a macroeconomic equilibrium in which real

**FIGURE 7.10**

## Economic Growth and Inflation

Economic growth is the persistent increase in potential GDP. Economic growth is shown as an ongoing rightward movement in the *LAS* curve. Inflation is the persistent rise in the price level. Inflation occurs when aggregate demand increases by more than the increase in long-run aggregate supply.

GDP exceeds potential GDP. The amount by which real GDP exceeds potential GDP is called an **inflationary gap**. This name reminds us that a gap has opened up between real GDP and potential GDP and that this gap creates inflationary pressure.

The above full-employment equilibrium shown in Fig. 7.11(c) occurs where the aggregate demand curve $AD_2$ intersects the short-run aggregate supply curve $SAS_2$ at a real GDP of $7.2 trillion and a price level of 110. There is an inflationary gap of $0.2

trillion. The U.S. economy was in a situation similar to that depicted in part (c) in 1988–1990.

The economy moves from one type of equilibrium to another as a result of fluctuations in aggregate demand and in short-run aggregate supply. These fluctuations produce fluctuations in real GDP and the price level. Figure 7.11(d) shows how real GDP fluctuates around potential GDP.

Let's now look at some of the sources of these fluctuations around potential GDP.

---

**FIGURE 7.11**

## The Business Cycle

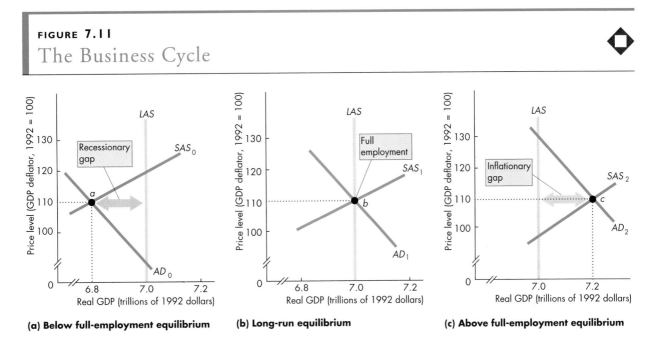

**(a) Below full-employment equilibrium**  **(b) Long-run equilibrium**  **(c) Above full-employment equilibrium**

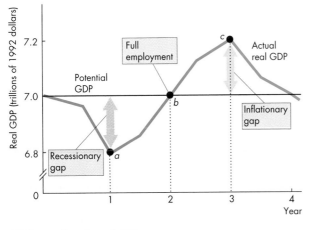

**(d) Fluctuations in real GDP**

Part (a) shows a below full-employment equilibrium in year 1; part (b) shows a long-run equilibrium in year 2; part (c) shows an above full-employment equilibrium in year 3. Part (d) shows how real GDP fluctuates around potential GDP in a business cycle. In year 1, there is a recessionary gap and the economy is at point *a* (in parts a and d). In year 2, there is long-run equilibrium and the economy is at point *b* (in parts b and d). In year 3, there is an inflationary gap and the economy is at point *c* (in parts c and d).

## Fluctuations in Aggregate Demand

One reason real GDP fluctuates around potential GDP is that aggregate demand fluctuates. Let's see what happens when aggregate demand increases.

Figure 7.12(a) shows an economy in long-run equilibrium. The aggregate demand curve is $AD_0$, the short-run aggregate supply curve is $SAS_0$, and the long-run aggregate supply curve is $LAS$. Real GDP equals potential GDP at $7 trillion, and the price level is 110.

Now suppose that the world economy expands and that the demand for U.S.-made goods increases in Japan and Europe. The increase in U.S. exports increases aggregate demand, and the aggregate demand curve shifts rightward from $AD_0$ to $AD_1$ in Fig. 7.12(a).

Faced with an increase in demand, firms increase production and raise prices. Real GDP increases to $7.5 trillion, and the price level rises to 115. The economy is now in an above full-employment equilibrium. Real GDP exceeds potential GDP, there is an inflationary gap.

The increase in aggregate demand has increased the prices of all goods and services. Faced with higher prices, firms have increased their output rates. At this stage, prices of goods and services have increased but wage rates have not changed. (Recall that as we move along a short-run aggregate supply curve, wage rates are constant.)

The economy cannot produce in excess of potential GDP forever. Why not? What are the forces at work that bring real GDP back to potential GDP?

Because the price level has increased and wage rates are unchanged, workers have experienced a fall in the buying power of their wages and firms' profits have increased. In these circumstances, workers demand higher wages and firms, anxious to maintain their employment and output levels, meet those demands. If firms do not raise wage rates, they will either lose workers or have to hire less productive ones.

As wage rates rise, the short-run aggregate supply curve begins to shift leftward. In Fig. 7.12(b), the short-run aggregate supply curve moves from $SAS_0$

### FIGURE 7.12

## An Increase in Aggregate Demand

**(a) Short-run effect**

An increase in aggregate demand shifts the aggregate demand curve from $AD_0$ to $AD_1$. In the short-run equilibrium, real GDP is $7.5 trillion and the price level rises to 115 in part (a). In this situation, there is an inflationary gap. The money wage rate rises, and the short-run aggregate supply curve shifts

**(b) Long-run effect**

leftward from $SAS_0$ to $SAS_1$ in part (b). As it shifts, it intersects the aggregate demand curve $AD_1$ at higher price levels and lower real GDP levels. Eventually, the price level rises to 125 and real GDP decreases to $7.0 trillion—potential GDP.

toward $SAS_1$. The rise in wages and the shift in the *SAS* curve produce a sequence of new equilibrium positions. Along the adjustment path, real GDP falls and the price level rises. The economy moves up along its aggregate demand curve as shown by the arrowheads in the figure.

Eventually, wage rates rise by the same percentage as the price level. At this time, the aggregate demand curve $AD_1$ intersects $SAS_1$ at a new long-run equilibrium. The price level has risen to 125, and real GDP is back where it started, at potential GDP.

A decrease in aggregate demand has similar but opposite effects to those of an increase in aggregate demand. That is, a decrease in aggregate demand shifts the aggregate demand curve leftward. Real GDP decreases to less than potential GDP, and a recessionary gap emerges. Firms cut prices. The lower price level increases the purchasing power of wages and increases firms' costs relative to their output prices because wages remain unchanged. Eventually, the slack economy leads to falling wage rates and the short-run aggregate supply curve shifts rightward. But wage rates change slowly, so real GDP slowly returns to potential GDP and the price level falls slowly.

Let's now work out how real GDP and the price level change when aggregate supply changes.

## Fluctuations in Aggregate Supply

Fluctuations in short-run aggregate supply can bring fluctuations in real GDP around potential GDP. Suppose that initially real GDP equals potential GDP. Then there is a large but temporary rise in the price of oil. What happens to real GDP and the price level?

Figure 7.13 answers this question. The aggregate demand curve is $AD_0$, the short-run aggregate supply curve is $SAS_0$, and the long-run aggregate supply curve is *LAS*. Equilibrium real GDP is $7 trillion, which equals potential GDP, and the price level is 110. Then the price of oil rises. Faced with higher energy and transportation costs, firms decrease production. Short-run aggregate supply decreases, and the short-run aggregate supply curve shifts leftward to $SAS_1$. The price level rises to 120, and real GDP decreases to $6.5 trillion. Because real GDP decreases, the economy experiences recession. Because the price level increases, the economy experiences inflation. A combination of recession and inflation, called *stagflation*, actually occurred in the United States in the mid-1970s and early 1980s. But events like this are not common.

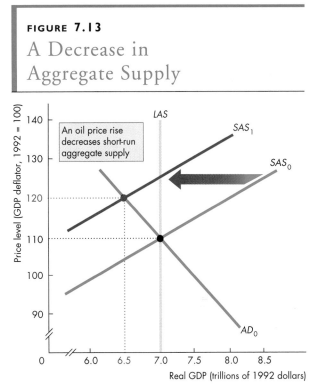

**FIGURE 7.13**

## A Decrease in Aggregate Supply

An increase in the price of oil decreases short-run aggregate supply and shifts the short-run aggregate supply curve from $SAS_0$ to $SAS_1$. Real GDP decreases from $7.0 trillion to $6.5 trillion, and the price level rises from 110 to 120. The economy experiences both recession and inflation—stagflation.

## REVIEW

- Increases in long-run aggregate supply bring economic growth, and bigger increases in aggregate demand than in *LAS* bring inflation.
- There are three types of short-run macroeconomic equilibrium: (1) below full-employment equilibrium (potential GDP exceeds real GDP and there is a recessionary gap); (2) long-run equilibrium (real GDP equals potential GDP); and (3) above full-employment equilibrium (real GDP exceeds potential GDP and there is an inflationary gap).
- Fluctuations in aggregate demand and short-run aggregate supply bring fluctuations in real GDP around potential GDP.

Let's put our new knowledge of aggregate supply and aggregate demand to work and see how we can explain recent U.S. macroeconomic performance.

# U.S. Economic Growth, Inflation, and Cycles

THE ECONOMY IS CONTINUALLY CHANGING. If you imagine the economy as a video, then an aggregate supply–aggregate demand figure such as Fig. 7.13 is a freeze-frame. We're going to run the video (instant replay) but keep our finger on the freeze-frame button and look at some important parts of the previous action. Let's run the video from 1960.

Figure 7.14 shows the state of the economy in 1960 at the point of intersection of its aggregate demand curve $AD_{60}$ and short-run aggregate supply curve $SAS_{60}$. Real GDP was \$2.3 trillion, and the GDP deflator was 23.3 (about a fifth of its 1996 level). In 1960, real GDP equaled potential GDP—the economy was on $LAS_{60}$.

By 1996, the economy had reached the point marked by the intersection of aggregate demand curve $AD_{96}$ and short-run aggregate supply curve $SAS_{96}$. Real GDP was \$7 trillion, and the GDP

deflator was 111. Also in 1996, the economy was on $LAS_{96}$, with real GDP equal to potential GDP.

The path traced by the blue and red dots in Fig. 7.14 has three key features:

- Economic growth
- Inflation
- Business cycles

## Economic Growth

Over the years, real GDP grows—shown in Fig. 7.14 by the rightward movement of the points. The faster real GDP grows, the larger is the horizontal distance between successive dots in the figure. The forces that generate economic growth are those that increase potential GDP. Potential GDP grows because the quantity of labor grows, we accumulate physical and human capital, and our technologies advance.

These forces that bring economic growth were stronger during the 1960s and mid-1980s than at other times. During the 1970s, growth was slow.

**FIGURE 7.14**

## Aggregate Supply and Aggregate Demand: 1960–1996

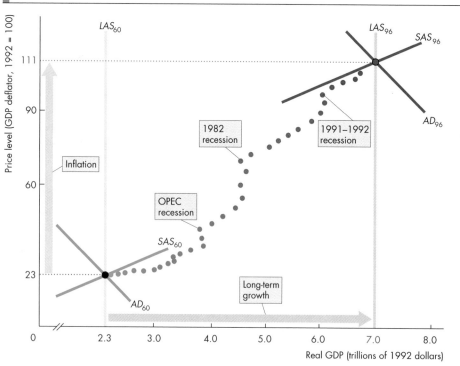

Each point shows the GDP deflator and real GDP in a given year. In 1960, these variables were determined by the aggregate demand curve $AD_{60}$ and the short-run aggregate supply curve $SAS_{60}$. Each point is generated by the gradual shifting of the AD and SAS curves. By 1996, the curves were $AD_{96}$ and $SAS_{96}$. Real GDP grew, and the price level increased. Real GDP grew quickly and inflation was moderate in the 1960s; real GDP growth sagged in 1974–1975 and again in 1982. Inflation was rapid in the 1970s but slowed after the 1982 recession. The period from 1982 to 1989 was one of strong, persistent expansion. A recession began in 1991, and a further expansion then followed.

## Inflation

The price level rises over the years—shown in Fig. 7.14 by the upward movement of the points. The larger the rise in the price level, the larger is the vertical distance between successive dots in the figure. The main force generating the persistent increase in the price level is a tendency for aggregate demand to increase at a faster pace than the increase in long-run aggregate supply. All of the factors that increase aggregate demand and shift the aggregate demand curve influence the pace of inflation. But one factor—the growth of the quantity of money—is the main source of *persistent* increases in aggregate demand and persistent inflation.

## Business Cycles

Over the years, the economy grows and shrinks in cycles—shown in Fig. 7.14 by the wavelike pattern made by the points, with the recessions highlighted. The cycles arise because both the expansion of short-run aggregate supply and the growth of aggregate demand do not proceed at a fixed, steady pace. Although the economy has cycles, recessions do not usually follow quickly on the heels of their predecessors; "double-dip" recessions like the one in the cartoon are rare.

## The Evolving Economy: 1960–1996

During the 1960s, real GDP growth was rapid and inflation was low. This was a period of rapid increases in aggregate supply and of moderate increases in aggregate demand.

The mid-1970s were years of rapid inflation and recession—of stagflation. The major source of these developments was a series of massive oil price increases that shifted the short-run aggregate supply curve leftward and rapid increases in the quantity of money that shifted the aggregate demand curve rightward. Recession occurred because the short-run aggregate supply curve shifted leftward at a faster pace than the aggregate demand curve shifted rightward.

The rest of the 1970s saw high inflation—the price level increased quickly—and only moderate growth in real GDP. By 1980, inflation was a major problem and the Fed decided to take strong action against it. It permitted interest rates to rise to previously unknown levels. Consequently, aggregate demand decreased. By 1982, the decrease in aggregate demand put the economy in a deep recession.

*"Please stand by for a series of tones. The first indicates the official end of the recession, the second indicates prosperity, and the third the return of the recession."*

*Drawing by Mankoff; © 1991 The New Yorker Magazine, Inc.*

During the years 1982 to 1990, capital accumulation and steady technological advance resulted in a sustained rightward shift of the long-run aggregate supply curve. Wage growth was moderate, and the short-run aggregate supply curve also shifted rightward. Aggregate demand growth kept pace with the growth of aggregate supply. Sustained but steady growth in aggregate supply and aggregate demand kept real GDP growing and inflation steady. The economy moved from a recession with real GDP less than potential GDP in 1981 to above full-employment in 1990. It was in this condition when a decrease in aggregate demand led to the 1991 recession. The economy again embarked on a path of expansion through 1996. The expansion took real GDP back to potential GDP and returned employment to full employment.

◆ The aggregate supply–aggregate demand model explains economic growth, inflation, and the business cycle. The model is a useful one because it enables us to keep our eye on the big picture. But it lacks detail. It does not tell us as much as we need to know about the deeper forces that lie behind aggregate supply and aggregate demand. The chapters that follow begin to fill in the details. We begin with the supply side and study the forces that make our economy grow. But before you embark on this next stage, take a look at *Reading Between the Lines* on pages 158–159, which gives you a look at the U.S. economy in 1997.

# Policy
## WATCH

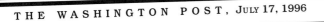

## Aggregate Supply and Aggregate Demand in Action

**Essence** of
**THE STORY**

■ In mid-1996, real GDP was growing at a rate of 4 percent a year. The unemployment rate was at its lowest in six years.

■ Investors expected the Fed to raise interest rates to check inflation.

■ The Fed had raised interest rates in early July when the unemployment rate fell to 5.3 percent and wages increased by 0.8 percent.

■ But stock prices fell in mid-July 1996.

■ The lower stock prices might be sign of lower profits and might weaken consumer confidence and decrease consumer spending.

■ Interest rates decreased with the news of the stock price drop and the announcement of a 0.1 percent increase in consumer prices.

THE WASHINGTON POST, July 17, 1996

# Apply 1 Stock Drop and Watch the Economy Cool

BY JOHN M. BERRY

The 6.5 percent slide in stock prices this month could turn out to be a cloud with a silver lining.

That decline, a direct sign of weaker corporate earnings, could be a bit of a blow to consumers' confidence and dampen their spending somewhat in coming months, a number of analysts said.

Normally, such developments wouldn't be regarded as good news at all. But with economic growth running at a 4 percent pace recently, unemployment at its lowest level in six years and many investors braced for a Federal Reserve boost in short-term interest rates to head off any rise in inflation, a little cooling could be just what the doctor ordered.

Some investors appear to be interpreting the market's drop in exactly that fashion. Interest rates soared early this month when the Labor Department said payroll jobs had increased briskly in June, the unemployment rate had fallen to 5.3 percent and average hourly earnings had jumped 0.8 percent. Since then, the drop in stock prices and some other favorable news—including a report yesterday that consumer prices rose a scant 0.1 percent last month—have unwound much of the earlier rise in rates. ...

In a revised forecast, the administration predicted the economy would grow 2.6 percent from last year's fourth quarter to this year's, rather than the 2.2 percent expected at the beginning of this year. Nevertheless, the higher figure still assumes that growth will slow down in the second half of the year and that the unemployment rate will move back up to 5.6 percent. The forecast for consumer price inflation was revised upward slightly, from 3.1 percent to 3.2 percent.

Reprinted with permission.

# Economic

## A N A L Y S I S

■ Figure 1 shows that real GDP was above potential GDP at the end of 1994—an inflationary gap—below potential GDP at the end of 1995 and beginning of 1996—a recessionary gap—and equal to potential GDP in 1996. (Potential GDP is the author's estimate.)

■ Figure 2 shows that inflation increased in 1995 and decreased in 1996.

■ The increase in the inflation rate during 1995 was caused by the 1994 inflationary gap. The decrease in the inflation rate during late 1995 and 1996 was caused by the recessionary gap present during those years.

■ Figure 3 shows the U.S. economy in 1997 and explains the fears expressed in the news article in terms of the aggregate supply–aggregate demand model.

■ In the second quarter of 1996, real GDP was $6.9 trillion and the price level was 110.

■ You can see these values at the intersection of the aggregate demand curve $AD_{96}$ and the short-run aggregate supply curve $SAS_{96}$.

■ The economy is at full-employment equilibrium. Real GDP equals potential GDP on the long-run aggregate supply curve $LAS_{96}$.

■ Many people feared that aggregate demand was growing quickly in 1996 and that, with no action from the Fed, the aggregate demand curve might shift rightward to $AD'$.

■ If the aggregate demand curve did shift rightward to $AD'$, an inflationary gap would emerge and the inflation rate would begin to rise again.

■ And if an inflationary gap is expected, it is a good bet that the Fed will increase interest rates in an attempt to hold aggregate demand growth back.

■ But if households expect lower future incomes because business profits are down, perhaps aggregate demand growth will slow with no action by the Fed.

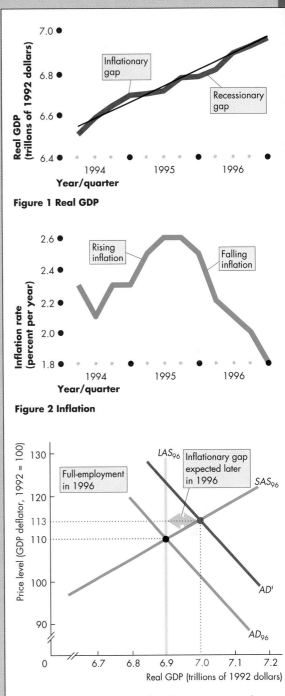

**Figure 1 Real GDP**

**Figure 2 Inflation**

**Figure 3 Aggregate demand and aggregate supply**

## You're

### THE VOTER

■ During a two-week period in July 1996, the Fed first increased and then decreased interest rates. How do you think the economy responds to this type of action by the Fed?

■ Would you support an increase in interest rates to keep inflation in check?

■ Would you support a decrease in interest rates to lower unemployment?

# SUMMARY

## Key Points

### Aggregate Supply (pp. 142–146)

- In the long run, the quantity of real GDP supplied is potential GDP, which is independent of the price level. The long-run aggregate supply curve is vertical.

- In the short run, the money wage rate is constant, so a rise in the price level increases the quantity of real GDP supplied. The short-run aggregate supply curve is upward sloping.

- A change in potential GDP changes both long-run and short-run aggregate supply. A change in the money wage rate or resource prices changes only short-run aggregate supply.

### Aggregate Demand (pp. 147–150)

- A rise in the price level decreases the quantity of real GDP demanded, other things remaining the same.

- The reason is that the higher price level decreases the quantity of *real* wealth, raises the interest rate, and raises the cost of domestic goods compared with foreign goods.

- Changes in expected future incomes, profits, and inflation, changes in fiscal policy and monetary policy, and changes in world real GDP and the foreign exchange rate change aggregate demand.

### Macroeconomic Equilibrium (pp. 150–155)

- In the short run, real GDP and the price level are determined by aggregate demand and short-run aggregate supply.

- In the long run, real GDP equals potential GDP and aggregate demand determines the price level and the money wage rate.

- Economic growth occurs because potential GDP increases.

- Inflation occurs because aggregate demand grows more quickly than potential GDP.

- Business cycles occur because aggregate demand and aggregate supply fluctuate.

### U.S. Economic Growth, Inflation, and Cycles (pp. 156–157)

- U.S. potential GDP grew fastest during the 1960s and mid-1980s and slowest during the 1970s.

- U.S. inflation persists because aggregate demand grows faster than potential GDP.

- U.S. business cycles occur because aggregate supply and aggregate demand change at an uneven pace.

## Key Figures

## Key Terms

## QUESTIONS

1. What are the three factors that determine the quantity of real GDP supplied?
2. What is the relationship between potential GDP and full employment?
3. Name and distinguish between two macroeconomic time frames and two concepts of aggregate supply.
4. Distinguish between movements along the short-run and the long-run aggregate supply curves.
5. Consider the following events:
   a. Potential GDP increases
   b. The money wage rate rises
   c. The price level rises
   d. The money wage rate and the price level rise by the same percentages

   Say which of these events, if any, change:
   (1) Long-run aggregate supply but not short-run aggregate supply.
   (2) Short-run aggregate supply but not long-run aggregate supply.
   (3) Both short-run aggregate supply and long-run aggregate supply.

   Also say which of these events, if any, bring a movement along
   (4) The long-run aggregate supply curve.
   (5) The short-run aggregate supply curve.
   (6) Both the short-run and long-run aggregate supply curves.
6. Distinguish between aggregate demand and the quantity of real GDP demanded.
7. Which of the following do not affect aggregate demand?
   a. Quantity of money
   b. Interest rates
   c. Technological change
   d. Human capital
8. Define short-run macroeconomic equilibrium.
9. Distinguish between a recessionary equilibrium and full-employment equilibrium.
10. Work out the short-run and long-run effects of an increase in the quantity of money on the price level and real GDP.
11. Work out the short-run effect of an increase in the price of oil on the price level and real GDP.
12. What are the main factors generating growth, inflation, and cycles in the U.S. economy?

## PROBLEMS

1. The following events occur that influence the economy of Toughtimes:
   - A deep recession hits the world economy.
   - Oil prices rise sharply.
   - Businesses expect huge losses in the near future.
   a. Use the *AS–AD* model to explain the separate effects of each event on real GDP and the price level in Toughtimes, starting from long-run equilibrium.
   b. Use the *AS–AD* model to explain the combined effects of these events on real GDP and the price level in Toughtimes, starting from long-run equilibrium.
   c. Explain what the Toughtimes government or central bank can do to overcome the problems faced by the economy.
2. The following events occur that influence the economy of Coolland:
   - The world economy experiences a strong expansion.
   - Businesses expect huge profits in the near future.
   - The Coolland government cuts its purchases of goods and services.
   a. Use the *AS–AD* model to explain the separate effects of each event on real GDP and the price level in Coolland, starting from long-run equilibrium.
   b. Use the *AS–AD* model to explain the combined effects of these events on real GDP and the price level in Coolland, starting from long-run equilibrium.
   c. Explain why the Coolland government or central bank might want to take action to influence the Coolland economy.
3. The economy of Mainland has the following aggregate demand and supply schedules:

| Price level | Real GDP demanded | Real GDP supplied in the short run |
|---|---|---|
| | (trillions of 1992 dollars) | |
| 90 | 4.5 | 3.5 |
| 100 | 4.0 | 4.0 |
| 110 | 3.5 | 4.5 |
| 120 | 3.0 | 5.0 |
| 130 | 2.5 | 5.5 |
| 140 | 2.0 | 6.0 |

a.   Plot the aggregate demand curve and short-run aggregate supply curve in a figure.
b.   What are the values of real GDP and the price level in Mainland in a short-run macroeconomic equilibrium?
c.   Mainland's potential GDP is $5.0 trillion. Plot the long-run aggregate supply curve in the same figure in which you answered part (a).

4.   In problem 3, aggregate demand increases by $1 trillion. What are the changes in real GDP and the price level in the short run?

5.   In problem 3, aggregate supply decreases by $1 trillion. What is the new short-run macroeconomic equilibrium?

6.   In the economy shown in the figure below, short-run aggregate supply is $SAS_0$ and aggregate demand is $AD_0$. Then some events change aggregate demand and the aggregate demand curve shifts rightward to $AD_1$. Later, some further events change aggregate supply, and the short-run aggregate supply curve shifts leftward to $SAS_1$.

a.   What is the initial equilibrium point?
b.   What is the equilibrium point after the change in aggregate demand?
c.   What is the equilibrium point after the change in aggregate supply?
d.   What events could have changed aggregate demand from $AD_0$ to $AD_1$?
e.   What events could have changed aggregate supply from $SAS_0$ to $SAS_1$?
f.   After the increase in aggregate demand but before the decrease in aggregate supply, is the real GDP greater than or less than potential GDP?

## CRITICAL THINKING

1.   After you have studied the account of the U.S. economic expansion during the 1990s in *Reading Between the Lines* on pp. 532–533:
a.   Describe the main features of the economy in 1996 that worried economists.
b.   In which periods was there a recessionary gap and in which was there an inflationary gap?
c.   Use the *AS-AD* model to show the economy in 1996 if the Fed increased interest rates by too much and created a recession.
d.   Use the *AS-AD* model to show the economy in 1996 if the Fed cut interest rates to stimulate aggregate demand and avoid a recession.

2.   You are the President's economic advisor and have the following forecasts of aggregate demand and aggregate supply for next year:

| Price level | Real GDP demanded | Real GDP supplied | Potential GDP |
|---|---|---|---|
| | | (trillions of 1992 dollars) | |
| 100 | 8.3 | 5.3 | 7 |
| 105 | 7.8 | 6.3 | 7 |
| 110 | 7.3 | 7.3 | 7 |
| 115 | 6.8 | 8.3 | 7 |

This year, real GDP is $6.8 trillion, potential GDP is also $6.8 trillion, and the price level is 107. The President wants answers to the following questions:
a.   What is your forecast of next year's real GDP?
b.   What is your forecast of next year's price level?
c.   What is your forecast of the inflation rate?
d.   What is your forecast of the growth rate of real GDP?
e.   What is your forecast of the growth rate of potential GDP?
f.   Will there be a recessionary gap or an inflationary gap? By how much?

3.   Carefully draw some figures similar to those in this chapter and use the information in question 2 to explain:
a.   What policy actions can bring real GDP to potential GDP.
b.   What the inflation rate is if aggregate demand is changed by policy to achieve potential GDP.

# Expanding the Frontier

Economics is about how we cope with scarcity. We cope by making choices that balance marginal benefits and marginal costs so that we use our scarce resources efficiently. ◆ These choices determine how much work we do, how hard we work at school to learn the mental skills that form our human capital and that determine the kinds of jobs we get and the incomes we earn, and how much we save for future big ticket expenditures. These choices also determine how much businesses and governments spend on new capital—on auto assembly lines, computers and fiber cables for improved Internet services, shopping malls, highways, bridges, and tunnels—and how intensively existing capital and natural resources are used and therefore how quickly they wear out or are used up. Most significant of all, these choices determine the problems that scientists, engineers, and other inventors work on to develop new technologies. ◆ All the choices we've just described determine two vital measures of economic performance:

- Real GDP
- Economic growth

Real GDP is determined by the quantity of labor, the quantity of capital, and the state of technological knowledge. And economic growth—the growth rate of real GDP—is determined by growth in the quantity of labor, capital accumulation, and technological advances. ◆ Economic growth, maintained at a steady rate over a number of decades, is the single most powerful influence on any society. It brings a transformation that continues to amaze thoughtful people. Economic growth, maintained at a rapid rate, can transform a society in years, not decades. Such transformations are taking place right now in many Asian countries. These transformations are economic miracles. ◆ The three chapters in this part study the miracle of rapid economic growth and the forces that shape our capacity to produce goods and services. ◆ In Chapter 8, you will learn about our choices in the labor market that determine the quantity of labor and the levels of employment and unemployment. ◆ In Chapter 9, you will study the process of capital accumulation and the saving and investment decisions that govern it. You'll discover that some countries don't save enough to pay for the capital they accumulate and others save more than they need. And you'll see how international capital markets move savings to where they can obtain the highest possible return. ◆ In Chapter 10, you will study economic growth. You will learn about some economic miracles and some problems, especially the problem of the growth slowdown in the United States during the 1970s and 1980s. ◆ But first, we'll spend some time with Joseph Schumpeter and Paul Romer, two economists who have revolutionized the way we think about economic growth.

# Economic Growth

## The Economist: Joseph Schumpeter

Joseph Schumpeter, the son of a textile factory owner, was born in Austria in 1883. He moved from Austria to Germany during the tumultuous 1920s when those two countries experienced hyperinflation. And in 1932, in the depths of the Great Depression, he came to the United States and became a professor of economics at Harvard University.

This creative economic thinker wrote on economic growth and development, business cycles, political systems, and economic biography. He was a person of strong opinions who expressed them strongly and delighted in verbal battles.

Schumpeter has become the unwitting founder of modern growth theory. He saw the development and diffusion of new technologies by profit-seeking entrepreneurs as the source of economic progress. But he saw economic progress as a process of creative destruction—the creation of new profit opportunities and the destruction of currently profitable businesses. For Schumpeter, economic growth and the business cycle were a single phenomenon.

When Schumpeter died in 1950, he had achieved his self-expressed life's ambition: He was regarded as the world's greatest economist.

> *"Economic progress, in capitalist society, means turmoil."*
>
> JOSEPH SCHUMPETER
>
> *CAPITALISM, SOCIALISM AND DEMOCRACY*

## The Issues and Ideas

Technological change, capital accumulation, and population growth all interact to produce economic growth. But what is cause and what is effect, and can we expect productivity and income per person to keep growing?

The classical economists of the eighteenth and nineteenth centuries believed that technological advances and capital accumulation were the engines of growth. But they also believed that no matter how successful people were at inventing more productive technologies and investing in new capital, they were destined to live at the subsistence level. These economists based their conclusion on the belief that productivity growth causes population growth, which in turn causes productivity to decline. These classical economists believed that whenever economic growth raises incomes above the subsistence level, the population will increase. And they went on to reason that the increase in population brings diminishing returns that lower productivity. As a result, incomes must always return to the subsistence level. Only when incomes are at the subsistence level is population growth held in check.

A new approach, called neoclassical growth theory, was developed by Robert Solow of MIT during the 1950s. Solow, who was one of Schumpeter's students, received the Nobel Prize for Economic Science for this work.

Solow challenged the conclusions of the classical economists. But the new theories of economic growth developed during the 1980s and 1990s went further. They stand the classical belief on its head. Today's theory of population growth is that rising income slows the population growth rate because it increases the opportunity cost of having children and lowers the opportunity cost of investing in children and equipping them with more human capital, which makes them more productive. Productivity and income grow because technology advances and the scope for further productivity growth, which is stimulated by the search for profit, is practically unlimited.

Flemish farmers in the fifteenth century. With newly developed horse-drawn plows, harrows, and planters, farmers could plant more wheat than they could harvest. But despite big efforts, no one had been able to make a machine that could replicate the swing of a scythe. Then in 1831, 22-year-old Cyrus McCormick built a machine that worked. It scared the horse that pulled it, but it did in a matter of hours what three men could accomplish in a day. Technological change has increased productivity on farms and brought economic growth. Do the facts about productivity growth mean that the classical economists, who believed that diminishing returns would push us relentlessly back to a subsistence living standard, were wrong?

increase agricultural productivity. In the foreseeable future, we might have superconductors that revolutionize the use of electric power, virtual reality theme parks and training facilities, pollution-free hydrogen cars, wristwatch telephones, and optical computers that we can talk to. With these new technologies, our ability to create yet more dazzling technologies increases. Technological change begets technological change in an (apparently) unending process and makes us ever more productive and brings ever higher incomes.

## THEN...

In 1830, a strong and experienced farm worker could harvest three acres of wheat in a day. The only capital employed was a scythe to cut the wheat, which had been used since Roman times, and a cradle on which the stalks were laid, which had been invented by

## ...AND NOW

Today's technologies are expanding our horizons beyond the confines of our planet and are expanding our minds. Geosynchronous satellites bring us global television, voice and data communication, and more accurate weather forecasts, which incidentally

**The revolution in the way economists think about economic growth has been led by Paul Romer, a professor of economics at Stanford University, whom you can meet on the following pages.**

**Paul Romer** is Professor of Economics at the Graduate School of Business at Stanford University and the Royal Bank Fellow of the Canadian Institute for Advanced Research. Born in 1955 in Denver, Colorado, he earned his B.S. in Mathematics (1977) and his Ph.D. in Economics (1983) from the University of Chicago.

Professor Romer has transformed the way economists think about economic growth. He believes that sustained economic growth arises from competition among firms. Firms try to increase their profits by devoting resources to creating new products and developing new ways of making existing products.

Michael Parkin talked with Professor Romer about his work, how he was influenced by Joseph Schumpeter and Robert Solow, and the insights economic growth offers us.

**Professor Romer, why did you decide to become an economist?**

As an undergraduate, I studied math and physics and was interested in becoming a cosmologist. During my senior year, I concluded that job prospects in physics were not very promising, so I decided to go to law school. I was an undergraduate at the University of Chicago, where the law and economics movement first emerged. In the fall of my senior year, I took my first economics course to prepare for law school. My economics professor, Sam Peltzman, presented a simple piece of economic analysis that changed my life. He argued that the demand for economists was likely to grow for decades. The government, which employs economists, would grow in size. Businesses that deal with the government would want their own economists. The legal profession that serves businesses would also need more economists. Because of all these demands, many students would want to take economics courses. This meant that there would be many job openings for economists at universities. Moreover, he claimed, being a professor of economics was a lot like being a cosmologist and far more fun than being a lawyer. I could take fragmentary bits of evidence and try to make sense of them using mathematical equations. So I tore up my law school applications, applied to graduate school in economics, and never looked back.

**What are the truly important lessons we've learned about the causes of economic growth?**

As a physics major, I felt that the description economists used for growth violated a basic law of physics: the conservation of mass. Economists seemed to be saying that GDP, the output of a nation, was a bunch of stuff that was "produced" and that the quantity of stuff produced has grown steadily over time and will continue to do so. But this can't be right. We have the same amount of stuff, or elements from the periodic table, that we had 100,000 years ago because there are many more people now. In terms of kilograms of matter per person, we know that we are vastly poorer than our ancestors were 100,000 years ago. Yet we clearly have a higher standard of living. How could this be? This basic question indicates that thinking about growth as a production process that generates stuff is a dead-end. Instead, economic growth has to be about rearranging the fixed amount of matter that we have to work with and making new combinations that seem a lot more valuable. The key insight is that economic growth comes from increases in value, not increases in the amount of matter.

**Can you give us an example of what you mean by an increase in value?**

For tens of thousands of years, we treated iron oxide, ordinary rust, like dirt. When we lived in caves, we learned how to use it as a pigment for decorating cave walls. We took the low-value dirt and put it to the higher-valued use of making cave paintings. Later, we learned how to extract the iron from iron ore to make bridges and rails. Later still, we learned how to arrange the iron atoms together with carbon atoms and make steel. Recently, we learned how to take iron oxide and put it on magnetic tape and use it to store sound and pictures. The iron, oxygen, and carbon atoms have always been here. We have a higher standard of living because we have learned how to take these atoms and arrange them in ways that we find more valuable.

**What kind of policy implications does this kind of thinking lead to?**

Policy makers must encourage institutions to become more efficient at discovering new recipes to rearrange matter. Consider the transistor as an example. We take silicon and mix it with a few impurities and some metal in just the right way, and we get a computer chip worth thousands of times what the raw ingredients were worth. Research grants, subsidies for education, and institutions like the nonprofit private university encourage the production of new recipes or ideas. But so

*We take silicon and mix it with a few impurities and some metal in just the right way, and we get a computer chip worth thousands of times what the raw ingredients were worth.*

do venture capitalists who help new-technology startups, competitive markets that allow the firms with better instructions or ideas to quickly displace existing firms, and labor laws that let inefficient firms lay off workers when more efficient new firms come on the scene. We must let firms like Digital Electronics or Wang Computers shrink, maybe even fail, if we want to make room for new firms like Intel to enter the scene and thrive.

**Were the classical economists wrong in their view that population growth and diminishing returns are the dominant long-term influences** on production and incomes? Or is the current global population explosion part of a process that will ultimately prove them correct?

Classical economists like Malthus and Ricardo were right when they argued that we have a fixed amount of natural resources to work with. Malthus pointed out that resource scarcity will lead to falling standards of living if we continue to work with the same set of recipes or instructions for using our resources. Where he went wrong was in assuming that there was little scope for us to find new recipes for taking resources such as land, water, carbon dioxide, nitrogen, and sunshine and converting them into carbohydrates and proteins that we can eat.

The classical economists got half of the story right. We do live in a world with scarce resources. What they missed was the other half. There is an incomprehensibly large number of different formulas or recipes we can use to recombine these scarce resources into things we value, such as protein or entertainment.

Scarcity is a very important part of economics and our lives. For example, we know that there is an absolute limit on the number of people who can live on the earth. One way or another, we know that the rate of population growth will slow down. It's only a question of how and when. But will this ultimately lead to a period when standards of living fall as Malthus predicted? I doubt it. As countries get rich, population growth slows. As a larger fraction of the worldwide population becomes educated, these people will help us to discover new things, like plants that are more efficient at taking carbon dioxide out of the atmosphere, wires that are superconductors at high temperatures, and more efficient distribution systems. With these discoveries, standards of living for all humans will continue to improve.

**During the past decade, China and several other economies in East Asia have experienced rapid, unheralded growth rates. Why?**

These countries took some of the recipes, formulas, and instructions for generating value that already existed in the advanced countries of the world and put them to use within their borders. It's the same process that the Japanese followed after the Meiji restoration at the end of the last century. These countries noticed that other people in the world knew a lot about how to create value and realized that by trading with the people who possessed all this knowledge, they could share in the gains.

**What lessons from East Asia can, in principle, be applied in Africa and Central Europe?**

The basic insight is that there are huge potential gains from trade. Poor countries can supply their natural and human resources. Rich countries can supply their know-how. When these are combined, everyone can be better off. The challenge is for a country to arrange its laws and institutions so that both sides can profitably engage in trade. If there are barriers to trade or if the government cannot protect basic property rights and prevent crime, trade can't take place. For example, the Japanese have been able to borrow many ideas about manufacturing and design and even to improve on some of these ideas. But because they have barriers that limit entry of foreign firms into the retail sector, they still waste vast quantities of resources on a very inefficient distribution system.

**What does today's thinking about economic growth owe to the work of Joseph Schumpeter and Robert Solow?**

Schumpeter worked at a time before most economists had learned to work with equations. He coined the phrase "creative destruction," which describes the process by which companies like Wang shrink or go out of business when new firms come in. He also described in words how important monopoly profits are in the process of innovation. There were many other economists, including Alfred Marshall, who described these same issues in verbal terms and also struggled with the challenge of expressing these ideas in terms of equations.

Robert Solow was part of the post–World War II generation of economists who truly mastered the use of equations and wrote eloquently using both words and equations. As a result, his ideas have been far more influential than Schumpeter's. Many economists in the 1950s were trying to get a grasp on the economic effects of knowledge, formulas, recipes, and instructions. Solow called these things "technology" and gave us a wonderfully concise and workable way to think about how technology interacts with other economic inputs such as capital and labor. He also linked the methods that he and several economists were using to measure technology with this framework for thinking about the behavior of the economy as a whole. His work on growth was a masterful piece of invention, synthesis, and exposition.

In the last 15 years, economists have taken the mathematical framework that Solow gave us and extended it to bring in some of the elements that Schumpeter described in words, things like creative destruction and monopoly power. One of the great things about ideas is that they build on each other. In Isaac Newton's famous phrase, those of us working on growth today are "able to see farther because we stand on the shoulders of giants." Newton was another person who was pretty good with equations and could also turn a good phrase.

> *If you can learn how to write readable prose and use the basic tools of mathematics, you can do almost anything in today's world.*

**Is economics a worthwhile subject to major in today? What can a person do with an economics degree?**

Economics is an excellent training ground for developing mathematical and verbal skills. But students should supplement the courses in economics with courses in mathematics and science that force them to practice working with equations, graphs, and numbers. In learning a skill, there is no substitute for practice. Innate ability is far less important than most students think.

They should also take courses that force them to write, revise, and edit. I took an English course in college that taught me the basics of how to edit, and it is one of the best investments I made. You can't tell what you will end up doing or what skills you will need later in life. But if you can learn how to write readable prose and use the basic tools of mathematics, you can do almost anything in today's world.

# Chapter 8

# Employment and Unemployment

## Vital Signs

Each month, we chart the course of the unemployment rate as a measure of U.S. economic health. How do we measure unemployment? What does it tell us? Is it a reliable vital sign for the economy? ◆ June 1992 was a month in which unemployment peaked at almost 10 million. How can such a large number of people be unemployed? How do people become unemployed? Do most of them get fired, or do most quit their jobs to look for better ones? How long do spells of unemployment last for most people—a week, two weeks, or several months? And how does the length of unemployment spells vary over the business cycle? ◆ You probably know that unemployment is more common among young people than among older people. It is also more common among minorities than among whites. Why are some groups more frequently unemployed than others? ◆ We also chart every month the number of people working. This number fluctuates as the unemployment rate fluctuates, but it also trends upward. At the start of 1997, more than 127 million people in the United States had jobs. What does this vital sign tell us about the health of the U.S. economy? Does the number of jobs grow quickly enough to keep pace with increases in the population? ◆ Yet other signs of economic health are the hours people work and the wages they receive. Are work hours growing as quickly as the number of people with jobs? Are most of the new jobs full time or part time? Also, are most new jobs high-wage or low-wage jobs? ◆ These are the questions we study in this chapter. You will discover that a lot of ideas that people have about the U.S. labor market are just plain wrong. The economy has created millions of jobs, including good jobs that pay high wages and provide good benefits. But most people have seen a slowdown in their rate of wage increase, and many have seen their wages fall. We begin by looking at the key labor market indicators and the way they are measured.

## After studying this chapter, you will be able to:

■ Define the unemployment rate, the labor force participation rate, the employment-to-population ratio, and aggregate hours

■ Describe the trends and fluctuations in the indicators of labor market performance

■ Describe the sources of unemployment, its duration, and the groups that are most affected by it

■ Explain how employment and wage rates are determined by demand and supply in the labor market

## Employment and Wages

THE QUANTITY OF REAL GDP SUPPLIED DEPENDS on the quantities of labor and capital and on the state of technology. And potential GDP depends on the quantity of capital and the state of technology and on the quantity of labor employed at *full employment*. In this chapter, we study the forces that determine the quantity of labor employed and the concept of full employment. We begin by learning how the state of the labor market is observed and measured.

### Population Survey

Every month, the U.S. Census Bureau surveys 60,000 households and asks a series of questions about the age and job market status of its members. This survey is called the Current Population Survey. The Census Bureau uses the answers to describe the anatomy of the labor force.

Figure 8.1 shows the population categories used by the Census Bureau and the relationships among the categories. It divides the population into two groups: the working-age population and others who are too young to work or who live in institutions and are unable to work. The **working-age population** is the total number of people aged 16 years and over who are not in jail, hospital, or some other form of institutional care. The Census Bureau divides the working-age population into two groups: those in the labor force and those not in the labor force. It also divides the labor force into two groups: the employed and the unemployed. So the **labor force** is the sum of the employed and the unemployed.

To be counted as employed in the Current Population Survey, a person must have either a full-time job or a part-time job. To be counted as *un*employed, a person must be available for work and must be in one of three categories:

1. Without work but has made specific efforts to find a job within the previous four weeks
2. Waiting to be called back to a job from which he or she has been laid off
3. Waiting to start a new job within 30 days

Anyone surveyed who satisfies one of these three criteria is counted as unemployed. People in the working-age population who are neither employed nor unemployed are classified as not in the labor force.

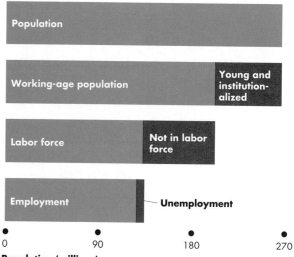

### FIGURE 8.1
## Population Labor Force Categories

The population is divided into the working-age population and the young and institutionalized. The working-age population is divided into the labor force and those not in the labor force. The labor force is divided into the employed and the unemployed.

*Source: Economic Report of the President, 1997.*

In 1996, the population of the United States was 265.5 million. There were 64.9 million people under 16 years of age or living in institutions. The working-age population was 200.6 million. Of this number, 66.7 million were not in the labor force. Most of these people were in school full time or had retired from work. The remaining 133.9 million people made up the U.S. labor force. Of these, 126.7 million were employed and 7.2 million were unemployed.

### Three Labor Market Indicators

The Census Bureau calculates three indicators of the state of the labor market, which are shown in Fig. 8.2. They are:

- The unemployment rate
- The labor force participation rate
- The employment-to-population ratio

**The Unemployment Rate**   The amount of unemployment is an indicator of the extent to which people who want jobs can't find them. The **unemployment rate** is the percentage of the people in the labor force who are unemployed. That is,

$$\text{Unemployment rate} = \frac{\text{Number of people unemployed}}{\text{Labor force}} \times 100,$$

and

$$\text{Labor force} = \text{Number of people employed} + \text{Number of people unemployed.}$$

In 1996, the number of people employed was 126.7 million and the number unemployed was 7.2 million. By using the above equations, you can verify that the labor force was 133.9 million (126.7 million plus 7.2 million) and the unemployment rate was 5.4 percent (7.2 million divided by 133.9 million, multiplied by 100).

Figure 8.2. shows the unemployment rate (orange line) and two other labor market indicators between 1960 and 1996. The average unemployment rate has been 6 percent, and it reached peak values during the OPEC recession and the recessions of 1982 and 1990–1991.

**The Labor Force Participation Rate**   The number of people who join the labor force is an indicator of the willingness of people of working age to take jobs. The **labor force participation rate** is the percentage of the working-age population who are members of the labor force. That is,

$$\frac{\text{Labor force}}{\text{participation rate}} = \frac{\text{Labor force}}{\text{Working-age population}} \times 100.$$

In 1996, the labor force was 133.9 million and the working-age population was 200.6 million. By using the above equation, you can calculate the labor force participation rate. It was 66.7 percent (133.9 million divided by 200.6 million, multiplied by 100).

The labor force participation rate (graphed in red and plotted on the left scale) has followed an upward trend and has increased from 59 percent during the early 1960s to 67 percent during the 1990s. It has also had some mild fluctuations. They result from unsuccessful job seekers becoming discouraged

**FIGURE 8.2**

Employment, Unemployment, and the Labor Force: 1960–1996

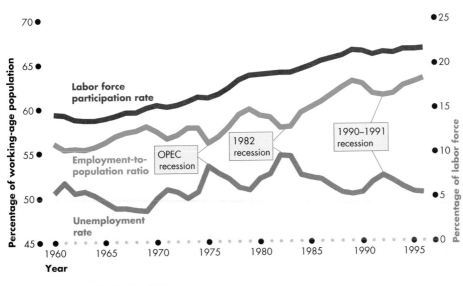

The unemployment rate increases in recessions and decreases in expansions. The labor force participation rate and the employment-to-population ratio have upward trends and fluctuate with the business cycle. The employment-to-population ratio fluctuates more than the labor force participation rate and reflects cyclical fluctuations in the unemployment rate. Fluctuations in the labor force participation rate arise mainly because of discouraged workers.

*Source: Economic Report of the President, 1997.*

workers. **Discouraged workers** are people who are available and willing to work but have not made specific efforts to find a job within the previous four weeks. These workers often temporarily leave the labor force during a recession and reenter during an expansion and become active job seekers.

**The Employment-to-Population Ratio** The number of people of working age who have jobs is an indicator of both the availability of jobs and the degree of match between people's skills and jobs. The **employment-to-population ratio** is the percentage of people of working age who have jobs. That is,

$$\text{Employment-to-population ratio} = \frac{\text{Number of people employed}}{\text{Working-age population}} \times 100.$$

In 1996, employment was 126.7 million and the working-age population was 200.6 million. By using the above equation, you can calculate the employment-to-population ratio. It was 63.2 percent (126.7 million divided by 200.6 million, multiplied by 100).

The employment-to-population ratio (graphed in blue and plotted against the left scale) has increased from 55 percent during the early 1960s to 63 percent during the 1990s. The increase in the employment-to-population ratio means that the U.S. economy has created jobs at a faster rate than the working-age population has grown. This labor market indicator also fluctuates, and its fluctuations coincide with but are opposite to those in the unemployment rate. It falls during a recession and increases during an expansion.

Why have the labor force participation rate and the employment-to-population ratio increased? The main reason is an increase in the number of women in the labor force. Figure 8.3 shows this increase. Between 1960 and 1996, the female labor force participation rate increased from 38 percent to 59 percent. Shorter work hours, higher productivity, and an increased emphasis on white-collar jobs have expanded the job opportunities and wages available to women. At the same time, technological advances have increased productivity in the home and freed up women's time to take jobs outside the home.

Figure 8.3 also shows another remarkable trend in the U.S. labor force: The labor force participation rate and the employment-to-population ratio for men have *decreased*. Between 1960 and 1996, the male labor force participation rate decreased from

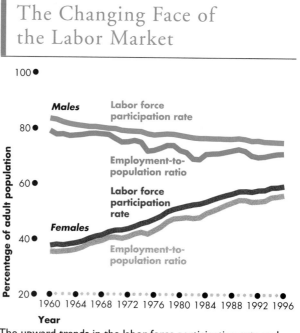

### FIGURE 8.3
## The Changing Face of the Labor Market

The upward trends in the labor force participation rate and the employment-to-population ratio are accounted for mainly by the increasing participation of women in the labor market. The male labor force participation rate and employment-to-population ratio have decreased.

*Source: Economic Report of the President, 1997.*

83 percent to 75 percent. It has decreased because increasing numbers of men are remaining in school longer and because some are retiring earlier.

### Aggregate Hours

The three labor market indicators that we've just examined are useful signs of the health of the economy and directly measure what matters to most people: jobs. But they don't tell us the quantity of labor used to produce GDP, and we cannot use them to calculate the productivity of labor. The productivity of labor is significant because it influences the wages people earn.

The reason why the number of people employed does not measure the quantity of labor employed is that jobs are not all the same. People in part-time jobs might work just a few hours a week. People in full-time jobs work around 35 to 40 hours a week.

And some people regularly work overtime. For example, a 7-11 store might hire six students who work for three hours a day each. Another 7-11 store might hire two full-time workers who work nine hours a day each. The number of people employed in these two stores is eight, but the total hours worked by six of the eight is the same as the total hours worked by the other two. To determine the total amount of labor used to produce GDP, we measure labor in hours rather than in jobs. **Aggregate hours** are the total number of hours worked by all the people employed, both full time and part time, during a year.

Figure 8.4(a) shows aggregate hours in the U.S. economy from 1960 to 1996. Like the employment-to-population ratio, aggregate hours have an upward trend. But aggregate hours have not grown as quickly as have the number of people employed. Between 1960 and 1996, the number of people employed in the U.S. economy increased by 90 percent. During that same period, aggregate hours increased by only 70 percent. Why the difference? Because average hours per worker decreased.

Figure 8.4(b) shows average hours per worker. After hovering at almost 39 hours a week during the early 1960s, average hours per worker decreased to about 34 hours a week during the 1990s. This shortening of the average workweek has arisen partly because of a decrease in the average hours worked by full-time workers but mainly because the number of part-time jobs has increased faster than the number of full-time jobs.

Fluctuations in aggregate hours and average hours per worker line up with the business cycle. Figure 8.4 highlights the past three recessions, during which aggregate hours decreased and average hours per worker decreased more quickly than trend.

## Wage Rates

The **real wage rate** is the quantity of goods and services that an hour's work can buy. It is equal to the money wage rate (dollars per hour) divided by the price level. If we use the GDP deflator to measure the price level, the real wage rate is expressed in 1992 dollars because the GDP deflator is 100 in 1992. The real wage is a significant economic variable because it measures the reward for labor.

What has happened to the real wage rate in the United States? Figure 8.5 answers this question. It shows four measures of the average hourly real wage rate in the U.S. economy between 1960 and 1996.

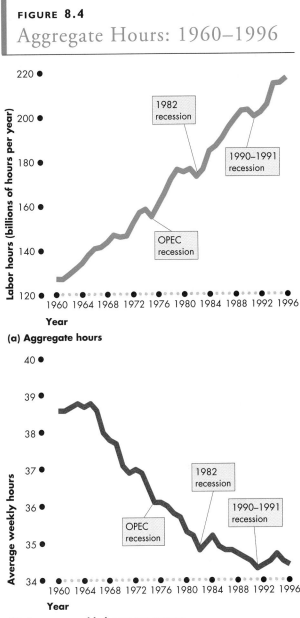

**FIGURE 8.4**

Aggregate Hours: 1960–1996

**(a) Aggregate hours**

**(b) Average weekly hours per person**

Aggregate hours (part a) measure the total labor used to produce real GDP more accurately than does the number of people employed because an increasing proportion of jobs are part time. Between 1960 and 1996, aggregate hours increased by an average of 1.5 percent a year. Fluctuations in aggregate hours coincide with business cycle fluctuations. Aggregate hours have increased at a slower rate than the number of jobs because the average workweek has shortened (part b).

*Source: Economic Report of the President, 1997, and the author's calculations.*

**FIGURE 8.5**

## Real Wage Rates: 1960–1996

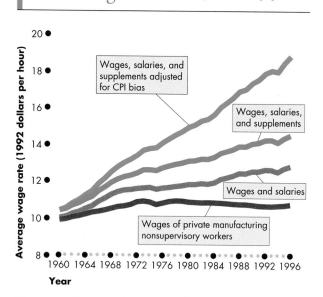

The average hourly real wage rate of private manufacturing nonsupervisory workers peaked in 1978 and then fell through 1993. Broader measures of the average hourly real wage rate increased. All the official measures show a productivity growth slowdown during the 1970s. An unofficial view is that inflation has been overestimated by 1.1 percent a year and the real wage rate has increased at roughly a constant rate.

Source: *Economic Report of the President*, 1997, and the author's calculations and assumptions.

The first measure of the real wage rate is the Department of Labor's calculation of the average hourly earnings of private manufacturing nonsupervisory workers. This measure increased to a maximum of $11.16 in 1978 (in 1992 dollars) and then followed a fifteen-year downward trend.

The second measure of the real wage rate is calculated by dividing total wages and salaries in the national income accounts by aggregate hours. This measure is broader than the first and includes the incomes of all types of labor, whether their rate of pay is calculated by the hour or not. This broader measure did not follow a downward trend, but its growth rate slowed during the mid-1970s and remained low through the early 1980s. It then speeded up during the late 1980s and 1990s.

An increasing proportion of labor compensation takes the form of fringe benefits such as pension contributions and the payment by employers of health insurance premiums. Figure 8.5 shows a third measure of the hourly real wage rate that reflects this trend. It is *total labor compensation*—wages, salaries, and benefits—divided by aggregate hours. This measure is the most comprehensive one available, and it shows that the real wage rate has increased. But it also shows that no matter how we measure the wage rate, the productivity growth slowdown also slowed real wage rate growth.

The decline in the average wage rate of manufacturing nonsupervisory workers and the slowdown in the growth rate of the broader measures of the average wage rate coincide with the *productivity growth slowdown* that you saw in Chapter 5. This productivity growth slowdown is the main reason for this behavior of average real wage rates. But whether this slowdown actually occurred depends on what actually happened to the price level. The three measures of real wages that we've just described are based on the official measure of inflation. If inflation has been overestimated by the 1.1 percent that the Boskin Commission (see Chapter 6, p. 131) estimates it has, then real wages have grown at a constant rate, as shown by the fourth line in Fig. 8.5.

## REVIEW

- The labor force participation rate and the employment-to-population ratio have an upward trend; the unemployment rate and employment-to-population ratio fluctuate with the business cycle.
- The female labor force participation rate has increased, but the male labor force participation rate has decreased.
- Aggregate hours have not grown as quickly as the number of people employed because the average workweek has shortened.
- Average hourly real wage rates have grown, but their growth rate slowed with the productivity growth slowdown of the 1970s.

Potential GDP depends on the full-employment quantity of labor. But at full employment, there is always some unemployment. Let's take a closer look at unemployment and see what determines its rate.

# Unemployment and Full Employment

How do people become unemployed, how long do they remain unemployed, and who is at greatest risk to become unemployed? Let's answer these questions by looking at the anatomy of unemployment.

## The Anatomy of Unemployment

People become unemployed if they:

1. Lose their jobs and search for another job
2. Leave their jobs and search for another job
3. Enter or reenter the labor force to search for a job

People end a spell of unemployment if they:

1. Are hired or recalled
2. Withdraw from the labor force

People who are laid off, either permanently or temporarily, from their jobs are called **job losers**. Some job losers become unemployed, but some immediately withdraw from the labor force. People who voluntarily quit their jobs are called **job leavers**. Like job losers, some job leavers become unemployed and search for a better job, while others withdraw from the labor force temporarily or permanently retire from work. People who enter or reenter the labor force are called **entrants** and **reentrants**. Entrants are mainly people who have just left school. Some entrants get a job right away and are never unemployed, but many spend time searching for their first job, and during this period they are unemployed. Reentrants are people who have previously withdrawn from the labor force. Most of these people are formerly discouraged workers. Figure 8.6 shows these labor market flows.

Let's see how much unemployment arises from the three different ways in which people can become unemployed.

**The Sources of Unemployment**   Figure 8.7 shows unemployment by reason for becoming unemployed. Job losers are the biggest source of unemployment. Also, their number fluctuates a great deal. In the recession of 1990–1991, on any given day, more

## FIGURE 8.6
## Labor Market Flows

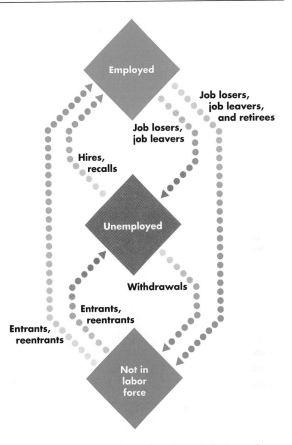

Unemployment results from employed people losing or leaving their jobs (job losers and job leavers) and from people entering the labor force (entrants and reentrants). Unemployment ends because people get hired or recalled or because they withdraw from the labor force.

than 5 million of the 9.4 million people who were unemployed were job losers. In contrast, in the peak year of 1989, fewer than 3 million of the 6.5 million people who were unemployed were job losers.

Entrants and reentrants also are a large component of the unemployed, and their number fluctuates mildly. On any given day, between 2.5 million and 3 million unemployed people are entrants and reentrants.

Job leavers are the smallest and most stable source of unemployment. On any given day, fewer than 1 million people are unemployed because they

FIGURE **8.7**

## Unemployment by Reasons

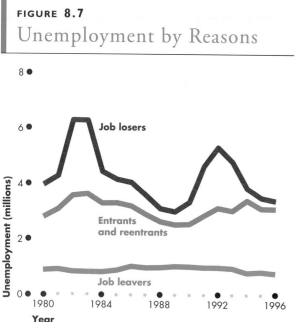

Everyone who is unemployed is either a job loser, a job leaver, or an entrant or reentrant into the labor force. Most of the unemployment that exists results from job loss. The number of job losers fluctuates more closely with the business cycle than do the numbers of job leavers and entrants and reentrants. Entrants and reentrants are the second most commonly unemployed people. Their number fluctuates with the business cycle because of discouraged workers. Job leavers are the least common unemployed people.

*Source: Economic Report of the President, 1997.*

FIGURE **8.8**

## Unemployment by Duration

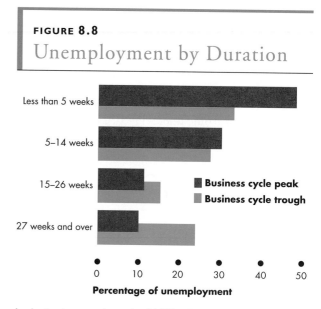

In the business cycle peak of 1989, when the unemployment rate was 5.3 percent, 49 percent of unemployment lasted for less than 5 weeks and 30 percent lasted for 5 to 14 weeks. So 79 percent of unemployment lasted for less than 15 weeks, and 21 percent lasted for 15 weeks or more. In the business cycle trough of 1983, when the unemployment rate was 9.7 percent, 33 percent of unemployment lasted for less than 5 weeks and 27 percent lasted for 5 to 14 weeks. So 60 percent of unemployment lasted for less than 15 weeks, and 40 percent lasted for 15 weeks or more.

*Source: Economic Report of the President, 1997.*

are job leavers. The number of job leavers is remarkably constant, although to the extent that it fluctuates, it does so in line with the business cycle: A slightly larger number of people leave their jobs in good times than in bad times.

**The Duration of Unemployment**   Some people are unemployed for a week or two, and others are unemployed for periods of a year or more. The longer the spell of unemployment, the greater the personal cost to the unemployed. The average duration of unemployment varies over the business cycle. Figure 8.8 compares the duration of unemployment in a business cycle peak in 1989, when the unemployment rate was low with that at the business cycle trough of 1983 when the unemployment rate was high. In 1989, when the unemployment rate hit a low of 5.3 percent, almost 50 percent of the unemployed were in that state

for less than 5 weeks and only 21 percent of the unemployed were jobless for longer than 15 weeks. In 1983, when unemployment reached a high of 9.7 percent, only 33 percent of the unemployed found a new job in less than 5 weeks and 40 percent were unemployed for more than 15 weeks. At both low and high unemployment rates, about 30 percent of the unemployed take between 5 weeks and 14 weeks to find a job.

**The Demographics of Unemployment**   Figure 8.9 shows unemployment for different demographic groups. The figure shows that high unemployment rates occur among young workers and also among blacks. In the business cycle trough in 1992, the unemployment rate of black teenagers was almost 40 percent. Even in 1996, when the unemployment rate was 5.4 percent, the rates for black teenagers barely fell. The unemployment rates for white teenagers are less than half those of black teenagers.

## FIGURE 8.9

# Unemployment by Demographic Group

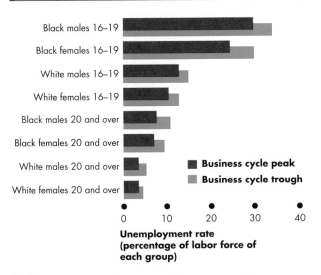

Black teenagers experience unemployment rates that average three times those of white teenagers, and the unemployment rates of teenagers are much higher than those of people aged 20 years and over. Even in a business cycle trough, when unemployment is at its highest rate, only 6 percent of whites aged 20 years and over are unemployed.

*Source: Economic Report of the President, 1997.*

The racial differences also exist for workers aged 20 years and over. The highest unemployment rates that whites 20 years and over experience are less than the lowest rates experienced by the other groups.

Why are unemployment rates of teenagers so high? There are three reasons. First, young people are still in the process of discovering what they are good at and trying different lines of work. So they leave their jobs more frequently than older workers do. Second, firms sometimes hire teenagers on a short-term or trial basis. So the rate of job loss is higher for teenagers than for other people. Third, most teenagers are not in the labor force but are in school. This fact means that the percentage of the teenage population that is unemployed is much lower than the percentage of the teenage labor force that is unemployed. In 1996, for example, 1,306,000 teenagers were unemployed and 6,499,000 were employed, and the teenage unemployment rate (all races) was 20 percent. But 11,000,000 teenagers were

in school. The ratio of teenage unemployment to the teenage population is less than 7.5 percent. That is, 20 percent of the teenage labor force or 7.5 percent of the teenage population is unemployed.

## Types of Unemployment

Unemployment is classified into three types that are based on its causes. They are:

- Frictional
- Structural
- Cyclical

**Frictional Unemployment    Frictional unemployment** is the unemployment that arises from normal labor turnover—from people entering and leaving the labor force and from the ongoing creation and destruction of jobs. Frictional unemployment is a permanent and healthy phenomenon in a dynamic, growing economy.

The unending flow of people into and out of the labor force and the processes of job creation and job destruction create the need for people to search for jobs and for businesses to search for workers. Always there are businesses with unfilled jobs and people seeking jobs. Look in your local newspaper, and you will see that there are always some jobs being advertised. Businesses don't usually hire the first person who applies for a job, and unemployed people don't usually take the first job that comes their way. Instead, both firms and workers spend time searching out what they believe will be the best match available. By this process of search, people can match their own skills and interests with the available jobs and find a satisfying job and income. While these unemployed people are searching, they are frictionally unemployed.

The amount of frictional unemployment depends on the rate at which people enter and reenter the labor force and on the rate at which jobs are created and destroyed. During the 1970s, the amount of frictional unemployment increased as a consequence of the postwar baby boom that began during the late 1940s. By the late 1970s, the baby boom had created a bulge in the number of people leaving school. As these people entered the labor force, the amount of frictional unemployment increased.

The amount of frictional unemployment is influenced by unemployment benefits. The greater the number of unemployed people covered by unemployment insurance and the more generous the unemployment benefit they receive, the longer is the average time taken in job search and the greater is the amount of frictional unemployment. In the United States in 1996, 36 percent of the unemployed received unemployment benefits. And the average benefit check was $160 a week. Canada and Western Europe have more generous benefits than those in the United States and have higher unemployment rates.

**Structural Unemployment**    **Structural unemployment** is the unemployment that arises when changes in technology or international competition change the skills needed to perform jobs or change the locations of jobs. Structural unemployment usually lasts longer than frictional unemployment because workers must usually retrain and possibly relocate to find a job. For example, when a steel plant in Gary, Indiana, is automated, some jobs in that city are destroyed. Meanwhile, new jobs for security guards, life-insurance salespeople, and retail clerks are created in Chicago, Indianapolis, and other cities. The unemployed former steelworkers remain unemployed for several months until they move, retrain, and get one of these jobs. Structural unemployment is painful, especially for older workers for whom the best available option might be to retire early but with a lower income than they had expected.

At some times, the amount of structural unemployment is modest. At other times, it is large, and at such times, structural unemployment can become a serious long-term problem. It was especially large during the late 1970s and early 1980s. During those years, oil price hikes and an increasingly competitive international environment destroyed jobs in traditional U.S. industries, such as auto and steel, and created jobs in new industries, such as electronics and bioengineering, as well as in banking and insurance. Structural unemployment was also present during the early 1990s as many businesses and governments "downsized."

**Cyclical Unemployment**    **Cyclical unemployment** is the fluctuating unemployment over the business cycle. Cyclical unemployment increases during a recession and decreases during an expansion. An auto worker who is laid off because the economy is in a recession and who gets rehired some months later when the expansion begins has experienced cyclical unemployment.

Figure 8.10, illustrates cyclical unemployment in the United States between 1980 and 1996. Part (a)

shows the fluctuations of real GDP around potential GDP. Part (b) shows fluctuations in the unemployment rate around a line labeled "Natural rate of unemployment." The **natural rate of unemployment** is the unemployment rate when there is no cyclical unemployment or, equivalently, when all the unemployment is frictional and structural. The divergence of the unemployment rate from the natural rate is cyclical unemployment. Notice that cyclical unemployment is *negative* at a business cycle peak. Total unemployment is less than the sum of frictional and structural unemployment.

In Fig. 8.10, the unemployment rate fluctuates around the natural rate of unemployment (part b) just as real GDP fluctuates around potential GDP (part a). When the unemployment rate equals the natural rate of unemployment, real GDP equals potential GDP. When the unemployment rate is less than the natural rate of unemployment, real GDP is greater than potential GDP. And when the unemployment rate is greater than the natural rate of unemployment, real GDP is less than potential GDP.

### Full Employment

There is always *some* unemployment—someone looking for a job or laid off and waiting to be recalled. So what do we mean by *full employment*? **Full employment** occurs when the unemployment rate equals the natural rate of unemployment.

There can be a lot of unemployment at full employment, and the term "full employment" is an example of a technical economic term that does not correspond with everyday language. The term "natural rate of unemployment" is another example of a technical economic term that does not correspond with everyday language. For most people—especially for unemployed workers—there is nothing *natural* about unemployment.

So why are do economists call a situation with a lot of unemployment one of full employment? And why is the unemployment at full employment "natural"?

The reason is that the complex machine that we call the U.S. economy undergoes constant changes in its players, structure, and direction. This process of change creates frictions and dislocations that are unavoidable. And they create unemployment.

In 1996, the U.S. economy employed 127 million people. More than 2.5 million retired during

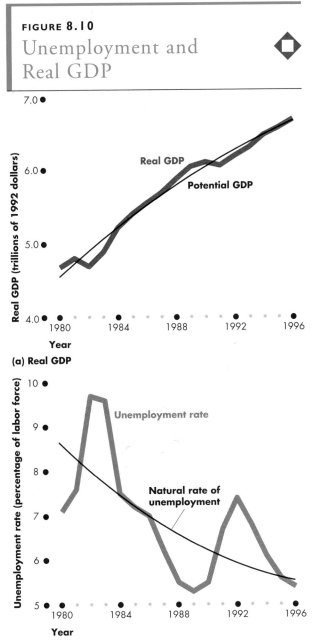

**FIGURE 8.10**

## Unemployment and Real GDP

(a) Real GDP

(b) Unemployment rate

As real GDP fluctuates around potential GDP (part a), the unemployment rate fluctuates around the natural rate of unemployment (part b). In the deep recession of 1982, unemployment reached almost 10 percent. In the milder recession of 1990–1991, the unemployment rate peaked at less than 8 percent. The natural rate of unemployment decreased during the 1980s and 1990s.

*Source: Economic Report of the President,* 1997, and the author's assumptions.

that year, and more than 3 million new workers entered the labor force. All these people worked in some 20 million businesses, some of which downsized and failed and others of which expanded. All these people and businesses produced goods and services valued at almost $7 trillion. The amount of unemployment that arises from the frictions and structural changes is "natural" unemployment.

There is not much controversy about the existence of a natural rate of unemployment. Nor is there much controversy that it fluctuates. The natural rate of unemployment arises from the existence of frictional and structural unemployment, and it fluctuates because the frictions and the amount of structural change fluctuate. But there is controversy about the magnitude of the natural rate of unemployment and the extent to which it fluctuates. Some economists believe that the natural rate of unemployment fluctuates frequently and that at times of rapid demographic and technological change, its rate can be high. Others think that it changes slowly.

In Fig. 8.10(b), the natural rate of unemployment is 8.5 percent in 1980 and it falls steadily through the 1980s and 1990s to less than 6 percent by 1996. This estimate of the natural rate of unemployment in the United States is one that many, but not all economists would accept.

### REVIEW

■ The people who become unemployed are job losers, job leavers, and labor force entrants or reentrants.

■ Unemployment can be *frictional* (normal labor market turnover), *structural* (a long-lasting decline in a region or industry), or *cyclical* (in line with the business cycle).

■ When all the unemployment is frictional and structural (when there is no cyclical unemployment), the unemployment rate equals the *natural rate of unemployment.*

■ When the unemployment rate is equal to the *natural rate of unemployment,* there is full employment.

We're now going to turn from describing to *explaining* the trends and fluctuations in employment, wage rates, and unemployment. We begin by explaining the trends in employment and wage rates.

## Explaining Employment and Wage Rates

WE CAN UNDERSTAND THE AMOUNT OF EMPLOY-ment and the wage rate by applying the model of demand and supply to the labor market.

### Demand and Supply in the Labor Market

Figure 8.11 illustrates the U.S. labor market at the beginning of 1995, when there was full employment. The *x*-axis measures the quantity of labor employed as *aggregate hours*—billions of hours per year. The *y*-axis measures the real wage rate. The figure has two curves: a labor demand curve and a labor supply curve. In the labor market, firms demand labor and households supply labor.

The **labor demand curve** shows the quantity of labor that firms plan to hire at each possible real wage rate. The lower the real wage rate, the greater is the quantity of labor that firms plan to hire. That is, the labor demand curve slopes downward, just like the demand curves you studied in Chapter 4 (on p. 70). The reason why the quantity of labor demanded depends on the *real* wage rate is that firms care only about the amount they pay for labor relative to the amount they get for their output. If money wages and prices change in the same proportion, the quantity of labor that firms plan to hire is unaffected.

The **labor supply curve** shows the quantity of labor that households plan to supply at each possible real wage rate. The higher the real wage rate, the greater is the quantity of labor that households plan to supply. That is, the labor supply curve slopes upward like the supply curves in Chapter 4 (on pp. 74–75). The reason why the quantity of labor supplied depends on the *real* wage rate is that households care only about the amount they are paid for their labor relative to the price they must pay for the things they buy. If money wages and prices change in the same proportion, the quantity of labor that households plan to supply is unaffected.

The reason why the quantity of labor demanded increases as the real wage rate decreases—why the labor demand curve slopes downward—is that firms strive to maximize profit. If the wage rate at which firms can hire labor falls relative to the price they can get for their output, the real wage rate decreases and

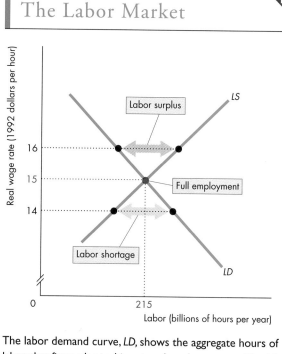

**FIGURE 8.11**

## The Labor Market

The labor demand curve, *LD*, shows the aggregate hours of labor that firms plan to hire at each real wage rate. The labor supply curve, *LS*, shows the aggregate hours that households plan to work at each real wage rate. In equilibrium, the real wage rate is $15 an hour and 215 billion hours of labor are employed.

they have an incentive to expand production and hire more labor. The reason why the quantity of labor supplied increases as the real wage rate increases—why the labor supply curve slopes upward—is that households strive to use their scarce time in the most efficient way. If the wage rate they are offered rises relative to the prices they must pay for goods and services, the real wage rate increases and they have a stronger incentive to work.

Labor demand and labor supply determine the level of employment, unemployment, and real wage rate. In Fig. 8.11, at wage rates below $15 an hour, for example at $14 an hour, there is a labor shortage. People find jobs easily, but businesses are short of labor. But this situation doesn't last long. Firms offer higher wage rates to attract labor, and the real wage rate rises toward the equilibrium of $15 an hour.

At wage rates above $15 an hour, for example at $16 an hour, there is a labor surplus. People have a hard time finding jobs, and businesses can easily hire all the labor they want. Firms now offer lower wages, and the real wage rate falls toward the equilibrium wage rate of $15 an hour.

At a wage rate of $15 an hour, the quantity demanded equals the quantity supplied. There is neither a shortage nor a surplus of labor.

## The Trends in Employment and Wage Rates

We can use the model of labor demand and labor supply to understand the long-term trends in aggregate hours and real wage rates. We saw in Fig. 8.4 that aggregate hours have increased steadily over the years. In 1960, aggregate hours were 18 billion, and in 1996, they were 218 billion. We also saw in Fig. 8.5 that the real wage rate has increased. The economy-wide average real wage rate including supplements increased from $11 an hour in 1960 to $15 an hour in 1996.

Figure 8.12 shows how these changes came about. In 1960, the labor demand curve was $LD_{60}$ and the labor supply curve was $LS_{60}$. The equilibrium real wage rate was $11 an hour, and 18 billion hours of labor were employed.

Throughout the period since 1960, labor has become more and more productive. The reason is that capital per worker has increased and technology has advanced. We will explore these reasons for this increased productivity in Chapter 10. But regardless of the reasons, the effect of an increase in labor productivity is an increase in the demand for labor. If an hour of labor can produce more output, firms are willing to pay a higher wage rate to hire that hour of labor. This increase in demand is shown by a rightward shift in the labor demand curve from $LD_{60}$ to $LD_{96}$.

At the same time as labor became more productive and the demand for it increased, the population grew and so did the working-age population. With a larger working-age population, the supply of labor increased. This increase is shown by the rightward shift in the labor supply curve from $LS_{60}$ to $LS_{96}$.

To predict the effects of an increase in *both* demand and supply, we need to know which had the larger increase. In this case, the increase in the demand for labor was larger than the increase in supply. As a result, both the quantity of labor employed and the average real wage rate increased.

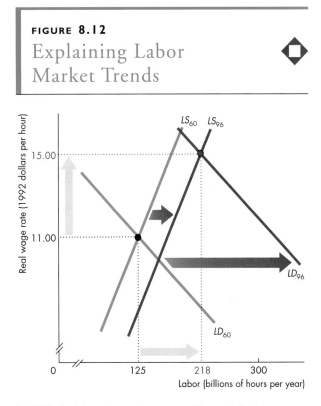

### FIGURE 8.12
## Explaining Labor Market Trends

In 1960, the labor demand curve was $LD_{60}$ and the labor supply curve was $LS_{60}$. The equilibrium real wage rate was $11 an hour, and 125 billion hours of labor were employed. Over the years, advances in technology increased the productivity of labor and increased the demand for labor. The demand curve shifted rightward to $LD_{96}$. At the same time, an increase in the working-age population increased the supply of labor and the labor supply curve shifted rightward to $LS_{96}$. But the labor supply curve shifted by less than the labor demand curve. Because both labor demand and labor supply increased, the quantity of labor employed increased. And because labor demand increased by more than labor supply, the real wage rate increased.

## Changes in the Distribution of Jobs and Wage Rates

When we looked at the trends in wage rates, we saw that while total hourly compensation has grown, the average hourly wage rates of manufacturing non-supervisory workers has decreased. These changes have brought relative economic hardship to a large number of families. Why have these changes in wage rates occurred?

Figure 8.13 helps us to answer this question. It shows how structural change has increased some wages and employment opportunities and decreased others. The figure describes the U.S. labor market during the 1980s and 1990s. Part (a) shows the labor market in manufacturing industries—those that produce goods—and part (b) shows the labor market in service industries. In each part, the $y$-axis measures the real wage rate and the $x$-axis measures the quantity of labor in terms of workers, not hours.

In 1980, the labor supply curve in manufacturing was $LS_M$ and in services it was $LS_{80}$. The labor demand curve in each sector was $LD_{80}$. In manufacturing, the average real wage rate was $12.60 an hour and 20 million people had jobs. In services, the average real wage rate was $10.00 an hour and 18 million people had jobs.

During the 1980s and through 1996, technological change and international competition brought a decrease in the demand for labor in manufacturing. The demand curve shifted leftward to become $LD_{96}$ in part (a). With no change (assumed) in supply, the real wage rate fell to $11.80 and the number of people with jobs in manufacturing decreased to 18 million. The 2 million people who lost their jobs had to search for a job in the service industries.

The same technological change and international competition that destroyed jobs in manufacturing created jobs in services. The demand for labor in services increased, and the labor demand curve shifted rightward. By 1996, the demand curve had become $LD_{96}$ in part (b).

As people who had lost their jobs in manufacturing looked for jobs in services and as the growing population entered the labor market, the supply of labor in services increased. The labor supply curve shifted rightward. By 1996, the supply curve had become $LS_{96}$ in part (b).

The increase in labor supply was smaller than the increase in labor demand. As a result, the real wage rate increased to $10.80 and the number of people with jobs in services increased to 30 million.

The changes that we've just looked at break the labor market into just two sectors. In reality, it has many sectors and reallocations of labor take place among the many sectors. Even while the total number of jobs in services was increasing, some service jobs were being destroyed. For example, jobs for directory assistance operators and television service engineers virtually disappeared, while jobs for telephone sales persons and ATM service engineers increased.

**FIGURE 8.13**

## Labor Force Reallocation

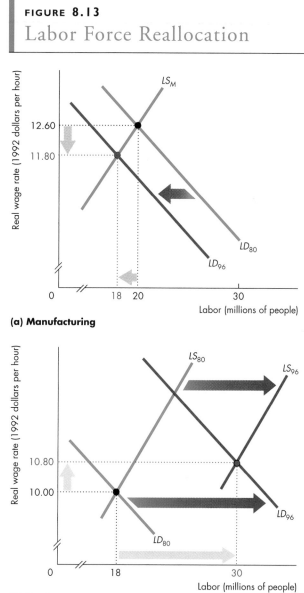

**(a) Manufacturing**

**(b) Services**

Between 1980 and 1996, the demand for labor in manufacturing decreased (part a) and the labor demand curve shifted leftward from $LD_{80}$ to $LD_{96}$. In services (part b), the demand for labor increased and the demand curve shifted rightward from $LD_{80}$ to $LD_{96}$. In manufacturing, the supply of labor was constant (an assumption) at $LS_M$, but in services the supply of labor increased and the supply curve shifted rightward from $LS_{80}$ to $LS_{96}$. In manufacturing, employment and the real wage rate decreased. In services, demand increased by more than supply, so both employment and the real wage rate increased.

## REVIEW

- The labor demand curve shows the quantity of labor that firms plan to hire at each real wage rate. The labor demand curve slopes downward because a fall in the real wage rate gives firms a stronger incentive to increase production and hire more labor.
- The labor supply curve shows the quantity of labor that households plan to supply at each real wage rate. The labor supply curve slopes upward because a rise in the real wage rate gives households a stronger incentive to work.
- Labor demand and labor supply curves interact to determine the level of employment and the real wage rate.
- Both the real wage rate and employment have increased because labor demand and labor supply have increased but labor demand has increased by more than labor supply.

We've now studied the main trends in employment and wage rates, and we have seen how the demand and supply model can help us to understand those trends. Our next task is to explain unemployment.

## Explaining Unemployment

WE'VE DESCRIBED HOW PEOPLE BECOME unemployed—they lose jobs, leave jobs, and enter or reenter the labor force—and we've classified unemployment—it can be frictional, structural, and cyclical. But describing and classifying unemployment do not *explain* it. Why is there always some unemployment? Why does its rate fluctuate? Why was the unemployment rate lower during the 1960s than during the 1980s and early 1990s?

If we want to design policies that can reduce unemployment, we must answer these questions. We must understand the forces that generate unemployment and that cause its rate to change. Unemployment is ever present, and its rate fluctuates for three reasons:

- Job search
- Job rationing
- Sticky wages

## Job Search

**Job search** is the activity of people looking for acceptable vacant jobs. There might be as many jobs as there are people looking for jobs, but there are always some people who have not yet found suitable jobs. The reason is that the labor market is in a constant state of change. Jobs are destroyed and created as businesses fail and new businesses start up and as new technologies and new markets evolve. In the process, people lose jobs. Other people enter or reenter the labor market. Still other people leave their jobs to look for better ones, and others retire. This constant churning in the labor market means that there are always some people looking for jobs, and these people are the unemployed. Job search takes place even when the quantity of labor demanded equals the quantity supplied. In this situation, some people have not yet found a job and some jobs have not yet been filled.

Job search explains frictional, structural, and cyclical unemployment. All three types of unemployment occur because job losers, job leavers, and labor force entrants and reentrants don't know about all the jobs available to them, so they must take time to *search* for an acceptable one. This search takes time, and the average amount of time varies. When there is a small amount of structural change and when the economy is close to a business cycle peak, search times are low and the unemployment rate is low. But when structural change is rapid and when the economy is in a recession, search times increase and the unemployment rate increases.

Although job search is cyclical, it also has slower changes that bring changes in the natural rate of unemployment. The main sources of these slower changes are:

- Demographic change
- Unemployment benefits
- Structural change

**Demographic Change**   An increase in the proportion of the population that is of working age brings an increase in the entry rate into the labor force and an increase in the unemployment rate. This factor has been important in the U.S. labor market in recent years. The bulge in the birth rate that occurred in the late 1940s and early 1950s increased the proportion of new entrants into the labor force during the 1970s and brought an increase in the unemployment rate.

As the birth rate declined, the bulge moved into higher age groups and the proportion of new entrants declined during the 1980s. During this period, the natural rate of unemployment decreased.

Another demographic trend is an increase in the number of households with two paid workers. When unemployment comes to one of these workers, it is possible, with income still flowing in, to take longer to find a new job. This factor might have increased frictional unemployment.

**Unemployment Benefits**  The length of time that an unemployed person spends searching for a job depends, in part, on the opportunity cost of job search. With no income during a period of unemployment, an unemployed person faces a high opportunity cost of job search. In this situation, search is likely to be short and an unattractive job is likely to be accepted as a better alternative to continuing a costly search process. With generous unemployment insurance benefits, the opportunity cost of job search is low. In this situation, search is likely to be prolonged. An unemployed worker will hold out for the ideal job.

The opportunity cost of job search fell during the late 1960s and 1970s as unemployment benefits were extended to larger groups. As a result, the natural rate of unemployment increased during those years.

**Structural Change**  Labor market flows and unemployment are influenced by the pace and direction of technological change. Sometimes, technological change brings a *structural slump*, a condition in which some industries die and some regions suffer while other industries are born and other regions flourish. When these events occur, labor turnover is high—the flows between employment and unemployment increase and the pool of those unemployed increases. The decline of industries in the "Rust Belt" and the rapid expansion of industries in the "Sun Belt" illustrate the effects of technological change and were a source of the increase in unemployment during the 1970s and early 1980s. The analysis of the changes in the reallocation of the U.S. labor force from manufacturing to services (Fig. 8.13) is also an example of the effects of technological change. While these changes were taking place, the natural rate of unemployment increased.

Job search unemployment is present even when the quantity of labor demanded equals the quantity supplied. The other possible explanations of unemployment are based on the view that the quantity of labor demanded does not always equal the quantity supplied.

## Job Rationing

**Job rationing** is the practice of paying employed people a wage that creates an excess supply of labor and a shortage of jobs and increases the natural rate of unemployment. When there is job rationing, there are fewer available jobs than there are people looking for jobs. Three reasons why jobs might be rationed are:

- Efficiency wages
- Insider interest
- The minimum wage

**Efficiency Wages**  Some firms can increase their labor productivity by paying wages above the competitive wage rate. The higher wage attracts a higher quality of labor, encourages greater work effort, and cuts down on the firm's labor turnover rate and recruiting costs. But the higher wage also adds to the firm's costs. So a firm offers a wage rate that balances productivity gains and additional costs. The wage rate that maximizes profit is called the **efficiency wage**.

The efficiency wage might be higher than the competitive equilibrium wage. The wage cannot be lower than the competitive wage because competition for labor would bid the wage up. With an efficiency wage above the competitive wage, some labor is unemployed and employed people have an incentive to perform well to avoid being fired.

**Insider Interest**  Why don't firms cut their wage costs by offering jobs to unemployed workers for a lower wage rate than that paid to existing workers? One explanation, called **insider-outsider theory**, is that to be productive, new workers—outsiders—must receive on-the-job training from existing workers—insiders. If insiders train outsiders who are paid a lower wage, the insiders' bargaining position is weakened. So insiders will train outsiders only if everyone receives the same rate of pay.

When bargaining for a pay deal, unions represent the interests of insiders only. The agreed-on wage exceeds the competitive wage and there are always outsiders who are unable to find work. So the pursuit of rational self-interest by insiders is a further reason why the natural rate of unemployment is not zero.

**The Minimum Wage**  A minimum wage is a wage rate legislated by the federal government. The minimum wage is usually set at a rate that is higher than what the market would determine. As a result, the quantity of labor supplied exceeds the quantity demanded. The minimum wage explains why the unemployment rate of young people is high.

Job rationing is a possible reason why the natural rate of unemployment is high. It is a source of persistent and possibly large amount of frictional unemployment. The distinction between unemployment that arises from job search and that which arises from job rationing can be illustrated by musical chairs. If there are equal numbers of chairs (jobs) and players (people who want jobs), when the music stops and everyone searches for a chair, everyone finds one. If there are more players than chairs, when the music stops and everyone searches for a chair, some players can't find one. The chairs are rationed.

Job rationing is a source of long-term frictional unemployment. The final explanation of unemployment—sticky wages—is one reason why unemployment is cyclical.

## FIGURE 8.14
## Sticky Wages and Unemployment

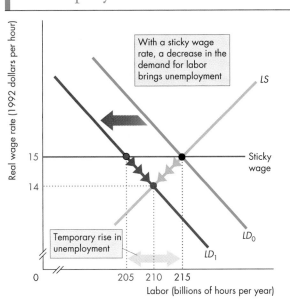

When the demand for labor is $LD_0$ and the supply of labor is $LS$, employment is 215 billion hours and the real wage rate is $15 an hour. The demand for labor decreases and the demand curve shifts leftward to $LD_1$, but the real wage rate is sticky at $15 an hour. Employment decreases to 205 billion hours, and there is a surplus of 10 billion hours—10 billion hours of labor are unemployed. Eventually, the real wage rate falls to $14 an hour and employment increases to 210 billion hours.

## Sticky Wages

Wages do not change as often as prices do. So if the demand for labor decreases, the equilibrium real wage rate falls, but the actual real wage rate does not change immediately. Rather, it gradually falls toward its new equilibrium, and it takes some time to get there. During this process of gradual wage adjustment, there is a surplus of labor and unemployment is temporarily high.

Figure 8.14 illustrates this type of unemployment. Initially, the demand for labor is $LD_0$ and the supply of labor is $LS$. The equilibrium level of employment is 215 billion hours, and the real wage rate is $15 an hour. The demand for labor then decreases, and the demand curve shifts leftward to $LD_1$. But the real wage rate is temporarily sticky at $15 an hour. At this real wage rate and in the new conditions, firms are willing to hire only 205 billion hours of labor. So there is a surplus of 10 billion hours and unemployment is created.

Eventually, as prices and wages change, the real wage rate falls to its equilibrium level. In this example, when the real wage rate has fallen to $14 an hour, the quantity of labor demanded equals the quantity supplied and the surplus of labor vanishes.

## R E V I E W

■ Unemployment is always present because of job search.

■ The natural rate of unemployment depends on the age distribution of the population, unemployment benefits, and structural change.

■ Some unemployment results from job rationing and sticky wages.

◆ You have now completed your study of labor markets. Before you leave this topic, take a look at *Reading Between the Lines* on pp. 186–187, which examines how the computer and information revolution of the 1980s and 1990s has changed wages and employment.

You now know how the quantity of labor is determined. Your next task is to study the factors that influence the quantity of capital. Capital is accumulated as a result of saving and investment decisions. We study these decisions in Chapter 9.

# Policy
## WATCH

## Technological Change and Jobs

## Essence of THE STORY

■ Job cuts surged in July 1996, despite labor shortages in some industries.

■ According to a Chicago-based placement firm, job cuts increased by 79.7 percent from July 1995 to July 1996.

■ Job cuts in the first seven months of 1996 numbered 312,356, an increase of 32.5 percent over the same period in 1995.

■ The number of job cuts in July was partially attributable to 7,000 job cuts at Digital Equipment Corp. and 6,100 job cuts at AlliedSignal Inc.

■ Hardest hit in July was the computer industry, which cut 8,804 jobs.

THE DALLAS MORNING NEWS, AUGUST 8, 1996

# July Job Cuts Rise 80 Percent

Despite labor shortages in some industries, announced job cuts in July continued to surge, Challenger, Gray & Christmas, Inc. said Wednesday.

The Chicago-based outplacement firm's latest report on layoffs said last month's total of job cuts was 41,843, up 79.7 percent from 23,283 in July 1995, and up 4.2 percent from 40,163 in June of this year.

July represented the largest number of job cuts since January, when AT&T announced massive job cuts.

The firm said that from January through July, job cuts averaged 44,622 per month, 32.6 percent higher than the monthly average of 33,654 for the same period in 1995. The monthly job cut average for the first seven months of 1993, the largest job cut year of the decade, was 50,516.

On average, there were 2,096 job cuts per business day between Jan. 2 and July 31, the firm said.

The increase in July job cuts comes on the heels of stunning figures from the first half of the year which showed job cuts rising sharply from 1995. Including the July data, the total for the first seven months of this year was 312,356, 32.5 percent higher than 235,582 in the same period last year. The total 12-month figure in 1995 was 439,882.

The tally of jobs lost in July was boosted by Digital Equipment Corp. and Allied-Signal Inc., which announced 7,000 and 6,100 job cuts, respectively, Challenger said.

The industry hardest hit in July was the computer industry, with 8,804 casualties.

# Economic

## A N A L Y S I S

■ Most of the job cuts reported in the news article create *structural* unemployment.

■ Figure 1 shows the rate of job destruction in U.S. manufacturing industries during the 1980s. These data are compiled infrequently and are not yet available for the 1990s. But the 1980s data tell us a lot.

■ The rate of job destruction fluctuates with the business cycle. But on the average, about 1 percent of jobs get destroyed each month.

■ Much of the job destruction arises because technological advances enable companies to produce more output with fewer workers. This process has been going on almost uninterrupted since the Industrial Revolution around 1760.

■ With a normal rate of job destruction, more than a million people would lose their jobs during July 1996.

■ The announced job cutbacks reported in this news article (and frequently reported in the media) are a tiny proportion of total job losses.

The reported job cuts are the losses in big companies that are shedding labor in large numbers.

■ Most job losses and most new jobs that are created are unreported because they happen in small companies.

■ Job cuts are serious for the people whom they affect. But they would be even more serious if jobs were not being created in even larger numbers.

■ Figure 1 also shows the rate of job creation and the net change in the number of jobs in manufacturing. In most years, more jobs were destroyed than created in the manufacturing industries. But (not shown in the figure) more jobs were created in services than the number lost in manufacturing.

■ Technological change creates more jobs than it destroys. It increases the productivity of labor and leads to an increase in the demand for labor.

■ Figure 2 shows the total amount of job creation and job destruction in manufacturing during the 1980s and the relationship between this number and the unem-

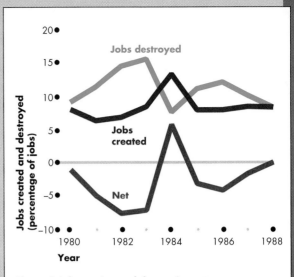

Figure 1 Job creation and destruction rates

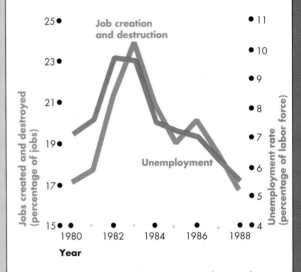

Figure 2 Job creation and destruction and unemployment

ployment rate. It shows that the total amount of job creation and job destruction fluctuates in line with fluctuations in the unemployment rate.

## You're

### THE VOTER

■ What policy actions, if any, can the government take to protect people from job losses?

■ List all the policy actions you can think of, and attach to each policy its pros and cons.

## SUMMARY

## Key Points

### Employment and Wages (pp. 170–174)

- The labor force participation rate and the employment-to-population ratio have an upward trend, and fluctuate with the business cycle.
- The labor force participation rate has increased for females and decreased for males.
- Aggregate hours have an upward trend, and they fluctuate with the business cycle.
- Based on the CPI, real hourly wage rates in manufacturing fell after 1973. Broader real wage measures did not fall, but their growth rates slowed.

### Unemployment and Full Employment (pp. 175–179)

- People are constantly entering and leaving the state of unemployment.
- The duration of unemployment fluctuates over the business cycle. But the demographic patterns of unemployment are constant.
- Unemployment can be frictional, structural, and cyclical.
- When all the unemployment is frictional and structural, unemployment is at its natural rate and there is *full employment*. The natural rate of unemployment fluctuates because of fluctuations in frictional and structural unemployment.

### Explaining Employment and Wage Rates (pp. 180–183)

- The higher the real wage rate, the smaller is the quantity of labor demanded and the greater is the quantity of labor supplied.
- Labor demand and labor supply determine the level of employment and the real wage rate.
- The average real wage rate and employment increase because labor demand increases by more than labor supply.
- Labor demand increases because capital accumulation and technological change make labor more productive. Labor supply increases because the working-age population grows.

### Explaining Unemployment (pp. 183–185)

- Unemployment arises from job search, job rationing, and sticky wages.
- Job search unemployment changes slowly because of changes in demographic trends, unemployment benefits, and the pace of structural change.
- Job rationing can arise from efficiency wages, insider interest, and the minimum wage.

## Key Figures ◆

## Key Terms

# QUESTIONS

1. What are the categories that the Census Bureau uses in its monthly survey to classify the population?
2. Define the unemployment rate, the labor force participation rate, and the employment-to-population ratio.
3. What do the unemployment rate, the labor force participation rate, and the employment-to-population ratio tell us about labor market performance?
4. What are discouraged workers? Does the official unemployment measure include them?
5. Define aggregate hours. Why might aggregate hours be a more accurate measure of the quantity of labor than the number of people employed?
6. Name four measures of the average hourly real wage rate and describe how each one changed between 1970 and 1996. Which of them increased fastest?
7. How do people become unemployed? What is the most common way and what is the one that fluctuates most?
8. How does the duration of unemployment vary over the business cycle?
9. Which groups of the population experience the highest unemployment rates?
10. Distinguish between frictional, structural, and cyclical unemployment.
11. What is the natural rate of unemployment, what is full employment, and how are the two related?
12. What is the relationship between the unemployment rate and real GDP over the business cycle?
13. Explain how demand and supply in the labor market determine the level of employment and the real wage rate.
14. What are the main changes in demand and supply in the labor market that have brought employment growth?
15. What are the main changes in demand and supply in the labor market that have brought a slowdown in the rate of increase in real wage rates and a fall in some real wage rates?
16. What are the three main explanations of unemployment?

# PROBLEMS

1. The Census Bureau measured the following numbers in December 1996: labor force, 135 million; employment, 127.9 million; working-age population, 201.6 million. Calculate for that month the:
   a. Unemployment rate.
   b. Labor force participation rate.
   c. Employment-to-population ratio.
2. During 1996, the working-age population increased by 2.1 million, employment increased by 2.8 million, and the labor force increased by 2.6 million. What happened to the level of unemployment and what do you believe happened to the number of discouraged workers?
3. In January 1996, the unemployment rate was 5.7 percent. In December 1996, the unemployment rate was 5.3 percent. What do you believe happened in 1996 to the numbers of:
   a. Job losers?
   b. Job leavers?
   c. Labor force entrants and reentrants?
4. The labor market in an economy is described by the figure. Initially, demand is $LD_0$, but then it decreases to $LD_1$.

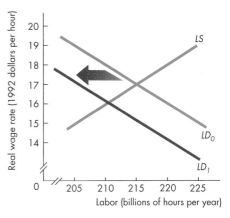

   a. What, initially, are the employment hours and real wage rate?
   b. What factors could have changed to decrease the demand for labor?
   c. When the demand for labor decreases, does the supply of labor change? Explain your answer
   d. When the demand for labor decreases, does the quantity of labor supplied change? Explain your answer.

e. When the demand for labor decreases, what are the new level of employment hours and the new real wage rate if wages are flexible?

5. Suppose that the labor market shown in the figure in problem 4 is that in manufacturing. Suppose that the labor market for services is exactly like that for manufacturing except that the demand for labor increases by exactly the same amount as the decrease in demand in manufacturing.
   a. Draw the new demand curve and answer the same questions as in problem 4.
   b. What do you predict will happen to the unemployment rate during the time the labor markets for manufacturing and services adjust to the changes in demand?

6. Suppose in problem 4 that when the demand for labor decreases, the real wage rate is sticky and does not change.
   a. What is the level of employment hours?
   b. What is the quantity of employment hours supplied?
   c. What is the number of hours that are unemployed?
   d. During the time that the real wage rate is stuck above its equilibrium level, is the unemployment rate greater than, less than, or equal to the natural rate of unemployment?

7. You are told the following facts about the economy of Big Time: All the people work in either fishing, Big Time's traditional economic activity, or video game production, Big Time's new-found bonanza industry. The working-age population is growing by 1 million people a year and the number of jobs is growing by 1.2 million a year. But jobs in fishing are disappearing at a rate of 2 million a year, and jobs are being created in video game production at a rate of 3.2 million a year. What do you predict is happening to wage rates, employment, and unemployment in Big Time both in total and in its two industries. Draw two labor market figures, one for the fishing industry and one for the video games industry, and show how the demand and supply curves are shifting and how wage rates and employment levels are changing.

http://hepg.awl.com/parkin/econ100

# CRITICAL THINKING

1. Study *Reading Between the Lines* on pp. 186–187 and then answer the following questions:
   a. What types of jobs have been destroyed and created in the United States in the past 15 years?
   b. What types of businesses create and destroy jobs? Do all the jobs created get reported in the newspapers? Explain why or why not.
   c. What information would you need that is not supplied in the news article to determine whether the job losses reported will create frictional, structural, or cyclical unemployment?
   d. Which fluctuates most, the rate of job creation or the rate of job destruction?

2. Visit the Web site of the Bureau of Labor Statistics at http://stats.bls.gov and click on the "Regional Information" button. You will see a map that enables you to find labor market data for your own region.
   a. What have been the trends in employment, unemployment, and labor force participation in your own region during the past two years?
   b. Based on what you know about your own region, how would you set about explaining these trends?
   c. Try to identify those industries that have expanded most and those that have shrunk.
   d. What are the problems with your own regional labor market that you think need state government action to resolve?
   e. What actions do you think your state government must take to resolve them? Answer this question by using the demand and supply model of the labor market and predict the effects of the actions you prescribe.
   f. Compare the labor market performance of your own region with that of the nation as a whole.
   g. If your region is performing better than the national average, to what do attribute the success? If your region is performing worse than the national average, to what do attribute its problems? What federal actions are needed in your regional labor market?

# Chapter 9

# Capital, Investment, and Saving

The 1996 Olympic Games in Atlanta were watched, as they happened, by more than two billion people (two fifths of the world's population). This media event was made possible by an enormous investment in a global video network. An even larger investment in a vast network of computers, telecommunications equipment, and databases enables a grade school student in Alice Springs, Australia, to click her mouse button and surf the Internet or send an e-mail message to her "pen-friend" in Akron, Ohio. How do businesses make the investment decisions that create the amazing tools that are building a global village? ◆ Each one of us decides how much income to save and how much to spend on consumption goods and services. Some of us spend everything we earn and can't wait for the next payday to come around. Others of us save large amounts of income. How do people make their saving decisions? ◆ Investment and saving decisions combine to determine interest rates and the long-term growth of potential GDP. Fluctuations in investment create cycles in real GDP. How do investment and saving decisions influence the interest rate you pay on your credit card balance and the interest rate you'll pay when you take a mortgage to buy a home? How do they influence the size of your pension when you retire? ◆ In this chapter, we study the decisions that determine the amount of capital in the economy and the return—the interest rate—that capital earns. When you have completed your study of this topic, you will be ready to learn about the forces that make potential GDP grow, which are explained in Chapter 10. ◆ We begin by looking at some facts about investment, capital, and interest rates in the United States and around the world.

## Building the Global Village

### After studying this chapter, you will be able to:

■ Describe the growth and fluctuations of investment and the capital stock

■ Describe the fluctuations in the real interest rate

■ Explain how investment decisions are made

■ Explain how household saving decisions are made

■ Explain how investment and saving determine the real interest rate

■ Explain how government influences the real interest rate, saving, and investment

■ Explain how international borrowing and lending are determined

## Capital and Interest

THE TOTAL QUANTITY OF PLANT, EQUIPMENT, buildings, and inventories is the economy's **capital stock**. The purchase of new capital, called **gross investment**, increases the capital stock, and the wearing out and scrapping of existing capital, called **depreciation**, decreases the capital stock. The capital stock increases by the amount of **net investment,** which equals gross investment minus depreciation. (See Chapter 6, p. 118.)

Figure 9.1 shows investment and capital in the United States from 1970 through 1996. In part (a), you can see that gross investment has grown and fluctuated. In the recession years (1975, 1982, and 1991), gross investment decreased, and in the expansion years, it grew quickly. Part of gross investment replaces worn-out capital. The green line labeled "Replacement investment" in Fig. 9.1(a) shows this amount. This component of investment has grown steadily, and it does not fluctuate much.

Figure 9.1(a) also shows net investment, the addition to the capital stock. Net investment has fluctuated like gross investment. In the recession years, net investment falls. It was $0.2 trillion in 1991, a recession year, but was almost $0.5 trillion in 1996, an expansion year.

Figure 9.1(b) shows how the capital stock has changed over the years. It has grown every year and increased from about $8 trillion in 1970 to almost $17 trillion in 1996. The growth of the capital stock slowed during the recessions, but the growth rate has always been positive.

The reason why the capital stock has grown every year is that net investment has been positive. The reason why the fluctuations in the growth rate of the capital stock are small is that net investment is small relative to the capital stock. When net investment decreases during a recession, the capital stock almost stops growing. When net investment increases during an expansion, the capital stock grows at about 3 percent a year. On the average, the capital stock has grown at around 2.5 percent a year.

Figure 9.1 shows both private and government investment and the privately owned and government-owned capital stock. Private investment is business investment plus investment in new homes and additions to inventories. Government investment is the part of government purchases that creates *social infrastructure capital.* The most basic component of social

FIGURE **9.1**

## Investment and the Capital Stock: 1970–1996

**(a) Investment**

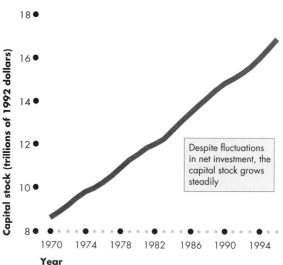

**(b) Capital stock**

Net investment fluctuates between less than $0.2 trillion a year in a recession and almost $0.5 trillion a year in an expansion. The capital stock has grown steadily to almost $17 trillion in 1996.

*Source:* U.S. Department of Commerce, *National Income and Product Accounts of the United States* and *The Capital Stock of the United States,* and author's assumptions and calculations.

infrastructure capital is the courts and the justice system that establish and enforce property rights. Without this social infrastructure our economy could not have developed. Other social infrastructure capital, for example, highways, dams and canals, schools, and state universities, increase potential GDP. National defense capital is also included in government investment.

## Investment Around the World

Figure 9.2 compares investment in the United States with that in other parts of the world. Here, investment includes both business investment and government investment. And so that we can make comparisons, we measure investment as a percentage of GDP—called the investment rate.

### FIGURE 9.2

## Investment in the United States and World: 1970–1995

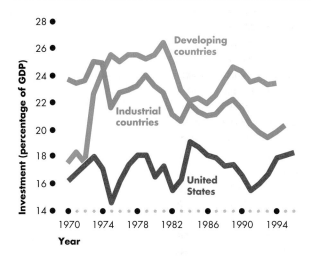

Here, investment includes business investment and government investment. Investment in the United States fluctuates between 15 percent and 19 percent of GDP. The United States has invested a smaller percentage of GDP than many other countries have. Since 1975, the developing countries have invested a larger percentage of GDP than have the industrial countries.

*Sources:* U.S. Department of Commerce, *National Income and Product Accounts of the United States* and *International Financial Statistics, Yearbook,* 1996.

Figure 9.2 shows that the investment rate in the United States has fluctuated and, throughout the period shown in the figure, has been less than the investment rate in the other industrial countries and the developing countries. The industrial countries are Canada, Japan, Australia, New Zealand, and 18 rich countries in Western Europe. The developing countries comprise the rest of the world.

Investment in the industrial countries has fluctuated and has been on a downward trend. Investment in the developing countries has fluctuated and has followed two distinct trends: an upward trend from 1970 through 1981 and a downward trend through the 1980s. Since 1975, the investment rate in the developing countries has exceeded that in the industrial countries.

Within the developing economies, those in Asia (such as China, Korea, Taiwan, and Malaysia) have the highest investment rates and those in Africa and Central and South America have the lowest investment rates. But most of these countries have higher investment rates than that of the United States.

## Interest Rates

When we studied labor in Chapter 8, we discovered that both the quantity of labor and the real wage rate per hour of labor have increased over the years. We've seen that the capital stock has grown steadily over time. But what has happened to the return on capital? Has it grown also? To find out, we must first define the return on capital.

The return on capital is the **real interest rate**, which is equal to the *nominal* interest rate adjusted for inflation. The nominal interest rate is the interest rate expressed in terms of money.

The real interest rate is approximately equal to the nominal interest rate minus the inflation rate. But the exact calculation allows for the change in the purchasing power of the interest as well as the amount of the loan.[1]

Suppose the nominal interest rate is 6 percent a year and there is no inflation. The real interest rate is also 6 percent a year. Now suppose the inflation rate is 4 percent a year. In this situation, prices are rising and

---

[1] To calculate the real interest rate, subtract the inflation rate from the nominal interest rate and divide that number by (1 + Inflation rate/100). If the nominal interest rate is 10.24 percent and the inflation rate is 4 percent, the real interest rate is $(10.24 - 4) \div (1 + 0.04) = 6$ percent.

money is losing value at a rate of 4 percent a year. If the real interest rate remains at 6 percent a year, the nominal interest rate must rise to 10.24 percent a year.

To see why the nominal interest rate is 10.24 percent when inflation is 4 percent and the real interest rate is 6 percent, think about the following example. You borrow $1,000 for one year. If the real interest rate is 6 percent a year, the people who loaned you the money must be able to buy goods and services valued in today's prices at $1,060 when you repay them. But after a year in which prices rise by 4 percent, they need $1,102.40 to buy goods and services that today cost $1060. So if you pay them $1,102.40, you are paying them only $1,060 in today's prices and the *real* interest paid is $60—6 percent a year.

In the world economy, there are thousands of different interest rates. The real interest rate at which homebuyers and risky businesses can borrow is higher than the rate at which large corporations can borrow. And large corporations pay a higher interest rate than the U.S. government pays. But all real interest rates tend to move up and down together.

One real interest rate that fluctuates with many others is the real interest rate at which big U.S. corporations borrow. This rate is higher than that at which the U.S government can borrow but lower than the rate that you must pay on a bank loan or credit card balance. But it moves up and down in the same way as all these other interest rates.

Figure 9.3 shows the real interest rate paid by big U.S. corporations from 1970 through 1996. The average real interest rate during these years is 4 percent a year. The real interest rate does not rise steadily like the real wage rate rises. It fluctuates around a constant level.

Four subperiods are striking:

1. The 1970s—low (and negative in 1975)
2. Between 1980 and 1985—increased to exceed 8 percent
3. Between 1985 and 1989—decreased to about 5 percent
4. The 1990s—steady between 4 percent and 6 percent

The 1970s were years of economic turmoil that resulted from huge oil price hikes. The 1980s began with a deep recession but then went into a long expansion. The 1990s also began in recession and then had a long expansion. We'll learn in this chapter *why* these events influenced the real interest rate.

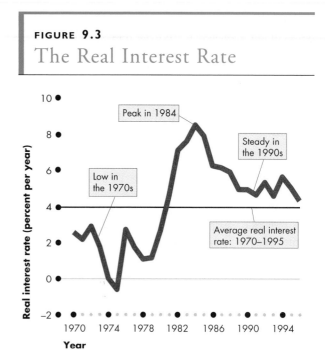

**FIGURE 9.3**

## The Real Interest Rate

The real interest rate (here, the rate at which big U.S. corporations can borrow) was low during the 1970s and negative in 1975. It increased strongly between 1980 and 1984 and then decreased through 1989. It has been relatively steady at between 4 percent and 6 percent a year during the 1990s.

*Source: Economic Report of the President, 1996, and the author's calculations.*

## REVIEW

■ Net investment (gross investment minus depreciation) increases the capital stock.

■ Net investment fluctuates but is usually positive, so the capital stock grows every year. Fluctuations in the growth of the capital stock are small because net investment is small relative to the capital stock.

■ Government purchases include investment in social infrastructure capital.

■ The U. S. investment rate (the percentage of GDP invested) is less than the rate in many other countries, especially the developing countries.

■ The return on capital is the real interest rate.

How do businesses make investment decisions and what determines their demand for investment? We answer those questions next.

# Investment Decisions

INVESTMENT CONSISTS OF PRIVATE INVESTMENT and government investment. We'll look at the role of government later in this chapter and first focus on private investment decisions.

How does Chrysler decide how much to spend on a new car assembly plant? How does AT&T decide how much to spend on fiber-optic cables? Business investment decisions are influenced by:

- The expected profit rate
- The real interest rate

To decide whether to invest in a new assembly line, Chrysler compares the expected profit rate with the real interest rate. The real interest rate is the opportunity cost of an investment. Let's look more closely at the expected profit rate and the real interest rate.

## The Expected Profit Rate

Other things remaining the same, the greater the expected profit rate from new capital, the greater is the amount of investment.

Imagine that Chrysler is trying to decide whether to build a new $100 million automobile assembly line that will produce cars for one year and then be scrapped. Chrysler expects a net revenue of $120 million from operating the plant. Net revenue is equal to total revenue from sales minus the cost of labor and materials. The firm's expected profit from this assembly line is $20 million, which equals $120 million (net revenue) minus $100 million (cost of the plant). The expected *profit rate* is 20 percent a year—($20 million ÷ $100 million) × 100.

Of the many influences on the expected profit rate, the three that stand out are:

1. The phase of the business cycle
2. Advances in technology
3. Taxes

The phase of the business cycle influences the expected profit rate because sales fluctuate over the business cycle. In an expansion, an increase in sales brings a higher profit rate. In a recession, a decrease in sales brings a lower profit rate.

As technologies advance, profit expectations change. When a new technology first becomes available, firms expect to be on a learning curve and so expect a modest profit rate from the new technology. But as firms gain experience with a new technology, they expect costs to fall and the profit rate to increase.

It is the *after-tax* profit rate that a firm receives, so changes in tax rates influence the firm's after-tax profit rate. Firms go to extreme lengths to avoid taxes, and for multinational firms, the decision about *where* to invest often turns on the effect of taxes on profit.

## The Real Interest Rate

Other things remaining the same, the lower the real interest rate, the greater is the amount of investment.

The funds used to finance investment might be borrowed, or they might be the financial resources of the firm's owners (the firm's retained earnings). But regardless of the source of the funds, the opportunity cost of the funds is the real interest rate. The real interest paid on borrowed funds is an obvious cost. The real interest rate is also the cost of using retained earnings because these funds could be loaned to another firm. The real interest income forgone is the opportunity cost of using retained earnings to finance an investment project.

In the Chrysler example, the expected profit rate is 20 percent a year. So it is profitable for Chrysler to invest as long as the real interest rate is less than 20 percent a year. That is, at real interest rates below 20 percent a year, Chrysler will build this assembly line, and at real interest rates in excess of 20 percent a year, it will not. Some projects are profitable at higher real interest rates, but other projects are profitable only at low real interest rates. Consequently, the higher the real interest rate, the smaller is the number of projects that are worth undertaking and the smaller is the amount of investment.

We summarize the influences on investment decisions in an investment demand curve.

## Investment Demand

If the real interest rate rises, other things remaining the same, investment decreases. The table in Fig. 9.4 shows an example of this relationship. It lists the levels of investment that occur at three real interest rates and with three expected profit rates. The relationship between investment and the real interest rate, other things remaining the same, is called **investment demand**.

Figure 9.4(a) shows an investment demand curve when the expected profit rate is average. Each point (*a* through *c*) corresponds to a row in the table. If the real interest rate is 6 percent a year, investment is $1 trillion. A change in the real interest rate brings a movement along the investment demand curve. If the real interest rate rises to 8 percent a year, investment decreases to $0.8 trillion; there is a movement up the investment demand curve. If the real interest rate falls to 4 percent a year, investment increases to $1.2 trillion; there is a movement down the investment demand curve.

Figure 9.4(b) shows how investment demand depends on the expected rate of profit. When firms expect an average profit rate, the investment demand curve is $ID_0$, the same as in part (a). But when the expected profit rate increases, investment demand increases and the investment demand curve shifts rightward to $ID_1$. When the expected profit rate decreases, investment demand decreases and the investment demand curve shifts leftward to $ID_2$. Fluctuations in the expected profit rate are the main source of fluctuations in investment demand.

Let's now see how the investment demand curve helps us to understand the changes in investment in the United States.

**FIGURE 9.4**

## Investment Demand

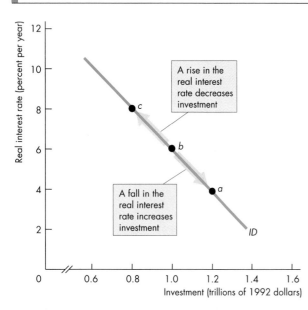

(a) The effect of a change in the real interest rate

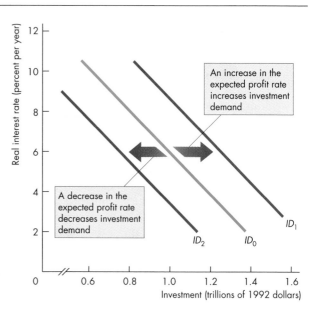

(b) The effect of a change in the expected profit rate

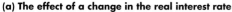

|   | Real interest rate (percent per year) | Investment (trillions of 1992 dollars) | | |
|---|---|---|---|---|
|   |   | **Expected profit rate** | | |
|   |   | **Low** | **Average** | **High** |
| *a* | 4 | 1.0 | 1.2 | 1.4 |
| *b* | 6 | 0.8 | 1.0 | 1.2 |
| *c* | 8 | 0.6 | 0.8 | 1.0 |

The table shows the level of investment for three different expected profit rates—low, average, and high—and three different interest rates. When the real interest rate is 6 percent a year and the expected profit rate is average, investment is $1.0 trillion. Part (a) shows the investment demand curve, *ID*, for an average expected profit rate. A change in the interest rate brings a movement along the investment demand curve. In part (b), a high expected profit rate shifts the curve rightward to $ID_1$ and a low expected profit rate shifts it leftward to $ID_2$.

## Investment Demand in the United States

Investment fluctuates because of fluctuations in the real interest rate and in the expected profit rate. Figure 9.5 shows the relative importance of these two factors in the United States. The dots in the figure show the gross investment and the real interest rate in the United States each year from 1981 to 1996. The figure also shows two U.S. investment demand curves—$ID_0$ and $ID_1$.

During the early 1980s, the investment demand curve was $ID_0$. Rising interest rates in 1982 brought a decrease in investment and a movement along the investment demand curve. The expected profit rate increased during the expansion in 1983 and 1984, and investment demand increased. This increase is shown by the rightward shift in the investment demand curve to $ID_1$. During the late 1980s, the expected profit rate decreased and the investment demand curve began to shift leftward. By 1991, the investment demand curve had shifted leftward back to $ID_0$. The expected profit rate increased again in the expansion of 1992–1994, and investment demand increased. Investment increased further in 1995 and 1996 as a lower real interest rate brought a movement along the investment demand curve $ID_1$.

You can see in Fig. 9.5 that investment fluctuates for two reasons: The real interest rate changes, which brings movements along an investment demand curve, and the expected profit rate changes, which shifts the investment demand curve.

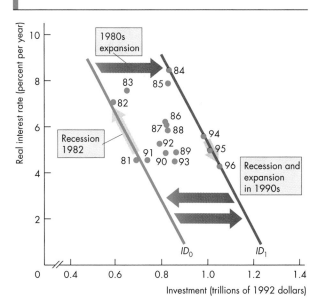

**FIGURE 9.5**

## Investment Demand in the United States

The blue dots show gross investment and the real interest rate in the United States for each year between 1981 and 1996. When the expected profit rate was low in the recession of the early 1980s, the investment demand curve was $ID_0$. As the real interest rate increased, investment decreased in 1982. During the 1980s, the expected profit rate increased and the investment demand curve shifted rightward. By 1984, it had shifted to $ID_1$. When the expected profit rate decreased in the late 1980s and the recession of 1991, the investment demand curve shifted leftward to $ID_0$. Then as the expected profit rate increased again through 1994, the investment demand curve shifted rightward to $ID_1$. As the real interest rate fell during 1995 and 1996, investment increased. Both swings in the expected profit rate and changes in interest rates bring fluctuations in gross investment.

*Source:* U.S. Department of Commerce, *National Income and Product Accounts of the United States,* and the author's assumptions.

---

### R E V I E W

- Investment depends on the expected profit rate and the real interest rate.

- Other things remaining the same, if the real interest rate falls, investment increases and if the real interest rate rises, investment decreases. A change in the interest rate brings a movement along the investment demand curve.

- When the expected profit rate increases, the investment demand curve shifts rightward; when the expected profit rate decreases, the $ID$ curve shifts leftward.

- Changes in the real interest rate and the expected profit rate play a role in creating fluctuations in U.S. investment, but changes in the expected profit rate have the larger effect.

Next, we study the decisions that create the funds that finance investment: saving and consumption decisions.

# Saving Decisions

PRIVATE INVESTMENT IS FINANCED BY NATIONAL saving and by borrowing from the rest of the world (see Chapter 6, p. 122). **National saving** is the sum of private saving and government saving. We first study private saving. Later in the chapter, we'll see how government actions influence the saving decisions.

Households must decide how to allocate their *disposable income* between saving and consumption. Of the many factors that influence a household's saving decision, the more important ones are:

- The real interest rate
- Disposable income
- Purchasing power of net assets
- Expected future income

## The Real Interest Rate

Other things remaining the same, the lower the real interest rate, the smaller is the amount of saving and the greater is the amount of consumption. The real interest rate is the opportunity cost of consumption. A dollar consumed is a dollar not saved, so the interest that could have been earned on that saving is forgone. This opportunity cost arises regardless of whether a person is a lender or a borrower. For a lender, saving less this year means receiving less interest next year. For a borrower, saving less this year means paying less off a loan this year and paying more interest next year.

You can see why the real interest rate influences saving by thinking about student loans. If the real interest rate on student loans jumped to 20 percent a year, students would save more (buying cheaper food and finding lower-rent accommodations) to pay off their loans as quickly as possible. If the real interest rate on student loans fell to 1 percent a year, students would save less and take larger loans.

## Disposable Income

The greater a household's disposable income, other things remaining the same, the greater is its saving. For example, a student works during the summer and earns a disposable income of $10,000. She spends the entire $10,000 on consumption during the year and saves nothing. When she graduates as an economics

major, her disposable income jumps to $20,000 a year. She now saves $4,000 and spends $16,000 on consumption. The increase in disposable income of $10,000 has increased saving by $4,000.

## Purchasing Power of Net Assets

A household's assets are what it *owns*, and its debts are what it *owes*. A household's *net assets* are its assets minus its debts. The purchasing power of a household's net assets is the *real* value of its net assets. It is the quantity of goods and services that its net assets can buy. The greater the purchasing power of a household's net assets, other things remaining the same, the less is its saving.

Patty is a department store executive who earns a disposable income of $30,000 a year. She has been saving and now has $15,000 in the bank and no debts. Patty's colleague, Tony, also earns a disposable income of $30,000, but he has no money in the bank. Patty decides that this year, she will take a vacation and save only $1,000 each year. But Tony decides to skip a vacation and save $5,000.

## Expected Future Income

The lower a household's expected future income, other things remaining the same, the greater is its saving. That is, if two households have the same disposable income in the current year, the household with the larger expected future income will spend a larger portion of current disposable income on consumption goods and services.

Look at Patty and Tony again. Patty has just been promoted and will receive a $10,000 pay raise next year. Tony has just been told that he will be laid off at the end of the year. On receiving this news, Patty buys a new car—increases her consumption expenditure—and Tony sells his car and takes the bus—decreases his consumption expenditure.

Every young household expects to have a higher future income for some years and then to have a lower income during retirement. Because of this pattern of income over the life cycle, young people save a small amount, middle-aged people save a lot, and retired people gradually spend their accumulated savings.

We've studied households' saving decisions so that we can see how their saving decisions interact with firms' investment decisions to determine the real interest rate, investment, and saving. The next step is to learn about the saving supply curve.

## Saving Supply

If the real interest rate rises, other things remaining the same, saving increases. The relationship between saving and the real interest rate, other things remaining the same, is called **saving supply**.

Figure 9.6 illustrates saving supply. The table shows a saving supply schedule, and the graph shows the saving supply curve. The points *a* through *c* on the saving supply curve *SS* in Fig. 9.6(a) correspond to the rows of the table. For example, point *b* indicates that when the real interest rate is 6 percent a year, saving is $1.0 trillion. If the real interest rate

rises from 6 percent a year to 8 percent a year, saving increases from $1 trillion to $1.1 trillion and there is a movement along the saving supply curve from *b* to *c*. If the real interest rate falls from 6 percent a year to 4 percent a year, saving decreases from $1 trillion to $0.9 trillion and there is a movement along the saving supply curve from *b* to *a*.

Along the saving supply curve, all other influences on saving remain the same. A change in any influence on saving other than the real interest rate changes saving supply and shifts the saving supply curve. An increase in disposable income, a decrease in the purchasing power of net assets, or a decrease

---

**FIGURE 9.6**

# Saving Supply

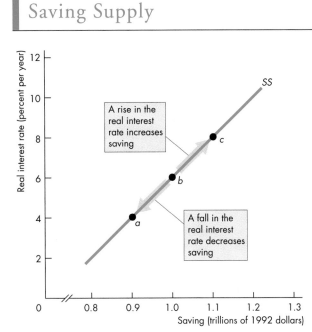

**(a) The effect of a change in the real interest rate**

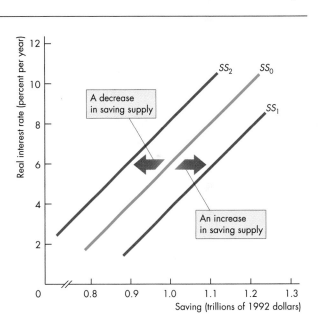

**(b) The effects of other influences on saving**

The table shows saving at three real interest rates. Part (a) shows the saving supply curve. Along the saving supply curve, the real interest rate changes but all other influences on saving remain the same. In part (b) an increase in disposable income (or a decrease in the purchasing power of net assets or a decrease in expected future income) increases saving and shifts the saving supply curve rightward from $SS_0$ to $SS_1$. A decrease in disposable income (or an increase in the purchasing power of net assets or an increase in expected future income) decreases saving and shifts the saving supply curve leftward from $SS_0$ to $SS_2$.

| | Real interest rate (percent per year) | Saving (trillions of 1992 dollars) |
|---|---|---|
| *a* | 4 | 0.9 |
| *b* | 6 | 1.0 |
| *c* | 8 | 1.1 |

in expected future income increases saving supply and shifts the saving supply curve rightward from $SS_0$ to $SS_1$. Changes in these factors in the opposite direction decrease saving and shift the saving supply curve leftward from $SS_0$ to $SS_2$.

Let's now see how the saving supply curve helps us to understand changes in saving in the United States.

## Saving Supply in the United States

All the influences on saving that we have isolated—the real interest rate, disposable income, the purchasing power of net assets, and expected future income—combine to determine fluctuations in saving in the United States.

Figure 9.7 shows the U.S. saving supply curve. Each point identified by a blue dot represents saving and the real interest rate for a particular year. In 1970, the saving supply curve was $SS_0$. The curve indicates that when the real interest rate rises, saving increases. But a large change in the real interest rate brings a small change in saving.

Over time, the saving supply curve has shifted rightward because disposable income has increased. Between 1970 and 1974, the saving supply curve shifted rightward to $SS_1$. But from 1974 through 1983, saving supply did not change much. A rising expected future income encouraged consumption rather than saving. But saving increased during these years because the real interest rate increased, and there was a movement along the saving supply curve $SS_1$.

During the rest of the 1980s, rising disposable income increased saving supply again and the saving supply curve shifted rightward. By 1996, it had shifted to $SS_2$.

Changes in other influences have decreased saving. During the 1980s, the purchasing power of net assets and expected future incomes both increased. With a booming stock market and increasing personal wealth, people saved less. Expectations of continued rapid economic expansion, which increased expected future incomes, reinforced the effect of increasing personal wealth. The result was an increase in consumption expenditure that almost equaled the increase in disposable income and a tiny increase in saving.

We've now studied the decisions that determine investment and saving and seen that both sets of decisions depend on the real interest rate. Next, we're going to see how the real interest rate, investment, and saving are simultaneously determined.

**FIGURE 9.7**

## Saving Supply in the United States: 1970–1996

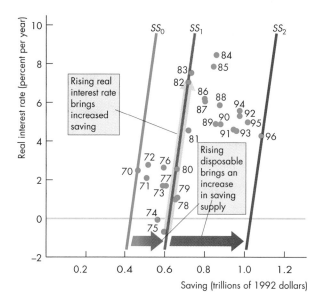

Each blue dot represents saving and the real interest rate for a particular year from 1970 through 1996. The blue curve $SS_0$ is an estimate of the saving supply curve for 1970. As disposable income increased, saving supply increased and the saving supply curve shifted rightward through $SS_1$ to $SS_2$. Saving supply did not change much between 1974 and 1983 because a rising stock market and rising expected future income encouraged consumption and discouraged saving.

*Source:* U.S. Department of Commerce, *National Income and Product Accounts of the United States*, and the author's assumptions.

## REVIEW

■ Saving decisions are influenced by the real interest rate, disposable income, the purchasing power of net assets, and expected future income.

■ The saving supply curve is the relationship between saving and the real interest rate, other things remaining the same. The higher the real interest rate, the greater is the level of saving, other things remaining the same.

■ The U.S. saving supply curve shifted rightward during the 1970s and between 1990 and 1996; but during the early 1980s, saving stagnated.

## Equilibrium in the World Economy

WE ARE NOW GOING TO SEE HOW INVESTMENT decisions and saving decisions determine the real interest rate. To do so, we study the economy of the entire world. The reason is that there is a single world capital market. Capital is free to roam the globe and seek the highest possible real rate of return. In 1996, for example, $244 billion of private funds flowed into the developing countries, $52 billion of which flowed into China. So the saving of one country is not always used to finance the investment of that country.

Real interest rates are not the same in every country because some countries are riskier than others. The riskier countries have higher real interest rates. But interest rates move up and down together. If two countries with equal risk had different interest rates, people would want to borrow in the country with a low interest rate and lend in the country with a high interest rate. But no one would want to lend in the country with a low interest rate, so its interest rate would rise. And no one would want to borrow in the country with a high interest rate, so its interest rate would fall. Interest rates would quickly become equal in the two countries. The real interest rate in the world economy is determined by global investment and global saving.

### Determining the Real Interest Rate

In Fig. 9.8 the world investment demand curve is *ID* and the world saving supply curve is *SS*. The higher the real interest rate, the greater is the amount of saving and the smaller is the amount of investment.

In the figure, when the real interest rate exceeds 6 percent a year, saving exceeds investment. Borrowers have an easy time finding the loans they want, but lenders are unable to lend all the funds they have available. The real interest rate falls, and as it does so, investment increases and saving decreases. The interest rate continues to fall until saving equals investment.

Alternatively, when the interest rate is less than 6 percent a year, saving is less than investment. Borrowers can't find the loans they want, but lenders are able to lend all the funds they have available. So the real interest rate rises. As the real interest rate rises, investment decreases and saving increases. The interest rate continues to rise as long as saving exceeds investment.

**FIGURE 9.8**

## Equilibrium in the World Capital Market

| | Real interest rate (percent per year) | Investment | Saving |
|---|---|---|---|
| | | (trillions of 1992 dollars) | |
| a | 4 | 8 | 5 |
| b | 6 | 6 | 6 |
| c | 8 | 4 | 7 |

The table shows world investment and saving at three interest rates, and the figure shows the world investment demand curve, *ID*, and world saving supply curve, *SS*. If the real interest rate is 4 percent a year, investment exceeds saving. There is a shortage of saving, and the real interest rate rises. If the real interest rate is 8 percent a year, investment is less than saving. There is a surplus of saving, and the real interest rate falls. When the real interest rate is 6 percent a year, investment equals saving. There is neither a shortage nor a surplus of saving, and the real interest rate is at its equilibrium level.

The real interest rate changes and is pulled toward an equilibrium level. In Fig. 9.8, this equilibrium is 6 percent a year. At this interest rate, there is neither a surplus nor a shortage of saving. Investors can get the funds they demand, and savers can lend all the funds they have available. The plans of savers and investors are consistent with each other.

Let's use the global saving supply and investment demand curves to explain changes in the real interest rate in the world economy.

### Explaining Changes in the Real Interest Rate

In 1996, the real interest rate paid on long-term loans by the biggest and safest U.S. corporations was about 4 percent a year. It was much more than 4 percent a year for homebuyers and risky businesses. Twelve years earlier, in 1984, the real interest rate was more than twice its 1996 level. In that year, it reached a peak level for big companies of 8.4 percent a year. In

contrast, 20 years earlier in 1975, the real interest rate was *negative*. Big companies could borrow at about 9 percent a year, and the inflation rate was about 10 percent a year. So the real interest rate was close to *minus* 1 percent a year.

Figure 9.9 explains why these changes in the real interest rate occurred. Each dot represents world investment and world saving and the real interest rate for a particular year. In 1973 (in part a), the saving supply curve was $SS_{73}$ and the investment demand curve was $ID_{73}$. The real interest rate was 2 percent a year, and the amount of saving and investment in the world economy was $3.7 trillion.

In 1973, a huge rise in the price of oil increased the incomes and saving of oil producers and exporters.

---

**FIGURE 9.9**

## Explaining Changes in the Real Interest Rate

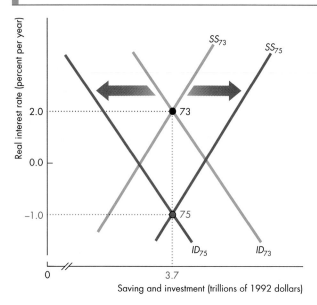

**(a) Onset of growth slowdown**

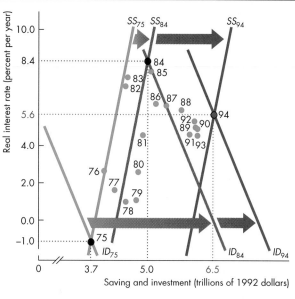

**(b) 1975–1994**

In 1973 (part a), world saving supply was $SS_{73}$ and world investment demand was $ID_{73}$. The real interest rate was 2 percent a year. A large increase in the world price of oil increased world saving supply and decreased world investment demand. By 1975, world saving supply was $SS_{75}$ and world investment demand was $ID_{75}$, and the real interest rate was negative. By 1984 (part b), a strong economic expansion was under way

and investment demand had increased to $ID_{84}$, but saving supply had not increased by much and was $SS_{84}$. The real interest rate increased and reached a peak of 8.4 percent in 1984. During the rest of the 1980s, saving supply increased by more than investment demand, and by 1994, the saving supply curve was $SS_{94}$ and the investment demand curve was $ID_{94}$. The real interest rate had fallen to 5.6 percent a year.

*Sources:* "The Penn World Table: An Expanded Set of International Comparisons, 1950–1988," *Quarterly Journal of Economics*, May 1991, pp. 327–368, New computer diskette, Mark 5.6a, *International Financial Statistics, Yearbook*, 1996, *Economic Report of the President*, 1997, and the author's assumptions and calculations.

By 1975, the world saving supply curve had shifted rightward to $SS_{75}$. Oil users and importers faced steep cost increases and a collapse of profits, which decreased investment demand. The world investment demand curve shifted leftward to $ID_{75}$. So by 1975, world saving supply had increased, world investment demand had decreased, and the real interest rate fell to –1 percent a year.

Figure 9.9(b) takes up the story at this point. Gradually, investment demand recovered and, except for severe recession in 1982, increased each year. By 1984, the investment demand curve had shifted rightward to $ID_{84}$. Through these same years, saving supply increased slowly. In 1984, the saving supply curve was similar to that in 1977. The reasons for slow saving growth are complex. But one factor at work, which we examine later in this chapter, was the emergence of large government deficits, which must be subtracted from private saving to determine total saving. The combination of a large increase in investment demand and a small increase in saving supply increased the real interest rate to 8.4 percent a year in 1984, and world investment and world saving increased to $5 trillion.

The rest of the 1980s and the 1990s saw a continued growth in the supply of saving relative to the increase in investment demand. By 1994, the investment demand curve had shifted rightward to $ID_{94}$ and the saving supply curve had shifted to $SS_{94}$. As a result of these changes, the real interest rate fell to 5.6 percent a year.

---

### R E V I E W

- The real interest rate is determined by world saving supply and world investment demand.
- A world oil price explosion of 1973–1974 increased saving supply and decreased investment demand. The real interest rate fell to a low point.
- The 1980s expansion increased investment demand, but saving supply grew by less and the real interest rate rose.
- During the late 1980s, investment demand increased less than saving supply and the real interest rate fell.

So far in our study of investment, saving, and the real interest rate, we've ignored government saving. Let's now bring government saving into the picture.

## The Role of Government

PART OF THE CAPITAL STOCK ARISES FROM government investment. And investment is financed by total saving, which is made up of private saving plus government saving. So government actions influence investment, saving, and the real interest rate. To complete our study of the forces that determine the quantity of capital and the real interest rate, we must investigate the role played by governments.

But because the real interest rate is determined in the *world* capital market, it is the *aggregate* investment and saving of all governments that matters, not the investment and saving of one individual government.

Most governments are tiny, and many U.S. corporations have a bigger impact on the world capital market than some governments do. Even the biggest governments make a relatively small difference to the world capital market. For example, the net saving of the U. S. government, which is one of the largest, is around 3 percent of world saving.

But governments in aggregate are large. World aggregate government net saving is close to 20 percent of total saving. And the direction of that saving is negative. Government saving is *negative*!

Let's see why government saving is negative and how government investment and saving influence total investment, saving, and the real interest rate.

### Government Budgets

You learned in Chapter 6 (p. 121) that GDP equals the sum of consumption expenditure, $C$, investment, $I$, government purchases $G$, and net exports. We'll ignore net exports for the moment and consider only a closed economy (such as the world economy). So in a closed economy,

$$GDP = C + I + G.$$

GDP also equals the sum of consumption expenditure, saving, $S$, and net taxes, $T$. That is,

$$GDP = C + S + T.$$

By combining these two ways of looking at GDP, you can see that

$$I = S + T - G.$$

■ If net taxes, *T*, exceed government purchases, *G*, the government has a budget surplus and government saving is positive.

■ If government purchases exceed net taxes, the government has a budget deficit and government saving is negative.

When the government has a budget surplus, it contributes toward financing investment. Its saving must be added to private saving. But when the government has a budget deficit, it competes with businesses for private saving. In this situation, government saving must be subtracted from private saving.

Government saving can influence the world capital market in two ways, one direct and one indirect. We'll begin with the direct effect.

### Direct Effect of Government Saving

The direct influence of government arises because government saving is part of total saving. So we must add government saving and private saving together to determine total saving. Figure 9.10 shows the effects of governments that have a large deficit. The investment demand curve, *ID*, is the same as the one you met in Fig. 9.8. The *private* saving supply curve, *PSS*, shows the relationship between private saving and the real interest rate. The saving supply curve *SS* shows the sum of private saving and government saving.

The horizontal distance between the private saving curve and the saving supply curve is government saving. In this example, government saving is a negative $2 trillion. That is, the governments of all the nations have a total budget deficit of $2 trillion. (This number is larger than the actual deficit in the world economy in the mid-1990s.)

The effect of government negative saving, which is also called *dissaving*, is to increase the real interest rate and to decrease investment. In this example, the real interest rate rises from 6 percent a year to 7.3 percent a year, and investment decreases from $6 trillion to $4.7 trillion.

Investment does not decrease by the full amount of the government deficit because the higher real interest rate induces an increase in private saving. In this example, private saving increases by $0.7 to $6.7 trillion. In reality, the increase in private saving might be quite small, at least in the short term.

The tendency for a government budget deficit to decrease investment is called a **crowding-out effect**. By raising the real interest rate, the government

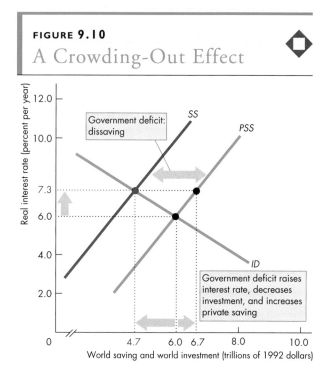

**FIGURE 9.10**

## A Crowding-Out Effect

The world investment demand curve is *ID*, and the world private saving supply curve, *PSS*. With balanced government budgets, the real interest rate is 6 percent a year and investment equals saving at $6 trillion a year. A government budget deficit is negative government saving (dissaving). We subtract the government deficit from private saving to determine the saving supply curve *SS*. The real interest rate rises, investment decreases (is crowded out) and private saving increases.

deficit crowds out private investment and slows the rate of economic growth.

A government surplus has the opposite effect: It increases saving, lowers the real interest rate, and stimulates investment and economic growth.

We've just studied the direct effect of government saving on the world capital market. But there is an indirect effect that we must also take into account.

### Indirect Effect of Government Saving

Government saving has an indirect effect on the world capital market because it influences private saving. In the crowding-out story we've just told, the *quantity of private saving* changes because the real interest rate changes. There is a movement along the *PSS* curve. But private saving supply does not change. That is, the *PSS* curve does not shift. The indirect effect arises from the possibility that a change in government saving changes private saving supply and shifts the *PSS* curve. In an extreme version of this effect, private saving changes to offset the government deficit and the deficit has no effect on the real interest rate or investment. Let's look at this extreme case.

**The Barro-Ricardo Effect** So named because it was first suggested by the English economist David Ricardo in the eighteenth century and refined by Robert J. Barro of Harvard University during the 1980s, the Barro-Ricardo effect holds that a government budget deficit has no effect on the real interest rate or investment. Another way of stating this view is that financing government purchases by taxes or by borrowing is equivalent.

The reasoning behind the Barro-Ricardo effect is the following. A government that runs a deficit must sell bonds to pay for the goods and services that are not paid for by taxes. And the government must pay interest on those bonds. It must also collect more taxes *in the future* to pay the interest on the larger quantity of bonds that are outstanding. Taxpayers are rational and have good foresight. They can see that their taxes will be higher in the future so their disposable income will be smaller. With a smaller expected future disposable income, saving increases. And if taxpayers want to neutralize the effects of the government deficit on their own consumption plans, they increase their saving by the same amount that the government is dissaving through its deficit.

Figure 9.11 shows this outcome. The private saving supply curve initially is $PSS_0$. The government has a balanced budget—neither a deficit nor a surplus—so saving supply is also $PSS_0$. With investment demand *ID*, the equilibrium real interest rate is 6 percent a year and investment and saving are $6 trillion.

Governments now run deficits that total $2 trillion. But these deficits induce an increase in private saving. Here, the increase is the full amount of the government deficit. So the private saving supply curve shifts rightward to $PSS_1$. Total saving supply remains at $PSS_0$, so the real interest rate remains at 6 percent a year. Investment also remains at $6 trillion a year. Private saving increases to $8 trillion.

The outcome shown in Fig. 9.11 is extreme and probably does not actually occur. Taxpayers probably respond in the *direction* suggested by Ricardo and Barro but not in the *amount* they suggest. So the effect of government deficits probably lies between the two cases shown in Figs. 9.10 and 9.11. That is,

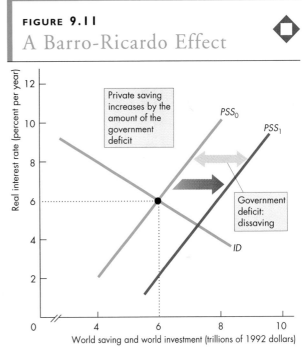

**FIGURE 9.11**

## A Barro-Ricardo Effect

The world investment demand curve is *ID*, and initially, the world private saving supply curve, $PSS_0$. With balanced government budgets, the real interest rate is 6 percent a year and investment equals saving at $6 trillion a year. Government budget deficits induce an increase in private saving. The *PSS* curve shifts rightward to $PSS_1$, and the real interest rate, investment, and *total* saving remain constant.

a government deficit increases the real interest rate and partly crowds out investment, but it also induces a partial increase in private saving in anticipation of lean times later when the tax bill rises to pay the interest on a rising debt.

## Government Deficits Today

Government deficits have been large in recent years and have probably been responsible for the high real interest rates of the 1990s. Figure 9.12 shows the deficits of the United States, the industrial countries, and the developing countries from 1988 through 1995 and projected deficits for 1996 and 1997.

During the early 1990s, deficits in the United States and the other industrial countries increased to more than 4 percent of GDP. For the world as a whole, a deficit of this magnitude exceeds $1 trillion. But after 1993, government deficits in the industrial countries decreased.

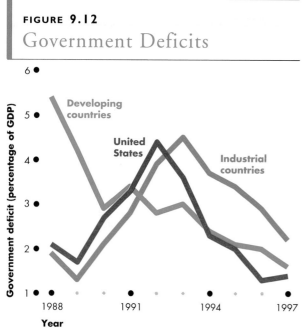

**FIGURE 9.12**

Government Deficits

The government deficit of the United States increased through 1992 and then decreased. The other industrial countries followed a similar pattern but peaked in 1993. The deficit of the developing countries has been on a downward trend throughout the period shown here.

*Source: World Economic Outlook* (Washington D.C.: International Monetary Fund, October 1996).

Government deficits in the developing countries have fallen steadily, and by 1992, they represented a smaller percentage of GDP than the deficits of the industrial countries. Developing countries have decreased their deficits because doing so has been a condition for receiving loans from their banks, most notably the World Bank. (The World Bank is an international organization that finances development projects in developing countries and that uses funds paid to it by the industrial countries.)

During the 1990s, real interest rates are higher than average. The basic reason is that investment demand is high relative to saving supply. The 1990s is a time when investment opportunities are large and saving rates are low compared with average times. Figure 9.3 shows that real interest rates averaged 4 percent between 1970 and 1995. But even this number is above the long-term average, which over the past 100 years is 2 percent a year. If government deficits continue to decrease, real interest rates will also decrease (other things remaining the same).

## REVIEW

- Total saving equals private saving plus government saving. Government saving equals net taxes minus government purchases.
- A government budget deficit decreases total saving, increases the real interest rate, decreases investment, and increases private saving.
- In the mid-1990s, government deficits were large but decreasing.

So far, we've looked at investment and saving in the world economy. Next we look at the national economy.

## Saving and Investment in the National Economy

SAVING SUPPLY AND INVESTMENT DEMAND IN THE world economy determine the world real interest rate. At the equilibrium real interest rate, world saving equals world investment.

Although saving equals investment in the world economy, it does not necessarily do so in a national economy. In a nation, investment is financed by *national* saving plus borrowing from the rest of the world (see Chapter 6, p. 122). Nations in which investment exceeds national saving borrow from the rest of the world, and nations in which national saving exceeds investment lend to the rest of the world. For the world as a whole, international borrowing equals international lending.

But as you also learned in Chapter 6, a nation's international lending equals its net exports. So a nation that has a net export surplus is also one that lends to the rest of the world. A nation whose imports exceed its exports has negative net exports and borrows from the rest of the world. Whether a nation has a surplus or deficit in its international trade depends on whether its national saving exceeds or falls short of its investment.

Let's take a closer look at the role played by national saving and investment decisions and see how they determine international borrowing. There are two channels of influence to consider.

First, each nation contributes to world saving and investment and so influences the world real interest rate. The larger the country, the greater is that influence. For example, investment and saving decisions in the United States, the European Union, and Japan have a big impact on world investment demand and world saving supply. So they have a big influence on the world real interest rate. The investment and saving of other nations individually have a small impact on world investment demand and world saving supply. So they have a negligible influence on the world real interest rate.

Second, a nation's saving and investment decisions, along with the world real interest rate, determine the amount the nation borrows from or lends to the rest of the world. They also, equivalently, determine a nation's net exports.

Figure 9.13 shows the determination of a nation's international borrowing and net exports. The nation's investment demand curve is *ID*, and its saving supply curve (including any government saving) is *SS*. The world real interest rate is 6 percent a year. At this real interest rate, investment is $1.5 trillion and saving is $1.0 trillion. International borrowing fills the gap between investment and saving. In the example in Fig. 9.13, investment exceeds saving, so the nation borrows from the rest of the world. If, at the world real interest rate, saving exceeds investment, the nation lends to the rest of the world.

## Government Saving and International Borrowing

The greater the amount of government saving, other things remaining the same, the greater is national saving. And the greater the national saving, the smaller is international borrowing (or the larger is international lending). An increase in the government deficit decreases national saving and increases international borrowing.

You can now see why U.S. net exports have been negative for the past 20 years. It is because U.S. national saving has been less than investment. Government dissaving (a government budget deficit) has contributed to the shortfall. A low private saving rate has also contributed.

You can also see that one popular view about the U.S. budget deficit is incorrect. Because the capital market is a global market and the U.S. government is a small player, the U.S. government deficit cannot cause much damage to growth by crowding out investment. But it does damage the growth of U.S disposable incomes because it increases international borrowing and increases the interest payments that we must make to the rest of the world.

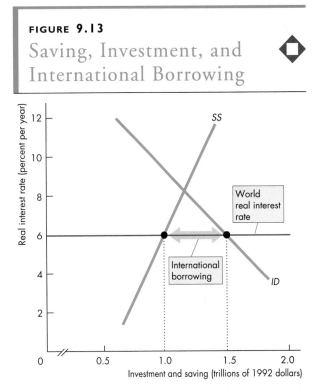

**FIGURE 9.13**

## Saving, Investment, and International Borrowing

A nation's investment demand curve is *ID*, and its saving supply curve (including government saving) is *SS*. The world real interest rate is 6 percent a year. At this interest rate, investment, which is $1.5 trillion, exceeds saving, which is $1.0 trillion. The nation borrows $0.5 trillion from the rest of the world.

---

## REVIEW

▦ If investment exceeds saving at the world real interest rate, net exports are negative and the nation borrows from the rest of the world.

▦ An increase in the government deficit increases international borrowing, but it does not crowd out investment.

◆ In this chapter, we've seen that the quantity of capital depends on investment and saving; and we've seen how the real interest rate is determined in the world capital market. Your next task is to see how technological change brings capital accumulation and economic growth.

Before embarking on this task, take a look at *Reading Between the Lines* on pp. 208–209, which examines the private saving performance of the United States in recent years.

# Policy
## WATCH

### Saving in the United States

WINSTON-SALEM JOURNAL, OCTOBER 6, 1996

## Seniors Aren't As Thrifty As Believed

BY STEVEN PEARLSTEIN
THE WASHINGTON POST

For some time, the economist's mantra has gone something like this: A falling savings rate has led to falling investment, and falling investment has led to slow erosion in the average American's standard of living.

But what accounts for this declining savings rate, which has fallen from more than 11 percent of household income in the 1950s and '60s to less than 4 percent in the 1990s?

During the 1980s, one favorite explanation was that profligate baby boomers were spending on BMWs, expensive suits and high-priced houses. ...

But a controversial new study by Laurence Kotlikoff of Boston University, John Sabelhaus of the Congressional Budget Office and Jagadeesh Gokhale of the Federal Reserve Bank of Cleveland concludes that it is really grandma and grandpa who have been living high on the hog.

In 1960, the typical 70-year-old American spent about 71 cents for every dollar spent by a 30-year-old.

By the late 1980s, it was the oldster who was the bigger spender, shelling out $1.18 for every dollar spent by the typical 30-year-old.

One obvious reason for this shift was the dramatic increase in health-care spending. ...

But even with medical costs factored out, the analysts still found that seniors have been on a spending spree these past 30 years. ...

[Gokhale, Kotlikoff and Sabelhaus] concluded that the elderly have been garnering an ever-increasing share of the country's resources and have been spending that increase rather than saving it.

The transfer of wealth and income from young to old—what economists call intergenerational transfers—has been well documented. ... The primary factors there are Social Security and Medicare benefits, the values of which have been rising faster than the incomes of working Americans. ...

In a world where people receive entitlements for life, they are more likely to spend down their savings knowing they can always fall back on annuities if they live longer than average and draw down their entire savings. ...

Of course, Social Security, Medicare and private pensions have been around for a long time. But whereas these annuities represented 16 percent of income received by the elderly in 1960, they represent 40 percent of the income received by the elderly today. ...

■ Household saving has fallen from 11 percent of income during the 1950s and 1960s to less than 4 percent during the 1990s.

■ In 1960, seniors spent 71 cents for every dollar spent by younger adults. By the late 1980s, seniors spent $1.18 for every dollar spent by younger adults.

■ In 1960, 16 percent of seniors' income came from Social Security and Medicare. Now the amount is 40 percent.

■ When people expect to receive pensions and benefits throughout their lives, they spend more and save less.

# Economic

## A N A L Y S I S

■ Figure I shows two measures of personal saving in the United States. The left scale (red line) shows national saving as a percentage of gross national product. The right scale (blue line) shows personal saving as a percentage of disposable income.

■ Both measures show a similar downward trend. But this trend raises two questions: What caused it, and what are its consequences?

■ Private saving depends on the real interest rate, disposable income, the purchasing power of net assets, and expected future income.

■ Figure 2 shows the private saving supply curve in 1963, $PSS_{63}$. The real interest rate was 3 percent a year and the average family saved $2,000 (measured in terms of 1992 prices), which is a point on $PSS_{63}$.

■ Disposable income in the United States has increased over the last 30 years.

■ Other things remaining the same, the increase in disposable income increases saving. By 1992, the increase in disposable income might have shifted the saving supply curve rightward to $PSS'_{92}$.

■ But the average family saved only $1,200 in 1992. And the real interest rate in that year was 5 percent, a higher rate than in 1962.

■ So the private saving supply curve in 1992 had actually shifted leftward to $PSS_{92}$. The 1992 saving per family of $1,200 at the real interest rate of 5 percent a year is a point on this curve.

■ The main factor that decreased saving, according to the research reported in the news article, is the increase in Social Security and Medicare. These programs give people a higher expected income during retirement and induce them to save less and consume more.

■ What are the consequences of decreased saving?

■ The United States is a large part of the world, so lower U.S. saving means a significant decrease in world saving and a higher real interest rate.

■ It also means a larger amount of U.S. borrowing from the rest of the world and imports that exceed exports.

Figure 1 Saving rates

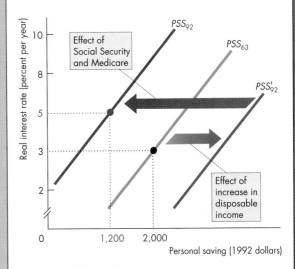

Figure 2 Saving supply curves

## You're

### THE VOTER

■ What do you think the federal government should do about the low U.S. saving rate?

■ If the study reported in the news article is correct, cutting Social Security and Medicare would increase private saving. What are the pros and cons of making such cuts?

■ What, if any, tax reforms would increase saving?

■ Would you vote for tax incentives, a cut in Social Security, neither, or both? Explain why.

# SUMMARY

## Key Points

### Capital and Interest (pp. 192–194)

- The capital stock grows steadily because net investment is usually positive.
- The return on capital is the real interest rate—the nominal interest rate adjusted for inflation.

### Investment Decisions (pp. 195–197)

- Other things remaining the same, the lower the real interest rate or the higher the expected profit rate, the greater is the amount of investment.
- Investment demand is the relationship between investment and the real interest rate, other things remaining the same. Investment demand changes when the expected profit rate changes.

### Saving Decisions (pp. 198–200)

- Other things remaining the same, the higher the real interest rates, the greater is saving.
- Saving supply is the relationship between saving and the real interest rate, other things remaining the same.
- Saving supply changes when disposable income, the purchasing power of net assets, expected future income changes.

### Equilibrium in the World Economy (pp. 201–203)

- Because capital is free to move internationally to seek the highest possible real rate of return, the real interest rate is determined in a global market.
- The equilibrium real interest rate makes world saving equal to world investment.

### The Role of Government (pp. 203–206)

- National saving equals private saving plus government saving.
- Government saving equals net taxes minus government purchases.

- A government budget deficit might increase the real interest rate and crowd out private investment.
- A government budget deficit might also increase private saving supply because it decreases expected future disposable income.

### Saving and Investment in the National Economy (pp. 206–207)

- In the national economy, foreign borrowing fills the gap between national saving and investment.
- An increase in the government budget deficit decreases national saving and increases foreign borrowing, but it does not decrease investment.

## Key Figures

Figure 9.4    Investment Demand, 196
Figure 9.6    Saving Supply, 199
Figure 9.8    Equilibrium in the World Capital Market, 201
Figure 9.10   A Crowding-Out Effect, 204
Figure 9.11   A Barro-Ricardo Effect, 205
Figure 9.13   Saving, Investment, and International Borrowing, 207

## Key Terms

Capital stock, 192
Crowding-out effect, 204
Depreciation, 192
Gross investment, 192
Investment demand, 195
National saving, 198
Net investment, 192
Real interest rate, 193
Saving supply, 199

# QUESTIONS

1. Which component of gross investment fluctuates the most, net investment or replacement investment?
2. Why does the capital stock grow smoothly when net investment fluctuates?
3. What is the real interest rate?
4. Describe how the real interest rate has changed since 1975.
5. What determines investment?
6. Why does a fall in the real interest rate increase investment?
7. How is investment influenced by the expected rate of profit?
8. What is the investment demand curve, what brings a movement along the investment demand curve, and what makes it shift?
9. What have been the main changes in investment demand in the United States in recent years?
10. What are the main influences on saving?
11. Why does a rise in the real interest rate increase saving?
12. How do disposable income, the purchasing power of net assets, and expected future income influence saving?
13. What is the saving supply curve, what brings a movement along the saving supply curve, and what makes it shift?
14. What have been the main changes in saving supply in the United States in recent years?
15. Explain how the real interest rate is determined.
16. What have been the main influences on the real interest rate during the 1980s and 1990s?
17. How does government saving influence national saving?
18. How does government saving influence the real interest rate, investment, and private saving?
19. What happens to the real interest rate, investment, and private saving if government deficits around the world increase?
20. What determines U.S. international borrowing?
21. How does a government budget deficit in the United States influence investment, saving, and U.S. international borrowing?

# PROBLEMS

1. A cellular phone assembly plant costs $10 million and has a life of one year. The firm will have to hire labor at a cost of $3 million and buy parts and fuel at a cost of a further $3 million. If the firm builds the plant, it will be able to produce cellular telephones that will sell for $17 million. Does it pay the firm to invest in this new production line at the following real interest rates:
   a. 5 percent a year?
   b. 10 percent a year?
   c. 15 percent a year?
2. Suppose the phone producer in problem 1 expects its total revenue to increase to $17.5 million with unchanged costs. What now is the highest real interest rate at which it will undertake the investment? How does the firm's investment demand curve change as a result of an increase in its expected profit rate?
3. In 1997, the Batman family (Batman and Robin) had a disposable income of $50,000, net assets of $100,000, and an expected future income of $50,000 a year. At an interest rate of 4 percent a year, the Batmans would save $10,000. At an interest rate of 6 percent a year, they would save $12,500. And at an interest rate of 8 percent a year, they would save $15,000.
   a. Draw a graph of the Batman family's saving supply curve for 1997.
   b. In 1998, everything remained the same as the year before except that the Batmans expected their future income to rise to $60,000 a year. Show the influence of this change on the Batman family's saving supply curve.
   c. In 1999, everything remained the same as the year before except that the Batmans disposable income increased to the $60,000 a year they expected it would the year before. The Batmans now expect their income to remain at $60,000 a year. Show the influence of this change on the Batman family's saving supply curve.
   d. In 2000, the stock market boomed and the Batmans' assets increased by 50 percent. Show the influence of this change on the Batman family's saving supply curve.

4. The year is 3053. The economy of Alpha Centura, still isolated from all other planets, has the following saving supply and investment demand:

| Real interest rate (percent per year) | Saving | Investment (trillions of 3050 zips) |
|:---:|:---:|:---:|
| 4 | 2 | 7 |
| 5 | 6 | 6 |
| 6 | 10 | 5 |
| 7 | 14 | 4 |
| 8 | 18 | 3 |

Alpha Centura's government budget is balanced.
  a. What is the equilibrium real interest rate?
  b. What is equilibrium investment?
  c. What is equilibrium saving?

5. The government of Alpha Centura spends big on a space program and incurs a deficit of 5 trillion zips. The Alpha Centurans have not heard of Ricardo and keep spending as if there were no government deficit.
  a. What is the new equilibrium real interest rate?
  b. What is the new equilibrium investment and saving?

6. Alpha Centura's space program pays off. The Alpha Centurans and Earth people discover each other and begin to pursue intergalactic economic trade, borrowing, and lending. The real interest rate on Earth is 6 percent a year. On Alpha Centura, it is the number you calculated for problem 5.
  a. Which planet borrows from the other?
  b. Do investment and saving on Alpha Centura increase or decrease?
  c. Do investment and saving on Earth increase or decrease?

7. Suppose that before Alpha Centura and Earth discover each other, the Alpha Centurans begin to realize that the government deficit is going to mean that their taxes will rise. They discover and apply the Barro-Ricardo principle.
  a. What happens to their saving supply curve?
  b. What happens to their investment demand curve?
  c. What happens to the real interest rate and investment?

## CRITICAL THINKING

1. Study *Reading Between the Lines* on pp. 208–209 and then answer the following questions:
  a. What has happened to the saving rate in the United States during the past 30 years?
  b. How does the saving behavior of older Americans compare with that of younger Americans?
  c. What are the main reasons you can think of that might account for the patterns that you describe in your answers to parts (a) and (b)?
  d. What are the likely effects of a decrease in U.S. saving supply? Explain the effects on national saving, investment, the world real interest rate, and U.S. international borrowing and lending.
  e. If the U.S. saving rate increases during the 2000s, how will that change influence the U.S. and world quantity of capital by 2010?

2. Suppose the U.S. government cuts the tax rate on business profits.
  a. How do you think this tax cut will influence firm's investment plans?
  b. How will the tax cut influence private saving decisions?
  c. How will the tax cut influence the real interest rate?
  d. How will the tax cut influence U.S. international borrowing?
  For each part, draw a figure to illustrate the effects. Then go on to think about and answer the following questions:
  e. Who would benefit from such a tax cut?
  f. Who would pay for such a tax cut?
  g. On balance, do you favor or oppose such a tax cut? Why?

3. Use the latest *World Economic Outlook*, published twice a year by the International Monetary Fund, to get data on government budget deficits. (The data are *not* on the IMF World Wide Web site.)
  a. What are the trends in deficits? Are they the same as or different from those in Fig. 9.12 on p. 206?
  b. What influence do you expect the deficits to have on the real interest rate and investment next year?

# Chapter 10

# Economic Growth

Real GDP per person in the United States has doubled between 1960 and 1996. If you live in a dorm, chances are it was built during the 1960s and equipped with two electricity outlets, one for a desk lamp and one for a bedside lamp. Today, with the help of a power bar (or two), your room bulges with a television and VCR, CD player, microwave, refrigerator, coffee maker, toaster, computer—and the list goes on. What has brought about this growth in production and incomes? What can be done to speed up economic growth? ◆ We see greater extremes of economic growth if we look at modern Asia. On the banks of the Li River in Southern China, Songman Yang breeds cormorants, amazing birds that he trains to fish

## Transforming People's Lives

and to deliver their catch to a basket on his simple bamboo raft. Songman's work, the capital equipment and technology he uses, and the income he earns are similar to those of his ancestors going back some 2,000 years. Yet all around Songman, in China's bustling villages, towns, and cities, people are participating in an economic miracle. They are creating businesses, investing in new technologies, developing local and global markets, and experiencing income growth of more than 6 percent a year. Similar rapid economic growth is taking place in Hong Kong, South Korea, and Taiwan. In these countries, real GDP has doubled *three times*—an eightfold increase—between 1960 and 1996. Why have incomes in these Asian economies grown so rapidly? What makes an economic miracle? ◆ In this chapter, we study the forces that make real GDP grow, that make some countries grow faster than others, and that make our own growth rate sometimes slow down and sometimes speed up. We'll also look at policies for achieving faster economic growth.

## After studying this chapter, you will be able to:

- ■ Describe the long-term growth trends in the United States and other countries and regions

- ■ Identify the main sources of long-term of real GDP growth

- ■ Explain the productivity growth slowdown in the United States during the 1970s

- ■ Explain the rapid economic growth rates being achieved in East Asia

- ■ Explain the theories of economic growth

- ■ Describe the policies that might be used to speed up economic growth

# Long-Term Growth Trends

THE LONG-TERM GROWTH TRENDS THAT WE study in this chapter are the trends in *potential GDP*. We are interested in long-term growth primarily because it brings rising incomes *per person*. So we begin by looking at some facts about the level and growth rate of real GDP per person in the United States and around the world. Let's look first at real GDP per person in the United States over the past hundred years.

## Growth in the U.S. Economy

Figure 10.1 shows real GDP per person in the United States for the hundred years from 1896 to 1996. The average growth rate over this period is 2 percent a year. But the long-term growth rate has varied from a low of 1.1 percent a year between 1973 and 1984 to a high of 3 percent a year during the 1920s and the 1960s.

Figure 10.1 shows you the recent productivity growth slowdown in a longer perspective. It also shows that productivity growth slowdowns have occurred before. The early years of the 1900s and the mid-1950s had even slower growth than we have today. The rapid growth of the 1960s was not unusual either. The decade of the 1920s was a period of similarly rapid growth.

In the middle of the graph are two extraordinary events: the Great Depression of the 1930s and World War II of the 1940s. The fall in real GDP during the Depression and the bulge during the war obscure any changes in the long-term growth trend that might have occurred within these years. But between 1930 and 1950, averaging out the Depression and the war, the long-term growth rate was 2.2 percent a year.

A major goal of this chapter is to explain why our economy grows and why the long-term growth rate varies. A related goal is to explain variations in the economic growth rate across countries. Let's look at some facts about these variations.

---

**FIGURE 10.1**

## A Hundred Years of Economic Growth in the United States

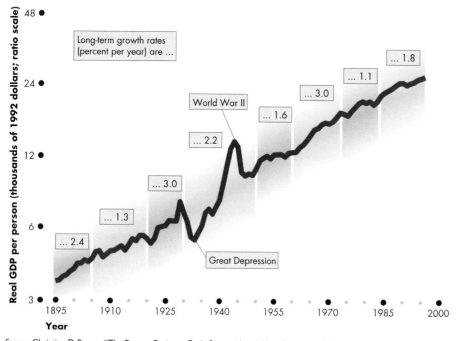

During the 100 years from 1896 to 1996, real GDP per person in the United States grew by 2 percent a year, on the average. The growth rate was above average during the 1920s and 1960s, and it was below average in 1903–1920, the 1950s, and 1973–1996.

*Source:* Christina D. Romer "The Prewar Business Cycle Reconsidered: New Estimates of Gross National Product, 1869–1908," *Journal of Political Economy* Vol. 97 (1989); *National Income and Product Accounts of the United States; Historical Statistics of the United States Colonial Times to 1957* (U.S. Department of Commerce, 1960); and *Economic Report of the President,* 1997.

## Real GDP Growth in the World Economy

Figure 10.2 shows real GDP growth in the United States and in some other countries since 1960. The data shown in this figure are in 1985 dollars. Part (a) looks at the richest countries. The United States has the highest real GDP per person, and Canada has the second highest. But up to 1989, Canada grew faster than the United States and so was catching up.

Until 1985, the third richest countries were France, Germany, Italy, and the United Kingdom. Figure 10.2(a) shows them as Europe Big 4. But in 1985, the fastest-growing rich country, Japan, caught up with Europe Big 4. All the countries shown in Fig. 10.2(a) are catching up with the United States. Japan has caught up most, Canada has got closest, and Europe Big 4 has caught up least.

Not all countries are growing faster than, and catching up with, the United States. Figure 10.2(b) looks at some of these. Africa and Central and South America were stagnating, not growing, during the 1980s. As a result, the gap between them and the United States widened. Western Europe other than the Big 4 countries grew during the 1970s and 1980s but at a rate that was roughly equal to that of the United States. So the gap remained constant. The former Communist countries of Central Europe grew faster than the United States until the late 1980s and then stagnated.

The data used in Fig. 10.2 are not currently available beyond 1992. But other data (not shown in Fig. 10.2) suggest that after 1992, real GDP per person shrank in some of the countries of Central Europe as they went through a process of traumatic political change.

---

**FIGURE 10.2**

## Economic Growth Around the World: Catch-Up or Not?

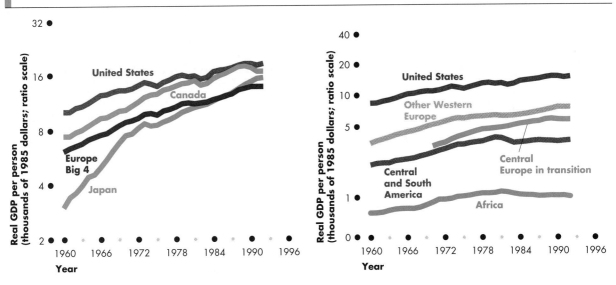

**(a) Catch up?**

**(b) No catch up?**

Real GDP per person has grown throughout the world economy. Among the rich industrial countries (part a), real GDP growth has been faster in Canada, the big four Western European countries (France, Germany, Italy, and the United Kingdom), and Japan than in the United States and they are catching up. The most spectacular growth was in Japan during the 1960s. The income level in Canada has also become closest to the U.S. income level. Among a wider range of countries (part b), there is less sign of convergence. The gaps between the income levels of the United States, other Western European countries, Central Europe, Central and South America, and Africa have remained remarkably constant.

*Source:* Robert Summers and Alan Heston, New Computer Diskette (Mark 5.6a), January 15, 1995 , distributed by the National Bureau of Economic Research to update "The Penn World Table: An Expanded Set of International Comparisons, 1950–1988," *Quarterly Journal of Economics,* May 1991, 327–368.

Taking both parts of Fig. 10.2 together, we can see that the catch-up in real GDP per person that is visible in part (a) is not a global phenomenon. Some rich countries are catching up with the United States, but the gaps between the United States and many poor countries are not closing.

Another group of countries that in 1960 had low levels of real GDP per person are catching up with the United States in a dramatic way. These are Hong Kong, Singapore, Taiwan, and Korea. Figure 10.3 shows how these countries are catching up with the

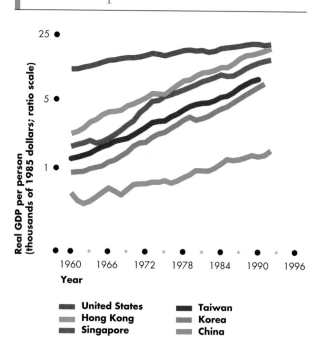

### FIGURE 10.3
## Catch-Up in Asia

The clearest examples of catch-up have occurred in five economies in Asia. Starting out in 1960 with incomes as little as one tenth of that in the United States, four Asian economies (Hong Kong, Singapore, Taiwan, and Korea) have substantially narrowed the gap on the United States. And from being a very poor developing country in 1960, China's income level now exceeds the income level that Hong Kong had in 1960. China is growing at a rate that is enabling it to continue to catch up with the United States.

*Source:* Robert Summers and Alan Heston, New Computer Diskette (Mark 5.5), June 15 1993, distributed by the National Bureau of Economic Research to update "The Penn World Table (Mark 5): An Expanded Set of International Comparisons, 1950–1988," *Quarterly Journal of Economics*, May 1991, 327–368.

United States. The figure also shows that China is catching up, but more slowly and from a very long way behind. In 1960, China's real GDP per person was one twentieth that of the United States, but by 1990, it was one twelfth.

The four small Asian countries shown in Fig. 10.3 are like fast trains running on the same track at similar speeds and with a roughly constant gap between them. Hong Kong is the lead train and runs about 12 years in front of Korea, which is the last train. Real GDP per person in Korea in 1990 was similar to that in Hong Kong in 1978, 12 years earlier. During the 30 years between 1960 and 1990, Hong Kong transformed itself from a poor developing country into one of the world's richest countries.

China is now doing what Hong Kong has done. If China continues its rapid growth, the world economy will become a dramatically different place. Because China is equivalent to more than 200 countries the size of Hong Kong. Whether China will continue on its current path of rapid growth is impossible to predict.

### REVIEW

- Over the hundred years between 1896 and 1996, real GDP per person in the United States grew at an average rate of 2 percent a year. Slow growth occurred during the early 1900s, mid-1950s, and 1973–1996, and rapid growth occurred during the 1920s and 1960s.
- Some rich countries are catching up with the United States, but the gaps between the United States and many poor countries are not closing.
- Hong Kong, Korea, Singapore, and Taiwan are catching up fastest. China is also catching up but more slowly and from a long way behind.

The facts about economic growth in the United States and around the world raise some big questions that we're now going to answer. We'll study the causes of economic growth in three stages. First, we'll look at the preconditions for growth and the activities that sustain it. Second, we'll learn how economists measure the relative contributions of the sources of growth—an activity called *growth accounting*. Third, we'll study three theories of economic growth that seek to explain how the influences on growth interact to determine the growth rate. Let's take our first look at the causes of economic growth.

# The Causes of Economic Growth: A First Look

MOST HUMAN SOCIETIES HAVE LIVED FOR centuries and even thousands of years like Songman Yang, with no economic growth. The key reason is that they have lacked some fundamental social institutions and arrangements that are essential preconditions for economic growth. Let's see what these preconditions are.

## Preconditions for Economic Growth

The most basic precondition for economic growth is an appropriate *incentive* system. Three institutions are crucial to the creation of incentives. They are:

1. Markets
2. Property rights
3. Monetary exchange

Markets enable buyers and sellers to get information and to do business with each other, and market prices send signals to buyers and sellers that create incentives to increase or decrease the quantities demanded and supplied. Markets enable people to specialize and trade and to save and invest. But for markets to work, we need property rights and monetary exchange.

Property rights are the social arrangements that govern the ownership, use, and disposal of resources and goods and services. They include the rights to physical property (land, buildings, and capital equipment), to financial property (claims by one person against another), and to intellectual property (such as inventions). Clearly established and enforced property rights give people an assurance that a capricious government will not confiscate their income or savings.

Monetary exchange facilitates transactions of all kinds, including the orderly transfer of private property from one person to another. Property rights and monetary exchange create incentives for people to specialize and trade, to save and invest, and to discover new technologies.

No unique political system is necessary to deliver the preconditions for economic growth. Liberal democracy, founded on the fundamental principle of the rule of law, is the system that does the best job. It provides a solid base on which property rights can be established and enforced. But authoritarian political systems have sometimes provided an environment in which economic growth has occurred.

Early human societies, based on hunting and gathering, did not experience economic growth because they lacked these preconditions. Economic growth began when societies evolved the three key institutions that create incentives. But the presence of an incentive system and the institutions that create it does not guarantee that economic growth will occur. It permits economic growth but does not make that growth inevitable.

The simplest way in which growth happens when the appropriate incentive system exists is that people begin to specialize in the activities at which they have a comparative advantage and trade with each other. You saw in Chapter 3 how everyone can gain from such activity. By specializing and trading, everyone can acquire goods and services at the lowest possible cost. Equivalently, people can obtain a greater volume of goods and services from their labor.

As an economy moves from one with little specialization to one that reaps the gains from specialization and exchange, its production and consumption grow. Real GDP per person increases, and the standard of living rises.

But for growth to be persistent, people must face incentives that encourage them to pursue three activities that generate ongoing economic growth. These activities are:

- Saving and investment in new capital
- Investment in human capital
- Discovery of new technologies

These three sources of growth, which interact with each other, are the primary sources of the extraordinary growth in productivity during the past 200 years. Let's look at each in turn.

## Saving and Investment in New Capital

Saving and investment in new capital increase the amount of capital per worker and increase real GDP per hour of labor—labor productivity. Labor productivity took the most dramatic upturn when the amount of capital per worker increased during the Industrial Revolution. Production processes that use hand tools can create beautiful objects, but production methods that use large amounts of capital per worker, such as auto plant assembly lines, are much more productive.

The accumulation of capital on farms, in textile factories, in iron foundries and steel mills, in coal mines, on building sites, in chemical plants, in auto plants, in banks and insurance companies, and in shopping malls has added incredibly to the productivity of our economy. The next time you see a Western movie, look carefully at the small amount of capital around. Try to imagine how productive you would be in such circumstances compared with your productivity today.

## Investment in Human Capital

Human capital—the accumulated skill and knowledge of human beings—is the most fundamental source of economic growth. It is a source of both increased productivity and technological advance.

The development of one of the most basic human skills, writing, was the source of some of the earliest major gains in productivity. The ability to keep written records made it possible to reap ever-larger gains from specialization and exchange. Imagine how hard it would be to do any kind of business if all the accounts, invoices, and agreements existed only in people's memories.

Later, the development of mathematics laid the foundation for the eventual extension of knowledge about physical forces and chemical and biological processes. This base of scientific knowledge was the foundation for the technological advances of the Industrial Revolution 200 years ago and of today's Information Revolution.

But much human capital that is extremely productive is much more humble. It takes the form of millions of individuals learning and repetitively doing simple production tasks and becoming remarkably more productive in the tasks.

One carefully studied example illustrates the importance of this kind of human capital. Between 1941 and 1944 (during World War II), U.S. shipyards produced some 2,500 units of a cargo ship, called the Liberty Ship, to a standardized design. In 1941, it took 1.2 million person-hours to build a ship. By 1942, it took 600,000, and by 1943, it took only 500,000. Not much change occurred in the capital employed during these years. But an enormous amount of human capital was accumulated. Thousands of workers and managers learned from experience and accumulated human capital that more than doubled their productivity in two years.

## Discovery of New Technologies

Saving and investment in new capital and the accumulation of human capital have made a large contribution to economic growth. But the contribution of technological change—of the discovery and the application of new technologies and new goods—has made an even greater contribution.

People are many times more productive today than they were a hundred years ago. We are not more productive because we have more steam engines per person and more horse-drawn carriages per person. Rather, it is because we have the engines and transportation equipment that use technologies that were unknown a hundred years ago and that are more productive than the old technologies were. Technological change makes an enormous contribution to our increased productivity. It arises from formal research and development programs and from informal trial and error, and it involves discovering new ways of getting more out of our resources.

To reap the benefits of technological change, capital must increase. Some of the most powerful and far-reaching fundamental technologies are embodied in human capital—for example, language, writing, and mathematics. But most technologies are embodied in physical capital. For example, to reap the benefits of the internal combustion engine, millions of horse-drawn carriages and horses had to be replaced by automobiles; more recently, to reap the benefits of computerized word processing, millions of typewriters had to be replaced by PCs and printers.

## REVIEW

- Economic growth cannot occur without institutions that create incentives to specialize and exchange, save and invest, and develop new technologies.
- The most significant sources of economic growth are saving and investment in new capital, the growth of human capital, and the discovery of new technologies. These sources interact: Human capital creates new technologies, which are embodied in both human and physical capital.

What is the quantitative contribution of the sources of economic growth? To answer this question, economists use growth accounting.

# Growth Accounting

THE QUANTITY OF REAL GDP SUPPLIED ($Y$) depends on three factors:

1. The quantity of labor ($N$)
2. The quantity of capital ($K$)
3. The state of technology ($T$)

The purpose of **growth accounting** is to calculate how much real GDP growth results from growth of labor and capital and how much is attributable to technological change.

The key tool of growth accounting is the **aggregate production function**, which is written as the equation:

$$Y = F(N, K, T).$$

In words, the quantity of real GDP supplied is determined by (is a function $F$ of) the quantities of labor and capital and of the state of technology. The larger $N$, $K$, or $T$, the greater is $Y$. And the faster $N$ and $K$ grow and the faster $T$ advances, the faster $Y$ grows.

So understanding what makes labor and capital grow and technology advance is the key to understanding economic growth. Labor growth depends primarily on population growth. And the growth rate of capital and the pace of technological advance determine the growth rate of labor productivity.

## Labor Productivity

**Labor productivity** is real GDP per hour of work. It is calculated by dividing real GDP by aggregate labor hours. That is, labor productivity equals $Y$ divided by $N$.

Labor productivity determines how much income an hour of labor generates. Figure 10.4 shows labor productivity for the period 1960–1996. You can see in this figure that productivity growth was most rapid during the 1960s and that it slowed down in 1973. You can also see that it speeded up again after 1983, but not to the pace of the 1960s.

Why did productivity grow fastest during the 1960s? Why did it slow down during the 1970s and then speed up again during the 1980s? Growth accounting answers these questions by dividing the

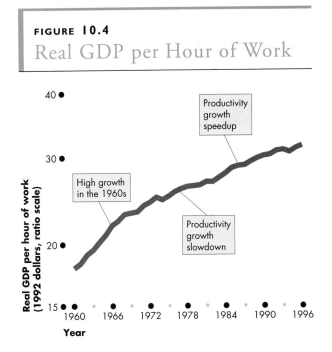

**FIGURE 10.4**

Real GDP per Hour of Work

Real GDP divided by aggregate hours equals real GDP per hour of work, which is a broad measure of productivity. During the 1960s, the productivity growth rate was high. It slowed during the 1970s and speeded up again after 1983.

Sources: U.S. Department of Commerce, *National Income and Product Accounts of the United States* (Washington, D.C.: U.S. Government Printing Office); U.S. Department of Labor, *Current Population Survey* (Washington, D.C.: U.S. Government Printing Office).

growth in labor productivity into two components and then measuring the contribution of each. The components are:

- Growth in capital per hour of labor
- Technological change

Technological change includes everything that contributes to labor productivity growth that is not included in growth in capital per hour. In particular, it includes human capital growth. Human capital growth and technological change are intimately related. Technology advances because knowledge advances. And knowledge is part of human capital. So "technological change" is a broad catchall concept.

The analytical engine of growth accounting is a relationship called the productivity function. Let's learn about this relationship and see how it is used.

## The Productivity Function

The **productivity function** is a relationship that shows how real GDP per hour of labor changes as the amount of capital per hour of labor changes with a given state of technology. Figure 10.5 illustrates the productivity function. Capital per hour of work is measured on the *x*-axis, and real GDP per hour of work is measured on the *y*-axis. The figure shows *two* productivity functions. One is the curve labeled $PF_0$, and the other is the curve labeled $PF_1$.

An increase in the quantity of capital per hour of labor increases real GDP per hour of labor, which is shown by a movement along a productivity function. For example, on $PF_0$, when capital per hour of labor is $30, real GDP per hour of labor is $20. If capital per hour of labor increases to $60, real GDP per hour of labor increases to $25.

Technological change increases the amount of GDP per hour of labor that can be produced by a given amount of capital per hour of labor. It is shown by an upward shift of the productivity function. For example, if capital per hour of work is $30 and a technological change increases real GDP per hour of work from $20 to $25, the productivity function shifts upward from $PF_0$ to $PF_1$ in Fig. 10.5. Similarly, if capital per hour of work is $60, the same technological change increases real GDP per hour of work from $25 to $32 and shifts the productivity function upward from $PF_0$ to $PF_1$.

To calculate the contributions of capital growth and technological change to productivity growth, we need to know the shape and slope of the productivity function. The shape of the productivity function reflects a fundamental economic law—the law of diminishing returns. The **law of diminishing returns** states that as the quantity of one input increases with the quantities of all other inputs remaining the same, output increases but by ever smaller increments. For example, in a factory that has a given amount of capital, as more labor is hired, production increases. But each *additional* hour of labor produces less *additional* output than the previous hour produced. Two typists working with one computer type fewer than twice as many pages per day as one typist working with one computer.

Applied to capital, the law of diminishing returns states that if a given number of hours of labor use more capital (with the same technology), the *additional* output that results from the *additional* capital gets smaller as the amount of capital increases. One typist working with two computers types fewer than

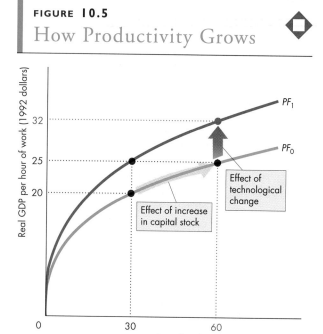

**FIGURE 10.5**

## How Productivity Grows

Productivity is measured by real GDP per hour of work, and it can grow for two reasons: (1) Capital per hour of work increases, and (2) technological advances occur. The productivity function, $PF_0$, shows the effects of an increase in capital per hour of work on productivity. Here, when capital per hour of work increases from $30 to $60, real GDP per hour of work increases from $20 to $25 along the productivity curve $PF_0$. Technological advance shifts the productivity function upward. Here, an advance in technology shifts the productivity function from $PF_0$ to $PF_1$. With this technological advance, real GDP per hour of work increases from $25 to $32 when there is $60 of capital per hour of work.

twice as many pages per day as one typist working with one computer. More generally, one hour of labor working with $60 of capital produces less than twice the output of one hour of labor working with $30 of capital. But how much less? The answer is given by the *one third rule*.

**The One Third Rule** Robert Solow of MIT estimated a production function from U.S. data. He discovered that on the average, with no change in technology, a 1 percent increase in capital per hour of labor brings a *one third of 1 percent* increase in real GDP per hour of labor. This one third rule is used to calculate the contributions of an increase in capital per hour of work and technological change to the growth of real GDP. Let's do such a calculation.

Suppose that capital per hour of work grows by 3 percent a year and real GDP per hour of work grows by 2.5 percent a year. The one third rule tells us that capital growth has contributed one third of 3 percent, which is 1 percent. The rest of the 2.5 percent growth of real GDP comes from technological change. That is, technological change has contributed 1.5 percent, which is the 2.5 percent growth of real GDP per hour of work minus the estimated 1 percent contribution of capital growth.

## Accounting for the Productivity Growth Slowdown and Speedup

We can use the one third rule to study U.S. productivity growth and the productivity growth slowdown. Figure 10.6 tells the story, starting in 1960.

**1960 to 1973** In 1960, capital per hour of work was $49 and real GDP per hour of work was $18 at the point marked 60 on $PF_0$. During the next 13 years, real GDP per hour of work expanded by 39 percent to $25. At the same time, capital per hour of work increased by 24 percent to $61. With no change in technology, the economy would have moved to point $a$ on $PF_0$ in Fig. 10.6, where real GDP per hour of work has increased by 8 percent ($1/3$ of 24 percent). But rapid technological change shifted the productivity curve upward to $PF_1$, and the economy moved to the point marked 73 on that curve.

**1973 to 1983** During the 10 years from 1973 to 1983, real GDP per hour of work expanded by 8 percent to $27. At the same time, capital per hour of work increased by 15 percent to $70. With no change in technology, the economy would have moved to point $b$ on $PF_1$ in Fig. 10.6, where real GDP per hour of work has increased by 5 percent ($1/3$ of 15 percent). But a tiny amount of technological change shifted the productivity curve upward to $PF_2$, and the economy moved to the point marked 83 on that curve.

We've now isolated the reason for the productivity growth slowdown. It occurred because the contribution of technological change to real GDP growth slowed.

**1983 to 1995** During the 12 years from 1983 to 1996, real GDP per hour of work expanded by 18.5 percent to $32. At the same time, capital per hour of work increased by 11 percent to $78. With no change

**FIGURE 10.6**

# Growth Accounting and the Productivity Growth Slowdown

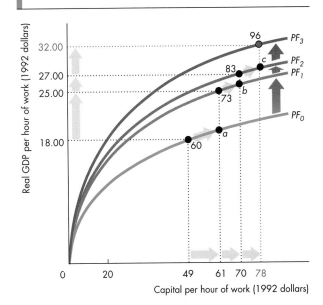

Between 1960 and 1973, which was a period of rapid productivity growth, capital per hour of work increased from $49 to $61, and technological progress shifted the productivity function upward from $PF_0$ to $PF_1$. Between 1973 and 1983, when potential GDP grew slowly, capital per hour of work increased from $61 to $70 and the productivity function barely shifted to $PF_2$. The effect of technological change was offset by oil price shocks. Between 1983 and 1995, capital per hour of work increased from $70 to $78 and technological progress shifted the productivity function upward from $PF_2$ to $PF_3$. Although productivity growth was not as rapid as in the 1960s, the productivity growth rate did increase.

*Sources:* U.S. Department of Commerce, *National Income and Product Accounts of the United States* (Washington, D.C.: U.S. Government Printing Office); U.S. Department of Labor, *Current Population Survey* (Washington, D.C.: U.S. Government Printing Office); and the author's calculations.

in technology, the economy would have moved to point $c$ on $PF_2$ in Fig. 10.6, where real GDP per hour of work has increased by 3.7 percent ($1/3$ of 11 percent). But a return of more rapid technological change shifted the productivity curve upward to $PF_3$, and the economy moved to the point marked 96 on that curve. Although technological change resumed, its pace was slower than during the 1960s.

## Technological Change During the Productivity Growth Slowdown

Technological change did not stop during the productivity growth slowdown. On the contrary, there was a lot of it. But the technological change that occurred did not increase productivity. Instead, it was directed toward coping with two other problems. They are:

- Energy price shocks
- The environment

**Energy Price Shocks**   Energy prices increased sharply in 1973–1974 and again in 1979–1980. One effect of higher energy prices was an increase in the rate at which gas-guzzling automobiles, airplanes, and heating systems were scrapped. This effect would be shown as a leftward movement along the productivity function as capital per hour of labor decreases. But another effect of increases in oil prices is that technological change is directed toward saving energy rather than enhancing productivity. For example, airplanes became more fuel efficient, but they didn't operate with smaller crews. Real GDP per gallon of fuel increased a lot, but real GDP per hour of labor increased slowly.

**The Environment**   The 1970s saw an expansion of laws and resources devoted to protecting the environment and improving the quality of the workplace. The benefits of these actions—cleaner air and water and safer factories—are not counted as real GDP. So the growth of these benefits is not measured as part of productivity growth. If these items were included in real GDP, the productivity function would have shifted upward during the 1970s and the growth slowdown would have been less severe.

## R E V I E W

- Growth accounting isolates the contributions of capital growth and technological change to productivity growth by using the *one third* rule—a 1 percent increase in capital per hour of work brings a one third of 1 percent increase in real GDP per hour of work.

- The productivity growth slowdown of the 1970s occurred because technological change made almost no contribution to productivity growth.

# Growth Theory

WE'VE SEEN THAT REAL GDP GROWS WHEN THE quantities of labor and capital grow and when technology (which includes human capital) advances. Does this mean that the growth of labor and capital and technological advances *cause* economic growth? It might. But there are other possibilities. *One* of these factors might be the cause of real GDP growth and the others the *effect*. We must try to discover how the influences on economic growth interact with each other to make some economies grow quickly and others grow slowly. And we must probe the reasons why a country's long-term growth rate sometimes speeds up and sometimes slows.

We're going to look at three theories of economic growth. All three theories contain some germs of truth—some fundamental insights into the process of economic growth. But none gives a firm and sure answer to the basic questions of what causes growth and makes growth rates vary. The three theories are:

- Classical growth theory
- Neoclassical growth theory
- New growth theory

## Classical Growth Theory

**Classical growth theory** is the view that real GDP growth is temporary and that when real GDP per person rises above the subsistence level, a population explosion eventually brings real GDP per person back to the subsistence level. Adam Smith, Thomas Robert Malthus, and David Ricardo, the leading economists of the late eighteenth century and early nineteenth century, were the first to suggest this theory, but the theory is most closely associated with the name of Malthus and is sometimes called the *Malthusian theory*.

Many people today are Malthusians. They point to the world population explosion—5 billion today and (they predict) 11 billion by 2200—and speculate that we will run out of resources and return to a primitive standard of living if we do not take action to contain the population growth.

To understand classical growth theory, let's transport ourselves back to the world of 1776, when Adam Smith is first explaining the idea. Most of the 2.5 million people who live in the newly independent

United States of America work on farms or on their own land and perform their tasks using simple tools and animal power. They earn about 2 shillings (a little less than $12 dollars in today's money) for working a ten-hour day. Then advances in farming technology bring new types of plows and seeds that increase farm productivity. As farm productivity increases, farm production increases and some farm workers move from the land to the cities, where they get work producing and selling the expanding range of farm equipment. Incomes rise, and the people seem to be prospering. But will the prosperity last? Classical growth theory says it will not.

Figure 10.7 illustrates the start of growth according to the classical growth theory. Before growth begins, the economy is in the situation shown in the figure. The labor demand curve is $LD_0$, and the labor supply curve is $LS_0$. There is equilibrium in the labor market: The quantity of labor demanded equals the quantity supplied at a real wage rate of 2 shillings a day, and 2 million people are employed. (We will use constant 1776 prices in this example to keep it in its historical context.)

Advances in technology—in both agriculture and industry—lead to investment in new capital, which makes labor more productive. More and more businesses start up and try to hire the now more productive labor. So the demand for labor increases and the labor demand curve shifts rightward to $LD_1$. With this greater demand for labor, the real wage rate rises to 4 shillings a day, and this higher wage rate brings an increase in the quantity of labor supplied (a movement along the labor supply curve). In the new situation, 3 million people are employed.

At this stage, economic growth has occurred and everyone has benefited from it. Real GDP has increased, and the real wage rate has increased. But the classical economists believe that this new situation can't last because it will induce a population explosion.

**Classical Theory of Population Growth**   The classical theory of population growth is based on the idea of a subsistence real wage rate. The **subsistence real wage rate** is the minimum real wage rate needed to maintain life. By its definition, if the actual real wage rate is less than the subsistence real wage rate, some people cannot survive and the population decreases. But in classical theory, whenever the real wage rate exceeds the subsistence real wage rate, the population grows. This assumption, combined with diminishing returns to labor, has a very dismal implication—one that resulted in economics being called the *dismal science*. This implication is that no matter how much investment and technological change occurs, real wage rates are always pushed back toward the subsistence level.

Figure 10.8 shows this process. Here, the subsistence real wage rate is (by assumption) 2 shillings a day. The actual real wage rate, at the intersection of $LS_0$ and $LD_1$, is 4 shillings a day. Because the actual real wage rate exceeds the subsistence real wage rate, the population grows and the labor supply increases. The labor supply curve shifts rightward to $LS_1$. As it does so, the real wage rate falls and the quantity of labor demanded increases. Eventually, in the absence of further technological change, the economy comes to rest at the subsistence real wage rate of 2 shillings a day, and 5 million people are employed.

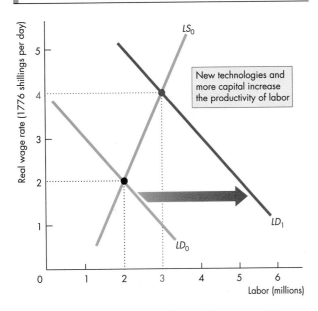

**FIGURE 10.7**
## Classical Growth Begins

Initially, the demand for labor is $LD_0$, and the supply of labor is $LS_0$. There are 2 million people employed, and they earn 2 shillings (1776 shillings) a day. An advance in technology and an increase in capital increase the productivity of labor, and the demand for labor increases to $LD_1$. The real wage rate rises to 4 shillings a day, and the quantity of labor supplied increases to 3 million.

## FIGURE 10.8

# A Dismal Outcome

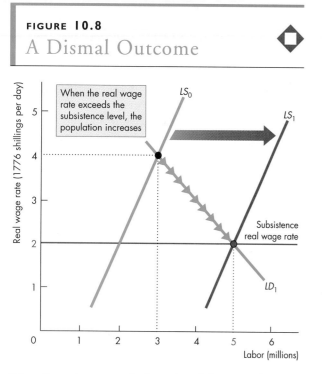

When the real wage rate is above the subsistence real wage rate, which in this example is 2 shillings a day, the population begins to increase. With an increase in population the supply of labor increases, and the labor supply curve shifts rightward to $LS_1$. As it does so, the real wage rate falls and the quantity of labor employed increases. The population stops growing when the real wage rate is back at the subsistence level.

The economy has grown, real GDP has increased, but a larger population is earning only the subsistence real wage rate.

### The Modern Theory of Population Growth

When the classical economists were developing their ideas about population growth, a population explosion was under way. In Britain and other Western European countries, improvements in diet and hygiene had lowered the death rate while the birth rate remained high. For several decades, population growth was extremely rapid. For example, after being relatively stable for several centuries, the population of Britain increased by 40 percent between 1750 and 1800 and by a further 50 percent between 1800 and 1830. At the same time, an estimated 1 million people (about 20 percent of the 1750 population) left Britain for America and Australia before 1800, and

outward migration continued on a similar scale through the nineteenth century. Population growth on this scale alarmed Malthus and the other classical economists and was the empirical basis for their theory of population growth.

But eventually, the birth rate fell, and while the population continued to increase, its rate of increase was moderate. This slowdown in the population growth rate seemed to make the classical theory increasingly less relevant. It also eventually led to the development of a modern economic theory of population growth.

The population growth rate is influenced by economic factors. Key among them is the opportunity cost of women's time. As women's wage rates have increased and their job opportunities have expanded, the opportunity cost of having children has increased. Faced with a higher opportunity cost, families have chosen to have a smaller number of children and the birth rate has fallen. Also, the death rate has fallen as greater investment has been made in advances in medicine.

If there is a connection between income levels and population growth, it is the opposite of that feared by the classical economists. As incomes rise, the population growth rate falls. This historical trend not only contradicts the views of the classical economists but it also calls into question the modern doomsday conclusion that we will be one day swamped with too many people for the planet to feed.

But despite the influence of economic factors on population growth, the influence is weak. And to a good approximation, the rate of population growth is independent of the rate of economic growth.

### Neoclassical Growth Theory

**Neoclassical growth theory** is the proposition that that real GDP per person grows because technological change induces saving and investment. Technological change is the fundamental cause of growth. Robert Solow of MIT suggested this theory during the 1950s. In the neoclassical theory, the rate of technological change influences the rate of economic growth, but economic growth does not influence the pace of technological change. It is assumed that technological change results from chance. When we get lucky, we have rapid technological change, and when bad luck strikes, the pace of technological advance slows.

At the heart of the neoclassical growth theory is the stock of capital per unit of labor and the *productivity function*—the relationship between capital per unit of labor and output per unit of labor. To keep things as simple as possible, the theory assumes that people work a fixed number of hours and that everyone works. So labor equals population. Also, the population grows at a constant rate. The model then can concentrate on the effects of technological change on saving, investment, and real GDP per person.

**Zero Growth**   Suppose that initially real GDP per person is constant. The quantity of capital is worth $10 trillion (1992 dollars). Each year, 10 percent of the capital stock wears out and is replaced. Investment and saving are $1 trillion. This amount is just sufficient to replace capital that wears out, so the quantity of capital remains constant at $10 trillion. With a constant labor force (which we are assuming), constant capital, and no technological change, real GDP is constant. There is no growth in this economy.

**Saving and Investment**   Figure 10.9 shows the investment demand curve and saving supply in the economy we've just described. (For a refresher on investment demand and saving supply, check back to Chapter 9, pp. 195–200.) The downward-sloping investment demand curve is $ID_0$. Along this curve, as the real interest rate falls, other things remaining the same, investment increases. The upward-sloping saving supply curve is $SS_0$. Along this curve, as the real interest rate rises, other things remaining the same, the supply of saving increases.

The real interest rate adjusts to achieve equilibrium. In Fig. 10.9, on $ID_0$ and $SS_0$, investment equals saving at a real interest rate of 4 percent a year with saving and investment equal to $1 trillion.

**A Technological Advance**   Now suppose that a technological advance occurs. This advance increases the productivity of capital and increases the expected profit rate. So businesses increase their investment demand. The investment demand curve shifts rightward to $ID_1$. The greater investment demand raises the real interest rate to 6 percent a year, and the higher real interest rate brings forth an increase in saving—a movement along the saving supply curve $SS_0$. Investment increases to $1.5 trillion.

Real GDP per person is now growing. Investment exceeds the amount needed to replace capital

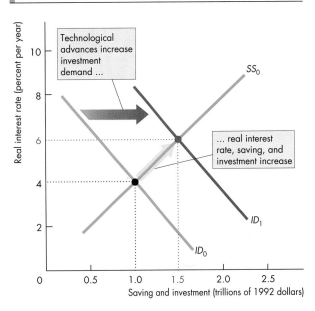

**FIGURE 10.9**

## Neoclassical Growth Begins

In neoclassical growth theory, economic growth results from technological change. Initially, investment demand is $ID_0$ and saving supply is $SS_0$. Investment is $1 trillion a year, and the real interest rate is 4 percent a year. This investment level replaces worn out capital and the quantity of capital is constant, so real GDP is also constant. A technological advance increases expected profits and increases investment demand. Investment demand increases to $ID_1$. The real interest rate rises to 6 percent a year, and investment increases to $1.5 trillion. As a result, the quantity of capital and real GDP begin to grow.

that is wearing out, so the quantity of capital increases. And with an increasing quantity of capital, real GDP increases.

**Saving and Investment in the Growing Economy**
Now that real GDP is growing, rising disposable income and a rising capital stock induce changes in saving and investment—cause shifts in the saving supply curve and the investment demand curve.

We cannot keep track of all these changes by using the investment demand–saving supply figure. Instead, we look at the demand for the entire stock of capital and the supply of the stock of capital. (Investment demand is the demand for *newly produced* capital in a given time period. Saving supply is the supply of funds to buy newly produced capital in a given time period.)

Figure 10.10 shows the demand for the stock of capital $KD_0$. This demand curve slopes downward. The lower the real interest rate, the greater is the quantity of capital demanded.

At a given moment, the supply of capital is given. It is the vertical line $KS_0$. In the long run, the supply of capital depends on saving decision. The neoclassical theory holds that if the real interest rate exceeds a target rate, the supply of capital increases; if the real interest rate is less that a target rate, the supply of capital decreases; and if the real interest rate equals a target rate, the supply of capital is constant. In Fig. 10.10, the target real interest rate is 4 percent a year and the long-run capital supply curve is $LKS$.

Initially, equilibrium is at point *a*, where $KD_0$ and $KS_0$ intersect and where the real interest rate is 4 percent a year—its target rate. The capital stock is $10 trillion. Neoclassical growth begins from this point.

A technological advance now increases the productivity of capital and the demand for capital curve shifts rightward to $KD_1$. The expected rate of profit increases, which brings an increase in investment demand (shown in Fig. 10.9). With higher investment, the supply of capital increases and the $KS$ curve begins to shift rightward. As it does so, the real interest rate falls.

**Zero Growth Again**  The capital stock continues to increase and the real interest rate continues to fall until the economy reaches point *b* in Fig. 10.10. Here the real interest rate is back at its long-run target rate of 4 percent a year and the capital stock has grown to $20 trillion. With no further capital growth, real GDP stops growing, and in the absence of another technological advance, growth has ended. In this new zero-growth situation, investment and saving are $2 trillion—just sufficient to replace 10 percent of the larger capital stock that wears out each year.

Throughout the process you've just studied, real GDP grows, but the growth rate gradually decreases and eventually growth ends. Ongoing exogenous technology advances are constantly increasing the demand for capital, raising the real interest rate, and inducing saving. The process that we've just examined repeats as long as technology advances, creating an ongoing process of long-term economic growth. The growth rate fluctuates because technological progress occurs at a variable rate.

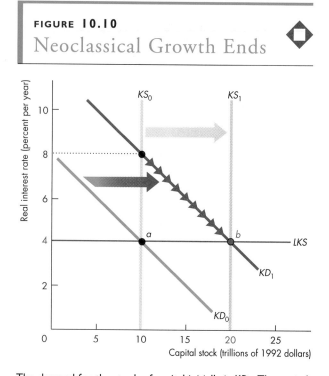

**FIGURE 10.10**

## Neoclassical Growth Ends

The demand for the stock of capital initially is $KD_0$. The capital stock is fixed in the short run and initially is $KS_0$. The long-run supply of capital is $LKS$. A technological advance increases the productivity of capital and increases the demand for capital to $KD_1$. The real interest rate rises. But so do investment and saving. The capital stock also increases. As the capital stock increases, the $KS$ curve shifts rightward toward $KS_1$. The real interest rate falls. When the real interest rate has fallen to its long-run target rate, the supply of capital stops increasing, the capital stock is constant at $20 trillion, and growth ends.

**Problem with Neoclassical Growth Theory**  All economies have access to the same technologies, and capital is free to roam the globe seeking the highest available rate of return. So neoclassical growth theory implies that growth rates and income levels per person around the globe converge. While there is some sign of convergence among the rich countries (shown in Fig. 10.2a), convergence is slow and it does not appear to be imminent for all countries (as we saw in Fig. 10.2b).

New growth theory attempts to overcome this shortcoming of neoclassical growth theory. It also attempts to explain how the rate of technological change is determined.

## New Growth Theory

**New growth theory** holds that real GDP per person grows because of the choices that people make in the pursuit of profit and that growth can persist indefinitely.

The theory begins with two facts about market economies:

- Discoveries result from choices and actions.
- Discoveries bring profit, and competition destroys profit.

**Discoveries and Choices**  When people discover a new product or technique, they think of themselves as being lucky. They are right. But the pace at which new discoveries are made—the pace at which technology advances—is not determined by chance. It depends on how many people are looking for a new technology and how intensively they are looking.

**Discoveries and Profits**  Profit is the spur to technological change. The forces of competition squeeze profits, so to increase profit, people constantly seek either lower-cost methods of production or new and better products for which people are willing to pay a higher price. Inventors can maintain a profit for several years by taking out a patent or copyright. But eventually, a new discovery is copied and profits disappear.

Two further facts play a key role in the new growth theory:

- Discoveries can be used by many people at the same time.
- Physical activities can be replicated.

**Discoveries Used by All**  Once a profitable new discovery has been made, everyone can use it. And one person's use of a new discovery does not prevent others from using it. This fact means that as the benefits of a new discovery spread, free resources become available. These resources are free because nothing is given up when they are used. They have a zero opportunity cost.

**Replicating Activities**  Production activities can be replicated. For example, there might be two, three, or fifty-three identical firms making fiber-optic cable using an identical assembly line and production technique. If one firm increases output, that firm experiences diminishing returns. But the economy can increase the output of fiber-optic cable by adding

another identical factory, and the economy does not experience diminishing returns.

The implication of this simple and appealing idea is astonishing. Unlike neoclassical theory, with its diminishing returns to capital, which eventually lowers the real interest rate to the target real interest rate, new growth theory has no such mechanism. Real GDP per person increases and does so indefinitely as long as people can undertake research and development that yields a higher return than the target real interest rate.

New growth theory sees the economy as a kind of perpetual motion mechanism. Economic growth is driven by our insatiable wants that lead us to pursue profit and innovate. The result of this process is new and better products. But new and better products result in new firms starting up and old firms going out of business. In this process, jobs are created and destroyed. The outcome is new and better jobs, more leisure, and more consumption. All this adds up to a higher standard of living. But our insatiable wants are still there, so the process continues, going round and round a circle of wants, profits, innovation, new products, and higher living standards.

The growth rate depends on people's ability to innovate and the rate of return to innovation. Over the years, this ability has changed. The invention of language and writing (the two most basic human capital tools), and later the development of the scientific method and the establishment of universities and research institutions, brought a huge increase in the rate of return to innovation. Today, a deeper understanding of genes is bringing profit in a growing biotechnology industry. And astonishing advances in computer technology are creating an explosion of profit opportunities in a wide range of new information age industries.

Figure 10.11 shows how the new growth theory works. Like Fig. 10.10, it shows the demand for and supply of the *stock* of capital. But unlike Fig. 10.10, here the marginal product of capital does not diminish as the quantity of capital increases. The demand curve for capital is horizontal at the real interest rate equal to the expected rate of profit.

The supply of capital is fixed in the short run and is shown by a vertical supply curve such as $KS_0$. The long-run capital supply curve is horizontal at the target real interest rate and is *LKS*.

Initially, the rate of return on capital is 2 percent a year, so the demand for capital is shown by the line $KD_0$ in Fig. 10.11. This rate of return is below the

## FIGURE 10.11
## New Growth Theory

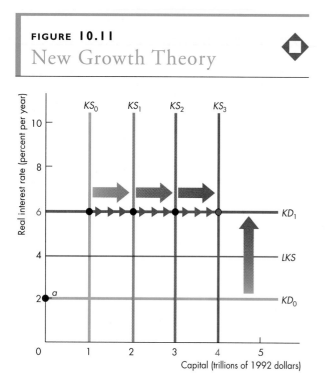

In new growth theory, economic growth results from technological change. The returns to capital do not diminish, and growth proceeds indefinitely. Initially, the rate of return on capital is 2 percent a year and the demand for capital is $KD_0$. The stock of capital is zero, and the economy is stuck at point $a$. The development of the scientific method increases the rate of return on capital to 6 percent a year and the demand for capital increases to $KD_1$. With a real interest rate greater than the target real interest rate, saving increases and the supply of capital increases. The capital supply curve shifts rightward successively through $KS_1, KS_2, KS_3$, and so on. As capital grows, real GDP grows but the real interest rate does not fall because there are no diminishing returns. Real GDP growth continues indefinitely.

target real interest rate, so no one has an incentive to save. The economy is stuck at point $a$.

The development of basic human capital tools such as mathematics and physics increases the return to capital and innovation and the demand for capital curve shifts upward to $KD_1$. The return to saving and investment now exceeds the target real interest rate. So investment and saving increase and the quantity of capital grows. As it does so, the supply of capital curve shifts rightward through $KS_1, KS_2, KS_3$, and so on. The capital stock grows, real GDP grows, and the rate of return on capital does not diminish.

Economic growth continues indefinitely as long as the real interest rate exceeds the target real interest rate.

Figure 10.11 shows the process we've just described. The target real interest rate is 4 percent a year, and the rate of return on capital is 6 percent a year. With positive saving, the capital supply curve shifts rightward indefinitely. The speed with which it shifts rightward depends on the extent to which the real interest rate exceeds the target real interest rate. The higher the real return on capital, the more the real interest rate exceeds that target real interest rate, and the faster the capital supply curve shifts rightward. So the faster the economy grows.

### Sorting Out the Theories

Which theory is correct? Probably none is exactly correct. But they all teach us something of value. The classical theory reminds us that our physical resources are limited and that with no advances in technology, we must eventually hit diminishing returns. Neoclassical theory reaches essentially the same conclusion, but not because of a population explosion. Instead, it emphasizes potentially diminishing returns to capital and reminds us that we cannot necessarily keep growth going just by accumulating capital. New growth theory emphasizes the possible capacity of human resources to innovate at a pace that offsets diminishing returns.

## R E V I E W

▧ Economic growth arises from increases in the capital stock, and advances in technology (which includes improvements in human capital).

▧ In classical growth theory, population explosions keep returning real GDP per person to the subsistence level because of diminishing returns to labor.

▧ In neoclassical growth theory, growth results from technological advances determined by chance.

▧ In new growth theory, the pursuit of profit brings persistent innovation and increased capital does not bring diminishing returns.

Your final task in this chapter is to examine the policy actions that might be taken to speed up the growth rate.

# Achieving Faster Growth

To ACHIEVE FASTER ECONOMIC GROWTH, WE MUST either increase the growth rate of capital per hour of work or increase the pace of technological advance (which includes improving human capital).

The main suggestions for achieving these objectives are:

- Stimulate saving
- Stimulate research and development
- Target high-technology industries
- Encourage international trade
- Improve the quality of education

**Stimulate Saving**    Saving finances investment, which brings capital accumulation and economic growth. So stimulating saving can stimulate economic growth. China, Hong Kong, Japan, Korea, Singapore, and Taiwan have the highest growth rates. They also have the highest saving rates. Some countries of Africa have the lowest growth rates. They also have the lowest saving rates. The saving rates in the United States and the other rich countries are modest.

The most obvious way in which saving could be increased is by providing tax incentives. Some incentives already exist, but more effective measures are possible. For example, instead of taxing incomes (which means taxing both consumption and saving), we could tax only consumption. Such a tax would encourage additional saving and most likely increase the economy's growth rate.

**Stimulate Research and Development**    Patents protect inventors and provide incomes that give incentives to research and development. But everyone can use the fruits of *basic* research and development efforts. For example, VisiCalc invented the basic idea of the spreadsheet. It did not take long for Lotus Corporation to use this idea and create the famous and immensely productive 1-2-3. And soon after, Microsoft Corporation created a Lotus 1-2-3 look-alike, Excel. Because basic inventions can be copied, the inventor's profit is limited, and the resources that a firm will allocate to making an invention or innovation are also limited. For this reason, the free market allocates too few resources to basic research.

This situation is one in which government subsidies might help. By using public funds to finance basic research and development that bring public benefits, it might be possible to encourage an efficient level of research. However, this solution is not foolproof. The main problem is that some mechanism must be designed for allocating the public funds. At present, universities and public research institutions such as NASA are the main channels through which public funds get used to finance research.

**Target High-Technology Industries**    Some people argue that by providing public funds to high-technology firms and industries, a country can become the first to exploit a new technology and can earn above-average profits for a period while others are busy catching up. This strategy is risky and just as likely to use resources inefficiently as to speed growth.

**Encourage International Trade**    Free international trade stimulates growth by extracting all the available gains from specialization and exchange. It is no accident that the fastest-growing nations today are those with the fastest-growing international trade—both exports and imports.

**Improve the Quality of Education**    Education, like basic research, brings benefits beyond those valued by the people who receive the education. And by its nature, education is a good the value of which people only appreciate fully *after* receiving it. So the free market produces too little education. By funding basic education and by ensuring high standards in basic skills such as language, mathematics, and science, governments can contribute to a nation's growth potential. Education can also be stimulated and improved by using tax incentives to encourage an increased scale of private provision.

◆ Economic growth is the single most decisive factor in influencing a country's living standard, but it is not the only one. Another is the extent to which the country fully employs its scarce resources, especially its labor. In recent years, the United States has enjoyed full employment and steady growth. But the business cycle is almost certainly not dead. And unemployment has become a severe problem for many countries. In Part 9, we study the fluctuations of real GDP and employment and unemployment around their long-term trends. But before embarking on this new topic, take a look at *Reading Between the Lines* on pages 230–231 and see how the Internet is contributing to the growth of our economy today.

# Growth in the Virtual Economy

The Wall Street Journal, October 17, 1996

## The Internet Economy

BY TAKUMA AMANO AND
ROBERT BLOHM

Belying the pessimism of limits-to-growth advocates, the U.S. economy grew at a seemingly robust annualized rate of 4.8% in this year's second quarter despite frequently reported downsizings or restructurings of U.S. corporations—even causing the Federal Reserve Board to consider tightening monetary policy. This healthy economic growth and a declining unemployment rate haven't been accompanied by inflationary pressure; the most recent annual increase of the producer price index was just 2.6%.

While President Clinton takes credit for this happy turn of events, and Bob Dole pooh-poohs it, what both men overlook is that the single most important factor behind this economic performance is the Internet. Conceived by the Defense Department in the mid-1960s and beefed up by the Reagan administration to provide massive computing capability for Star Wars and backup in case of war, the Internet was accessible until the end of the 1980s only by a limited number of government and academic users.

With the end of the Cold War, the advantages of the Internet for individual users soon became apparent and a new products market developed—both for Internet access, browsers and search and directory guides, such as Netscape and Yahoo!, and for computer networking equipment, like the electronic message switching systems and routers of Cisco Systems Inc. ...

Beyond the development of physical capital, there is also the development of metaphysical capital ... in the form of the new entrepreneurial talent being created by folks whose creative lives have become enmeshed in the Web. Once, a substantial percentage of young graduates with degrees in science and engineering would start their careers in defense-related industries. Now many go directly into young software and hardware companies.

The Internet market represents a successful shift of this country's most important economic resource—the human brain—to the highest value-added sector of the economy, demonstrating the optimum resource allocation inherent in our free market. ...

Barring another oil crisis, or excessive government spending, the Internet market will continue pushing the U.S. economy into a growth era qualitatively different from the past ...

## Essence of THE STORY

■ During the second quarter of 1996, the Internet was the single most important source of strong U.S. economic growth.

■ A few years ago, new science and engineering graduates found jobs in defense-related industries. Today, many get jobs in the computer industry.

■ The market economy is moving human capital to its highest-valued use.

■ The Internet will move the U.S. economy into a new growth era.

# Economic

## A N A L Y S I S

■ The growth of the Internet and the World Wide Web has been remarkable.

■ Figure 1 shows this growth. Measured by the number of host computers, the Internet grew from 1.3 million hosts at the end of 1992 to 9.5 million at the end of 1995, a growth rate of 5.7 percent *per month*.

■ The World Wide Web has grown even faster, from nothing in 1993 to more than half a million sites at the end of 1996, a growth rate of 22.7 percent *per month*! At this growth rate, the Web more than doubles in size every three months.

■ The news article says that the growth of the Internet is the main source of economic growth in the United States. But this claim is probably too strong. Let's see why.

■ Figure 2 shows real GDP from 1986 to 1996. The growth rate of real GDP was 2.19 percent a year between 1986 and 1992 (before the Web). It was 2.45 percent a year between 1993 and 1996 (after the Web).

■ Although real GDP growth increased slightly after 1993, there is no sign

that potential GDP growth increased. It might have done, but it is too early to tell because of the business cycle. In 1992, the economy was still recovering from the 1990–1991 recession and the unemployment rate was more than 7 percent. By 1996, the unemployment rate had fallen to 5.5 percent. We will not be able to say whether the *growth rate* of potential GDP has increased until we can see the current business cycle in a longer-term perspective.

■ Although we cannot determine whether the *growth rate* of potential GDP growth has increased, it is undeniable that the Internet has had a positive effect on the *level* of potential GDP.

■ The new technologies that are making the Internet grow are available for everyone to use. The opportunity cost of using these technologies is low.

■ Also, these forms of capital probably are not yet experiencing diminishing returns and perhaps will not do so for a long time.

■ It is possible that these new technologies have increased the rate of profit. If they have done so,

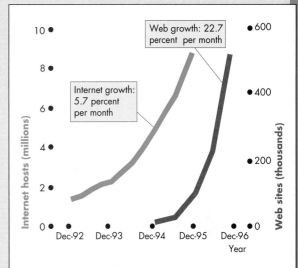

Figure 1 Growth of the Internet

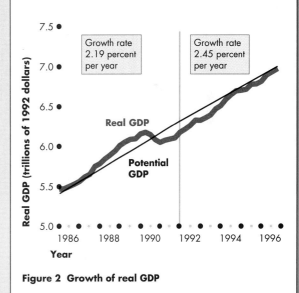

Figure 2 Growth of real GDP

they might have created a new growth environment in which the U.S. economy will expand at a more rapid rate than previously.

■ The evidence is not yet present in the GDP data. But real GDP growth might understate the true growth rate.

---

# SUMMARY

## Key Points

### Long-Term Growth Trends (pp. 214–216)

▣ Between 1896 to 1996, real GDP per person in the United States grew at an average rate of 2 percent a year. Growth was fastest during the 1920s and 1960s.

▣ The real GDP gaps between the United States and Africa as well as Central and South America have widened. The gaps between the United States and Hong Kong, Korea, Taiwan, and China have narrowed.

### The Causes of Economic Growth: A First Look (pp. 217–218)

▣ Economic growth occurs when an *incentive* system, which is created by markets, property rights, and monetary exchange, encourages saving, investment in physical and human capital, and the discovery of new technologies.

### Growth Accounting (pp. 219–222)

▣ Growth accounting measures the contributions of capital accumulation and technological change to productivity growth.

▣ Growth accounting uses the productivity function and the *one third rule*: a 1 percent increase in capital per hour of work brings a one third of 1 percent increase in real GDP per hour of work.

▣ During the productivity growth slowdown of the 1970s, technological change made almost no contribution to real GDP growth.

### Growth Theory (pp. 222–228)

▣ In classical theory, when the real wage rate exceeds the *subsistence* real wage rate, a population explosion brings diminishing returns to labor and real GDP per person returns to the subsistence level.

▣ In neoclassical growth theory, when the capital stock increases, the return to capital diminishes. Without technological change, growth ends.

▣ In new growth theory, the growth rate depends on the benefits and costs of developing new technologies.

▣ In new growth theory, the return to capital does not diminish when the capital stock increases.

### Achieving Faster Growth (p. 229)

▣ To achieve faster economic growth, we must increase the growth of capital per hour of work or increase the pace of technological advance.

▣ It might be possible to achieve faster growth by stimulating saving, subsidizing research and development, targeting (and possibly subsidizing) high-technology industries, and encouraging more international trade and more education.

## Key Figures

## Key Terms

# QUESTIONS

1. What was the average growth rate of real GDP per person in the United States between 1896 and 1996?

2. Which countries have grown fastest and which have grown slowest?

3. Have levels of real GDP per person across countries converged?

4. What are the three necessary preconditions for economic growth to occur?

5. What three activities can create ongoing economic growth?

6. Explain how economic growth can occur even in the absence of investment and new technologies.

7. What is growth accounting?

8. What is the main concept used in growth accounting?

9. How are the effects of capital accumulation and technological change separated by growth accounting techniques?

10. What is the one third rule and how is it used?

11. Explain the main sources of economic growth in the United States.

12. What were the main sources of the productivity growth slowdown in the United States during the 1970s?

13. Why did technological advances not increase productivity during the 1970s?

14. What are the main theories of economic growth?

15. What are the key assumptions of classical growth theory?

16. What are the key assumptions of neoclassical growth theory?

17. What are the key assumptions of new growth theory?

18. Contrast neoclassical growth theory and new growth theory.

19. What are the main policy actions that governments might take to increase the growth rate?

# PROBLEMS

1. The following information has been discovered about the economy of Longland: The economy's productivity function is:

| Capital per hour of work (1992 dollars per hour) | Real GDP per hour of work (1992 dollars per hour) |
|---|---|
| 10 | 3.80 |
| 20 | 5.40 |
| 30 | 6.80 |
| 40 | 8.00 |
| 50 | 9.00 |
| 60 | 9.80 |
| 70 | 10.40 |
| 80 | 10.80 |

Does this economy conform to the one third rule? If so, explain why. If not, explain why not and also explain what rule, if any, it does conform to.

2. The figure illustrates the productivity function of Lotus Land in 1989 and 1996.

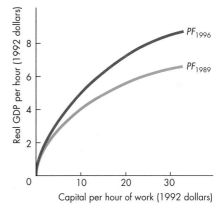

In 1989, capital per hour of work was $10, and in 1996 it was $25.

a. Does Lotus Land experience diminishing returns? Explain why or why not.

b. Use growth accounting to find the contribution of the change in capital between 1989 and 1996 to the growth of productivity in Lotus Land.

c. Use growth accounting to find the contribution of technological change between 1989 and 1996 to the growth of productivity in Lotus Land.

🖥 3. The following information has been discovered about the economy of Cape Despair. The subsistence real wage rate is $7 an hour. When the real wage rate rises above this level, the population grows; and when the real wage rate falls below this level, the population falls. With its current population, the demand and supply schedules for labor in Cape Despair are:

| Real wage rate (1992 dollars per hour) | Quantity of labor demanded (billions of hours per year) | Quantity of labor supplied (billions of hours per year) |
|:---:|:---:|:---:|
| 3 | 8 | 4 |
| 5 | 7 | 5 |
| 7 | 6 | 6 |
| 9 | 5 | 7 |
| 11 | 4 | 8 |
| 13 | 3 | 9 |
| 15 | 2 | 10 |
| 17 | 1 | 11 |

Initially, the labor force of Cape Despair is constant, and the real wage is at its subsistence level. Then a technological advance increases the amount that firms are willing to pay for labor by $2 at each level of employment.
   a.   What are the initial level of employment and real wage rate in Cape Despair?
   b.   What happens to the real wage rate immediately following the technological advance?
   c.   What happens to the population growth rate following the technological advance?
   d.   What is the employment level when Cape Despair returns to a long-run equilibrium?

4. Martha's Island is an economy that behaves according to the neoclassical growth model. The target real interest rate on capital is 3 percent a year. A technological advance increases the demand for capital and raises the interest rate to 5 percent a year. Describe what happens on Martha's Island.

🖥 5. Romeria is a country that behaves according to the predictions of new growth theory. The target real interest rate on capital is 3 percent a year. A technological advance increases the demand for capital and raises the interest rate to 5 percent a year. Describe what happens in Romeria and contrast it with the events in Martha's Island.

⊕   http://hepg.awl.com/parkin/econ100

# CRITICAL THINKING

1. After studying *Reading Between the Lines* on pp. 230–231, answer the following questions:
   a.   How quickly is the Internet growing compared with the growth of real GDP?
   b.   Are the measures of growth of the Internet and the World Wide Web in Fig. 1 comparable with the measure of the growth of real GDP in Fig. 2? (Think about what real GDP measures.)
   c.   What information would you need about Internet growth to determine how quickly its output is increasing?
   d.   Suppose that the Internet really does increase the growth rate of potential GDP. What, according to each of the three economic growth theories—classical, neoclassical, and new—will happen in the longer term?
   e.   Which of the three economic growth theories—classical, neoclassical, and new—does the author of the news article seem to believe is relevant in the United States today?

⊕ 2. Visit the Penn World Table Web site (linked from the Parkin site) and obtain data on real GDP per person for the United States, China, South Africa, and Mexico since 1960.
   a.   Draw a graph of the data.
   b.   Which country has the lowest real GDP per person and which has the highest?
   c.   Which country has experienced the fastest growth rate since 1960 and which the slowest?
   d.   Explain why the growth rates in these four countries are ranked on the order you have discovered.
   e.   Return to the Penn World Table Web site and obtain data for four other countries that interest you. Describe and explain the patterns that you find for these countries.

3. Write a memo to your Congress member in which you set out the policies you believe the U.S. government must follow to speed up the growth rate of real GDP in the United States.

4. Is faster economic growth always a good thing? Argue the case for faster growth and for slower growth and then reach a conclusion on whether growth should be increased or decreased.

# Aggregate Demand and Inflation

# Money Chasing Goods

Aggregate demand fluctuations bring recessions and expansions. If aggregate demand expands more rapidly than long-run aggregate supply, we get inflation. So understanding the forces that determine aggregate demand helps us to understand both the business cycle and inflation. ◆ It took economists a long time to achieve this knowledge, and we still don't know enough about aggregate demand to be able to forecast it more than a few months ahead. But we do know the basic factors that influence aggregate demand. And we know a lot about how those factors interact to send shock waves rippling through the economy. ◆ Fundamentally, aggregate demand is a monetary phenomenon. The quantity of money is the single most significant influence on aggregate demand. This insight was first outlined more than 200 years ago by David Hume, a Scottish philosopher and close friend of Adam Smith. Said Hume, "In every Kingdom into which money begins to flow in greater abundance than formerly, every thing takes a new face: labor and industry gain life; the merchant becomes more enterprising, the manufacturer more diligent and skilful, and even the farmer follows his plow with greater alacrity and attention." Milton Friedman and other economists known as *monetarists* also emphasize the central role of money. Money lies at the center of Keynes' theory of aggregate demand as well. But Keynes also called attention to the power of independent changes in government purchases, taxes, and business investment to influence aggregate demand. In the modern world, we also recognize the effect of changes in exports on aggregate demand. ◆ The chapters in this part explain the factors that influence aggregate demand and help you to understand how they interact to bring multiplier effects on aggregate expenditure. Chapter 11 explains the effects of changes in business investment and the multiplier effect it has on consumption expenditure and aggregate expenditure. This chapter also explain how changes in business inventories trigger changes in production and incomes. Chapter 12 looks at fiscal policy and applies the model of Chapter 11 to study the effects of changes in government purchases and taxes. Chapter 13 brings money into the picture and explains exactly what money is and how banks create it. Chapter 14 shows you how the Fed controls the quantity of money and thereby influences interest rates and expenditure. Chapter 15 returns to the aggregate supply–aggregate demand framework and explains inflation. It shows you how the trends in inflation are determined by the trend in the money supply and how fluctuations in aggregate demand bring fluctuations in inflation, employment and unemployment. ◆ Before you begin your study of aggregate demand and inflation, we'll spend some time with Milton Friedman, an economist who has advanced our knowledge in this field. And we'll talk with one of today's leading macroeconomists, Bennett McCallum of Carnegie Mellon University.

# Money and Inflation

## The Economist: Milton Friedman

Milton Friedman was born into a poor immigrant family in New York City in 1912. He was an undergraduate at Rutgers and graduate student at Columbia University during the Great Depression. Today, Professor Friedman is a Senior Fellow at the Hoover Institution at Stanford University. But his reputation was built between 1946 and 1983, when he was a leading member of the "Chicago School," an approach to economics developed at the University of Chicago and based on the views that free markets allocate resources efficiently and that stable and low money supply growth delivers macroeconomic stability.

Friedman has advanced our understanding of the forces that determine aggregate demand and clarified the effects of the quantity of money. For this work, he was awarded the (much overdue in the opinion of his many admirers) 1977 Nobel Prize for Economic Science.

By reasoning from basic economic principles, Friedman predicted that persistent demand stimulation would *not* increase output but *would* cause inflation. When output growth slowed and inflation broke out in the 1970s, Friedman seemed like a prophet and, for a time, his policy prescription, known as "monetarism," was embraced around the world.

> *"Inflation is always and everywhere a monetary phenomenon."*
>
> MILTON FRIEDMAN
>
> *THE COUNTER-REVOLUTION IN MONETARY THEORY*

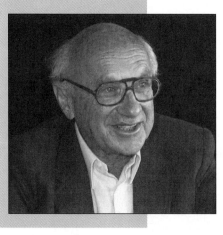

## The Issues and Ideas

The combination of history and economics has taught us a lot about the causes of inflation. Severe inflation—hyperinflation—arises from a breakdown of the normal fiscal policy processes at times of war or political upheaval. Tax revenues fall short of government spending, and newly printed money fills the gap between them. As inflation increases, the quantity of money needed to make payments increases, and a shortage of money can even result. So the rate of money growth increases yet further, and prices rise yet faster. Eventually, the monetary system collapses. Such was the experience of Germany during the 1920s and Brazil during the 1990s.

In earlier times, when commodities were used as money, inflation resulted from the discovery of new sources of money. The most recent occurrence of this type of inflation was at the end of the nineteenth century when gold, then used as money, was discovered in Australia, the Klondike, and South Africa.

In modern times, inflation has resulted from increases in the money supply that has accommodated increases in costs. The most dramatic of such inflations occurred during the 1970s when the Fed and other central banks around the world accommodated oil price increases.

To avoid inflation, money supply growth must be held in check. But at times of severe cost pressure, central banks feel a strong tug in the direction of avoiding recession and accommodating the cost pressure.

Yet some countries have avoided inflation more effectively than others have. One source of success is central bank independence. In low-inflation countries such as Germany and Japan, the central bank decides how much money to create and at what level to set interest rates and does not take instructions from the government. In high-inflation countries, such as the United Kingdom and Italy, the central bank takes direct orders from the government about interest rates and money supply growth. The architects of a new monetary system for the European Community have noticed this connection between central bank independence and inflation, and they are modeling the European Central Bank on Germany's Bundesbank.

## THEN ...

When inflation is especially rapid, as it was in Germany in 1923, money becomes almost worthless. In Germany at that time, bank notes were more valuable as fire kindling than as money, and the sight of people burning Reichmarks was a common one. To avoid having to hold money for too long, wages were paid and spent twice a day. Banks took deposits and made loans, but at interest rates that compensated both depositors and the bank for the falling value of money—interest rates that could exceed 100 percent a month.

The price of a dinner would increase during the course of an evening, making lingering over coffee a very expensive pastime.

## ... AND NOW

In 1994, Brazil had a computer-age hyperinflation, an inflation rate that was close to 50 percent a month. Banks installed ATMs on almost every street corner and refilled them several times an hour. Brazilians tried to avoid holding

currency. As soon as they were paid, they went shopping and bought enough food to get them through to the next payday. Some shoppers filled as many as six carts on a single monthly trip to the supermarket. Also, instead of using currency, Brazilians used credit cards whenever possible. But they paid their card balances off quickly because the interest rate on unpaid balances was 50 percent a month. Only at such a high interest rate did it pay banks to lend to cardholders, because banks themselves were paying interest rates of 40 percent a month to induce depositors to keep their money in the bank.

Many economists today are working on aggregate demand and inflation. One distinguished contributor, whom you can meet on the following pages, is Bennett McCallum of Carnegie Mellon University.

# Talking with

**Bennett T. McCallum** is
Professor of Economics at
Carnegie Mellon University. He was
born in Poteet, Texas, in 1935. As
an undergraduate, he attended
Rice University, where he earned a
degree in chemical engineering in
1958. He earned an MBA from
Harvard Business School in 1963
and a Ph.D. in economics from Rice
University in 1969.

Professor McCallum's research
interests include monetary theory
and policy, macroeconomic dynam-
ics, and applied econometrics.
Much of his research is aimed
toward improving monetary policy,
and Professor McCallum's advice is
sought by central banks around the
world. He has recently spent time
at the Reserve Bank of New
Zealand as well as the central bank
of the Phillipines.

Michael Parkin talked with
Professor McCallum about his
work, how it connects with the
work of other great economists,
and his insights on monetary policy.

**Professor McCallum, how did you become interested in Economics?**

I majored in chemical engineering in
college and later worked for three years
as a process design engineer for a petro-
chemical firm in Houston, Texas.
Then, at my wife's urging, I earned an
MBA at Harvard University. While
attending Harvard, I took as many economics, statistics, and operations
research courses as possible. I enjoyed
these courses and, as a result, decided
to enroll in a Ph.D. program in economics.

What I found attractive about economics is its fascinating—even beautiful—theoretical structure combined
with its emphasis on thinking analytically about public policy issues. The
usual noneconomist approach to policy
issues that one gets from the media and
other sources seems to consist mostly
of moralizing on the basis of the effects
that a policy might have on some particular social group, which is very different from thinking analytically.

**Many economists of your generation were heavily influenced by John Maynard Keynes. Looking back now on the work of Keynes, what do you think his legacy amounts to?**

Keynes was by all accounts an exceptionally brilliant person and very good
at his chosen subject of economics.
But he was principally interested in
the practical side of economics and
government policy. During World War
II, for instance, he contributed greatly
to Britain's wartime finance policy and
to the design of the Bretton Woods
system that governed international
monetary relations from 1945 to 1971.
Thus for Keynes, economic theory was
something that he did to persuade others of insights that he had. As a consequence, his theoretical work was, in
my opinion, badly flawed. His famous
*General Theory* contains numerous theoretical mistakes. It nevertheless did
make a big contribution to the way

> *What I found attractive about economics is its fascinating—even beautiful—theoretical structure combined with its emphasis on thinking analytically about public policy issues.*

that economic analysis is done, primarily by helping to persuade economists to be interested in short-run rather than just long-run analysis. That was actually a major reorientation in thinking. It was like saying, "Hey, guys, let's pay attention to short-run effects. They're important."

**Immediately following Keynes, economists began to emphasize that we can and should use fiscal policy to manipulate aggregate demand. What do we actually know about the ability of governments to manipulate aggregate expenditure using fiscal policy?**

If there is a major sustained increase in government spending, starting from a deep recession such as in the 1930s, there will be major effects, as in 1940 to 1944. But if resources are fully employed, then the main real effect will be to shift consumption to the government from households and businesses. If, instead, the government imposes a tax change that's financed by bonds, by borrowing more or less, then the effects will be smaller. From a business cycle point of view, the most important fiscal policy considerations involve the automatic stabilizers, since, at least in the United States, the legislature typically isn't able to take actions promptly enough to be very helpful for any particular economic boom or slump.

**What do we know about the Fed's ability to manipulate aggregate expenditure by using monetary policy?**

The Fed can act much more quickly, and changes in its policy stance almost certainly affect nominal expenditures, or GDP in dollar terms. In other words, when the central bank pursues a more expansionary policy, the rate of aggregate expenditures will increase. But that is in money terms. What the real effects are depends on how wage and price adjustments occur, and our understanding in that respect is very far from complete. Indeed, my opinion is that the most serious weakness in our understanding of macro and monetary issues is the mechanism by which changes in monetary policy affect real variables such as employment or price-level-adjusted GDP. Although there is a lot of good work going on right now, we don't have agreement on the nature of the wage and price adjustment process.

**Can we continue to use monetary policy to prevent inflation? If we can, how? And is Greenspan's current monetary policy on the right track?**

Certainly monetary policy can be used to prevent inflation. You just cannot have a serious long-lasting inflation unless the central bank is creating money rapidly. As for gauging whether monetary policy is tight or not, I think the best single measure is the rate of growth of the monetary base, by which we mean currency plus bank reserves.

As for recent federal reserve policy, I think it's been quite good over the period since Greenspan became chairman, but nevertheless, I think that the United States would benefit from legislation stating that the prevention of inflation is the Fed's main objective. Currently, the law fails to state the main responsibility of the Fed. Although Greenspan has been quite consistent on this dimension himself, it's not a good idea to have a system that relies so much on the judgments of a single person. The next Fed chairman might not be so reasonable. Legislation clearly mandating prevention of inflation as the Fed's main responsibility would make it more difficult for Congress to pressure the Fed toward other objectives, which are less suitable.

**What should the Fed be doing to minimize the risk of inflation and recession?**

There's no question that Fed policies have substantial effects on output and employment, but these effects are temporary. From my perspective, the extent to which the Fed can usefully contribute to reducing cyclical fluctuation is rather limited. So I think the Fed should try to keep total spending, one measure of which would be nominal GDP, growing smoothly at a rate that is basically noninflationary. For example, if the objective is to keep inflation at about 2 percent per year, then the Fed ought to keep nominal GDP growing rather smoothly at about 4 1/2 percent (since real GDP will in any case grow at about 2 1/2 percent, on the average).

In conducting this policy, in which the Fed tightens or loosens depending on whether nominal GDP is growing faster or slower than 4 1/2 percent, you have to use some measure to determine whether you are in fact tightening or loosening, and I would favor looking at the growth rate of the monetary base. Now the Fed does not do that; instead, it looks at the federal funds interest rate. The problem with that approach is that from the perspective of short-run analysis, a high interest rate means tight money, but from the perspective of long-run analysis, a high interest rate reflects loose money (fast money growth). So gauging monetary conditions on the basis of an interest rate is a rather tricky and difficult thing to do. That's why I would prefer to look at a very narrow, controllable monetary measure, such as the monetary base.

**What is your assessment of the U.S. deficit? Are deficits inflationary?**
Government deficits per se are not all that important at the macroeconomic level. More important is the extent of goods and services that are consumed by the government, rather than the private sector. Deficits are going to be inflationary if the central bank responds to them by creating money in an attempt to keep interest rates from rising. This often happens, especially in countries with poorly developed tax systems. But in the United States, the Fed has not been printing money to finance the deficit. Instead, the Fed has forced the Treasury to finance the deficit by borrowing from the public. So we've not had an accommodating policy from the Fed, and as a result, we've not had much inflation. Much the same has been true in Europe and in many of the developed economies over the last 10 to 15 years.

**Who historically are the big contributors to our understanding of aggregate fluctuations? Who are today's big contributors?**
There were several macroeconomists who took John Maynard Keynes' general body of reasoning and his idea of focusing on short-run phenomena and made something fairly coherent out them. Economists such as Patinkin, Modigliani, and Hicks developed Keynesian economics as opposed to thoughts that Keynes had himself begun with. What about before Keynes? His teacher, Alfred Marshall, viewed the generation of business cycles in a manner rather consistent with Keynes' views, but he did not give so much attention to that topic. Irving Fisher believed that if you stabilized price levels, it would tend to prevent the problems that create recessions. Marshall believed fairly much the same thing.

Robert Lucas has been easily the most productive economist of the last 25 years, certainly in the area of macroeconomics. Although his information-based theory of fluctuations has not prevailed, he nevertheless set the tone and direction for today's research.

There are two important lessons from Lucas's work. First, is the basic idea of rational expectations—that although people can't forecast the future perfectly, they can and do strive to avoid systematic expectational errors. This implies that in designing macroeconomic policy, governments should not rely on the presumption that people are going to make the same mistakes over and over again. The second main lesson from Lucas's work is that we should focus on long-run and long-lasting effects of policy actions rather than the temporary, short-term effects emphasized by the Keynesian approach of the 1950s and 1960s. We should try to design good institutions and good rules for policy making rather than being distracted by the alleged crisis of the day. In these teachings, as in many other ways, Lucas was further developing the general approach of Milton Friedman.

**Is an economics major a good thing to pursue at the end of the twentieth century?**
Although only a small fraction of students studying economics will go on to become professional economists, it's an excellent subject to take for preparing for other careers—including business and the law—because of the disciplined, analytical thinking that it teaches.

I'm of the belief that an undergraduate should take subjects that are interesting to him or her. Find something that's enjoyable to you, that you're interested in, and then work hard on that. It doesn't have to be economics. What's unfortunate is for students to just go through the paces while they're undergraduates and miss the opportunity to gain a foundation in some field that will allow them to start off on an intellectually satisfying life.

> *I'm of the belief that an undergraduate should take subjects that are interesting to him or her. Find something that's enjoyable to you, that you're interested in, and then work hard on that.*

# 11

# Expenditure Multipliers

In the Red Rocks Amphitheater in Denver, Bonnie Raitt sings into a microphone in a barely audible whisper. Moving to a louder passage, she increases the volume of her voice and now, through the magic of electronic amplification, booms across the stadium, drowning out every other sound. ◆ Dennis Archer, the mayor of Detroit, and a secretary are being driven to a business meeting along one of the city's less well-repaired highways. (There are some badly potholed highways in Detroit.) The car's wheels are bouncing and vibrating over some of the worst highways in the nation, but its passengers are completely undisturbed and the secretary's notes are written without a ripple, thanks to the car's efficient shock absorbers. ◆ Investment and exports fluctuate like the volume of Bonnie Raitt's voice and the uneven surface of a Detroit highway. How does the economy react to those fluctuations? Does it react like Dennis Archer's limousine, absorbing the shocks and providing a smooth ride for the economy's passengers? Or does it behave like Bonnie Raitt's amplifier, blowing up the fluctuations and spreading them out to affect the many millions of participants in an economic rock concert? ◆ You will explore these questions in this chapter. You will learn how a recession or a recovery begins when a change in investment or exports triggers a larger change in *aggregate* expenditure and real GDP—like Bonnie Raitt's amplifier. You will also learn how imports and income taxes have lowered the power of the amplifier. Finally, you will discover that in contrast to the initial amplification effect, the economy's shock absorbers, which are price and wage changes, pull real GDP back toward potential GDP. ◆ To achieve these objectives, we use a model called the *aggregate expenditure model*. This model explains changes in aggregate expenditure in a very short time frame during which prices do not change.

## Amplifier or Shock Absorber?

## After studying this chapter, you will be able to:

- Explain how expenditure plans are determined

- Explain how real GDP is determined when the price level is fixed

- Explain the multiplier

- Explain how imports and taxes influence the multiplier

- Explain how recessions and expansions begin

- Explain the relationship between aggregate expenditure and aggregate demand

- Explain how the multiplier gets smaller as the price level changes

# Fixed Prices and Expenditure Plans

MOST FIRMS ARE LIKE YOUR LOCAL SUPERMARKET. They set their prices, advertise their products and services, and sell the quantities their customers are willing to buy. If firms persistently sell a greater quantity than they plan to and are constantly running out of inventory, they eventually raise their prices. And if firms persistently sell a smaller quantity than they plan to and have inventories piling up, they eventually cut their prices. But in the very short term, their prices are fixed. They hold the prices they have set, and the quantities they sell depend on demand, not supply.

## The Aggregate Implications of Fixed Prices

Fixed prices have two immediate implications for the economy as a whole:

1. Because each firm's price is fixed, the *price level* is fixed.
2. Because demand determines the quantities that each firm sells, *aggregate demand* determines the aggregate quantity of goods and services sold, which equals real GDP.

So to understand the fluctuations in real GDP when the price level is fixed, we must understand aggregate demand fluctuations. The aggregate expenditure model explains fluctuations in aggregate demand by identifying the forces that determine expenditure plans.

## Expenditure Plans

The components of aggregate expenditure are:

■ Consumption expenditure
■ Investment
■ Government purchases of goods and services
■ Net exports (exports *minus* imports)

These four components of aggregate expenditure sum to real GDP (see Chapter 6, pp. 119–121). **Aggregate planned expenditure** is equal to *planned* consumption expenditure plus *planned* investment plus *planned* government purchases plus *planned* exports minus *planned* imports.

In the very short term, *planned* investment, *planned* government purchases, and *planned* exports are fixed. But *planned* consumption expenditure and *planned* imports are not fixed. They depend on the level of real GDP itself.

**A Two-Way Link Between Aggregate Expenditure and GDP** Because real GDP influences consumption expenditure and imports, and because consumption expenditure and imports are components of aggregate expenditure, there is a two-way link between aggregate expenditure and GDP. Other things remaining the same,

■ An increase in real GDP increases aggregate planned expenditure
■ An increase in aggregate expenditure increases real GDP

You are going to learn how this two-way link between aggregate expenditure and real GDP determines real GDP when the price level is fixed. The starting point is to consider the first piece of the two-way link: the influence of real GDP on planned consumption expenditure and saving.

## Consumption Function and Saving Function

Consumption and saving are influenced by several factors. The more important ones are:

■ Real interest rate
■ Disposable income
■ Purchasing power of net assets
■ Expected future income

Chapter 9 (see p. 198) explains how consumption and saving are influenced by these factors. Here, we are going to focus on the relationship between consumption and disposable income when the other factors (the real interest rate, the purchasing power of net assets, and expected future income) are constant. The reason for this focus is that disposable income and consumption are interrelated. Each influences the other.

**Consumption and Saving Plans** The table in Fig. 11.1 shows an example of the relationship among planned consumption expenditure, planned saving, and disposable income. It lists the consumption expenditure and the saving that people plan to undertake at each level of disposable income. Notice that at each level of disposable income, consumption expenditure plus saving always equals disposable income. The reason is that households can only consume or save their disposable income. So planned consumption plus planned saving always equals disposable income.

The relationship between consumption expenditure and disposable income, other things remaining the same, is called the **consumption function.** The relationship between saving and disposable income, other things remaining the same, is called the **saving function**. Let's beginning by studying the consumption function.

---

## Consumption Function and Saving Function

**(a) Consumption function**

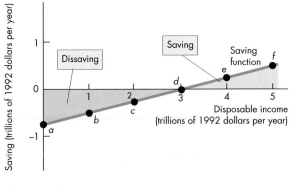

**(b) Saving function**

| | Disposable income | Planned consumption expenditure | Planned saving |
|---|---|---|---|
| | (trillions of 1992 dollars per year) | | |
| a | 0 | 0.75 | −0.75 |
| b | 1 | 1.50 | −0.50 |
| c | 2 | 2.25 | −0.25 |
| d | 3 | 3.00 | 0 |
| e | 4 | 3.75 | 0.25 |
| f | 5 | 4.50 | 0.50 |

The table shows consumption expenditure and saving plans at various levels of disposable income. Part (a) of the figure shows the relationship between consumption expenditure and disposable income (the consumption function). The height of the consumption function measures consumption expenditure at each level of disposable income. Part (b) shows the relationship between saving and disposable income (the saving function). The height of the saving function measures saving at each level of disposable income. Points *a* through *f* on the consumption and saving functions correspond to the rows of the table. The height of the 45° line in part (a) measures disposable income. So, along the 45° line, consumption expenditure equals disposable income. Consumption expenditure plus saving equals disposable income. When the consumption function is above the 45° line, saving is negative (dissaving occurs). When the consumption function is below the 45° line, saving is positive. At the point where the consumption function intersects the 45° line, all disposable income is consumed and saving is zero.

**Consumption Function** Figure 11.1(a) shows a consumption function. The *y*-axis measures consumption expenditure, and the *x*-axis measures disposable income. Along the consumption function, the points labeled *a* through *f* correspond to the rows of the table. For example, point *e* shows that when disposable income is $4 trillion, consumption expenditure is $3.75 trillion. Along the consumption function, as disposable income increases, consumption expenditure also increases.

At point *a* on the consumption function, consumption expenditure is $0.75 trillion even though disposable income is zero. This consumption expenditure is called *autonomous consumption*, and it is the amount of consumption expenditure that would take place in the short run, even if people had no current income. Consumption expenditure in excess of this amount is called *induced consumption*, which is expenditure that is induced by an increase in disposable income.

**45° Line** Figure 11.1(a) also contains a 45° line, the height of which measures disposable income. At each point on this line, consumption expenditure equals disposable income. In the range over which the consumption function lies above the 45° line—between *a* and *d*—consumption expenditure exceeds disposable income. In the range over which the consumption function lies below the 45° line—between *d* and *f*—consumption expenditure is less than disposable income. And at the point at which the consumption function intersects the 45° line—at point *d*—consumption expenditure equals disposable income.

**Saving Function** Figure 11.1(b) shows a saving function. The *x*-axis is exactly the same as that in part (a). The *y*-axis measures saving. Again, the points marked *a* through *f* correspond to the rows of the table. For example, point *e* shows that when disposable income is $4 trillion, saving is $0.25 trillion. Along the saving function, as disposable income increases, saving also increases. At disposable income less than $3 trillion (point *d*), saving is negative. Negative saving is called *dissaving*. At disposable income greater than $3 trillion, saving is positive, and at $3 trillion, saving is zero.

Notice the connection between the two parts of Fig. 11.1. When consumption expenditure exceeds disposable income in part (a), saving is negative in part (b). When disposable income exceeds consumption expenditure in part (a), saving is positive in part (b). And when consumption expenditure equals disposable income in part (a), saving is zero in part (b).

When saving is negative (when consumption expenditure exceeds disposable income), past savings are used to pay for current consumption. Such a situation cannot last forever, but it can occur if disposable income falls temporarily.

### Marginal Propensities to Consume and Save

The extent to which consumption expenditure changes when disposable income changes depends on the marginal propensity to consume. The **marginal propensity to consume** (*MPC*) is the fraction of a *change* in disposable income that is consumed. It is calculated as the *change* in consumption expenditure ($\Delta C$) divided by the *change* in disposable income ($\Delta YD$) that brought it about. That is,

$$MPC = \frac{\Delta C}{\Delta YD}.$$

In the table in Fig. 11.1, when disposable income increases from $3 trillion to $4 trillion, consumption expenditure increases from $3 trillion to $3.75 trillion. The $1 trillion increase in disposable income increases consumption expenditure by $0.75 trillion. The *MPC* is $0.75 trillion divided by $1 trillion, which equals 0.75.

The **marginal propensity to save** (*MPS*) is the fraction of a *change* in disposable income that is saved. It is calculated as the *change* in saving ($\Delta S$) divided by the *change* in disposable income ($\Delta YD$) that brought it about. That is,

$$MPS = \frac{\Delta S}{\Delta YD}.$$

In the table in Fig. 11.1, an increase in disposable income from $3 trillion to $4 trillion increases saving from zero to $0.25 trillion. The $1 trillion increase in disposable income increases saving by $0.25 trillion. The *MPS* is $0.25 trillion divided by $1 trillion, which equals 0.25.

The marginal propensity to consume plus the marginal propensity to save always equals 1. They sum to 1 because consumption expenditure and saving exhaust disposable income. Part of each dollar increase in disposable income is consumed, and the remaining part is saved. You can see that these two marginal propensities sum to 1 by using the equation

$$\Delta C + \Delta S = \Delta YD.$$

Divide both sides of the equation by the change in disposable income to obtain

$$\frac{\Delta C}{\Delta YD} + \frac{\Delta S}{\Delta YD} = 1.$$

$\Delta C/\Delta YD$ is the *marginal propensity to consume* (*MPC*), and $\Delta S/\Delta YD$ is the *marginal propensity to save* (*MPS*), so

$$MPC + MPS = 1.$$

## Slopes and Marginal Propensities

The slopes of the consumption function and the saving function are the marginal propensities to consume and save. Figure 11.2(a) shows the *MPC* as the slope of the consumption function. A $1 trillion increase in disposable income from $3 trillion to $4 trillion is the base of the red triangle. The increase in consumption expenditure that results from this increase in income is $0.75 trillion and is the height of the triangle. The slope of the consumption function is given by the formula "slope equals rise over run" and is $0.75 trillion divided by $1 trillion, which equals 0.75—the *MPC*.

Figure 11.2(b) shows the *MPS* as the slope of the saving function. A $1 trillion increase in disposable income from $3 trillion to $4 trillion (the base of the red triangle) increases saving by $0.25 trillion (the height of the triangle). The slope of the saving function is $0.25 trillion divided by $1 trillion, which equals 0.25—the *MPS*.

## Other Influences on Consumption Expenditure and Saving

You've seen that a change in disposable income leads to changes in consumption expenditure and saving. A change in disposable income brings movements along the consumption function and saving function.

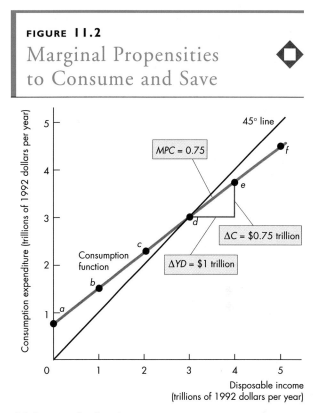

FIGURE 11.2

# Marginal Propensities to Consume and Save

**(a) Consumption function**

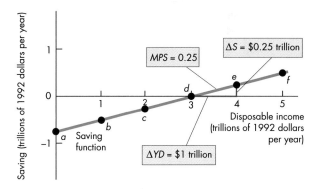

**(b) Saving function**

The marginal propensity to consume, *MPC*, is equal to the change in consumption expenditure divided by the change in disposable income, other things remaining the same. It is measured by the slope of the consumption function. In part (a), the *MPC* is 0.75. The marginal propensity to save, *MPS*, is equal to the change in saving divided by the change in disposable income, other things remaining the same. It is measured by the slope of the saving function. In part (b), the *MPS* is 0.25.

Along the consumption function and saving function, all other influences on consumption expenditure and saving (such as the real interest rate, expected future income, and the purchasing power net assets) are fixed. A change in any of these other influences shifts both the consumption function and the saving function.

When the real interest rate falls or when the purchasing power of net assets or expected future income increases, consumption expenditure increases and saving decreases. Figure 11.3 shows the effects of these changes on the consumption function and the saving function. The consumption function shifts upward from $CF_0$ to $CF_1$, and the saving function shifts downward from $SF_0$ to $SF_1$. Such shifts commonly occur during the expansion phase of the business cycle because, at such times, expected future income increases.

When the real interest rate rises or when the purchasing power of net assets or expected future income decreases, consumption expenditure decreases and saving increases. Figure 11.3 also shows the effects of these changes on the consumption function and the saving function. The consumption function shifts downward from $CF_0$ to $CF_2$, and the saving function shifts upward from $SF_0$ to $SF_2$. Such shifts often occur when a recession begins because at such a time, expected future income decreases.

We've studied the theory of the consumption function. Let's now see how that theory applies to the U.S. economy.

## The U.S. Consumption Function

Figure 11.4 shows the U.S. consumption function. Each point identified by a blue dot represents consumption expenditure and disposable income for a particular year. (The dots are for the years 1970–1996, and the even-numbered years are identified in the figure.) The line labeled $CF_0$ is an estimate of the U.S. consumption function in 1970, and the line labeled $CF_1$ is an estimate of the U.S. consumption function in 1996.

The slope of the consumption function in Fig. 11.4 is 0.75, which means that a $1 trillion increase in disposable income brings a $0.75 trillion increase in consumption expenditure. This slope, which is an estimate of the marginal propensity to consume, is an assumption that is in the middle of the range of values that economists have estimated for the marginal propensity to consume.

**FIGURE 11.3**

## Shifts in the Consumption and Saving Functions

**(a) Consumption function**

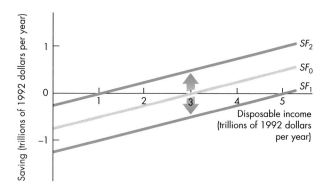

**(b) Saving function**

A fall in the real interest rate, an increase in the purchasing power of net assets, or an increase in expected future income increases consumption expenditure and decreases saving. It shifts the consumption function upward from $CF_0$ to $CF_1$ and shifts the saving function downward from $SF_0$ to $SF_1$. A rise in the real interest rate or a decrease in either the purchasing power of net assets or expected future income shifts the consumption function downward from $CF_0$ to $CF_2$ and shifts the saving function upward from $SF_0$ to $SF_2$.

The consumption function shifts upward over time as other influences on consumption expenditure. Of these other influences, the real interest rate and the purchasing power of net assets fluctuate and so bring upward and downward shifts in the consumption function. But rising expected future income brings a steady upward shift in the consumption function. As the consumption function shifts upward, autonomous consumption expenditure increases.

## Consumption as a Function of Real GDP

You've seen that consumption expenditure changes when disposable income changes. Disposable income changes when either real GDP changes or net taxes change. If tax rates don't change, real GDP is the only influence on disposable income. So consumption depends not only on disposable income but also on real GDP. We use this link between consumption and real GDP to determine equilibrium expenditure. But before we do so, we need to look at one further component of aggregate expenditure: imports. For like consumption expenditure, imports also are influenced by real GDP.

## Import Function

U.S. imports are determined by many factors, but in the short run, one factor dominates: U.S. real GDP. Other things remaining the same, the greater the U.S. real GDP, the larger is the quantity of U.S. imports.

The relationship between imports and real GDP is determined by the marginal propensity to import. The **marginal propensity to import** is the fraction of an increase in real GDP that is spent on imports. It is calculated as the change in imports divided by the change in real GDP that brought it about, other things remaining the same. For example, if a $1 trillion increase in real GDP increases imports by $0.25 trillion, the marginal propensity to import is 0.25.

In recent years, since the North American Free Trade Agreement was implemented, U.S. imports have surged. For example, in 1996, real GDP increased by $300 billion and imports increased by $60 billion. Assuming that other factors had a negligible influence on imports in 1996, the marginal propensity to import in that year was 0.2. The U.S. marginal propensity to import has been increasing.

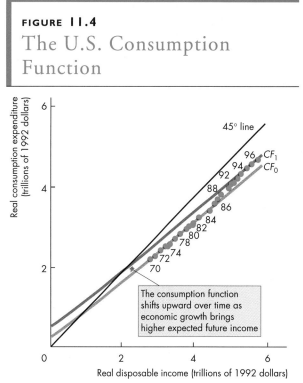

**FIGURE 11.4**

## The U.S. Consumption Function

Each blue dot shows consumption expenditure and disposable income for a particular year. The lines $CF_0$ and $CF_1$ are estimates of the U.S. consumption function in 1970 and 1996, respectively. Here, the (assumed) marginal propensity to consume is 0.75.

---

### R E V I E W

▨ Consumption expenditure and imports are influenced by real GDP.

▨ The marginal propensity to consume is the proportion of an increase in disposable income that is consumed.

▨ The effects of real GDP on consumption expenditure and imports are determined by the marginal propensity to consume and the marginal propensity to import.

Real GDP influences consumption and imports. But consumption and imports along with investment, government purchases, and exports influence real GDP. Your next task is to study this second piece of the two-way link between aggregate expenditure and real GDP and see how all the components of aggregate planned expenditure interact to determine real GDP.

## Real GDP with a Fixed Price Level

YOU ARE NOW GOING TO DISCOVER HOW AGGREGATE expenditure plans interact to determine real GDP when the price level is fixed. First we will study the relationship between aggregate planned expenditure and real GDP. Second, we'll learn about the key distinction between *planned* expenditure and *actual*

expenditure. And third, we'll study equilibrium expenditure, a situation in which aggregate planned expenditure and actual expenditure are equal.

The relationship between aggregate planned expenditure and real GDP can be described by either an aggregate expenditure schedule or an aggregate expenditure curve. The *aggregate expenditure schedule* lists aggregate planned expenditure generated at each level of real GDP. The *aggregate expenditure curve* is a graph of the aggregate expenditure schedule.

FIGURE 11.5

# Aggregate Planned Expenditure

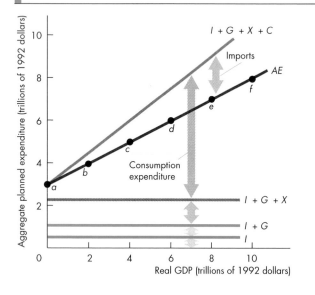

The aggregate expenditure schedule shows the relationship between aggregate planned expenditure and real GDP. Aggregate planned expenditure is the sum of planned consumption expenditure, investment, government purchases of goods and services, and exports minus imports. For example, in row *b* of the table, when real GDP is $2 trillion, planned consumption expenditure is $2.25 trillion, planned investment is $0.5 trillion, planned government purchases of goods and services are $0.55 trillion, planned exports are $1.2 trillion, and planned imports are $0.5 trillion. Thus when real GDP is $2 trillion, aggregate planned expenditure is $4 trillion ($2.25 + $0.5 + $0.55 + $1.2 − $0.5). The schedule shows that aggregate planned expenditure increases as real GDP increases. This relationship is graphed as the aggregate expenditure curve *AE*, the line *af*. The components of aggregate expenditure that increase with real GDP are consumption expenditure and imports. The other components—investment, government purchases, and exports—do not vary with real GDP.

| | Real GDP (Y) | Planned expenditure | | | | | Aggregate planned expenditure (AE = C + I + G + X − M) |
| | | Consumption expenditure (C) | Investment (I) | Government purchases (G) | Exports (X) | Imports (M) | |
|---|---|---|---|---|---|---|---|
| | | | | (trillions of 1992 dollars) | | | |
| a | 0 | 0.75 | 0.5 | 0.55 | 1.2 | 0.0 | 3 |
| b | 2 | 2.25 | 0.5 | 0.55 | 1.2 | 0.5 | 4 |
| c | 4 | 3.75 | 0.5 | 0.55 | 1.2 | 1.0 | 5 |
| d | 6 | 5.25 | 0.5 | 0.55 | 1.2 | 1.5 | 6 |
| e | 8 | 6.75 | 0.5 | 0.55 | 1.2 | 2.0 | 7 |
| f | 10 | 8.25 | 0.5 | 0.55 | 1.2 | 2.5 | 8 |

## Aggregate Planned Expenditure and Real GDP

The table in Fig. 11.5 sets out an aggregate expenditure schedule together with the components of aggregate planned expenditure. To calculate aggregate planned expenditure at a given real GDP, we add the various components together. The first column of the table shows real GDP, and the second column shows the consumption expenditure generated by each level of real GDP. A $2 trillion increase in real GDP generates a $1.50 trillion increase in consumption expenditure—the *MPC* is 0.75.

The next two columns show investment and government purchases of goods and services. Investment depends on the real interest rate and the expected rate of profit (see Chapter 9, p. 195). At a given point in time, these factors generate a particular level of investment. Suppose this level of investment is $0.5 trillion. Also, suppose that government purchases of goods and services are $0.55 trillion.

The next two columns show exports and imports. Exports are influenced by events in the rest of the world, prices of foreign-made goods and services relative to the prices of similar U.S.-made goods and services, and foreign exchange rates. But exports are not directly affected by real GDP in the United States. Exports are a constant $1.2 trillion. Imports increase as real GDP increases. A $2 trillion increase in real GDP generates a $0.5 trillion increase in imports—the marginal propensity to import is 0.25.

The final column shows aggregate planned expenditure—the sum of planned consumption expenditure, investment, government purchases of goods and services, and exports minus imports.

Figure 11.5 plots an aggregate expenditure curve. Real GDP is shown on the *x*-axis, and aggregate planned expenditure is shown on the *y*-axis. The aggregate expenditure curve is the red line *AE*. Points *a* through *f* on that curve correspond to the rows of the table. The *AE* curve is a graph of aggregate planned expenditure (the last column) plotted against real GDP (the first column).

Figure 11.5 also shows the components of aggregate expenditure. The constant components—investment (*I*), government purchases of goods and services (*G*), and exports *(X)*—are shown by the horizontal lines in the figure. Consumption expenditure (*C*) is the vertical gap between the lines labeled *I + G + X* and *I + G + X + C* .

To construct the *AE* curve, subtract imports (*M*) from the *I + G + X + C* line. Aggregate expenditure is expenditure on U.S.-made goods and services. But the components of aggregate expenditure—*C, I,* and *G*—include expenditure on imported goods and services. For example, a student's purchase of a new motor bike is part of consumption expenditure. But if that motor bike is a Honda made in Japan, expenditure on it must be subtracted from consumption expenditure to find out how much is spent on goods and services produced in the United States—on U.S. real GDP. Money paid to Honda for motor bike imports from Japan does not add to aggregate expenditure on U.S.-made goods and services.

Figure 11.5 shows that aggregate planned expenditure increases as real GDP increases. But as real GDP increases, only some of the components of aggregate planned expenditure increase. These components are consumption expenditure and imports. The sum of the components of aggregate expenditure that vary with real GDP is called **induced expenditure**. The sum of the components of aggregate expenditure that are not influenced by real GDP is called **autonomous expenditure**. The components of autonomous expenditure are investment, government purchases, exports, and autonomous consumption—that part of consumption expenditure that does not vary with real GDP. That is, autonomous expenditure is equal to the level of aggregate planned expenditure when real GDP is zero. In Fig. 11.5, autonomous expenditure is $3 trillion. And as real GDP increases from zero to $2 trillion, aggregate expenditure increases from $3 trillion to $4 trillion. Induced expenditure is $1 trillion—$4 trillion minus $3 trillion.

The aggregate expenditure curve summarizes the relationship between aggregate *planned* expenditure and real GDP. But what determines the point on the aggregate expenditure curve at which the economy operates? What determines *actual* aggregate expenditure?

## Actual Expenditure, Planned Expenditure, and Real GDP

*Actual* aggregate expenditure is always equal to real GDP, as we saw in Chapter 6 (p. 121). But aggregate *planned* expenditure is not necessarily equal to actual aggregate expenditure and therefore is not necessarily equal to real GDP. How can actual expenditure and planned expenditure differ from each other? Why don't expenditure plans get implemented? The main reason is that firms might end up with more inventories than planned or with less inventories than planned. People carry out their consumption expenditure plans, the government implements its planned purchases of goods and services, and net exports are as planned. Firms carry out their plans to purchase new buildings, plant, and equipment. But one component of investment is the change in firms' inventories of goods. If aggregate planned expenditure is less than real GDP, firms don't sell all the goods they produce and they end up with inventories they hadn't planned. If aggregate planned expenditure exceeds real GDP, firms sell more than they produce and inventories decrease below the level that firms had planned.

# FIGURE 11.6
## Equilibrium Expenditure

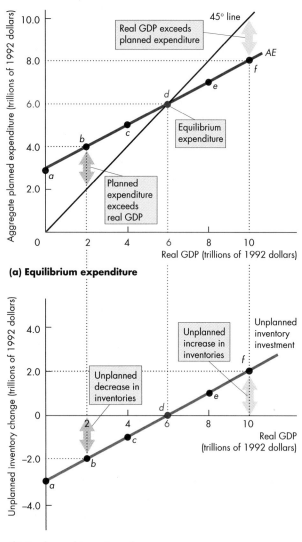

(a) Equilibrium expenditure

(b) Unplanned inventory changes

| | Real GDP (Y) | Aggregate planned expenditure (AE) | Unplanned inventory change (Y – AE) |
|---|---|---|---|
| | | (trillions of 1992 dollars) | |
| a | 0 | 3 | –3 |
| b | 2 | 4 | –2 |
| c | 4 | 5 | –1 |
| d | 6 | 6 | 0 |
| e | 8 | 7 | 1 |
| f | 10 | 8 | 2 |

The table shows expenditure plans at different levels of real GDP. When real GDP is $6 trillion, aggregate planned expenditure equals real GDP. Part (a) of the figure illustrates equilibrium expenditure, which occurs when aggregate planned expenditure equals real GDP at the intersection of the 45° line and the AE curve. Part (b) of the figure shows the forces that bring about equilibrium expenditure. When aggregate planned expenditure exceeds real GDP, inventories decrease—for example, point b in both parts of the figure. Firms increase production, and real GDP increases. When aggregate planned expenditure is less than real GDP, inventories increase—for example, point f in both parts of the figure. Firms decrease production, and real GDP decreases. When aggregate planned expenditure equals real GDP, there are no unplanned inventory changes and real GDP remains constant at equilibrium expenditure.

## Equilibrium Expenditure

**Equilibrium expenditure** is the level of aggregate expenditure that occurs when aggregate *planned* expenditure equals real GDP. It is a level of aggregate expenditure and real GDP at which everyone's spending plans are fulfilled. When the price level is fixed, equilibrium expenditure determines real GDP. When aggregate planned expenditure and actual aggregate expenditure are unequal, a process of convergence toward equilibrium expenditure occurs. And throughout this convergence process, real GDP adjusts. Let's examine equilibrium expenditure and the process that brings it about.

Figure 11.6(a) illustrates equilibrium expenditure. The table sets out aggregate planned expenditure at various levels of real GDP. These values are plotted as points *a* through *f* along the *AE* curve. The 45° line shows all the points at which aggregate planned expenditure equals real GDP. Thus where the *AE* curve lies above the 45° line, aggregate planned expenditure exceeds real GDP; where the *AE* curve lies below the 45° line, aggregate planned expenditure is less than real GDP; and where the *AE* curve intersects the 45° line, aggregate planned expenditure equals real GDP. Point *d* illustrates equilibrium expenditure. At this point, real GDP is $6 trillion.

## Convergence to Equilibrium

What are the forces that move aggregate expenditure toward its equilibrium level? To answer this question, we must look at a situation in which aggregate expenditure is away from its equilibrium level. Suppose that in Fig. 11.6, real GDP is $2 trillion. With real GDP at $2 trillion, actual aggregate expenditure is also $2 trillion. But aggregate *planned* expenditure is $4 trillion (point *b* in Fig. 11.6a). Aggregate planned expenditure exceeds *actual* expenditure. When people spend $4 trillion and firms produce goods and services worth $2 trillion, firms' inventories fall by $2 trillion (point *b* in Fig. 11.6b). Because the change in inventories is part of investment, *actual* investment is $2 trillion less than *planned* investment.

Real GDP doesn't remain at $2 trillion for very long. Firms have inventory targets based on their sales. When inventories fall below target, firms increase production to restore inventories to the target level. To increase inventories, firms hire additional labor and increase production. Suppose that they increase production in the next period by $2 trillion. Real GDP increases by $2.0 trillion to $4.0 trillion. But again, aggregate planned expenditure exceeds real GDP. When real GDP is $4.0 trillion, aggregate planned expenditure is $5 trillion (point *c* in Fig. 11.6a). Again, inventories decrease, but this time by less than before. With real GDP of $4.0 trillion and aggregate planned expenditure of $5 trillion, inventories decrease by $1 trillion (point *c* in Fig. 11.6b). Again, firms hire additional labor, and production increases; real GDP increases yet further.

The process that we have just described— planned expenditure exceeds real GDP, inventories decrease, and production increases to restore the level of inventories—ends when real GDP has reached $6 trillion. At this real GDP, there is an equilibrium. There are no unplanned inventory changes, and firms do not change their production.

You can do an experiment similar to the one we've just done but starting with a level of real GDP greater than equilibrium expenditure. In this case, planned expenditure is less than actual expenditure, inventories pile up, and firms cut production. As before, real GDP keeps on changing (decreasing this time) until it reaches its equilibrium level of $6.0 trillion.

## R E V I E W

- Equilibrium expenditure occurs when aggregate planned expenditure equals real GDP.
- Equilibrium expenditure results from an adjustment in real GDP.
- If real GDP and aggregate expenditure are less than their equilibrium levels, an unplanned fall in inventories leads firms to increase production and real GDP increases.
- If real GDP and aggregate expenditure are greater than their equilibrium levels, an unplanned rise in inventories leads firms to decrease production and real GDP decreases.

We've learned that when the price level is fixed, real GDP is determined by equilibrium expenditure. And we have seen how unplanned changes in inventories and the production response they generate bring a convergence toward equilibrium. We're now going to study *changes* in equilibrium and discover an economic amplifier called the *multiplier*.

# The Multiplier

INVESTMENT AND EXPORTS CAN CHANGE FOR many reasons. A fall in the real interest rate might induce firms to increase their planned investment. A wave of innovation, such as occurred with the spread of multimedia computers in the 1990s, might increase expected future profits and lead firms to increase their planned investment. An economic boom in Western Europe and Japan might lead to a large increase in their expenditure on U.S.-produced goods and services—on U.S. exports. These are all examples of increases in autonomous expenditure.

When autonomous expenditure increases, aggregate expenditure increases, and so does equilibrium expenditure and real GDP. But the increase in real GDP is *larger* than the change in autonomous expenditure. The **multiplier** is the amount by which a change in autonomous expenditure is magnified or multiplied to determine the change in equilibrium expenditure and real GDP.

It is easiest to get the basic idea of the multiplier if we work with an example economy in which there are no income taxes and no imports. So we'll first assume that these factors are absent. Then, when you understand the basic idea, we'll bring these factors back into play and see what difference they make to the multiplier.

## The Basic Idea of the Multiplier

Suppose that investment increases. The additional expenditure by businesses means that aggregate expenditure and real GDP increase. The increase in real GDP increases disposable income and with no income taxes, real GDP and disposable income increase by the same amount. The increase in disposable income brings an increase in consumption expenditure. And the increased consumption expenditure adds even more to aggregate expenditure. Real GDP and disposable income increase further, and so does consumption expenditure. The initial increase in investment brings an even bigger increase in aggregate expenditure because it induces an increase in consumption expenditure. The magnitude of the increase in aggregate expenditure that results from an increase in autonomous expenditure is determined by the *multiplier*.

The table in Fig. 11.7 sets out aggregate planned expenditure. Initially, when real GDP is $5 trillion,

aggregate planned expenditure is $5.25 trillion. For each $1 trillion increase in real GDP, aggregate planned expenditure increases by $0.75 trillion. This aggregate expenditure schedule is shown in the figure as the aggregate expenditure curve $AE_0$. Initially, equilibrium expenditure is $6 trillion. You can see this equilibrium in row $b$ of the table and in the figure where the curve $AE_0$ intersects the 45° line at the point marked $b$.

Now suppose that autonomous expenditure increases by $0.5 trillion. What happens to equilibrium expenditure? You can see the answer in Fig. 11.7. When this increase in autonomous expenditure is added to the original aggregate planned expenditure, aggregate planned expenditure increases by $0.5 trillion at each level of real GDP. The new aggregate expenditure curve is $AE_1$. The new equilibrium expenditure, highlighted in the table (row $d'$), occurs where $AE_1$ intersects the 45° line and is $8 trillion (point $d'$). At this real GDP, aggregate planned expenditure equals real GDP.

## The Multiplier Effect

In Fig. 11.7, the increase in autonomous expenditure of $0.5 trillion increases equilibrium expenditure by $2 trillion. That is, the change in autonomous expenditure leads, like Bonnie Raitt's music-making equipment, to an amplified change in equilibrium expenditure. This amplified change is the *multiplier effect*—equilibrium expenditure increases by *more than* the increase in autonomous expenditure. The multiplier is greater than 1.

Initially, when autonomous expenditure increases, aggregate planned expenditure exceeds real GDP. As a result, inventories decrease. Firms respond by increasing production so as to restore their inventories to the target level. As production increases, so does real GDP. With a higher level of real GDP, *induced expenditure* increases. Thus equilibrium expenditure increases by the sum of the initial increase in autonomous expenditure and the increase in induced expenditure. In this example, induced expenditure increases by $1.5 trillion, so equilibrium expenditure increases by $2 trillion.

Although we have just analyzed the effects of an *increase* in autonomous expenditure, the same analysis applies to a decrease in autonomous expenditure. If initially the aggregate expenditure curve is $AE_1$, equilibrium expenditure and real GDP are $8

## Why Is the Multiplier Greater Than 1?

We've seen that equilibrium expenditure increases by more than the increase in autonomous expenditure. This makes the multiplier greater than 1. How come? Why does equilibrium expenditure increase by more than the increase in autonomous expenditure?

The multiplier is greater than 1 because of induced expenditure—an increase in autonomous expenditure *induces* further increases in expenditure. If General Motors spends $10 million on a new car assembly line, aggregate expenditure and real GDP immediately increase by $10 million. But that is not the end of the story. Engineers and construction workers now have more income, and they spend part of the extra income on cars, microwave ovens, vacations, and a host of other goods and services. Real GDP now rises by the initial $10 million plus the extra consumption expenditure induced by the $10 million increase in income. The producers of cars, microwave ovens, vacations, and other goods now have increased incomes, and they, in turn, spend part of the increase in their incomes on consumption goods and services. Additional income induces additional expenditure, which creates additional income.

We have seen that a change in autonomous expenditure has a multiplier effect on real GDP. But how big is the multiplier effect?

## The Size of the Multiplier

Suppose that the economy is in a recession. Profit prospects start to look better, and firms are making plans for large increases in investment. The world economy is also heading toward expansion, and exports are increasing. The question on everyone's lips is: How strong will the expansion be? This is a hard question to answer. But an important ingredient in the answer is working out the size of the multiplier.

The *multiplier* is the amount by which a change in autonomous expenditure is multiplied to determine the change in equilibrium expenditure that it generates. To calculate the multiplier, we divide the change in equilibrium expenditure by the change in autonomous expenditure. Let's calculate the multiplier for the example in Fig. 11.7. Initially, equilibrium expenditure is $6 trillion. Then autonomous expenditure increases by $0.5 trillion, and equilibrium expenditure increases by $2 trillion to $8 trillion.

---

**FIGURE 11.7**

# The Multiplier

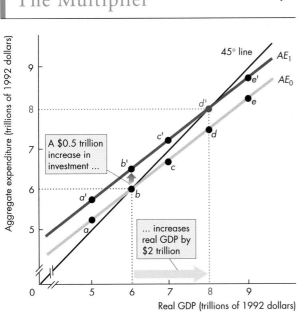

| Real GDP (Y) | Aggregate planned expenditure | | |
|---|---|---|---|
| | Original (AE₀) | | New (AE₁) |
| | (trillions of 1992 dollars) | | |
| 5 | a | 5.25 | a'  5.75 |
| **6** | **b** | **6.00** | b'  6.50 |
| 7 | c | 6.75 | c'  7.25 |
| 8 | d | 7.50 | **d'  8.00** |
| 9 | e | 8.25 | e'  8.75 |

A $0.5 trillion increase in autonomous expenditure shifts the AE curve upward by $0.5 trillion from AE₀ to AE₁. Equilibrium expenditure increases by $2 trillion, from $6 trillion to $8 trillion. The increase in equilibrium expenditure is 4 times the increase in autonomous expenditure, so the multiplier is 4.

---

trillion. A decrease in autonomous expenditure of $0.5 trillion shifts the aggregate expenditure curve downward by $0.5 trillion to AE₀. Equilibrium expenditure decreases from $8 trillion to $6 trillion. The decrease in equilibrium expenditure ($2 trillion) is larger than the decrease in autonomous expenditure that brought it about ($0.5 trillion). The multiplier is 4.

The multiplier is

$$\text{Multiplier} = \frac{\text{Change in equilibrium expenditure}}{\text{Change in autonomous expenditure}}$$

$$= \frac{\$2 \text{ trillion}}{\$0.5 \text{ trillion}} = 4.$$

## The Multiplier and the Marginal Propensity to Consume and Save

What determines the magnitude of the multiplier? The answer is the marginal propensity to consume. The larger is the marginal propensity to consume, the larger is the multiplier. To see why, let's do a calculation.

Aggregate expenditure and real GDP change because consumption expenditure changes and investment changes. The change in real GDP ($\Delta Y$) equals the change in consumption expenditure ($\Delta C$) plus the change in investment ($\Delta I$). That is,

$$\Delta Y = \Delta C + \Delta I.$$

But the change in consumption expenditure is determined by the change in real GDP and the marginal propensity to consume. It is

$$\Delta C = MPC \times \Delta Y.$$

Now substitute $MPC \times \Delta Y$ for $\Delta C$ in the previous equation to give

$$\Delta Y = (MPC \times \Delta Y) + \Delta I.$$

Now, solve for $\Delta Y$ as

$$(1 - MPC) \times \Delta Y = \Delta I.$$

and rearranging gives

$$\Delta Y = \frac{\Delta I}{\left(1 - MPC\right)}.$$

Finally, divide both sides of the previous equation by $\Delta I$ to give

$$\text{Multiplier} = \frac{\Delta Y}{\Delta I} = \frac{1}{(1 - MPC)}.$$

Using the numbers for Fig. 11.7, the $MPC$ is 0.75 so the multiplier is

$$\text{Multiplier} = \frac{1}{(1 - 0.75)} = \frac{1}{0.25} = 4.$$

There is another formula for the multiplier. Because the marginal propensity to consume ($MPC$) plus the marginal propensity to save ($MPS$) sum to 1, the term ($1 - MPC$) equals $MPS$. Therefore another formula for the multiplier is

$$\text{Multiplier} = \frac{1}{MPS}.$$

Again using the numbers in Fig. 11.7, we have

$$\text{Multiplier} = \frac{1}{0.25} = 4.$$

Because the marginal propensity to save ($MPS$) is a fraction—a number between 0 and 1—the multiplier is greater than 1.

Figure 11.8 illustrates the multiplier process. In round 1, autonomous expenditure increases by $0.5 trillion (shown by the green bar). At this time, induced expenditure does not change, so aggregate expenditure and real GDP increase by $0.5 trillion. In round 2, the larger real GDP induces more consumption expenditure. Induced expenditure increases by 0.75 times the increase in real GDP, so the increase in real GDP of $0.5 trillion induces a further increase in expenditure of $0.375 trillion. This change in induced expenditure (the green bar in round 2), when added to the previous increase in expenditure (the blue bar in round 2), increases aggregate expenditure and real GDP by $0.875 trillion. The round 2 increase in real GDP induces a round 3 increase in expenditure. The process repeats through successive rounds. Each increase in real GDP is 0.75 times the previous increase. The cumulative increase in real GDP gradually approaches $2 trillion.

So far, we've ignored imports and income taxes. Let's now see how these two factors influence the multiplier.

### Imports and Income Taxes

The multiplier is determined, in general, not only by the marginal propensity to consume but also by the marginal propensity to import and by the marginal tax rate. Imports make the multiplier smaller than it otherwise would be. To see why, think about what

**FIGURE 11.8**

# The Multiplier Process ◆

■ Increase in current round

■ Cumulative increase from previous rounds

Autonomous expenditure increases in round 1 by $0.5 trillion. As a result, real GDP increases by the same amount. With a marginal propensity to consume of 0.75, each additional dollar of real GDP induces an additional 0.75 of a dollar of aggregate expenditure. The round 1 increase in real GDP induces an increase in consumption expenditure of $0.375 trillion in round 2. At the end of round 2, real GDP has increased by $0.875 trillion. The extra $0.375 trillion of real GDP in round 2 induces a further increase in consumption expenditure of $0.281 trillion in round 3. Real GDP increases yet further to $1.156 trillion. This process continues with real GDP increasing by ever-smaller amounts. When the process comes to an end, real GDP has increased by a total of $2 trillion.

happens following an increase in investment. An increase in investment increases real GDP, which in turn increases consumption expenditure. But part of the increase in investment and consumption expenditure is expenditure on imported goods and services, not U.S.-produced goods and services. Only expenditure on U.S.-produced goods and services increases U.S. real GDP. The larger the marginal propensity to import, the smaller is the change in U.S. real GDP.

Income taxes also make the multiplier smaller than it otherwise would be. Again, think about what happens following an increase in investment. An increase in investment increases real GDP. But because income taxes increase, disposable income increases by less than the increase in real GDP. Consequently, consumption expenditure increases by less than it would do if taxes had not changed. The larger is the marginal tax rate, the smaller is the change in disposable income and real GDP.

The marginal propensity to import and the marginal tax rate together with the marginal propensity to consume determine the multiplier. And their combined influence depends on the slope of the *AE* curve. The multiplier is equal to 1 divided by 1 minus the slope of the *AE* curve. Figure 11.9 compares two situations. In Fig. 11.9(a), there are no imports and no taxes. The slope of the *AE* curve equals the marginal propensity to consume, which is 0.75, and the multiplier is 4. In Fig. 11.9(b), imports and income taxes decrease the slope of the *AE* curve to 0.5. In this case, the multiplier is 2.

Over time, the value of the multiplier changes as tax rates change and as the marginal propensity to consume and the marginal propensity to import change. These ongoing changes make the multiplier hard to predict. But they do not change the fundamental fact that an initial change in autonomous expenditure leads to a magnified change in aggregate expenditure and real GDP.

Now that we've studied the multiplier and the factors that influence its magnitude, let's use what we've learned to gain some insights into business cycle turning points.

## Business Cycle Turning Points

At business cycle turning points, the economy moves from expansion to recession or from recession to expansion. Economists understand these turning points as seismologists understand earthquakes. They know quite a lot about the forces and mechanisms that produce them, but they can't predict them. The forces that bring business cycle turning points are the swings in autonomous expenditure such as investment and exports. The mechanism that gives momentum to the economy's new direction is the multiplier. Let's use what we've now learned to examine these turning points.

### FIGURE 11.9

# The Multiplier and the Slope of the *AE* Curve

**(a) Multiplier is 4**

**(b) Multiplier is 2**

Imports and income taxes make the *AE* curve less steep and reduce the value of the multiplier. In part (a), with no imports and income taxes, the slope of the *AE* curve is 0.75 (the marginal propensity to consume) and the multiplier is 4. But with

imports and income taxes, the slope of the *AE* curve is less than the marginal propensity to consume. In part (b), the slope of the *AE* curve is 0.5. In this case, the multiplier is 2.

**An Expansion Begins**  An expansion is triggered by an increase in autonomous expenditure that increases aggregate planned expenditure. At the moment the economy turns the corner into expansion, aggregate planned expenditure exceeds real GDP. In this situation, firms see their inventories taking an unplanned dive. The expansion now begins. To meet their inventory targets, firms increase production, and real GDP begins to increase. This initial increase in real GDP brings higher incomes that stimulate consumption expenditure. The multiplier process kicks in, and the expansion picks up speed.

**A Recession Begins**  The process we've just described works in reverse at a business cycle peak. A recession is triggered by a decrease in autonomous expenditure that decreases aggregate planned expenditure. At the moment the economy turns the corner into recession, real GDP exceeds aggregate planned

expenditure. In this situation, firms see unplanned inventories piling up. The recession now begins. To reduce their inventories, firms cut production, and real GDP begins to decrease. This initial decrease in real GDP brings lower incomes that cut consumption expenditure. The multiplier process reinforces the initial cut in autonomous expenditure, and the recession takes hold.

**The Next U.S. Recession?**  Since 1991, the U.S. economy has been in a business cycle expansion. The last real GDP trough was in the first quarter of 1991. The science of macroeconomics cannot predict when the next recession will begin. A recession seemed possible in 1995 following a rapid buildup of inventories during 1994. But firms planned this inventory buildup. At the beginning of 1997, there was still no immediate prospect of the next recession. But it will surely come. And when it does, the mechanism you've just studied will operate.

> ### R E V I E W
>
> ▧ A change in autonomous expenditure changes real GDP by an amount determined by the multiplier.
> ▧ The multiplier is larger, the greater the marginal propensity to consume, the smaller the marginal propensity to import, and the smaller the marginal tax rate.
> ▧ Fluctuations in autonomous expenditure bring business cycle turning points.

The economy's potholes are changes in investment and exports. And the economy does not operate like the shock absorbers on Dennis Archer's car. While the price level is fixed, the effects of the economic potholes are not smoothed out. Instead, they are amplified like Bonnie Raitt's voice. But we've considered only the adjustments in spending that occur in the very short term when the price level is fixed. What happens after a long enough time lapse for the price level to change? Let's answer this question.

# The Multiplier and the Price Level

WHEN FIRMS CAN'T KEEP UP WITH SALES AND their inventories fall below target, they increase production, but at some point, they raise their prices. Similarly, when firms find unwanted inventories piling up, they decrease production, but eventually, they cut their prices. So far, we've studied the macroeconomic consequences of firms changing their production levels when their sales change, but we haven't looked at the effects of price changes. When individual firms change their prices, the economy's price level changes.

To study the simultaneous determination of real GDP and the price level, we use the *aggregate supply–aggregate demand model*, which is explained in Chapter 7. But to understand how aggregate demand adjusts, we need to work out the connection between the aggregate supply–aggregate demand model and the equilibrium expenditure model that we've used in this chapter.

The key to understanding the relationship between these two models is the distinction between the aggregate *expenditure* and aggregate *demand* and the related distinction between the aggregate *expenditure curve* and the aggregate *demand curve*.

## Aggregate Expenditure and Aggregate Demand

The aggregate expenditure curve is the relationship between the aggregate planned expenditure and real GDP, all other influences on aggregate planned expenditure remaining the same. The aggregate demand curve is the relationship between the aggregate quantity of goods and services demanded and the price level, all other influences on aggregate demand remaining the same. Let's explore the links between these two relationships.

## Aggregate Expenditure and the Price Level

When the price level changes, aggregate planned expenditure changes and the quantity of real GDP demanded changes. The aggregate demand curve slopes downward. Why? There are two main reasons:

1. Wealth effect
2. Substitution effects

**Wealth Effect** Other things remaining the same, the higher the price level, the smaller is the purchasing power of people's assets. For example, suppose you have $100 in the bank and the price level is 110. If the price level rises to 130, your $100 buys fewer goods and services. You are less wealthy. With less wealth, you will probably want to try to spend a bit less and save a bit more. Aggregate planned expenditure is lower the higher the price level, other things remaining the same.

**Substitution Effects** A rise in the price level today, other things remaining the same, makes current goods and services more costly relative to future goods and services and results in a delay in purchases—an *intertemporal substitution*. A rise in the price level, other things remaining the same, makes U.S.-produced goods more expensive relative to foreign-produced goods and services and increases imports and decreases exports—an *international substitution*.

When the price level rises, each of these effects reduces aggregate planned expenditure at each level of real GDP. As a result, when the price level rises, the aggregate expenditure curve shifts downward. A fall in the price level has the opposite effect. When the price level falls, the aggregate expenditure curve shifts upward.

Figure 11.10(a) shows the shifts of the *AE* curve. When the price level is 110, the aggregate expenditure curve is $AE_0$, which intersects the 45° line at point *b*. Equilibrium expenditure is $7 trillion. If the price level increases to 130, the aggregate expenditure curve shifts downward to $AE_1$, which intersects the 45° line at point *a*. Equilibrium expenditure is $6 trillion. If the price level decreases to 90, the aggregate expenditure curve shifts upward to $AE_2$, which intersects the 45° line at point *c*. Equilibrium expenditure is $8 trillion.

We've just seen that when the price level changes, other things remaining the same, the aggregate expenditure curve shifts and the equilibrium expenditure changes. And when the price level changes, other things remaining the same, there is a movement along the aggregate demand curve. Figure 11.10(b) shows these movements along the aggregate demand curve. At a price level of 110, the aggregate quantity of goods and services demanded is $7 trillion—point *b* on the aggregate demand curve *AD*. If the price level rises to 130, the aggregate quantity of goods and services demanded decreases to $6 trillion. There is a movement along the aggregate demand curve to point *a*. If the price level falls to 90, the aggregate quantity of goods and services demanded increases to $8 trillion. There is a movement along the aggregate demand curve to point *c*.

Each point on the aggregate demand curve corresponds to a point of equilibrium expenditure. The equilibrium expenditure points *a*, *b*, and *c* in Fig. 11.10(a) correspond to the points *a*, *b*, and *c* on the aggregate demand curve in Fig. 11.10(b).

When the price level changes, other things remaining the same, the aggregate expenditure curve shifts and there is a movement along the aggregate demand curve. When any other influence on aggregate planned expenditure changes, *both* the aggregate expenditure curve and the aggregate demand curve shift. For example, an increase in investment or in exports increases both aggregate planned expenditure and aggregate demand and shifts both the *AE* curve and the *AD* curve. Figure 11.11 illustrates the effect of such an increase.

Initially, the aggregate expenditure curve is $AE_0$ in part (a) and the aggregate demand curve is $AD_0$ in part (b). The price level is 110, real GDP is $7 trillion, and the economy is at point *a* in both parts of the figure. Now suppose that investment increases by $1 trillion. At a constant price level of 110, the aggregate expenditure curve shifts upward to $AE_1$. This curve intersects the 45° line at an equilibrium

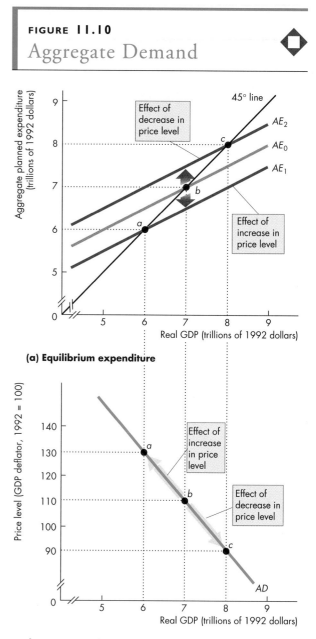

**FIGURE 11.10**

## Aggregate Demand

**(a) Equilibrium expenditure**

**(b) Aggregate demand**

A change in the price level shifts the *AE* curve and results in a *movement along* the *AD* curve. When the price level is 110, the *AE* curve is $AE_0$, and equilibrium expenditure is $7 trillion at point *b*. When the price level rises to 130, the *AE* curve is $AE_1$, and equilibrium expenditure is $6 trillion at point *a*. When the price level falls to 90, the *AE* curve is $AE_2$, and equilibrium expenditure is $8 trillion at point *c*. Points *a*, *b*, and *c* on the *AD* curve in part (b) correspond to the equilibrium expenditure points *a*, *b*, and *c* in part (a).

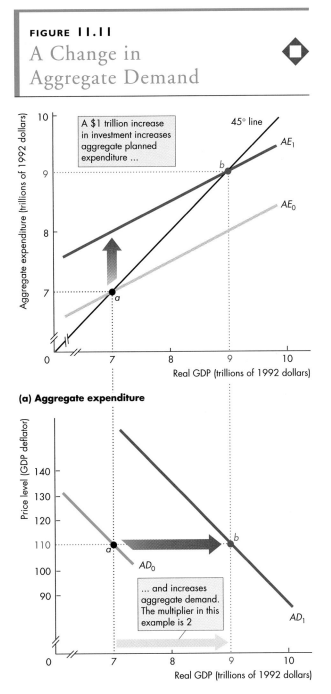

**FIGURE 11.11**

## A Change in Aggregate Demand

**(a) Aggregate expenditure**

**(b) Aggregate demand**

The price level is 110. When the aggregate expenditure curve is $AE_0$ (part a), the aggregate demand curve is $AD_0$ (part b). An increase in autonomous expenditure shifts the $AE$ curve upward to $AE_1$. In the new equilibrium, real GDP is $9 trillion (at $b$). Because the quantity of real GDP demanded at a price level of 110 increases to $9 trillion, the $AD$ curve shifts rightward to $AD_1$.

expenditure of $9 trillion (point $b$). This equilibrium expenditure of $9 trillion is the aggregate quantity of goods and services demanded at a price level of 110, as shown by point $b$ in part (b). Point $b$ lies on a new aggregate demand curve. The aggregate demand curve has shifted rightward to $AD_1$.

But how do we know by how much the $AD$ curve shifts? The multiplier determines the answer. The larger the multiplier, the larger is the shift in the aggregate demand curve that results from a given change in autonomous expenditure. In this example, the multiplier is 2. A $1 trillion increase in investment produces a $2 trillion increase in the aggregate quantity of goods and services demanded at each price level. That is, a $1 trillion increase in autonomous expenditure shifts the aggregate demand curve rightward by $2 trillion.

A decrease in autonomous expenditure shifts the aggregate expenditure curve downward and shifts the aggregate demand curve leftward. You can see these effects by reversing the change that we've just studied. Suppose that the economy is initially at point $b$ on the aggregate expenditure curve $AE_1$ and the aggregate demand curve $AD_1$. A decrease in autonomous expenditure shifts the aggregate planned expenditure curve downward to $AE_0$. The aggregate quantity of goods and services demanded falls from $9 trillion to $7 trillion, and the aggregate demand curve shifts leftward to $AD_0$.

Let's summarize what we have just discovered:

If some factor other than a change in the price level increases autonomous expenditure, the $AE$ curve shifts upward and the $AD$ curve shifts rightward.

The size of the $AD$ curve shift depends on the change in autonomous expenditure and the multiplier.

## Equilibrium GDP and the Price Level

In Chapter 7, we learned that aggregate demand and short-run aggregate supply determine equilibrium real GDP and the price level. We've now put aggregate demand under a more powerful microscope and have discovered that a change in investment (or in any component of autonomous expenditure) changes aggregate demand and shifts the aggregate demand curve. The magnitude of the shift depends on the multiplier. But whether a change in autonomous expenditure results ultimately in a change in real GDP, a change in the price level, or a combination of the two depends on aggregate supply. There are two time frames to consider, the short run and the long run. First we'll see what happens in the short run.

**An Increase in Aggregate Demand in the Short Run**   Figure 11.12 describes the economy. In part (a), the aggregate expenditure curve is $AE_0$, and equilibrium expenditure is $7 trillion—point $a$. In part (b), aggregate demand is $AD_0$, and the short-run aggregate supply curve is $SAS$. (Look at Chapter 7 if you need to refresh your understanding of this curve.) Equilibrium is at point $a$, where the aggregate demand and short-run aggregate supply curves intersect. The price level is 110, and real GDP is $7 trillion.

Now suppose that investment increases by $1 trillion. With the price level fixed at 110, the aggregate expenditure curve shifts upward to $AE_1$. Equilibrium expenditure increases to $9 trillion—point $b$ in part (a). In part (b), the aggregate demand curve shifts rightward by $2 trillion, from $AD_0$ to $AD_1$. How far the aggregate demand curve shifts is determined by the multiplier when the price level is fixed. But with this new aggregate demand curve, the price level does not remain fixed. The price level rises, and as it does so the aggregate expenditure curve shifts downward. The short-run equilibrium occurs when the aggregate expenditure curve has shifted downward to $AE_2$ and the new aggregate demand curve, $AD_1$, intersects the short-run aggregate supply curve. Real GDP is $8.6 trillion, and the price level is 116 (at point $c$).

When price level effects are taken into account, the increase in investment still has a multiplier effect on real GDP, but the effect is smaller than it would be if the price level were fixed. The steeper the slope of the short-run aggregate supply curve, the larger is the increase in the price level and the smaller is the multiplier effect on real GDP.

**An Increase in Aggregate Demand in the Long Run**   Figure 11.13 illustrates the long-run effect of an increase in aggregate demand. In the long run, real GDP equals potential GDP and there is full employment. Potential GDP is $7 trillion, and the long-run aggregate supply curve is $LAS$. Initially, the economy is at point $a$ (parts a and b).

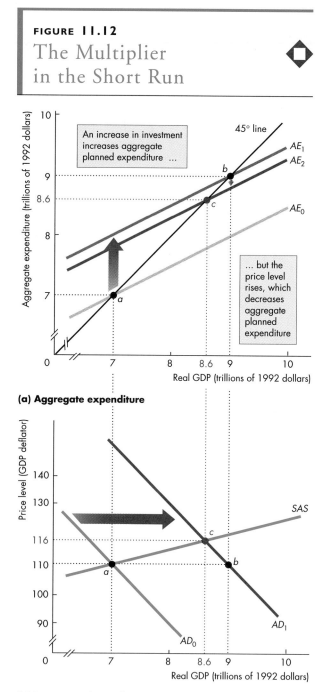

FIGURE 11.12

The Multiplier in the Short Run

**(a) Aggregate expenditure**

**(b) Aggregate demand**

An increase in investment shifts the AE curve from $AE_0$ to $AE_1$ (part a) and the AD curve from $AD_0$ to $AD_1$ (part b). The price level does not remain at 110 but rises. The higher price level shifts the AE curve downward from $AE_1$ to $AE_2$. The economy moves to point c in both parts. In the short run, the multiplier effect is smaller than when the price level is fixed.

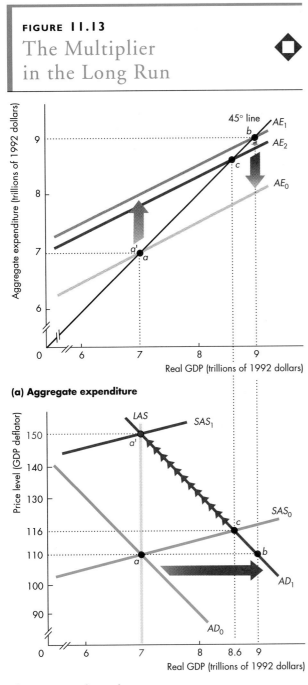

**FIGURE 11.13**

The Multiplier
in the Long Run

**(a) Aggregate expenditure**

**(b) Aggregate demand**

Starting from point *a*, an increase in investment shifts the *AE* curve to *AE₁* and the *AD* curve to *AD₁*. In the short run, the economy moves to point *c*. In the long run, the money wage rate rises, the *SAS* curve shifts to *SAS₁*, the *AE* curve shifts back to *AE₀*, the price level rises, and real GDP falls. The economy moves to point *a'*, and in the long run, the multiplier is zero.

Investment increases by $1 trillion. The aggregate expenditure curve shifts to $AE_1$ and the aggregate demand curve shifts to $AD_1$. With no change in the price level, the economy would move to point *b* and real GDP would increase to $9 trillion. But in the short run, the price level rises to 116 and real GDP increases to only $8.6 trillion. With the higher price level, the $AE$ curve shifts from $AE_1$ to $AE_2$. The economy is now in a short-run equilibrium at point *c*. Real GDP is now above potential GDP. The labor force is more than fully employed, and shortages of labor increase the money wage rate. The higher money wage rate increases costs, which decreases short-run aggregate supply and shifts the *SAS* curve leftward to $SAS_1$. The price level rises further, and real GDP decreases. There is a movement along $AD_1$, and the $AE$ curve shifts downward from $AE_2$ toward $AE_0$. When the money wage rate and the price level have increased by the same percentage, real GDP is again equal to potential GDP and the economy is at point *a'*. In the long run, the multiplier is zero.

---

## R E V I E W

◼ A change in the price level shifts the *AE* curve and brings a movement along the *AD* curve.

◼ A change in autonomous expenditure that is not caused by a change in the price level shifts both the *AE* curve and the *AD* curve, and the multiplier determines the magnitude of the shift in the *AD* curve.

◼ In the short run, the increase in real GDP that results from an increase in autonomous expenditure is smaller than the increase in aggregate demand.

◼ In the long run, an increase in aggregate demand leaves real GDP unchanged but increases the price level. In the long run, the multiplier is zero.

◆ You are now ready to build on what you've learned about expenditure fluctuations and study the roles of fiscal policy and monetary policy in smoothing the business cycle. In Chapter 12, we study fiscal policy—government purchases, taxes, and the deficit—and in Chapters 13 and 14, we study monetary policy—interest rates and the quantity of money. But before you leave the current topic, look at *Reading Between the Lines* on pages 262–263 and see the model you've studied in this chapter in action in the U.S. economy.

## Recession Watch

THE SEATTLE TIMES, DECEMBER 22, 1996

# Polishing Up Those Forecasts

BY STEPHEN H. DUNPHY

This is the time of year when economists around the nation put the finishing touches on their forecasts for next year. ...

The consensus seems to be that the economy will experience slow growth next year with an outside chance of tipping into an outright recession. Most economists are pegging growth at about 2 percent to 2.5 percent for the year.

That's now being called a soft landing, engineered by the Federal Reserve. Of course, that used to be called a growth recession in which the economy grew, but not fast enough to create many new jobs. Soft landing sounds better than growth recession, but it is all the same.

Some signs are pointing toward a business slowdown. Among them: a bigger-than-expected drop in home construction, tepid retail revenue, falling auto sales, declining industrial home production and a slump in U.S. exports. Boeing sales could help that latter category as its production lines gear up for the recent spurt in orders.

Here is what economists watch for as danger signs of recession:

—A spike in inflation brought on by shortages in energy or labor. Oil prices have risen in recent months, but that remains a volatile commodity. Tight labor conditions in many regions—including the Seattle area—are threatening to push wages higher.

This is the area to watch: Most recessions in recent years have come from the Fed raising interest rates to slow or stop inflation.

—Inventory buildups. If sales slow, goods begin to build up on the shelf. That leads to production cuts and job losses. But some economists say "just-in-time" manufacturing techniques make inventories less important.

Business inventories rose less than 1 percent in the third quarter, while sales rose more than 1 percent. That suggests underlying economic conditions are still solid.

—Unexpected jolts. Something unexpected could trigger a recession. The Gulf War had that effect. Ditto the Arab oil embargo. There is nothing on the horizon now.

"We do believe that growth has slowed," said economists for DRI/McGraw Hill, a major economic forecasting company. "But the economy is not shifting into recession. ...

Reprinted with permission.

## Essence of THE STORY

■ The consensus among economists (at the end of 1996) is that real GDP will grow by 2 percent to 2.5 percent during 1997.

■ The chance of a recession is seen as small.

■ Decreases in home construction, auto sales, industrial production, and U.S. exports and slow retail sales all point to a slowdown.

■ Danger signs of a recession include a spike in inflation brought on by shortages of labor and inventory buildups.

■ In 1997, there are signs of a labor shortage, but inventories have not built up.

# Economic

## A N A L Y S I S

■ Inventory investment fluctuates, and when recession begins, an *unplanned* inventory buildup occurs.

■ But not all increases in inventories are unplanned.

■ Figure 1 shows the changes in inventories between 1990 and 1996. The last recession, in 1990–1991, was preceded by an unplanned increase in inventories. But the most recent large increase in inventories, in 1994, was planned and did not lead to recession.

■ Figure 1 also shows that inventories increased during 1996. We do not know whether this increase is unplanned or planned.

■ Planned inventory changes are part of planned investment and so are part of aggregate planned expenditure.

■ Figure 2 shows two possible scenarios for 1997. In the first scenario, aggregate planned expenditure is $AE_{97}$. At point $a$, $AE_{97}$ intersects the 45° line and aggregate planned expenditure equals real GDP at $7 trillion, which (we'll assume) equals potential GDP.

■ Figure 2(b) shows the relationship between real GDP and unplanned inventory changes as the line labeled $UI_{97}$. At the equilibrium real GDP of $7 trillion, shown at point $a'$, there is no unplanned change in inventory.

■ In the second scenario, aggregate planned expenditure decreases and the $AE$ curve shifts downward to $AE'$. The new equilibrium occurs at point $b$.

■ In Fig. 2(b), the unplanned inventory curve shifts to $UI'$.

■ With real GDP at $7 trillion, there is now an unplanned increase in inventories, shown in Fig. 2(b).

■ Firms decrease production, and real GDP decreases. In Fig. 2(a), the economy moves to point $b$.

■ Unplanned inventory changes return to zero when aggregate planned expenditure equals real GDP, at point $b'$ in Fig. 2(b).

■ At the beginning of 1997, no events had occurred to make the second outcome predictable.

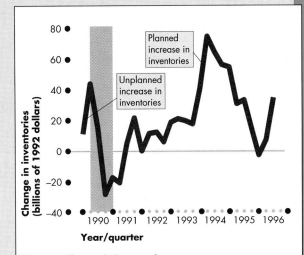

Figure 1 Change in inventories

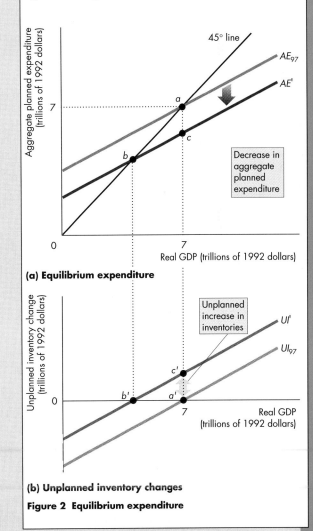

(a) Equilibrium expenditure

(b) Unplanned inventory changes

Figure 2 Equilibrium expenditure

# SUMMARY

## Key Points

### Fixed Prices and Expenditure Plans (pp. 242–247)

▓ When the price level is fixed, expenditure plans determine real GDP.

▓ Consumption expenditure is determined by disposable income, and the marginal propensity to consume (*MPC*) determines the change in consumption expenditure brought about by a change in disposable income. Real GDP determines disposable income.

▓ Imports are determined by real GDP, and the marginal propensity to import determines the change in imports brought about by a change in real GDP.

### Real GDP with a Fixed Price Level (pp. 248–251)

▓ Aggregate *planned* expenditure depends on real GDP.

▓ Equilibrium expenditure occurs when aggregate planned expenditure equals actual expenditure and real GDP.

### The Multiplier (pp. 252–257)

▓ The multiplier is the magnified effect of a change in autonomous expenditure on real GDP.

▓ The multiplier is influenced by the marginal propensity to consume, the marginal propensity to import, and the marginal income tax rate.

### The Multiplier and the Price Level (pp. 257–261)

▓ The aggregate demand curve is the relationship between the quantity of real GDP demanded and the price level, other things remaining the same.

▓ The aggregate expenditure curve is the relationship between aggregate planned expenditure and real GDP, other things remaining the same.

▓ At a given price level, there is a given aggregate expenditure curve. A change in the price level changes aggregate planned expenditure and shifts the aggregate expenditure curve. A change in the price level also creates a movement along the aggregate demand curve.

▓ A change in autonomous expenditure that is not caused by a change in the price level shifts the aggregate expenditure curve and shifts the aggregate demand curve. The magnitude of the shift of the aggregate demand curve depends on the multiplier and on the change in autonomous expenditure.

▓ The multiplier decreases as the price level changes, and in the long run the multiplier is zero.

## Key Figures

## Key Terms

# QUESTIONS

1. What is the main influence on consumption expenditure and saving in the short term?
2. What are the consumption function and the saving function? What is the relationship between them?
3. What is the marginal propensity to consume? Why is it less than 1?
4. Explain the relationship between the marginal propensities to consume and to save.
5. What determines the slope of the consumption function?
6. What is the marginal propensity to import?
7. What are the aggregate expenditure schedule and the aggregate expenditure curve?
8. Distinguish between induced expenditure and autonomous expenditure.
9. How is equilibrium expenditure determined?
10. Explain how a recovery gets going when aggregate planned expenditure exceeds real GDP.
11. Explain why an increase in autonomous expenditure shifts the aggregate expenditure curve.
12. What is the multiplier?
13. Explain the multiplier process.
14. What determines the size of the multiplier?
15. Explain the influences of the marginal propensity to consume, imports, and taxes on the size of the multiplier.
16. Describe the relationship between the aggregate expenditure curve and the aggregate demand curve.
17. Explain why the aggregate expenditure curve shifts downward when the price level increases.
18. What happens to the aggregate expenditure curve and the aggregate demand curve when the price level changes and everything else is constant?
19. Explain why an increase in autonomous expenditure increases aggregate demand.
20. Explain why the multiplier is larger when the price level is fixed than when it changes.
21. Explain why the multiplier is zero in the long run.

# PROBLEMS

1. You are given the following information about the economy of Heron Island:

| Disposable income (millions of dollars per year) | Consumption expenditure (millions of dollars per year) |
|---|---|
| 0 | 5 |
| 10 | 10 |
| 20 | 15 |
| 30 | 20 |
| 40 | 25 |

Calculate Heron Island's
a. Marginal propensity to consume.
b. Saving at each level of disposable income.
c. Marginal propensity to save.

2. Turtle Island has no imports or exports, the people of Turtle Island pay no incomes taxes, and the price level is fixed. The figure illustrates the components of aggregate planned expenditure on Turtle Island.

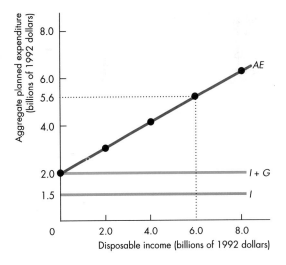

On Turtle Island, what is:
a. Autonomous expenditure?
b. The marginal propensity to consume?
c. Aggregate planned expenditure when real GDP is $6 billion?
d. If real GDP is $4 billion, what is happening to inventories?

e. If real GDP is $6 billion, what is happening to inventories?

f. What is the multiplier?

3. You are given the following information about the economy of Zeeland: Autonomous consumption expenditure is $100 billion, and the marginal propensity to consume is 0.9. Investment is $460 billion, government purchases of goods and services are $400 billion, and net taxes are a constant $400 billion—they do not vary with income.

a. What is the consumption function?

b. What is the equation that describes the aggregate expenditure curve?

c. Calculate equilibrium expenditure.

d. If investment falls to $360 billion, what is the change in equilibrium expenditure and what is the size of the multiplier?

4. Suppose that in problem 3, the price level is 100 and real GDP equals potential GDP.

a. If investment increases by $100 billion, what happens to the quantity of real GDP demanded?

b. In the short run, does equilibrium real GDP increase by more than, less than, or the same amount as the increase in the quantity of real GDP demanded?

c. In the long run, does equilibrium real GDP increase by more than, less than, or the same amount as the increase in the quantity of real GDP demanded?

d. In the short run, does the price level in Zeeland rise, fall, or remain unchanged?

e. In the long run, does the price level in Zeeland rise, fall, or remain unchanged?

# CRITICAL THINKING

1. Study *Reading Between the Lines* on pp. 262–263, and then answer the following questions:

a. The 1994 investment in inventories seems to have been a *planned* investment. What are the implications of a planned investment in business inventories for real GDP, aggregate expenditure, and inventory investment? Use a figure similar to Fig. 2 on p. 637 to answer this question.

b. The 1990 investment in inventories seems to have been an *unplanned* investment. What are the implications of an unplanned investment in business inventories for real GDP, aggregate expenditure, and inventory investment? Use a figure similar to Fig. 2 on p. 637 to answer this question.

c. What do you think will happen to real GDP, aggregate expenditure, and inventory investment in 1997? What clues do you get from the news article?

d. Is a buildup of business inventories a cause or a consequence of recession?

2. Visit the Penn World Table Web site (linked from the Parkin site) and obtain data on real GDP per person and consumption as a percentage of real GDP for the United States, China, South Africa, and Mexico since 1960.

a. In a spreadsheet, multiply your real GDP data by the consumption percentage and divide by 100 to obtain data on real consumption expenditure per person.

b. Make graphs like Fig. 11.4 that show the relationship between consumption and real GDP for these four countries.

c. Based on the numbers you've obtained, in which country do you expect the multiplier to be largest (other things being equal)?

d. What other data would you need in order to calculate the multipliers for these countries?

e. You are a research assistant in the office of the President's Council of Economic Advisors. You've been asked to draft a note for the President that explains the power and limitations of the multiplier. The President wants only 250 words of crisp, clear, jargon-free explanation together with a lively example.

http://hepg.awl.com/parkin/econ100

# Chapter 12

# Fiscal Policy

In 1997, the federal government planned to spend $1,631 billion, or 23 cents of every dollar that Americans earn. What are the effects of government spending on the economy? Does it create jobs? Or does it destroy them? And does a dollar spent by the government on goods and services have the same effect as a dollar spent by someone else? ◆ Although the federal government planned to *spend* 23 cents of every dollar earned, it did not plan to tax us by that amount. Its plans were for tax revenues of $1,505 billion or 21 cents of every dollar earned. What are the effects of taxes on the economy? Do taxes harm employment and economic growth? ◆ The plan to have tax revenues fall short of expenditures is not new on Capitol Hill. The last time the federal

## Balancing Acts on Capitol Hill

government budget was in surplus was 1969. Over the 28 years since then, and using constant 1992 dollars, the federal government's debt has increased from $1,000 billion to $3,500 billion. If these numbers are too big to mean anything, divide them by the U.S. population to find *your* share. Government

debt per person was more than $13,000 in 1997. Does it matter if the government doesn't balance its books? What are the effects of an ongoing government deficit and accumulating debt? Does it slow economic growth? Does it impose a burden on future generations—on you and your children? What must be done to balance the budget? Can spending cuts do it? Or must taxes be increased? Or can spending be cut so severely that taxes can also be cut? ◆ These are the fiscal policy issues that you will study in this chapter. We'll begin by describing the federal budget and the process of creating it. We'll also look at the recent history of the budget. We'll then use the multiplier analysis of Chapter 11 and the aggregate supply–aggregate demand model of Chapter 7 to study the effects of the budget on the economy.

## After studying this chapter, you will be able to:

- Describe the federal budget process

- Describe the recent history of federal expenditures, tax revenues, and the budget deficit

- Distinguish between automatic and discretionary fiscal policy

- Define and explain the fiscal policy multipliers

- Explain the effects of fiscal policy in the short run and in the long run

- Distinguish between and explain the demand-side and supply-side effects of fiscal policy

# The Federal Budget

THE ANNUAL STATEMENT OF THE EXPENDITURES and tax revenues of the government of the United States together with the laws and regulations that approve and support those expenditures and taxes make up the **federal budget**. The federal budget has two purposes:

1. To finance the activities of the federal government

2. To stabilize the economy

The first purpose of the federal budget was its only purpose before the Great Depression years of the 1930s. The second purpose of the federal budget arose as a reaction to the Great Depression. The use of the federal budget to achieve macroeconomic objectives such as full employment, sustained economic growth, and price level stability is called **fiscal policy**. It is on this second purpose that we focus in this chapter.

## The Institutions and Laws

Fiscal policy is made by the President and Congress on an annual time line that is shown in Figure 12.1.

**The Roles of the President and Congress**  The President *proposes* a budget to Congress each February and, after Congress has passed the budget acts in September, either signs those acts into law or vetoes them. Until recently, the President approved or vetoed an entire budget bill. The President did not have veto power to eliminate specific items in a budget bill and approve others—a *line-item veto*. Many state governors have long had a line-item veto, and the President of the United States received this power in 1996. But a court challenge has put the veto in doubt. Although the President proposes and ultimately approves the budget, the task of making the tough decisions on spending and taxes rests with Congress.

Congress begins its work on the budget with the President's proposal. The House of Representatives and the Senate develop their own budget ideas in their respective House and Senate Budget Committees. Formal conferences between the two houses eventually resolve differences of view, and a series of spending acts and an overall budget act are usually passed by both houses before the start of the fiscal year. A *fiscal year* is a year that runs from October 1 to September

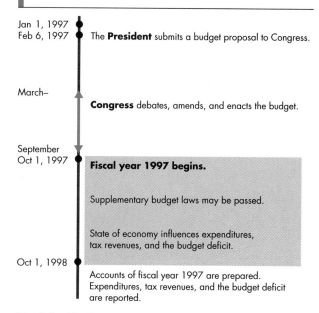

**FIGURE 12.1**

## The Federal Budget Time Line in 1997–98

The federal budget process begins with the President's proposals in February. Congress debates and amends these proposals and enacts a budget before the start of the fiscal year on October 1. The President signs the budget acts into law but may exercise a line-item veto. Throughout the fiscal year, Congress might pass supplementary budget laws. The budget outcome is calculated after the end of the fiscal year.

30 in the next calendar year. *Fiscal 1997* is the fiscal year that *begins* on October 1, 1997.

During a fiscal year, Congress often passes supplementary budget laws, and the budget outcome is influenced by the evolving state of the economy. For example, if a recession begins, tax revenues fall and welfare payments increase.

**The Employment Act of 1946**  Fiscal policy operates within the framework of the landmark **Employment Act of 1946**, in which Congress declared that

> it is the continuing policy and responsibility of the Federal Government to use all practicable means … to coordinate and utilize all its plans, functions, and resources … to promote maximum employment, production, and purchasing power.

This act recognized a role for government actions to keep unemployment low, keep the economy expanding, and keep inflation in check. The *Full Employment and Balanced Growth Act of 1978*, more commonly known as the *Humphrey-Hawkins Act*, went further than the 1946 employment act and set a specific target of 4 percent for the unemployment rate. Most economists regard this target as unattainable and it has no operational significance. Under the 1946 Act, the President must describe the current economic situation and the policies he believes are needed in an annual *Economic Report of the President*, which is written by the Council of Economic Advisers.

**The Council of Economic Advisers**   The President's **Council of Economic Advisers** (CEA) was established in 1946 by the Employment Act. The Council consists of a Chair and two other members, all of whom are economists on leave from their regular university or public service jobs. Members typically serve for two to three years. In 1997, the Chair of President Clinton's Council of Economic Advisers was Janet Yellen of the University of California at Berkeley, and the two members were Jeffrey A. Frankel, also of Berkeley, and Alicia H. Munnell. The

main work of the Council is to monitor the economy and to keep the President and the public well informed about the current state of the economy and the best available forecasts of where it is heading. This economic intelligence activity is one source of data that informs the budget-making process.

Let's look at the most recent federal budget.

### Highlights of the 1997 Budget

Table 12.1 shows the main items in the federal budget proposed by President Clinton in 1997. The numbers are projected amounts for the fiscal year beginning on October 1, 1997—fiscal 1997. Notice the three main parts of the table: *Tax revenues* are the government's receipts, *expenditures* are the government's outlays, and the *deficit* is the amount by which the government's expenditures exceed its tax revenues.

**Tax Revenues**   Tax revenues were projected to be $1,505 billion in fiscal 1997. These revenues come from four sources:

1. Personal income taxes
2. Social insurance taxes
3. Corporate income taxes
4. Indirect taxes

The largest source of revenue is *personal income taxes*, which in 1997 were expected to be $673 billion. These are the taxes paid by individuals on their incomes. The second largest source is *social insurance taxes*. These are the taxes paid by workers and their employers to finance the government's social security programs. Third in size are *corporate income taxes*. These are the taxes paid by companies on their profits. Finally, the smallest source of revenue comes from *indirect taxes*. These are taxes on the sale of gasoline, alcoholic drinks, and a few other items.

**Expenditures**   Expenditures are classified in three categories:

1. Transfer payments
2. Purchases of goods and services
3. Debt interest

The largest item of expenditure, *transfer payments*, are payments to individuals, businesses, other levels of government, and the rest of the world.

---

**TABLE 12.1**

## Federal Budget in Fiscal 1997

| Item | Projections (billions of dollars) | |
|---|---|---|
| **Tax Revenues** | **1,505** | |
| Personal income taxes | | 673 |
| Social insurance taxes | | 536 |
| Corporate income taxes | | 176 |
| Indirect taxes | | 120 |
| **Expenditures** | **1,631** | |
| Transfer payments | | 1,060 |
| Purchases of goods and services | | 324 |
| Debt interest | | 247 |
| **Deficit** | **126** | |

Source: *Economic Report of the President*, 1997, Table B-78.

In 1997, this item was expected to be $1,060 billion. It includes Social Security benefits, Medicare and Medicaid, unemployment checks, welfare payments, farm subsidies, grants to state and local governments, aid to developing countries, and dues to international organizations such as the United Nations. Transfer payments, especially those on Medicare and Medicaid, are sources of persistent growth in government expenditures and are a major source of political debate.

*Purchases of goods and services* are expenditures on final goods and services, and in 1997, they were expected to total $324 billion. These expenditures, which include those on national defense, the NASA space program, research on cures for AIDS and other diseases, computers for the Internal Revenue Service, government cars and trucks, federal highways, and dams, have decreased in recent years. This component of the federal budget is included in *government purchases of goods and services* that appears in the circular flow of expenditure and income and in the National Income and Product Accounts (see Chapter 6, pp. 122–123).

*Debt interest* is the interest on the government debt. In 1997, this item was expected to be $247 billion—some 15 percent of total expenditure. This interest payment is large because the government has a debt of almost $4 trillion, which has arisen from large and persistent budget deficits.

**Deficit**   The government's budget balance is

Budget balance = Tax revenues – Expenditures.

If tax revenues exceed expenditures, the government has a **budget surplus**. If expenditures exceed tax revenues, the government has a **budget deficit**. If tax revenues equal expenditures, the government has a **balanced budget**. In fiscal 1997, with projected expenditures of $1,631 billion and tax revenues of $1,505 billion, the government projected a budget deficit of $126 billion.

Big numbers like these are hard to visualize and hard to compare over time. To get a better sense of the magnitude of taxes, spending, and the deficit, we often express them as percentages of GDP. Expressing them this way lets us to see how large the government is relative to the size of the economy and also helps us to study *changes* in the scale of government over time.

How typical is the federal budget of 1997? Let's look at its recent history.

### The Budget in Historical Perspective

Figure 12.2 shows the government's tax revenues, expenditures, and budget deficit since 1978. Throughout this period, there was a budget deficit.

---

**FIGURE 12.2**

## The Budget Deficit

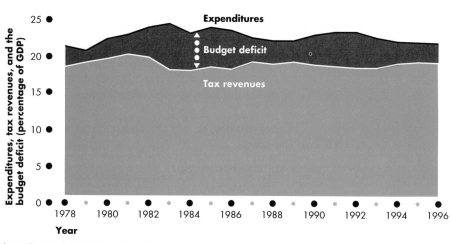

The figure records the federal government's expenditures, tax revenues, and budget deficit from 1978 to 1996. During the late 1970s, the deficit was small and decreasing, but during the 1980s, it became large and persisted. The budget deficit arose from the combination of a decrease in tax revenues and an increase in expenditures.

*Source: Economic Report of the President, 1997.*

The deficit was small and decreasing between 1978 and 1979, but it then increased and reached a peak in 1983 of 6.3 percent of GDP. It declined from 1983 through 1989 but averaged more than 4 percent of GDP through the entire decade of the 1980s. The deficit climbed again during the 1990–1991 recession and then decreased during the 1990s expansion.

Why did the government deficit grow in the early 1980s and remain high? The immediate answer is that expenditures increased and tax revenues

decreased. But which components of expenditures increased and which sources of tax revenues decreased? Let's look at tax revenues and expenditures in a bit more detail.

**Tax Revenues**   Figure 12.3(a) shows the components of tax revenues as percentages of GDP between 1978 and 1996. Total tax revenues increased between 1978 and 1981 and then declined through 1986. Most of the decline was in corporate and personal

---

**FIGURE 12.3**

## Federal Government Tax Revenues and Expenditures

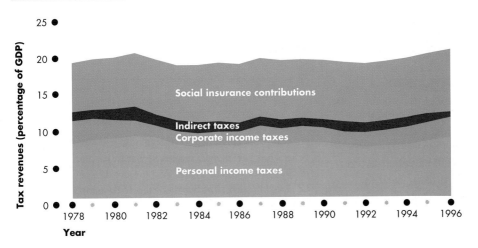

**(a) Tax revenues**

Part (a) shows the four components of government tax revenues: personal income taxes, corporate income taxes, indirect taxes, and social insurance contributions. Revenues from personal and corporate income taxes declined during the early 1980s, remained fairly steady from 1983 to 1991, and then increased. The other two components of tax revenues remained steady.

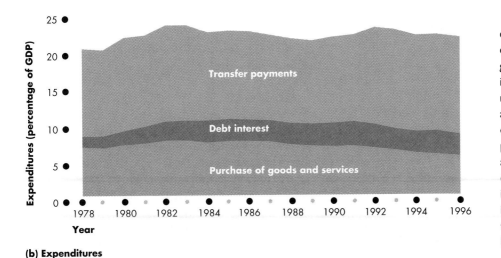

**(b) Expenditures**

*Source: Economic Report of the President, 1997.*

Part (b) shows three components of government expenditures: purchases of goods and services, debt interest, and transfer payments. Purchases of goods and services fluctuated but did not increase. Transfer payments fluctuated most and did increase, especially during the early 1980s and in 1991–1992. Debt interest increased steadily during the 1980s and 1990s as the budget deficit fed on itself.

income taxes, and the decline resulted from tax cuts passed in the Economic Recovery Tax Act of 1981. From 1986 through 1991, tax revenues did not change much as a percentage of GDP. But they increased after 1992 through 1996.

**Expenditures**    Figure 12.3(b) shows the components of government expenditures as percentages of GDP, between 1978 and 1996. Total expenditures decreased between 1978 and 1979 and then increased sharply between 1979 and 1983. Expenditures then declined slightly through 1989 before increasing again until 1992. After 1992, total expenditures decreased. Both purchases of goods and services and transfer payments fluctuated. The item that increased most persistently was debt interest. To understand why, we need to see the connection between the deficit and government debt.

**Deficit and Debt**    The government borrows to finance its deficit. And **government debt** is the total amount of government borrowing. It is the sum of past deficits minus the sum of past surpluses. When the government has a deficit, its debt increases. Once a persistent deficit emerged during the 1980s, the deficit began to feed on itself. The deficit led to increased borrowing; increased borrowing led to larger interest payments; and larger interest payments led to a larger deficit. That is the story of the increasing deficit of the 1980s.

Figure 12.4 shows the history of government debt since 1945. At the end of World War II, debt (as a percentage of GDP) was at an all-time high of 114 percent. Huge wartime deficits had increased debt to the point that it exceeded real GDP. Postwar budget surpluses lowered the debt to GDP ratio through 1974, by which time it stood at 24 percent, its lowest point since World War II. Small deficits increased the debt to GDP ratio slightly through the 1970s, and large deficits increased it dramatically between 1981 and 1986. During the late 1980s, the ratio continued to increase but at a more moderate rate. It grew quickly again during the 1990–1991 recession, but the debt to GDP ratio fell when the economy recovered during 1993 and 1995.

**Debt and Capital**    When individuals and businesses incur debts, they usually do so to buy capital—assets that yield a return. In fact, the main point of debt is to enable people to buy assets that will earn a return that exceeds the interest paid on the debt.

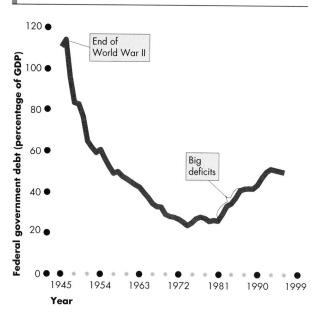

FIGURE 12.4

The Federal Government Debt

Federal government debt (the accumulation of past budget deficits less past budget surpluses) was more than 100 percent of GDP at the end of World War II. Debt as a percentage of GDP fell through 1974 but then started to increase. After a further brief decline during the late 1970s, it exploded during the 1980s and continued to increase through 1993.

Source: Economic Report of the President, 1997.

The government is similar to individuals and businesses in this regard. Much government expenditure is on public assets that yield a return. Highways, major irrigation schemes, public schools and universities, public libraries, and the stock of national defense capital all yield a social rate of return that probably far exceeds the interest rate that the government pays on its debt.

But total government debt, which is almost $4 trillion, is more than twice the value of the public capital stock. So some government debt has been incurred to finance public consumption expenditure. This expenditure does not have an ongoing social return.

How does the U.S. government deficit compare with deficits in other countries?

## The Budget Deficit in Global Perspective

Is the United States unusual in running a budget deficit? Do other countries have budget deficits or do they have budget surpluses? Figure 12.5 answers these questions. Almost all countries have budget deficits in today's world. To make the deficits comparable across countries, we measure the deficits as percentages of GDP. The biggest deficits relative to GDP are found in Japan, the Middle East, and the countries of Central Europe that are making a transition from a heavily regulated economy to a market economy. The

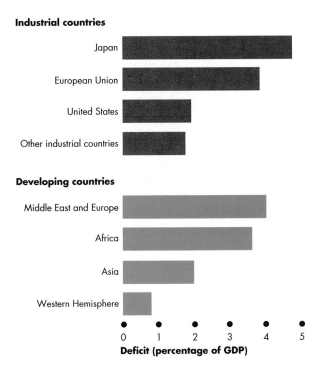

**FIGURE 12.5**

Government Deficits Around the World in 1996

**Industrial countries**

**Developing countries**

**Deficit (percentage of GDP)**

Governments in most countries have budget deficits. The largest ones are in Japan, the Middle East, and Europe, and the smallest are in the developing countries in the Western Hemisphere—Central and South America. The U.S. federal government deficit is at the low end of the scale.

*Source: World Economic Outlook* (Washington, D.C.: International Monetary Fund, May 1996), Tables A14 and A19.

smallest deficits relative to GDP are found in the developing countries of the Western Hemisphere. The U.S. budget deficit is *smaller* than that of most countries. It is smaller than Japan's and the average of the rich industrial countries in Europe.

## State and Local Budgets

The *total government* sector of the United States includes state and local governments as well as the federal government. In 1997, when federal government expenditures were $1,631 billion, state and local expenditures were $1,050 billion. Most of these expenditures were on public schools, colleges, and universities ($350 billion), local police and fire services, and roads.

It is the total government sector that influences the aggregate economy. But state and local budgets are not designed, as the federal budget is, with the specific goal of stabilizing the aggregate economy. On the contrary, sometimes, when the aggregate economy needs an injection of additional expenditures, state and local governments cut their expenditures and deficits. Such changes in expenditures occurred during the 1990–1991 recession when many states both cut their expenditures and increased taxes.

### REVIEW

- Fiscal policy is created by Congress and the President and is a key tool designed to influence employment and economic activity.
- Each year, the budget is proposed by the President in February and amended and enacted by Congress. The fiscal year begins on October 1.
- For many years, the federal government has run a budget deficit and federal debt has grown.

Now that you know what the federal budget is and what the main items of revenue and expenditure are, it is time to study the *effects* of fiscal policy. We'll begin by learning about its effects on expenditure plans when the price level is fixed. You will see that fiscal policy has multiplier effects like the expenditure multipliers explained in Chapter 11. Then we'll study the influences of fiscal policy on both aggregate demand and aggregate supply and look at its short-run and long-run effects on real GDP and the price level.

# Fiscal Policy Multipliers

FISCAL POLICY ACTIONS CAN BE EITHER AUTOMATIC or discretionary. **Automatic fiscal policy** is a change in fiscal policy that is triggered by the state of the economy. For example, an increase in unemployment triggers an *automatic* increase in payments to the unemployed. A fall in incomes triggers an *automatic* decrease in tax receipts. That is, this type of fiscal policy adjusts automatically. **Discretionary fiscal policy** is a policy action that is initiated by an act of Congress. It requires a change in tax laws or in some spending program. For example, an increase in the income tax rate and an increase in defense spending are discretionary fiscal policy actions. That is, discretionary fiscal policy is a deliberate policy action.

We begin by studying the effects of *discretionary* changes in government spending and taxes. To focus on the essentials, we'll initially study a model economy that is simpler than the one in which we live. In our model economy, there is no international trade and the taxes are all lump sum. **Lump-sum taxes** are taxes that do not vary with real GDP. The government fixes them, and they change when the government changes them. But they do not vary automatically with the state of the economy.

The main example of a lump-sum tax is the *property tax*. This tax varies across individuals and depends on the value of the property a person occupies. But unlike the income tax, it does not change simply because a person's income changes.

We use lump-sum taxes in our model economy because they make the principles we are studying easier to understand. Once we've grasped the principles, we'll explore our real economy with its international trade and income taxes—taxes that *do* vary with real GDP.

Like our real economy, the model economy we study is bombarded by spending fluctuations. Business investment in new building, plant and equipment, and inventories fluctuates because of swings in profit expectations and interest rates. These fluctuations set up multiplier effects that start a recession or an expansion. If a recession takes hold, unemployment increases and incomes fall. If an expansion becomes too strong, inflationary pressures build up. To minimize the effects of these swings in spending, the government might change either its purchases of goods and services or taxes. By changing either of these items, the government can influence aggregate

expenditure and real GDP. But it also changes its budget deficit or surplus. An alternative fiscal policy action is to change both purchases and taxes together so that the budget balance does not change. We are going to study the initial effects of these discretionary fiscal policy actions in the very short run when the price level is fixed. Each of these actions creates a multiplier effect on real GDP. These multipliers are:

- The government purchases multiplier
- The lump-sum tax multiplier

## The Government Purchases Multiplier

The **government purchases multiplier** is the magnification effect of a change in government purchases of goods and services on equilibrium expenditure and real GDP.

Government purchases are a component of aggregate expenditure. So when government purchases change, aggregate expenditure and real GDP change. The change in real GDP induces a change in consumption expenditure, which brings a further change in aggregate expenditure. A multiplier process ensues. This multiplier process is like the one described in Chapter 11 (pp. 252–257). Let's look at an example.

**Cape Canaveral Multiplier** Before the National Aeronautics and Space Administration (NASA) built a major space launching facility at Cape Canaveral in Florida in the 1960s, the Cape was a quiet place. The injection of government purchases to build the space launching and research facility created jobs in the region. Because construction workers and NASA workers spent most of their incomes locally, consumption expenditure increased. Retail stores and hotels and motels opened and hired yet more people and, in the process, created yet bigger incomes. These incomes were also spent in the area, so spending and incomes rose still further. Eventually, expenditures and incomes stopped rising but remained at their new higher levels.

**The Size of the Multiplier** Table 12.2 illustrates the government purchases multiplier with a numerical example. The first column lists various possible levels of real GDP. Our task is to find equilibrium expenditure and the change in real GDP when government purchases change. The second column shows taxes.

**TABLE 12.2**

# The Government Purchases Multiplier

| | Real GDP (Y) | Taxes (T) | Disposable income (Y – T) | Consumption expenditure (C) | Investment (I) | Initial government purchases (G) | Initial aggregate planned expenditure (AE = C + I + G) | New government purchases (G') | New aggregate planned expenditure (AE' = C + I + G') |
|---|---|---|---|---|---|---|---|---|---|
| | | | | | (trillions of dollars) | | | | |
| a | 5.0 | 0.5 | 4.5 | 3.75 | 1.0 | 0.5 | 5.25 | 1.0 | 5.75 |
| b | 6.0 | 0.5 | 5.5 | 4.50 | 1.0 | 0.5 | 6.00 | 1.0 | 6.50 |
| c | 7.0 | 0.5 | 6.5 | 5.25 | 1.0 | 0.5 | 6.75 | 1.0 | 7.25 |
| d | 8.0 | 0.5 | 7.5 | 6.00 | 1.0 | 0.5 | 7.50 | 1.0 | 8.00 |
| e | 9.0 | 0.5 | 8.5 | 6.75 | 1.0 | 0.5 | 8.25 | 1.0 | 8.75 |

They are fixed at $0.5 trillion, regardless of the level of real GDP. (This is an assumption that keeps your attention on the key idea and makes the calculations easier to do.) The third column calculates disposable income. Because taxes are a lump sum, disposable income equals real GDP minus the $0.5 trillion of taxes. For example, in row *b*, real GDP is $6 trillion and disposable income is $5.5 trillion. The next column shows consumption expenditure. In this example, the *marginal propensity to consume* is 0.75. That is, a $1 increase in disposable income brings a 75-cent increase in consumption expenditure. Check this fact by calculating the increase in consumption expenditure when disposable income increases by $1 trillion from row *b* to row *c*. Consumption expenditure increases by $0.75 trillion. The next column shows investment, which is a constant of $1 trillion. The next column shows the initial level of government purchases, which is $0.5 trillion. Aggregate planned expenditure is the sum of consumption expenditure, investment, and government purchases.

Equilibrium expenditure and real GDP occur when aggregate planned expenditure equals actual expenditure. In this example, equilibrium expenditure is $6 trillion (highlighted in row *b* of the table.)

The final two columns of the table show what happens when government purchases increase by $0.5 trillion to $1 trillion. Aggregate planned expenditure increases by $0.5 trillion at each level of real GDP. At the initial real GDP of $6 trillion (row *b*), aggregate planned expenditure increases to $6.5 trillion.

Because aggregate planned expenditure now exceeds real GDP, inventories decrease and firms increase production. Output, incomes, and expenditure increase. Increased incomes induce a further increase in expenditure. But the induced increase in aggregate planned expenditure is less than the increase in income, and eventually a new equilibrium is reached. The new equilibrium is at a real GDP of $8 trillion (highlighted in row *d* ).

A $0.5 trillion increase in government purchases has increased equilibrium expenditure and real GDP by $2 trillion. Therefore the government purchases multiplier is 4. The size of the multiplier depends on the marginal propensity to consume, which in this example is 0.75. The following formula shows the connection between the government purchases multiplier and the marginal propensity to consume (*MPC*):

$$\text{Government purchase multiplier} = \frac{1}{1 - MPC}.$$

Let's check this formula by using the numbers in the above example. The marginal propensity to consume is 0.75, so the government purchases multiplier is 4.

Figure 12.6 illustrates the government purchases multiplier. Initially, aggregate planned expenditure is shown by the curve labeled $AE_0$. The points on this curve, labeled *a* through *e,* correspond with the rows of Table 12.2. This aggregate expenditure curve intersects the 45° line at the equilibrium level of real GDP, which is $6 trillion.

**FIGURE 12.6**

# The Government Purchases Multiplier

Initially, the aggregate expenditure curve is $AE_0$ and real GDP is $6 trillion (at point b). An increase in government purchases of $0.5 trillion increases aggregate planned expenditure at each level of real GDP by $0.5 trillion. The aggregate expenditure curve shifts upward from $AE_0$ to $AE_1$—a parallel shift. At the initial real GDP of $6 trillion, aggregate planned expenditure is now $6.5 trillion. Because aggregate planned expenditure is greater than real GDP, real GDP increases. The new equilibrium is reached when real GDP is $8 trillion—the point at which the $AE_1$ curve intersects the 45° line (at d'). In this example, the government purchases multiplier is 4.

When government purchases increase by $0.5 trillion, the aggregate expenditure curve shifts upward by that amount to $AE_1$. With this new aggregate expenditure curve, equilibrium real GDP increases to $8 trillion. The increase in real GDP is 4 times the increase in government purchases. The government purchases multiplier is 4.

You've seen that in the very short term, when the price level is fixed, an increase in government purchases increases real GDP. But to produce more output, more people must be employed. So in the short term, an increase in government purchases can create jobs.

Increasing its purchases of goods and services is one way in which the government can try to stimulate the economy. A second way in which the government might act to increase real GDP in the very short run is by decreasing lump-sum taxes. Let's see how this action works.

## The Lump-Sum Tax Multiplier

The **lump-sum tax multiplier** is the magnification effect of a change in lump-sum taxes on equilibrium expenditure and real GDP. An *increase* in taxes *decreases* disposable income, which *decreases* consumption expenditure. The amount by which consumption expenditure initially changes is determined by the marginal propensity to consume. In our example, the marginal propensity to consume is 0.75, so a $1 tax cut increases disposable income by $1 and increases aggregate expenditure initially by 75 cents.

This initial change in aggregate expenditure has a multiplier just like the government purchases multiplier. We've seen that the government purchases multiplier is $1/(1 - MPC)$. Because a tax *increase* leads to a *decrease* in expenditure, the lump-sum tax multiplier is *negative*. And because a change in lump-sum taxes changes aggregate expenditure initially by only $MPC$ multiplied by the tax change, the lump-sum tax multiplier is equal to

$$\text{Lump-sum tax multiplier} = \frac{-MPC}{1 - MPC}.$$

In our example, the marginal propensity to consume is 3/4, so the lump-sum tax multiplier is

$$\text{Lump-sum tax multiplier} = \frac{-\frac{3}{4}}{1 - \frac{3}{4}} = -3.$$

Figure 12.7 illustrates the lump-sum tax multiplier. Initially, the aggregate expenditure curve is $AE_0$, and equilibrium expenditure is $8 trillion. Taxes increase by $1 trillion, and disposable income falls by that amount. With a marginal propensity to consume of 3/4, aggregate expenditure decreases initially by $0.75 trillion and the aggregate expenditure curve shifts downward by that amount to $AE_1$. Equilibrium expenditure and real GDP fall by $3 trillion to $5 trillion. The lump-sum tax multiplier is –3.

**FIGURE 12.7**

# The Lump-Sum
# Tax Multiplier

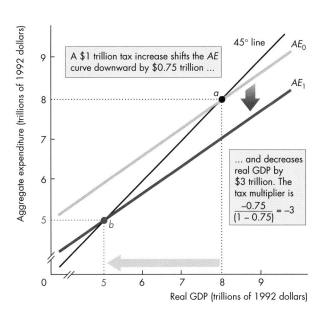

A \$1 trillion tax increase shifts the *AE* curve downward by \$0.75 trillion ...

... and decreases real GDP by \$3 trillion. The tax multiplier is $\dfrac{-0.75}{(1-0.75)} = -3$

Initially, the aggregate expenditure curve is $AE_0$ and equilibrium expenditure is \$8 trillion. The marginal propensity to consume is 0.75. Lump-sum taxes increase by \$1 trillion, so disposable income falls by \$1 trillion. The decrease in aggregate expenditure is found by multiplying this change in disposable income by the marginal propensity to consume and is \$1 trillion x 0.75 = \$0.75 trillion. The aggregate expenditure curve shifts *downward* by this amount to $AE_1$. Equilibrium expenditure decreases by \$3 trillion, from \$8 trillion to \$5 trillion. The lump-sum tax multiplier is –3.

**Lump-Sum Transfer Payments**  The lump-sum tax multiplier also tells us the effects of a change in lump-sum transfer payments. Transfer payments are like negative taxes, so an increase in transfer payments works like a decrease in taxes. Because the tax multiplier is negative, a decrease in taxes increases expenditure. An increase in transfer payments also increases expenditure. So the lump-sum transfer payments multiplier is positive. It is

$$\text{Lump-sum transfer} \atop \text{payments multiplier} = \frac{MPC}{1-MPC}.$$

## Induced Taxes and Entitlement Spending

In the examples we've studied so far, taxes are lump-sum taxes. But in reality, net taxes (taxes minus transfer payments) vary with the state of the economy.

On the revenue side of the budget, tax laws define tax *rates* to be paid, not tax *dollars* to be paid. Tax *dollars* paid depend on tax *rates* and incomes. But incomes vary with real GDP, so tax *revenues* depend on real GDP. Taxes that vary with real GDP are called **induced taxes.** When the economy expands, induced taxes increase because real GDP increases. When the economy is in a recession, induced taxes decrease because real GDP decreases.

On the outlay side of the budget, the government creates programs that entitle suitably qualified people and businesses to receive benefits. The spending on such programs is called **entitlement spending,** and it results in transfer payments that depend on the economic state of individual citizens and businesses. When the economy is in a recession, unemployment is high, the number of people experiencing economic hardship increases, and a larger number of firms and farms experience hard times. Entitlement spending increases. When the economy expands, entitlement spending decreases.

Induced taxes and entitlement payments decrease the multiplier effects of changes in government purchases and lump-sum taxes. The reason is that they weaken the link between real GDP and disposable income and so dampen the effect of a change in real GDP on consumption expenditure. When real GDP increases, induced taxes increase and entitlement payments decrease, so disposable income does not increase by as much as the increase in real GDP. As a result, consumption expenditure does not increase by as much as it otherwise would have done and the multiplier effect is reduced.

The extent to which induced taxes and entitlement payments decrease the multiplier depends on the *marginal tax rate*. The marginal tax rate is the proportion of an additional dollar of real GDP that flows to the government in net taxes (taxes minus transfer payments). The higher the marginal tax rate, the larger is the proportion of an additional dollar of real GDP that is paid to the government and the smaller is the induced change in consumption expenditure. The smaller the change in consumption expenditure induced by a change in real GDP, the smaller is the multiplier effect of a change in government purchases or lump-sum taxes.

## International Trade and Fiscal Policy Multipliers

Not all expenditure in the United States is on U.S.-produced goods and services. Some of it is on imports—on foreign-produced goods and services. Imports affect the fiscal policy multipliers in exactly the same way that they influence the investment multiplier, as explained in Chapter 11 (see pp. 254–255), and there is no new principle involved. The extent to which an additional dollar of real GDP is spent on imports is determined by the *marginal propensity to import*. Expenditure on imports does not generate U.S. real GDP and does not lead to an increase in U.S. consumption expenditure. The larger the marginal propensity to import, the smaller is the increase in consumption expenditure induced by an increase in real GDP and the smaller are the government purchases and lump-sum tax multipliers.

So far, we've studied *discretionary* fiscal policy. Let's now look at *automatic* stabilizers.

## Automatic Stabilizers

**Automatic stabilizers** are mechanisms that stabilize real GDP without explicit action by the government. Their name is borrowed from engineering and conjures up images of shock absorbers, thermostats, and sophisticated devices that keep airplanes and ships steady in turbulent air and seas. Automatic fiscal stabilizers are a consequence of income taxes and transfer payments that automatically fluctuate with real GDP. If real GDP begins to decrease, tax revenues fall and transfer payments rise. These changes in taxes and transfer payments affect the economy and the government's budget deficit. Let's study the budget deficit over the business cycle.

**Budget Deficit Over the Business Cycle** Figure 12.8 shows the business cycle and fluctuations in the budget deficit since 1975. Part (a) shows the fluctuations of real GDP around potential GDP. Part (b) shows the federal budget deficit. Both parts highlight recessions by shading those periods. By comparing the two parts of the figure, you can see the relationship between the business cycle and the budget deficit. As a rule, when the economy is in the expansion phase of a business cycle, the budget deficit declines. (In the figure, a declining deficit means a deficit that is getting closer to zero.) As the expansion slows before the recession begins, the budget deficit

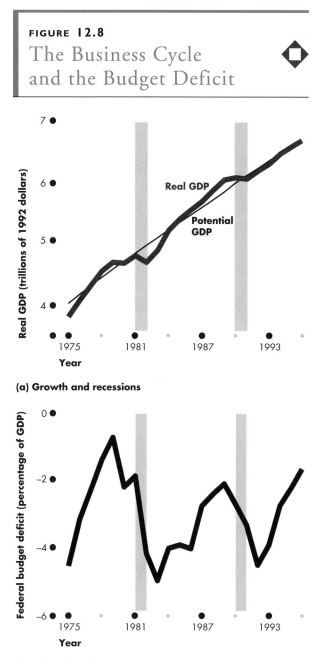

**FIGURE 12.8**

# The Business Cycle and the Budget Deficit

**(a) Growth and recessions**

**(b) Federal budget deficit**

As real GDP fluctuates around potential GDP (part a), the budget deficit fluctuates (part b). During a recession (shaded years), tax revenues decrease, transfer payments increase, and the budget deficit increases. The deficit also increases *before* a recession as real GDP growth slows and *after* a recession before real GDP growth speeds up.

*Source: Economic Report of the President, 1997, and the author's calculations.*

increases. It continues to increase during the recession and for a further period after the recession is over. Then, when the expansion is well under way, the budget deficit declines again.

The budget deficit fluctuates with the business cycle because both tax revenues and expenditures fluctuate with real GDP. As real GDP increases during an expansion, tax revenues increase and transfer payments decrease, so the budget deficit automatically decreases. As real GDP decreases during a recession, tax revenues decrease and transfer payments increase, so the budget deficit automatically increases.

Fluctuations in investment and exports have a multiplier effect on real GDP. But automatic fluctuations in tax revenues (and the budget deficit) act as an automatic stabilizer. They decrease the swings in disposable income and make the multiplier effect smaller. They dampen both expansions and recessions.

**Balanced Budget Amendment**   Some economists and politicians want to introduce a **balanced budget amendment** that requires the federal budget to be balanced. And such an amendment came close to passing during 1996.

A law that requires the federal budget to be balanced is probably infeasible. The budget might be balanced on the average over a number of years and perhaps balanced over a business cycle. But the budget is an annual event, and it is impossible, even if it were desirable, to balance the budget year by year. Most revenues and a large part of expenditures are determined not only by laws but also by the state of the economy. Further, a budget that was balanced every year would not have the automatic stabilizing properties that a cyclically unbalanced budget has.

Because the budget deficit increases when the economy is in recession and decreases when the economy is in an expansion, economists have developed a modified deficit concept called the cyclically adjusted deficit. The **cyclically adjusted deficit** is the budget deficit that would occur if the economy were at full employment.

**The Cyclically Adjusted Deficit**   The cyclically adjusted deficit is a measure for judging whether the budget deficit is cyclical or structural. The budget deficit is cyclical only if it is present because real GDP is below potential GDP. In this state, taxes are temporarily low and transfer payments are temporarily high. The budget deficit is structural—there is a **structural deficit**—if government expenditures

exceed tax revenues when real GDP equals potential GDP. The two terms "cyclically adjusted deficit" and "structural deficit" are equivalent.

Figure 12.9 illustrates the deficit and the concept of the structural deficit. The blue curve shows government expenditures. The expenditures curve slopes downward because the higher level of real GDP, the lower is the level of transfer payments, so the lower is the level of government expenditures. The green curve shows tax revenues. The tax revenues curve slopes upward because most components of tax revenues increase as incomes and real GDP increase.

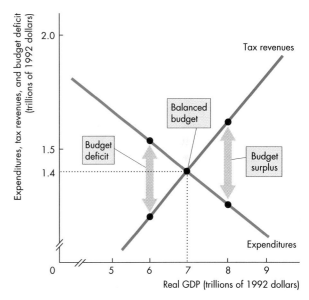

**FIGURE 12.9**

## Cyclical and Structural Deficits

Federal expenditures (blue line) decrease as real GDP increases because transfer payments decrease. Tax revenues (green line) increase as real GDP increases because most taxes are linked to income and expenditures. If real GDP is $7 trillion, the government has a *balanced budget.* If real GDP is less than $7 trillion, expenditures exceed tax revenues and the government has a budget deficit. If real GDP exceeds $7 trillion, expenditures are less than tax revenues and the government has a budget surplus. If potential GDP is $7 trillion, there is no structural deficit—the budget deficits and surpluses are cyclical. But if potential GDP is less than $7 trillion, there is a structural deficit.

In Fig. 12.9, if real GDP is $7 trillion, the government has a *balanced budget.* Expenditures and tax revenues each equal $1.4 trillion. If real GDP is less than $7 trillion, expenditures exceed tax revenues and there is a budget deficit. And if real GDP is greater than $7 trillion, expenditures are less than tax revenues and there is a budget surplus.

To determine whether there is a structural deficit, we need to know potential GDP. First, suppose that potential GDP is $7 trillion. In this case, the structural deficit is zero. As real GDP fluctuates over the business cycle, the budget fluctuates around zero and alternates between a surplus and a deficit.

Second, suppose that potential GDP is $6 trillion. In this case, the budget is in deficit at full employment: There is a structural deficit. In a recession, the deficit increases, and in an expansion, the deficit decreases. But even at the peak of a business cycle, the budget might still be in deficit. The deficit cycles with the business cycle, but it rarely, perhaps never, gets into surplus. The deficit in this example behaves like the U.S. deficit shown in Fig. 12.8.

Finally, suppose that potential GDP is $8 trillion. In this case, the budget is in surplus at full employment: There is a structural surplus. In a recession, the surplus decreases, and in an expansion, the surplus increases. Even at the trough of a business cycle, there might still be a surplus. The government budget balance cycles with the business cycle, but the budget rarely, perhaps never, goes into deficit.

## R E V I E W

■ When the price level is fixed, a change in government purchases or lump-sum taxes has a multiplier effect on real GDP.

■ The multiplier effect of a change in government purchases is greater than that of a change in lump-sum taxes because a dollar of taxes initially changes aggregate expenditure by less than a dollar.

■ The presence of income taxes and international trade reduces the fiscal policy multipliers.

■ Income taxes and entitlement programs work as automatic stabilizers to dampen the business cycle.

Your next task is to see how, with the passage of more time and with some price level adjustments, these multiplier effects change.

## Fiscal Policy Multipliers and the Price Level

WE'VE SEEN HOW REAL GDP RESPONDS TO changes in fiscal policy when the price level is fixed and all the adjustments that take place are in spending, income, and production. The period over which this response occurs is very short. Once production starts to change, regardless of whether it increases or decreases, prices also start to change. The price level and real GDP change together, and the economy moves to a new short-run equilibrium.

To study the simultaneous changes in real GDP and the price level that result from fiscal policy, we use the aggregate supply–aggregate demand model of Chapter 7. In the long run, both the price level and the money wage rate respond to fiscal policy. As these further changes take place, the economy gradually moves toward a new long-run equilibrium. We also use the aggregate supply–aggregate demand model to study these adjustments.

We begin by looking at the effects of fiscal policy on aggregate demand and the aggregate demand curve.

### Fiscal Policy and Aggregate Demand

You learned about the relationship between aggregate demand, aggregate expenditure, and equilibrium expenditure in Chapter 11. You are now going to use what you learned there to work out what happens to aggregate demand, the price level, real GDP, and jobs when fiscal policy changes. We'll start by looking at the effects of a change in fiscal policy on aggregate demand.

Figure 12.10 shows the effects of an increase in government purchases on aggregate demand. Initially, the aggregate expenditure curve is $AE_0$ in part (a), and the aggregate demand curve is $AD_0$ in part (b). The price level is 110, real GDP is $7 trillion, and the economy is at point $a$ in both parts of the figure. Now suppose that government purchases increase by $0.5 trillion. At a constant price level of 110, the aggregate expenditure curve shifts upward to $AE_1$. This curve intersects the 45° line at an equilibrium expenditure of $9 trillion at point $b$. This amount is the aggregate quantity of goods and services demanded at a price level of 110, as shown by point $b$ in part (b). Point $b$

## FIGURE 12.10

## Government Purchases and Aggregate Demand

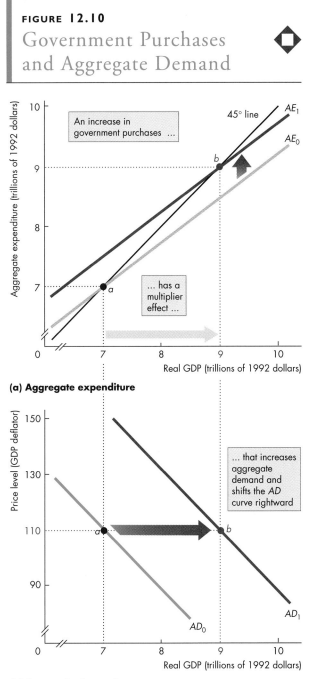

**(a) Aggregate expenditure**

**(b) Aggregate demand**

The price level is 110, aggregate planned expenditure is $AE_0$ (part a), and aggregate demand is $AD_0$ (part b). An increase in government purchases shifts the $AE$ curve to $AE_1$ and equilibrium real GDP increases to $9 trillion. The aggregate demand curve shifts rightward to $AD_1$.

lies on a new aggregate demand curve. The aggregate demand curve has shifted rightward to $AD_1$.

The government purchases multiplier determines the distance by which the aggregate demand curve shifts rightward. The larger the multiplier, the larger is the shift in the aggregate demand curve resulting from a given change in government purchases. In this example, a $0.5 trillion increase in government purchases produces a $2 trillion increase in the aggregate quantity of goods and services demanded at each price level. The multiplier is 4. So the $0.5 trillion increase in government purchases shifts the aggregate demand curve rightward by $2 trillion.

Figure 12.10 shows the effects of an increase in government purchases. But a similar effect occurs for *any* expansionary fiscal policy. An **expansionary fiscal policy** is an increase in government purchases or a decrease in tax revenues. But the distance the $AD$ curve shifts is smaller for a tax cut than for a government purchases increase of the same size.

Figure 12.10 can also be used to illustrate the effects of a **contractionary fiscal policy**—a decrease in government purchases or an increase in tax revenues. In this case, start at point $b$ in each part of the figure and decrease government purchases or increase taxes. Aggregate demand decreases from $AD_1$ to $AD_0$.

**Equilibrium GDP and the Price Level in the Short Run** We've seen how an increase in government purchases increases aggregate demand. Let's now see how it changes real GDP and the price level. Figure 12.11(a) describes the economy. Aggregate demand is $AD_0$, and the short-run aggregate supply curve is $SAS$. (Check back to Chapter 7 if you need to refresh your understanding of the $SAS$ curve.) Equilibrium is at point $a$, where the aggregate demand and short-run aggregate supply curves intersect. The price level is 110, and real GDP is $7 trillion.

An increase in government purchases of $0.5 trillion shifts the aggregate demand curve rightward from $AD_0$ to $AD_1$. While the price level is fixed at 110, the economy moves toward point $b$ and real GDP increases toward $9 trillion. But during the adjustment process, the price level does not remain constant. It gradually rises, and the economy moves along the short-run aggregate supply curve to the point of intersection of the short-run aggregate supply curve and the new aggregate demand curve— point $c$. The price level rises to 126, and real GDP increases to only $8.6 trillion.

## FIGURE 12.11
## Fiscal Policy, Real GDP, and the Price Level

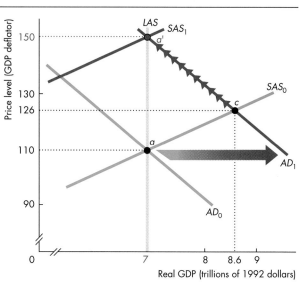

**(a) Fiscal policy with unemployment**

An increase in government purchases shifts the *AD* curve from $AD_0$ to $AD_1$. With a fixed price level, the economy would have moved to point *b*. But the price level rises, and in the short run, the economy moves to point *c*. The price level increases to 126, and real GDP increases to $8.6 trillion.

**(b) Fiscal policy with full employment**

At point *c*, real GDP exceeds potential GDP and unemployment is below the natural rate. The wage rate rises, and short-run aggregate supply decreases. The *SAS* curve shifts leftward to $SAS_1$, and in the long run, the economy moves to point *a'*. The price level rises to 150, and real GDP returns to $7 trillion.

When we take the price level effect into account, the increase in government purchases still has a multiplier effect on real GDP, but the effect is smaller than it would be if the price level remained constant. Also, the steeper the slope of the short-run aggregate supply curve, the larger is the increase in the price level, the smaller is the increase in real GDP, and the smaller is the government purchases multiplier. But the multiplier is not zero.

In the long run, real GDP equals potential GDP—the economy is at full-employment equilibrium. When real GDP equals potential GDP, an increase in aggregate demand has the same short-run effect as we've just worked out, but its long-run effect is different. The increase in aggregate demand raises the price level, but in the long run, it leaves real GDP unchanged at potential GDP.

To study this case, let's see what happens if the government embarks on an expansionary fiscal policy when real GDP equals potential GDP.

## Fiscal Expansion at Potential GDP

Suppose that real GDP is equal to potential GDP, which means that unemployment is equal to the natural rate of unemployment. But suppose also that the unemployment rate and the natural rate are high and that most people, including the government, mistakenly think that the unemployment rate exceeds the natural rate. In this situation, the government tries to lower the unemployment rate by using an expansionary fiscal policy.

Figure 12.11(b) shows the effect of an expansionary fiscal policy when real GDP equals potential GDP. In this example, potential GDP is $7 trillion. Aggregate demand increases, and the aggregate demand curve shifts rightward from $AD_0$ to $AD_1$. The short-run equilibrium, point *c*, is an above full-employment equilibrium. The labor force is more than fully employed, and there are shortages of labor. Wage rates begin to increase. Higher wage rates increase costs, and short-run aggregate supply decreases. The *SAS* curve begins to shift leftward from $SAS_0$ to $SAS_1$. The economy moves up the aggregate demand curve $AD_1$ toward point $a'$.

Eventually, when all adjustment to wage rates and the price level have been made, the price level is 150 and real GDP is again at potential GDP of $7 trillion. The multiplier in the long run is zero. There has been a temporary decrease in the unemployment rate during the process you've just looked at, but not a permanent decrease. But the price level rise is permanent.

## Limitations of Fiscal Policy

Because the short-run fiscal policy multipliers are not zero, expansionary fiscal policy can be used to increase real GDP and decrease the unemployment rate in a recession. Contractionary fiscal policy can also be used if the economy is overheating to decrease real GDP and help to keep inflation in check. But the use of fiscal policy is limited by two factors.

First, the legislative process is slow, which means that it is difficult to take fiscal policy actions in a timely way. The economy might be able to benefit from fiscal stimulation right now, but it will take Congress many months, perhaps more than a year, to act. By the time the action is taken, the economy might need an entirely different fiscal medicine.

Second, it is not always easy to tell whether real GDP is below (or above) potential GDP. A change in aggregate demand can move real GDP away from potential GDP, or a change in aggregate supply can change real GDP and change potential GDP. This difficulty is a serious one because, as you've seen, fiscal stimulation at full employment leads to a rise in the price level and has no long-run effect on real GDP.

## R E V I E W

- Changes in the price level decrease the effect of the fiscal policy multiplier on real GDP.
- In the long run, when real GDP equals potential GDP, fiscal policy influences only the price level. The multiplier effect on real GDP is zero.

So far in this chapter, we've ignored any potential effects of fiscal policy on aggregate supply. Yet many economists believe the supply-side effects of fiscal policy are large. Let's now look at these effects.

# Fiscal Policy and Aggregate Supply

DURING THE 1980s, WHEN RONALD REAGAN WAS President, a group of economists known as *supply-siders* became prominent. Supply-siders believed that tax cuts would strengthen incentives and increase aggregate supply. Their ideas were called "voodoo economics" by George Bush, and many other people are skeptical about supply-siders' claims. But these claims remain part of the political debate today. They are the main rationale for a flat tax that some economists and politicians have advocated.

Using the concepts of the *AS-AD* model, the supply-siders' claim is that tax cuts increase potential GDP. Is this claim correct?

There is no disagreement among economists that taxes create disincentives and decrease potential GDP. The disagreements are about numbers. Supply-siders say the effects are large. Others suspect that the effects are small, possibly too small to bother about.

Let's study the effects of taxes on potential GDP and then see how the supply effects and demand effects together influence real GDP and the price level.

## Fiscal Policy and Potential GDP

Potential GDP depends on the full-employment quantity of labor, the quantity of capital, and the state of technology. Taxes can influence all three of these factors. The main tax to consider is the income tax. By taxing the incomes people earn when they work or save, the government weakens the incentives to work and save. The result is a smaller quantity of labor and capital and a lower potential GDP. Also, the income tax weakens the incentive to develop new technologies that increase income. So the pace of technological change might be slowed, which slows the growth rate of potential GDP. Let's look at the effect of the income tax on both the quantity of labor and the quantity of capital.

**Labor and the Income Tax**  The quantity of labor is determined by demand and supply in the labor market (see Chapter 8, pp. 180–181). Figure 12.12(a) shows a labor market. The demand for labor is *LD*, and the supply is *LS*. With no income tax, this labor market achieves equilibrium at a real wage rate of $14 an hour and 230 billion hours of labor per year are employed.

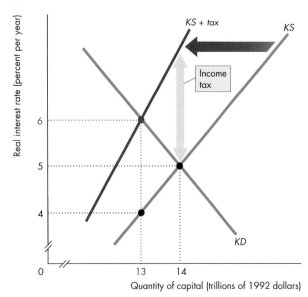

**FIGURE 12.12**

## Supply-Side Effects of the Income Tax

**(a) The labor market**

**(b) The capital market**

In part (a), the income tax shifts the supply of labor curve, LS, leftward to LS + tax. The before-tax wage rate rises, the after-tax wage rate falls, and the quantity of labor employed decreases. In part (b), the income tax shifts the supply of capital curve, KS, leftward to KS + tax. The before-tax interest rate rises, the after-tax interest rate falls, and the quantity of capital decreases. With less labor and less capital, potential GDP falls.

Now suppose an income tax is introduced. The income tax weakens the incentive to work and decreases the supply of labor. The supply curve shifts leftward to *LS + tax*. With this new lower supply of labor, the *before-tax* wage rate rises to $15 an hour and the quantity of labor employed decreases to 210 billion hours a year. The before-tax wage rate rises, but the *after-tax* wage rate falls. In Fig. 12.12(a), it falls to $10 an hour.

**Capital and the Income Tax**   The quantity of capital is determined by demand and supply in the capital market (see Chapter 9, pp. 201–203). Figure 12.12(b) shows the capital market. The demand for capital is *KD*, and the supply is *KS*. With no income tax, the capital market achieves equilibrium at a real interest rate of 5 percent a year and $14 trillion of capital is available.

Now consider the effects of a tax on income from capital. The income tax, which weakens the incentive to save, decreases the supply of capital. The supply curve shifts leftward to *KS + tax*. The *before-tax* interest rate rises to 6 percent a year and the quantity of capital decreases to $13 trillion. The before-tax interest rate rises, but the *after-tax* interest rate falls. In Fig. 12.12, it falls to 4 percent a year.

**Potential GDP and *LAS***   Because the income tax decreases the equilibrium quantities of labor and capital, it also decreases potential GDP. But potential GDP determines long-run aggregate supply. So the income tax decreases long-run aggregate supply and shifts the *LAS* curve leftward.

### Supply Effects and Demand Effects

Let's now bring the supply effects and demand effects of fiscal policy together. Figure 12.13(a) shows the most likely effects of a tax cut. The tax cut increases aggregate demand and shifts the *AD* curve rightward, just as before. But a tax cut that increases the incentive to work and save also increases aggregate supply. It shifts the long-run and short-run aggregate supply curves rightward. Here we focus on the short-run and show the effect on the *SAS* curve, which shifts rightward to $SAS_1$. In this example, the tax cut has a large effect on aggregate demand and a small effect on aggregate supply. The aggregate demand curve shifts rightward by a larger amount than the rightward shift in the short-run aggregate supply curve. The outcome is a rise in the price level and an increase in real GDP.

# Two Views of the Supply-Side Effects of Fiscal Policy

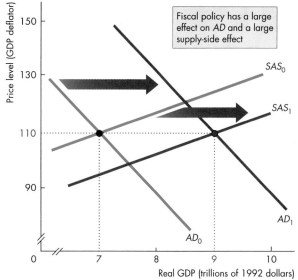

**(a) The traditional view**

A tax cut increases aggregate demand and shifts the AD curve rightward from $AD_0$ to $AD_1$ (both parts). Such a policy change also has a supply-side effect. If the supply-side effect is small, the SAS curve shifts rightward from $SAS_0$ to $SAS_1$ in part (a). The demand-side effect dominates the supply-side effect, real GDP increases, and the price level rises.

**(b) The supply-side view**

If the supply-side effect of a tax cut is large, the SAS curve shifts to $SAS_1$ in part (b). In this case, the supply-side effect is as large as the demand-side effect. Real GDP increases, and the price level remains constant. But if the supply-side effect were larger than the demand-side effect, the price level would actually fall.

But notice that the price level rises by *less* and real GDP increases by *more* than would occur if there were no supply-side effects.

Figure 12.13(b) shows the effects that supply-siders believe to occur. A tax cut still has a large effect on aggregate demand, but it has a similarly large effect on aggregate supply. The aggregate demand curve and the short-run aggregate supply curve shift rightward by similar amounts. In this particular case, the price level remains constant and real GDP increases. A slightly larger increase in aggregate supply would have brought a fall in the price level, a possibility that some supply-siders believe could occur.

The general point that everyone agrees with is that a tax cut that strengthens incentives increases real GDP by more and is less inflationary than an equal-sized expansionary fiscal policy that does not change incentives or that weakens them.

## REVIEW

■ The income tax has incentive effects on the supply of labor and the supply of capital, and a cut in the income tax rate increases potential GDP.

■ A tax cut increases both aggregate supply and aggregate demand. There is disagreement about which effect is larger. A tax cut increases real GDP, but it can either raise or lower the price level.

◆ You've seen how fiscal policy influences the way real GDP fluctuates and how it influences potential GDP. *Reading Between the Lines* on pp. 286–287 looks further at the 1997 budget and President Clinton's fiscal policy. Your next task is to study monetary policy. We begin in the next chapter by describing the monetary system of a modern economy.

# Policy
## WATCH

**Deficit Reduction**

LOS ANGELES TIMES, FEBRUARY 7, 1997

# Clinton's Budget Plan

BY ART PINE

WASHINGTON—Never mind balancing the budget by fiscal year 2002, as President Clinton and top congressional leaders are promising. The real question is, what about 2003 and beyond? ...

That issue is troubling government and private budget analysts as political leaders from both parties rally around Clinton's newfound willingness—and that of Republican congressional leaders—to eliminate the federal budget deficit five years from now. ...

Revised estimates by the Congressional Budget Office show that lawmakers will have to cut only $154 billion more to erase the deficit that year—far less than the $285 billion forecast a year ago. Much of the $154-billion cut will come from lower interest rates.

The real problem will come after 2002—especially in 2008 and beyond, analysts said, when members of the baby-boom generation start to reach retirement age and the cost of Medicare, Medicaid and Social Security begins to explode.

Robert D. Reischauer, a Brookings Institution budget expert who headed the CBO from 1989 to 1995, warned that, unless lawmakers soon begin to make far

more sweeping long-term changes than Clinton is asking, the deficit will come back quickly after 2002 with a vengeance.

CBO figures show that, barring a major restructuring of Medicare, Medicaid and Social Security, the budget deficit could mushroom from zero in 2002 to 4.5% of the gross domestic product—the output of the U.S. economy—by 2010 and 9.5% by 2025. (It was 1.4% in fiscal 1996.) ...

Moreover, analysts said that Medicare, Medicaid and Social Security are not the only big federal spending programs Congress needs to tackle to put the nation's fiscal house in order for the longer run. Another is defense, which many budget experts regard as a time bomb. ...

Finally, Brookings' Reischauer warned that, without major changes in Medicare and Social Security, the cutbacks in the remainder of the domestic budget—from environmental spending to highway programs—will have to be so deep that it is simply unrealistic to count on them. ...

To avoid widening the deficit after 2002, Congress must either slash spending on Medicare, Medicaid and Social Security or raise taxes to a level that is likely to be politically unacceptable. ...

■ President Clinton and Republican Congress leaders want to eliminate the federal budget deficit by 2002.

■ Congressional Budget Office (CBO) figures show that without a restructuring of Medicare, Medicaid, and Social Security, the budget deficit could grow from zero in 2002 to 4.5 percent of GDP by 2010 and 9.5 percent by 2025. The budget deficit was 1.4 percent of GDP in 1996.

■ To avoid a growing deficit after 2002, Congress must either reduce spending or raise taxes.

■ Some budget experts say the budget cannot be balanced after 2002 unless Medicare and Medicaid are overhauled.

# Economic

## A N A L Y S I S

■ Figure 1 shows two federal deficit projections, one before and one after the 1997 proposed budget. With no changes, the deficit would have fallen slightly from 1.5 percent of GDP in 1997 to 1.0 percent of GDP in 2002. The changes proposed in the 1997 budget eliminate the deficit by 2002.

■ Figure 1 also shows that compared with the projection made a year earlier, the deficit does not change in 1997 and 1998 and that in 1999, it falls by only 0.2 percent of GDP ($22 billion). The big reductions occur in 2000, 2001, and 2002.

■ Figure 1 also shows that most of the deficit reduction planned comes from spending cuts. There is a small decrease in debt interest and, in 2002, a one-time revenue from selling rights to broadcasters and mobile phone companies to use the airwaves.

■ Figure 2 shows what the government says will happen in 2000. Potential GDP will be $7.5 trillion and the long-run aggregate supply curve will be $LAS_0$. The short-run aggregate supply curve will be $SAS_0$

and the aggregate demand curve will be $AD_0$. Real GDP will be $7.5 trillion and the price level will be 122.

■ The decreases in spending on defense, Medicare, and Medicaid in 2000 will decrease aggregate planned expenditure and, with a multiplier effect, will decrease aggregate demand.

■ The aggregate demand curve shifts leftward to $AD_1$. With no other changes in planned expenditure in 2000, the economy would move to below full employment at point $a$.

■ The government forecasts that private spending will increase and keep aggregate demand at $AD_0$, so full employment will prevail despite the government cuts.

■ The government's forecasts for 2001 and 2002 are similar. That is, despite cuts in government purchases, increases in private expenditure will maintain full employment.

■ The forecasts for beyond 2003 are for a rise in the deficit unless taxes rise or social programs are radically restructured.

**Figure 1  The projections**

**Figure 2  AS–AD in 2000**

## You're

### THE VOTER

■ Do you think the deficit should be eliminated more quickly or more slowly than the government plans?

■ Do you think the deficit should be eliminated with greater tax increases than spending cuts?

■ What do you believe are the options after 2002 in light of the predictions about the growth of Medicaid and Medicare spending reported in the news article?

# SUMMARY

## Key Points

### The Federal Budget (pp. 268–273)

- The federal budget finances the activities of the government and is used to stabilize real GDP.
- Federal tax revenues come from personal income taxes, social insurance taxes, corporate income taxes, and indirect taxes. Federal expenditures include transfer payments, purchases of goods and services, and debt interest.
- When government expenditures exceed tax revenues, the government has a budget deficit.

### Fiscal Policy Multipliers (pp. 274–280)

- Fiscal policy actions are discretionary or automatic.
- The government purchases multiplier equals $1/(1 - MPC)$. The lump-sum tax multiplier equals $-MPC/(1 - MPC)$. The transfer payments multiplier is equal in magnitude to the lump-sum tax multiplier but is positive.
- Income taxes and entitlement payments bring fluctuations in tax revenues and transfer payments over the business cycle and act as automatic stabilizers.

### Fiscal Policy Multipliers and the Price Level (pp. 280–283)

- An expansionary fiscal policy increases aggregate demand and shifts the aggregate demand curve rightward. It increases real GDP and raises the price level. (A contractionary fiscal policy has the opposite effects.)
- Price level changes dampen fiscal policy multiplier effects.
- At potential GDP, an expansionary fiscal policy raises the price level and in the long run leaves real GDP unchanged. The fiscal policy multipliers in the long run are zero.

### Fiscal Policy and Aggregate Supply (pp. 283–285)

- Fiscal policy has supply-side effects because the increases in taxes weaken the incentives to work, save, and invest.
- A tax cut increases both aggregate demand and aggregate supply. It increases real GDP but has an ambiguous effect on the price level.

## Key Figures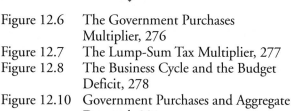

## Key Terms

# QUESTIONS

1. Describe the main purposes of the federal budget.
2. Describe the process that creates a federal budget.
3. List the four main sources of federal tax revenues and the three main components of federal expenditures.
4. List the main changes in taxes and government expenditures that are associated with the increase in the federal government deficit during the 1980s.
5. Compare the U.S. federal deficit with deficits in other regions and countries.
6. Explain the link between the deficit and government debt.
7. How has the federal government debt as a percentage of GDP changed since 1945?
8. Distinguish between automatic and discretionary fiscal policy.
9. Explain why an increase in government purchases has a multiplier effect on real GDP when the price level is fixed.
10. Explain why the lump-sum tax multiplier is smaller than the government purchases multiplier.
11. Explain why real GDP increases when both taxes and government purchases increase by the same amount.
12. Explain how induced taxes and entitlement spending influence the fiscal policy multipliers.
13. Explain how international trade influences the fiscal policy multipliers.
14. Explain how the deficit fluctuates over the business cycle and define the structural deficit.
15. Explain how the multiplier effect is modified in the short run when the price level begins to change.
16. Explain what happens following an increase in government purchases if real GDP equals potential GDP.

# PROBLEMS

1. In the economy of Zapland, the marginal propensity to consume is 0.9, investment is $50 billion, government purchases of goods and services are $40 billion, and lump-sum taxes are $40 billion. Zapland has no exports and no imports.
   a. The government cuts its purchases of goods and services to $30 billion. What is the change in equilibrium expenditure?
   b. What is the value of the government purchases multiplier?
   c. The government continues to purchase $40 billion worth of goods and services and cuts lump-sum taxes to $30 billion. What is the change in equilibrium expenditure?
   d. What is the value of the lump-sum tax multiplier?
   e. The government simultaneously cuts both its purchases of goods and services and lump-sum taxes to $30 billion. What is the change in equilibrium expenditure?

2. Suppose that the price level in the economy of Zapland as described in problem 1 is 100. The economy is also at full employment.
   a. If the government of Zapland increases its purchases of goods and services by $10 billion, what happens to the quantity of real GDP demanded?
   b. How does Zapland's aggregate demand curve change? Draw a two-part diagram that is similar to Fig. 12.10 to illustrate the change in both the *AE* curve and the *AD* curve.
   c. In the short run, does equilibrium real GDP increase by more than, less than, or the same amount as the increase in the quantity of real GDP demanded?
   d. In the long run, does equilibrium real GDP increase by more than, less than, or the same amount as the increase in the quantity of real GDP demanded?
   e. In the short run, does the price level in Zapland rise, fall, or remain unchanged?
   f. In the long run, does the price level in Zapland rise, fall, or remain unchanged?

🖥 3. In the figure below, aggregate demand is initially $AD_0$ and short-run aggregate supply is initially $SAS_0$. A tax cut increases aggregate demand to $AD_1$. This same tax cut influences incentives and increases aggregate supply. At first, there is no supply-side effect. Then short-run aggregate supply increases to $SAS_1$. Eventually, short-run aggregate supply increases to $SAS_2$.

Use the letters in the figure and the values on the axes to trace the path of the economy and to answer the following questions.
  a. What are the initial equilibrium values of real GDP and the price level before the tax cut occurs?
  b. What is the immediate effect of the tax cut before its supply-side effects begin to occur?
  c. How do real GDP and the price level change when short-run aggregate supply increases to $SAS_1$?
  d. How do real GDP and the price level change when short-run aggregate supply increases to $SAS_2$?

🌐 http://hepg.awl.com/parkin/econ100

# CRITICAL THINKING

1. Study *Reading Between the Lines* on pp. 286–287 and then:
  a. Describe the plan to eliminate the federal budget deficit by 2002.
  b. Explain what the Congressional Budget Office is predicting about the budget after 2002.
  c. Lay out the options for keeping the budget balanced after 2002.
  d. Explain why lower government expenditures are not predicted to lower real GDP. What else is expected to occur that will enable full employment to be maintained?
  e. Suppose the government was to cut spending even more than planned and turn its deficit into a surplus. What do you predict would be the short-run and long-run effects of such an action?

2. Thinking about the supply-side effects of tax cuts:
  a. What would be the main effects of lower income tax rates on potential GDP?
  b. How would lower income taxes influence the real wage rate and the real interest rate?
  c. What are the main costs of lower income taxes?

🌐 3. Visit the Web site of National Center for Policy Analysis Idea House at http://www.public-policy.org/~ncpa/pi/taxes/tax71.html and click on Dick Armey Flat Tax and Jerry Brown's Tax Plan. When you've studied these two pages, answer the following questions:
  a. What are the main features of the plans?
  b. What do you predict would be the main effects of each proposal?
  c. Which proposal appeals more to you and why?

🌐 4. Visit the U.S. government budget Web site at http://cher.eda.doc.gov/BudgetFY97/index.html. Use the information that you can find at this site to compare the levels of government expenditure in the main industrial countries. Then use the fiscal policy multiplier analysis that you've learned about in this chapter to predict which countries have the strongest automatic stabilizers and which have the weakest. Explain the reasons for your predictions.

# Money

Money, like fire and the wheel, has been around for a very long time. An incredible array of items have served as money. Wampum (beads made from shells) was used by North American Indians, whale's teeth were used by Fijians, and tobacco was used by early American colonists. Cakes of salt served as money in Ethiopia and Tibet. Today, when we want to buy something, we use coins or bills, write a check, or present a credit card. Tomorrow, we'll use a "smart card" that keeps track of spending and that our pocket computer can read. Are all these things money? ◆ When we deposit some coins or notes into a bank, is that still money? And what happens when the bank lends the money in our deposit account to someone else? How can we get our money back

## Money Makes the World Go Around

if it's been lent out? Does lending by banks create money—out of thin air? ◆ In the 1970s, you had either a savings deposit that earned interest or a checking deposit that did not. Today, there are accounts that provide the convenience of a checking deposit and the income of a savings deposit. Why were these new kinds of bank deposits introduced? ◆ During the 1970s, the quantity of money in the United States increased quickly, but during the 1980s and 1990s, it increased at a slower pace. In Russia and in some Latin American countries, the quantity of money is increasing at an extremely rapid pace. In Switzerland and Germany, the quantity of money has increased at a slower pace. Does the rate of increase in the quantity of money matter? What are the effects of an increasing quantity of money on our economy? ◆ In this chapter, we'll study that useful invention: money. We'll look at its functions and the way it is measured in the United States today. We'll explain how banks and other financial institutions create money. Finally, we'll examine the effects of money on the economy.

## After studying this chapter, you will be able to:

- Define money and describe its functions

- Explain the economic functions of banks and other financial institutions

- Describe the financial innovations of the 1980s and 1990s

- Explain how banks create money

- Explain why the quantity of money is an important economic magnitude

- Explain the quantity theory of money

# What Is Money?

WHAT DO WAMPUM, TOBACCO, AND NICKELS AND dimes have in common? Why are they all examples of money? To answer these questions, we need a definition of money. **Money** is any commodity or token that is generally acceptable as the means of payment. A **means of payment** is a method of settling a debt. When a payment has been made, there is no remaining obligation between the parties to a transaction. So what wampum, tobacco, and nickels and dimes have in common is that they have served (or still do serve) as the means of payment. But money has three other functions:

- Medium of exchange
- Unit of account
- Store of value

## Medium of Exchange

A *medium of exchange* is an object that is generally accepted in exchange for goods and services. Money acts as such a medium. Without money, it would be necessary to exchange goods and services directly for other goods and services—an exchange called **barter**. For example, if you want to buy a hamburger, you offer the paperback novel you've just finished reading in exchange for it. Barter requires a *double coincidence of wants*, a situation that occurs when Erika wants to buy what Kazia wants to sell and Kazia wants to buy what Erika wants to sell. To get your hamburger, you must find someone who's selling hamburgers and who wants your paperback novel. Money guarantees that there is a double coincidence of wants because people with something to sell will always accept money in exchange for it. Money acts as a lubricant that smoothes the mechanism of exchange.

## Unit of Account

A *unit of account* is an agreed measure for stating the prices of goods and services. To get the most out of your budget, you have to figure out whether seeing one more movie is worth its opportunity cost. But that cost is not dollars and cents. It is the number of ice-cream cones, sodas, and cups of coffee that you must give up. It's easy to do such calculations when

all these goods have prices in terms of dollars and cents (see Table 13.1). If a movie costs $6 and a six-pack of soda costs $3, you know right away that seeing one movie costs you 2 six-packs of soda. If jelly beans are 50¢ a pack, a movie costs 12 packs of jelly beans. You need only one calculation to figure out the opportunity cost of any pair of goods and services.

But imagine how troublesome it would be if your local movie theater posted its price as 2 six-packs of soda, and if the convenience store posted the price of a six-pack of soda as 2 ice-cream cones, and if the ice-cream shop posted the price of a cone as 3 packs of jelly beans, and if the candy store priced a pack of jelly beans as 2 cups of coffee! Now how much running around and calculating do you have to do to figure out how much that movie is going to cost you

---

**TABLE 13.1**

## The Unit of Account Function of Money Simplifies Price Comparisons

| Good | Price in money units | Price in units of another good |
|---|---|---|
| Movie | $6.00 each | 2 six-packs of soda |
| Soda | $3.00 per six-pack | 2 ice-cream cones |
| Ice cream | $1.50 per cone | 3 packs of jelly beans |
| Jelly beans | $0.50 per pack | 2 cups of coffee |
| Coffee | $0.25 per cup | 1 local phone call |

*Money as a unit of account*: The price of a movie is $6 and the price of a cup of coffee is 25¢, so the opportunity cost of a movie is 24 cups of coffee ($6.00 ÷ 25¢ = 24).

*No unit of account*: You go to a movie theater and learn that the price of a movie is 2 six-packs of soda. You go to a candy store and learn that a pack of jelly beans costs 2 cups of coffee. But how many cups of coffee does seeing a movie cost you? To answer that question, you go to the convenience store and find that a six-pack of soda costs 2 ice-cream cones. Now you head for the ice-cream shop, where an ice-cream cone costs 3 packs of jelly beans. Now you get out your pocket calculator: 1 movie costs 2 six-packs of soda, or 4 ice-cream cones, or 12 packs of jelly beans, or 24 cups of coffee!

in terms of the soda, ice cream, jelly beans, or coffee that you must give up to see it? You get the answer for soda right away from the sign posted on the movie theater. But for all the other goods you're going to have to visit many different stores to establish the price of each commodity in terms of another and then calculate prices in units that are relevant for your own decision. Cover up the column labeled "price in money units" in Table 13.1 and see how hard it is to figure out the number of local phone calls it costs to see one movie. It's enough to make a person swear off movies! How much simpler it is if all the prices are expressed in dollars and cents.

### Store of Value

Any commodity or token that can be held and exchanged later for goods and services is called a *store of value*. Money acts as a store of value. If it did not, it would not be acceptable in exchange for goods and services. The more stable the value of a commodity or token, the better it can act as a store of value, and the more useful it is as money. No store of value is completely safe. The value of a physical object, such as a house, a car, or a work of art, fluctuates over time. The value of commodities and tokens used as money also fluctuate, and when there is inflation, they persistently fall in value.

### Money in the United States Today

In the United States today, money consists of:

■ Currency
■ Deposits at banks and other financial institutions

**Currency**    The bills and coins that we use in the United States today are known as **currency**. Bills are money because the government declares them so with the words "This note is legal tender for all debts, public and private." You can see these words on every dollar bill.

**Deposits**    Deposits at banks and other financial institutions such as savings and loan associations (S&Ls) are also money. Deposits are money because they can be converted into currency and because they are used to settle debts.

**Official Measures of Money**    The two main official measures of money in the United States today are known as M1 and M2. Figure 13.1 shows the items that make up these two measures. **M1** consists of currency and traveler's checks plus checking deposits owned by individuals and businesses. M1 does *not* include currency held by banks, and it does not include currency and checking deposits owned by the U.S. government. **M2** consists of M1 plus saving deposits and time deposits. Time deposits are deposits that have a fixed term to maturity. (There is a third official measure of money, M3, which consists of M2 plus large-scale time deposits and term deposits.)

---

**FIGURE 13.1**

## Two Measures of Money ◆

|  | $ billions |
|---|---|
| **M2** | **$3,826** |
| Money market mutual funds and other deposits | $529 |
| Time deposits | $949 |
| Savings deposits | $1,271 |
| **M1** | $1,077 |
| Checking deposits | $673 |
| Currency and traveler's checks | $404 |

M1    ■ Currency held outside banks and traveler's checks
       ■ Checking deposits at commercial banks, S&Ls, savings banks, and credit unions

M2    ■ M1
       ■ Savings deposits
       ■ Time deposits
       ■ Money market mutual funds and other deposits

*Source: Economic Report of the President, 1997.*

**Are M1 and M2 Really Money?** Money is the means of payment. So the test of whether an asset is money is whether it serves as a means of payment. Currency passes the test. But what about deposits? Checking deposits are money because they can be transferred from one person to another by writing a check. Such a transfer of ownership is equivalent to handing over currency. Because M1 consists of currency plus checking deposits and each of these is a means of payment, *M1 is money*.

But what about M2? Some of the savings deposits in M2 are just as much a means of payment as the checking deposits in M1. You can use the ATM at the grocery store checkout or gas station and transfer funds directly from your saving account to pay for your purchase. But other saving deposits are not means of payment. These deposits are known as *liquid assets*. **Liquidity** is the property of being instantly convertible into a means of payment with little loss in value. Because most of the deposits in M2 are quickly and easily converted into currency or checking deposits, they are operationally similar to M1, but they are not means of payment.

**Deposits Are Money but Checks Are Not** In defining money, we include, along with currency, deposits at banks and other financial institutions. But we do not count the checks that people write as money. Why are deposits money and checks not?

To see why deposits are money but checks are not, think about what happens when Colleen buys some roller blades for $200 from Rocky's Rollers. When Colleen goes to Rocky's shop, she has $500 in her deposit account at the Laser Bank. Rocky has $1,000 in his deposit account—at the same bank, as it happens. The total deposits of these two people is $1,500. Colleen writes a check for $200. Rocky takes the check to the bank right away and deposits it. Rocky's bank balance rises from $1,000 to $1,200, and Colleen's balance falls from $500 to $300. The total deposits of Colleen and Rocky are still the same as before: $1,500. Rocky now has $200 more, and Colleen has $200 less than before.

This transaction has transferred money from Colleen to Rocky. The check itself was never money. There wasn't an extra $200 worth of money while the check was in circulation. The check instructs the bank to transfer money from Colleen to Rocky.

In the example, Colleen and Rocky use the same bank. The same story, but with additional steps, describes what happens if Colleen and Rocky use

different banks. Rocky's bank credits the check to Rocky's account and then takes the check to a check-clearing center. The check is then sent to Colleen's bank, which pays Rocky's bank $200 and then debits Colleen's account $200. This process can take a few days, but the principles are the same as when two people use the same bank.

**Credit Cards Are Not Money** So checks are not money. But what about credit cards? Isn't having a credit card in your wallet and presenting the card to pay for your roller blades the same thing as using money? Why aren't credit cards somehow valued and counted as part of the quantity of money?

When you pay by check, you are frequently asked to prove your identity by showing your driver's license. It would never occur to you to think of your driver's license as money. It's just an ID card. A credit card is also an ID card but one that lets you take a loan at the instant you buy something. When you sign a credit card sales slip, you are saying, "I agree to pay for these goods when the credit card company bills me." Once you get your statement from the credit card company, you must make the minimum payment due (or clear your balance). To make that payment, you need money—you need to have currency or a checking deposit to pay the credit card company. So although you use a credit card when you buy something, the credit card is not the *means of payment*, and it is not money.

---

R E V I E W

- Money is the means of payment and has three functions: medium of exchange, unit of account, and store of value.
- A commodity can serve as money, but modern societies use currency and deposits.
- The main component of money in the United States today is deposits at banks and other financial institutions.
- Checks and credit cards are not money.

We've seen that the main component of money in the United States is deposits at banks and other financial institutions. Let's take a closer look at these institutions.

# Financial Intermediaries

A FIRM THAT TAKES DEPOSITS FROM HOUSEHOLDS and firms and makes loans to other households and firms is called a **financial intermediary**. The deposits of four types of financial intermediaries make up the nation's money:

- Commercial banks
- Savings and loan associations
- Savings banks and credit unions
- Money market mutual funds

## Commercial Banks

A **commercial bank** is a firm, licensed by the Comptroller of the Currency (in the U.S. Treasury) or by a state agency to receive deposits and make loans. Close to 13,000 commercial banks operate in the United States today. A commercial bank's business is summarized in its balance sheet.

A bank's *balance sheet* lists its assets, liabilities, and net worth. *Assets* are what the bank *owns, liabilities* are what the bank *owes*, and *net worth*, which is equal to assets minus liabilities, is the value of the bank to its stockholders—its owners. A bank's balance sheet is described by the equation

Liabilities + Net worth = Assets.

Among a bank's liabilities are the deposits that are part of the nation's money. Your deposit at the bank is a liability to your bank (and an asset to you) because the bank must repay your deposit (and sometimes the interest on it too) whenever you decide to take your money out of the bank.

**Profit and Prudence: A Balancing Act**   The aim of a bank is to maximize the net worth of its stockholders. To achieve this objective, the interest rate at which a bank lends exceeds that rate at which it borrows. But a bank must perform a delicate balancing act. Lending is risky, and the more a bank ties up its deposits in high-risk, high-interest rate loans, the bigger is its chance of not being able to repay its depositors. And if depositors perceive a high risk of not being repaid, they withdraw their funds and create a crisis for the bank. So a bank must be prudent in the way it uses its deposits, balancing security for the depositors against profit for its stockholders.

**Reserves and Loans**   To achieve security for its depositors, a bank divides its funds into two parts: reserves and loans. **Reserves** are cash in a bank's vault plus its deposits at Federal Reserve banks. (We'll study the Federal Reserve banks in Chapter 14.) The cash in a bank's vaults is a reserve to meet its depositor's demand for currency. It keeps the ATM replenished every time you and your friends have raided it for cash for a midnight pizza. The account of a bank at the Federal Reserve is similar to your own bank account. Commercial banks use these accounts to receive and make payments. A commercial bank deposits cash into or draws cash out of its account at the Federal Reserve and writes checks on that account to settle debts with other banks.

If a bank kept all its deposits as reserves, it wouldn't make any profit. In fact, it keeps only a small fraction of its funds in reserves and lends the rest. A bank has three types of assets. They are as follows:

1. *Liquid assets* are U.S. government Treasury bills and commercial bills. These assets are the banks' first line of defense if they need cash. They can be sold and instantly converted into cash with virtually no risk of loss. Because liquid assets are virtually risk free, they have a low interest rate.

2. *Investment securities* are longer-term U.S. government bonds and other bonds. These assets can be sold quickly and converted into cash but at prices that fluctuate. Because their prices fluctuate, these assets are riskier than liquid assets, but they also have a higher interest rate.

3. *Loans* are commitments of fixed amounts of money for agreed-upon periods of time. Most banks' loans are made to corporations to finance the purchase of capital equipment and inventories and to households—personal loans—to finance consumer durable goods, such as cars or boats. The outstanding balances on credit card accounts are also bank loans. Loans are the riskiest assets of a bank because they cannot be converted into cash until they are due to be repaid. And some borrowers default and never repay. Because they are the riskiest of a bank's assets, they also carry the highest interest rate.

Commercial bank deposits are one component of the nation's money. But other financial intermediaries also take deposits that form part—an increasing part—of the nation's money. The largest of these other financial intermediaries are the S&Ls.

## Savings and Loan Associations

A **savings and loan association** (S&L) is a financial intermediary that receives checking deposits and savings deposits and that makes personal, commercial, and home-purchase loans.

## Savings Banks and Credit Unions

A **savings bank** is a financial intermediary owned by its depositors that accepts savings deposits and makes mostly home-purchase loans. Savings banks perform functions similar to those of S&Ls. The key difference is that savings banks, also called *mutual* savings banks, are owned by their depositors.

A **credit union** is a financial intermediary owned by its depositors that accepts savings deposits and makes mostly consumer loans. The key difference between a savings bank and a credit union is that a credit union is owned by a social or economic group such as a firm's employees.

## Money Market Mutual Funds

A **money market mutual fund** is a financial institution that obtains funds by selling shares and uses these funds to buy highly liquid assets such as U.S. Treasury bills. Money market mutual fund shares act like the deposits at commercial banks and other financial intermediaries. Shareholders can write checks on their money market mutual fund accounts. But there are restrictions on most of these accounts. For example, the minimum deposit accepted might be $2,500, and the smallest check a depositor is permitted to write might be $500.

## The Economic Functions of Financial Intermediaries

All financial intermediaries make a profit from the spread between the interest rate they pay on deposits and the interest rate at which they lend. Why can financial intermediaries get deposits at a low interest rate and lend at a higher one? What services do they perform that make their depositors willing to put up with a low interest rate and their borrowers willing to pay a higher one?

Financial intermediaries provide four main services that people are willing to pay for:

- Creating liquidity
- Minimizing the cost of obtaining funds
- Minimizing the cost of monitoring borrowers
- Pooling risk

**Creating Liquidity**   Financial intermediaries create liquidity. *Liquid* assets are those that are easily and with certainty convertible into money. Some of the liabilities of financial intermediaries are themselves money; others are highly liquid assets that are easily converted into money.

Financial intermediaries create liquidity by borrowing short and lending long. Borrowing short means taking deposits but standing ready to repay them on short notice (and on even no notice in the case of checking deposits). Lending long means making loan commitments for a prearranged, and often quite long, period of time. For example, when a person makes a deposit with a savings and loan association, that deposit can be withdrawn at any time. But the S&L makes a lending commitment for perhaps more than 20 years to a homebuyer.

**Minimizing the Cost of Borrowing**   Finding someone from whom to borrow can be a costly business. Imagine how troublesome it would be if there were no financial intermediaries. A firm that was looking for $1 million to buy a new production plant would probably have to hunt around for several dozen people from whom to borrow in order to acquire enough funds for its capital project. Financial intermediaries lower those costs. The firm needing $1 million can go to a single financial intermediary to obtain those funds. The financial intermediary has to borrow from a large number of people, but it's not doing that just for this one firm and the million dollars it wants to borrow. The financial intermediary can establish an organization that is capable of raising funds from a large number of depositors and can spread the cost of this activity over a large number of borrowers.

**Minimizing the Cost of Monitoring Borrowers** Lending money is a risky business. There's always a danger that the borrower may not repay. Most of the money lent gets used by firms to invest in projects that they hope will return a profit. But sometimes those hopes are not fulfilled. Checking up on the activities of a borrower and ensuring that the best possible decisions are being made for making a profit and avoiding a loss are costly and specialized activities. Imagine how costly it would be if each household that lent money to a firm had to incur the costs of monitoring that firm directly. By depositing funds with a financial intermediary, households avoid those costs. The financial intermediary performs the monitoring activity by using specialized resources that have a much lower cost than what each household would incur if it had to undertake the activity individually.

**Pooling Risk** As we noted above, lending money is risky. There is always a chance of not being repaid—of default. Lending to a large number of different individuals can reduce the risk of default. In such a situation, if one person defaults on a loan, it is a nuisance but not a disaster. In contrast, if only one person borrows and that person defaults on the loan, the entire loan is a write-off. Financial intermediaries enable people to pool risk in an efficient way. Thousands of people lend money to any one financial intermediary, and, in turn, the financial intermediary re-lends the money to hundreds, perhaps thousands, of individual firms. If any one firm defaults on its loan, that default is spread across all the depositors with the intermediary, and no individual depositor is left exposed to a high degree of risk.

---

## R E V I E W

- Money consists of currency (including travelers' checks) and deposits owned by individuals and businesses. M1 is currency plus checking deposits. M2 is M1 plus savings deposits, small time deposits, and money market mutual funds.
- Most of the nation's money consists of deposits in commercial banks, savings and loan associations, savings banks, credit unions, and money market mutual funds.
- The main economic functions of financial intermediaries are to create liquidity, to minimize the cost of obtaining funds and of monitoring borrowers, and to pool risk.

We are interested in banks and other financial intermediaries because they create money. But these firms are highly regulated, and this regulation limits their ability to create money. So next, we'll examine these regulations. We'll also look at the deregulation and innovation that have occurred in the financial sector during the past 20 years.

## Financial Regulation, Deregulation, and Innovation

FINANCIAL INTERMEDIARIES ARE HIGHLY REGULATED institutions. But regulation is not static, and in the 1980s, some important changes in their regulation as well as deregulation took place. Also, the institutions are not static. In their pursuit of profit, they constantly seek lower-cost ways of obtaining funds, monitoring borrowers, pooling risk, and creating liquidity. They also are inventive in seeking ways to avoid the costs imposed on them by financial regulation. Let's look at regulation, deregulation, and innovation in the financial sector in recent years.

### Financial Regulation

Financial intermediaries face two types of regulation:

- Deposit insurance
- Balance sheet rules

**Deposit Insurance** The deposits of most financial intermediaries are insured by the Federal Deposit Insurance Corporation (FDIC). The FDIC is a federal agency that receives its income from compulsory insurance premiums paid by commercial banks and other financial intermediaries. The FDIC operates two separate insurance funds: the Bank Insurance Fund (BIF), which insures deposits in commercial banks, and the Saving Association Insurance Fund (SAIF), which insures the deposits of S&Ls, savings banks, and credit unions. Each of these funds insures deposits of up to $100,000.

The existence of deposit insurance provides protection for depositors in the event that a financial intermediary fails. But it also limits the incentive for the owner of a financial intermediary to make safe investments and loans. Some economists believe that deposit insurance played an important role in creating a crisis for S&Ls during the 1980s. Depositors did not worry about risk because their deposits were insured. The S&L owners made high-risk loans because they knew they were making a one-way bet. If their loans paid off, they made a high rate of return. If they failed and could not meet their obligations to the depositors, the insurance fund would step in. Bad loans were good business!

Because of this type of problem, all financial intermediaries face regulation of their balance sheets.

**Balance Sheet Rules**   The most important balance sheet regulations are:

- Capital requirements
- Reserve requirements
- Deposit rules
- Lending rules

*Capital requirements* are the minimum amount of an owner's own financial resources that must be put into an intermediary. This amount must be sufficiently large to discourage owners from making loans that are too risky.

*Reserve requirements* are rules setting out the minimum percentages of deposits that must be held in currency or other safe, liquid assets. These minimum percentages vary across the different types of intermediaries and deposits; they are largest for checking deposits and smallest for long-term savings deposits.

*Deposit rules* are restrictions on the different types of deposits that an intermediary can accept. These are the rules that historically have created the sharpest distinctions between the various institutions. For example, in the past, commercial banks provided checking accounts while other institutions provided only savings accounts.

*Lending rules* are restrictions on the proportions of different types of loans that an intermediary may make. Like deposit rules, these rules also helped to create sharp distinctions between the various institutions. Before 1980, commercial banks were the only intermediaries that were permitted to make commercial loans, and S&Ls and savings banks were restricted to making mostly mortgage loans to home buyers.

To enable S&Ls and savings banks to compete with commercial banks for funds, a ceiling was imposed on the interest rates that banks could pay on deposits. This interest ceiling regulation was known as *Regulation Q*. Also, commercial banks were not permitted to pay interest on checking deposits.

## Deregulation in the 1980s

In 1980, Congress passed the Depository Institutions' Deregulation and Monetary Control Act (DIDMCA). The DIDMCA removed many of the distinctions between commercial banks and other financial intermediaries. It permitted nonbank financial intermediaries to compete with commercial banks in a wider range of lending business. At the same time it permitted the payment of interest on checking deposits so that NOW accounts and ATS accounts could be offered by all deposit-taking institutions—banks and nonbanks.[1] It also extended the powers of the Federal Reserve to place reserve requirements on all depository institutions. Despite the general direction of deregulation, this move brought a greater measure of central control over the financial system than had previously existed and represented a strengthening of the Fed's control.

The ability of S&Ls and savings banks to compete for lending business with commercial banks was further strengthened in 1982 with the passage of the Garn-St. Germain Depository Institutions Act. This legislation further eased restrictions on the scale of commercial lending that S&Ls and savings banks could undertake.

Another important regulatory change occurred in 1986: the abolition of Regulation Q. With the abolition of Regulation Q, a fiercely competitive environment was created. This environment encouraged rapid innovation in the types of deposits offered and rapid growth in money market mutual funds.

## Financial Innovation

The development of new financial products—of new ways of borrowing and lending—is called **financial innovation**. The aim of financial innovation is to lower the cost of deposits or to increase the return from lending or, more simply, to increase the profit from financial intermediation. There are three main influences on financial innovation:

- Economic environment
- Technology
- Regulation

The pace of financial innovation was remarkable during the 1980s and 1990s, and all three of these forces played a role.

---

[1] A NOW account is a Negotiable Order of Withdrawal account; "negotiable order of withdrawal" is another name for a check. An ATS account is an Automatic-Transfer Savings account—a savings account that is linked to a checking account. Funds are automatically tranferred between the two accounts.

**Economic Environment**   Some of the innovation was a response to high inflation and high interest rates. An important example is the development of variable interest rate mortgages. Traditionally, house purchases have been financed by mortgage loans at a guaranteed interest rate. Rising interest rates brought rising borrowing costs for S&Ls, and because they were committed to fixed interest rates on their mortgages, the industry incurred severe losses. The creation of variable interest rate mortgages has taken some of the risk out of long-term lending for house purchases.

**Technology**   Other financial innovations resulted from technological change, most notably that associated with the decreased cost of computing and long-distance communication. The spread in the use of credit cards and the development of international financial markets—for example, the increased importance of Eurodollars—are consequences of technological change.[2]

**Regulation**   A good deal of financial innovation takes place to avoid regulation. For example, Regulation Q, which prevented banks from paying interest on checking deposits, gave the impetus to devising new types of deposits on which checks could be written and interest paid, thereby getting around the regulation.

### Deregulation, Innovation, and Money

Deregulation and financial innovation that have led to the development of new types of deposit accounts have brought important changes in the composition of the nation's money. In 1960, M1 consisted of only currency and checking deposits at commercial banks. In the 1990s, other new types of checking deposits have expanded while traditional checking deposits have declined. Similar changes have taken place in the composition of M2. Savings deposits have declined, while time deposits and money market mutual funds have expanded.

---

[2] Eurodollars are U.S. dollar bank accounts held in other countries, mainly in Europe. They were "invented" during the 1960s when the Soviet Union wanted the security and convenience of holding funds in U.S. dollars but were unwilling to place deposits in U.S. banks.

## REVIEW

- Financial intermediaries are required to insure their deposits, and their lending is regulated.
- The 1980s saw a wave of financial deregulation that blurred the distinction between commercial banks and other financial institutions.
- Financial intermediaries constantly seek new ways of making a profit and react to the changing economic environment, new technologies, and regulations.
- Deregulation and innovation have brought new types of deposits that changed the composition of the nation's money.

We're now ready to learn how banks create money. In the following section, we'll use the term *banks* to refer to all the depository institutions whose deposits are part of the money supply. Let's see how money gets created.

## How Banks Create Money

BANKS CREATE MONEY. BUT THIS DOESN'T MEAN that they have smoke-filled back rooms in which counterfeiters are busily working. Remember, most money is deposits, not currency. What banks create is deposits, and they do so by making loans. But the amount of deposits they can create is limited by their reserves.

### Reserves: Actual and Required

We've seen that banks don't have $100 in bills for every $100 that people have deposited with them. In fact, a typical bank today has reserves of $6.00 for every $100 of deposits. No need for panic. These reserve levels are adequate for ordinary business needs.

The fraction of a bank's total deposits that are held in reserves is called the **reserve ratio**. The reserve ratio changes when a bank's customers make a deposit or withdrawal. Making a deposit increases the reserve ratio, and making a withdrawal decreases the reserve ratio.

The **required reserve ratio** is the ratio of reserves to deposits that banks are required, by regulation, to hold. A bank's *required reserves* are equal to its deposits multiplied by the required reserve ratio. Actual reserves minus required reserves are **excess reserves**. Whenever banks have excess reserves, they are able to create money.

To see how banks create money, we'll look at two model banking systems. In the first, there is only one bank; in the second, there are many banks.

### Creating Deposits by Making Loans in a One-Bank Economy

In the model banking system that we'll study first, there is only one bank and its required reserve ratio is 25 percent. That is, for each dollar deposited, the bank keeps 25¢ in reserves and lends the rest. The balance sheet of One-and-Only Bank is shown in Fig. 13.2(a). On January 1, its deposits are $400 million and its reserves are 25 percent of this amount—$100 million. Its loans are equal to deposits minus reserves and are $300 million.

The story begins with Al Capone, who has decided to end his career of crime. He has been holding all his money in currency and has a nest egg of $1 million. On January 2, Al decides to put his $1 million on deposit at the One-and-Only Bank. On the day that Al makes his deposit, the One-and-Only Bank's balance sheet changes. The new situation is shown in Fig. 13.2(b). The bank now has $101 million in reserves and $401 million in deposits. It still has loans of $300 million.

The bank now has *excess reserves*. With reserves of $101 million, the bank would like to have deposits of $404 million and loans of $303 million. Because it is the One-and-Only Bank, the manager knows that the reserves will remain at $101 million. That is, she knows that when she makes a loan, the amount lent remains on deposit at the One-and-Only Bank. She knows, for example, that all the suppliers of Sky's-the-Limit Construction are also depositors of One-and-Only. So she knows that if she makes the loan that Sky's-the-Limit has just requested, the deposit she lends will never leave One-and-Only. When Sky's-the-Limit uses part of its new loan to pay $100,000 to I-Dig-It Excavating Company for some excavations, the One-and-Only Bank simply moves the funds from Sky's-the-Limit's checking account to I-Dig-It's checking account.

So on January 3, the manager of One-and-Only calls Sky's-the-Limit's accountant and offers to lend

the maximum that she can. How much does she lend? She lends $3 million. By lending $3 million, One-and-Only's balance sheet changes to the one shown in Fig. 13.2(c). Loans increase by $3 million to $303 million. The loan shows up in Sky's-the-Limit's deposit initially, and total deposits increase to $404 million—$400 million plus Al Capone's deposit of $1 million plus the newly created deposit of $3 million. The bank now has no excess reserves and has reached the limit of its ability to create money.

---

**FIGURE 13.2**

## Creating Money at the One-and-Only Bank

**(a) Balance sheet on January 1**

| Assets<br>(millions of dollars) | | Liabilities<br>(millions of dollars) | |
|---|---|---|---|
| Reserves | $100 | Deposits | $400 |
| Loans | $300 | | |
| Total | $400 | Total | $400 |

**(b) Balance sheet on January 2**

| Assets<br>(millions of dollars) | | Liabilities<br>(millions of dollars) | |
|---|---|---|---|
| Reserves | $101 | Deposits | $401 |
| Loans | $300 | | |
| Total | $401 | Total | $401 |

**(c) Balance sheet on January 3**

| Assets<br>(millions of dollars) | | Liabilities<br>(millions of dollars) | |
|---|---|---|---|
| Reserves | $101 | Deposits | $404 |
| Loans | $303 | | |
| Total | $404 | Total | $404 |

In part (a) the One-and-Only Bank has deposits of $400 million, loans of $300 million, and reserves of $100 million. The bank's required reserve ratio is 25 percent. When the bank receives a deposit of $1 million (part b), it has excess reserves. It lends $3 million and creates a further $3 million of deposits. Deposits increase by $3 million, and loans increase by $3 million (in part c).

## The Deposit Multiplier

The **deposit multiplier** is the amount by which an increase in bank reserves is multiplied to calculate the increase in bank deposits. That is,

$$\text{Deposit multiplier} = \frac{\text{Change in deposits}}{\text{Change in reserves}}.$$

In the example we've just worked through, the deposit multiplier is 4. The $1 million increase in reserves created a $4 million increase in deposits. The deposit multiplier is linked to the required reserve ratio by the following equation

$$\text{Deposit multiplier} = \frac{1}{\text{Required reserve ratio}}.$$

In the example the required reserve ratio is 25 percent, or 0.25. That is,

$$\text{Deposit multiplier} = \frac{1}{0.25}$$

$$= 4.$$

## Creating Deposits by Making Loans with Many Banks

If you told the loans officer at your own bank that she creates money, she wouldn't believe you. Bankers see themselves as lending the money they receive from others, not creating money. But in fact, even though each bank lends only what it receives, the banking *system* creates money. To see how, let's look at another example.

Figure 13.3 is going to keep track of what is happening in the process of money creation by a banking system in which each bank has a required reserve ratio of 25 percent. The process begins when Art decides to decrease his currency holding and put $100,000 on deposit. Now Art's bank has $100,000 of new deposits and $100,000 of additional reserves. With a required reserve ratio of 25 percent, the bank keeps $25,000 on reserve and lends $75,000 to Amy. Amy writes a check for $75,000 to buy a copy-shop franchise from Barb. At this point, Art's bank has a new deposit of $100,000, new loans of $75,000, and new reserves of $25,000. You can see this situation in Fig. 13.3 as the first row of the "running tally."

For Art's bank, that is the end of the story. But it's not the end of the story for the entire banking system. Barb deposits her check for $75,000 in another bank, which has an increase in deposits and reserves of $75,000. This bank puts 25 percent of its increase in deposits ($18,750) into reserve and lends $56,250 to Bob. And Bob writes a check to Carl to pay off a business loan. The current state of play is seen in the second row of the "running tally" in Fig. 13.3. Now total bank reserves have increased by $43,750 ($25,000 plus $18,750), total loans have increased by $131,250 ($75,000 plus $56,250), and total deposits have increased by $175,000 ($100,000 plus $75,000).

When Carl takes his check to his bank, its deposits and reserves increase by $56,250, $14,063 of which it keeps in reserve and $42,187 of which it lends. This process continues until there are no excess reserves in the banking system. But the process takes a lot of further steps. One additional step is shown in Fig. 13.3. The figure also shows the final tallies—reserves increase by $100,000, loans increase by $300,000, and deposits increase by $400,000.

The sequence in Fig. 13.3 is the first four stages of the process. To figure out the entire process, look closely at the numbers in the figure. At each stage, the loan is 75 percent (0.75) of the previous loan and the deposit is 0.75 of the previous deposit. Call that proportion $L$ ($L = 0.75$). The complete sequence is

$$1 + L + L^2 + L^3 + \dots .$$

Remember, $L$ is a fraction, so at each stage in this sequence the amount of new loans gets smaller. The total number of loans made at the end of the process is the above sum, which is[3]

$$\frac{1}{(1 - L)}.$$

---

[3] Both here and in the expenditure multiplier process in Chapter 28, the sequence of values is called a convergent geometric series. To find the sum of a series such as this, begin by calling the sum $S$. Then write out the sum as
$$S = 1 + L + L^2 + L^3 + \dots.$$
Multiply by $L$ to get
$$LS = L + L^2 + L^3 + \dots$$
and then subtract the second equation from the first to get
$$S(1 - L) = 1$$
or
$$S = \frac{1}{(1 - L)}.$$

## FIGURE 13.3

## The Multiple Creation of Bank Deposits

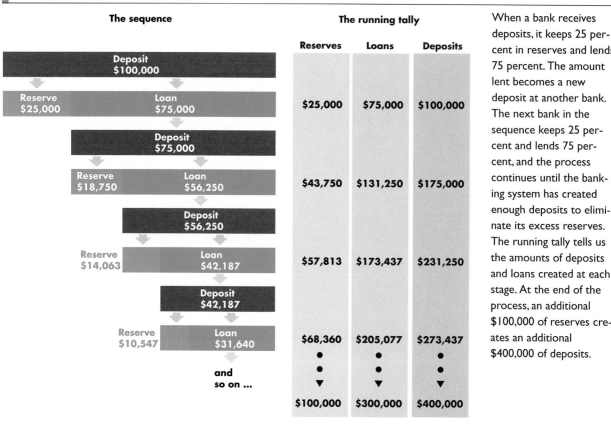

When a bank receives deposits, it keeps 25 percent in reserves and lends 75 percent. The amount lent becomes a new deposit at another bank. The next bank in the sequence keeps 25 percent and lends 75 percent, and the process continues until the banking system has created enough deposits to eliminate its excess reserves. The running tally tells us the amounts of deposits and loans created at each stage. At the end of the process, an additional $100,000 of reserves creates an additional $400,000 of deposits.

If we use the numbers from the example, the total increase in deposits is

$100,000 + 75,000 + 56,250 + 42,190 + ...$

$= \$100,000 (1 + 0.75 + 0.5625 + 0.4219 + ...)$

$= \$100,000 (1 + 0.75 + 0.75^2 + 0.75^3 + ...)$

$= \$100,000 \times \dfrac{1}{(1 - 0.75)}$

$= \$100,000 \times \dfrac{1}{(0.25)}$

$= \$100,000 \times 4$

By using the same method, you can check that the totals for reserves and loans are the ones shown in Fig. 13.3.

So even though each bank lends only the money it receives, the banking system as a whole does create money by making loans. The amount created is exactly the same in a multibank system as in a one-bank system.

### The Deposit Multiplier in the United States

The deposit multiplier in the United States works in the same way as the deposit multiplier we've just worked out for a model economy. But the deposit multiplier in the United States differs from the one we've just calculated for three reasons. First, the required reserve ratio of U.S. banks is smaller than the 25 percent we used here. Second, U.S. banks sometimes choose to hold excess reserves. Third, not all the loans made by banks return to them in the form of reserves. Some of the loans remain outside the banks and are held as currency. The smaller required reserve ratio makes the U.S. multiplier larger than the multiplier in the above example. But the other two factors make the U.S. multiplier smaller.

---

## REVIEW

▨ Banks create deposits by making loans, and their reserves and the required reserve ratio determine the amount they can lend.

▨ Each time a bank makes a loan, both deposits at other banks and required reserves increase.

▨ When deposits are at a level that makes required reserves equal to actual reserves, the banks have reached the limit of their ability to create money.

▨ A change in reserves brings about a multiple change in deposits, and the deposit multiplier equals 1 divided by the required reserve ratio.

Now that we know what money is and how banks create it, let's see how the amount of money created by the banks influences the economy. We'll discover that this influence is powerful.

---

## Money, Real GDP, and the Price Level

YOU NOW KNOW THAT IN A MODERN ECONOMY such as that of the United States today, most of the money is bank deposits. You've seen that banks actually create money by making loans. Does the quantity of money created by the banking and financial system matter? What effect does money have? Does it matter whether the quantity of money increases quickly or slowly? In particular, how does the quantity of money influence real GDP, the price level, and the inflation rate?

We're going to answer these questions first by using the aggregate supply–aggregate demand model, which explains how money affects real GDP and the price level in the short run. Then we're going to study a theory called the quantity theory of money, which explains how money growth influences inflation in the long run. We'll also look at some historical and international evidence on the relationship between money growth and inflation.

## The Short-Run Effects of a Change in the Quantity of Money

Figure 13.4 illustrates the *AS-AD* model that explains how real GDP and the price level are determined in the short run. (For a full explanation of the *AS-AD* model, see Chapter 7, pp. 142–155.) We are going to use this model to study the short-run effects of a change in the quantity of money on real GDP and the price level. Potential GDP is $7 trillion, and the long-run aggregate supply curve is *LAS*. The short-run aggregate supply curve is *SAS*. Initially, the aggregate demand curve is $AD_0$. Equilibrium real GDP is $6.8 trillion, and the price level is 107 at the intersection of the *AD* curve and the *SAS* curve.

---

**FIGURE 13.4**

## Short-Run Effects of Change in Quantity of Money

Real GDP is less than potential GDP. An increase in the quantity of money increases aggregate demand and shifts the aggregate demand curve rightward from $AD_0$ to $AD_1$. The price level rises to 110, and real GDP expands to $7 trillion. The increase in the quantity of money increases real GDP to potential GDP.

Banks, flush with excess reserves, make loans, and the loans create money. This increase results from the process of money creation we've just studied. With more money in their bank accounts and more loans, people plan to increase their consumption expenditure and businesses plan to increase their investment. Aggregate demand increases, and the aggregate demand curve shifts rightward to $AD_1$. A new equilibrium emerges at the intersection point of $AD_1$ and $SAS$. Real GDP expands to $7 trillion, and the price level rises to 110. Real GDP now equals potential GDP, and there is full employment. This increase in the quantity of money has increased both real GDP and the price level.

Now imagine the reverse situation. Real GDP is initially $7 trillion, and the price level is 110 at the intersection point of $AD_1$ and $SAS$. The quantity of money *decreases*. With *less* money in their bank accounts, people and businesses plan to decrease their expenditures. Aggregate demand decreases, and the aggregate demand curve shifts leftward to $AD_0$. A recession occurs as real GDP shrinks to $6.8 trillion, and the price level falls to 107.

These influences of the quantity of money on real GDP and the price level are *short-run* effects. In the long run, a change in the quantity of money, perhaps surprisingly, has no effect on real GDP. All its effects are on the price level. Let's see why this outcome occurs.

## The Long-Run Effects of a Change in the Quantity of Money

Figure 13.5 explains how real GDP and the price level are determined in both the short run and the long run. Again, potential GDP is $7 trillion and the long-run aggregate supply curve is *LAS*. The short-run aggregate supply curve is $SAS_1$. Initially, the aggregate demand curve is $AD_1$. Equilibrium real GDP is $7 trillion, and the price level is 110. So real GDP equals potential GDP, and there is full employment.

Now suppose the quantity of money increases. Aggregate demand increases, and the aggregate demand curve shifts rightward to $AD_2$. The new short-run equilibrium is at the intersection point of $AD_2$ and $SAS_1$. The price level rises to 113, and real GDP expands to $7.2 trillion. This short-run adjustment has put real GDP above potential GDP and has decreased unemployment below the natural rate. A

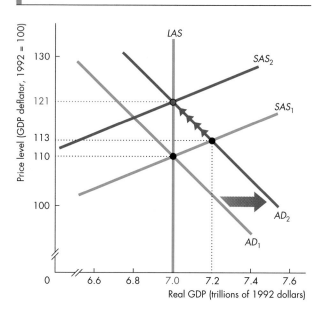

**FIGURE 13.5**

## Long-Run Effects of Change in Quantity of Money

Real GDP equals potential GDP. An increase in the quantity of money shifts the aggregate demand curve from $AD_1$ to $AD_2$. In the short run, the price level rises to 113, and real GDP increases to $7.2 trillion. Real GDP exceeds potential GDP, and the money wage rate rises. Short-run aggregate supply decreases, and the SAS curve shifts leftward from $SAS_1$ to $SAS_2$. Real GDP returns to potential GDP, and the price level rises to 121. In the long run, the increase in the quantity of money increases the price level and has no effect on real GDP.

shortage of labor makes the money wage rate rise. As the money wage rate rises, short-run aggregate supply decreases and the *SAS* curve shifts leftward toward $SAS_2$. As short-run aggregate supply decreases, the price level rises to 121 and real GDP decreases back to potential GDP at $7 trillion.

Thus from one full-employment equilibrium to another, an increase in the quantity of money increases the price level and has no effect on real GDP. This relationship between the quantity of money and the price level at full employment is made more precise by the quantity theory of money, which tells us about the quantitative link between money growth and inflation.

## The Quantity Theory of Money

The **quantity theory of money** is the proposition that in the long run, an increase in the quantity of money brings an equal percentage increase in the price level. The original basis of the quantity theory of money is a concept known as *the velocity of circulation* and an equation called *the equation of exchange*.

The **velocity of circulation** is the average number of times a dollar of money is used annually to buy the goods and services that make up GDP. GDP is equal to the price level ($P$) multiplied by real GDP ($Y$); that is,

$$GDP = PY.$$

Call the quantity of money $M$. The velocity of circulation, $V$, is determined by the equation

$$V = PY/M.$$

For example, if GDP is $6.0 trillion and the quantity of money is $3 trillion, the velocity of circulation is

2. On the average, each dollar of money circulates twice in its use to purchase the final goods and services that make up GDP; that is, each dollar of money is used twice in a year to buy GDP.

Figure 13.6 shows the history of the velocity of circulation of both M1 and M2, the two main official definitions of money. You can see that the velocity of circulation of M1 increased between 1945 and 1980 and fluctuated through the 1980s and 1990s. In contrast, the velocity of circulation of M2 has been remarkably stable. The reason why the velocity of M1 has increased is that deregulation and financial innovation have created new types of deposits and payments technologies that are substitutes for M1. As a result, the quantity of M1 per dollar of GDP has decreased, and equivalently, the velocity of circulation of M1 has increased. The reason why the velocity of M2 has been almost constant is that the new types of deposits that have replaced M1 are part of M2. So the ratio of M2 to GDP and the velocity of circulation of M2 have been much more stable.

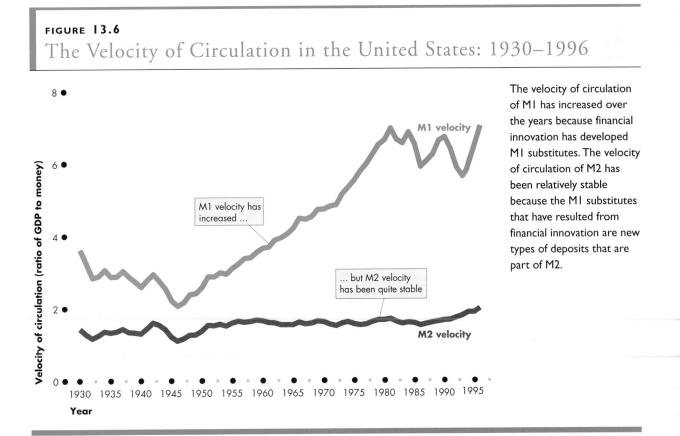

**FIGURE 13.6**

The Velocity of Circulation in the United States: 1930–1996

The velocity of circulation of M1 has increased over the years because financial innovation has developed M1 substitutes. The velocity of circulation of M2 has been relatively stable because the M1 substitutes that have resulted from financial innovation are new types of deposits that are part of M2.

The **equation of exchange** states that the quantity of money ($M$) multiplied by the velocity of circulation ($V$) equals GDP, or

$$MV = PY.$$

Given the definition of the velocity of circulation, this equation is always true—it is true by definition. With $M$ equal to $3 trillion and $V$ equal to 2, $MV$ is equal to $6.0 trillion, the value of GDP.

The equation of exchange becomes the quantity theory of money by making two assumptions:

1. The velocity of circulation is not influenced by the quantity of money.
2. Potential GDP is not influenced by the quantity of money.

If these two assumptions are true, the equation of exchange tells us that a change in the quantity of money brings about an equal proportional change in the price level. You can see why by solving the equation of exchange for the price level. Dividing both sides of the equation by real GDP ($Y$) gives

$$P = (V/Y)M.$$

In the long run, real GDP ($Y$) equals potential GDP, so if potential GDP and velocity are not influenced by the quantity of money, the relationship between the change in the price level ($\Delta P$) and the change in the quantity of money ($\Delta M$) is

$$\Delta P = (V/Y)\,\Delta M.$$

Divide this equation by the previous one, $P = (V/Y)M$, to get

$$\Delta P/P = \Delta M/M.$$

($\Delta P/P$) is the proportional increase in the price level, and ($\Delta M/M$) is the proportional increase in the quantity of money. So this equation is the quantity theory of money: In the long run, the percentage increase in the price level equals the percentage increase in the quantity of money.

## The Quantity Theory and the AS-AD Model

The quantity theory of money can be interpreted in terms of the *AS-AD* model. The aggregate demand curve is a relationship between the quantity of real GDP demanded ($Y$) and the price level ($P$), other things remaining constant. We can obtain such a relationship from the equation of exchange,

$$MV = PY.$$

Dividing both sides of this equation by real GDP ($Y$) gives

$$P = MV/Y.$$

This equation may be interpreted as describing an aggregate demand curve. In Chapter 7 (pp. 147–148), you saw that the aggregate demand curve slopes downward: As the price level increases, the quantity of real GDP demanded decreases. The above equation also shows such a relationship between the price level and the quantity of real GDP demanded. For a given quantity of money ($M$) and a given velocity of circulation ($V$), the higher the price level ($P$), the smaller is the quantity of real GDP demanded ($Y$).

In general, when the quantity of money changes, the velocity of circulation might also change. But the quantity theory asserts that velocity is not influenced by the quantity of money. If this assumption is correct, an increase in the quantity of money increases aggregate demand and shifts the aggregate demand curve upward by the same amount as the percentage change in the quantity of money.

The quantity theory of money also asserts that real GDP, which in the long run equals potential GDP, is not influenced by the quantity of money. This assertion is true in the *AS-AD* model in the long run when the economy is on its long-run aggregate supply curve. Figure 13.5 shows the quantity theory result in the *AS-AD* model. Initially, the economy is on the long-run aggregate supply curve *LAS* and at the intersection of the aggregate demand curve $AD_1$ and the short-run aggregate supply curve $SAS_1$. A 10 percent increase in the quantity of money shifts the aggregate demand curve from $AD_1$ to $AD_2$. This shift, measured by the vertical distance between the two demand curves, is 10 percent. In the long run, wages rise (also by 10 percent) and shift the *SAS* curve leftward to $SAS_2$. A new long-run equilibrium occurs at the intersection of $AD_2$ and $SAS_2$. Real GDP remains at potential GDP of $7 trillion, and the price level rises to 121. The new price level is 10 percent higher than the initial one ($121 - 110 = 11$, which is 10 percent of 110).

So the *AS-AD* model predicts the same outcome as the quantity theory of money. The *AS-AD* model also predicts a less precise relationship between the quantity of money and the price level in the short run than in the long run. For example, Fig. 13.4 shows that if we start out at a below-full employment equilibrium, an increase in the quantity of money increases real GDP. In this case, a 10 percent increase in the money supply increases the price level from 107 to 110—a 2.8 percent increase. That is, the price level increases by a smaller percentage than the percentage increase in the quantity of money.

How good a theory is the quantity theory of money? Let's answer this question by looking at the relationship between money and the price level, both historically and internationally.

## Historical Evidence on the Quantity Theory of Money

The percentage increase in the price level is the inflation rate, and the percentage increase in the quantity of money is the money supply growth rate. So the quantity theory predictions can be cast in terms of money growth and inflation. The quantity theory predicts that at a given level of potential GDP and in the long run, the inflation rate will equal the money growth rate. But over time, potential GDP expands. Taking this expansion into account, the quantity theory predicts that in the long run, the inflation rate will equal the money growth rate minus the growth rate of potential GDP.

We can test the quantity theory of money by looking at the historical relationship between money growth and inflation in the United States. Figure 13.7 shows two views of this relationship for the years between 1930 and 1996. In both parts of the figure, the inflation rate is the percentage change in the GDP deflator, and the two alternative money growth rates are based on M1 and M2. Part (a) shows year-to-year changes in money and the price level. These changes show the short-run relationship between money growth and inflation. Part (b) shows decade average changes. These changes average out the year-to-year fluctuations and enable us to see the long-run relationship between the variables. If the quantity theory is a reasonable guide to reality, there should be a strong correlation between inflation and money growth in the decade average data and a weak correlation in the year-to-year data.

The data are broadly consistent with the quantity theory. The money growth rate and the inflation rate are correlated, but the relationship is not precise. During World War II, money growth increased sharply while inflation remained low. After the war, inflation exploded while money growth remained

steady. Between 1950 and 1995, the inflation rate fluctuated less than the fluctuations in the money growth rate. The year-to-year fluctuations in money growth and inflation, which contain short-run influences (in part a), show a weak correlation, and the decade average fluctuations in money growth and inflation (in part b) show a stronger correlation.

## International Evidence on the Quantity Theory of Money

Another way to test the quantity theory of money is to look at the cross-country relationship between money growth and inflation. Figure 13.8 shows this relationship for 60 countries during the 1980s. By looking at a decade average, we again are smoothing out the short-run effects of money growth and focusing on the long-run effects. There is in these data an unmistakable tendency for high money growth to be associated with high inflation. The evidence is strongest for the high-inflation countries, which are shown in Fig. 13.8(a), but it is also present for the low-inflation countries, which are shown in Fig. 13.8(b).

## Correlation, Causation, and Other Influences

Both the historical evidence for the United States and the international data tell us that in the long run, money growth and inflation are correlated. But the correlation between money growth and inflation does not tell us that money growth causes inflation. Money growth might cause inflation; inflation might cause money growth; or some third variable might simultaneously cause inflation and money growth.

According to the quantity theory and according to the *AS-AD* model, causation runs from money growth to inflation. But neither theory denies the possibility that at different times and places, causation might run in the other direction or that some third factor might be the root cause of both rapid money growth and inflation. One possible third factor is a large and persistent government budget deficit that gets financed by creating money.

But some occasions give us an opportunity to test our assumptions about causation. One of these is World War II and the years immediately following it. Rapid money growth during the war years was accompanied by controls that held prices down dur-

**FIGURE 13.7**

Money Growth and Inflation in the United States

**(a) Year-to-year change in money supply and the price level**

Year-to-year fluctuations in money growth and inflation (part a) are loosely correlated, but decade average fluctuations in money growth and inflation (part b) are closely correlated. The burst of postwar inflation was caused by rapid money growth during World War II, and the rise in inflation during the 1970s was caused by more rapid money growth during the 1960s.

**(b) Decade average change in money supply and the price level**

Sources: *Historical Statistics of the United States, Economic Report of the President,* 1996, and the author's calculations.

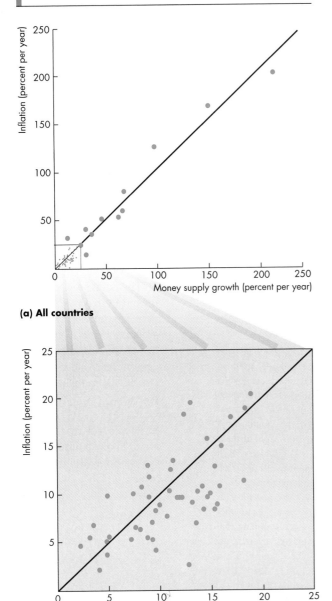

**FIGURE 13.8**

## Money Growth and Inflation in the World Economy

**(a) All countries**

**(b) Low-inflation countries**

Inflation and money growth in 60 countries (in part a) and low-inflation countries (in part b) show a clear positive relationship between money growth and inflation.

*Source:* Federal Reserve Bank of St. Louis, *Review*, May/June 1988, p. 15.

ing the war but allowed them to rise immediately after the war. The inflationary consequences of wartime money growth was delayed by price controls but not removed. It is inconceivable that this was an example of reverse causation—of postwar inflation causing wartime money growth. Another is the late 1960s and 1970s. Rapid money growth that began during the 1960s almost certainly caused the high and persistent inflation of the 1970s. The combination of historical and international correlations between money growth and inflation and independent evidence about the direction of causation leads to the conclusion that the quantity theory is correct in the long run. It explains the long-term fundamental source of inflation. But the quantity theory is not correct in the short run. To understand the short-term fluctuations in inflation, the joint effects of a change in the quantity of money on real GDP, the velocity of circulation, and the price level must be explained. The *AS-AD* model provides this explanation. It also points to the possibility of other factors that influence both aggregate supply and aggregate demand influencing the inflation rate independently of the money growth rate in the short run.

### R E V I E W

- The quantity of money influences the price level and real GDP.
- In the short run, an increase in the quantity of money increases aggregate demand and increases both the price level and real GDP.
- In the long run, when real GDP equals potential GDP, an increase in the quantity of money brings an equal percentage increase in the price level (the quantity theory of money).
- The long-run historical and international evidence on the relationship between money growth and inflation supports the quantity theory.

◆ Before you leave the subject of this chapter, look at *Reading Between the Lines* on pp. 310–311 and see how rapid money growth has brought inflation in Serbia. In the next chapter, we'll learn how the Fed influences the quantity of money and interest rates in its attempt to steer the course of the economy. Then, in Chapter 15, we'll return to the problem of inflation and explore more deeply its causes and consequences and ways of keeping it under control.

# The Quantity Theory in Action

*THE NEW YORK TIMES, DECEMBER 15, 1996*

## Serbia Tries to Buy Social Peace with Back Pay

By CHRIS HEDGES

BELGRADE, Serbia, Dec. 14—Business is brisk on the corner of Goce Delceva and Bulever Lenjina streets. And when business here prospers, the rest of Serbia suffers.

"We can't sell German marks fast enough," said Predrag Aleksic, who stood with a cluster of nine other black market money vendors.

"People cash their pension or salary checks at the bank and come out here to get at least some of it in foreign currency. We are seeing more and more new dinar bills, which means our Government is probably printing lots of money."

Serbia's economy, in a tailspin following decades of Communism and years of mismanagement and sanctions, seems headed for a new crisis.

After a year of relative stability, the local currency, the dinar, has begun to plummet in value. The Government of President Slobodan Milosevic, in an apparent bid to mute public unrest over the government's cancellation of election results, which has triggered huge demonstrations on the streets here every day for the last three weeks, has promised to pay pensions, salaries, student grants and social welfare payments that have been in arrears.

But economists say that to carry out this program, which requires hundreds of million of dollars, the government has begun to print money without the reserves to back it.

They also worry that the infusion of cash into the shaky economy has already triggered a devaluation that may snowball into hyperinflation by next year. …

This morning, as tens of thousands of students and opposition politicians again marched through central Belgrade, lines of elderly pensioners, many in threadbare coats, gathered at a branch of Jugobanka in the city's New Belgrade section. Most worked for three or four decades in state-owned companies and now live on pensions of less than $100 a month.

For the first time in 12 months, these men and women received full pension checks today, although the payment covered only the month of October. The Government has promised to pay all pension payments for this year by the end of this month. …

Economists fear that the days of disastrous hyperinflation in 1993, which saw the value of the currency drop by 10 or 20 percent in a single day, could return. …

Street vendors, who clogged the sidewalks selling everything from eggs to videotapes outside the Merkator shopping mall, said sales had fallen by half over the last month.

"People aren't buying," said Nikola Suskavcevic, as he stood next to an array of cheap household goods spread out over the hood of his small car. "Everyone is scared about what will happen next." …

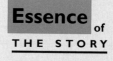

## Essence of THE STORY

■ The government of Serbia is creating money at a rapid rate and prices are rising rapidly.

■ To avoid losses, people cash their checks at the bank and then sell their dinars for foreign currency on the black market.

■ The government has promised to pay arrears of pensions, salaries, student grants, and social welfare, but economists say the government will create the money to make these payments.

■ People fear that injecting even more money into the economy will cause hyperinflation.

# Economic

## A N A L Y S I S

■ Current economic data for Serbia are not available. But data for Yugoslavia (of which present day Serbia is a part) are.

■ Figure 1 shows the inflation rate in Yugoslavia from 1986 through 1992 and the money supply growth rate through 1990. (Note that these growth rates are *thousands* of percent per year!)

■ Hyperinflation is defined as an inflation rate greater than 50 percent per month or 12,875 percent per year. Serbia doesn't have hyperinflation, but its inflation rate is high.

■ Figure 1 shows that money growth and inflation tend to move in a similar direction.

■ The quantity theory of money can be used to explain the movements in money growth and inflation.

■ The table contains some relevant data: inflation rate, real GDP

growth, money growth, and the change in velocity for 1986, 1987, and 1988. (These are the last three years for which we have GDP data for this country.)

■ Velocity changes, but on the average, over a number of years, it is remarkably stable. Also, real GDP growth does not change much. But as the money supply growth rate changes, so also does the inflation rate change.

■ Between 1985 and 1988, money growth and inflation were 136 percent a year each and real GDP and velocity barely changed. With numbers like these, it is clear that money growth generates inflation.

■ When inflation is as high and variable as it has been in Serbia, money ceases to work well as a medium of exchange, a unit of account, or a store of value.

■ So people don't want to hold Serbian dinars. They prefer to hold German

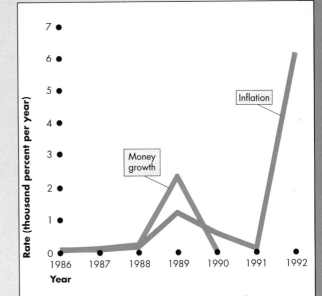

Figure 1  Inflation and money growth in Yugoslavia

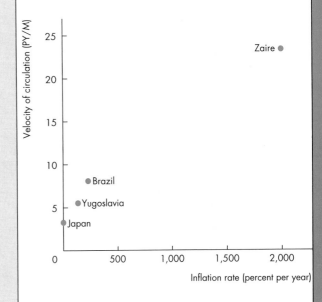

Figure 2  Inflation and velocity

marks, a currency that has stable buying power. So the velocity of circulation of dinars is high.

■ The higher the inflation rate, the more quickly people try to spend their income and the higher is the velocity of circulation. Figure 2 shows that in low-inflation Japan, the velocity is

less than in Yugoslavia. And in high-inflation Brazil and hyperinflation Zaire, the velocity is greater than in Yugoslavia.

■ Serbian money growth occurs not because the government is trying to cause inflation but because it has no way of financing its deficit other than by money printing.

|      | Inflation rate | Real GDP growth | Money growth | Change in velocity |
|------|------|------|------|------|
|      | *(percent per year)* | | | |
| 1986 | 88.4  | 3.5  | 110.4 | −7.3 |
| 1987 | 125.0 | −1.0 | 99.5  | 11.7 |
| 1988 | 211.8 | −2.0 | 215.1 | −3.0 |
| **Average** | **136.4** | **0.1** | **136.5** | **0.1** |

*Source: International Financial Statistics Yearbook, 1995, (Washington D.C.: International Monetary Fund).*

# SUMMARY

## Key Points

### What Is Money? (pp. 292–294)

■ Money is the means of payment, a medium of exchange, a unit of account, and a store of value.

■ M1 consists of currency, travelers' checks, and checking deposits), and M2 consists of M1 plus savings deposits, time deposits, and money market mutual funds.

### Financial Intermediaries (pp. 295–297)

■ Commercial banks, S&Ls, savings banks, credit unions, and money market mutual funds are financial intermediaries whose liabilities are money.

■ Financial intermediaries provide four main economic services: They create liquidity, minimize the cost of obtaining funds, minimize the cost of monitoring borrowers, and pool risks.

### Financial Regulation, Deregulation, and Innovation (pp. 297–299)

■ Financial regulation to protect depositors includes deposit insurance, minimum capital rules, and required reserves.

■ Deregulation during the 1980s removed the distinctions between banks and nonbank intermediaries.

■ The search for profit leads to the creation of new types of deposits and loans, which change the composition of the nation's money supply.

### How Banks Create Money (pp. 299–303)

■ Banks create money by making loans.

■ The total quantity of deposits that can be supported by a given amount of reserves (the deposit multiplier) is determined by the required reserve ratio.

### Money, Real GDP, and the Price Level (pp. 303–309)

■ An increase in the quantity of money increases aggregate demand and, in the short run, increases both the price level and real GDP.

■ In the long run, an increase in the quantity of money bring increases in the price level and no change in real GDP.

■ Like the *AS–AD* model, the quantity theory of money predicts no long-run relationship between money and real GDP.

## Key Figures ◆

## Key Terms

# QUESTIONS

1. What is money? What are its functions?

2. What are the two main measures of money in the United States today?

3. Why aren't checks money?

4. Why aren't credit cards money?

5. What is a financial intermediary?

6. What are the types of financial intermediaries in the United States whose deposits are part of the nation's money?

7. What are the economic functions of financial intermediaries?

8. How do banks make a profit and how do they create money?

9. Describe the main types of financial regulation that a financial intermediary faces.

10. Describe the deregulation of financial intermediaries that took place in the 1980s.

11. What is financial innovation? Explain the financial innovation that took place in the 1980s.

12. Define the deposit multiplier.

13. Explain why the deposit multiplier equals 1 divided by the required reserve ratio.

14. What does the aggregate supply–aggregate demand model predict about the effects of a change in the quantity of money on the price level and real GDP when the economy is initially
    a. In a recession?
    b. At full employment?

15. What is the equation of exchange and the velocity of circulation? What assumptions are necessary to make the equation of exchange the quantity theory of money?

16. What is the U.S. historical evidence on the quantity theory of money?

17. What is the international evidence on the quantity theory of money?

# PROBLEMS

1. In the United States today, money includes which of the following items?
   a. Federal Reserve banknotes in the Bank of America's cash machines
   b. Your Visa card
   c. The quarters inside public phones
   d. U.S. dollar bills in your wallet
   e. The check you have just written to pay for your rent
   f. The loan you took out last August to pay for your school fees

2. Which of the following items are money? Which are deposit money?
   a. Checking deposits at Citicorp
   b. IBM stock held by individuals
   c. The Susan B. Anthony dollar coin
   d. U.S. government securities
   e. NOW accounts

   Explain your answer by referring to the three basic functions of money.

3. Sara withdraws $1,000 from her savings account at the Lucky S&L, keeps $50 in cash, and deposits the balance in her checking account at the Bank of America. What is the immediate change in M1 and M2?

4. The commercial banks in Desertland have:

   | | |
   |---|---|
   | Reserves | $250 million |
   | Loans | $1,000 million |
   | Deposits | $2,000 million |
   | Total assets | $2,500 million |

   a. Construct the commercial banks' balance sheet. If you are missing any assets, call them "other assets"; if you are missing any liabilities, call them "other liabilities."
   b. Calculate the banks' reserve ratio.
   c. If banks hold no excess reserves, calculate the deposit multiplier.

5. An immigrant arrives in New Transylvania with $1,200. The $1,200 is put into a bank deposit. All the banks in New Transylvania have a required reserve ratio of 10 percent.
   a. What is the initial increase in the quantity of money of New Transylvania?

b. What is the initial increase in the quantity of bank deposits when the immigrant arrives?

c. How much does the immigrant's bank lend out?

d. Set out the transactions that take place and calculate the amount lent and the amount of deposits created if all the funds lent are returned to the banking system in the form of deposits.

e. By how much has the quantity of money increased after the banks have made 20 loans?

f. What is the total increase in the quantity of money, in bank loans, and in bank deposits?

6. Quantecon is a country in which the quantity theory of money operates. The country has a constant population, capital stock, and technology. In year 1, real GDP was $400 million, the price level was 200, and the velocity of circulation of money was 20. In year 2, the quantity of money was 20 percent higher than in year 1.

a. What was the quantity of money in year 1?

b. What was the quantity of money in year 2?

c. What was the price level in year 2?

d. What was the level of real GDP in year 2?

e. What was the velocity of circulation in year 2?

# CRITICAL THINKING

1. Study *Reading Between the Lines* on pp. 310–311 and then answer the following questions:

a. How has Serbia coped with the problem of finding a stable unit of account?

b. What has happened to the velocity of circulation of money in Serbia?

c. How do people protect themselves from a falling value of money in Serbia?

d. Why has Serbia's inflation rate been higher than its money supply growth rate in some years? Does this fact contradict the quantity theory of money?

2. Rapid inflation in Brazil caused the cruzeiro to lose its ability to function as money. Which of these commodities do you think would be most likely to take the place of the cruzeiro in the Brazilian economy?

a. Tractor parts

b. Packs of cigarettes

c. Loaves of bread

d. Impressionist paintings

e. Baseball trading cards

3. Visit Mark Bernkopf's Central Banking Resource Center on the World Wide Web at http://adams.patriot.net/~bernkopf/ (or use the link on the Parkin Web site) and read the short article on Electronic Cash. Also read "The End of Cash" by James Gleick (first published in the *New York Times Magazine*, June 16, 1996). Then answer the following questions:

a. What is e-cash?

b. Mark Bernkopf asks: "Will 'e-cash' enable private currencies to overturn the ability of governments to make monetary policy?" What do you think?

c. When you buy an item on the Internet and pay by using a form of e-cash, are you using money? Explain why or why not.

d. In your opinion, is the concern about e-cash a real concern or hype?

# Monetary Policy

In 1987, William Greider's *Secrets of the Temple: How the Federal Reserve Runs the Country* made the *New York Times* best-seller list. This book was popular partly because it was (and is) a good read and partly because it let its reader in on some secrets—the secrets of the mysterious Fed. What exactly is the Fed? What tools does it possess? And how does it use them? ◆ One thing the Fed does is to manage the nation's money. The amount of money in existence is surprisingly large. An unknown quantity of U.S. bills circulates abroad, especially in Russia and the rest of Eastern Europe. But there are enough coins and bills circulating in the United States today for every person to have a wallet stuffed with more than $1,000. In addition, enough money is deposited in banks and other financial institutions for every person to have a deposit of more than $12,500. What determines the amount of currency and bank deposits in existence? How does the Fed change the amount of money floating around the economy? And why do individuals and businesses hold so much money? ◆ Through 1996, interest rates were remarkably stable. But toward the year's end, more and more people began to wonder when the Fed would push them upward, and by how much. Then, in March 1997, the Fed finally acted and increased interest rates. But was that the only interest rate increase we would see in 1997? Or would there be more interest rate increases? And how does the Fed change interest rates? How do interest rates influence the economy? How do higher interest rates keep inflation in check? ◆ In this chapter, you will learn about the Fed and monetary policy. You will learn how the Fed influences interest rates and how interest rates influence the economy. You'll discover that interest rates depend, in part, on the amount of money in existence. You will also discover how the Fed influences the quantity of money to influence interest rates as it attempts to smooth the business cycle and keep inflation in check.

## Temple of Secrets

## After studying this chapter, you will be able to:

- Describe the structure of the Federal Reserve System (the Fed)

- Describe the tools used by the Fed to conduct its monetary policy

- Explain what an open market operation is and how it works

- Explain how an open market operation changes the money supply

- Explain what determines the demand for money

- Explain how the Fed influences interest rates

- Explain how interest rates influence the economy

# The Federal Reserve System

THE CENTRAL BANK OF THE UNITED STATES IS the **Federal Reserve System**. A **central bank** is a bank's bank and a public authority that regulates a nation's financial institutions and markets. As the banks' bank, the Fed provides banking services to commercial banks such as Citibank and the Bank of America. A central bank is not a citizens' bank. That is, the Fed does not provide general banking services for businesses and individual citizens.

The Fed conducts the nation's **monetary policy**, which means that it adjusts the quantity of money in circulation. The Fed's goals are to keep inflation in check, maintain full employment, moderate the business cycle, and contribute toward achieving long-term growth. Complete success in the pursuit of these goals is impossible, and the Fed's more modest goal is to improve the performance of the economy and to get closer to the goals than a "hands off" approach would achieve. Whether the Fed succeeds in improving economic performance is a matter on which there is a range of opinion.

This chapter examines the tools available to the Fed in its conduct of monetary policy and looks at the effects of the Fed's actions on the economy. We begin by describing the structure of the Fed.

## The Structure of the Federal Reserve System

The key elements in the structure of the Federal Reserve System are:

- The Board of Governors
- The Regional Federal Reserve Banks
- The Federal Open Market Committee

**The Board of Governors**  The Board of Governors has seven members, who are appointed by the President of the United States and confirmed by the Senate, each for a 14-year term. The terms are staggered so that one seat on the board becomes vacant every two years. The President appoints one of the board members as Chairman for a term of four years, which is renewable.

**The Federal Reserve Banks**  There are 12 Federal Reserve banks, one for each of 12 Federal Reserve districts shown in Fig. 14.1. Each Federal Reserve bank has nine directors, three of who are appointed by the Board of Governors and six of who are elected by the commercial banks in the Federal Reserve district. The directors of the regional Federal Reserve banks appoint the bank's president, and the Board of Governors approves this appointment.

The Federal Reserve Bank of New York (known as the New York Fed) occupies a special place in the Federal Reserve System because it implements some of the Fed's most important policy decisions.

**The Federal Open Market Committee**  The **Federal Open Market Committee** (FOMC) is the main policy-making organ of the Federal Reserve System. The FOMC consists of the following voting members:

- The chairman and other six members of the Board of Governors
- The president of the Federal Reserve Bank of New York
- The presidents of the other regional Federal Reserve banks (of whom, on a yearly rotating basis, only four vote)

The FOMC meets approximately every six weeks to review the state of the economy and to decide the actions to be carried out by the New York Fed.

## The Fed's Power Center

A description of the formal structure of the Fed gives the impression that power in the Fed resides with the Board of Governors. In practice, it is the chairman of the Board of Governors who has the largest influence on the Fed's monetary policy actions, and some remarkable individuals have held this position. One of these is Paul Volcker, who was appointed in 1979 by President Carter and reappointed in 1983 by President Reagan. Volcker eradicated inflation but helped to create one of the most severe postwar recessions. Another is Alan Greenspan, who was appointed by President Reagan in 1987 and reappointed by President Bush in 1992 and again for another term by President Clinton in 1996.

The chairman's power and influence stem from three sources. First, it is the chairman who controls the agenda and who dominates the meetings of the FOMC. Second, day-to-day contact with a large staff of economists and other technical experts provides the chairman with detailed background briefings on monetary policy issues. Third, the chairman is the spokesperson for the Fed and the Fed's

FIGURE 14.1

## The Federal Reserve System

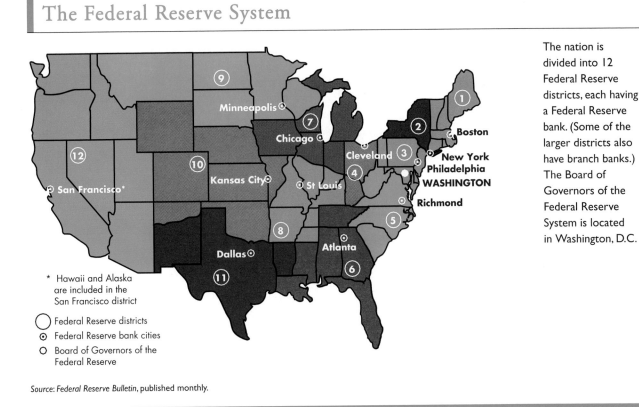

The nation is divided into 12 Federal Reserve districts, each having a Federal Reserve bank. (Some of the larger districts also have branch banks.) The Board of Governors of the Federal Reserve System is located in Washington, D.C.

* Hawaii and Alaska are included in the San Francisco district

◯ Federal Reserve districts
⊙ Federal Reserve bank cities
◯ Board of Governors of the Federal Reserve

Source: *Federal Reserve Bulletin*, published monthly.

main point of contact with the President and government and with foreign central banks and governments.

### The Fed's Policy Tools

The Federal Reserve System has many responsibilities, but we'll examine its single most important one: regulating the amount of money floating around in the United States. How does the Fed control the money supply? It does so by adjusting the reserves of the banking system. It is also by adjusting the reserves of the banking system and by standing ready to make loans to banks that the Fed is able to prevent bank failures. The Fed uses three main policy tools to achieve its objectives:

- Required reserve ratios
- Discount rate
- Open market operations

**Required Reserve Ratios**   All depository institutions in the United States are required to hold a minimum

percentage of deposits as reserves. This minimum percentage is known as a *required reserve ratio*. The Fed determines a required reserve ratio for each type of deposit. In 1997, banks were required to hold minimum reserves equal to 3 percent of checking deposits up to $49 million and 10 percent of these deposits in excess of $49 million. The required reserves on other types of deposits were zero.

**Discount Rate**   The **discount rate** is the interest rate at which the Fed stands ready to lend reserves to commercial banks. A change in the discount rate is proposed to the FOMC by the Board of Directors of at least one of the 12 Federal Reserve banks and is approved by the Board of Governors.

**Open Market Operations**   An **open market operation** is the purchase or sale of government securities—U.S. Treasury bills and bonds—by the Federal Reserve System in the open market. When the Fed conducts an open market operation, it makes a transaction with a bank or some other business but it does not transact with the federal government.

The structure and policy tools of the Federal Reserve System are summarized in Fig. 14.2. To understand how open market operations work, we need to know about the Fed's balance sheet.

## The Fed's Balance Sheet

The balance sheet of the Federal Reserve System for December 1996 is set out in Table 14.1. The assets on the left side are what the Fed owns, and the liabilities on the right side are what it owes. The Fed's three main assets are:

1. Gold and foreign exchange
2. U.S. government securities
3. Loans to banks

The Fed's holdings of gold and foreign exchange are its international reserves. Most of the Fed's foreign exchange consists of deposits by the Fed at other central banks. The Fed's holdings of U.S. government securities are the backing for dollar bills and banks' deposits at the Fed. The Fed sometimes makes loans to banks on which the Fed charges them the discount rate. (These loans were negligible in December 1996.)

The Fed's two main liabilities are:

1. Federal Reserve notes in circulation
2. Banks' deposits

The Federal Reserve notes in circulation are the dollar bills that we use in our daily transactions. Some of these bills are in circulation with the public; others are in the tills and vaults of banks and other financial institutions. Banks' deposits are the deposits of commercial banks, which are part of the reserves of those banks.

You might be wondering why Federal Reserve notes are considered a liability of the Fed. When bank notes were invented, they gave their owner a claim on the gold reserves of the issuing bank. Such notes were *convertible paper money*. The holder of such a note could convert the note on demand into gold (or some other commodity such as silver) at a guaranteed price. Thus when a bank issued a note, it was holding itself liable to convert that note into gold or silver. Modern bank notes are nonconvertible. A *nonconvertible note* is a bank note that is not convertible into any commodity and that obtains its value by government fiat—hence the term "fiat money." Such notes are the legal liability of the bank that issues them, and they are backed by holdings of securities and loans. Federal Reserve notes are backed by the Fed's holdings of U.S. government securities.

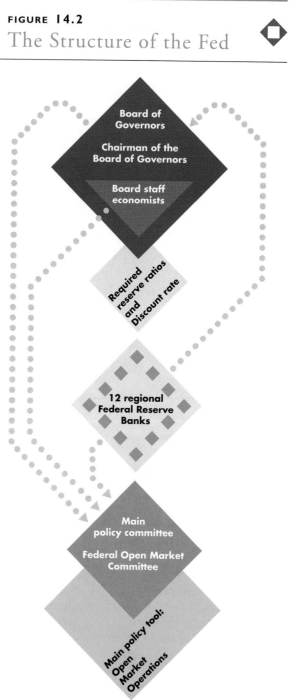

**FIGURE 14.2**

## The Structure of the Fed

The Board of Governors sets required reserve ratios and, on the proposal of the 12 Federal Reserve banks, sets the discount rate. The Board of Governors and presidents of the regional Federal Reserve banks sit on the FOMC to determine open market operations.

**TABLE 14.1**

# The Fed's Balance Sheet, December 1996

| Assets (billions of dollars) | | Liabilities (billions of dollars) | |
|---|---|---|---|
| Gold and foreign exchange | 21 | Federal Reserve notes | 427 |
| U.S. government securities | 460 | Banks' deposits | 25 |
| Loans to banks | 0 | Other liabilities (net) | 29 |
| Total assets | 481 | Total liabilities | 481 |

Source: Federal Reserve Bulletin (March 1997).

The Fed's liabilities, together with coins in circulation (coins are issued by the Treasury and are not liabilities of the Fed), make up the monetary base. That is, the **monetary base** is the sum of Federal Reserve notes, coins, and banks' deposits at the Fed. The monetary base is so called because it acts like a base that supports the nation's money supply. The larger the monetary base, the greater is the quantity of money.

## R E V I E W

- The Federal Reserve System is the central bank of the United States.
- A central bank conducts a nation's monetary policy and supervises the financial system.
- The Fed's policy tools are required reserve ratios, the discount rate, and open market operations.
- The Board of Governors sets required reserve ratios.
- It also sets the discount rate on the recommendation of the regional Federal Reserve banks.
- The Federal Open Market Committee (FOMC) determines open market operations.

Next, we're going to see how the Fed controls the money supply. We'll see how the Fed's monetary policy instruments change the monetary base and how changes in the monetary base change the quantity of money in circulation.

# Controlling the Money Supply

THE FED CONSTANTLY MONITORS AND ADJUSTS the quantity of money in the economy. To change the quantity of money, the Fed can use any of its three tools: required reserve ratios, the discount rate, and open market operations. Required reserve ratios are changed infrequently. The discount rate and open market operations are used more frequently. Let's see how these tools work.

## How Required Reserve Ratios Work

When the Fed *increases* the required reserve ratio, the banks must hold more reserves. To increase their reserves, the banks must *decrease* their lending, which *decreases* the quantity of money. When the Fed *decreases* the required reserve ratio, the banks may hold less reserves. To decrease their reserves, the banks *increase* their lending, which *increases* the quantity of money.

## How the Discount Rate Works

When the Fed *increases* the discount rate, the banks must pay a higher price for any reserves that they borrow from the Fed. Faced with higher cost of reserves, the banks try to get by with smaller reserves. But with a given required reserve ratio, the banks must also *decrease* their lending to decrease their borrowed reserves. So the quantity of money *decreases*. When the Fed *decreases* the discount rate, the banks pay a lower price for any reserves that they borrow from the Fed. Faced with lower cost of reserves, the banks are willing to borrow more reserves and *increase* their lending. So the quantity of money *increases*.

## How an Open Market Operation Works

When the Fed *buys* securities in an open market operation, the monetary base *increases*, banks *increase* their lending, and the quantity of money *increases*. When the Fed *sells* securities in an open market operation, the monetary base *decreases*, banks *decrease* their lending, and the quantity of money *decreases*. Open market operations are used more frequently than the other two tools and are the most complex in their operation. So we'll study this tool in greater detail than the other two.

When the Fed conducts an open market operation, the reserves of the banking system (a component of the monetary base) change. To see why, we'll trace the effects of an open market operation when the Fed *buys* securities. (The effects of a sale of securities is the reverse of what we'll see here.)

**The Fed Buys Securities**   Suppose the Fed buys $100 million of U.S. government securities in the open market. There are two cases to consider: when the Fed buys from a commercial bank and when it buys from the public (a person or business that is not a commercial bank). The outcome is essentially the same in either case, but you might need to be convinced of this fact, so we'll study the two cases, starting with the simplest case, in which the Fed buys from a commercial bank.

*Buys from Commercial Bank*   When the Fed buys $100 million of securities from the Manhattan Commercial Bank, two things happen:

1. The Manhattan Commercial Bank has $100 million less securities, and the Fed has $100 million more securities.
2. The Fed pays for the securities by crediting the Manhattan Commercial Bank's deposit account at the Fed with $100 million.

Figure 14.3(a) shows the effects of these actions on the balance sheets of the Fed and the Manhattan Commercial Bank. Ownership of the securities passes from the commercial bank to the Fed, so the bank's assets decrease by $100 million and the Fed's assets increase by $100 million, as shown by the blue arrow running from the Manhattan Commercial Bank to the Fed. The Fed pays for the securities by crediting the Manhattan Commercial Bank's deposit account— its reserves—at the Fed with $100 million, as shown by the green arrow running from the Fed to the Manhattan Commercial Bank. This action increases the monetary base and increases the reserves of the banking system.

The Fed's assets increase by $100 million, and its liabilities also increase by $100 million. The commercial bank's total assets remain constant, but their composition changes. Its holdings of government securities decrease by $100 million, and its deposits at the Fed increase by $100 million. So the bank has additional reserves, which it can use to make loans.

---

**FIGURE 14.3**

## The Fed Buys Securities in the Open Market

**(a) The Fed buys securities from a commercial bank**

**The Federal Reserve Bank of New York**

| Assets | Liabilities |
|---|---|
| Securities   +$100 | Reserves of Manhattan Commercial Bank   +$100 |

The Fed buys securities from a commercial bank ...

... and pays for the securities by increasing the reserves of the commercial bank

**The Manhattan Commercial Bank**

| Assets | Liabilities |
|---|---|
| Securities   −$100 | |
| Reserves   +$100 | |

**(b) The Fed buys securities from the public**

**The Federal Reserve Bank of New York**

| Assets | Liabilities |
|---|---|
| Securities   +$100 | Reserves of Manhattan Commercial Bank   +$100 |

The Fed buys securities from Goldman Sachs, a member of the general public ...

**Goldman Sachs**

| Assets | Liabilities |
|---|---|
| Securities   −$100 | ... and pays for the securities by writing a check that is deposited to Goldman Sachs's account at the Manhattan Commercial Bank and that increases the reserves of the commercial banks |
| Deposits at Manhattan Commercial Bank   +$100 | |

**The Manhattan Commercial Bank**

| Assets | Liabilities |
|---|---|
| Reserves   +$100 | Goldman Sachs's deposit   +$100 |

We've just seen that when the Fed buys government securities from a bank, the bank's reserves increase. But what happens if the Fed buys government securities from the public—say from Goldman Sachs, a financial services company?

**Buys from Public**   When the Fed buys $100 million of securities from Goldman Sachs, three things happen:

1. Goldman Sachs has $100 million less securities, and the Fed has $100 million more securities.
2. The Fed pays for the securities with a check for $100 million drawn on itself, which Goldman Sachs deposits in its account at the Manhattan Commercial Bank.
3. The Manhattan Commercial Bank collects payment of this check from the Fed, and $100 million is deposited in Manhattan's deposit account at the Fed.

Figure 14.3(b) shows the effects of these actions on the balance sheets of the Fed, Goldman Sachs, and the Manhattan Commercial Bank. Ownership of the securities passes from Goldman Sachs to the Fed, so Goldman Sachs's assets decrease by $100 million and the Fed's assets increase by $100 million, as shown by the blue arrow running from Goldman Sachs to the Fed. The Fed pays for the securities with a check payable to Goldman Sachs, which Goldman Sachs deposits in the Manhattan Commercial Bank. This payment increases Manhattan's reserves by $100 million, as shown by green arrow running from the Fed to Manhattan Commercial Bank. It also increases Goldman Sachs's deposit at the Manhattan Commercial Bank by $100 million, as shown by the red arrow running from the Manhattan Commercial Bank to Goldman Sachs. Just as when the Fed buys from a bank, this action increases the monetary base and increases the reserves of the banking system.

Again, the Fed's assets increase by $100 million, and its liabilities also increase by $100 million. Goldman Sachs has the same total assets as before, but their composition has changed. It now has more money and fewer securities. The Manhattan Commercial Bank's total assets increase, and so do its liabilities. Its deposits at the Fed—its reserves—increase by $100 million, and its deposit liability to Goldman Sachs increases by $100 million. Because its reserves have increased by the same amount as its deposits, the bank has excess reserves, which it can use to make loans.

We've studied what happens when the Fed *buys* government securities from either a bank or the public. When the Fed *sells* securities, all the transactions and events you've just studied work in reverse. (Trace the process again but with the Fed selling and the banks or public buying securities.)

The effects of an open market operation on the balance sheets of the Fed and the banks that we've just described are not the end of the story—they are just the beginning. With an increase in their reserves, the banks are able to make more loans, which increases the quantity of money. With a decrease in reserves, the banks must cut back on their loans and the quantity of money decreases.

A change in the monetary base that results from an open market operation has ripple effects through the economy. First, it has a multiplier effect on the quantity of money. Second, it changes interest rates. Third, it changes aggregate expenditure and real GDP. We are going to study these ripple effects in the rest of this chapter. We begin by studying the multiplier effect of an open market operation on the quantity of money. To do so, we build on the link between bank reserves and bank deposits that you studied in Chapter 13. But first we examine a related broader link between the monetary base and the quantity of money.

## Monetary Base and Bank Reserves

We've defined the *monetary base* as the sum of Federal Reserve notes, coins, and banks' deposits at the Fed. The monetary base is held either by banks as *reserves* or outside the banks as currency in circulation. When the monetary base increases, both bank reserves and currency in circulation increase. But only the increase in bank reserves can be used by banks to make loans and create additional money. An increase in currency held outside the banks is called a **currency drain**. A currency drain reduces the amount of additional money that can be created from a given increase in the monetary base.

The **money multiplier** is the amount by which a change in the monetary base is multiplied to determine the resulting change in the quantity of money. It is related to, but differs from, the deposit multiplier that we studied in Chapter 13. The *deposit multiplier* is the amount by which a change in bank reserves is multiplied to determine the change in the bank deposits.

Let's now look at the money multiplier.

### The Multiplier Effect of an Open Market Operation

Figure 14.4 shows the multiplier effect of an open market purchase of securities from the banks. Initially, the banks' reserves increase but the quantity of money does not change. The banks have excess reserves, and the following sequence of events takes place:

■ Banks lend excess reserves.

■ The money supply increases.

■ New deposits are used to make payments.

■ Some of the new money is held as currency— a *currency drain*.

■ Some of the new money remains on deposit in banks.

■ Banks' required reserves increase.

■ Excess reserves decrease but remain positive.

The sequence repeats in a series of rounds, but each round begins with a smaller quantity of excess reserves than did the previous one. The process continues until excess reserves have finally been eliminated.

Figure 14.5 keeps track of the increases in reserves, loans, deposits, currency, and money that results from an open market operation of $100,000. In this figure, the *currency drain* is 33.33 percent and the *required reserve ratio* is 10 percent. These numbers are assumed to keep the arithmetic simple.

The Fed buys $100,000 of securities from the banks. The banks' reserves increase by this amount, but deposits do not change. The banks have excess reserves of $100,000, and they lend those reserves. When the banks lend $100,000 of excess reserves, $66,667 remains in the banks as deposits and $33,333 drains off and is held outside the banks as currency. The quantity of money has now increased by $100,000—the increase in deposits plus the increase in currency holdings.

The increased bank deposits of $66,667 generates an increase in required reserves of 10 percent of that amount, which is $6,667. Actual reserves have

---

**FIGURE 14.4**

## A Round in the Multiplier Process Following an Open Market Operation

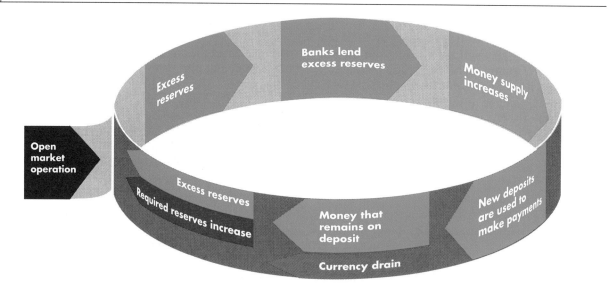

An open market operation increases bank reserves and creates excess reserves. Banks lend the excess reserves, and new loans are used to make payments. Households and firms receiving payments keep some of the receipts in the form of currency— a currency drain—and place the rest on deposit in banks. The increase in bank deposits increases banks' reserves but also increases banks' required reserves. Required reserves increase by less than actual reserves, so the banks still have some excess reserves, though less than before. The process repeats until excess reserves have been eliminated.

FIGURE 14.5

The Multiplier Effect of an Open Market Operation

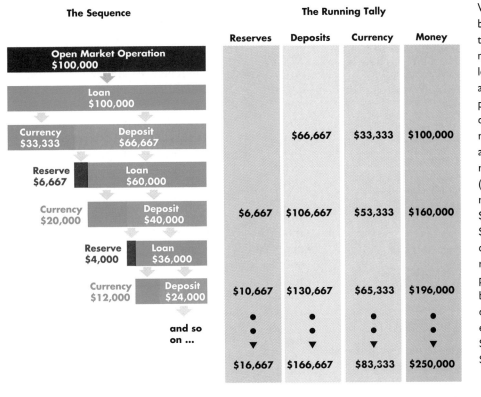

When the Fed provides the banks with $100,000 of additional reserves in an open market operation, the banks lend those reserves. Of the amount lent, $33,333 (33.33 percent) leaves the banks in a currency drain and $66,667 remains on deposit. With additional deposits, required reserves increase by $6,667 (10 percent required reserve ratio) and the banks lend $60,000. Of this amount, $20,000 leaves the banks in a currency drain and $40,000 remains on deposit. The process repeats until the banks have created enough deposits to eliminate their excess reserves. An additional $100,000 of reserves creates $250,000 of money.

increased by the same amount as the increase in deposits—$66,667. So the banks now have excess reserves of $60,000. At this stage, we have gone once around the circle shown in Fig. 14.4. The process we've just described repeats but begins with excess reserves of $60,000. Figure 14.5 shows the next two rounds. At the end of the process, the quantity of money has increased by a multiple of the increase in the monetary base. In this case, the increase is $250,000, which is 2.5 times the increase in the monetary base.

An open market *sale* works similarly to an open market purchase, but it *decreases* the quantity of money. (Trace the process again but with the Fed selling and the banks or public buying securities.)

When the Fed undertakes an open market operation, it is trying to influence the course of the economy. But the Fed's influence is indirect. You've now studied the initial effect of the Fed's actions, which is to change the quantity of money.

### REVIEW

▨ When the Fed buys securities in the open market, the monetary base and bank reserves increase and banks have excess reserves. When the Fed sells securities in the open market, the monetary base and bank reserves decrease and banks have a shortage of reserves.

▨ With excess reserves, the banks increase their lending and the quantity of money increases.

▨ With a shortage of reserves, the banks decrease their lending and the quantity of money decreases.

When the Fed changes the quantity of money, it sets off a ripple effect, the next part of which is a change in interest rates. Why do interest rates change when the quantity of money changes? We'll discover the answer by studying the demand for money.

# The Demand for Money

THE AMOUNT OF MONEY WE RECEIVE EACH WEEK in payment for our labor is income—a flow. The amount of money that we hold in our wallet or in a deposit account at the bank is an inventory—a stock. There is no limit to how much income we would like to receive each week. But there is a limit to how big an inventory of money each of us would like to hold on to and not spend.

## The Influences on Money Holding

The quantity of money that people choose to hold depends on four main factors:

- The price level
- The interest rate
- Real GDP
- Financial innovation

Let's look at each of them.

**The Price Level** The quantity of money measured in dollars is called the quantity of *nominal money*. The quantity of nominal money demanded is proportional to the price level, other things remaining the same. That is, if the price level (GDP deflator) increases by 10 percent, people will want to hold 10 percent more nominal money than before, other things being equal. What matters is not the number of dollars that you hold but their buying power. If you hold $20 to buy your weekly movies and soda, you will increase your money holding to $22 if the prices of movies and soda—and your wage rate—increase by 10 percent.

The quantity of money measured in constant dollars (for example, in 1992 dollars) is called *real money*. Real money is equal to nominal money divided by the price level. It is the quantity of money measured in terms of what it will buy. In the above example, when the price level rises by 10 percent and you increase your average cash holding by 10 percent, you are keeping your *real* cash holding constant. Your $22 at the new price level buys the same quantity of goods and is the same quantity of *real money* as your $20 at the original price level. The quantity of real money held does not depend on the price level.

**The Interest Rate** A fundamental principle of economics is that as the opportunity cost of something increases, people try to find substitutes for it. Money is no exception. The higher the opportunity cost of holding money, other things being equal, the lower is the quantity of real money demanded. But what is the opportunity cost of holding money? It is the interest rate that you can earn by holding money minus the interest rate that you must forgo on other assets that you could hold instead of money.

The interest rate that you earn on currency and some checking deposits is zero. So the opportunity cost of holding these items is the interest rate on other assets such as a savings bond or Treasury bill. By holding money instead, you forgo the interest that you otherwise would have received. This forgone interest is the opportunity cost of holding money.

Money loses value because of inflation. So, why isn't the inflation rate part of the cost of holding money? It is: Other things being equal, the higher the expected inflation rate, the higher are interest rates and the higher, therefore, is the opportunity cost of holding money. (The forces that make interest rates change to reflect changes in the expected inflation rate are described in Chapter 15 on pp. 354–355.)

**Real GDP** The quantity of money that households and firms plan to hold depends on the amount they are spending, and the quantity of money demanded in the economy as a whole depends on aggregate expenditure—real GDP.

Again, suppose that you hold an average of $20 to finance your weekly purchases of movies and soda. Now imagine that the prices of these goods and of all other goods remain constant but that your income increases. As a consequence, you now spend more, and you also keep a larger amount of money on hand to finance your higher volume of expenditure.

**Financial Innovation** Technological change and the arrival of new financial products change the quantity of money held. The major financial innovations are the widespread use of:

1. Daily interest checking deposits
2. Automatic transfers between checking and savings deposits
3. Automatic teller machines
4. Credit cards

These innovations have occurred because of the development of computing power that has lowered the cost of calculations and record keeping.

We summarize the effects of the influences on money holding by using the demand for money curve.

## The Demand for Money Curve

The *demand for money* is the relationship between the quantity of real money demanded and the interest rate, when all other influences on the amount of money that people wish to hold remain the same. Figure 14.6 shows a demand for money curve, *MD*. When the interest rate rises, everything else remaining the same, the opportunity cost of holding money rises and the quantity of money demanded decreases—there is a movement along the demand for money curve. Similarly, when the interest rate falls, the opportunity cost of holding money falls, and the quantity of money demanded increases—there is a downward movement along the demand for money curve.

## Shifts in the Demand Curve for Real Money

A change in real GDP or financial innovation changes the demand for money and shifts the demand curve for real money. Figure 14.7 illustrates the change in the demand for money. A decrease in real GDP decreases the demand for money and shifts the demand curve leftward from $MD_0$ to $MD_1$. An increase in real GDP has the opposite effect. It increases the demand for money and shifts the demand curve rightward from $MD_0$ to $MD_2$.

The influence of financial innovation on the demand for money curve is more complicated. It might increase the demand for some types of deposits, decrease the demand for others, and decrease the demand for currency. We'll look at the effects of financial innovation by studying the demand for money in the United States.

### FIGURE 14.6
## The Demand for Money

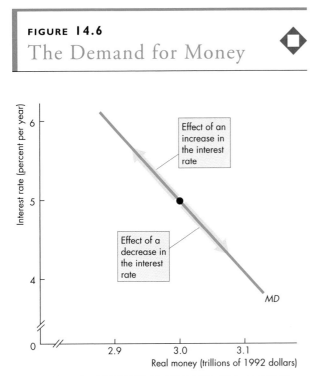

### FIGURE 14.7
## Changes in the Demand for Money

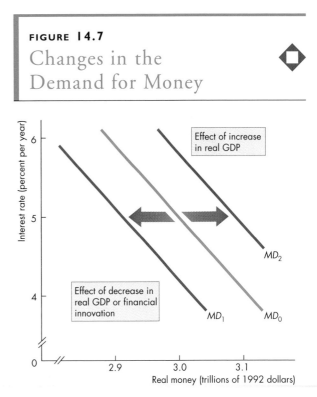

The demand for money curve, *MD*, shows the relationship between the quantity of money that people plan to hold and the interest rate, other things remaining the same. The interest rate is the opportunity cost of holding money. A change in the interest rate brings a movement along the demand curve.

A decrease in real GDP decreases the demand for money and shifts the demand curve leftward from $MD_0$ to $MD_1$. An increase in real GDP increases the demand for money and shifts the demand curve rightward from $MD_0$ to $MD_2$. Financial innovation generally decreases the demand for money.

### The Demand for Money in the United States

Figure 14.8 shows the relationship between the interest rate and the quantity of real money demanded in the United States between 1970 and 1996. Each dot shows the interest rate and the amount of real money held in a given year. In 1970, the demand for M1 (shown in part a) was $MD_{70}$. During the early 1970s, the spread of credit cards decreased the demand for M1 (currency and checking deposits) and this financial innovation shifted the demand for M1 curve leftward to $MD_{76}$. But over the years, real GDP growth increased the demand for M1, and by 1994, the demand for M1 curve had shifted rightward to $MD_{94}$.

Further financial innovation, probably arising from the further increased use of credit cards, decreased the demand for M1 and shifted the demand curve leftward again.

In 1970, the demand for M2 (shown in part b) was $MD_{70}$. The spread of credit cards that decreased the demand for M1 during the period did not decrease demand for M2. The reason is that most of the new financial products were M2 deposits. So from 1970 through 1989, the demand for M2 increased and the demand for M2 curve shifted rightward to $MD_{89}$. But in the period after 1989, the main innovations were in financial products that compete with deposits of all kinds. So the demand for M2 decreased, and the demand for M2 curve shifted leftward to $MD_{96}$.

---

**FIGURE 14.8**

## The Demand for Money in the United States

**(a) M1 demand**

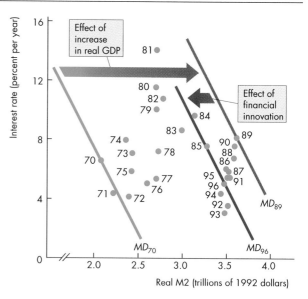

**(b) M2 demand**

The dots show the quantity of real money and the interest rate in each year between 1970 and 1996. In 1970, the demand for M1 was $MD_{70}$ in part (a). The demand for M1 decreased during the early 1970s because of financial innovation, and the demand curve shifted leftward to $MD_{76}$. But the demand for M1 has increased because of real GDP growth, and by 1994, the demand curve had shifted rightward to $MD_{94}$. Further financial

innovation decreased the demand for M1 in 1995 and 1996 and shifted the demand curve leftward again to $MD_{96}$. In 1970, the demand for M2 curve was $MD_{70}$ in part (b). The growth of real GDP increased the demand for M2, and by 1989, the demand curve had shifted rightward to $MD_{89}$. During the 1990s, new substitutes for M2 decreased the demand for M2 and the demand curve shifted leftward to $MD_{96}$.

*Source: Economic Report of the President, 1997, and the author's calculations and assumptions.*

◾ The demand for money curve shows the relationship between the quantity of real money demanded and the interest rate with all other influences on money holding unchanged.

◾ An increase in the interest rate decreases the quantity of money demanded and brings a movement along the demand curve for real money.

◾ Other influences on the quantity of real money demanded are real GDP and financial innovation.

◾ An increase in real GDP increases the demand for money and shifts the demand curve rightward.

◾ Financial innovations have decreased the demand for M1. These innovations initially increased the demand for M2, but later the demand for M2 also decreased.

We now know what determines the demand for money. And we've seen that a key factor is the interest rate—the opportunity cost of holding money. But what determines the interest rate? Let's find out.

## Interest Rate Determination

AN INTEREST RATE IS THE PERCENTAGE YIELD on a financial security such as a *bond* or a *stock*. The higher the price of a financial asset, other things remaining the same, the lower is the interest rate. An example will make this relationship clear. Suppose the federal government sells a bond that promises to pay $10 a year. If the price of the bond is $100, the interest rate is 10 percent per year—$10 is 10 percent of $100. If the price of the bond is $50, the interest rate is 20 percent—$10 is 20 percent of $50. And if the price of the bond is $200, the interest rate is 5 percent—$10 is 5 percent of $200.

You've just seen the link between the price of a bond and the interest rate. People divide their wealth between bonds (and other interest-bearing financial assets) and money, and the amount they hold as money depends on the interest rate. We can study the forces that determine the interest rate either in the market for bonds or the market for money. Because the Fed can influence the *supply* of money, we focus on the market for money.

## Money Market Equilibrium

The interest rate is determined by the supply of and demand for money. The quantity of money supplied is determined by the actions of the banking system and the Fed. On any given day, the supply of money is a fixed quantity. The *real* quantity of money supplied is equal to the nominal quantity supplied divided by the price level. At a given moment in time, there is a particular price level, and so the quantity of real money supplied is also a fixed amount. The supply curve of real money is shown in Fig. 14.9 as the vertical line labeled *MS*. The quantity of real money supplied is $3.0 trillion.

**FIGURE 14.9**

## Money Market Equilibrium ◆

Money market equilibrium occurs when the interest rate has adjusted to make the quantity of money demanded equal to the quantity supplied. Here, equilibrium occurs at an interest rate of 5 percent. At interest rates above 5 percent, the quantity of money demanded is less than the quantity supplied, so people buy bonds, and the interest rate falls. At interest rates below 5 percent, the quantity of real money demanded exceeds the quantity supplied, so people sell bonds and the interest rate rises. Only at 5 percent is the quantity of real money in existence willingly held.

On any given day, all the influences on the demand for money except for the interest rate are constant. But the lower the interest rate, the greater is the quantity of money demanded. Figure 14.9 shows a demand for money curve, *MD*.

**Equilibrium**   When the quantity of money supplied equals the quantity of money demanded, the money market is in equilibrium. Figure 14.9 illustrates equilibrium in the money market. Equilibrium is achieved by changes in the interest rate. If the interest rate is too high, people demand a smaller quantity of money than the quantity supplied. They are holding too much money. In this situation, they try to get rid of money by buying bonds. As they do so, the price of a bond rises and the interest rate falls to the equilibrium rate. Conversely, if the interest rate is too low, people demand a larger quantity of money than the quantity supplied. They are holding too little money. In this situation, they try to get more money by selling bonds. As they do so, the price of a bond falls and the interest rate rises to the equilibrium rate. Only when the interest rate is at the level at which people are holding the quantity of money supplied do they willingly hold the money and take no actions that change the interest rate.

## Changing the Interest Rate

Suppose that the economy is overheating and the Fed fears inflation. It decides to take action to decrease aggregate demand and spending. To do so, it wants to raise interest rates and discourage borrowing and expenditure on goods and services. What does the Fed do?

The Fed sells securities in the open market. As it does so, it mops up bank reserves and induces the banks to cut their lending. The banks make a smaller quantity of new loans each day until the stock of loans outstanding has fallen to a level that is consistent with the new lower level of reserves. The money supply decreases.

Suppose that the Fed undertakes open market operations on a sufficiently large scale to decrease the money supply from $3.0 trillion to $2.9 trillion. As a consequence, the supply curve of real money shifts leftward, as shown in Fig. 14.10, from $MS_0$ to $MS_1$.

The demand for money is shown by *MD*. With an interest rate of 5 percent and $2.9 trillion of money in the economy, firms and households are now holding less money than they wish to hold. They attempt to increase their money holding by selling financial

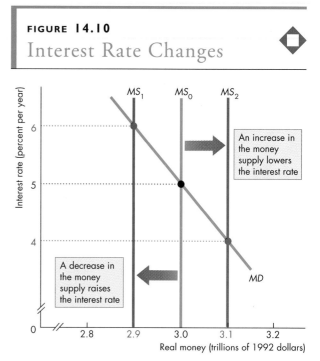

**FIGURE 14.10**

## Interest Rate Changes

An open market sale of securities shifts the money supply curve leftward to $MS_1$ and the interest rate rises to 6 percent. An open market purchase of securities shifts the money supply curve rightward to $MS_2$ and the interest rate falls to 4 percent.

assets. As they do so, the prices of bonds fall and the interest rate rises. When the interest rate has increased to 6 percent, people are willing to hold the smaller $2.9 trillion of money that the Fed and the banks have created.

Conversely, suppose that the Fed fears recession and decides to stimulate spending by increasing the money supply. If the Fed increases the real money supply to $3.1 trillion, the supply of money curve shifts rightward from $MS_0$ to $MS_2$. Equilibrium occurs when the interest rate has fallen to 4 percent.

## R E V I E W

■ Short-term interest rates are determined by the demand for and supply of money. When the quantity of money demanded equals the quantity supplied, the interest rate is at its equilibrium level.

■ To increase the interest rate, the Fed sells securities and decreases the money supply. To decrease the interest rate, the Fed buys securities and increases the money supply.

## Monetary Policy

YOU HAVE NOW LEARNED A GREAT DEAL ABOUT the Fed, the monetary policy actions it can take, and the effects of those actions on short-term interest rates. Most of the "secrets of the temple" have been revealed. But you are possibly thinking: All this sounds nice in theory, but does it really happen? Does the Fed actually do the things we've learned about in this chapter? Indeed, it does happen, sometimes with dramatic effect.

To see the Fed in action, we'll do two things. First, we'll look at the fluctuations in short-term interest rates in the United States since 1970 and see how the Fed has influenced those fluctuations. Second, we'll focus on two episodes in the life of the Fed. One is from the turbulent years of the early 1980s when the Fed was struggling to eradicate a stubborn inflation. The other is from the period since a stock market crash of 1987 during which the Fed tried to keep inflation in check without killing economic growth.

### The Fed in Action

You've seen that the immediate effect of the Fed's actions is a change in the short-term interest rate. Figure 14.11 shows the course of four short-term interest rates since 1970:

1. The 3-month Treasury bill rate, which is the interest rate paid by the federal government on 3-month loans

2. The 6-month commercial bill rate, which is the interest rate paid by large corporations on 6-month loans

3. The discount rate, which is the interest rate charged to banks by the Fed when the banks borrow reserves

4. The federal funds rate, which is the interest rate that the banks charge each other on overnight loans of reserves

Notice how closely these four interest rates move together. The interest rate that the Fed directly controls is the discount rate, and the rate that it closely

---

**FIGURE 14.11**

## Short-Term Interest Rates

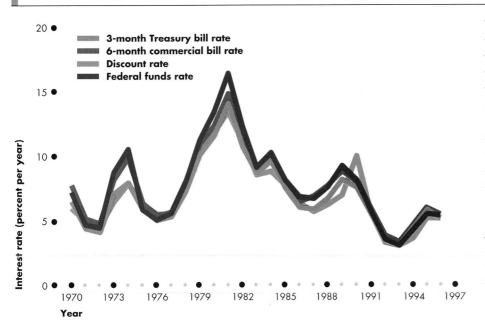

**3-month Treasury bill rate**
**6-month commercial bill rate**
**Discount rate**
**Federal funds rate**

The Fed directly determines the discount rate (the rate at which the Fed lends reserves to banks) and closely monitors the federal funds rate (the rate at which banks lend reserves to each other). All short-term interest rates move up and down together, so the Fed influences all short-term rates such as the 3-month Treasury bill rate (the rate at which the federal government borrows in the short term) and the 6-month commercial bill rate (the rate at which big corporations borrow in the short term).

Source: *Economic Report of the President, 1997*

monitors is the federal funds rate, but because the short-term rates all move up and down together, the Fed is effectively able to influence all these rates.

Do short-term interest rates rise and fall in response to changes in the quantity of money, as the theory we've just studied predicts? Mostly they do, but not quite always. Figure 14.12 illustrates this connection. It shows the federal funds rate and a measure of the quantity of money. This measure of money is M2 expressed as a percentage of GDP. The reason for looking at M2 is that it is this measure of money that the Fed has placed greatest emphasis on. The reason for expressing M2 as a percentage of GDP is that we can see both the supply-side and demand-side effects on interest rates in a single measure. Interest rates rise if the quantity of money decreases. Interest rates also rise if the demand for money increases. But the demand for money increases if GDP increases. So the ratio of M2 to GDP rises either if the supply of money increases (M2 increases) or the demand for money decreases (GDP decreases).

You can see by studying Fig. 14.12 that between 1970 and 1990, the rises and falls in the interest rate were exactly matched by decreases and increases in the ratio of M2 to GDP. An increase in the supply of money relative to the demand for money brought a fall in the interest rate (1970–1972, 1974–1977, and 1981–1986). A decrease in the supply of money relative to the demand for money brought a rise in the interest rate (1972–1974, 1977–1981, and 1986–1989).

You can also see in Fig. 14.12 that after 1990, the relationship between money and interest rates broke down. When the interest rate fell through 1993, the M2 to GDP ratio did not increase. The reason is that the demand for M2 fell because of the availability of some new substitute ways of holding wealth—bond and equity mutual funds. These funds were growing through the 1980s, but they grew more quickly during the 1990s, and their growth disturbed the traditional relationship between M2 and short-term interest rates. Consequently, after 1990, the Fed began to pay less attention to M2.

**FIGURE 14.12**

## Money and Interest Rates

When the ratio of M2 to GDP (measured on the left scale) rises, either the supply of money increases or the demand for money decreases. The result, before 1990, is a fall in the federal funds rate (measured on the right scale). Similarly, when the ratio of M2 to GDP falls, either the supply of money has decreased or the demand for money has increased and (again before 1990) the federal funds rate rises. After 1990, the relationship between M2 and interest rates broke down because new substitutes for M2 decreased the demand for M2.

Source: *Economic Report of the President,* 1997, and the author's calculations.

You've now seen that we can explain short-term interest rate fluctuations as arising from fluctuations in the supply of money relative to the demand for money. But this relationship doesn't tell us whether actions by the Fed or fluctuations in GDP brought the fluctuations in the M2 to GDP ratio. Do the Fed's own actions move interest rates around? Let's look at the Fed in action.

**Paul Volcker's Fed**  At the start of Paul Volcker's term of office as chairman of the Fed, which began in August 1979, the United States was locked in the grips of double-digit inflation. Volcker ended that inflation. He did so by forcing interest rates sharply upward from 1979 through 1981. This increase in interest rates resulted from the Fed using open market operations and increases in the discount rate to keep the banks short of reserves, which in turn held back the growth in the supply of loans and of money relative to the growth in their demand.

As we saw in Fig. 14.10, to increase interest rates, the Fed has to cut the real money supply. In practice, because the economy is growing and because prices are rising, a *slowdown* in nominal money supply growth is enough to increase interest rates. It is not necessary to actually *cut* the nominal money supply.

When Volcker became chairman of the Fed, the money supply was growing at more than 8 percent a year. Volcker slowed down that money supply growth to 6.5 percent in 1981. As a result, interest rates increased. The Treasury bill rate—the rate at which the government borrows—increased from 10 percent to 14 percent. The rate at which big corporations borrow increased from 9 percent to 14 percent. Mortgage rates—the rates at which homebuyers borrow—increased from 11 percent to 15 percent. The economy went into recession. The money supply growth slowdown and interest rate hike cut back the growth rate of aggregate demand. Real GDP fell, and the inflation rate slowed down.

**Alan Greenspan's Fed**  Alan Greenspan became chairman of the Fed in August 1987. In the two preceding years, the money supply had grown at a rapid pace, interest rates had tumbled, and the stock market had boomed. Then, suddenly and with no warning, stock prices fell, bringing fears of economic calamity and recession. This was Alan Greenspan's first test as Fed chairman.

The Fed's immediate reaction to the new situation was to emphasize the flexibility and sensitivity of the financial system and to make reserves plentiful to avoid any fear of a banking crisis. But as the months passed, it became increasingly clear that the economy was not heading for any kind of a recession. Unemployment continued to fall, income growth continued to be strong, and the fears that emerged were of inflation, not recession.

Seeking to avoid a serious upturn in inflation, the Fed slowed money growth and, just as Paul Volcker had done eight years earlier, forced interest rates sharply upward. Open market operations were targeted toward creating a shortage of reserves in the banking system to slow the money supply growth rate. As a consequence, during the year from May 1988 to May 1989, the M1 measure of the money supply was virtually constant and the M2 measure grew by only 2.4 percent, both down from growth rates of around 5 percent a year earlier and down from around 10 percent a year before the stock market crash. The slowdown in money supply growth increased interest rates throughout 1988. The interest rate on U.S. government 3-month Treasury bills increased from less than 6 percent a year at the start of 1988 to almost 9 percent a year by early 1989.

As 1989 advanced, concern about inflation remained, but renewed fears of recession returned as an increasing number of signs of a slowing economy emerged. Interest rates were gradually lowered, and the money supply was permitted to grow more quickly. By 1990, recession had become a reality. At first, the Fed's reaction was to adopt a neutral position, waiting for signs of recovery from an increase in investment and consumption expenditure. But as the months passed and recovery seemed elusive, the Fed eventually began to stimulate spending with a series of interest rate cuts. During 1991, interest rates declined by three percentage points as the Fed tried to encourage an increase in borrowing and spending.

By mid-1991, the recovery had begun and real GDP expanded. By 1997, this expansion was still going strong and set to break a record to become the longest peacetime expansion. The Fed played a role in keeping the expansion alive and in holding inflation in check. It did so by trying to anticipate unwanted deviations in either direction. Through 1992 and 1993, the Fed permitted rapid money growth and kept interest rates low. During 1994, the Fed slowed money growth and pushed interest rates upward. It permitted rates to fall again during 1996 and nudged them up slightly in the first quarter of 1997.

## Profiting by Predicting the Fed

Every day, the Fed influences interest rates by its open market operations. By buying securities and increasing the money supply, the Fed can lower interest rates; by selling securities and lowering the money supply, the Fed can increase interest rates. Sometimes such actions are taken to offset other influences and keep interest rates steady. At other times, the Fed moves interest rates up or down. The higher the interest rate, the lower is the price of a bond; the lower the interest rate, the higher is the price of a bond. Thus predicting interest rates is the same as predicting bond prices. Predicting that interest rates are going to fall is the same as predicting that bond prices are going to rise—a good time to buy bonds. Predicting that interest rates are going to rise is the same as predicting that bond prices are going to fall—a good time to sell bonds.

Because the Fed is the major player whose actions influence interest rates and bond prices, predicting the Fed is profitable and a good deal of effort goes into that activity. But people who anticipate that the Fed is about to increase the money supply buy bonds right away, pushing their prices upward and pushing interest rates downward *before* the Fed acts. Similarly, people who anticipate that the Fed is about to decrease the money supply sell bonds right away, pushing their prices downward and pushing interest rates upward before the Fed acts. In other words, bond prices and interest rates change as soon as the Fed's actions are foreseen. By the time the Fed actually takes its actions, if those actions are correctly foreseen, they have no effect. The effects occur in anticipation of the Fed's actions. Only changes in the money supply that are not foreseen change the interest rate at the time that those changes occur.

growth and inflation. The mechanism through which aggregate demand changes involves several channels. Higher interest rates bring a decrease in consumption expenditure and investment. Tighter bank credit brings fewer loans and reinforces the effects of higher interest rates on consumption expenditure and investment.

Higher interest rates bring an increase in the exchange rate that makes U.S. exports more expensive and makes imports less costly. So net exports decrease. The decreases in consumption, investment, and net exports all combine to decrease aggregate demand, which in turn slows the growth rate of real GDP and the inflation rate. Schematically, the effects of the Fed's actions ripple through the economy in the following way:

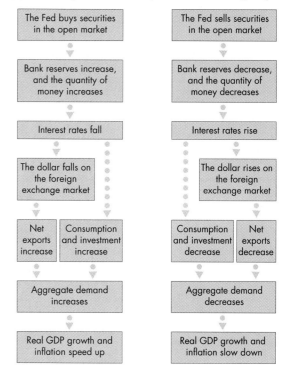

## The Ripple Effects of Monetary Policy

You've now seen that the Fed's actions do indeed change interest rates and that the Fed tries to influence the course of the economy. These monetary policy measures work by changing aggregate demand. When the Fed slows money growth and pushes interest rates up, it decreases aggregate demand, which in turn slows both real GDP growth and inflation. When the Fed speeds money growth and lowers interest rates, it increases aggregate demand, which in turn speeds real GDP

## Interest Rates and the Business Cycle

You've seen the connection between the Fed's actions and interest rates in Fig. 14.12. What about the ripple effects that we've just described? Do they really occur? Do changes in interest rates ultimately influence the real GDP growth rate? Yes they do. You can see these effects in Fig. 14.13. The blue line in this figure shows the short-term interest rate minus the long-term interest rate. The short-term interest rate is influenced by the Fed in the way that you studied

## FIGURE 14.13
## Interest Rates and Real GDP Growth

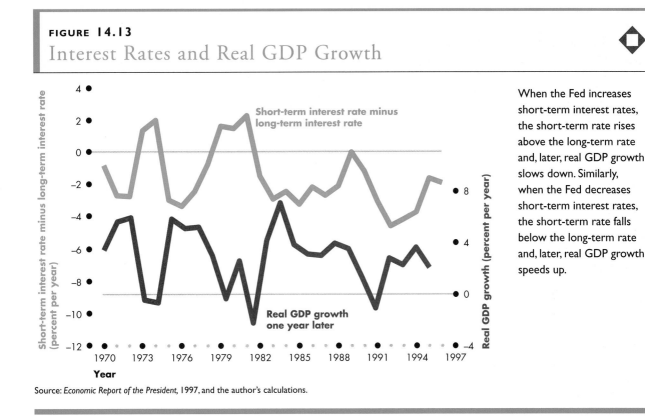

When the Fed increases short-term interest rates, the short-term rate rises above the long-term rate and, later, real GDP growth slows down. Similarly, when the Fed decreases short-term interest rates, the short-term rate falls below the long-term rate and, later, real GDP growth speeds up.

Source: *Economic Report of the President,* 1997, and the author's calculations.

earlier in this chapter. And changes in short-term rates have some influence on the long-term interest rate. But this influence is small, and the long-term interest rate is determined by saving and investment plans (see Chapter 9, pp. 201–203) and by long-term inflation expectations (see Chapter 15, pp. 354–355). The red line in Fig. 14.13 is the real GDP growth rate *one year later.* You can see that when short-term interest rates rise or long-term interest rates fall, the real GDP growth rate slows down in the following year. Long-term interest rates fluctuate less than short-term rates, so when short-term rates rise above long-term rates, it is because the Fed has pushed short-term rates upward. And when short-term rates fall below long-term rates, it is because the Fed has pushed short-term rates downward. So when the Fed stimulates aggregate demand (pushes short-term rates downward), the GDP growth rate speeds up, and when the Fed lowers aggregate demand (pushes short-term rates upward), the real GDP growth rate slows down. The inflation rate also increases and decreases in sympathy with these fluctuations in real GDP growth.

### REVIEW

- The Fed directly controls the discount rate, closely monitors the federal funds rate, and influences all short-term interest rates.
- Fluctuations in short-term interest rates usually mirror fluctuations in the ratio of M2 to GDP.
- When the money supply change is *un*anticipated, interest rates change at the same time as the change in the money supply. When a money supply change is *anticipated*, interest rates change ahead of the change in the money supply.
- When the Fed lowers (raises) interest rates, aggregate demand increases (decreases) and real GDP growth and inflation speed up (slow down).

◆ *Reading Between the Lines* on pages 334–335 looks at the Fed in action during 1996. Now that you know how the Fed determines the quantity of money and interest rates, we're going to explore the influence of money (and other factors) on inflation.

# Policy
## WATCH

The Fed in Action

Essence of
THE STORY

THE DENVER POST, DECEMBER 20, 1996

## Fed Won't Hike Rates, Experts Say

WASHINGTON—The Federal Reserve will leave the economy on autopilot in 1997, barring any blips on its radar screen that indicate inflation is taking off.

The vast majority of Wall Street economists say the Fed remains more likely to raise interest rates in the new year than lower them. But at present, there is little evidence that price pressures are on an upward trajectory, leaving the Fed with a steady flight path for monetary policy in the months ahead.

"The Fed is absolutely, flatly, and firmly on hold for a while," said John Williams, chief economist at Bankers Trust Co.

Earlier this week, the Federal Open Market Committee left its monetary policy unchanged, signaling it is comfortable with U.S. economic conditions. That marked the seventh consecutive time the FOMC took no action on rates.

That lack of a rate action reflects a consensus among policy makers that inflation hasn't risen enough to necessitate tighter credit conditions, observers said. The Fed's steady policy also suggests policy makers are satisfied with the extent to which growth has moderated since the second quarter of 1996, when gross domestic product expanded at a 4.7 percent annual pace.

Dow Jones News Service. Reprinted with permission.

- At the end of 1996, it was expected that the Fed would not increase interest rates in the immediate future.

- For the seventh consecutive meeting, the FOMC decided against making any changes to monetary policy.

- Policy makers agree that inflation has not increased enough to require tighter credit conditions.

# Economic

## A N A L Y S I S

■ Approximately every 6 weeks, the FOMC meets to review the state of the economy and set policy guidelines for open market operations. For most of 1996, the FOMC made no policy changes.

■ Figure 1 shows the economy in 1995 and 1996.

■ In 1995, real GDP was $6.7 trillion and the price level was 108, at the intersection of the aggregate demand curve $AD_{95}$ and the short-run aggregate supply curve $SAS_{95}$. Also, real GDP was equal to potential GDP—the economy was on long-run aggregate supply curve $LAS_{95}$.

■ By 1996, real GDP had increased to $6.9 trillion and the price level had increased to 110, at the intersection of the aggregate demand curve $AD_{96}$ and the short-run aggregate supply curve $SAS_{96}$. Real GDP remained at potential GDP—the economy was on long-run aggregate supply curve $LAS_{96}$.

■ Looking forward to 1997, the Fed was comfortable with the state of the U.S. economy. Figure 2 shows the Fed's forecast of aggregate demand for 1997 as $AD_{97}$ and short-run aggregate supply curve $SAS_{97}$. The Fed expected real GDP to grow to $7.05 trillion and the price level to rise to 113.

■ If aggregate demand increases to $AD_0$, we will have an inflationary gap. Inflation and real GDP will increase. To counter such an increase, the Fed might tighten money and raise interest rates.

■ If aggregate demand increases to $AD_1$, we will have a recessionary gap. Inflation and real GDP will decrease. To counter such an increase, the Fed might loosen money and lower interest rates.

■ You can see the dilemma the Fed faces every year. If aggregate demand increases by too much, the Fed must try to dampen the economy. If aggregate demand increases by too little, the Fed must try to stimulate the economy. But to be effective, the Fed must anticipate the change in aggregate demand correctly.

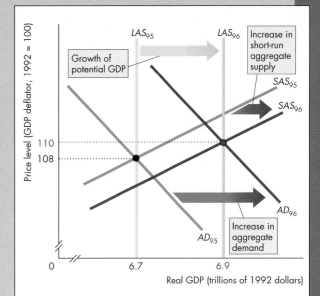

**Figure 1  The economy in 1995 and 1996**

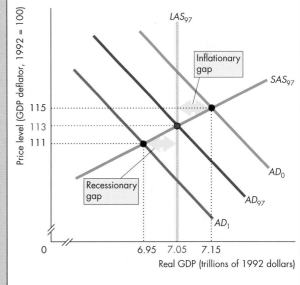

**Figure 2  Some scenarios for 1997**

## You're

### THE VOTER

■ Why did the Fed believe that no monetary policy action was needed during 1996?

■ Did the Fed change interest rates in 1997? If so, by how much, in which direction, and why?

■ What should the Fed do if a recession appears to be likely? What should the Fed do if inflation appears to be likely?

# SUMMARY

## Key Points

### The Federal Reserve System (pp. 316–319)

- The Federal Reserve System is the central bank of the United States.
- The Fed influences the economy by setting the required reserve ratio for banks, by setting the discount rate—the interest rate at which it is willing to lend reserves to the banking system—and by open market operations.

### Controlling the Money Supply (pp. 319–323)

- By buying government securities in the market (an open market purchase), the Fed is able to increase the monetary base and the reserves available to banks.
- There follows an expansion of bank lending and the quantity of money increases.
- By selling government securities, the Fed is able to decrease the monetary base and bank reserves and decrease the quantity of money.

### The Demand for Money (pp. 324–327)

- The quantity of money demanded is the amount of money that people plan to hold.
- The quantity of real money equals the quantity of nominal money divided by the price level.
- The quantity of real money demanded depends on the interest rate and real GDP. A higher interest rate induces a smaller quantity of real money demanded.

### Interest Rate Determination (pp. 327–328)

- Changes in interest rates achieve equilibrium in the markets for money and financial assets.
- Money market equilibrium achieves an interest rate (and an asset price) that makes the quantity of real money available willingly held.
- If the quantity of real money is increased by the actions of the Fed, the interest rate falls and the prices of financial assets rise.

### Monetary Policy (pp. 329–333)

- The Fed directly controls the discount rate and closely targets the federal funds rate, but all short-term rates fluctuate together and the Fed influences all short-term interest rates.
- People attempt to profit by predicting the actions of the Fed. To the extent that they can predict the Fed, interest rates and the price of financial assets move in anticipation of the Fed's actions rather than in response to them.
- Consequently, interest rates change when the Fed changes the money supply only if the Fed catches people by surprise. Anticipated changes in the money supply produce interest rate changes by themselves.
- When the Fed lowers interest rates, it increases aggregate demand, which speeds real GDP growth and inflation. And when the Fed raises interest rates, it decreases aggregate demand, which slows real GDP growth and inflation.

## Key Figures

## Key Terms

# QUESTIONS

1. What is the Federal Reserve System?
2. What are the three main components in the structure of the Federal Reserve System?
3. What are the three policy tools of the Fed? Which of these is the Fed's most frequently used tool?
4. What is the effect of a change in required reserves?
5. What is the effect of a change in the discount rate?
6. What is the effect of an open market operation?
7. If the Fed wants to decrease the quantity of money, does it buy or sell U.S. government securities in the open market?
8. Trace the events that follow an open market purchase of securities by the Fed from a commercial bank.
9. Trace the events that follow an open market purchase of securities by the Fed from the public.
10. Trace the events that follow an open market sale of securities by the Fed to a commercial bank.
11. Trace the events that follow an open market sale of securities by the Fed to the public.
12. What is the money multiplier?
13. Why does an open market operation have a multiplier effect on the quantity of money?
14. Distinguish between nominal money and real money.
15. What is the opportunity cost of holding money?
16. What do we mean by the demand for money?
17. What determines the demand for money?
18. What happens to the interest rate on a bond if the price of the bond increases?
19. How does equilibrium come about in the money market?
20. What happens to the interest rate if the money supply increases?
21. Trace the ripple effects of the Fed's actions when it increases the interest rate.
22. Explain why it pays people to try to predict the Fed's actions.

# PROBLEMS

1. You are given the following information about the economy of Nocoin: The banks have deposits of $300 billion. Their reserves are $15 billion, two thirds of which is in deposits with the central bank. There are $30 billion notes outside the banks. There are no coins in Nocoin!
   a. Calculate the monetary base.
   b. Calculate the currency drain.
   c. Calculate the money supply.
   d. Calculate the money multiplier.
2. Suppose that the Bank of Nocoin, the central bank, undertakes an open market purchase of securities of $0.5 million. What happens to the money supply? Explain why the change in the money supply is not equal to the change in the monetary base.
3. You are given the following information about the economy of Miniland: For each $1 increase in real GDP, the demand for money increases by one quarter of a dollar, other things remaining the same. Also, if the interest rate increases by 1 percentage point (for example, from 4 percent to 5 percent), the quantity of real money demanded falls by $50. If real GDP is $4,000 and the price level is 1,
   a. At what interest rate is no money held?
   b. How much real money is held at an interest rate of 10 percent a year?
   c. Draw a graph of the demand for money.
4. Given the demand for money in Miniland, if the price level is 1, real GDP is $4,000, and the real money supply is $750,
   a. What is the equilibrium interest rate?
   b. What is the equilibrium quantity of real money held?
5. Suppose that the Bank of Miniland, the central bank, wants to lower the interest rate by 1 percentage point. By how much would it have to change the real money supply to achieve that objective?

6. The figure shows the demand for real money in Upland.

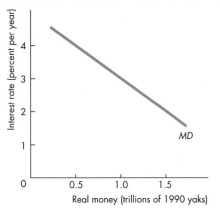

a. In the figure, draw the supply of money curve if the interest rate in Upland is 3 percent a year.

b. Suppose that the Bank of Upland (the central bank) wants to lower the interest rate by 1 percentage point. By how much must it change the real money supply to achieve that objective? Draw the new supply of money curve.

c. Suppose that to change the quantity of money in part (b), the Bank of Upland uses open market operations. Does the Bank of Upland make an open market purchase or an open market sale of securities?

7. Starting from above full-employment equilibrium, briefly explain with the aid of a figure the short-run effect on the price level and real GDP of an open market sale of securities by the Fed. Does such an action help to avoid inflation? Does such an action lower real GDP in the long run?

http://hepg.awl.com/parkin/econ100

# CRITICAL THINKING

1. Study *Reading Between the Lines* on pp. 334–335 and then answer the following questions:
   a. Why did the Fed repeatedly *not* increase interest rates during 1996?
   b. What does the Fed look at when it is deciding whether to change interest rates?
   c. What are the risks from the Fed raising interest rates and from not raising interest rates? Which is the more risky in your opinion and why?
   d. When the Fed does raise interest rates, what actions does it take?

2. Could the Volcker Fed have brought inflation under control without creating a deep recession? If you think the answer is "no," do you think it was wise to lower inflation? If you think the answer is "yes," what would the Fed have had to do differently?

3. Visit the World Wide Web site of the Fed at http://www.bog.frb.fed.us/ (or by using the link on the Parkin Web site) and obtain the latest data on M1, M2, and some short-term interest rates. Then answer the following questions.
   a. Is the Fed trying to slow the economy or speed it up? How can you tell which?
   b. What open market operations do you think the Fed has undertaken during the past month?
   c. Skim the latest minutes of the FOMC, which you can find at the Fed's Web site, and see whether you can discover the open market operations planned.
   d. In the light of the Fed's recent actions, what ripple effects do you expect over the coming months?
   e. What do you think the effects of the Fed's recent actions will be on bond prices and stock prices?

4. Visit the World Wide Web site of the Fed at http://www.bog.frb.fed.us/ (or by using the link on the Parkin Web site) and look at the current economic conditions described in the Beige Book. On the basis of current forecasts by the Fed, do you predict that the Fed will raise interest rates, lower interest rates, or hold interest rates steady? Write a brief summary of your predictions and reasons.

# 15

# Inflation

At the end of the third century A.D., Roman Emperor Diocletian struggled to contain an inflation that raised prices by more than 300 percent a year. At the end of the twentieth century, Russian President Boris Yeltsin struggled to contain a severe inflation that raised prices at a rate of close to 1,000 percent a year. But the most rapid recent inflations have been in Brazil, where the inflation rate hit 40 percent *per month* in 1994, and in Zaire, which had an inflation rate of 75 percent *per month*. What causes rapid inflation? ◆ In comparison with the cases just described, the United States has had remarkable price stability. Nevertheless, during the 1970s, the U.S. price level more than doubled—an inflation of more than 100 percent over the decade. Today, along with the other rich industrial countries, the United States has a low inflation rate at about 2.5 percent a year.

## From Rome to Russia

Why do some countries have a low inflation rate? And why did a more serious inflation break out in the United States during the 1970s? ◆ Most of life's big economic decisions—whether to buy or rent a home, whether to save more for retirement—turn on what is going to happen to inflation. Will inflation increase so our savings buy less? Will inflation decrease so our debts are harder to repay? To make good decisions, we need good forecasts of inflation, and not for just next year but for many years into the future. How do people try to forecast inflation? And how do expectations of inflation influence the economy? ◆ As the inflation rate rises and falls, the unemployment rate and interest rates also fluctuate. What are the links between inflation and the economy that make unemployment and interest rates fluctuate when inflation fluctuates? ◆ In this chapter, you will learn about the forces that generate inflation, the effects of inflation, and the way in which people try to forecast inflation. You will pull together several of the threads you have been following through your study of macroeconomics. And again, you will use the *AS-AD* model of Chapter 7. But first, let's recall what inflation is and how it is measured.

## After studying this chapter, you will be able to:

- **Distinguish between inflation and a one-time rise in the price level**

- **Explain the different ways in which inflation can be generated**

- **Describe how people try to forecast inflation**

- **Explain the short-run and long-run relationships between inflation and unemployment**

- **Explain the short-run and long-run relationships between inflation and interest rates**

## Inflation and the Price Level

WE DON'T HAVE MUCH INFLATION TODAY, BUT during the 1970s it was a major problem. **Inflation** is a process in which the *price level is rising* and *money is losing value.*

If the price level rises persistently, then people need more and more money to make transactions. Incomes rise, so firms must pay out more in wages and other payments to resource owners. And prices rise, so consumers must take more money with them when they go shopping. But the value of money gets smaller and smaller.

A change in one price is not inflation. For example, if the price of hot dogs jumps to $25 and all other money prices fall slightly so that the price level remains constant, there is no inflation. Instead, the relative price of hot dogs has increased. If the price of hot dogs and all other prices rise by a similar percentage, there is inflation.

But a one-time jump in the price level is not inflation. Instead, inflation is an ongoing *process.* Figure 15.1 illustrates this distinction. The red line shows the price level rising continuously. That is inflation. The blue line shows a one-time jump in the price level. This economy is not experiencing inflation. Its price level is constant most of the time.

Inflation is a serious problem, and preventing inflation is the main task of monetary policy and the actions of the Fed. We are going to learn how inflation arises and see how we can avoid the situation shown in the cartoon. But first, let's see how we calculate the inflation rate.

To measure the inflation *rate,* we calculate the annual percentage change in the price level. For example, if this year's price level is 126 and last year's

*"I told you the Fed should have tightened."*

*Drawing by Mankoff; © 1997 The New Yorker Magazine, Inc.*

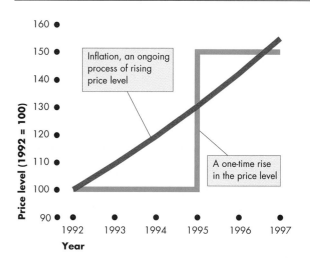

**FIGURE 15.1**

## Inflation Versus a One-Time Rise in the Price Level

Along the red line, an economy experiences inflation because the price level is rising persistently. Along the blue line, an economy experiences a one-time rise in the price level.

price level was 120, the inflation rate is 5 percent per year. That is,

$$\text{Inflation rate} = \frac{126 - 120}{120} \times 100$$

$$= 5 \text{ percent per year.}$$

This equation shows the connection between the *inflation rate* and the *price level.* For a given price level last year, the higher the price level in the current year, the higher is the inflation rate. If the price level is *rising,* the inflation rate is *positive.* If the price level rises at a *faster* rate, the inflation rate *increases.* Also, the higher the new price level, the lower is the value of money, and the higher is the inflation rate.

Inflation can result from either an increase in aggregate demand or a decrease in aggregate supply. These two sources of impulses that can get inflation started are called:

■ Demand pull

■ Cost push

We'll first study a demand-pull inflation.

## Demand-Pull Inflation

AN INFLATION THAT RESULTS FROM AN INITIAL increase in aggregate demand is called **demand-pull inflation**. Such an inflation can arise from any factor that increases aggregate demand such as an:

1. Increase in the money supply
2. Increase in government purchases
3. Increase in exports

### Inflation Effect of an Increase in Aggregate Demand

Suppose that last year the price level was 110 and real GDP was $7 trillion. Potential GDP was also $7 trillion. Figure 15.2(a) illustrates this situation. The aggregate demand curve is $AD_0$, the short-run

aggregate supply curve is $SAS_0$, and the long-run aggregate supply curve is $LAS$.

In the current year, aggregate demand increases to $AD_1$. Such a situation arises if, for example, the Fed loosens its grip on the money supply, or the government increases its purchases of goods and services, or exports increase.

With no change in potential GDP, and with no change in the money wage rate, the long-run aggregate supply curve and the short-run aggregate supply curve remain at $LAS$ and $SAS_0$.

The price level and real GDP are determined at the point where the aggregate demand curve $AD_1$ intersects the short-run aggregate supply curve. The price level rises to 113, and real GDP increases above potential GDP to $7.5 trillion. The economy experiences a 2.7 percent rise in the price level (a price level of 113 compared with 110) and a rapid expansion of real GDP. Unemployment falls below the natural rate. The next step in the unfolding story is a rise in wages.

**FIGURE 15.2**
## A Demand-Pull Rise in the Price Level

**(a) Initial effect**

**(b) Wages adjust**

In part (a), the aggregate demand curve is $AD_0$, the short-run aggregate supply curve is $SAS_0$, and the long-run aggregate supply curve is $LAS$. The price level is 110, and real GDP is $7 trillion, its long-run level. Aggregate demand increases to $AD_1$ (because, for example, the Fed increases the money supply, or the government increases its purchases of goods and services,

or exports increase). The new equilibrium occurs where $AD_1$ intersects $SAS_0$. The price level rises to 113, and real GDP increases to $7.5 trillion. In part (b), starting from above full employment, wages begin to rise and the short-run aggregate supply curve shifts leftward toward $SAS_1$. The price level rises further, and real GDP returns to its long-run level.

## Wage Response

Real GDP cannot remain above potential GDP forever. With unemployment below its natural rate, there is a shortage of labor. In this situation, wages begin to rise. As they do so, short-run aggregate supply decreases and the SAS curve starts to shift leftward. The price level rises further, and real GDP begins to decrease.

With no further change in aggregate demand—the aggregate demand curve remains at $AD_1$—this process ends when the short-run aggregate supply curve has shifted to $SAS_1$ in Fig. 15.2(b). At this time, the price level has increased to 121 and real GDP has returned to potential GDP of $7 trillion, the level from which it started.

## A Demand-Pull Inflation Process

The process we've just studied eventually ends when, for a given increase in aggregate demand, wages have adjusted enough to restore the real wage rate to its full-employment level. We've studied a one-time rise in the price level like that described in Fig. 15.1(b). For inflation to proceed, aggregate demand must persistently increase.

The only way in which aggregate demand can persistently increase is if the quantity of money persistently increases. Suppose the government has a large budget deficit that it finances by selling bonds to the Fed. When the Fed buys these bonds, it creates more money. In this situation, aggregate demand increases year after year. The aggregate demand curve keeps shifting rightward. This persistent increase in aggregate demand puts continual upward pressure on the price level. The economy now experiences demand-pull inflation.

Figure 15.3 illustrates the process of demand-pull inflation. The starting point is the same as that shown in Fig. 15.2. The aggregate demand curve is $AD_0$, the short-run aggregate supply curve is $SAS_0$, and the long-run aggregate supply curve is $LAS$. Real GDP is $7 trillion, and the price level is 110. Aggregate demand increases, shifting the aggregate demand curve to $AD_1$. Real GDP increases to $7.5 trillion, and the price level rises to 113. The economy is at an above full-employment equilibrium. There is a shortage of labor, and the wage rate rises, shifting the short-run aggregate supply curve to $SAS_1$. The price level rises to 121, and real GDP returns to potential GDP.

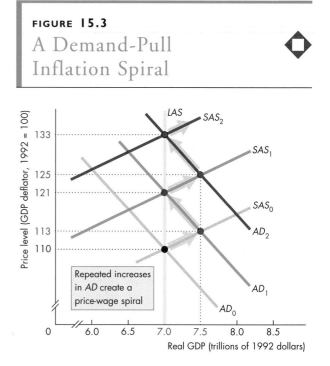

**FIGURE 15.3**

## A Demand-Pull Inflation Spiral

Each time the money supply increases, aggregate demand increases, and the aggregate demand curve shifts rightward from $AD_0$ to $AD_1$ to $AD_2$, and so on. Each time real GDP goes above potential GDP and unemployment goes below the natural rate, the money wage rate rises and the short-run aggregate supply curve shifts leftward from $SAS_0$ to $SAS_1$ to $SAS_2$, and so on. As aggregate demand continues to increase, the price level rises from 110 through 113, 121, 125, to 133, and so on. There is a perpetual demand-pull inflation. Real GDP fluctuates between $7 trillion and $7.5 trillion.

But the money supply increases again, and aggregate demand continues to increase. The aggregate demand curve shifts rightward to $AD_2$. The price level rises further to 125, and real GDP again exceeds potential GDP at $7.5 trillion. Yet again, the wage rate rises and decreases short-run aggregate supply. The $SAS$ curve shifts to $SAS_2$, and the price level rises further to 133. As the money supply continues to grow, aggregate demand increases and the price level rises in an ongoing demand-pull inflation process.

The process you have just studied generates inflation—an ongoing process of a rising price level.

**Demand-Pull Inflation in Kalamazoo**   You may better understand the inflation process that we've just described by considering what is going on in an individual part of the economy, such as a Kalamazoo soda-bottling plant. Initially, when aggregate demand increases, the demand for soda increases and the price of soda rises. Faced with a higher price, the soda plant works overtime and increases production. Conditions are good for workers in Kalamazoo, and the soda factory finds it hard to hang onto its best people. To do so, it has to offer higher wages. As wages increase, so do the soda factory's costs.

What happens next depends on what happens to aggregate demand. If aggregate demand remains constant (as in Fig. 15.2b), the firm's costs are increasing but the price of soda is not increasing as quickly as its costs. Production is scaled back. Eventually, wages and costs increase by the same percentage as the price of soda. In real terms, the soda factory is in the same situation as initially—before the increase in aggregate demand. The plant produces the same amount of soda and employs the same amount of labor as before the increase in demand.

But if aggregate demand continues to increase, so does the demand for soda, and the price of soda rises at the same rate as wages. The soda factory continues to operate above full employment, and there is a persistent shortage of labor. Prices and wages chase each other upward in an unending spiral.

**Demand-Pull Inflation in the United States**   A demand-pull inflation like the one you've just studied occurred in the United States during the 1960s. In 1960, inflation was a moderate 2 percent a year, but its rate increased slowly to 3 percent by 1966. Then, in 1967, a large increase in government purchases on the Vietnam War and an increase in spending on social programs, together with an increase in the growth rate of the money supply, increased aggregate demand more quickly. Consequently, the rightward shift of the aggregate demand curve speeded up and the price level increased more quickly. Real GDP increased above potential GDP, and the unemployment rate fell below the natural rate.

With unemployment below the natural rate, the money wage rate started to rise more quickly and the short-run aggregate supply curve shifted leftward. The Fed responded with a further increase in the money supply growth rate, and a demand-pull inflation spiral unfolded. By 1970, the inflation rate had reached 6 percent a year.

For the next three years, aggregate demand continued to grow quickly and the inflation rate remained around 6 percent a year.

R E V I E W

■ Demand-pull inflation begins when an increase in aggregate demand increases real GDP and increases the price level.
■ At above full employment, the wage rate rises, short-run aggregate supply decreases, real GDP decreases, and the price level rises further.
■ If aggregate demand keeps increasing, wages chase prices in an unending inflation spiral.

Next, let's see how shocks to aggregate supply can create cost-push inflation.

## Cost-Push Inflation

AN INFLATION THAT RESULTS FROM AN INITIAL increase in costs is called **cost-push inflation**. The two main sources of increases in costs are:

1. An increase in money wage rates
2. An increase in the money prices of raw materials

At a given price level, the higher the cost of production, the smaller is the amount that firms are willing to produce. So if money wage rates rise or if the prices of raw materials (for example, oil) rise, firms decrease their supply of goods and services. Aggregate supply decreases, and the short-run aggregate supply curve shifts leftward.[1] Let's trace the effects of such a decrease in short-run aggregate supply on the price level and real GDP.

### Initial Effect of a Decrease in Aggregate Supply

Suppose that last year the price level was 110 and real GDP was $7 trillion. Potential real GDP was also $7 trillion. Figure 15.4 illustrates this situation. The aggregate demand curve was $AD_0$, the short-run aggregate supply curve was $SAS_0$, and the long-run aggregate supply curve was $LAS$. In the current year, the world's oil producers form a price-fixing organization

[1] Some cost-push forces, such as an increase in the price of oil accompanied by a decrease in the availability of oil, can also decrease long-run aggregate supply. We'll ignore such effects here and examine cost-push factors that change only short-run aggregate supply.

### FIGURE 15.4

## A Cost-Push Rise in the Price Level

Initially, the aggregate demand curve is $AD_0$, the short-run aggregate supply curve is $SAS_0$, and the long-run aggregate supply curve is $LAS$. A decrease in aggregate supply (for example, resulting from an increase in the world price of oil) shifts the short-run aggregate supply curve to $SAS_1$. The economy moves to the point where the short-run aggregate supply curve $SAS_1$ intersects the aggregate demand curve $AD_0$. The price level rises to 117, and real GDP decreases to $6.5 trillion. The economy experiences inflation and a contraction of real GDP—*stagflation*.

that strengthens their market power and increases the relative price of oil. They raise the nominal price of oil, and this action decreases short-run aggregate supply. The short-run aggregate supply curve shifts leftward to $SAS_1$. The price level rises to 117, and real GDP decreases to $6.5 trillion. The combination of a rise in the price level and a decrease in real GDP is called **stagflation**.

This event is a one-time rise in the price level like that in Fig. 15.1(b). It is not inflation. In fact, a supply shock on its own cannot cause inflation. Something more must happen to enable a one-time supply shock to be converted into a process of money supply growth and ongoing inflation. The money supply must persistently increase. And it often does increase, as you will now see.

### Aggregate Demand Response

When real GDP falls, the unemployment rate rises above the natural rate. In such a situation, there is usually an outcry of concern and a call for action to restore full employment. Suppose that the Fed increases the money supply. Aggregate demand increases. In Fig. 15.5, the aggregate demand curve shifts rightward to $AD_1$. The increase in aggregate demand has restored full employment. But the price level rises to 121, a 10 percent increase over the initial price level.

### A Cost-Push Inflation Process

The oil producers now see the prices of everything that they buy increase by 10 percent. So they increase the price of oil again to restore its new high relative price. Figure 15.6 continues the story.

### FIGURE 15.5

## Aggregate Demand Response to Cost Push

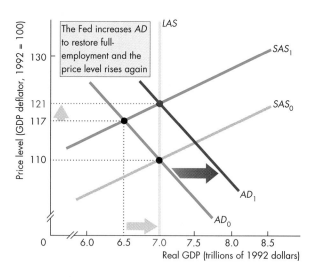

Following a cost-push increase in the price level, real GDP is below potential GDP and unemployment is above the natural rate. If the Fed responds by increasing aggregate demand to restore full employment, the aggregate demand curve shifts rightward to $AD_1$. The economy returns to full employment, but at the expense of more inflation. The price level rises to 121.

The short-run aggregate supply curve now shifts to $SAS_2$, and another bout of stagflation ensues. The price level rises further to 129, and real GDP falls to $6.5 trillion. Unemployment increases above its natural rate. If the Fed responds yet again with an increase in the money supply, aggregate demand increases and the aggregate demand curve shifts to $AD_2$. The price level rises even higher—to 133—and full employment is again restored. A cost-push inflation spiral results. But if the Fed does not respond, the economy remains below full employment.

You can see that the Fed has a dilemma. If it increases the money supply to restore full employment, it invites another oil price hike that will call forth yet a further increase in the money supply.

### FIGURE 15.6
## A Cost-Push Inflation Spiral

When a cost increase (for example, an increase in the world oil price) decreases short-run aggregate supply from $SAS_0$ to $SAS_1$, the price level rises to 117 and real GDP decreases to $6.5 trillion. The Fed responds with an increase in the money supply that shifts the aggregate demand curve from $AD_0$ to $AD_1$. The price level rises again to 121, and real GDP returns to $7 trillion. A further cost increase occurs, which shifts the short-run aggregate supply curve again, this time to $SAS_2$. Stagflation is repeated, and the price level now rises to 129. The Fed responds again, and the cost-price inflation spiral continues.

Inflation will rage along at a rate decided by the oil-exporting nations. If the Fed keeps the lid on money supply growth, real GDP remains below potential GDP.

**Cost-Push Inflation in Kalamazoo** What is going on in the Kalamazoo soda-bottling plant when the economy is experiencing cost-push inflation? When the oil price increases, so do the costs of bottling soda. These higher costs decrease the supply of soda, increasing its price and decreasing the quantity produced. The soda plant lays off some workers. This situation will persist until either the Fed increases aggregate demand or the price of oil falls. If the Fed increases aggregate demand, as it did in the mid-1970s, the demand for soda increases and so does its price. The higher price of soda brings higher profits, and the bottling plant increases its production. The soda factory rehires the laid-off workers.

**Cost-Push Inflation in the United States** A cost-push inflation like the one you've just studied occurred in the United States during the 1970s. It began in 1974 when the Organization for Petroleum Exporting Countries (OPEC) raised the price of oil fourfold. The higher oil price decreased aggregate supply, which caused the price level to rise more quickly and real GDP to shrink. The Fed then faced a dilemma. Would it increase the quantity of money and accommodate the cost-push forces or would it keep aggregate demand growth in check by limiting money growth? In 1975, 1976, and 1977, the Fed repeatedly allowed the money supply to grow quickly, and inflation proceeded at a rapid rate. In 1979 and 1980, OPEC was again able to push oil prices higher. On that occasion, the Fed decided not to respond to the oil price hike with an increase in the money supply. The result was a recession but also, eventually, a fall in inflation.

### R E V I E W

■ Cost-push inflation starts with an increase in the money wage rate or in the money price of a raw material that decreases aggregate supply.
■ Real GDP decreases, and the price level rises—*stagflation* occurs.
■ If the Fed increases aggregate demand to restore full employment, freewheeling cost-push inflation ensues.

# Effects of Inflation

REGARDLESS OF WHETHER INFLATION IS DEMAND-pull or cost-push, the failure to correctly *anticipate* it results in unintended consequences. These unintended consequences impose costs in both labor markets and capital markets. Let's examine these costs.

## Unanticipated Inflation in the Labor Market

Unanticipated inflation has two main consequences for the operation of the labor market:

- Redistribution of income
- Departure from full employment

**Redistribution of Income**    Unanticipated inflation redistributes income between employers and workers. Sometimes employers gain at the expense of workers, and sometimes they lose. If an unexpected increase in aggregate demand increases the inflation rate, then wages will not have been set high enough. Profits will be higher than expected, and wages will buy fewer goods than expected. In this case, employers gain at the expense of workers. But if aggregate demand is expected to increase at a rapid rate and it fails to do so, workers gain at the expense of employers. With a high inflation rate anticipated, wages are set too high and profits are squeezed. Redistribution between employers and workers creates an incentive for both firms and workers to try to forecast inflation correctly.

### Departures from Full Employment
Redistribution brings gains to some and losses to others. But departures from full employment impose costs on everyone. To see why, let's return to the soda-bottling plant in Kalamazoo.

If the bottling plant and its workers do not anticipate inflation, but inflation occurs, the money wage rate does not rise to keep up with inflation. The real wage rate falls, and the firm tries to hire more labor and increase production. But because the real wage rate has fallen, the firm has a hard time attracting the labor it wants to employ. It pays overtime rates to its existing work force, and because it runs its plant at a faster pace, it incurs higher plant maintenance and parts replacement costs. But also, because the real wage rate has fallen, workers begin to quit the bottling plant to find jobs that pay a real wage rate that is closer to one that prevailed before the outbreak of inflation. This labor turnover imposes additional costs on the firm. So even though its production increases, the firm incurs additional costs, and its profits do not increase as much as they otherwise would. The workers incur additional costs of job search, and those who remain at the bottling plant wind up feeling cheated. They've worked overtime to produce the extra output, and when they come to spend their wages, they discover that prices have increased, so their wages buy a smaller quantity of goods and services than expected.

If the bottling plant and its workers anticipate a high inflation rate that does not occur, they increase the money wage rate by too much, and the real wage rate rises. At the higher real wage rate, the firm lays off some workers and the unemployment rate increases. Those workers who keep their jobs gain, but those who become unemployed lose. Also, the bottling plant loses because its output and profits fall.

## Unanticipated Inflation in the Capital Market

Unanticipated inflation has two consequences for the operation of the capital market. They are:

- Redistribution of income
- Too much or too little lending and borrowing

**Redistribution of Income**    Unanticipated inflation redistributes income between borrowers and lenders. Sometimes borrowers gain at the expense of lenders, and sometimes they lose. When inflation is unexpected, interest rates are not set high enough to compensate lenders for the falling value of money. In this case, borrowers gain at the expense of lenders. But if inflation is expected and then fails to occur, interest rates are set too high. In this case, lenders gain at the expense of borrowers. Redistributions of income between borrowers and lenders create an incentive for both groups to try to forecast inflation correctly.

### Too Much or Too Little Lending and Borrowing
If the inflation rate turns out to be either higher or lower than expected, the interest rate does not incorporate a correct allowance for the falling value of money and the real interest rate is either lower or higher than it otherwise would be. When the real

interest rate turns out to be too low, which occurs when inflation is *higher* than expected, borrowers wish they had borrowed more and lenders wish they had lent less. Both groups would have made different lending and borrowing decisions with greater foresight about the inflation rate. When the real interest rate turns out to be too high, which occurs when inflation is *lower* than expected, borrowers wish they had borrowed less and lenders wish they had lent more. Again, both groups would have made different lending and borrowing decisions with greater foresight about the inflation rate.

So unanticipated inflation imposes costs regardless of whether the inflation turns out to be higher or lower than anticipated. The presence of these costs gives everyone an incentive to forecast inflation correctly. Let's see how people go about this task.

## Forecasting Inflation

Inflation is difficult to forecast. The reasons are, first, there are several sources of inflation—the demand-pull and cost-push sources you've just studied. Second, the speed with which a change in either aggregate demand or aggregate supply translates into a change in the price level varies. This speed of response also depends, as you will see below, on the extent to which the inflation is anticipated.

Because inflation is costly and difficult to forecast, people devote considerable resources to improving inflation forecasts. Some people specialize in forecasting, and others buy forecasts from specialists. The specialist forecasters are economists who work for public and private macroeconomic forecasting agencies and for banks, insurance companies, labor unions, and large corporations. The returns these specialists make depend on the quality of their forecasts, so they have a strong incentive to forecast as accurately as possible. The most accurate forecast possible is the one that is based on all the relevant information and is called a **rational expectation**.

A rational expectation is not a correct forecast. It is simply the best forecast available. It will often turn out to be wrong, but no other forecast that could have been made with the information available could be predicted to be better.

You've seen the effects of inflation when people fail to anticipate it. And you've seen why it pays to try to anticipate inflation. Let's now see what happens if inflation is correctly anticipated.

## Anticipated Inflation

In the demand-pull and cost-push inflations that we studied earlier in this chapter, money wages are sticky. When aggregate demand increases, either to set off a demand-pull inflation or to accommodate cost-push inflation, the money wage does not change immediately. But if people correctly anticipate increases in aggregate demand, they will adjust money wage rates so as to keep up with anticipated inflation.

In this case, inflation proceeds with real GDP equal to potential GDP and unemployment equal to the natural rate. Figure 15.7 explains why. Suppose that last year the price level was 110 and real GDP was $7 trillion, which is also potential GDP. The aggregate demand curve was $AD_0$, the aggregate supply curve was $SAS_0$, and the long-run aggregate supply curve was *LAS*.

Suppose that potential GDP does not change, so the *LAS* curve does not shift. Also suppose that aggregate demand is expected to increase and that the expected aggregate demand curve for this year is $AD_1$. In anticipation of this increase in aggregate demand, money wage rates rise and the short-run aggregate supply curve shifts leftward. If the money wage rate rises by the same percentage as the price level rises, the short-run aggregate supply curve for next year is $SAS_1$.

If aggregate demand turns out to be the same as expected, the aggregate demand curve is $AD_1$ and with the short-run aggregate supply curve $SAS_1$ the actual price level is 121. Between last year and this year, the price level increased from 110 to 121 and the economy experienced an inflation rate of 10 percent, the same as the inflation rate that was anticipated. If this anticipated inflation is ongoing, in the following year aggregate demand increases (as anticipated) and the aggregate demand curve shifts to $AD_2$. The money wage rate rises to reflect the anticipated inflation, and the short-run aggregate supply curve shifts to $SAS_2$. The price level rises by a further 10 percent to 133.

What has caused this inflation? The immediate answer is that because people expected inflation, wages were increased and prices increased. But the expectation was correct. Aggregate demand was expected to increase, and it did increase. Because aggregate demand was *expected* to increase from $AD_0$ to $AD_1$, the short-run aggregate supply curve shifted from $SAS_0$ to $SAS_1$. Because aggregate demand actually did increase by the amount that was expected, the actual aggregate demand curve shifted from $AD_0$

to $AD_1$. The combination of the anticipated and actual increases in aggregate demand produced an increase in the price level that was anticipated.

Only if aggregate demand growth is correctly forecasted does the economy follow the course described in Fig. 15.7. If the expected growth rate of aggregate demand is different from its actual growth rate, the expected aggregate demand curve shifts by an amount that is different from the actual aggregate demand curve. The inflation rate departs from its expected level, and to some extent, there is unanticipated inflation.

## FIGURE 15.7

# Anticipated Inflation

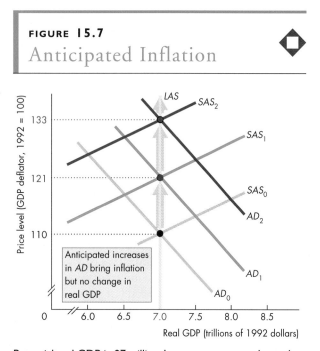

Potential real GDP is $7 trillion. Last year, aggregate demand was $AD_0$, and the short-run aggregate supply curve was $SAS_0$. The actual price level was the same as the expected price level—110. This year, aggregate demand is expected to increase to $AD_1$. The rational expectation of the price level changes from 110 to 121. As a result, wages rise and the short-run aggregate supply curve shifts to $SAS_1$. If aggregate demand actually increases as expected, the actual aggregate demand curve $AD_1$ is the same as the expected aggregate demand curve. Equilibrium occurs at a real GDP of $7 trillion and an actual price level of 121. The inflation is correctly anticipated. Next year the process continues with aggregate demand increasing as expected to $AD_2$ and wages rising to shift the short-run aggregate supply curve to $SAS_2$. Again, real GDP remains at $7 trillion, and the price level rises, as anticipated, to 133.

## Unanticipated Inflation

When aggregate demand increases by *more* than expected, there is some unanticipated inflation that looks just like the demand-pull inflation that you studied earlier. Some inflation is expected, and the money wage rate is set to reflect that expectation. The $SAS$ curve intersects the $LAS$ curve at the expected price level. Aggregate demand then increases, but by more than expected. So the $AD$ curve intersects the $SAS$ curve at a level of real GDP that exceeds potential GDP. With real GDP above potential GDP and unemployment below the natural rate, the money wage rate rises. So the price level rises further. If aggregate demand increases again, a demand-pull inflation spiral unwinds.

When aggregate demand increases by *less* than expected, there is some unanticipated inflation that looks like the cost-push inflation that you studied earlier. Again, some inflation is expected, and the money wage rate is set to reflect that expectation. The $SAS$ curve intersects the $LAS$ curve at the expected price level. Aggregate demand then increases, but by less than expected. So the $AD$ curve intersects the $SAS$ curve at a level of real GDP below potential GDP. Aggregate demand increases to restore full employment. But if aggregate demand is expected to increase by more than it actually does, wages again rise, short-run aggregate supply again decreases, and a cost-push spiral unwinds.

We've seen that only when inflation is unanticipated does real GDP depart from potential GDP. When inflation is anticipated, real GDP remains at potential GDP. Does this mean that an anticipated inflation has no costs?

## The Costs of Anticipated Inflation

The costs of an anticipated inflation depend on its rate. At a moderate rate of 2 or 3 percent a year, the cost is probably small. But as the anticipated inflation rate rises, so do its costs, and an anticipated inflation at a rapid rate can be extremely costly.

Anticipated inflation decreases potential GDP and slows economic growth. These adverse consequences arise for three major reasons:

■ Transactions costs

■ Tax effects

■ Increased uncertainty

**Transactions Costs**    The first transactions costs
are known as the "boot leather costs." These are costs
that arise from an increase in the velocity of circulation of money and an increase in the amount of running around that people do to try to avoid incurring
losses from the falling value of money.

When money loses value at a rapid anticipated
rate, it does not function well as a store of value and
people try to avoid holding money. They spend their
incomes as soon as they receive them, and firms pay
out incomes—wages and dividends—as soon as they
receive revenue from their sales. The velocity of circulation increases. During the 1920s, when inflation in
Germany reached *hyperinflation* levels (rates more
than 50 percent a month), wages were paid and
spent twice in a single day!

The range of estimates of the boot leather costs
is large. Some economists put the cost at close to
zero. Others estimate it to be as much 2 percent of
GDP for a 10 percent inflation. For a rapid inflation,
these costs are much more.

The boot leather costs of inflation are just one
of several transactions costs that are influenced by
the inflation rate. At high anticipated inflation rates,
people seek alternatives to money as a means of
payment and use tokens and commodities or even
barter, all of which are less efficient than money as a
means of payment. For example, in Israel during the
1980s, when inflation reached 1,000 percent a year,
the U.S. dollar started to replace the increasingly
worthless shekel. Consequently, people had to keep
track of the exchange rate between the shekel and
the dollar hour by hour and had to engage in many
additional and costly transactions in the foreign
exchange market.

Because anticipated inflation increases transactions
costs, it diverts resources from producing goods and
services and it decreases potential GDP. The faster the
anticipated inflation rate, the greater is the decrease
in potential GDP and the further leftward does the
*LAS* curve shift.

**Tax Effects**    Anticipated inflation interacts with
the tax system and creates serious distortions in
incentives. Its major effect is on real interest rates.

Anticipated inflation swells the dollar returns on
investments. But dollar returns are taxed, so the effective tax rate rises. This effect becomes serious at even
modest inflation rates. Let's consider an example.

Suppose the real interest rate is 4 percent a year
and the tax rate is 50 percent. With no inflation, the

nominal interest rate is also 4 percent a year and 50
percent of this rate is taxable. The real *after-tax* interest rate is 2 percent a year (50 percent of 4 percent).
Now suppose the inflation rate is 4 percent a year,
so the nominal interest rate is 8 percent a year. The
nominal *after-tax* rate is 4 percent a year (50 percent
of 8 percent). Now subtract the 4 percent inflation
rate from this amount, and you see that the *real after-
tax interest rate* is zero! The true tax rate on interest
income is 100 percent.

The higher the inflation rate, the higher is the
effective tax rate on income from capital. And the
higher the tax rate, the higher is the interest rate paid
by borrowers and the lower is the after-tax interest
rate received by lenders (see Chapter 12, p. 284).

With a low after-tax real interest rate, the incentive to save is weakened and the saving rate falls.
With a high cost of borrowing, the amount of investment decreases. And with a fall in saving and investment, the pace of capital accumulation slows and so
does the long-term growth rate of real GDP.

**Increased Uncertainty**    When the inflation rate
is high, there is increased uncertainty about the
long-term inflation rate. Will inflation remain high
for a long time or will price stability be restored?
This increased uncertainty makes long-term planning difficult and gives people a shorter-term focus.
Investment falls, and so the growth rate slows.

But this increased uncertainty also misallocates
resources. Instead of concentrating on the activities
at which they have a comparative advantage, people
find it more profitable to search for ways of avoiding
the losses that inflation inflicts. As a result, inventive
talent that might otherwise work on productive innovations works on finding ways of profiting from the
inflation instead.

The implications of inflation for economic
growth have been estimated to be enormous. Peter
Howitt of Ohio State University, building on work
by Robert Barro of Harvard University, has estimated
that if inflation is lowered from 3 percent a year to
zero, the growth rate of real GDP will rise by between
0.06 and 0.09 percentage points a year. These numbers might seem small. But they are growth rates.
After 30 years, real GDP would be 2.3 percent higher
and the present value of all the future output would
be 85 percent of current GDP—almost $6 trillion!
In the rapid anticipated inflations of Brazil and
Russia, the costs are much greater than the numbers
given here.

## REVIEW

▪ Wrong inflation forecasts are costly, and to minimize forecasting errors, people use all the available information and make a *rational expectation*.

▪ Anticipated changes in aggregate demand and aggregate supply result in anticipated inflation.

▪ A rapid anticipated inflation diverts resources from producing goods and services and decreases potential GDP.

You've seen that an increase in aggregate demand that is not fully anticipated increases both the price level and real GDP. It also decreases unemployment. Similarly, a decrease in aggregate demand that is not fully anticipated decreases the price level and real GDP. It also increases unemployment. Do these relationships mean that there is a tradeoff between inflation and unemployment? That is, does low unemployment always bring inflation and does low inflation bring high unemployment? We explore these questions next.

# Inflation and Unemployment: The Phillips Curve

The AGGREGATE SUPPLY–AGGREGATE DEMAND model focuses on the price level and real GDP. Knowing how these two variables change, we can work out what happens to the inflation rate and the unemployment rate. But the model does not place inflation and unemployment at the center of the stage.

A more direct way of studying inflation and unemployment uses a relationship called the Phillips curve. The Phillips curve approach uses the same basic ideas as the *AS-AD* model, but it focuses directly on inflation and unemployment. The Phillips curve is so named because New Zealand economist A.W. Phillips popularized it. A **Phillips curve** is a curve that shows a relationship between inflation and unemployment. There are two time frames for Phillips curves:

▪ The short-run Phillips curve
▪ The long-run Phillips curve

## The Short-Run Phillips Curve

The **short-run Phillips curve** is a curve that shows the tradeoff between inflation and unemployment, holding constant:

1. The expected inflation rate
2. The natural unemployment rate

You've just seen what determines the expected inflation rate. The natural rate of unemployment and the factors that influence it are explained in Chapter 8 on pp. 178, 183–185.

Figure 15.8 shows a short-run Phillips curve, *SRPC*. Suppose that the expected inflation rate is 10 percent a year and the natural unemployment rate is

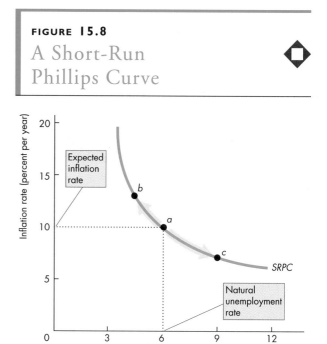

**FIGURE 15.8**

## A Short-Run Phillips Curve

The short-run Phillips curve (*SRPC*) shows the relationship between inflation and unemployment at a given expected inflation rate and given natural unemployment rate. With an expected inflation rate of 10 percent a year and a natural unemployment rate of 6 percent, the short-run Phillips curve passes through point *a*. An unanticipated increase in aggregate demand lowers unemployment and increases inflation—a movement up the short-run Phillips curve. An unanticipated decrease in aggregate demand increases unemployment and lowers inflation—a movement down the short-run Phillips curve.

6 percent, point *a* in the figure. A short-run Phillips curve passes through this point. If inflation rises above its expected rate, unemployment falls below its natural rate. This joint movement in the inflation rate and the unemployment rate is illustrated as a movement up the short-run Phillips curve from point *a* to point *b* in the figure. Similarly, if inflation falls below its expected rate, unemployment rises above the natural rate. In this case there is movement down the short-run Phillips curve from point *a* to point *c*.

This negative relationship between inflation and unemployment along the short-run Phillips curve is explained by the aggregate supply–aggregate demand model. Figure 15.9 shows the connection between the two approaches. Initially, the aggregate demand curve is $AD_0$, the short-run aggregate supply curve is $SAS_0$, and the long-run aggregate supply curve is *LAS*. Real GDP is $7 trillion, and the price level is 100. Aggregate demand is expected to increase, and the aggregate demand curve is expected to shift rightward to $AD_1$. Anticipating this increase in aggregate demand, the money wage rate rises, which shifts the short-run aggregate supply curve to $SAS_1$. What happens to actual inflation and real GDP depends on the *actual* change in aggregate demand.

First, suppose that aggregate demand actually increases by the amount expected, so the aggregate demand curve shifts to $AD_1$. The price level rises from 100 to 110, and the inflation rate is an anticipated 10 percent a year. Real GDP remains at potential GDP, and unemployment remains at the natural rate. The economy moves to point *a* in Fig. 15.9, and it can equivalently be described as being at point *a* on the short-run Phillips curve in Fig. 15.8.

Alternatively, suppose that aggregate demand is expected to increase to $AD_1$ but actually increases by more than expected to $AD_2$. The price level now rises to 113, a 13 percent inflation rate. Real GDP increases above potential GDP, and unemployment falls below the natural rate. We can now describe the economy as moving to point *b* in Fig. 15.9 or at point *b* on the short-run Phillips curve in Fig. 15.8.

Finally, suppose that aggregate demand is expected to increase to $AD_1$ but actually remains at $AD_0$. The price level now rises to 107, a 7 percent inflation rate. Real GDP falls below potential GDP, and unemployment rises above the natural rate. We can now describe the economy as moving to point *c* in Fig. 15.9 or at point *c* on the short-run Phillips curve in Fig. 15.8.

**FIGURE 15.9**

## *AS-AD* and the Short-Run Phillips Curve

If aggregate demand is expected to increase and shift the aggregate demand curve from $AD_0$ to $AD_1$, then the money wage rate rises by an amount that shifts the short-run aggregate supply curve from $SAS_0$ to $SAS_1$. The price level rises to 110, a 10 percent rise, and the economy is at point *a* in this figure and at point *a* on the short-run Phillips curve in Fig. 15.8. If, with the same expectations, aggregate demand increases and shifts the aggregate demand curve from $AD_0$ to $AD_2$, the price level rises to 113, a 13 percent rise, and the economy is at point *b* in this figure and at point *b* on the short-run Phillips curve in Fig. 15.8. If, with the same expectations, aggregate demand does not change, the price level rises to 107, a 7 percent rise, and the economy is at point *c* in this figure and at point *c* on the short-run Phillips curve in Fig. 15.8.

The short-run Phillips curve is like the short-run aggregate supply curve. A movement along the *SAS* curve that brings a higher price level and an increase in real GDP is equivalent to a movement along the short-run Phillips curve that brings an increase in the inflation rate and a decrease in the unemployment rate. (Similarly, a movement along the *SAS* curve that brings a lower price level and a decrease in real GDP is equivalent to a movement along the short-run Phillips curve that brings a decrease in the inflation rate and an increase in the unemployment rate.)

## The Long-Run Phillips Curve

The **long-run Phillips curve** is a curve that shows the relationship between inflation and unemployment when the actual inflation rate equals the expected inflation rate. The long-run Phillips curve is vertical at the natural unemployment rate. It is shown in Fig. 15.10 as the vertical line $LRPC$. The long-run Phillips curve tells us that any anticipated inflation rate is possible at the natural unemployment rate. This proposition is the same as the one you discovered in the *AS-AD* model. When inflation is anticipated, real GDP equals potential GDP. And with real GDP equal to potential GDP, unemployment is at the natural rate.

When the expected inflation rate changes, the short-run Phillips curve shifts. If the expected inflation rate is 10 percent a year, the short-run Phillips curve is $SRPC_0$. If the expected inflation rate falls to

7 percent a year, the short-run Phillips curve shifts downward to $SRPC_1$. The distance by which the short-run Phillips curve shifts downward when the expected inflation rate falls is equal to the change in the expected inflation rate.

To see why the short-run Phillips curve shifts when the expected inflation rate changes, let's do a thought experiment. There is full employment, and a 10 percent a year anticipated inflation is raging. The Fed now begins an attack on inflation by slowing money supply growth. Aggregate demand growth slows, and the inflation rate falls to 7 percent a year. At first, this decrease in inflation is *un*anticipated, so wages continue to rise at their original rate. The short-run aggregate supply curve shifts leftward at the same pace as before. Real GDP falls, and unemployment increases. In Fig. 15.10, the economy moves from point *a* to point *c* on $SRPC_0$.

If the actual inflation rate remains steady at 7 percent a year, this rate eventually comes to be expected. As this happens, wage growth slows and the short-run aggregate supply curve shifts leftward less quickly. Eventually, it shifts leftward at the same pace at which the aggregate demand curve is shifting rightward. The actual inflation rate equals the expected inflation rate, and full employment is restored. Unemployment is back at its natural rate. In Fig. 15.10, the short-run Phillips curve has shifted from $SRPC_0$ to $SRPC_1$ and the economy is at point *d*.

An increase in the expected inflation rate has the opposite effect to that shown in Fig. 15.10. Another important source of shifts in the Phillips curve is a change in the natural rate of unemployment.

## Changes in the Natural Unemployment Rate

The natural unemployment rate changes for many reasons (see Chapter 8, pp. 183–184). A change in the natural unemployment rate shifts both the short-run and long-run Phillips curves. Figure 15.11 illustrates such shifts. If the natural unemployment rate increases from 6 percent to 9 percent, the long-run Phillips curve shifts from $LRPC_0$ to $LRPC_1$, and if expected inflation is constant at 10 percent a year, the short-run Phillips curve shifts from $SRPC_0$ to $SRPC_1$. Because the expected inflation rate is constant, the short-run Phillips curve $SRPC_1$ intersects the long-run curve $LRPC_1$ (point *e*) at the same inflation rate at which the short-run Phillips curve $SRPC_0$ intersects the long-run curve $LRPC_0$ (point *a*).

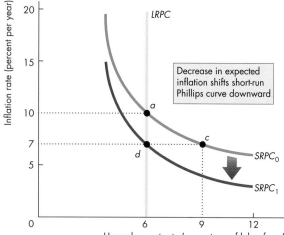

### FIGURE 15.10
## Short-Run and Long-Run Phillips Curves

The long-run Phillips curve is $LRPC$, a vertical line at the natural unemployment rate. A fall in expected inflation shifts the short-run Phillips curve downward. For example, when the expected inflation rate falls from 10 percent a year to 7 percent a year, the short-run Phillips curve shifts downward from $SRPC_0$ and $SRPC_1$. The new short-run Phillips curve intersects the long-run Phillips curve at the new expected inflation rate—point *d*. With the original expected inflation rate (of 10 percent), an actual inflation rate of 7 percent a year would occur at an unemployment rate of 9 percent, at point *c*.

## The U.S. Phillips Curve

Figure 15.12(a) is a scatter diagram of inflation and unemployment since 1960. The Phillips curve does not jump out of this figure. But we can interpret the data in terms of a shifting short-run Phillips curve as in Fig. 15.12(b). During the 1960s, the natural rate of unemployment was 5 percent and the expected inflation rate was 2 percent a year (point *a*), so the short-run Phillips curve was $SRPC_0$. During the 1970s and through 1981, the expected inflation rate and the natural unemployment rate increased and the short-run Phillips curve shifted rightward to $SRPC_1$, $SRPC_2$, and $SRPC_3$. During the 1980s and 1990s, the expected inflation rate and the natural unemployment rate decreased and the short-run Phillips curve shifted leftward. By the early 1990s, the curve was back at $SRPC_1$. And by 1996, the natural unemployment rate and the expected inflation rate were back around their 1960s levels, so the short-run Phillips curve was back at $SRPC_0$.

**FIGURE 15.12**

## Phillips Curves in the United States

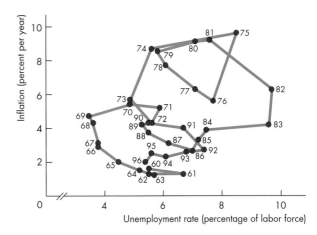

**(a) Time sequence**

**FIGURE 15.11**

## A Change in the Natural Unemployment Rate

A change in the natural unemployment rate shifts both the short-run and long-run Phillips curves. Here the natural unemployment rate increases from 6 percent to 9 percent, and the two Phillips curves shift right to $SRPC_1$ and $LRPC_1$. The new long-run Phillips curve intersects the new short-run Phillips curve at the expected inflation rate—point *e*.

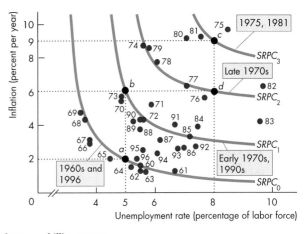

**(b) Four Phillips curves**

In part (a), each dot represents the combination of inflation and unemployment for a particular year in the United States. There is no clear relationship between the two variables. Part (b) interprets the data with a shifting short-run Phillips curve. The black dots *a*, *b*, *c*, and *d* show the combination of the natural rate of unemployment and the expected inflation rate in different periods. The short-run Phillips curve was $SRPC_0$ during the 1960s and in 1996. It was $SRPC_1$ during the early 1970s and 1990s, $SRPC_2$ during the late 1970s, and $SRPC_3$ (briefly) in 1975 and 1981.

- Unanticipated changes in the inflation rate bring movements along the short-run Phillips curve.

- An unanticipated increase in the inflation rate lowers the unemployment rate, and an unanticipated decrease in the inflation rate raises the unemployment rate.

- A change in the expected inflation rate shifts the short-run Phillips curve (upward for an increase in inflation and downward for a decrease in inflation) by an amount equal to the change in the expected inflation rate.

- A change in the natural unemployment rate shifts both the short-run and long-run Phillips curves (rightward for an increase in the natural rate and leftward for a decrease).

- The relationship between inflation and unemployment in the United States can be interpreted by a short-run Phillips curve that shifts.

So far, we've studied the effects of inflation on real GDP, real wages, employment, and unemployment. But inflation lowers the value of money and changes the real value of the amounts borrowed and repaid. As a result, interest rates are influenced by inflation. Let's see how.

# Interest Rates and Inflation

TODAY, BUSINESSES IN THE UNITED STATES CAN borrow at interest rates of around 6 percent a year. Businesses in Russia pay interest rates of 60 percent a year, and those in Turkey pay 75 percent a year. Although U.S. interest rates have never been as high as these two cases, during the 1980s, U.S. businesses faced interest rates of 16 percent or higher. Why do interest rates vary so much both across countries and over time? The answer is because the inflation rate varies. When the inflation rate changes, nominal interest rates change to make borrowers pay the amount that compensates lenders for the fall in the value of money. Let's see how inflation affects borrowers and lenders and how it leads to changes in interest rates.

## The Effects of Inflation on Borrowers and Lenders

The *nominal* interest rate is the price paid by a borrower to compensate a lender for two things: the amount loaned and the fall in the value of money that results from inflation. The *real* interest rate is the price paid by a borrower to compensate a lender only for the amount loaned. It is the real cost of a loan to the borrower and the real return on a loan to the lender. The forces of demand and supply determine an equilibrium real interest rate that does not depend on the inflation rate. These same forces also determine an equilibrium nominal interest rate that does depend on the inflation rate and that equals the equilibrium real interest rate plus the expected inflation rate.

To see why these outcomes occur, imagine that there is no inflation and that the nominal interest rate is 4 percent a year. The real interest rate is also 4 percent a year. The amount that businesses and people want to borrow equals the amount that businesses and people want to lend at this real interest rate. Walt Disney Corporation is willing to pay an interest rate of 4 percent a year to get the funds it needs to pay for its global investment in new theme parks. Sue and thousands of people like her are willing to lend Disney the amount it needs for its theme parks if they can get a *real* return of 4 percent a year. (Sue wants to buy a new car, and she plans to save enough to do so.)

Now suppose inflation breaks out at a steady 6 percent a year. All dollar prices and values, including theme park profits and car prices rise by 6 percent a year. If Disney was willing to pay a 4 percent interest rate when there was no inflation, it is now willing to pay 10 percent interest. The reason is that its profits are rising by 6 percent a year, so it is *really* paying only 4 percent. Similarly, if Sue was willing to lend at a 4 percent interest rate when there was no inflation, she is now willing to lend only if she gets 10 percent interest. The price of the car Sue is planning on buying is rising by 6 percent a year, so she is *really* getting only a 4 percent interest rate.

Because borrowers are willing to pay the higher rate and lenders are willing to lend only if they receive the higher rate, when inflation is anticipated, the *nominal interest rate* increases by an amount equal to the expected inflation rate. The *real interest rate* remains constant. The real interest rate might change because the supply of saving or investment demand has changed for some other reason. But a change in the expected inflation rate alone does not change the real interest rate.

Do the effects of inflation on interest rates that we've just described actually occur? Let's look at the U.S. experience.

### Inflation and Interest Rates in the United States

Figure 15.13 shows the relationship between inflation and nominal interest rates in the United States between 1960 and 1996. Each point represents a year. The interest rate is that paid by large corporations on 6-month loans. The blue line shows the relationship between the nominal interest rate and the inflation rate if the real interest rate is constant at 2.1 percent a year, which is its actual average value in this period. When the red dot lies above the blue line, the real interest rate exceeds 2.1 percent a year, and when the red dot lies below the blue line, the real interest rate is less than 2.4 percent a year.

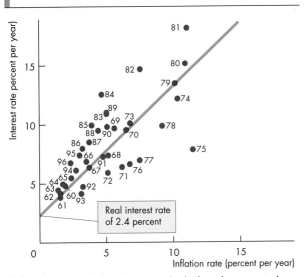

**FIGURE 15.13**

## Inflation and the Interest Rate

Other things remaining the same, the higher the expected inflation rate, the higher is the nominal interest rate. A graph showing the relationship between nominal interest rates and the actual inflation rate reveals that the influence of inflation on nominal interest rates is a powerful one.

*Source: Economic Report of the President, 1997.*

There is a positive relationship between the inflation rate and the interest rate, but the real interest rate has not been constant. During the 1960s, inflation and nominal interest rates were low. In the early 1970s, inflation began to increase, but it was not expected to increase much and certainly not to persist. As a result, nominal interest rates did not rise very much at that time. During the late 1970s and early 1980s, inflation of close to 10 percent a year came to be expected as an ongoing and highly persistent phenomenon. As a result, nominal interest rates increased to around 15 percent a year. Then in 1984 and 1985, the inflation rate fell—at first unexpectedly. Interest rates began to fall but not nearly as quickly as the inflation rate. Short-term interest rates fell more quickly than long-term interest rates because, at that time, it was expected that inflation would be lower in the short term but not as low in the longer term.

By the 1990s, inflation and the nominal interest rate had returned to their 1960s levels, and with inflation near its expected rate, the real interest rate was close to its long-term average of 2.1 percent a year.

The relationship between inflation and interest rates is even more dramatically illustrated by international experience. For example, in recent years, Chile has experienced an inflation rate of around 30 percent with nominal interest rates of about 40 percent. Brazil has experienced inflation rates and nominal interest rates of 40 percent a *month*. At the other extreme, countries such as Japan and Belgium have low inflation and low nominal interest rates.

## R E V I E W

- The real interest rate is equal to the nominal interest rate minus the inflation rate.
- An increase in the inflation rate brings an increase in the nominal interest rate.

◆ *Reading Between the Lines* on pages 356–357 looks at the current low inflation in the United States and the Fed's actions to keep it that way.

You have now completed your study of inflation. This material, together with that on economic growth (Chapter 10), gives a good overview of the long-term problems that confront a modern economy such as that of the United States. Our task in the following chapter is to focus more sharply on the problems of short-term fluctuations and the business cycle.

# Keeping Inflation Down

THE CINCINNATI ENQUIRER, JANUARY 22, 1997

## Greenspan Reports Economy Still Strong

BY LAURA COHN AND MICHAEL McKEE
BLOOMBERG NEWS

The U.S. economy remains strong with few signs of immediate inflationary pressures even as an era of low wage gains may be ending, Federal Reserve Chairman Alan Greenspan said Tuesday.

"The economy has retained considerable vigor, with few signs of the imbalances and inflationary tensions that have disrupted past expansions," Mr. Greenspan said. "By some important measures of price trends, inflation actually slowed a bit in 1996."

Analysts interpreted Mr. Greenspan's comments to the Senate Budget committee as suggesting the Fed's policy-making Open Market committee won't raise interest rates when it meets Feb. 4-5.

Still, the Fed chairman left the door ajar for action later if inflation accelerates because of rising wage levels. Though it has taken a while, tight labor markets are beginning to put upward pressure on wages.

"The relatively modest wage gains we've seen are a transitional rather than a lasting phenomenon," Mr. Greenspan said. "Indeed, the recent pickup in some measures of wages suggests that the transition may already be running its course."

If that's the case, the Fed chairman suggested the central bank will have to consider raising the federal funds rate on overnight bank loans it controls.

So far, wages have increased only at a modest pace and that has kept prices in check, according to Sung Won Sohn, chief economist at Norwest Corp. Mr. Greenspan "made it clear that we are probably at the end of that good luck period," Mr. Sohn said. "From here on, we should expect somewhat higher rate of wage gains and, therefore, inflation."

Mr. Sohn also said Mr. Greenspan's comments—as well as the overall economic outlook—suggest the Fed will raise the rate on overnight bank loans by about a quarter percent this spring from 5.25 percent. That's "likely to be followed by another couple of tightenings later this year," he said. ...

Bloomberg News. Reprinted with permission.

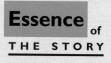

## Essence of THE STORY

■ The U.S. economy continues to expand with few signs of inflation. According to some measures, inflation slowed during 1996.

■ Wage gains were moderate during 1996, but the latest upswing in wage rates could indicate that inflation might accelerate.

■ To combat inflation, the Fed may raise interest rates in the spring and follow this with further increases later.

# Economic

## A N A L Y S I S

■ Figure 1 shows the inflation rate and the earnings growth rate from January 1995 to December 1996. Inflation has been on a slight upward trend since late 1995.

■ Figure 2 interprets the changes in inflation and unemployment by using the Phillips curve.

■ In January 1995, the long-run Phillips curve was $LRPC_0$ at the (assumed) natural unemployment rate of 5.7 percent. The short-run Phillips curve was $SRPC_0$, and unemployment was slightly below the natural rate.

■ With unemployment below the natural rate, inflation increased. The expected inflation rate also increased and the short-run Phillips curve shifted upward to $SRPC_1$.

■ In May 1995, the unemployment rate remained below the natural rate.

■ But during the rest of 1995 and the first half of 1996, the natural rate of unemployment decreased to (an assumed) 5.5 percent and the long-run Phillips curve shifted leftward to $LRPC_1$. The short-run Phillips curve also shifted leftward to $SRPC_2$.

■ In February 1996, unemployment was close to the new natural rate.

■ During the second half of 1996, the natural rate of unemployment remained at (an assumed) 5.5 percent but the actual unemployment rate decreased below the natural rate.

■ By September 1996, the inflation rate had increased to 3 percent a year.

■ The long-run Phillips curve remained at $LRPC_1$, but the expected inflation rate increased and by December 1996, the short-run Phillips curve shifted back to $SRPC_0$.

■ Whether inflation is going to continue to increase depends on how rapidly the money supply grows. The Fed is committed to maintaining non-inflationary money growth, and Fig. 3 shows that it is succeeding.

■ From April 1995 to March 1996, M2 growth increased. Through the rest of 1996, M2 growth has been steady at about 4 percent a year.

■ An M2 growth rate of this magnitude is likely to keep inflation low.

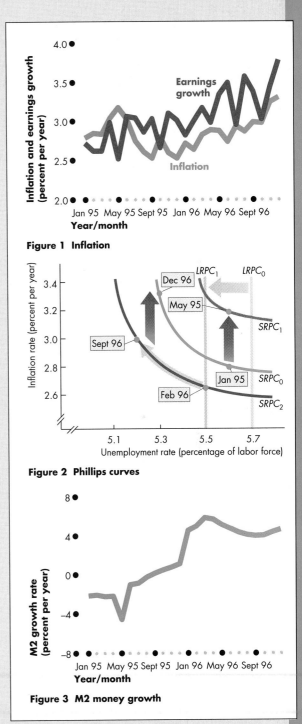

Figure 1  Inflation

Figure 2  Phillips curves

Figure 3  M2 money growth

357

# SUMMARY

## Key Points

### Inflation and the Price Level (p. 340)

- Inflation is a process of persistently rising prices and falling value of money.

### Demand-Pull Inflation (pp. 341–343)

- Demand-pull inflation arises from increasing aggregate demand.
- Its main sources are increases in the money supply or in government purchases.

### Cost-Push Inflation (pp. 343–345)

- Cost-push inflation can result from any factor that decreases aggregate supply.
- Its main sources are increasing wage rates and increasing prices of key raw materials.

### Effects of Inflation (pp. 346–350)

- Inflation is costly when it is unanticipated because it creates inefficiencies and redistributes income and wealth.
- People try to anticipate inflation to avoid its costs.
- Forecasts of inflation based on all the available relevant information are called rational expectations.
- A moderate anticipated inflation has a small cost. But a rapid anticipated inflation is costly because it decreases potential GDP and slows growth.

### Inflation and Unemployment: The Phillips Curve (pp. 350–354)

- The short-run Phillips curve shows the tradeoff between inflation and unemployment when the expected inflation rate and the natural unemployment rate are constant.
- The long-run Phillips curve, which is vertical, shows that when the actual inflation rate equals the expected inflation rate, the unemployment rate equals the natural unemployment rate.
- Unexpected changes in the inflation rate bring movements along the short-run Phillips curve.
- Changes in expected inflation shift the short-run Phillips curve.
- Changes in the natural unemployment rate shift both the short-run and long-run Phillips curves.

### Interest Rates and Inflation (pp. 354–355)

- The higher the expected inflation rate, the higher is the nominal interest rate.
- As the anticipated inflation rate rises, borrowers willingly pay a higher interest rate and lenders successfully demand a higher interest rate.
- The nominal interest rate adjusts to equal the real interest rate plus the expected inflation rate.

## Key Figures

## Key Terms

# QUESTIONS

1. What is inflation and how is its rate measured?
2. Distinguish between the price level and the inflation rate.
3. Distinguish between a one-time change in the price level and inflation.
4. Distinguish between demand-pull inflation and cost-push inflation.
5. What are the factors that can start a demand-pull inflation?
6. Explain the sequence of events that unfold when a demand-pull inflation spiral occurs.
7. What are the factors that can start a cost-push inflation?
8. Explain the sequence of events that unfold when a cost-push inflation spiral occurs.
9. Why is unanticipated inflation costly?
10. What are the losses that a person suffers in labor markets when inflation is unanticipated?
11. What are the losses that a person suffers in capital markets when inflation is unanticipated?
12. Explain why unanticipated inflation does not only redistribute income but also creates inefficiency.
13. Why do people devote resources to trying to forecast inflation?
14. What is a rational expectation?
15. What causes an anticipated inflation?
16. Describe the sequence of events that unfold during an anticipated inflation.
17. What are the costs of anticipated inflation?
18. What does the short-run Phillips curve show?
19. What is held constant when there is a movement along a short-run Phillips curve?
20. What does the long-run Phillips curve show?
21. What is held constant when there is a movement along a long-run Phillips curve?
22. What have been the main causes of shifts in the U.S. short-run Phillips curve during the 1970s, 1980s, and 1990s?
23. Why do nominal interest rates vary so much both across countries and over time?
24. What is the relationship between inflation and the nominal interest rate in the United States?

# PROBLEMS

1. Work out the effects on the price level of the following unexpected events:
   a. An increase in the money supply
   b. An increase in government purchases of goods and services
   c. An increase in income taxes
   d. An increase in investment demand
   e. An increase in the wage rate
   f. An increase in labor productivity
2. Work out the effects on the price level of the events listed in problem 1 when they are correctly anticipated.
3. The figure shows an economy's long-run aggregate supply curve, $LAS$, three aggregate demand curves, $AD_0$, $AD_1$, and $AD_2$, and three short-run aggregate supply curves, $SAS_0$, $SAS_1$, and $SAS_2$. The economy starts out on the curves $AD_0$ and $SAS_0$.

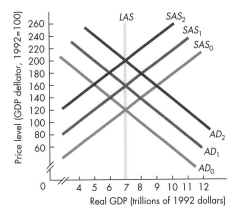

   Some events then occur that take the economy to the other aggregate demand curves and short-run aggregate supply curves.
   a. Describe the sequence of events in the figure if there is a demand-pull inflation.
   b. Describe the sequence of events in the figure if there is a cost-push inflation.
   c. Describe the sequence of events in the figure if there is an anticipated inflation.
4. In the economy in problem 3, aggregate demand unexpectedly increases to $AD_1$.
   a. What is the price level in the short run?
   b. What is real GDP in the short run?
   c. What is the price level in the long run?
   d. What is real GDP in the long run?

5. An economy has a natural unemployment rate of 4 percent when its expected inflation is 6 percent. Its inflation and unemployment history is as follows:

| Inflation rate (percent per year) | Unemployment rate (percent) |
|---|---|
| 10 | 2 |
| 8 | 3 |
| 6 | 4 |
| 4 | 5 |
| 2 | 6 |

a. Draw a diagram of this economy's short-run and long-run Phillips curves.

b. If the actual inflation rate rises from 6 percent a year to 8 percent a year, what is the change in the unemployment rate? Explain why it occurs.

c. If the natural unemployment rate rises to 5 percent, what is the change in the unemployment rate? Explain why it occurs.

d. Go back to part (b). If the expected inflation rate falls to 4 percent a year, what is the change in the unemployment rate? Explain why it occurs.

## CRITICAL THINKING

1. Study *Reading Between the Lines* on pp. 356–357 and then answer the following questions:
   a. What does Alan Greenspan say about the likelihood of inflation increasing?
   b. Is the news article describing a cost-push inflation or a demand-pull inflation or an anticipated inflation? Provide detailed reasons.
   c. If the Fed tightens money and raises interest rates, how do you think that action will influence inflation and unemployment in the short run?
   d. If the Fed tightens money and raises interest rates, how do you think that action will influence inflation and unemployment in the long run?
   e. If the Fed raises interest rates in 1997, does that make it likely that interest rates will be higher or lower than they otherwise would have been in 1998?

2. In light of what you have learned in this chapter, what do you think the Fed should do during 1998 to keep inflation in check?

3. If inflation rates of 10 percent a year (as we had during the 1970s) returned in the United States, who would benefit and who would lose?

4. "The Phillips curve is a menu from which the government must chose how much inflation and how much unemployment to buy." Evaluate this statement. Under what conditions is it true? Under what conditions is it false?

5. If the Fed aimed to use monetary policy to lower the unemployment rate to 3 percent, what do you predict would happen to:
   a. Unemployment in the short run?
   b. Unemployment in the long run?
   c. Inflation in the short run?
   d. Inflation in the long run?
   e. The short-run Phillips curve?
   f. The long-run Phillips curve?
   g. Potential GDP?
   h. The growth rate of potential GDP?

# Understanding and Smoothing the Business Cycle

To cure a disease, doctors must first understand how the disease responds to different treatments. It helps to understand the mechanisms that operate to cause the disease, but sometimes, a workable cure can be found even before the full story of the causes has been told. ◆ Curing economic ills is similar to curing our medical ills. We need to understand how the economy responds to the treatments we might prescribe for it. And sometimes, we want to try a cure, even though we don't fully understand the reasons for the problem we're trying to control. ◆ You have already encountered a lot of what is known about macroeconomic performance. You've seen how the pace of capital accumulation and technological change determine the long-term growth trend. You've learned how fluctuations around the long-term trend can be generated by changes in aggregate demand and aggregate supply. And you've learned about the key sources of fluctuations in aggregate demand and aggregate supply. ◆ The two chapters in this part build of everything you've studied in macroeconomics. The central tool they use is the AS–AD model. But they use it to explain the big picture or grand vision that different schools of thought hold concerning the way the economy operates and what is important. ◆ In Chapter 16, you will learn about alternative visions of the business cycle. All of these visions can be translated in the AS–AD model. And doing so helps us to compare and contrast the competing visions. But one theory of the cycle, the new *real business cycle (RBC)* theory, is more at home with the demand and supply model of microeconomics (Chapter 4) than the AS–AD model. Most economists have not embraced the real business cycle approach. It is an extreme view. But the method that real business cycle theory uses is here to stay. This method is to build a (mathematical) model of the entire economy and then see, in a computer simulation, what kind of cycle the model creates. The economy on the computer is then calibrated to the real economy and the cycles are compared. The computer model can be treated with a variety of 'medications' and their effects observed. This new style of business cycle research cannot be explained in detail without using advanced mathematical ideas. But the economics that underlies it can be explained and Chapter 16 shows you the nature of the model that real business cycle theorists have used. ◆ In Chapter 17, we turn to the policy debate. There, you will study the alternative approaches that have been proposed to speed growth, smooth the business cycle, and contain inflation. Again, the AS–AD model is the workhorse you will use to compare the effects of alternative policy strategies. ◆ Before we embark on the next two chapters, we're going to meet two economists whose ideas about business cycles and macroeconomic policy have been influential. They are Irving Fisher and Frederic S. Mishkin.

# Business Cycles

## The Economist: Irving Fisher

**Irving Fisher (1867–1947) is the greatest American-born economist. The son of a Congregational minister who died as Irving was finishing high school, he paid his way through Yale and earned enough money to support his mother and younger brother by tutoring his fellow students.**

**Irving Fisher came to economics by way of mathematics. He was Yale's first Ph.D. candidate in pure economics, but was a student in the math department!**

**The contributions that Fisher made to economics cover the entire subject. He is best known for his work on the quantity theory of money (Chapter 30, pp. 679–683) and the relation between interest rates and inflation (Chapter 32, pp. 728–729). But he also wrote on the business cycle. He believed that the Great Depression was caused because the fall in the price level increased the real burden of debts. He wrote from experience: He had borrowed heavily to buy stocks in the rising market of the late 1920s and lost a fortune of perhaps 10 million dollars in the crash of 1929.**

> *"…in the great booms and depressions, … the two big bad actors are debt disturbances and price level disturbances."*
>
> IRVING FISHER
>
> *"The Debt Deflation Theory of Depressions"*
>
> ECONOMETRICA, 1933

## The Issues and Ideas

Economic activity has fluctuated between boom and bust for as long as we've had records. And understanding the sources of economic fluctuations has turned out to be difficult. One reason is that there are no simple patterns. Every new episode of the business cycle is different from its predecessor in some way. Some cycles are long and some short, some are mild and some severe, some begin in the United States and some abroad. We never know with any certainty when the next turning point (down or up) is coming or what will cause it. A second reason is that the apparent waste of resources during a recession or depression seems to contradict the very foundation of economics: Resources are limited and people have unlimited wants—there is scarcity. A satisfactory theory of the business cycle must explain why scarce resources don't *always* get fully employed.

One theory is that recessions result from insufficient aggregate demand. The solution is to increase government spending, cut taxes, and cut interest rates. But demand stimulation must not be overdone. Countries that stimulate aggregate demand too much, such as Brazil, find their economic growth rates sagging, unemployment rising, and inflation accelerating.

Today's new theory, real

business cycle theory, predicts that fluctuations in aggregate demand have no effect on output and employment and change only the price level and inflation rate. But this theory ignores the real effects of financial collapse of the type that occurred in the 1930s. If banks fail on a large scale and people lose their wealth, other firms also begin to fail and jobs are destroyed. Unemployed people cut their spending, and output falls further. Demand stimulation may not be called for, but action to ensure that sound banks survive certainly is.

While economists are trying to understand the sources of the business cycle, the government and the Fed are doing the best they can to moderate the cycle. In the years since World War II, there appears to have been some success. Although the business cycle has not disappeared, it has become much less severe.

What happens to the economy when people lose confidence in banks? They withdraw their funds. These withdrawals feed on themselves, creating a snowball of withdrawals and, eventually, panic. Short of funds with which to repay depositors, banks call in loans and previously sound businesses are faced with financial distress. They close down and lay off workers. And recession deepens and turns into depression. Bank failures and the resulting decline in the nation's supply of money and credit were a significant factor in deepening and prolonging the Great Depression. But they taught us the importance of stable financial institutions and gave rise to the establishment of federal deposit insurance to prevent future financial collapse.

## ... AND NOW

How can a building designed as a shop have no better use than to be boarded up and left empty? Not enough aggregate demand, say the Keynesians. Not so, say the real business cycle theorists. Technological change has reduced the building's current productivity as a shop to

zero. But its expected future productivity is sufficiently high that it is not efficient to refit the building for some other purpose.

All unemployment, whether of buildings or people, can be explained in a similar way. For example, how can it be that during a recession, a person trained as a shop clerk is without work? Not enough aggregate demand is one answer. Another is that the current productivity of shop clerks is low, but their expected future productivity is sufficiently high that it does not pay an unemployed clerk to retrain for a job that is currently available.

It is now almost 70 years since the Great Depression. Although we've had many recessions since then, none compare with the severity of that event. Some credit for avoiding another major depression must go to the Federal Reserve board. You'll next meet Professor Frederick Mishkin, current VP and director of research at the Fed of New York.

**Frederic S. Mishkin** is currently an executive vice president and director of research at the Federal Reserve Bank of New York. He is on leave from the Graduate School of Business at Columbia University. Professor Mishkin was born in New York City in 1951. He received his Ph.D. from MIT in 1976 and has taught at the University of Chicago, Northwestern University, Princeton University, and Columbia University.

Professor Mishkin's research focuses on monetary policy and its impact on financial markets and the aggregate economy.

Michael Parkin talked with Professor Mishkin about his work, the role the Fed plays in monetary policy, and the legacy of Irving Fisher.

**Why are you an economist?**
The Great Depression was the most important event in my father's life, and we talked about it continually at the dinner table. We also talked about the stock market. These discussions piqued my interest in economics. When I went to college, I thought of becoming a physicist, but I realized that economics has many of same attributes. Both disciplines demand thinking logically and are consistently based on models. The real-world problems that were implicit in the study of economics proved much more interesting to me then. I realized that economics was my calling, and in fact, it was one of the best choices I've ever made.

**What are the most basic principles that you find yourself repeatedly returning to in your professional life, and especially in your life as the director of research at the New York Fed.**
A key principle is that incentives are everything. Particularly in today's world, where you need creativity, you cannot motivate people to do good research by just commanding them. You instead need to motivate them by saying, "Do your own work, figure it out yourself, but, on the other hand, I'm going to give you the right incentives." A second principle is the concept of backward induction. If you think about where you want to be and work backwards, you are frequently way ahead of the game. Not only are these two concepts extremely useful in thinking about real-world economic problems, they've been absolutely invaluable to me in managing the Fed's research group of 150 people. We have an annual evaluation process followed by a salary review, and promotions are determined by how well people are doing and how well they respond to incentives.

> *A key principle is that incentives are everything.*

**Does the work of Federal Reserve banks directly contribute to the quality of the monetary policy that is developed?**

In economics we never really have answers, but we are able to understand things better through research that initiates debate and makes good policy outcomes more likely. Many of the new ideas that are published in the academic journals have helped to guide policy makers. I have stressed the value of basic research here at the Federal Reserve Bank of New York and have emphasized our need to be at the very frontier of ideas. We also have to make decisions from day to day that involves much more nitty-gritty research. For example, we have to forecast the economy and try to understand what's going on in the inflation process.

**We are enjoying one of longest uninterrupted recoveries in U.S. economic history, and there's little sign of either serious inflation or a serious recession. To what do you attribute this successful run? What part do you think the Fed can take credit for, and where else would you allocate credit, if anywhere?**

There's a fair amount of credit due to the Fed, but I'm going to use an adage that my mother always said to me, "It's better to be lucky than good, but it's even better to be good and lucky." The Fed has been both good and lucky. The "good" part is that the Fed has acted in accordance with the results of economic research that indicates that good monetary policy is forward looking. There are lags from mon-etary policy to inflation on the order of two to three years. This indicates that monetary policy actions today have little effect on today's inflation but are highly relevant to what will happen to future inflation. We must look to the future if we are to promote a stable economic environment in which we have very low inflation. In February 1994, when the Fed

> *Monetary policy actions today have little effect on today's inflation but are highly relevant to what will happen to future inflation.*

started to raise interest rates, unemployment was close to the 7 percent range and inflation pressures were nonexistent. Yet, look-ing several years down the road, we realized that if we did not start to raise interest rates and tighten monetary policy, then we would eventually have an overheated economy with inflation out of control. The preemptive policy of raising interest rates was extremely successful because it helped the inflation rate to stay very low, and the economy continued to grow at a sustainable pace. Another benefit of pursuing a preemptive policy is that markets and businesses under-stand that the central bank will be serious about controlling inflation. That produces a much more stable environment because businesses know they can't solve their prob-lems by just raising prices. Instead, they have to be efficient and keep costs low. The Fed has also been "lucky." Even if the Fed is doing the right thing during a business cycle expansion, there may be a tendency for the economy to over-heat a little bit and a little bit of inflation to occur. This has not happened. The economy is about as good as it can get, and that requires not only good policy but also some luck.

**The traditional categories for dis-cussing policy involve terms such as *rules*, *discretion*, and *fixed rules* ver-sus *feedback rules*. Is that language of use in thinking about Fed policy?**

I think that there's a problem with the dichotomy between rules and discretion. One part of the litera-ture views rules as being critical to solving problems such as time inconsistency. Trying to do what looks good right now but not wor-rying about the future may result in a sequence of policies that lead to poor outcomes in the long run. You have to avoid the temptation to do what looks like the right thing today and ignore the long run. That's one of the reasons why people feel that rules are impor-tant. On the other hand, the criti-cism of rules is that they are too rigid, particularly for dealing with unexpected events. Rules can, in that situation, lead to a very bad outcome. An alternative is to pur-sue a policy that is basically con-strained discretion. It's rulelike, but without a rigid rule. For exam-ple, inflation-targeting regimes that have been pursued in many countries throughout the world in recent years are neither a rule nor discretion. They are, instead, con-strained discretion. My view is that a good monetary policy should always be rulelike; but, on the other hand, the idea of putting in fixed rules is probably not a good idea.

For the past 15 years the real business cycle research agenda has downplayed the role of money. How do you evaluate the recent real business cycle research program?

The real business cycle literature takes the view that monetary policy is not important to the actual short-term business cycle. I think that monetary policy is more important to the business cycle than real business cycle models give credit for. There is evidence that monetary policy has been important. For example, during the early 1980s, the Federal Reserve took very active steps to get inflation under control and the result was a quite severe recession, but eventually the tight monetary policy produced the right outcome, which was low inflation. I would also characterize the Great Depression as a period where monetary policy performed very poorly and contributed to the most severe economic contraction in the U.S. history. I think monetary policy actions were extremely important during that episode and extremely important during the period 1980 to 1982. On the other hand, real business cycle literature points out that the degree of control that monetary policy authorities can exert on the business cycle is indeed limited, and I am quite sympathetic to this view. The idea that the monetary authorities are able to tweak the business cycle at every turn is just not correct because the actual degree of certainty as to what will happen as a result of certain monetary policy actions is by no means clear. The real business cycle literature has made people aware that monetary policy cannot be fully in control of what

happens in the business cycle. On the other hand, I think that it's overstretching to say that monetary policy actions don't have real effects.

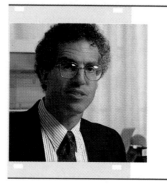

How can students help themselves to be more able to address interesting, real problems?

It is critical to get students to apply what they learn in class to their everyday lives. I tell my students that they must be reading newspapers such as *The Wall Street Journal, The Financial Times*, or *The New York Times* for business and financial news. I also tell students that they actually can use economic principles such as adverse selection and moral hazard to solve real-world problems every day. For example, if somebody's a rich person and is thinking about getting married, he or she faces an adverse selection problem: Does the other person love me because I'm wealthy rather than because I'm a lovable person?

In addition to managing the research group, I participate in the management committee of the bank. I've been able to actively contribute to the management of this bank because I can use economic principles to discuss what I think would be sensible solutions to problems. Economics is wonderful training for being able to

solve many problems that hit you every day.

What, for you, is the legacy of Irving Fisher?

Irving Fisher is one of the extraordinary American economists. He's famous for the quantity theory of money, which is extremely useful in thinking about the importance of money to the economy. He was a pioneer whose work on interest rates is still valuable today in thinking about how to conduct monetary policy. He also did path-breaking work for which he was not famous. For example, his paper "The Debt Deflation Theory of the Great Depression" has led to a much better understanding of financial crises in today's world.

What can an undergraduate gain from taking an economics course?

Economics is an important part of a liberal arts education and is essential for law and MBA students. For the first time in my life, I've actually been a manager, and one of the things that is really striking is how useful economic concepts have been to helping me to be effective. I now can go back to my MBA students and show them that many of these concepts are ones that I actually used in practice to make me a better manager.

Economics is not only useful in helping people become professionals, but also extremely useful in terms of making them better educated citizens. Yes, I do want to train people to help them be successful directly in their careers, but I also want to make them more successful, generally, as people. I think economics is a very powerful tool in achieving that.

# Chapter 16

# The Business Cycle

The 1920s were years of unprecedented prosperity for Americans. After the horrors of World War I (1914–1918), the economic machine was back at work, producing such technological marvels as cars and airplanes, telephones and vacuum cleaners. Houses and apartments were being built at a frantic pace. Then, almost without warning, in October 1929, came a devastating stock market crash. Overnight, the values of stocks and shares traded on Wall Street fell by 30 percent. During the four succeeding years, there followed the most severe economic contraction in recorded history. By 1933, real GDP had fallen by 30 percent, unemployment had increased to 25 percent of the labor force, and employment was down 20 percent.

## Must What Goes Up Always Come Down?

What caused the Great Depression? ◆ By the standard of the Great Depression, recent recessions have been mild. But recessions have not gone away. Our economy has experienced 15 recessions since 1920 and 10 since the end of World War II in 1945. For 16 months, from November 1973 through March 1975, real GDP fell by 5 percent. It fell again in 1980 and yet again in back-to-back recessions in 1981–1982. Most recently, real GDP decreased for 8 months in 1990–1991. Between these recessions, expansions took real GDP and income per person to new heights. Since the 1990–1991 recession, real GDP has grown steadily. By the end of 1996, it was some 15 percent higher than it had been in the 1990–1991 recession. What causes a repeating sequence of recessions and expansions in our economy? Must what goes up always come down? Will we have another recession? When? Before 2000? ◆ We are going to explore the business cycle in this chapter. You will see how all the strands of macroeconomics that you've been following come together and weave a complete picture of the forces and mechanisms that generate economic growth and fluctuations in production, employment and unemployment, and inflation.

## After studying this chapter, you will be able to:

- Distinguish among the different theories of the business cycle

- Explain the Keynesian and monetarist theories of the business cycle

- Explain the new classical and new Keynesian theories of the business cycle

- Explain real business cycle theory

- Describe the origins of and the mechanisms at work during two recent recessions and during the Great Depression

# Cycle Patterns, Impulses, and Mechanisms

YOU'VE LOOKED AT THE BUSINESS CYCLE AT several points in your study of macroeconomics. You met it first in Chapter 5, which defines the phases of the cycle and describes its history. You learned about a framework for studying the business cycle—the aggregate supply–aggregate demand model—in Chapter 7. In Chapter 8, you saw how unemployment fluctuates over the business cycle. In Chapter 11, you focused on business cycle turning points and the inventory changes and expenditure multiplier effects that operate as the economy swings from expansion to recession and from recession to expansion. In Chapter 12, you studied the ways in which fiscal policy influences and is influenced by the business cycle. Finally, you saw in Chapters 13 through 15 how money influences economic fluctuations and how inflation and the business cycle intertwine.

You've also looked at another type of economic fluctuation: the productivity growth slowdown of the 1970s. This slowdown is not classified as a business cycle event, but it has some similarities. It is part of an overall process of economic growth, the pace of which fluctuates. The processes of growth and of the business cycle are intimately connected. In fact, according to one view, they are all manifestations of the same phenomenon.

This chapter brings all these strands in your previous study of macroeconomics together and gives you an opportunity both to review what you have learned and to put it to work in a focused way in interpreting and making sense of particular episodes in our economic history.

We'll get moving by first returning to the facts about the business cycle and looking at the complex patterns it makes.

## Business Cycle Patterns

The business cycle is an irregular and nonrepeating up-and-down movement of business activity that takes place around a generally rising trend and that shows great diversity. Each recession, expansion, and turning point has been dated by the National Bureau of Economic Research (NBER). The NBER has identified 15 recessions and expansions since 1920. On the average, recessions have lasted for just over a

year and real GDP has fallen from peak to trough by more than 6 percent. Expansions have lasted for almost 4 years on the average, and real GDP has increased from trough to peak by an average of 22 percent. But these averages hide huge variations from one cycle to another.

Figure 16.1 shows the range of variation across the different recessions and expansions. It shows the total percentage change in real GDP during successive recessions and expansion. You can see that the Great Depression was much more severe than anything that followed it. Over a 43-month period, real GDP shrank by 33 percent. The second most severe recession was also in the 1930s. Another relatively severe recession occurred at the end of World War II in 1945. The only other recession that comes close to these is the OPEC recession of 1974–1975, which lasted for 16 months, during which real GDP fell by 5 percent. The other recessions since 1950, including the most recent 1990–1991 recession, have been much milder than those of the 1930s. The biggest expansion occurred during World War II. But the other two big expansions were in the 1960s and 1980s. There is no correlation between the length of an expansion and the length of the preceding recession.

With this enormous diversity of experience, there is no simple explanation for the business cycle. Also, there is no (currently available) way of forecasting when the next turning point will come. But there is a body of theory about the business cycle that helps us to understand its causes. A good place to begin studying this theory is to distinguish the possible ways in which cycles can be created.

## Cycle Impulses and Mechanisms

Cycles are a widespread physical phenomenon. In a tennis match, the ball cycles from one side of the court to the other and back again. Every day, the earth cycles from day to night and back to day. A child on a rocking horse creates a cycle as the horse swings back and forth.

The tennis ball cycle is the simplest. It is caused by the actions of the players. Each time the ball changes direction (at each turning point), the racket (an outside force) is applied. The day-night-day cycle is the most subtle. This cycle is caused by the rotation of the earth. No new force is applied each day to make the sun rise and set. It happens because of

FIGURE 16.1

Some Business Cycle Patterns

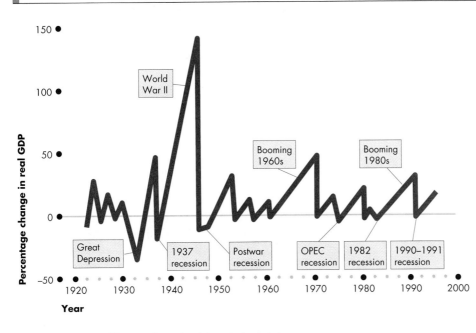

Recessions have lasted from 43 months during the Great Depression, when real GDP fell by 33 percent, to 6 months in 1980, when real GDP fell by 2.5 percent. The mildest recession lasted through most of 1970, when real GDP fell by 1 percent. Recessions have been less severe in the post-World War II period. Expansions have lasted from 6 months in 1980 to more than 100 months during the 1960s. Expansions have become longer and stronger during the post-World War II period.

*Source:* National Bureau of Economic Research and the author's calculations.

the design of the objects that interact to create the cycle. Nothing happens at a turning point (sunrise and sunset) that is any different from what is happening at other points except that the sun comes into or goes out of view. The child's rocking horse cycle is a combination of these two cases. To start the horse rocking, some outside force must be exerted (as in the tennis ball cycle). But once the horse is rocking, the to-and-fro cycle continues for some time with no further force being applied (as in the day-night-day cycle). The rocking horse cycle eventually dies out unless the horse is pushed again, and each time the horse is pushed, the cycle temporarily becomes more severe.

The economy is a bit like all three of these examples. It can be hit by shocks (like a tennis ball) that send it in one direction or another, it can cycle indefinitely (like the turning of day into night), and it can cycle in swings that get milder until another shock sets off a new burst of bigger swings (like a rocking horse). While none of these analogies is perfect, they all contain some insights into the business cycle.

Different theories of the cycle emphasize different outside forces (different tennis rackets) and different cycle mechanisms (different solar system and rocking horse designs).

Although there are several different theories of the business cycle, they all agree about one aspect of the cycle: the central role played by investment and the accumulation of capital.

## The Central Role of Investment and Capital

Whatever the shocks are that hit the economy, they hit one crucial variable: investment. Recessions begin when investment in new capital slows down, and they turn into expansions when investment speeds up. Investment and capital interact like the spinning earth and the sun to create an ongoing cycle.

In an expansion, investment proceeds at a rapid rate and the capital stock grows quickly. But rapid capital growth means that the amount of capital per hour of labor is growing. Equipped with more capital, labor becomes more productive. But the *law of diminishing returns* begins to operate. The law of diminishing returns states that as the quantity of capital increases, with the quantity of labor remaining the same, the gain in productivity from the additional units of capital eventually diminishes. Diminishing returns to capital bring a fall in the profit rate, and with a lower profit rate, the incentive to invest weakens. As a result, investment eventually falls. When it falls by a large amount, recession begins.

In a recession, investment is low and the capital stock grows slowly. In a deep recession, the capital stock might actually fall. Slow capital growth (or even a falling capital stock) means that the amount of capital per hour of labor is falling. With a low amount of capital per hour of labor, businesses begin to see opportunities for profitable investment and the pace of investment eventually picks up. As it does so, recession turns into expansion.

## The *AS-AD* Model

Investment and capital are a crucial part of the business cycle mechanism, but they are just one part. To study the broader business cycle mechanism, we need a broader framework. That framework is the *AS-AD* model of Chapter 7. All the theories of the business cycle can be described in terms of the *AS-AD* model. Theories differ both in what they identify as the impulse and in the cycle mechanism. But all theories can be thought of as making assumptions about the factors that make either aggregate supply or aggregate demand fluctuate and assumptions about how they interact with each other to create a business cycle. Business cycle impulses can affect either the supply side or the demand side of the economy or both. But there are no pure supply-side theories. We will classify all theories of the business cycle as either:

- Aggregate demand theories
- Real business cycle theory

We'll study the aggregate demand theories first. Then we'll study real business cycle theory, which is a more recent approach that isolates a shock that has both aggregate supply and aggregate demand effects.

## Aggregate Demand Theories of the Business Cycle

THREE TYPES OF AGGREGATE DEMAND THEORY OF the business cycle have been proposed. They are:

- Keynesian theory
- Monetarist theory
- Rational expectations theories

### Keynesian Theory

The **Keynesian theory of the business cycle** regards volatile expectations as the main source of economic fluctuations. This theory is distilled from Keynes' *General Theory of Employment, Interest, and Money*. We'll explore the Keynesian theory by looking at its main impulse and the mechanism that converts that impulse into a real GDP cycle.

**Keynesian Impulse** The *impulse* in the Keynesian theory of the business cycle is *expected future sales and profits*. A change in expected future sales and profits changes the demand for new capital and changes the level of investment.

Keynes had a sophisticated theory about *how* expected sales and profits are determined. He reasoned that these expectations would be volatile because most of the events that shape the future are unknown and impossible to forecast. So, he reasoned, news or even rumors about future tax rate changes, interest rate changes, advances in technology, global economic and political events, or any other of the thousands of relevant factors that influence sales and profits change expectations in ways that can't be quantified but that have large effects.

To emphasize the volatility and diversity of sources of changes in expected sales and profits, Keynes described these expectations as *animal spirits*. In using this term, Keynes was not saying that expectations are irrational. Rather, he meant that because future sales and profits are impossible to forecast, it might be rational to take a view about them based on rumors, guesses, intuition, and instinct. Further, it might be rational to *change* one's view of the future, perhaps radically, in the light of scraps of new information.

**Keynesian Cycle Mechanism** In the Keynesian theory, once a change in animal spirits has changed investment, a cycle mechanism begins to operate that has two key elements. First, the initial change in investment has a multiplier effect. The change in investment changes *aggregate* expenditure, real GDP, and disposable income. The change in disposable income changes consumption expenditure, and aggregate demand changes by a multiple of the initial change in investment. (This mechanism is described in detail in Chapter 11, pp. 252–259.) The aggregate demand curve shifts rightward in an expansion and leftward in a recession.

The second element of the Keynesian cycle mechanism is the response of real GDP to a change in aggregate demand. The short-run aggregate supply curve is horizontal (or nearly so). With a horizontal *SAS* curve, swings in aggregate demand translate into swings in real GDP with no changes in the price level. But the short-run aggregate supply curve depends on the money wage rate. If the money wage rate is fixed (sticky), the *SAS* curve does not move. And if the money wage rate changes, the *SAS* curve shifts. In the Keynesian theory, the response of the money wage rate to changes in aggregate demand are *asymmetric*.

On the downside, when aggregate demand decreases and unemployment rises, the money wage rate does not change. It is completely rigid in the downward direction. With a decrease in aggregate demand and no change in the money wage rate, the economy gets stuck in a below full-employment equilibrium. No natural forces operate to restore full employment. The economy remains in that situation until animal spirits are lifted and investment increases.

On the upside, when aggregate demand increases and unemployment falls below the natural rate, the money wage rate rises quickly. It is flexible in the upward direction. At above full employment, the horizontal *SAS* curve plays no role and only the vertical *LAS* curve is relevant. With an increase in aggregate demand and an accompanying rise in the money wage rate, the price level rises quickly to eliminate the shortages and bring the economy back to full employment. The economy remains in that situation until animal spirits fall and investment and aggregate demand decrease.

Figures 16.2 and 16.3 illustrate the Keynesian theory of the business cycle by using the aggregate supply–aggregate demand model. In Fig. 16.2, the economy is initially at full employment (point *a*) on the long-run aggregate supply curve (*LAS*), the aggregate demand curve (*AD$_0$*), and the short-run

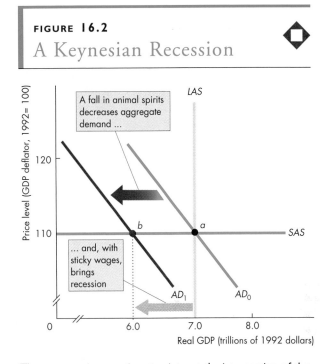

FIGURE 16.2

## A Keynesian Recession

The economy is operating at point *a* at the intersection of the long-run aggregate supply curve (*LAS*), the short-run aggregate supply curve (*SAS*), and the aggregate demand curve (*AD$_0$*). A Keynesian recession begins when a fall in animal spirits causes investment demand to decrease. Aggregate demand decreases, and the *AD* curve shifts leftward to *AD$_1$*. With sticky money wages, real GDP decreases to $6 trillion and the price level does not change. The economy moves to point *b*.

aggregate supply curve (*SAS*). A fall in animal spirits decreases investment, and a multiplier process decreases aggregate demand. The aggregate demand curve shifts leftward to *AD$_1$*. With a fixed money wage rate, real GDP falls to $6 trillion and the economy moves to point *b*. Unemployment has increased and there is a surplus of labor. But the money wage rate does not fall, and the economy remains at point *b* until some force moves it away.

That force is shown in Fig. 16.3. Here, starting out at point *b*, a rise in animal spirits increases investment. The multiplier process kicks in, and aggregate demand increases. The *AD* curve shifts to *AD$_2$*, and real GDP begins to increase. An expansion is under way. As long as real GDP remains below potential GDP ($7 trillion in this example), the money wage rate and the price level remain constant. But real

## FIGURE 16.3

# A Keynesian Expansion

Starting at point $b$, a Keynesian expansion begins when a rise in animal spirits causes investment demand to increase. Aggregate demand increases, and the $AD$ curve shifts rightward to $AD_2$. With sticky money wages, real GDP increases to $7 trillion. But the economy does not go all the way to point $c$. When full employment is reached, the money wage rate rises and the $SAS$ curve shifts upward toward $SAS_1$. The price level rises as the economy heads toward point $d$.

GDP never increases to point $c$, the point of intersection of $SAS_0$ and $AD_2$. The reason is that once real GDP exceeds potential GDP and unemployment falls below the natural rate, the money wage rate begins to rise and the $SAS$ curve starts to shift upward toward $SAS_1$. As the money wage rate rises, the price level also rises and real GDP growth slows. The economy follows a path like the one shown by the arrows connecting point $b$, the initial equilibrium, with point $d$, the final equilibrium.

The Keynesian business cycle is mainly like a tennis match. It is caused by outside forces—animal spirits—that change direction and set off a process that ends at an equilibrium that must be hit again by the outside forces to disturb it.

## Monetarist Theory

The **monetarist theory of the business cycle** regards fluctuations in the money stock as the main source of economic fluctuations. This theory is distilled from the writings of Milton Friedman and several other economists. We'll explore the monetarist theory as we did the Keynesian theory, by looking first at its main impulse and second at the mechanism that creates a cycle in real GDP.

**Monetarist Impulse** The *impulse* in the monetarist theory of the business cycle is the *growth rate of the quantity of money*. A speedup in money growth brings expansion, and a slowdown in money growth brings recession. The source of the change in the growth rate of the quantity of money is the monetary policy actions of the Fed.

**Monetarist Cycle Mechanism** In the monetarist theory, once the Fed has changed the money growth rate, a cycle mechanism begins to operate that, like the Keynesian mechanism, first affects aggregate demand. When the money growth rate increases, the quantity of real money in the economy increases. Interest rates fall, and real money balances increase. The foreign exchange rate also falls—the dollar loses value on the foreign exchange market. These initial financial market effects begin to spill over into other markets. Investment demand and exports increase, and consumers spend more on durable goods. These initial changes in expenditure have a multiplier effect, just as investment has in the Keynesian theory. Through these mechanisms, a speedup in money growth shifts the aggregate demand curve rightward and brings an expansion. Similarly, a slowdown in money growth shifts the aggregate demand curve leftward and brings a recession.

The second element of the monetarist cycle mechanism is the response of aggregate supply to a change in aggregate demand. The short-run aggregate supply curve is upward-sloping. With an upward-sloping $SAS$ curve, swings in aggregate demand translate into swings in both real GDP and the price level. But monetarists believe that real GDP deviations from full employment are temporary in both directions.

In monetarist theory, the money wage rate is only *temporarily sticky*. When aggregate demand decreases and unemployment rises, the money wage rate eventually begins to fall. As the money wage rate falls, so does the price level and after a period of adjustment, full employment is restored. When aggregate demand increases and unemployment falls below the natural rate, the money wage rate begins to rise. As the money wage rate rises, so does the price level. And through a period of adjustment, real GDP returns to potential GDP and the unemployment rate returns to the natural rate.

Figure 16.4 illustrates the monetarist theory. In part (a), the economy is initially at full employment (point *a*) on the long-run aggregate supply curve (*LAS*), the aggregate demand curve (*AD*$_0$), and the short-run aggregate supply curve (*SAS*$_0$). A slowdown in the money growth rate decreases aggregate

demand and the aggregate demand curve shifts leftward to *AD*$_1$. Real GDP decreases to $6.5 trillion, and the economy goes into recession (point *b*). Unemployment increases and there is a surplus of labor. The money wage rate begins to fall. As the money wage falls, the short-run aggregate supply curve starts to shift rightward toward *SAS*$_1$. The price level falls, and real GDP begins to expand as the economy moves to point *c*, its new full-employment equilibrium.

Figure 16.4(b) shows the effects of the opposite initial money shock—a speedup in money growth. Here, starting out at point *c*, a speedup in the money growth rate increases aggregate demand and shifts the *AD* curve to *AD*$_2$. Both real GDP and the price level

---

**FIGURE 16.4**

## A Monetarist Business Cycle

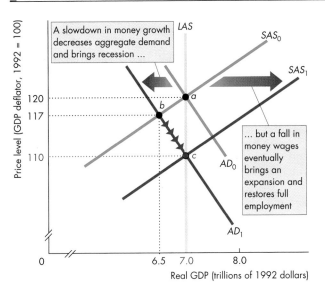

**(a) Recession**

A monetarist recession begins when a slowdown in money growth decreases aggregate demand. The *AD* curve shifts leftward from *AD*$_0$ to *AD*$_1$ (in part a). With sticky money wages, real GDP decreases to $6.5 trillion and the price level falls to 117 as the economy moves from point *a* to point *b*. With a surplus of labor, the money wage rate falls and the *SAS* curve shifts rightward to *SAS*$_1$. The price level falls further and real GDP returns to potential GDP at point *c*.

**(b) Expansion**

Starting at point *c* (part b), a monetarist expansion begins when an increase in money growth increases aggregate demand and shifts the *AD* curve rightward to *AD*$_2$. With sticky money wages, real GDP rises to $7.5 trillion, the price level rises to 113, and the economy moves to point *d*. With a shortage of labor, the money wage rate rises and the *SAS* curve shifts toward *SAS*$_2$. The price level rises and real GDP decreases to potential GDP as the economy heads toward point *e*.

increase as the economy moves to point $d$, the point of intersection of $SAS_1$ and $AD_2$. With real GDP above potential GDP and unemployment below the natural rate, the money wage rate begins to rise and the $SAS$ curve starts to shift leftward toward $SAS_2$. As the money wage rate rises, the price level also rises and real GDP decreases. The economy moves from point $d$ to point $e$, its new full-employment equilibrium.

The monetarist business cycle is like a rocking horse. It needs an outside force to get it going, but once going, it rocks back and forth (but just once). It doesn't matter in which direction the force initially hits. If it is a money growth slowdown, the economy cycles with a recession followed by expansion. If it is a money growth speedup, the economy cycles with an expansion followed by recession.

## Rational Expectations Theories

A **rational expectation** is a forecast that is based on all the available relevant information (see Chapter 15, p. 347). Rational expectations theories of the business cycle are theories based on the view that money wages are determined by a rational expectation of the price level. Two distinctly different rational expectations theories of the cycle have been proposed. A **new classical theory of the business cycle** regards *unanticipated* fluctuations in aggregate demand as the main source of economic fluctuations. This theory is based on the work of Robert E. Lucas, Jr., (see the part opener on pp. 91–96) and several other economists, including Thomas J. Sargent and Robert J. Barro. A different **new Keynesian theory of the business cycle** also regards *unanticipated* fluctuations in aggregate demand as the main source of economic fluctuations but it leaves room for *anticipated* demand fluctuations to play a role. We'll explore these theories as we did the Keynesian and monetarist theories, by looking first at the main impulse and second at the cycle mechanism.

**Rational Expectations Impulse**  The *impulse* that distinguishes the rational expectations theories from the other aggregate demand theories of the business cycle is the *unanticipated change in aggregate demand*. A larger than anticipated increase in aggregate demand brings an expansion, and a smaller than anticipated increase in aggregate demand brings a recession. Any factor that influences aggregate demand—for exam-ple, fiscal policy, monetary policy, or developments in the world economy that influence exports—whose change is not anticipated can bring a change in real GDP.

**Rational Expectations Cycle Mechanisms**  To describe the rational expectations cycle mechanisms, we'll deal first with the new classical version. When aggregate demand decreases, if the money wage rate doesn't change, real GDP and the price level both decrease. The fall in the price level increases the *real* wage rate, and employment decreases and unemployment increases. In the new classical theory, these events occur only if the decrease in aggregate demand is not anticipated. If the decrease in aggregate demand *is* anticipated, the price level is expected to fall and both firms and workers will agree to a lower money wage rate. By doing so, they can prevent the real wage from rising and avoid a rise in the unemployment rate.

Similarly, if firms and workers anticipate an increase in aggregate demand, they expect the price level to rise and will agree to a higher money wage rate. By doing so, they can prevent the real wage rate from falling and avoid a fall in the unemployment rate below the natural rate.

Only fluctuations in aggregate demand that are unanticipated and not taken into account in wage agreements bring changes in real GDP. *Anticipated* changes in aggregate demand change the price level, but they leave real GDP and unemployment unchanged and do not create a business cycle.

New Keynesian economists, like new classical economists, believe that money wages are influenced by rational expectations of the price level. But new Keynesians emphasize the long-term nature of most wage contracts. They say that *today's* money wages are influenced by *yesterday's* rational expectations. These expectations, which were formed in the past, are based on old information that might now be known to be incorrect. After they have made a long-term wage agreement, both firms and workers might anticipate a change in aggregate demand, which they expect will change the price level. But because they are locked into their agreement, they are unable to change money wages. So money wages are sticky in the new Keynesian theory, and with sticky money wages, even an *anticipated* change in aggregate demand changes real GDP.

New classical economists believe that long-term contracts are renegotiated when conditions change to make them outdated. So they do not regard long-term contracts as an obstacle to money wage flexibility, provided that both parties to an agreement recognize the changed conditions. If both firms and workers expect the price level to change, they will change the agreed money wage rate to reflect that shared expectation. In this situation, anticipated changes in aggregate demand change the money wage rate and the price level and leave real GDP unchanged.

The distinctive feature of both versions of the rational expectations theory of the business cycle is the role of unanticipated changes in aggregate demand. Figure 16.5 illustrates the effect of unanticipated changes on real GDP and the price level.

Potential GDP is $7 trillion, and the long-run aggregate supply curve is *LAS*. Aggregate demand is expected to be *EAD*. Given potential GDP and *EAD*, the money wage rate is set at the level that is expected to bring full employment. At this money wage rate, the short-run aggregate supply curve is *SAS*. Imagine that initially aggregate demand equals expected aggregate demand, so there is full employment. Real GDP is $7 trillion, and the price level is 110. Then, unexpectedly, aggregate demand turns out to be less than expected and the aggregate demand curve shifts leftward to $AD_0$ (in Fig. 16.5a). Many different aggregate demand shocks, such as a slowdown in the money growth rate or a collapse of exports, could have caused this shift. A recession

FIGURE 16.5

# A Rational Expectations Business Cycle

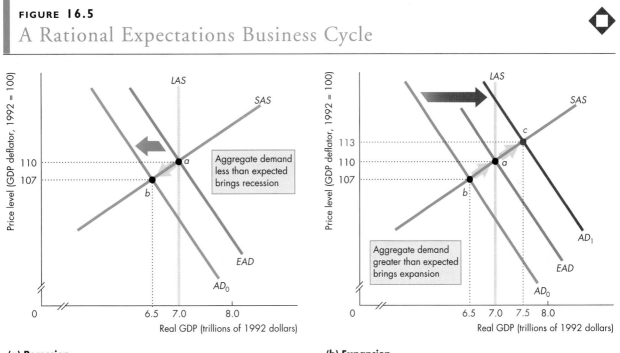

**(a) Recession**

The economy is expected to be at point *a* at the intersection of the long-run aggregate supply curve, *LAS*; the short-run aggregate supply curve, *SAS*; and the *expected* aggregate demand curve, *EAD*. A rational expectations recession begins when an unanticipated fall in aggregate demand shifts the *AD* curve leftward to $AD_0$. With money wage rates based on the expectation that aggregate demand will be *EAD*, real GDP falls to $6.5 trillion and the price level falls to 107 as the economy moves to point *b*. As long as aggregate demand is *expected* to

**(b) Expansion**

be *EAD*, there is no change in the money wage rate.

A rational expectations expansion begins when an unanticipated rise in aggregate demand shifts the *AD* curve rightward from $AD_0$ to $AD_1$. With money wage rates based on the expectation that aggregate demand will be *EAD*, real GDP increases to $7.5 trillion and the price level rises to 113 as the economy moves to point *c*. Again, as long as aggregate demand is *expected* to be *EAD*, there is no change in the money wage rate.

begins. Real GDP falls to $6.5 trillion, and the price level falls to 107. The economy moves to point *b*. Unemployment increases, and there is a surplus of labor. But aggregate demand is expected to be at *EAD*, so the money wage rate doesn't change and the short-run aggregate supply curve remains at *SAS*.

The recession ends when aggregate demand increases to its expected level. And a larger increase that takes aggregate demand to a level that exceeds *EAD* brings an expansion. In Fig. 16.5(b), the aggregate demand curve shifts rightward to $AD_1$. Such an increase in aggregate demand might be caused by a speedup in the money growth rate or an export boom. Real GDP now increases to $7.5 trillion, and the price level rises to 113. The economy moves to point *c*. Unemployment is now below the natural rate. But aggregate demand is expected to be at *EAD*, so the money wage rate doesn't change and the short-run aggregate supply curve remains at *SAS*.

Fluctuations in aggregate demand between $AD_0$ and $AD_1$ around expected aggregate demand *EAD* bring fluctuations in real GDP and the price level between points *b* and *c*.

The two versions of the rational expectations theory differ in their predictions about the effects of a change in expected aggregate demand. The new classical theory predicts that as soon as expected aggregate demand changes, the money wage rate also changes, so the *SAS* curve shifts. The new Keynesian theory predicts that the money wage rate changes only gradually when new contracts are made, so the *SAS* curve moves only slowly. This difference between the two theories is crucial for policy. According to the new classical theory, anticipated policy actions change the price level only and have no effect on real GDP and unemployment. The reason is that when policy is expected to change, the money wage rate changes, so the *SAS* curve shifts and offsets the effects of the policy action on real GDP. In contrast, in the new Keynesian theory, because the money wage rate changes only when new contracts are made, even anticipated policy actions change real GDP and can be used in an attempt to stabilize the cycle.

Like the monetarist business cycle, these rational expectations cycles are similar to rocking horses. They need an outside force to get them going, but once going, the economy rocks around its full employment point. The new classical horse rocks faster and comes to rest more quickly than the new Keynesian horse.

## AS-AD General Theory

All the theories of the business cycle that we've considered can be viewed as particular cases of the more general *AS-AD* theory. In this more general theory, the impulses of both the Keynesian and monetarist theories can change aggregate demand. A multiplier effect makes aggregate demand change by more than any initial change in one of its components. The money wage rate can be viewed as responding to changes in the expected price level. Even if the money wage is flexible, it will change only to the extent that price level expectations change. As a result, the money wage rate will adjust gradually.

Although in all three types of business cycle theory that we've considered, the cycle is caused by fluctuations in aggregate demand, the possibility that an occasional aggregate supply shock might occur is not ruled out. A recession could occur because aggregate supply falls. For example, a widespread drought that cuts agricultural production could cause a recession in an economy that has a large agricultural sector. But these aggregate demand theories of the cycle regard aggregate supply shocks as rare rather than normal events. Aggregate demand fluctuations are the normal ongoing sources of fluctuations.

### R E V I E W

- Keynesian theory says that the business cycle is caused by volatile expectations about future sales and profits—*animal spirits*—a multiplier effect, and sticky money wages.
- Monetarist theory says that the business cycle is caused by the Fed speeding up and slowing the growth rate of money, which changes spending plans.
- New classical and new Keynesian theories (rational expectations theories) say that the business cycle is caused by unanticipated fluctuations in aggregate demand.
- In the new classical theory, the money wage rate responds to price level expectations, and in the new Keynesian theory, the money wage rate is set by long-term contracts.

A new theory of the business cycle challenges the mainstream and traditional aggregate demand theories that you've just studied. It is called the real business cycle theory. Let's look at this new cycle theory.

# Real Business Cycle Theory

THE NEWEST THEORY OF THE BUSINESS CYCLE, known as **real business cycle theory** (or RBC theory), regards random fluctuations in productivity as the main source of economic fluctuations. These productivity fluctuations are assumed to result mainly from fluctuations in the pace of technological change, but they might also have other sources such as international disturbances, climate fluctuations, or natural disasters. The origins of real business cycle theory can be traced to the rational expectations revolution set off by Robert E. Lucas, Jr., but the first demonstration of the power of this theory was given by Edward Prescott and Finn Kydland and by John Long and Charles Plosser. Today, real business cycle theory is part of a broad research agenda called *dynamic general equilibrium analysis*, and hundreds of young macroeconomists do research on this topic.

Like our study of the aggregate demand theories, we'll explore RBC theory by looking first at its impulse and second at the mechanism that converts that impulse into a cycle in real GDP.

## The RBC Impulse

The *impulse* in RBC theory is the *growth rate of productivity* that results from *technological change*. RBC theorists believe this impulse to be generated mainly by the process of research and development that leads to the creation and use of new technologies. Sometimes, technological progress is rapid and productivity grows quickly; at other times, progress is slow and productivity grows moderately. Occasionally, technological change is so far-reaching that it makes a large amount of existing capital, especially human capital, obsolete. It also, initially, destroys jobs and shuts down businesses. These initial effects of far-reaching technological change *decrease* productivity and can trigger a recession. Ultimately, such technological change creates both jobs and businesses and brings massive gains in productivity. Other shocks, such as the world oil embargo of the mid-1970s, can temporarily decrease productivity.

To isolate the RBC theory impulse—the growth rate of productivity that results from technological change—economists use the tool of growth accounting, which is explained in Chapter 10, on pp. 219–221.

---

**FIGURE 16.6**
## The Real Business Cycle Impulse

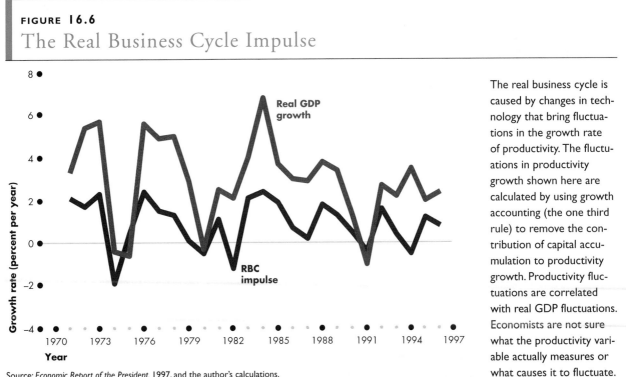

The real business cycle is caused by changes in technology that bring fluctuations in the growth rate of productivity. The fluctuations in productivity growth shown here are calculated by using growth accounting (the one third rule) to remove the contribution of capital accumulation to productivity growth. Productivity fluctuations are correlated with real GDP fluctuations. Economists are not sure what the productivity variable actually measures or what causes it to fluctuate.

Source: *Economic Report of the President*, 1997, and the author's calculations.

Figure 16.6 shows the RBC impulse for the United States from 1970 to 1996. The figure also shows that fluctuations in productivity growth are correlated with real GDP fluctuations. This RBC productivity variable is a catchall, and economists are not sure what it actually measures or what causes it to fluctuate.

## The RBC Mechanism

According to RBC theory, two immediate effects follow from a change in productivity that get an expansion or a contraction going:

1. Investment demand changes.
2. The demand for labor changes.

We'll study these effects and their consequences during a recession. In an expansion, they work in the direction opposite to what is described here.

A wave of technological changes makes some existing capital obsolete and temporarily lowers productivity. Firms expect the future profits to fall and see their labor productivity falling. With lower profit expectations, they cut back their purchases of new capital, and with lower labor productivity, they plan to lay off some workers. So the initial effect of a temporary fall in productivity is a decrease in investment demand and a decrease in the demand for labor.

Figure 16.7 illustrates these two initial effects of a decrease in productivity. Part (a) shows investment demand, $ID$, and saving supply, $SS$ (both of which are explained in Chapter 9, pp. 195–196 and 198–199). Initially, investment demand is $ID_0$ and the equilibrium investment and saving are $1 trillion at a real interest rate of 6 percent a year. A decrease in productivity decreases investment demand and the $ID$ curve shifts leftward to $ID_1$. The real interest rate falls to 4 percent, and investment and saving decrease to $0.7 trillion.

Part (b) shows the demand for labor, $LD$, and the supply of labor, $LS$ (which are explained in Chapter 8, p. 180). Initially, the demand for labor is $LD_0$, and equilibrium employment is 200 billion hours a year at a real wage rate of $15 an hour. The decrease in productivity decreases the demand for labor, and the $LD$ curve shifts leftward to $LD_1$.

Before we can determine the new level of employment and real wage rate, we need to take a ripple effect into account—the key ripple effect in RBC theory.

**The Key Decision: When to Work?** According to RBC theory, people decide *when* to work by doing a cost-benefit calculation. They compare the return from working in the current period with the *expected* return from working in a later period. You make such a comparison every day in school. Suppose your goal in this course is to get an A. To achieve this goal, you work pretty hard most of the time. But during the few days before the midterm and final exams, you work especially hard. Why? Because you believe that the return from studying close to the exam is greater than the return from studying when the exam is a long time away. So during the term, you take time off for the movies and other leisure pursuits, but at exam time, you work every evening and weekend.

Real business cycle theory says that workers behave like you. They work fewer hours, sometimes zero hours, when the real wage rate is temporarily low, and they work more hours when the real wage rate is temporarily high. But to properly compare the current wage rate with the expected future wage rate, workers must use the real interest rate. If the real interest rate is 6 percent a year, a real wage of $1 an hour earned this week will become $1.06 a year from now. If the real wage rate is expected to be $1.05 an hour next year, today's real wage of $1 looks good. By working longer hours now and shorter hours a year from now, a person can get a 1 percent higher real wage rate. But suppose the real interest rate is 4 percent a year. In this case, $1 earned now is worth $1.04 next year. Working fewer hours now and more next year is the way to get a 1 percent higher real wage rate.

So the when-to-work decision depends on the real interest rate. The lower the real interest rate, other things remaining the same, the smaller is the supply of labor. Many economists believe this *intertemporal substitution* effect to be of negligible size. RBC theorists believe that the effect is large, and it is the key element in the RBC mechanism.

You've seen in Fig. 16.7(a) that the decrease in investment demand lowers the real interest rate. This fall in the real interest rate lowers the return to current work and decreases the supply of labor. In Fig. 16.7(b), the labor supply curve shifts leftward to $LS_1$. The effect of a productivity shock on the demand for labor is larger than the effect of the fall in the real interest rate on the supply of labor. That is, the $LD$ curve shifts farther leftward than does the $LS$ curve. As a result, the real wage rate falls to $14.50 an hour and the level of employment falls to 195 billion hours. A recession has begun and is intensifying.

## FIGURE 16.7
# Capital and Labor Markets in a Real Business Cycle

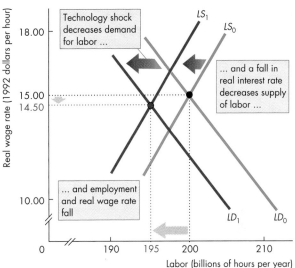

**(a) Investment, saving, and interest rate**

**(b) Labor and wage rate**

Saving supply is *SS* (part a), and initially, investment demand is $ID_0$. The real interest rate is 6 percent, and saving and investment are $1 trillion. In the labor market (part b), the demand for labor is $LD_0$ and the supply of labor is $LS_0$. The real wage rate is $15 an hour, and employment is 200 billion hours. A technological change temporarily decreases productivity, and both investment demand and the demand for labor decrease.

The two demand curves shift leftward to $ID_1$ and $LD_1$. In part (a), the real interest rate falls to 4 percent a year and investment and saving decrease. In part (b), the fall in the real interest rate decreases the supply of labor (the when-to-work decision) and the supply curve shifts leftward to $LS_1$. Employment falls to 195 billion hours, and the real wage rate falls to $14.50 an hour. A recession is under way.

**Real GDP and the Price Level** The next part of the RBC story traces the consequences of the changes you've just seen for real GDP and the price level. With a decrease in employment, aggregate supply decreases, and with a decrease in investment demand, aggregate demand decreases. Figure 16.8 illustrates these effects, using the *AS-AD* framework. Initially, the long-run aggregate supply curve is $LAS_0$, and the aggregate demand curve is $AD_0$. The price level is 110, and real GDP is $7 trillion. There is no short-run aggregate supply curve in this figure because in RBC theory, the *SAS* curve has no meaning. The labor market moves relentlessly toward its equilibrium, and the money wage rate adjusts freely (either upward or downward) to ensure that the real wage rate keeps the quantity of labor demanded equal to the quantity supplied. In RBC theory, unemploy-

ment is always at the natural rate, and the natural rate fluctuates over the business cycle because the amount of job search fluctuates.

The decrease in employment decreases total production and aggregate supply decreases. The *LAS* curve shifts leftward to $LAS_1$. The decrease in investment demand decreases aggregate demand, and the *AD* curve shifts leftward to $AD_1$. The price level falls to 107, and real GDP decreases to $6.8 trillion. The economy has gone through a recession.

**What Happened to Money?** The name *real* business cycle theory is no accident. It reflects the central prediction of the theory. Real things, not nominal or monetary things, cause the business cycle. If the quantity of money changes, aggregate demand changes. But if there is no real change—with no

FIGURE 16.8

## AS-AD in a Real Business Cycle

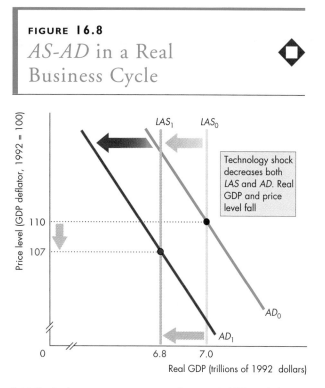

Initially, the long-run aggregate supply curve is $LAS_0$, and the aggregate demand curve is $AD_0$. Real GDP is $7 trillion (which equals potential GDP), and the price level is 110. There is no SAS curve in the real business cycle theory because the money wage rate is flexible. The technological change described in Fig. 16.7 temporarily decreases potential GDP, and the LAS curve shifts leftward to $LAS_1$. The fall in investment demand decreases aggregate demand, and the AD curve shifts leftward to $AD_1$. Real GDP decreases to $6.8 trillion, and the price level falls to 107. The economy has gone into recession.

change in the use of resources and no change in potential GDP—the change in money changes only the price level. In real business cycle theory, this outcome occurs because the aggregate supply curve is the LAS curve, which pins real GDP down at potential GD. So when AD changes, only the price level changes.

**Cycles and Growth**   The shock that drives the business cycle of RBC theory is the same as the force that generates economic growth: technological change. On the average, as technology advances, productivity grows. But it grows at an uneven pace. You saw this fact when you studied growth accounting in Chapter

10. There, we focused on slow-changing trends in productivity growth. Real business cycle theory uses the same idea but says that there are frequent shocks to productivity that are mostly positive but that are occasionally negative.

### Criticisms of Real Business Cycle Theory

RBC theory is controversial, and when economists discuss it, they often generate more heat than light. Its detractors claim that its basic assumptions are just too incredible. Money wages *are* sticky, they claim, so to assume otherwise is at odds with a clear fact. Intertemporal substitution is too weak, they say, to account for large fluctuations in labor supply and employment with small real wage changes.

But what really kills the RBC story, say most economists, is an implausible impulse. Technology shocks are not capable of creating the swings in productivity that growth accounting reveals. These swings in productivity are caused by something, they concede, but they are as likely to be caused by *changes in aggregate demand* as by technology. If the fluctuations in productivity are caused by aggregate demand fluctuations, then the traditional demand theories are needed to explain them. Fluctuations in productivity do not cause the cycle but are caused by it!

Building on this theme, the critics point out that the so-called productivity fluctuations that growth accounting measures are correlated with changes in the growth rate of money and other indicators of changes in aggregate demand.

### Defense of Real Business Cycle Theory

The defenders of RBC theory claim that the theory works. It explains the macroeconomic facts about the business cycle and is consistent with the facts about economic growth. In effect, a single theory explains *both growth and cycles*. The growth accounting exercise that explains slowly changing trends also explains the more frequent business cycle swings. Its defenders also claim that RBC theory is consistent with a wide range of *micro*economic evidence about labor supply decisions, labor demand and investment demand decisions, and information on the distribution of income between labor and capital.

RBC theorists acknowledge that money and the business cycle are correlated. That is, rapid money growth and expansion go together, and slow money growth and recession go together. But, they argue, causation does not run from money to real GDP as the traditional aggregate demand theories state. Instead, they view causation as running from real GDP to money—so-called reverse causation. In a recession, the initial fall in investment demand that lowers the interest rate decreases the demand for bank loans and lowers the profitability of banking. So banks increase their reserves and decrease their loans. The quantity of bank deposits and hence the quantity of money decrease. This reverse causation is responsible for the correlation between money growth and real GDP according to real business cycle theory.

Its defenders also argue that the RBC view is significant because it at least raises the possibility that the business cycle is efficient. The business cycle does not signal an economy that is misbehaving; it is business as usual. If this view is correct, it means that policy designed to smooth the cycle is misguided. Only by taking out the peaks can the troughs be smoothed out. But peaks are bursts of investment to take advantage of new technologies in a timely way. So smoothing the cycle means delaying the benefits of new technologies.

## R E V I E W

- Real business cycle (RBC) theory says that economic fluctuations are caused by technological change that makes productivity growth fluctuate.
- A fall in productivity decreases both investment demand and the demand for labor and lowers the real interest rate. The lower real interest rate decreases the supply of labor and employment, and the real wage rate falls.
- A fall in productivity decreases both long-run aggregate supply and aggregate demand and decreases both real GDP and the price level.

You've now reviewed the main theories of the business cycle. Your next task is to examine some actual business cycles. In pursuing this task, we will focus on the recession phase of the cycle. We'll do this mainly because it is the recessions that cause the most trouble. We begin by looking at two recent recessions.

# Two Recent Recessions

IN THE THEORIES OF THE BUSINESS CYCLE THAT you've studied, recessions can be triggered by a variety of forces, some on the aggregate demand side and some on the aggregate supply side. Let's identify the shocks that triggered two recent recessions: the OPEC recession of 1974–1975 and the 1990–1991 recession.

## The OPEC Recession

During the early 1970s, real GDP was on trend and growing at a rate similar to its long-run average growth rate. Unemployment ranged between 5 and 6 percent, and inflation ranged between 3 and 6 percent a year. More and more people were enjoying and sharing in the benefits of sustained economic expansion. But undercurrents were at work that would bring extraordinary change during the mid-1970s.

Toward the end of 1973, the U.S. and world economies were dealt a devastating blow. The Organization of Petroleum Exporting Countries (OPEC), which controlled 68 percent of world oil production (outside the Communist countries), imposed an oil embargo and increased the price of a barrel of oil from $2.60 to $11.65—a 348 percent increase. The price hike had dramatic macroeconomic effects. For the next two years, the U.S. economy went into a severe recession.

Figure 16.9 shows the severity of the OPEC recession and illustrates the forces that caused the recession by using the mainstream *AS-AD* framework. Before the oil price hike, the aggregate demand and short-run aggregate supply curves were $AD_{73}$ and $SAS_{73}$, respectively. Real GDP was $3.9 trillion, and the GDP deflator was 35.4. Through the subsequent two years, aggregate demand continued to increase and the aggregate demand curve shifted rightward to $AD_{75}$. When OPEC increased the price of crude oil, the prices of other fuels as well as the prices of many other raw materials also increased. The index of all commodity prices excluding fuel increased by 63 percent in 1973 and 24 percent in 1974. Labor costs also started to increase more quickly. As a result of these resource price increases, the short-run aggregate supply curve shifted leftward to $SAS_{75}$. This shift in the short-run aggregate supply curve, triggered by the oil price increase, was the single most significant event producing the OPEC recession. Real GDP fell to $3.87 trillion, and the GDP deflator increased to

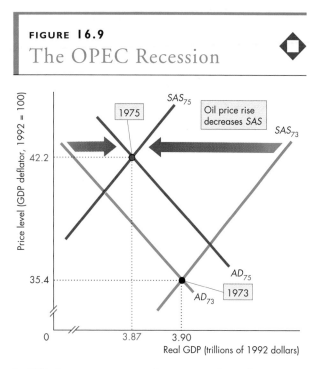

**FIGURE 16.9**

## The OPEC Recession

In 1973, the economy was on its aggregate demand curve, $AD_{73}$, and its short-run aggregate supply curve, $SAS_{73}$, with real GDP at $3.9 trillion and a GDP deflator of 35.4. Between 1973 and 1975, aggregate demand continued to increase at a moderate pace and the aggregate demand curve shifted to $AD_{75}$. In 1974, OPEC increased the price of oil by 348 percent. Other input prices and wages increased, and the short-run aggregate supply curve shifted to $SAS_{75}$. The large shift of the SAS curve combined with the moderate shift of the AD curve led to stagflation—a decrease in real GDP and rising inflation.

42.2—an almost 20 percent increase in the price level over the two years of recession. Thus during the OPEC recession, real GDP decreased and the inflation rate increased. This combination of events gave rise to a new word, *stagflation*, a combination of falling real GDP and rising inflation.

### The 1990–1991 Recession

At the beginning of 1990, the economy was at full employment. The unemployment rate was just above 5 percent, and inflation was steady at 4 percent a year. But the events of 1990 disturbed this situation and brought an end to the longest peacetime expansion in U.S. history.

The dominant events of 1990 were the Persian Gulf crisis and the ensuing Gulf War triggered by Saddam Hussein's invasion of Kuwait. The Gulf crisis brought shocks to both aggregate demand and aggregate supply. The aggregate demand shocks went in both directions. First, fiscal policy became less restrained as government purchases increased to cope with the military consequences of the crisis. The Gulf situation also increased uncertainty about expected sales and profits, which brought a fall in investment. With a fall in investment, aggregate demand decreased. Although fiscal policy was working in the direction opposite to this change in investment, it was not strong enough to prevent aggregate demand from decreasing.

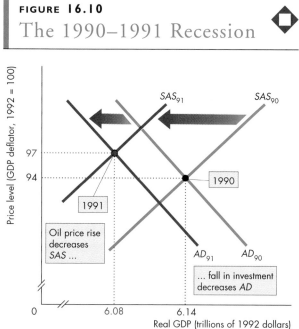

**FIGURE 16.10**

## The 1990–1991 Recession

In 1990, the economy was on its aggregate demand curve, $AD_{90}$, and its short-run aggregate supply curve, $SAS_{90}$, with real GDP at $6.14 trillion and a GDP deflator of 94. A large increase in oil prices decreased aggregate supply and shifted the short-run aggregate supply curve to $SAS_{91}$. Uncertainty surrounding the world economy lowered profit expectations, leading to a fall in investment and a decrease in aggregate demand. The aggregate demand curve shifted to $AD_{91}$. The combination of a decrease in both aggregate supply and aggregate demand puts the economy into recession.

On the supply side, the Gulf crisis put the world energy markets into turmoil yet again. Between April 1990 and October 1990, the price of crude oil more than doubled. This oil price increase operated in a way similar to that of the 1970s. It decreased short-run aggregate supply.

Figure 16.10 shows how the combined effects of these forces started the 1990–1991 recession. In mid-1990, the economy was on aggregate demand curve $AD_{90}$ and short-run aggregate supply curve $SAS_{90}$ with real GDP at \$6.14 trillion and the GDP deflator at 94. By mid-1991, the short-run aggregate supply curve had shifted to $SAS_{91}$, and investment uncertainty had shifted the aggregate demand curve to $AD_{91}$. Real GDP had decreased to \$6.08 trillion. The GDP deflator increased to 97, which slowed the inflation rate slightly to 3.2 percent over the year.

You've seen how aggregate demand and aggregate supply changed in two recent recessions. What happened in the labor market during these recessions?

## The Labor Market in the OPEC Recession

During the OPEC recession, the real wage rate fell from \$14.64 an hour in 1973 to \$14.49 an hour in 1975.[1] Aggregate hours decreased from 157 billion in 1973 to 155 billion in 1975. What caused this decrease in both employment and the real wage rate? We've seen that there are two views about the labor market. The traditional view is that the money wage rate is sticky and changes only gradually. The real business cycle view is that the money wage rate is flexible and adjusts to keep the labor market in equilibrium. Let's see how these two views explain the changes in the real wage rate and employment during the OPEC recession.

**Sticky Wage Theory** Figure 16.11 illustrates the labor market in 1973 and 1975 according to the sticky wage view. In 1973, the demand for labor was $LD_{73}$ and the supply of labor was $LS_{73}$. The real wage rate, \$14.64 an hour, and the level of employment, 157 billion hours, are determined at the intersection of these two curves. The unemployment rate in 1973

---

[1] The measure of real wage rates used here is aggregate wages, salaries, and benefits divided by aggregate hours—see Fig. 8.5, p. 174.

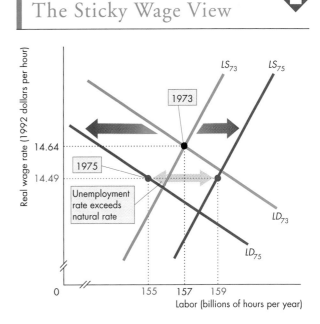

**FIGURE 16.11**

## The Sticky Wage View

In 1973, the demand for labor was $LD_{73}$ and the supply of labor was $LS_{73}$. If the quantity of labor demanded equaled the quantity supplied in 1973, the real wage rate of \$14.64 an hour and employment of 157 billion hours are at the point of intersection of $LD_{73}$ and $LS_{73}$. The OPEC oil price hike lowered the productivity of labor, so the demand for labor decreased and the demand for labor curve shifted leftward to $LD_{75}$. An increase in the population increased the supply of labor and shifted the supply curve rightward to $LS_{75}$. The real wage rate fell, but not by enough to bring about equality between the quantities of labor supplied and demanded. The quantity demanded was 155 billion hours, but the quantity supplied was 159 billion hours. Unemployment increased.

was 4.9 percent, which we will assume was equal to the natural rate, so there was full employment. (This is an assumption, not a fact.)

The OPEC oil price hike lowered labor productivity, which in turn decreased the demand for labor. The labor demand curve shifted leftward to $LD_{75}$. There were four main reasons for this decrease in labor productivity. First, OPEC restricted the supply of crude oil, which meant that some firms experienced temporary shortages of fuel and so had to slow down production. Second, faced with higher energy prices, firms economized on the use of energy. For example, transportation companies lowered truck speeds and airlines pruned schedules to get better payloads. Again, production per hour of labor fell. Third, labor resources that were previously used in production were redirected to designing and building more fuel-efficient equipment. For example, automakers designed smaller, more fuel-efficient cars. Yet again, production per work-hour fell. Fourth, gas-guzzling planes and road vehicles and energy-hungry furnaces and industrial equipment were scrapped at a more rapid than normal pace, a process that decreased the capital stock and so further cut labor productivity.

In the sticky wage view, the real wage rate is determined in the short run by the gradually changing money wage rate and the price level. Between 1973 and 1975, the money wage rate increased by 18 percent. But the price level increased by 19 percent, so the real wage rate fell by 1 percent, to $14.49. At this real wage rate and with the new demand for labor curve, employment decreased to 155 billion hours in 1975.

Through 1974 and 1975, the population increased, and as a result, the supply of labor increased. If there were no other influences on the supply of labor, the supply curve shifted rightward from $LS_{73}$ to $LS_{75}$. At the real wage rate of $14.49, the quantity of labor supplied was 159 billion hours. Unemployment increased above the natural rate. The unemployment rate increased from 4.9 percent in 1973 to 8.5 percent in 1975.

What were the forces preventing the real wage rate from falling in 1975? Given that both the money wage rate and the price level had increased by almost 20 percent, it seems hard to believe that the money wage was sticky. The flexible wage theory has an answer.

**Flexible Wage Theory**   The flexible wage theory is that the money wage rate adjusts to maintain equality between the quantity of labor demanded and the quantity supplied. Fluctuations in unemployment are fluctuations in the natural rate of unemployment. Let's examine the OPEC recession again and see how we can interpret it in terms of this alternative theory.

Figure 16.12 illustrates the flexible wage view of the OPEC recession. The 1973 demand and supply curves, $LD_{73}$ and $LS_{73}$, are identical to those in Fig. 16.11, and they determine the 1973 (assumed) full-employment equilibrium. Following the oil price hike, the demand for labor fell and the demand curve shifted leftward to $LD_{75}$, just as it did in Fig. 16.11.

So far, the flexible wage and sticky wage stories have been the same. The difference arises on the supply side of the labor market. An increase in the population increased the supply of labor. But a fall in the real interest rate—the when-to-work decision—decreased the supply of labor. The real interest rate, which had been around 1 percent a year in 1973, fell to almost *minus* 1 percent a year in 1975. With a low (negative) real interest rate, 1975 was for many people a good year in which to borrow and look for a better job rather than work. This factor was so strong, according to the flexible wage view, that it more than counteracted the increase in the population. So the supply of labor decreased. The labor supply curve shifted leftward to $LS_{75}$ in Fig. 16.12.

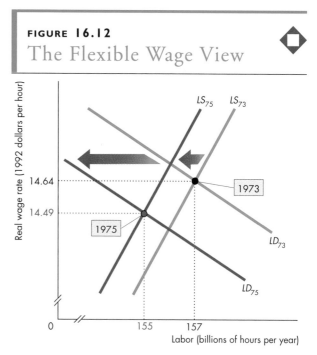

The Flexible Wage View

During the OPEC recession, the real wage rate fell from $14.64 an hour to $14.49 an hour and employment fell from 157 billion hours to 155 billion hours. These movements of the real wage rate and employment are consistent with the flexible wage theory. A fall in the real interest rate made 1975 a bad year for working and a good year for searching for a better job, so the supply of labor decreased. The supply of labor curve shifted leftward to $LS_{75}$, and the 1975 equilibrium is at the intersection of $LD_{75}$ and $LS_{75}$. According to the flexible wage theory, the increase in unemployment that occurred between 1973 and 1975 is interpreted as a temporary increase in the natural rate of unemployment.

The new supply of labor curve intersected the new demand for labor curve at a real wage rate of $14.49 an hour and an employment level of 155 billion hours. You can't see it in Fig. 16.12, but the natural rate of unemployment increased through 1975, according to the flexible wage view. In deciding not to work, more people searched for new and better jobs, so job search and unemployment increased. People who had previously worked in energy-using jobs looked for higher-paid energy-saving jobs.

We've interpreted the labor market in the OPEC recession in two ways. Can we also interpret the 1990–1991 recession in these same two ways?

## The Labor Market in the 1990–1991 Recession

During the 1990–1991 recession, the real wage rate *increased* from $17.32 an hour in 1990 to $17.45 an hour in 1991, and aggregate hours decreased from 203 billion in 1990 to 201 billion in 1992. Why did the real wage rate increase when hours decreased and the economy was in recession?

**Sticky Wage Theory** A sticky wage story can be told about money wages in the 1990–1991 recession that is based on the rational expectations theories of the business cycle. According to this view, the money wage rate in 1991 was determined by decisions made in 1990 based on the price level then expected for 1991. Prices had increased during 1990 by about 4.5 percent a year. Assuming that this rate would continue through 1991 and allowing for a small expected rise in labor productivity, employers and workers agreed to increase the money wage rate by almost 5 percent.

In reality, the inflation rate slowed in 1991 to less than 4 percent. As a result, the real wage rate increased by 1 percent. With an increase in the real wage rate, the quantity of labor demanded decreased and employment fell.

Can the flexible wage theory interpret the 1990–1991 change in employment and the real wage rate?

**Flexible Wage Theory** The flexible wage theory has a difficult time accounting for the events we've just described. For the real wage rate to rise and employment to fall, the supply of labor must have decreased and by more than the decrease in the demand for labor. But the influences on the supply

of labor worked in the wrong direction in 1991. The working-age population increased that year by almost 1 percent. More significant, though, the real interest rate *increased*. So the when-to-work decision and the population change both increased the supply of labor.

The failure of a simple flexible wage theory to explain the rise in the real wage rate and the fall in employment does not mean that the entire approach is invalid. Many economists believe that a more detailed microeconomic story about labor reallocation across sectors and changes in wage rates for individual jobs can explain even the 1990–1991 recession in terms of flexible wages.

Determining which of the two wage theories is correct is not just an academic curiosity. It is crucial for the design of antirecessionary policy. If the flexible wage theory is correct, there is only one aggregate supply curve—the vertical long-run aggregate supply curve. This fact means that any attempt to bring the economy out of recession by increasing aggregate demand—for example, by lowering interest rates and increasing the money supply or by fiscal policy measures—is doomed to failure and can result only in a higher price level (more inflation). Conversely, if the sticky wage theory is correct, then the short-run aggregate supply curve slopes upward. An increase in aggregate demand, although increasing the price level somewhat, increases real GDP and will bring the economy out of a recession.

### REVIEW

- The OPEC recession was triggered by a supply shock—an increase in the price of oil.
- The 1990–1991 recession was triggered by a supply shock—the Gulf crisis, which increased the price of oil—and a demand shock—increased uncertainty, which lowered investment demand.
- The labor market can be interpreted by using either the sticky wage theory or the flexible wage theory during the OPEC recession but by using only the sticky wage theory during the 1990–1991 recession.

You've now seen how business cycle theory can be used to interpret two recent recessions. But can we use business cycle theory to explain the greatest of recessions—the Great Depression? Let's find out.

## The Great Depression

THE LATE 1920S WERE YEARS OF ECONOMIC boom. New houses and apartments were built on an unprecedented scale, new firms were created, and the capital stock of the nation expanded. At the beginning of 1929, U.S. real GDP exceeded potential GDP and the unemployment rate was a low 3.2 percent. But as that eventful year unfolded, increasing signs of economic weakness began to appear. The most dramatic events occurred in October when the stock market collapsed, losing more than one third of its value in two weeks. The four years that followed were years of monstrous economic depression.

Figure 16.13 shows the dimensions of the Great Depression. On the eve of the Great Depression in 1929, the economy was on aggregate demand curve $AD_{29}$ and short-run aggregate supply curve $SAS_{29}$. Real GDP was $1,028 billion (1992 dollars), and the GDP deflator was 15.

In 1930, there was a widespread expectation that the price level would fall, and the money wage rate fell. With a lower money wage rate, the short-run aggregate supply curve shifted from $SAS_{29}$ to $SAS_{30}$. But increased pessimism and uncertainty decreased investment and the demand for consumer durables, and aggregate demand decreased to $AD_{30}$. In 1930, real GDP decreased to $936 billion (a 9 percent decrease) and the price level fell to 14.6 (a 3 percent fall).

In a normal recession, the economy might have remained below full employment for a year or so and then started to expand. But the recession of 1930 was not a normal one. In 1930 and the next two years, the economy was further bombarded with huge negative demand shocks (the sources of which we'll look at in a moment). The aggregate demand curve shifted leftward all the way to $AD_{33}$. With a depressed economy, the price level was expected to fall and wages fell in line with those expectations. The money wage fell from 55¢ an hour in 1930 to 44¢ an hour by 1933. As a result of lower wages, the aggregate supply curve shifted from $SAS_{30}$ to $SAS_{33}$. But the size of the shift of the short-run aggregate supply curve was much less than the decrease in aggregate demand. As a result, the aggregate demand curve and the short-run aggregate supply curve intersected in 1933 at a real GDP of $734 billion (a decrease of 29 percent from 1929) and a GDP deflator of 11.4 (a decrease of 24 percent from 1929).

**FIGURE 16.13**

## The Great Depression

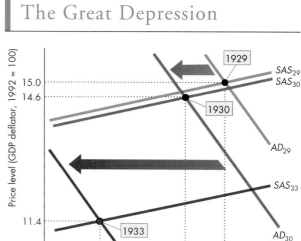

In 1929, real GDP was $1,028 billion and the GDP deflator was 15—at the intersection of $AD_{29}$ and $SAS_{29}$. Increased pessimism and uncertainty resulted in a decrease in investment and aggregate demand decreased to $AD_{30}$. The money wage rate decreased, so the short-run aggregate supply curve shifted to $SAS_{30}$. Real GDP and the price level fell. In the next three years, decreases in the money supply and investment decreased aggregate demand, shifting the aggregate demand curve to $AD_{33}$. Again, to some degree, the decrease in aggregate demand was anticipated, so wages fell and the short-run aggregate supply curve shifted to $SAS_{33}$. By 1933, real GDP had fallen to $734 billion (71 percent of its 1929 level) and the GDP deflator had fallen to 11.4 (76 percent of its 1929 level).

Although the Great Depression brought enormous hardship, the distribution of that hardship was uneven. Twenty-five percent of the work force had no jobs at all. Also at that time, there were virtually no organized social security and unemployment programs in place. So for many families there was virtually no income. But the pocketbooks of those who kept their jobs barely noticed the Great Depression. It is true that wages fell from 57¢ an hour in 1929 to 44¢ an hour in 1933. But at the same time, the price level fell by a larger percentage, so real wages actually increased. Thus people who had jobs became better off during the Great Depression.

You can begin to appreciate the magnitude of the Great Depression if you compare it with the two recessions that we studied earlier in this chapter. Between 1973 and 1975, real GDP fell by 1.8 percent. From mid-1990 to mid-1991, it fell by 1.6 percent. A hypothetical 1999 Great Depression would lower real GDP by 30 percent, to less than its 1979 level.

## Why the Great Depression Happened

The late 1920s were years of economic boom, but they were also years of increasing uncertainty. The main source of increased uncertainty was international. The world economy was going through tumultuous times. The patterns of world trade were changing as Britain, the traditional economic powerhouse of the world, began its period of relative economic decline and new economic powers such as Japan began to emerge. International currency fluctuations and the introduction of restrictive trade policies by many countries (see Chapter 18) further increased the uncertainty faced by firms. There was also domestic uncertainty arising from the fact that there had been such a strong boom in recent years, especially in the capital goods sector and housing. No one believed that this boom would last forever, but many people thought it had a lot farther to run and there was great uncertainty about how demand would change.

This environment of uncertainty led to a slowdown in consumer spending, especially on new homes and household appliances. By the fall of 1929, the uncertainty had reached a critical level and contributed to the stock market crash. The stock market crash, in turn, heightened people's fears about economic prospects in the foreseeable future. Fear fed fear. Investment collapsed. The building industry almost disappeared. An industry that had been operating flat out just two years earlier was now building virtually no new houses and apartments. It was this drop in investment and a drop in consumer spending on durables that led to the initial leftward shift of the aggregate demand curve from $AD_{29}$ to $AD_{30}$ in Fig. 16.13.

At this stage, what became the Great Depression was no worse than many previous recessions had been. What distinguishes the Great Depression from previous recessions are the events that followed between 1930 and 1933. But economists, even to

this day, have not come to agreement on how to interpret those events. One view, argued by Peter Temin,[2] is that spending continued to fall for a wide variety of reasons—including a continuation of increasing pessimism and uncertainty. According to Temin's view, the continued contraction resulted from a collapse of expenditure that was independent of the decrease in the quantity of money. The investment demand curve shifted leftward. Milton Friedman and Anna J. Schwartz have argued that the continuation of the contraction was almost exclusively the result of the subsequent worsening of financial and monetary conditions.[3] According to Friedman and Schwartz, it was a severe cut in the money supply that lowered aggregate demand, prolonging the contraction and deepening the depression.

Although there is disagreement about the causes of the contraction phase of the Great Depression, the disagreement is not about the elements at work but about the degree of importance attached to each. Everyone agrees that increased pessimism and uncertainty lowered investment demand, and everyone agrees that there was a massive contraction of the real money supply. Temin and his supporters assign primary importance to the fall in autonomous expenditure and secondary importance to the fall in the money supply. Friedman and Schwartz and their supporters assign primary responsibility to the money supply and regard the other factors as being of limited importance.

Let's look at the contraction of aggregate demand a bit more closely. Between 1930 and 1933, the nominal money supply decreased by 20 percent. This decrease in the money supply was not directly induced by the Fed's actions. The *monetary base* (currency in circulation and bank reserves) hardly fell at all. But the bank deposits component of the money supply suffered an enormous collapse. It did so primarily because a large number of banks failed. Before the Great Depression, fueled by increasing stock prices and booming business conditions, bank loans expanded. But after the stock market crash and the downturn, many borrowers found themselves in hard economic times. They could not pay the interest on

[2] Peter Temin, *Did Monetary Forces Cause the Great Depression?* (New York: W. W. Norton, 1976).
[3] Milton Friedman and Anna J. Schwartz developed this explanation in *A Monetary History of the United States: 1867–1960* (Princeton, N.J.: Princeton University Press, 1963), Chapter 7.

their loans, and they could not meet the agreed repayment schedules. Banks had deposits that exceeded the realistic value of the loans that they had made. When depositors withdrew funds from the banks, the banks lost reserves. Many of them simply couldn't meet their depositors' demands to be repaid.

Bank failures feed on themselves and create additional failures. Seeing banks fail, people become anxious to protect themselves and so take their money out of the banks. Such were the events of 1930. The quantity of notes and coins in circulation increased, and the volume of bank deposits declined. But the very action of taking money out of the bank to protect one's wealth accentuated the process of banking failure. Banks were increasingly short of cash and unable to meet their obligations.

What role did the stock market crash of 1929 play in producing the Great Depression? It certainly created an atmosphere of fear and panic and probably also contributed to the overall air of uncertainty that dampened investment spending. It also reduced the wealth of stockholders, encouraging them to cut back on their consumption spending. But the direct effect of the stock market crash on consumption, although a contributory factor to the Great Depression, was not the major source of the drop in aggregate demand. It was the collapse in investment arising from increased uncertainty that brought the 1930 decline in aggregate demand.

The stock market crash was a predictor of severe recession. It reflected the expectations of stockholders concerning future profit prospects. As those expectations became pessimistic, people sold their stocks. There were more sellers than buyers and the prices of stocks were bid lower and lower. That is, the behavior of the stock market was a consequence of expectations about future profitability, and those expectations were lowered as a result of increased uncertainty.

## Can It Happen Again?

Because we have an incomplete understanding of the causes of the Great Depression, we cannot be sure whether such an event will happen again. The economic turmoil of the 1920s that preceded the Depression certainly can happen again. But there are some significant differences between the economy of the 1990s and that of the 1930s that make a severe depression much less likely today than it was 60 years ago. The most significant features of the economy that make severe depression less likely today are:

- Bank deposit insurance
- The Fed's role as lender of last resort
- Taxes and government spending
- Multi-income families

Let's examine these in turn.

**Bank Deposit Insurance**   As a result of the Great Depression, the federal government established, in the 1930s, the Federal Deposit Insurance Corporation (FDIC). The FDIC insures bank deposits for up to $100,000 per deposit, so most depositors need no longer fear bank failure. If a bank fails, the FDIC pays the deposit holders. With federally insured bank deposits, the key event that turned a fairly ordinary recession into the Great Depression is most unlikely to occur. It was the fear of bank failure that caused people to withdraw their deposits from banks. The aggregate consequence of these individually rational acts was to cause the very bank failures that were feared. With deposit insurance, most depositors have nothing to lose if a bank fails and so have no incentive to take actions that are likely to give rise to that failure.

Some recent events reinforce this conclusion. With massive failures of S&Ls in the 1980s and with bank failures in New England in 1990 and 1991, there was no tendency for depositors to panic and withdraw their funds in a self-reinforcing run on similar institutions.

**Lender of Last Resort**   The Fed is the lender of last resort in the U.S. economy. If a single bank is short of reserves, it can borrow reserves from other banks. If the entire banking system is short of reserves, banks can borrow from the Fed. By making reserves available (at a suitable interest rate), the Fed is able to make the quantity of reserves in the banking system respond flexibly to the demand for those reserves. Bank failure can be prevented, or at least contained to cases in which bad management practices are the source of the problem. Widespread failures of the type that occurred in the Great Depression can be prevented.

It is now generally agreed that the Fed made a serious mistake in its handling of monetary policy during the Great Depression. With one eye on the international situation, the Fed *increased* the discount rate sharply from 1.5 percent to 3.5 percent just when the banks needed to borrow more. It was only long after the event, when Friedman and Schwartz examined the contraction years of the Great Depression, that economists came to realize that the Fed would have had to *decrease* the discount rate and *increase* the monetary base to have prevented the intensification of the contraction. Now that this lesson has been learned and there is such widespread agreement about the matter, there is at least some chance that the mistake will not be repeated.

The last time the Fed was confronted by a similar problem, although on a much smaller scale, was in October 1987. At that time, a severe stock market crash triggered fears of a new Great Depression. The Fed Chairman, Alan Greenspan, told the U.S. banking and financial community that the Fed had both the ability and the intent to maintain calm financial conditions and to supply sufficient reserves to ensure that the banking system did not begin to contract.

**Taxes and Government Spending**  The government sector was a much smaller part of the economy in 1929 than it has become today. On the eve of that earlier recession, government purchases of goods and services were less than 9 percent of GDP. Today, government purchases exceed 20 percent of GDP. Government transfer payments were less than 6 percent of GDP in 1929. Today, they exceed 15 percent of GDP.

A larger level of government purchases of goods and services means that when recession hits, a large component of aggregate demand does not decline. But government transfer payments are the most sensitive economic stabilizer. When the economy goes into recession and depression, more people qualify for unemployment benefits and social security. As a consequence, although disposable income decreases, the extent of the decrease is moderated by the existence of such programs. Consumption expenditure, in turn, does not decline by as much as it would in the absence of such government programs. The limited decline in consumption spending further limits the overall decrease in aggregate expenditure, thereby limiting the magnitude of an economic downturn.

**Multi-Income Families**  At the time of the Great Depression, families with more than one wage earner were much less common than they are today. The labor force participation rate in 1929 was around 55 percent. Today, it is 67 percent. Thus even if the unemployment rate increased to around 25 percent today, close to 50 percent of the adult population

would actually have jobs. During the Great Depression, less than 40 percent of the adult population had work. Multi-income families have greater security than single-income families do. The chance of both (or all) income earners in a family losing their jobs simultaneously is much lower than the chance of a single earner losing work. With greater family income security, family consumption is likely to be less sensitive to fluctuations in family income that are seen as temporary. Thus when aggregate income falls, it might not induce a cut in consumption. For example, during the OPEC recession, as real GDP fell, personal consumption expenditure actually increased. In 1990–1991, when real GDP fell by $60 billion, consumption expenditure fell by only $26 billion.

For the four reasons we have just reviewed, it appears that the economy has better shock-absorbing characteristics today than it had in the 1920s and 1930s. Even if there is a collapse of confidence, leading to a fall in investment, today's shock absorbers will not translate that initial shock into the large and prolonged fall in real GDP and rise in unemployment that occurred more than 60 years ago.

Because the economy is now more immune to severe recession than it was in the 1930s, even a stock market crash of the magnitude that occurred in 1987 had barely noticeable effects on spending. A crash of a similar magnitude in 1929 resulted in the near collapse of housing investment and consumer durable purchases. In the period following the 1987 stock market crash, investment and spending on durable goods hardly changed.

None of this is to say that there might not be a deep recession or even a Great Depression in the last half of the 1990s (or beyond). But it would take a very severe shock to trigger one.

◆ We have now completed our study of the business cycle. During an expansion, analysts use the theories you have studied to try to forecast the next recession. You can see an example of this activity in *Reading Between the Lines* on pp. 390–391.

We have also completed our study of the science of macroeconomics and learned about the influences on long-term economic growth and inflation as well as the business cycle. We have discovered that these issues pose huge policy challenges. How can we speed up the rate of economic growth while at the same time keeping inflation low and avoiding big swings of the business cycle? Our task in the next chapter is to study these macroeconomic policy challenges.

# The 1990s Expansion

THE ARIZONA REPUBLIC, DECEMBER 29, 1996

## Can Economic Expansion Keep From Faltering?

BY VIVIAN MARINO
THE ASSOCIATED PRESS

WASHINGTON—Just as the economy helped evict George Bush from the White House four years ago, it renewed Bill Clinton's lease in 1996.

Jobs were plentiful. Incomes rose. The stock market marched further into record territory. ...

How much of the credit does Clinton truly deserve? Will the economic expansion—the third longest in the country's history—continue during his second term, or through 1997, for that matter?

Only two other presidents this century—John F. Kennedy and Lyndon B. Johnson—have avoided recessions while in office. No two-term president has managed to escape one.

Some believe Clinton will rewrite history. Forty-four top economic forecasters surveyed recently by the National Association of Business Economists predicted the expansion that began in March 1991 would continue into the 21st century, with growth averaging 2.5 percent over the next five years.

Others believe the cycle is winding down. ...

Heading into 1997, the economy does appear to be moderating.

Recent data show new home sales plunged nearly 9 percent in October.

Unemployment climbed to a four-month high of 5.4 percent in November, after hovering near 5 percent in August.

The gross domestic product ... rose at a weaker-than-estimated 2 percent annual rate in the third quarter, less than half the nearly 5 percent pace in the April-to-June quarter.

Most economists believe the GDP will average 2.5 percent growth for all of 1996 and ease to between 2 percent and 2.25 percent in 1997. ...

The year ends with relatively low interest rates, around 7.5 percent for a 30-year fixed-rate mortgage, and low inflation, around 3 percent.

Other positive economic signs linger: Consumer confidence is at a seven-year high. The manufacturing sector of the economy remains at a five-month high in terms of growth. And the stock market has continued to break records, with the Dow Jones industrial average rising nearly 500 points in November alone. ...

Clinton takes credit for cutting the federal budget deficit in each year of office. It also was during his tenure that median household income rose for the first time in six years—2.7 percent in 1995. ...

The Associated Press. Reprinted with permission.

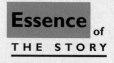

**Essence** of **THE STORY**

■ Three presidents this century have escaped recessions while in office: Kennedy, Johnson, and Clinton.

■ During President Clinton's first term, unemployment was low, household incomes increased, and the Dow Jones industrial index expanded.

■ Some economists believe the expansion that began in March 1991 will continue into the twenty-first century. Others believe the expansion is slowing.

■ Some recent data show that unemployment is climbing and GDP growth is slowing.

■ But consumer confidence is high, the manufacturing sector is at a five-month high in terms of growth, and the stock market continues to break records.

■ President Clinton takes credit for cutting the budget deficit during each year in office.

# Economic

## A N A L Y S I S

■ Presidents Kennedy and Johnson and, to date, President Clinton have all escaped recessions while holding office. But there are some significant differences between the two eras.

■ Figure 1 shows the economy during the Kennedy-Johnson era. When President Kennedy took office in 1960, real GDP was $2.3 trillion. At the end of President Johnson's term, real GDP was $3.3 trillion.

■ During these years, real GDP grew at a rate of 4.9 percent per year and the inflation rate was 2.2 percent per year.

■ In 1960, the economy was in a recessionary gap. Figure 1 shows this gap. The aggregate demand curve $AD_{60}$ intersects the short-run supply curve $SAS_{60}$ to the left of the long-run aggregate supply curve $LAS_{60}$.

■ In 1968, the economy was in an inflationary gap. Figure 1 shows this gap. The aggregate demand curve $AD_{68}$ intersects the short-run supply curve $SAS_{68}$ to the right of the long-run aggregate supply curve $LAS_{68}$.

■ In 1993, when President Clinton took office, the economy was in a recessionary gap similar to that inherited by President Kennedy. Figure 2 shows the situation. Real GDP was $6.2 trillion in 1992. In 1996, real GDP was $6.9 trillion, which equaled potential GDP.

■ During President Clinton's first term of office, real GDP growth was 2.8 percent per year and the inflation rate was 2.6 percent per year.

■ These episodes have contrasting policies. The Kennedy-Johnson period was one of expansionary fiscal policy. Government consumption expenditure increased by 4.7 percent per year.

■ In contrast during the first Clinton term, government consumption expenditure increased only 1 percent over the entire four-year period.

■ The Kennedy-Johnson period was also a period of rapid monetary growth. The M2 growth rate was almost 8 percent per year. In contrast, during President Clinton's first term, M2 grew by only 2.6 percent per year.

**Figure 1  Kennedy-Johnson years**

**Figure 2  Clinton years**

■ The economic expansion during the 1960s exceeded the expansion of potential GDP and was policy driven. President Johnson bears some of the responsibility for the 1960s expansion being too strong and starting the inflationary 1970s.

■ The economic expansion of the 1990s is an expansion of potential GDP and is not driven by policy. More likely, supply-side factors are at work, for which President Clinton can take limited credit.

| SUMMARY |
|---|

## Key Points

### Cycle Patterns, Impulses, and Mechanisms (pp. 368–370)

- Since 1920, there have been fifteen recessions and expansions.
- The Great Depression was the most severe contraction of real GDP, and the postwar recessions have been milder than the prewar recessions.

### Aggregate Demand Theories of the Business Cycle (pp. 370–376)

- Keynesian business cycle theory identifies volatile expectations about future sales and profits as the main source of economic fluctuations.
- Monetarist business cycle theory identifies fluctuations in the money stock as the main source of economic fluctuations.
- Rational expectations theory identifies unanticipated fluctuations in aggregate demand as the main source of economic fluctuations.

### Real Business Cycle Theory (pp. 377–381)

- In real business cycle (RBC) theory, economic fluctuations are caused by fluctuations in the influence of technological change on productivity growth.
- A temporary slowdown in the pace of technological change decreases investment demand and both the demand for labor and supply of labor decrease.

### Two Recent Recessions (pp. 381–385)

- The OPEC recession was triggered by an increase in the price of oil and an oil embargo, which decreased aggregate supply.
- The 1990–1991 recession resulted from the Gulf crisis, which increased the price of oil and decreased aggregate supply, and a decrease in investment, which decreased aggregate demand.

### The Great Depression (pp. 386–389)

- The Great Depression started with increased uncertainty, which brought a fall in investment (especially in housing) and spending on consumer durables.
- There then followed a near total collapse of the financial system. Banks failed and the money supply fell, resulting in a continued fall in aggregate demand.
- The Great Depression itself produced a series of reforms that make a repeat of such a depression much less likely.

## Key Figures ◆

## Key Terms

## QUESTIONS

1. Describe an average recession and expansion.

2. Have recessions been getting more severe or less severe?

3. Distinguish between a cycle impulse and a cycle mechanism, and identify the impulse and mechanism in three analogies given in this chapter.

4. What is the Keynesian theory of the business cycle? Carefully distinguish between its impulse and its mechanism.

5. What is the monetarist theory of the business cycle? Carefully distinguish between its impulse and its mechanism.

6. What are the rational expectations theories of the business cycle? Carefully distinguish between their impulses and their mechanisms.

7. What is the key difference between new classical theory and new Keynesian theory of the business cycle?

8. What is the impulse that causes economic fluctuations according to real business cycle theory?

9. In real business cycle theory, what happens to investment demand and the demand for labor if a technological change brings a large increase in productivity?

10. How is the labor supply decision influenced by the real interest rate?

11. Why is there no short-run aggregate supply curve in real business cycle theory?

12. List the main arguments against and in favor of real business cycle theory.

13. When did the Great Depression and the OPEC recession occur?

14. What triggered the OPEC recession and the 1990–1991 recession?

15. Which one of the OPEC recession and the 1990–1991 recession was a period of stagflation?

16. Describe the changes in employment and real wages in the OPEC recession. What is the sticky wage theory of these changes? What is the flexible wage theory of these changes?

## PROBLEMS

Use the figure on the next page, which shows the economy of Virtualreality, for all the following problems.

1. When the economy is in a long-run equilibrium, it is at points *b*, *e*, and *h*. When a recession occurs in Virtualreality, the economy moves away from these points to one of the two other points identified in each of the three parts of the figure.
   a. If the Keynesian theory is the correct explanation for the recession, to which points does the economy move?
   b. If the monetarist theory is the correct explanation for the recession, to which points does the economy move?
   c. If the new classical rational expectations theory is the correct explanation for the recession, to which points does the economy move?
   d. If the new Keynesian rational expectations theory is the correct explanation for the recession, to which points does the economy move?
   e. If real business cycle theory is the correct explanation for the recession, to which points does the economy move?

2. Suppose that when the recession occurs in Virtualreality, the economy moves to *a*, *f*, and *i*. Which, if any, theory of the business cycle explains this outcome?

3. Suppose that when the recession occurs in Virtualreality, the economy moves to *c*, *f*, and *i*. Which, if any, theory of the business cycle explains this outcome?

4. Suppose that when the recession occurs in Virtualreality, the economy moves to *a*, *d*, and *i*. Which, if any, theory of the business cycle explains this outcome?

5. Suppose that when the recession occurs in Virtualreality, the economy moves to *c*, *d*, and *i*. Which, if any, theory of the business cycle explains this outcome?

6. Suppose that when the recession occurs in Virtualreality, the economy moves to *a*, *f*, and *g*. Which, if any, theory of the business cycle explains this outcome?

**(a) Labor market**

**(b) AS-AD**

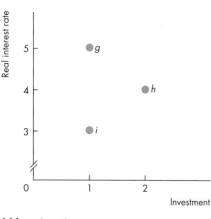

**(c) Investment**

# CRITICAL THINKING

1. Study *Reading Between the Lines* on pp. 390–391 and then answer the following questions:
   a. What are the alternative views about the U.S. economy expressed in the article?
   b. What is the relevance, if any, of the information given in the article about the number of presidents who have avoided recessions?
   c. What does the article regard as positive signs that point to continued expansion?
   d. What does the article regard as negative signs that point to recession?
   e. Can you detect any clues in the news article to tell you whether the author is a Keynesian, monetarist, new classical, new Keynesian, or real business cycle supporter?
   f. What policy actions, if any, do you think the Fed or Congress needs to take in 1997 and 1998 to keep the economy growing and to prevent a new recession?

2. Describe the changes in employment and real wages during the 1990–1991 recession. What is the sticky wage theory of these changes? What is the flexible wage theory of these changes?

3. Describe the changes in real GDP, employment and unemployment, and the price level that occurred during the Great Depression years of 1929–1933.

4. List all of the features of the U.S. economy during the current year that you can think of that are consistent with a pessimistic outlook for the next two years.

5. List all of the features of the U.S. economy during the current year that you can think of that are consistent with an optimistic outlook for the next two years.

6. How do you think the U.S. economy is going to evolve over the next year or two? Explain your predictions, drawing on the pessimistic and optimistic factors that you have listed in the previous two questions and on your knowledge of macroeconomic theory.

# 17

# Macroeconomic Policy Challenges

From 1991 through 1997, the U.S. economy performed well. Real GDP expanded by 2.6 percent a year, unemployment fell to below 5 percent, and the inflation rate remained below 3 percent a year. The United States was not alone in achieving a strong macroeconomic performance. Real GDP expanded in Canada by 2.5 percent a year and in the developing countries of Asia by 8 percent a year. But not all countries and regions shared in this solid growth. Japan's real GDP expanded by a lackluster 1 percent a year, and in Russia, real GDP shrank for five successive years to less than two thirds of its 1990 level. ◆ There were clouds, even in the U.S. economic sky. Interest rates remained relatively high, and the federal budget deficit stubbornly persisted. Also, there were questions about how fast U.S. real GDP could grow over the longer term. Had the potential GDP growth rate increased? Had the natural rate of unemployment decreased? Or was real GDP now above potential GDP? Was the economy overheating again? If it was overheating, was inflation about to increase? And when is the next recession coming? ◆ The variety of macroeconomic performance raises questions about macroeconomic policy. Can policy improve performance? Specifically, can the federal government use its fiscal policy to speed up long-term growth, keep inflation in check, and maintain a low unemployment rate? Can the Fed use its monetary policy to achieve any of these ends? Are some policy goals better achieved by fiscal policy and some by monetary policy? What specific policy actions do the best job? Are some ways of conducting policy better than others? ◆ In this chapter, we're going to study the challenges of achieving the highest sustainable long-term growth rate and low unemployment while avoiding inflation. At the end of the chapter, you will have a deeper understanding of the macroeconomic policy problems facing the United States today.

## What Can Policy Do?

## After studying this chapter, you will be able to:

- ■ Describe the goals of macroeconomic policy and the main features of fiscal policy and monetary policy since 1960

- ■ Explain how fiscal policy and monetary policy influence long-term economic growth

- ■ Evaluate fixed-rule and feedback-rule policies to stabilize the business cycle

- ■ Explain how fiscal policy influences the natural rate of unemployment

- ■ Explain why lowering inflation usually brings recession

## Policy Goals

MACROECONOMIC POLICY GOALS FALL INTO TWO big categories: domestic and international. We study international macroeconomic policy issues in Chapters 18 and 19. Here, we focus on domestic policy. The four main domestic macroeconomic policy goals are to:

- Achieve the highest sustainable rate of potential GDP growth
- Smooth out avoidable business cycle fluctuations
- Maintain low unemployment
- Maintain low inflation

### Potential GDP Growth

Rapid sustained real GDP growth can make a profound contribution to economic well being. With a growth rate of 2 percent a year, it takes more than 30 years for production to double. With a growth rate of 5 percent a year, production more than doubles in just 15 years. And with a growth rate of 10 percent a year, as some Asian countries are achieving, production doubles in just 7 years. The limits to *sustainable* growth are determined by the availability of natural resources, by environmental considerations, and by the willingness of people to save and invest in new capital and new technologies rather than consume everything they produce.

How fast can the economy grow over the long term? Between 1988 and 1995, through one complete business cycle, potential GDP grew at a rate of 2 percent a year.[1] But the U.S. population grows at about 1 percent a year, so the growth rate of real GDP per person was 1 percent a year, which means that output per person doubles every 70 years. Most economists believe that the U.S. economy can maintain a long-term growth rate of potential GDP of 2.5 percent a year. This growth rate would double output per person every 48 years. A few economists believe that with the right policies, sustainable growth of 5 percent a year is possible. This growth rate would double output per person every 18 years, increase it more than sixfold over 48 years, and increase it more than twelvefold in 70 years. So increasing the long-term growth rate is of critical importance.

---
[1] This number and the other numbers in this paragraph are based on the official measure of real GDP. If we take inflation bias into account, the growth rates might be as much as 1 percent per year more than these.

### The Business Cycle

Potential GDP probably does not grow at a constant rate. Fluctuations in the pace of technological advance and in the pace of investment in new capital bring fluctuations in potential GDP. So some fluctuations in real GDP represent fluctuations in potential GDP. But when real GDP grows less quickly than potential GDP, output is lost, and when real GDP grows more quickly than potential GDP, bottlenecks arise. Keeping real GDP growth steady and equal to potential GDP growth avoids these problems.

It is not known how smooth real GDP growth can be made. Real business cycle theory regards all the fluctuations in real GDP as fluctuations in potential GDP. The aggregate demand theories regard most of the fluctuations in real GDP as being avoidable deviations from potential GDP.

### Unemployment

When real GDP growth slows, unemployment rises above the natural rate of unemployment. The higher the unemployment rate, the longer is the time taken by unemployed people to find jobs. Productive labor is wasted, and there is a slowdown in the accumulation of human capital. If high unemployment persists, serious psychological and social problems arise for the unemployed workers and their families.

When real GDP growth speeds up, unemployment decreases and falls below the natural rate of unemployment. The lower the unemployment rate, the harder it becomes for expanding industries to get the labor they need to keep growing. If extremely low unemployment persists, serious bottlenecks and production dislocations occur.

Keeping unemployment at the natural rate avoids both of these problems. But just what is the natural rate of unemployment? Assessments vary. The actual average unemployment rate over the most recent business cycle—1988 to 1996—was 6 percent. Most economists would put the natural rate at about 5.5 percent. A few economists believe that the natural rate is lower than this, perhaps as low as 5 percent. At the other extreme, real business cycle theorists believe that the natural rate fluctuates and always equals the actual unemployment rate.

If the natural rate of unemployment becomes high, then a goal of policy becomes lowering the natural rate itself. This goal is independent of smoothing the business cycle.

## Inflation

When inflation fluctuates unpredictably, money becomes less useful as a measuring rod for conducting transactions. In extreme cases, it becomes useless and is abandoned as the means of payment. Borrowers and lenders and employers and workers must take on extra risks. Keeping the inflation rate steady and predictable avoids these problems.

What is the most desirable inflation rate? Some economists say that the *rate* of inflation doesn't matter much as long as the rate is *predictable*. But most economists believe that price stability, which they translate as an inflation rate between 0 and 3 percent a year, is desirable. The reason why zero is not the target is that some price increases are due to quality improvements—a measurement bias in the price index—so a *measured* inflation rate between 0 and 3 percent a year is equivalent to price stability.

**FIGURE 17.1**

## Macroeconomic Performance: Real GDP and Inflation

Real GDP growth and inflation fluctuate a great deal, and during the 1970s, inflation mushroomed (the height of the green shaded area) and real GDP growth slowed. This macroeconomic performance falls far short of the goals of a high and stable real GDP growth rate and low and predictable inflation.

*Source: The Economic Report of the President, 1997.*

## The Two Core Policy Indicators: Real GDP Growth and Inflation

Although macroeconomic policy pursues the four goals we've just considered, the goals are not independent ones. Three of these goals—increasing the real GDP growth rate, smoothing the business cycle, and maintaining low unemployment—are linked together. Real GDP growth tells us directly about the long-term goal of high sustainable growth and the business cycle. It also has a strong link to unemployment. If growth becomes too rapid, unemployment falls below the natural rate, and if growth becomes too slow, unemployment rises above the natural rate. So keeping real GDP growing steadily at its maximum sustainable rate is equivalent to avoiding business fluctuations and keeping unemployment at the natural rate.

There are some connections between real GDP growth and inflation, but over the long run, these two variables are largely independent. So two variables, real GDP growth and inflation, are the core policy targets.

Policy performance, judged by the two core policy targets—real GDP growth and inflation—is shown in Fig. 17.1. Here the red line shows real GDP growth. Real GDP growth averaged 4 percent a year during the 1960s, but after 1970, the growth rate fell to less than 2.5 percent a year. Real GDP growth has fluctuated between a high of 6.8 percent in 1984 and a low of –2.1 percent in 1982. The height of the green shaded area shows inflation. The inflation rate was low during the 1960s, exploded during the 1970s, and then fell through the 1980s. During the 1990s, inflation returned to its 1960s level.

### R E V I E W

- The goals of domestic macroeconomic policy are the highest sustainable rate of potential GDP growth, small business cycle fluctuations, low unemployment, and low inflation.
- Keeping real GDP growing steadily at its highest sustainable rate is equivalent to avoiding business cycle fluctuations and keeping unemployment at the natural rate.

We've examined the policy goals. Let's now look at the policy tools and the way they have been used.

## Policy Tools and Performance

THE TOOLS THAT ARE USED TO TRY TO ACHIEVE macroeconomic performance objectives are fiscal policy and monetary policy. **Fiscal policy**, which is described in Chapter 12, is the use of the federal budget to achieve macroeconomic objectives. The detailed fiscal policy tools are tax rates, benefit rates, and government purchases of goods and services. These tools work by influencing aggregate supply and aggregate demand in the ways explained in Chapter 7. **Monetary policy**, which is described in Chapter 14, is the adjustment of the quantity of money in circulation and interest rates by the Federal Reserve (the Fed) to achieve macroeconomic objectives. These tools work by changing aggregate demand. How have the tools actually been used in the United States? Let's answer this question by summarizing the main directions of fiscal and monetary policy over the years since 1960.

### Fiscal Policy Since 1960

Figure 17.2 gives a broad summary of fiscal policy since 1960. It shows the levels of government revenues and expenditures and the budget balance (each as a percentage of GDP). So that you can see the political context of fiscal policy, the figure also shows the terms of administrations and the names of the incumbent presidents.

Fiscal policy was mildly expansionary during the Kennedy years and strongly expansionary during the later Johnson years when the Vietnam War buildup occurred. During Nixon's presidency, spending growth was kept moderate. But under the pressure of the first OPEC oil shock, spending soared during Ford's presidency. The Carter years began with spending cuts, but then spending climbed to a new high. During the first Reagan term, spending continued to increase at first but it was later held in check, and then during the second Reagan term, spending was cut. During the Bush years, government purchases took an increased percentage of GDP but taxes took a smaller percentage. As the 1991 recession

**FIGURE 17.2**

## The Fiscal Policy Record: A Summary

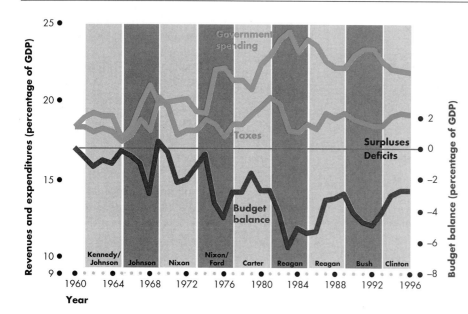

Fiscal policy is summarized here by the performance of government spending, taxes, and the budget balance. Spending has been on an upward trend, and because spending has increased more than taxes, a deficit has emerged. Cycles in spending and taxes have resulted in cycles in the deficit that often have been expansionary in the year before an election and contractionary in the year following an election.

*Source: The Economic Report of the President, 1997, and the author's calculations.*

intensified and the 1992 election drew closer, tax cuts became the rage, especially in Congress, and revenues decreased. But a tax bill in 1993 increased taxes, so revenues increased during the Clinton presidency. At the same time, spending was held in check and decreased as a percentage of GDP.

The budget balance tells an interesting story. During the terms of Johnson, Nixon, and Ford and the first Reagan term, the budget deficit decreased in the immediate postelection year and increased as the next election approached.

Let's now look at monetary policy.

## Monetary Policy Since 1960

Figure 17.3 shows three broad measures of monetary policy. They are the growth rate of M2, the federal funds rate, and the real federal funds rate. The M2 growth rate tells us how monetary policy was influencing an important determinant of aggregate demand. The federal funds rate tells us how the Fed was acting to change money growth. And the real federal funds rate tells us how the Fed was acting

on the opportunity cost of short-term funds that influences spending plans.

Figure 17.3 also identifies the election years, the presidents, and the Fed chairs. The Fed has had five chairs during this period. Notice that the term of a Fed chair does not coincide with the term of a president. William McChesney Martin was a long-serving chair whose term began in 1951. He retired in 1969 and was replaced by Arthur Burns, who served until 1977. William Miller had the shortest term and was replaced by Paul Volcker in 1979. The next chair, Alan Greenspan, was appointed by President Reagan in 1987 and has served under three presidents.

First, let's look at some of the monetary policy trends. During the 1960s, the M2 growth rate averaged 7 percent a year and ranged between a low of 4 percent in 1969 and a high of 9 percent in 1967. It then increased to average 10 percent a year between 1970 and 1983 and hit a peak of 14 percent in 1976. M2 growth fell steadily from 12 percent in 1983 to less than 1 percent in 1994 but then increased in 1995. The federal funds rate trended upward from 1960 through 1981 and then trended downward. The real federal funds rate fell through 1975 and

---

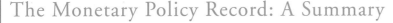

**FIGURE 17.3**

The Monetary Policy Record: A Summary

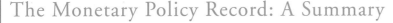

The monetary policy record is summarized here by the growth rate of M2 and the federal funds rate. Fluctuations in M2 growth have coincided with elections, the growth rate usually increasing in the year before an election. Important exceptions are 1979–1980 and 1991–1992, when monetary policy did not become expansionary and the incumbent President lost the election.

*Source: The Economic Report of the President, 1997.*

then increased and remained high through most of the 1980s. It fell during the early 1990s but then began to rise again through 1995.

The general upward trend in M2 growth brought the 1970s inflation, which brought rising *nominal* interest rates but, at first, falling real interest rates. The subsequent sharp downward trend in M2 growth brought falling inflation and falling nominal interest rates but was accompanied by high real interest rates.

Next, look at the cycles. The peaks and troughs in M2 growth more or less coincide with the opposite turning points in the federal funds rate. When the Fed cuts the federal funds rate, M2 growth speeds up; when the Fed increases the federal funds rate, M2 growth slows down. But notice also a remarkable fact about the monetary policy cycles. There is a tendency for the federal funds rate to rise and the M2 growth rate to decrease immediately following an election and for the federal funds rate to fall and the M2 growth rate to increase as the next election approaches. Usually, the incumbent president or his party's successor has won the election. There are two exceptions. In 1980, M2 growth increased, but not as quickly as the demand for money. Interest rates increased, the economy slowed, and Jimmy Carter lost his reelection bid. In 1992, M2 growth slowed, interest rates rose, and George Bush lost his reelection bids. A coincidence? Perhaps, but presidents take a keen interest in what the Fed is up to.

## R E V I E W

- The macroeconomic policy tools are fiscal policy and monetary policy.
- Fiscal policy was expansionary during the Kennedy, Johnson, Ford, and first Reagan terms; moderate during the Nixon and Bush terms; and contractionary during the Carter, second Reagan, and Clinton terms.
- Money supply growth increased at the end of the 1960s and remained high through the 1970s. It slowed through the 1980s and 1990s.

You've now studied the goals of policy and seen the broad trends and cycles in fiscal and monetary policy. Let's now study the ways in which policy might be used better to achieve its goals. We'll begin by looking at long-term growth policy.

# Long-Term Growth Policy

THE SOURCES OF THE LONG-TERM GROWTH OF potential GDP, which are explained in Chapter 10 (pp. 217–218), are the accumulation of physical and human capital and the advance of technology. Chapter 10 briefly examines the range of policies that might achieve faster growth. Here, we probe more deeply into the problem of boosting the long-term growth rate.

Monetary policy can contribute to long-term growth by keeping the inflation rate low. (Chapter 15, pp. 348–349 explains some connections between inflation on growth.) Fiscal policy and other policies can also contribute to growth by influencing the private decisions on which long-term growth depends in three areas. All growth policies increase:

- National saving
- Investment in human capital
- Investment in new technologies

## National Saving

National saving equals private saving plus government saving. Figure 17.4 shows national saving and its private and government components since 1960. From 1960 through 1982, national saving (green line) fluctuated around an average of 20 percent of GDP. There then began a steady slide that saw national saving sink to 14 percent of GDP in 1993 before beginning to rise again. Private saving (blue line) actually increased as a percentage of GDP between 1960 and 1984, when it peaked at 22 percent of GDP. Government saving (the vertical gap between the blue line and the green line) was generally positive before 1975 and became increasingly negative (government dissaving) during the 1980s.

The data you have just examined are for *gross* saving. Each year, national wealth grows by the amount of *net* saving, which equals gross saving minus the value of capital that is scrapped during the year. Figure 17.4 shows U.S. net saving as a percentage of GDP. You can see that net saving (red line) followed a falling trend through 1993. The reason is that capital depreciated at an increasing rate. During the 1960s, depreciation ranged between 10 percent and 14 percent of GDP. This percentage edged upward and was around 12 percent by the mid-1990s. In the 1982 recession, it reached 14 percent of GDP. As a result of the fall in gross saving and the increase in the depreciation rate, net saving in the United States sank to an all-time low of 2.4 percent of GDP in 1993. But since 1993, the net saving rate has been rising.

U.S. investment, one of the engines of growth, is not limited by U.S. saving. The reason is that foreign saving can be harnessed to finance U.S. investment. But boosting the U.S. saving rate can help to bring faster real GDP growth for two reasons. First, the U.S. economy is a significant proportion of the world economy, so an increase in U.S. saving would increase world saving and bring lower real interest rates around the world. With lower real interest rates, investment would be boosted everywhere. The U.S. economy and the world economy could grow faster. Second, with more domestic saving, there might be an increase in

domestic investment in high-risk–high-return new technologies that could boost U.S. growth.

How can national saving be increased? The two points of attack are:

■ Increasing government saving
■ Increasing private saving

**Increasing Government Saving**    Government saving has been negative since 1975, and its average during the 1990s has been –2.2 percent of GDP. Increasing government saving means reducing or eliminating the federal deficit. But as is explained in Chapter 12, achieving a substantial cut in the deficit will be hard work and will be achieved only by cuts in such sensitive areas as Social Security, Medicaid, and Medicare.

**Increasing Private Saving**    Private saving has fallen from its peak of the mid-1980s, but even in the low years of 1992 and 1993, private saving was the same percentage of GDP it had been in 1960. The main way in which government actions can boost private saving is by increasing the after-tax rate of return on saving. This is what government policy has sought to do, but on only one type of asset: individual retirement accounts (IRAs). By putting their savings into IRAs, people can avoid income tax on their interest income. But they cannot use their IRAs (without tax penalties) until they reach the age of 59 1/2. Also, there are limits to the amount that can be accumulated tax-free in an IRA. The Clinton administration has proposed expanding IRAs.

Private saving probably could be stimulated more effectively by cutting taxes on interest income and capital gains across the board and replacing the lost government revenue from such a tax cut with a national consumption tax or a national sales tax. Whether such restructuring of taxes is politically feasible or desirable is a question that goes beyond the scope of macroeconomics.

*Private Saving and Inflation*    Inflation erodes the value of money and other financial assets such as bonds, and uncertainty about future inflation discourages saving. One further policy, therefore, that increases the saving rate is a monetary policy that preserves stable prices and minimizes uncertainty about the future value of money. Chapter 15 (pp. 348–349) spells out the broader connection between inflation and real GDP and explains why low inflation brings greater output and faster growth.

**FIGURE 17.4**

## Saving Rates in the United States: 1960–1996

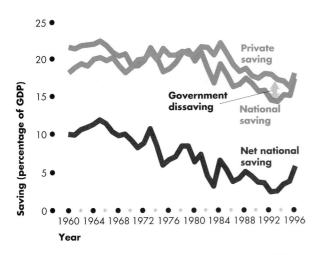

U.S. national saving (green line) peaked in 1979 and has fallen since that year. Both government saving and private saving have contributed to the fall. U.S. net saving (red line) has fallen even faster than national saving and has been on a downward trend since the mid-1960s. It hit an all-time low of 2.4 percent of GDP in 1993. It has increased since then.

*Source: The Economic Report of the President, 1997.*

## Investment in Human Capital

The accumulation of human capital plays a crucial role in economic growth, and two areas are relevant: schooling and on-the-job experience. Economic research shows that both schooling and on-the-job training pay. That is, on the average, the greater the number of years a person remains in school and the greater the number of years of work experience, the higher are that person's earnings. Furthermore, schooling and on-the-job experience yield one of the highest rates of return available.

If education and on-the-job training yield higher earnings, why does the government need a policy toward investment in human capital? Why can't people simply be left to get on with making their own decisions about how much human capital to acquire? The answer is that the *social* returns to human capital probably exceed the *private* returns. The extra productivity that comes from the *interactions* of well-educated and experienced people exceeds what each individual could achieve alone. So, left to ourselves, we would probably accumulate too little human capital. Let's look at some aspects of education and training policies.

**Education and Training Policies**   Governments attempt to increase human capital by subsidizing schooling. They also help to set the standards of achievement for the school system.

The United States has achieved a high standard on some dimensions of schooling but not on all dimensions. For example, in 1996, 63 percent of high school graduates enrolled in postsecondary education (one of the highest percentages in the world) but 13 percent of high school students dropped out and did not graduate.

The Goals 2000: Educate America Act of 1994 and President Clinton's second term education initiative are examples of attempts to improve the quality of schooling. The 1994 Act pays special attention to improving each child's state of preparation for school and performance in school, especially in mathematics and science, two areas in which U.S. schoolchildren are not leading the world. A further feature of Goals 2000 is to improve college access, especially for adults who can benefit from retraining.

The scope for government training programs is limited, but the government can set an example as an employer and it can encourage best-practice training programs for workers.

## Investment in New Technologies

Investment in new technologies is the third area in which policy can influence economic growth. As Chapter 10 explains, investment in new technologies is special for two reasons. First, it appears not to run into the problem of diminishing returns that plague the other types of capital and the other factors of production. Second, the benefits of new technologies spill over to influence all parts of the economy, not just the firms undertaking the investment. For these reasons, increasing the rate of investment in new technologies is a promising way of boosting long-term growth. But how can government policy influence the pace of technological change?

Government can fund and provide tax incentives for research and development activities. Through the National Science Foundation, the public universities, and various research establishments, governments fund a large amount of basic research. Also, the federal government encourages business research with a Research and Experiment Tax Credit (R&E credit). This credit is available to firms that spend more on research and development than some threshold amount. The idea is to stimulate more expenditure on these activities than would occur otherwise. The effectiveness of the R&E credit is not certain, but there is some evidence that it is a cost-effective way of boosting research.

### REVIEW

- Long-term growth policies focus on increasing saving and increasing investment in human capital and new technologies.
- The U.S. net saving rate has been on a negative trend since the mid-1970s. To increase the saving rate, government saving and the after-tax return on private saving must be increased and inflation must be kept in check.
- Human capital investment might be increased with improved education and on-the-job training programs.
- Investment in new technologies can be encouraged by government funding and tax incentives.

We've seen how government might use its fiscal and monetary policies to influence long-term growth. How can it influence the business cycle and unemployment? Let's now address this question.

## Business Cycle and Unemployment Policy

MANY DIFFERENT FISCAL AND MONETARY POLICIES can be pursued to stabilize the business cycle and cyclical unemployment. But all these polices fall into three broad categories:

- Fixed-rule policies
- Feedback-rule policies
- Discretionary policies

### Fixed-Rule Policies

A **fixed-rule policy** specifies an action to be pursued independently of the state of the economy. An everyday life example of a fixed rule is a stop sign. It says, "Stop regardless of the state of the road ahead— even if no other vehicle is trying to use the road." One fixed-rule policy, proposed by Milton Friedman, is to keep the quantity of money growing at a constant rate year in and year out, regardless of the state of the economy, to make the *average* inflation rate zero. Another fixed-rule policy is to balance the federal budget. Fixed rules are rarely followed in practice, but they have some merits in principle, and later in this chapter, we will study how they would work if they were pursued.

### Feedback-Rule Policies

A **feedback-rule policy** specifies how policy actions respond to changes in the state of the economy. A yield sign is an everyday feedback rule. It says, "Stop if another vehicle is attempting to use the road ahead, but otherwise, proceed." A macroeconomic feedback-rule policy is one that changes the money supply, interest rates, or even tax rates in response to the state of the economy. Some feedback rules guide the actions of policy makers. For example, the Fed's Federal Open Market Committee used a feedback rule when it kept pushing interest rates ever higher through 1994 in response to persistently falling unemployment and strong real GDP growth. Other feedback-rule policies are automatic. Examples are the automatic increase in tax revenues and decrease in transfer payments during an expansion and the automatic decrease in tax revenues and increase in transfer payments during a recession.

### Discretionary Policies

A **discretionary policy** responds to the state of the economy in a possibly unique way that uses all the information available, including perceived lessons from past "mistakes." An everyday discretionary policy occurs at an unmarked intersection. Each driver uses discretion in deciding whether to stop and how slowly to approach the intersection. Most macroeconomic policy actions have an element of discretion because every situation is to some degree unique. For example, through 1994, the Fed increased interest rates several times but by small increments. It might have delayed increasing rates until it was more sure that higher rates were needed and then increased them by a larger increment. The Fed used discretion based on lessons it had learned from earlier expansions. But despite the fact that all policy actions have an element of discretion, they can be regarded as modifications of a basic feedback-rule policy.

We'll study the effects of business cycle policy by comparing the performance of real GDP and the price level under a fixed rule and a feedback rule. Because the business cycle can result from demand shocks or supply shocks, we need to consider these two cases. We'll begin by studying demand shocks.

### Stabilizing Aggregate Demand Shocks

We'll study an economy that starts out at full employment and has no inflation. Figure 17.5 illustrates this situation. The economy is on aggregate demand curve $AD_0$ and short-run aggregate supply curve $SAS$. These curves intersect at a point on the long-run aggregate supply curve, $LAS$. The GDP deflator is 110, and real GDP is $7 trillion. Now suppose that there is an unexpected and temporary decrease in aggregate demand. Let's see what happens.

Perhaps investment decreases because of a wave of pessimism about the future, or perhaps exports decrease because of a recession in the rest of the world. Regardless of the origin of the decrease in aggregate demand, the aggregate demand curve shifts leftward, to $AD_1$ in Fig. 17.5. Aggregate demand curve $AD_1$ intersects the short-run aggregate supply curve, $SAS$, at a GDP deflator of 105 and a real GDP of $6.5 trillion. The economy is in a recession. Real GDP is less than potential GDP, and unemployment is above its natural rate.

FIGURE 17.5

## A Decrease in Aggregate Demand

The economy starts out at full employment on aggregate demand curve $AD_0$ and short-run aggregate supply curve $SAS$, the two curves intersecting on the long-run aggregate supply curve, $LAS$. Real GDP is $7 trillion, and the GDP deflator is 110. A fall in aggregate demand (due to pessimism about future profits, for example) unexpectedly shifts the aggregate demand curve to $AD_1$. Real GDP falls to $6.5 trillion, and the GDP deflator falls to 105. The economy is in a recession.

Suppose that the decrease in aggregate demand from $AD_0$ to $AD_1$ is temporary. As confidence in the future improves, firms' investment picks up, or as economic expansion proceeds in the rest of the world, exports gradually increase. As a result, the aggregate demand curve gradually returns to $AD_0$, but it takes some time to do so.

We are going to work out how the economy responds under two alternative policies during the period in which aggregate demand gradually increases to its original level: a fixed rule and a feedback rule.

**Fixed Rule: Monetarism**    The fixed rule that we'll study here is one in which government purchases of goods and services, taxes, and the money supply remain constant. Neither fiscal policy nor monetary policy responds to the depressed economy. This is the rule advocated by monetarists. A **monetarist** is

an economist who believes that fluctuations in the money stock are the main source of economic fluctuations—the monetarist theory of the business cycle (see Chapter 16, p. 372).

Figure 17.6(a) illustrates the response of the economy under a fixed rule when the decrease in aggregate demand to $AD_1$ is *temporary*. Gradually, aggregate demand returns to its original level and the aggregate demand curve shifts rightward to $AD_0$. As it does so, real GDP and the GDP deflator gradually increase. The GDP deflator gradually returns to 110 and real GDP to $7 trillion, as shown in Fig. 17.6(a). Throughout this process, the economy experiences more rapid growth than usual but beginning from a state in which real GDP is less than potential GDP. Also throughout the adjustment, unemployment remains above the natural rate.

Figure 17.6(b) illustrates the response of the economy under a fixed rule when the decrease in aggregate demand to $AD_1$ is *permanent*. Gradually, with unemployment above the natural rate, the money wage rate falls and the short-run aggregate supply curve shifts rightward to $SAS_1$. As it does so, real GDP gradually increases and the GDP deflator falls. Real GDP gradually returns to potential GDP of $7 trillion, and the GDP deflator gradually falls to 95, as shown in Fig. 17.6(b). Again, throughout the adjustment, real GDP is less than potential GDP and unemployment exceeds the natural rate.

Let's contrast the adjustment under a fixed-rule policy with that under a feedback-rule policy.

**Feedback Rule: Keynesian Activism**    The feedback rule that we'll study is one in which government purchases of goods and services increase, tax rates decrease, and the money supply increases when real GDP falls below potential GDP. In other words, both fiscal policy and monetary policy become expansionary when real GDP is less than potential GDP. When real GDP exceeds potential GDP, both policies operate in reverse, becoming contractionary. This rule is advocated by Keynesian activists. A **Keynesian activist** is an economist who believes that fluctuations in aggregate demand combined with sticky wages (and/or sticky prices) are the main source of economic fluctuations—the Keynesian and new Keynesian theories of the business cycle (see Chapter 16, pp. 370, 374).

Figure 17.6(c) illustrates the response of the economy under this feedback-rule policy. When aggregate demand decreases to $AD_1$, the expansionary fiscal and

**FIGURE 17.6**

# Two Stabilization Policies: Aggregate Demand Shock

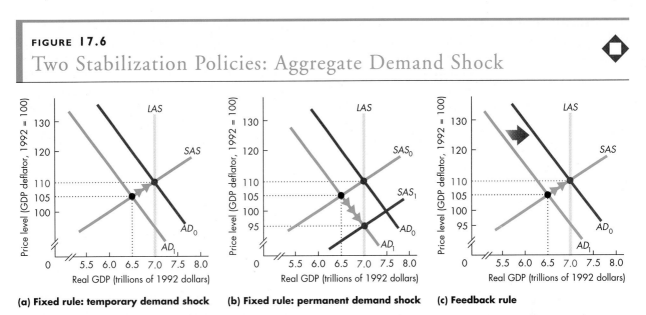

**(a) Fixed rule: temporary demand shock**  **(b) Fixed rule: permanent demand shock**  **(c) Feedback rule**

Aggregate demand has fallen from $AD_0$ to $AD_1$, and the economy is in a recession. Real GDP has fallen to $6.5 trillion, and the GDP deflator has fallen to 105. A fixed-rule stabilization policy (parts a and b) leaves aggregate demand at $AD_1$, so real GDP remains at $6.5 trillion and the GDP deflator remains at 105. If the aggregate demand shock is temporary (part a), aggregate demand subsequently returns to its original level and the aggregate demand curve shifts back to $AD_0$. As it does, real GDP increases back to $7 trillion and the GDP deflator increases to 110. If the demand shock is permanent (part b),

aggregate demand remains at $AD_1$. Eventually, because unemployment is above the natural rate, the money wage rate falls and the SAS curve shifts to $SAS_1$. The price level falls further (to a GDP deflator of 95), and real GDP returns to $7 trillion. Part (c) shows a feedback rule. With the economy in recession, expansionary fiscal and monetary policies increase aggregate demand and shift the aggregate demand curve from $AD_1$ to $AD_0$. Real GDP returns to $7 trillion and the GDP deflator returns 110.

monetary policies increase aggregate demand, shifting the aggregate demand curve immediately to $AD_0$. As other influences begin to increase aggregate demand, fiscal and monetary policies become contractionary and hold the aggregate demand curve steady at $AD_0$. Real GDP is held steady at $7 trillion, and the GDP deflator remains at 110.

**The Two Rules Compared**    Under a fixed-rule policy, the economy goes into a recession and stays there for as long as it takes for aggregate demand to increase again under its own steam. Only gradually does the aggregate demand curve return to its original position and the recession come to an end.

Under a feedback-rule policy, the economy is pulled out of its recession by the policy action. Once back at potential GDP, real GDP is held there by a gradual, policy-induced decrease in aggregate demand that exactly offsets the increase in aggregate demand coming from private spending decisions.

The price level and real GDP decrease and increase by exactly the same amounts under the two policies, but real GDP stays below potential GDP for longer with a fixed rule than it does with a feedback rule.

**The Fed's Feedback Rule: 1992–1996**    The Fed tries to operate a feedback rule like the one you've just studied. At the end of 1992, real GDP was below potential GDP and unemployment was above the natural rate. Through 1992, the Fed gradually lowered interest rates and speeded up money growth. The economy expanded. By 1994, real GDP was close to potential GDP and was growing faster than potential GDP. To prevent an outbreak of inflation, the Fed increased interest rates and slowed money growth. As the economy slowed during 1995, the Fed lowered interest rates and speeded up money growth. Real GDP growth again speeded up in 1996. And again, in early 1997, the Fed applied the monetary brake.

**So Feedback Rules Are Better?** Isn't it obvious that a feedback rule is better than a fixed rule? Can't the government and the Fed use feedback rules to keep the economy close to full employment with a stable price level? Of course, unforecasted events—such as a collapse in business confidence—will hit the economy from time to time. But by responding with a change in tax rates, spending, interest rates, and money supply, can't the government and the Fed minimize the damage from such a shock? It appears to be so from our analysis, and the Fed did a pretty good job during 1992–1996.

Despite the apparent superiority of a feedback rule, many economists remain convinced that a fixed rule stabilizes aggregate demand more effectively than a feedback rule does. These economists assert that fixed rules are better than feedback rules because:

- Potential GDP is not known.
- Policy lags are longer than the forecast horizon.
- Feedback-rule policies are less predictable than fixed-rule policies.

Let's look at these assertions.

**Knowledge of Potential GDP** To decide whether a feedback policy needs to stimulate or retard aggregate demand, it is necessary to determine whether real GDP is currently above or below potential GDP. But potential GDP is not known with certainty. It depends on a large number of factors, one of which is the level of employment when unemployment is at its natural rate. But uncertainty and disagreement exist about how the labor market works, so we can only estimate the natural rate of unemployment. As a result, there is uncertainty about the *direction* in which a feedback policy should be pushing the level of aggregate demand.

**Policy Lags and the Forecast Horizon** The effects of policy actions taken today are spread out over the following two years or even more. But no one is able to forecast accurately that far ahead. The forecast horizon of the policy makers is less than 1 year. Further, it is not possible to predict the precise timing and magnitude of the effects of policy actions. Thus feedback policies that react to today's economy may be inappropriate for the state of the economy at that uncertain future date when the policy's effects are felt.

For example, suppose that today the economy is in recession. The Fed reacts with an increase in the money supply growth rate. When the Fed puts on the monetary accelerator, the first reaction is a fall in interest rates. Some time later, lower interest rates produce an increase in investment and the purchases of consumer durable goods. Some time still later, this increase in expenditure increases income; higher income in turn induces higher consumption expenditure. Later yet, the higher expenditure increases the demand for labor, and eventually, wages and prices rise. The industries and regions in which spending increases occur vary, and so does the impact on employment. It can take from 9 months to 2 years for an initial action by the Fed to cause a change in real GDP, employment, and the inflation rate.

By the time the Fed's actions are having their maximum effect, the economy has moved on to a new situation. Perhaps a world economic slowdown has added a new negative effect on aggregate demand that is offsetting the Fed's expansionary actions. Or perhaps a boost in business confidence has increased aggregate demand yet further, adding to the Fed's own expansionary policy. Whatever the situation, the Fed can take the appropriate actions today only if it can forecast those future shocks to aggregate demand.

Thus to smooth the fluctuations in aggregate demand, the Fed needs to take actions today, based on a forecast of what will be happening over a period stretching 2 or more years into the future. It is no use taking actions a year from today to influence the situation that then prevails. By then it will be too late.

If the Fed is good at economic forecasting and bases its policy actions on its forecasts, then the Fed can deliver the type of aggregate-demand-smoothing performance that we assumed in the model economy that we studied earlier in this chapter. But if the Fed takes policy actions that are based on today's economy rather than on the forecasted economy a year into the future, then those actions will often be inappropriate ones.

When unemployment is high and the Fed puts its foot on the accelerator, it speeds the economy back to full employment. But the Fed might not be able to see far enough ahead to know when to ease off the accelerator and gently tap the brake, holding the economy at its full-employment point. Usually, the Fed keeps its foot on the accelerator for too long, and after the Fed has taken its foot off the accelerator pedal, the economy races through the full-employment point and starts to experience shortages and inflationary pressures. Eventually, when inflation increases and unemployment falls below its natural rate, the Fed steps on the brake, pushing the economy back below full employment.

According to advocates of fixed rules, the Fed's own reactions to the current state of the economy is one of the major sources of fluctuations in aggregate demand and the major factor that people have to forecast to make their own economic choices.

During 1994, the Fed tried hard to avoid the problems just described. It increased interest rates early in the expansion and by small increments. In 1995, after real GDP growth slowed down but before any serious signs of recession were on the horizon, it began to cut interest rates. And in 1997, before inflation turned seriously upward, the Fed squeezed the monetary brake. It is too early to tell whether the Fed now knows enough to avoid some of the mistakes of the past. But its actions during 1992–1996 were gentler and better timed than in previous cycles.

The problems for fiscal policy feedback rules are more severe than those for monetary policy because of the lags in the implementation of fiscal policy. The Fed can take actions relatively quickly. But before a fiscal policy action can be taken, the entire legislative process must be completed. Thus even before a fiscal policy action is implemented, the economy may have moved on to a new situation that calls for a different feedback policy from the one that is in the legislative pipeline.

**Predictability of Policies**  To make decisions about long-term contracts for employment (wage contracts) and for borrowing and lending, people have to anticipate the future course of prices—the future inflation rate. To forecast the inflation rate, it is necessary to forecast aggregate demand. And to forecast aggregate demand, it is necessary to forecast the policy actions of the government and the Fed.

If the government and the Fed stick to rock-steady, fixed rules for tax rates, spending programs, and money supply growth, then policy itself cannot be a contributor to unexpected fluctuations in aggregate demand.

In contrast, when a feedback rule is being pursued, there is more scope for the policy actions to be unpredictable. The main reason is that feedback rules are not written down for all to see. Rather, they have to be inferred from the behavior of the government and the Fed.

Thus with a feedback policy, it is necessary to predict the variables to which the government and Fed react and the extent to which they react. Consequently, a feedback rule for fiscal and monetary

policies can create more unpredictable fluctuations in aggregate demand than a fixed rule can.

Economists disagree about whether those bigger fluctuations offset the potential stabilizing influence of the predictable changes the Fed makes. No agreed measurements have been made to settle this dispute. Nevertheless, the unpredictability of the Fed in its pursuit of feedback policies is an important fact of economic life. And the Fed does not always go out of its way to make its reactions clear. Even in Congressional testimony, Federal Reserve Board chairmen are reluctant to make the Fed's actions and intentions entirely plain. (It has been suggested that two former chairmen of the Federal Reserve Board, the pipe-puffing Arthur Burns and the cigar-puffing Paul Volcker, carried their own smokescreens around with them, as if to exemplify the Fed's mysteriousness and unpredictability. The nonsmoking Alan Greenspan seems to be running a more open and predictable Fed.)

It is not surprising that the Fed seeks to keep *some* of its actions behind a smokescreen. First, the Fed wants to maintain as much freedom of action as possible and so does not want to state with too great a precision the feedback rules that it will follow in any given circumstances. Second, the Fed is part of a political process and, although legally independent of the federal government, is not immune to subtle influence. For at least these two reasons, the Fed does not specify feedback rules as precisely as the one we've analyzed in this chapter. As a result, the Fed cannot deliver an economic performance that has the stability that we generated in the model economy.

To the extent that the Fed's actions are discretionary and unpredictable, they lead to unpredictable fluctuations in aggregate demand. These fluctuations, in turn, produce fluctuations in real GDP, employment, and unemployment.

If it is difficult for the Fed to pursue a predictable feedback stabilization policy, it is probably impossible for Congress to do so. The stabilization policy of Congress is formulated in terms of spending programs and tax laws. Because these programs and laws are the outcome of a political process that is constrained only by the Constitution, there can be no effective way in which a predictable feedback fiscal policy can be adhered to.

We reviewed three reasons why feedback-rule policies might not be more effective than fixed-rule policies in controlling aggregate demand. But there is a fourth reason why some economists prefer fixed rules: Not all shocks to the economy are on the demand side. Most advocates of feedback rules believe that most fluctuations do come from aggregate demand. Some advocates of fixed rules believe that aggregate supply fluctuations are the dominant ones. Let's now see how aggregate supply fluctuations affect the economy under a fixed rule and a feedback rule. We will also see why the economists who believe that aggregate supply fluctuations are the dominant ones also favor a fixed rule rather than a feedback rule.

## Stabilizing Aggregate Supply Shocks

Real business cycle theorists believe that fluctuations in real GDP (and in employment and unemployment) are caused not by fluctuations in aggregate demand but by fluctuations in productivity growth. According to real business cycle theory, there is no useful distinction between long-run aggregate supply and short-run aggregate supply. Because wages are flexible, the labor market is always in equilibrium and unemployment is always at its natural rate. The vertical long-run aggregate supply curve is also the short-run aggregate supply curve. Fluctuations occur because of shifts in the long-run aggregate supply curve. Normally, the long-run aggregate supply curve shifts to the right—the economy expands. But the pace at which the long-run aggregate supply curve shifts to the right varies. Also, on occasion, the long-run aggregate supply curve shifts leftward, bringing a decrease in aggregate supply and a fall in real GDP.

If the real business cycle theory is correct, economic policy that influences the aggregate demand curve has no effect on real GDP. But it does affect the price level. If a feedback-rule policy is used to increase aggregate demand every time real GDP decreases, and if the real business cycle theory is correct, the feedback-rule policy will make price level fluctuations more severe than they otherwise would be. To see why, consider Fig. 17.7.

Imagine that the economy starts out on aggregate demand curve $AD_0$ and long-run aggregate supply curve $LAS_0$ at a GDP deflator of 110 and with real GDP equal to $7 trillion. Now suppose that the long-run aggregate supply curve shifts to $LAS_1$. An actual decrease in long-run aggregate supply can occur as a result of a severe drought or other natural catastrophe or perhaps as the result of a disruption of international trade such as the OPEC embargo of the 1970s.

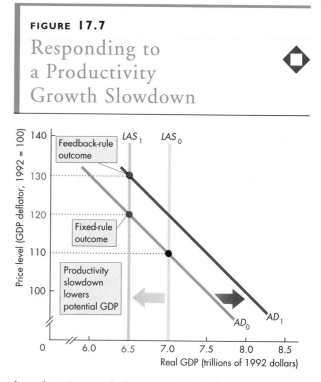

**FIGURE 17.7**

## Responding to a Productivity Growth Slowdown

A productivity growth slowdown shifts the long-run aggregate supply curve from $LAS_0$ to $LAS_1$. Real GDP decreases to $6.5 trillion, and the GDP deflator rises to 120. With a fixed rule, there is no change in the money supply, taxes, or government spending; aggregate demand stays at $AD_0$; and that is the end of the matter. With a feedback rule, the Fed increases the money supply and the Congress cuts taxes or increases spending, intending to increase real GDP. Aggregate demand shifts to $AD_1$, but the result is an increase in the price level—the GDP deflator rises to 130—with no change in real GDP.

**Fixed Rule** With a fixed rule, the fall in the long-run aggregate supply has no effect on the policies of the Fed or the government and no effect on aggregate demand. The aggregate demand curve remains $AD_0$. Real GDP decreases to $6.5 trillion, and the GDP deflator increases to 120.

**Feedback Rule** Now suppose that the Fed and the government use feedback rules. In particular, suppose that when real GDP decreases, the Fed increases the money supply and Congress enacts a tax cut to increase aggregate demand. In this example, the money supply and tax cut shift the aggregate demand curve to $AD_1$. The policy goal is to bring real GDP back to $7 trillion. But the long-run aggregate supply curve has shifted, and so potential GDP has decreased to $6.5 trillion. The increase in aggregate demand cannot bring forth an increase in output if the economy does not have the capacity to produce that output. So real GDP stays at $6.5 trillion, but the price level rises still further—the GDP deflator goes to 130. You can see that in this case, the attempt to stabilize real GDP using a feedback-rule policy has no effect on real GDP but generates a substantial price level increase.

We've now seen some of the shortcomings of using feedback rules for stabilization policy. Some economists believe that these shortcomings are serious and want to constrain Congress and the Fed so that they use fixed rules. Others, regarding the potential advantages of feedback rules as greater than their costs, advocate the continued use of such policies but with an important modification that we'll now look at.

## Nominal GDP Targeting

**Nominal GDP targeting** is an attempt to keep the growth rate of nominal GDP steady. This policy target was first proposed by a leading Keynesian activist, James Tobin of Yale University. It is a policy that recognizes the strengths of a fixed rule but that regards the monetarist fixed rule as inappropriate. Instead, nominal GDP targeting uses feedback rules for fiscal and monetary policy to hit a fixed nominal GDP growth target.

Because nominal GDP growth equals the real GDP growth rate plus the inflation rate, keeping nominal GDP growth steady does not directly target either real GDP growth or inflation. But nominal GDP usually grows quickly because the inflation rate is high. And nominal GDP usually grows slowly because real GDP growth is negative—the economy is in recession. So the idea is that, by keeping nominal GDP growth steady, both excessive inflation and severe recession might be avoided.

Nominal GDP targeting uses feedback rules. Expansionary fiscal and/or monetary actions increase aggregate demand when nominal GDP is below target and contractionary fiscal and/or monetary actions decrease aggregate demand when nominal GDP is above target. The main problem with nominal GDP targeting is that there are long and variable time lags between the identification of a need to change aggregate demand and the effects of the policy actions that are taken.

## Natural Rate Policies

The business cycle and unemployment policies we've considered have been directed at smoothing the business cycle and minimizing *cyclical unemployment*. It is also possible to pursue policies aimed at lowering the natural rate of unemployment. But there are no costless ways of lowering the natural rate of unemployment. Let's look at two possible ways.

One policy tool is unemployment insurance. To lower the natural rate of unemployment, the government might reduce the unemployment benefit, or shorten the period for which benefits are paid, or restrict benefits to people who undertake training programs that increase the likelihood of their finding jobs. With reduced benefits, an unemployed person would spend less time looking for a job and would accept a job even if it were not a good match for the person's skills. But such a policy might create hardship and have a cost that exceeds the cost of a high natural rate of unemployment.

The government might lower the minimum real wage rate. It could achieve a cut in the minimum wage either by holding the minimum money wage rate constant and letting inflation cut the minimum real wage rate or by cutting the minimum money wage rate. A lower minimum wage increases the quantity of labor demanded and lowers unemployment. The government faces a tradeoff between real wages and unemployment.

---

# R E V I E W

- Fixed-rule policies keep fiscal and monetary policy set steady and independent of the state of the economy.
- Feedback policies cut taxes, increase spending, and speed up money supply growth when the economy is in recession and reverse these measures when the economy is overheating.
- Successful feedback rules require knowledge of the source of shocks (demand side or supply side), an ability to forecast as far ahead as the policy actions have effects, and clarity about the feedback rules being used.

We've studied growth policy and business cycle and unemployment policy. Let's now study inflation policy.

## Inflation Policy

THERE ARE TWO INFLATION POLICY PROBLEMS. In times of price level stability, the problem is to prevent inflation from breaking out. In times of inflation, the problem is to reduce its rate and restore price stability. Preventing inflation from breaking out means avoiding both demand-pull and cost-push forces. Avoiding demand-pull inflation is the flip side of avoiding demand-driven recession and is achieved by stabilizing aggregate demand. So the business cycle and unemployment policy we've just studied is also an anti-inflation policy. But avoiding cost-push inflation raises some special issues that we need to consider. So we will look at two issues for inflation policy:

■ Avoiding cost-push inflation
■ Slowing inflation

### Avoiding Cost-Push Inflation

*Cost-push inflation* is inflation that has its origins in cost increases. In 1973–1974 and again in 1979, the world oil price exploded. Cost shocks such as these become inflationary if they are accommodated by an increase in the quantity of money. Such an increase in the quantity of money can occur if a monetary policy feedback rule is used. A fixed-rule policy for the money stock makes cost-push inflation impossible. Let's see why.

Figure 17.8 shows the economy at full employment. Aggregate demand is $AD_0$, short-run aggregate supply is $SAS_0$, and long-run aggregate supply is *LAS*. Real GDP is $7 trillion, and the GDP deflator is 110. Now suppose that OPEC tries to gain a temporary advantage by increasing the price of oil. The short-run aggregate supply curve shifts leftward from $SAS_0$ to $SAS_1$.

FIGURE 17.8

## Responding to an OPEC Oil Price Increase

**(a) Fixed rule**

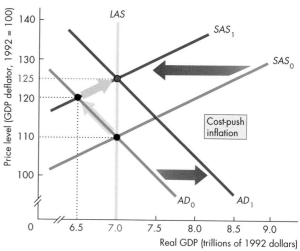

**(b) Feedback rule**

The economy starts out on $AD_0$ and $SAS_0$, with a GDP deflator of 110 and real GDP of $7 trillion. OPEC forces up the price of oil, and the short-run aggregate supply curve shifts to $SAS_1$. Real GDP decreases to $6.5 trillion, and the GDP deflator increases to 120. With a fixed-rule policy (part a), the Fed makes no change to aggregate demand. The economy stays in a recession until resource prices fall and the economy returns to its original position. With a feedback-rule policy (part b), the Fed injects additional money and the aggregate demand curve shifts to $AD_1$. Real GDP returns to $7 trillion (potential GDP), but the GDP deflator increases to 125. The economy is set for another round of cost-push inflation.

**Monetarist Fixed Rule**   Figure 17.8(a) shows what happens if the Fed follows a fixed rule for monetary policy and the government follows a fixed rule for fiscal policy. Suppose that the fixed rule is for zero money growth and no change in taxes or government purchases of goods and services. With these fixed rules, the Fed and the government pay no attention to the fact that there has been an increase in the price of oil. No policy actions are taken. The short-run aggregate supply curve has shifted to $SAS_1$, but the aggregate demand curve remains at $AD_0$. The GDP deflator rises to 120, and real GDP falls to $6.5 trillion. The economy has experienced *stagflation*. With unemployment above the natural rate, the money wage rate will eventually fall. The low level of real GDP and low sales will probably also bring a fall in the price of oil. These events will shift the short-run aggregate supply curve back to $SAS_0$. The GDP deflator will fall to 110, and real GDP will increase to $7 trillion. But this adjustment might take a long time.

**Keynesian Feedback Rule**   Figure 17.8(b) shows what happens if the Fed and government operate a feedback rule. The starting point is the same as before—the economy is on $SAS_0$ and $AD_0$ with a GDP deflator of 110 and real GDP of $7 trillion. OPEC raises the price of oil, and the short-run aggregate supply curve shifts to $SAS_1$. Real GDP decreases to $6.5 trillion, and the price level rises to 120.

A feedback rule is followed. With potential GDP perceived to be $7 trillion and with actual real GDP at $6.5 trillion, the Fed pumps money into the economy and the government increases its spending and lowers taxes. Aggregate demand increases, and the aggregate demand curve shifts rightward to $AD_1$. The price level rises to 125, and real GDP returns to $7 trillion. The economy moves back to full employment but at a higher price level. The economy has experienced *cost-push inflation*.

The Fed responded in the way we've just described to the first wave of OPEC price increases in the mid-1970s. OPEC sees the same advantage in forcing up the price of oil again. A new rise in the price of oil decreases aggregate supply, and the short-run aggregate supply curve shifts leftward once more. The Fed chases it with an increase in aggregate demand, and the economy is in a freewheeling inflation. Realizing this danger, the Fed did *not* respond in the early 1980s to the second wave of OPEC price increases as it had done before. Instead, the Fed held firm and even slowed down the growth of aggregate demand

to further dampen the inflation consequences of OPEC's actions.

**Incentives to Push Up Costs**   You can see that there are no checks on the incentives to push up *nominal* costs if the Fed accommodates price hikes. If some group sees a temporary gain from pushing up the price at which they are selling their resources and if the Fed always accommodates the increase to prevent unemployment and slack business conditions from emerging, then cost-push elements will have a free rein. But when the Fed pursues a fixed-rule policy, the incentive to attempt to steal a temporary advantage from a price increase is severely weakened. The cost of higher unemployment and lower output is a consequence that each group will have to face and recognize.

Thus a fixed rule can deliver steady inflation, while a feedback rule, in the face of cost-push pressures, leaves inflation free to rise and fall at the whim of whichever group believes a temporary advantage to be available from pushing up its price.

## Slowing Inflation

So far, we've concentrated on *avoiding* inflation. But often the problem is not to avoid inflation but to tame it. The United States was in such a situation during the late 1970s and early 1980s. How can inflation, once it has set in, be cured? We'll look at two cases:

- A surprise inflation reduction
- A credible announced inflation reduction

**A Surprise Inflation Reduction**   We'll use two equivalent approaches to study the problem of lowering inflation: the aggregate supply–aggregate demand model and the Phillips curve. The *AS-AD* model tells us about real GDP and the price level, while the Phillips curve, which is explained in Chapter 15 (pp. 350–354), lets us keep track of inflation and unemployment.

Figure 17.9 illustrates the economy at full employment with inflation raging at 10 percent a year. In part (a), the economy is on aggregate demand curve $AD_0$ and short-run aggregate supply curve $SAS_0$. Real GDP is $7 trillion, and the GDP deflator is 110. With real GDP equal to potential GDP on the *LAS* curve, the economy is at full employment. Equivalently, in part (b), the economy is on its long-run Phillips curve, *LRPC*, and short-run Phillips curve, $SRPC_0$. The

FIGURE 17.9

## Lowering Inflation

**(a) Aggregate demand and aggregate supply**

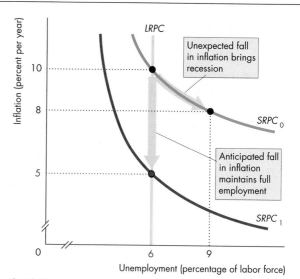

**(b) Phillips curves**

In part (a), aggregate demand is $AD_0$, short-run aggregate supply is $SAS_0$, and real GDP and potential GDP are $7 trillion on the long-run aggregate supply curve $LAS$. The aggregate demand curve is expected to shift and actually shifts to $AD_1$. The short-run aggregate supply curve shifts to $SAS_1$. The GDP deflator rises to 121, but real GDP remains at $7 trillion. Inflation is proceeding at a 10 percent a year, and this inflation rate is anticipated. In part (b), which shows this same situation, the economy on the short-run Phillips curve $SRPC_0$ and on the long-run Phillips curve $LRPC$. Unemployment is at the natural rate of 6 percent, and inflation is 10 percent a year. An unex-

pected slowdown in aggregate demand growth means that the aggregate demand curve shifts from $AD_0$ to $AD_2$, real GDP falls to $6.5 trillion, and inflation slows to 8 percent (GDP deflator is 118.8). Unemployment rises to 9 percent as the economy slides down $SRPC_0$. An anticipated, credible, announced slowdown in aggregate demand growth means that when the aggregate demand curve shifts from $AD_0$ to $AD_2$, the short-run aggregate supply curve shifts from $SAS_0$ to $SAS_2$. The short-run Phillips curve shifts to $SRPC_1$. Inflation slows to 5 percent, real GDP remains at $7 trillion, and unemployment remains at its natural rate of 6 percent.

inflation rate of 10 percent a year is anticipated, so unemployment is at its natural rate, 6 percent of the labor force.

Next year, aggregate demand is *expected* to increase and the aggregate demand curve in Fig. 17.9(a) is expected to shift rightward from $AD_0$ to $AD_1$. In expectation of this increase in aggregate demand, wages increase to shift the short-run aggregate supply curve from $SAS_0$ to $SAS_1$. If expectations are fulfilled, the GDP deflator rises to 121—a 10 percent inflation—and real GDP remains at potential GDP. In part (b), the economy remains at its original position—unemployment is at the natural rate, and the inflation rate is 10 percent a year.

Now suppose that no one is expecting the Fed to change its policy, but the Fed actually tries to slow

inflation. It raises interest rates and slows money growth. Aggregate demand growth slows, and the aggregate demand curve (in part a) shifts rightward from $AD_0$ not to $AD_1$, as people expect, but only to $AD_2$.

With no change in the expected inflation rate, wage rates rise by the same amount as before and the short-run aggregate supply curve shifts leftward from $SAS_0$ to $SAS_1$. Real GDP decreases to $6.5 trillion, and the GDP deflator rises to 118.8—an inflation rate of 8 percent a year. In Fig. 17.9(b), the economy moves along the short-run Phillips curve $SRPC_0$ as unemployment rises to 9 percent and inflation falls to 8 percent a year. The Fed's policy has succeeded in slowing inflation but at the cost of recession. Real GDP is below potential GDP, and unemployment is above its natural rate.

### A Credible Announced Inflation Reduction

Suppose that instead of simply slowing down the growth of aggregate demand, the Fed announces its intention ahead of its action and in a credible and convincing way so that its announcement is believed. That is, the Fed's policy is anticipated. Because the lower level of aggregate demand is expected, wages increase at a pace consistent with the lower level of aggregate demand. The short-run aggregate supply curve (in Fig. 17.9a) shifts leftward from $SAS_0$ but only to $SAS_2$. Aggregate demand increases by the amount expected, and the aggregate demand curve shifts from $AD_0$ to $AD_2$. The GDP deflator rises to 115.5—an inflation rate of 5 percent a year—and real GDP remains at potential GDP.

In Fig. 17.9(b), the lower expected inflation rate shifts the short-run Phillips curve downward to $SRPC_1$, and inflation falls to 5 percent a year, while unemployment remains at its natural rate of 6 percent.

A credible announced inflation reduction lowers inflation but with no accompanying loss of output or increase in unemployment.

### Inflation Reduction in Practice

When the Fed in fact slowed inflation in 1981, we paid a high price. The Fed's policy action was unpredicted. It occurred in the face of wages that had been set at too high a level to be consistent with the growth of aggregate demand that the Fed subsequently allowed. The consequence was recession—a decrease in real GDP and a rise in unemployment. Could the Fed have lowered inflation without causing recession by telling people far enough ahead of time that it did indeed plan to lower inflation?

The answer appears to be no. The main reason is that people expect the Fed to behave in line with its record, not with its stated intentions. How many times have you told yourself that it is your firm intention to take off 10 unwanted pounds or to keep within your budget and put a few dollars away for a rainy day, only to discover that, despite your very best intentions, your old habits win out in the end?

To form expectations of the Fed's actions, people look at the Fed's past *actions*, not its stated intentions. On the basis of such observations—called Fed-watching—they try to work out what the Fed's policy is, to forecast its future actions, and to forecast the effects of those actions on aggregate demand and inflation. The Greenspan Fed, like the Volcker Fed

that preceded it, has built a reputation for being anti-inflationary. That reputation is valuable because it helps the Fed to contain inflation and lowers the cost of eliminating inflation if it temporarily returns. The reason is that with a low expected inflation rate, the short-run Phillips curve is in a favorable position (like $SRPC_1$ in Fig. 17.9b). The Fed's action during the 1990s have been designed to keep inflation expectations low and prevent the gains made during the 1980s recession from being eroded.

### A Truly Independent Fed

A radical suggestion for strengthening the Fed's reputation as the guardian of price stability is to make the Fed more independent of government and to charge it with the single responsibility of achieving and maintaining price level stability. Some central banks are more independent than the Fed. The German and Swiss central banks are the best examples. Another example is the New Zealand central bank. All these central banks have the responsibility of stabilizing prices but not real GDP and of pursuing their objective without interference from the government. Recent research on central bank performance has strengthened the view that a more independent central bank can deliver a lower average inflation rate without creating either a higher unemployment rate or a lower real GDP growth rate.

### R E V I E W

- A fixed rule gives more effective protection against a cost-push inflation than a feedback rule does.
- When inflation is tamed, a recession usually results because people form policy expectations based on past policy actions.
- By establishing a reputation of being an inflation fighter, the Fed has strengthened the expectation that it will maintain low inflation and possibly lowered the cost of fighting inflation.

◆ *Reading Between the Lines* on pp. 414–415 looks at the challenges the Fed faced in 1997 as it sought to keep the economy expanding but avoid renewed inflation.

You've now completed your study of macroeconomics. In the remaining chapters we shift our focus to the international economy.

# Policy
## WATCH

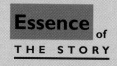

### Steering the Course

THE NEW YORK TIMES, *JANUARY 2, 1997*

# Outlook '97:
# Economy & Industry

**By LOUIS UCHITELLE**

The current economic recovery is nearly six years old, and the annual inflation rate is a meager 3.2 percent—the lowest level since World War II for an expansion this old. Economists are coming up with all sorts of explanations for the unusual milestone. And gradually many are concluding that inflation has become harder to explain.

The most striking aspect of this milestone is the scramble it is provoking among economists to repair the theory that they use to link unemployment and inflation. The theory, a keystone of economic policy, says that when the unemployment rate falls below a certain flash point, inflation soon accelerates. But the flash point foreseen in theory, 6 percent, was breached months ago, and nothing happened. The unemployment rate went as low as 5.1 percent, and still nothing happened. ...

The theoretical concept, known as the natural rate of unemployment, holds that at a certain level, the unemployment rate is just high enough to avoid labor shortages that would push up wages, prompting companies to raise prices to cover the additional labor costs. This equilibrium level, at which the inflation rate neither rises nor falls, has varied from decade to decade, but when the unemployment rate moves below what the Federal Reserve and the economists consider the natural rate, a series of responses develops that usually end in recession.

The Federal Reserve raises interest rates to discourage business activity. The unemployment rate then rises as people lose jobs, and the inflation rate falls. But instead of stopping at the natural rate, restoring an equilibrium, the unemployment rate often keeps rising as the economy slows. This sequence in the 1960's and the 1980's, the two other periods since World War II when a recovery has lasted as long as the current one, culminated in recessions. But with the natural rate theory so much in doubt today, the odds of a repeat performance are less. ...

Still, many forecasters and economists, particularly on Wall Street, where nervousness about inflation is part of the landscape, insist that the natural rate thesis remains valid and will show itself in 1997 in rising prices. "It is as important as ever," said Albert M. Wojnilower, senior economic adviser for Clipper Asset Management, "but no one is so sure anymore where the natural rate is." ...

**Essence** of
**THE STORY**

■ The current economic recovery is almost six years old, and the annual inflation rate is 3.2 percent.

■ The theory of the natural rate of unemployment holds that inflation will accelerate if unemployment falls below the natural rate. In the 1990s, the natural rate was believed to be 6 percent.

■ During 1996, the unemployment rate fell below 6 percent but inflation did not accelerate.

■ The 1960s and 1980s expansions ended when unemployment fell below the danger point, inflation broke out, and the Fed raised interest rates

■ Forecasters and economists are divided on the natural rate thesis.

# Economic

## A N A L Y S I S

■ The Fed faces a constant stabilization policy dilemma: whether to tighten or loosen its grip on money growth by raising or lowering short-term interest rates.

■ During 1996, the economy experienced slow growth and the unemployment rate averaged 5.4 percent. The Fed kept M2 money growth steady at around 4 percent per year.

■ Has the Fed done enough to stabilize the economy and prevent a return of inflation?

■ The theory of inflation predicts that the inflation rate rises if aggregate demand grows more quickly than potential GDP. Equivalently, the inflation rate rises if the unemployment rate falls below the natural rate.

■ The three figures show how the change in the inflation rate and the unemployment rate have been related since 1960.

■ In the 1960s, the natural rate of unemployment was about 5.4 percent (Fig. 1). In the 1970s, it was about 7.5 percent (Fig. 2), and in the late 1980s and 1990s, it fell to less than 6 percent (Fig. 3). (These are estimates of the natural rate.)

■ When the unemployment rate goes into the danger zone below the natural rate, the inflation rate usually increases. When the unemployment rate exceeds the natural rate, the inflation rate usually falls. (There were only two exceptions, in 1975 and 1987.)

■ By studying the shifting relationship between the change in the inflation rate and the unemployment rate, the Fed tries to estimate the natural rate and decide whether to tighten or loosen its monetary policy.

■ No one knows what the natural rate is. The natural rate keeps changing, and although we can estimate what it has been in the past, we cannot know its current and future levels.

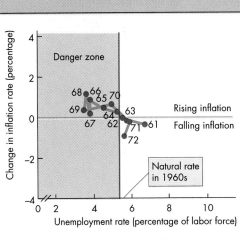

Figure 1 1960 to 1972

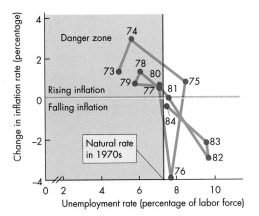

Figure 2 1973 to 1984

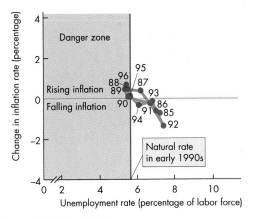

Figure 3 1985 to 1996

## You're

### THE VOTER

■ Why does the Fed need to estimate the natural rate of unemployment?

■ What are the main pros and cons of the Fed forgetting about the natural rate of unemployment and fixing the growth rate of M2?

■ What are the main pros and cons of the Fed raising interest rates every time the economy moves into the inflation danger zone?

415

# SUMMARY

## Key Points

### Policy Goals (pp. 396–397)

- The goals of macroeconomic policy are to achieve the highest sustainable rate of long-term real GDP growth, smooth unavoidable business cycle fluctuations, maintain low unemployment, and avoid inflation.

### Policy Tools and Performance (pp. 398–400)

- Fiscal policy was expansionary during the Kennedy years, the late 1960s and early 1970s, and the early Reagan 1980s. It was contractionary during the Carter, later Reagan, and Clinton years.
- The M2 growth rate increased during the 1970s, peaked in 1976, and then fell.

### Long-Term Growth Policy (pp. 400–402)

- Policies to increase the long-term growth rate focus on increasing saving and investment in human capital and new technologies.
- To increase the saving rate, government saving must increase or incentives for private saving must be strengthened by increasing after-tax returns.
- Human capital investment might be increased with improved education and by improving on-the-job training programs.
- Investment in new technologies can be encouraged by tax incentives.

### Business Cycle and Unemployment Policy (pp. 403–409)

- In the face of an aggregate demand shock, a fixed-rule policy takes no action. Real GDP and the price level fluctuate.
- In the face of an aggregate demand shock, a feedback-rule policy takes offsetting fiscal and monetary action. An ideal feedback rule keeps the economy at full employment, with stable prices.
- Some economists say that a feedback rule creates fluctuations because it requires greater knowledge of the economy than we have, operates with time lags that extend beyond the forecast horizon, and introduces unpredictability about policy reactions.
- In the face of a productivity growth slowdown, both rules have the same effect on output. A feedback rule brings a higher inflation rate than a fixed rule does.
- Nominal GDP targeting might avoid the extremes of inflation and recession.

### Inflation Policy (pp. 410–413)

- A fixed rule minimizes the threat of cost-push inflation. A feedback rule validates cost-push inflation and leaves the price level and inflation rate free to move to wherever they are pushed.
- Inflation can be tamed, at little or no cost in terms of lost output or excessive unemployment, by slowing the growth of aggregate demand in a credible and predictable way. But usually, when inflation is slowed down, a recession occurs.

## Key Figures

## Key Terms

1. What are the four goals of macroeconomic policy?
2. What are the two core goals of policy and why are they core?
3. Describe the main features of fiscal policy since 1960. In which periods did fiscal policy increase aggregate demand? In which periods did fiscal policy decrease aggregate demand?
4. Describe the main features of monetary policy since 1960. In which periods was monetary policy inflationary? In which periods did monetary policy fight inflation?
5. What three things can policy do to try to speed potential GDP growth?
6. What is the distinction between a fixed-rule policy, a feedback-rule policy, and discretionary policy? Provide an example of each type of policy both in everyday life and in macroeconomics.
7. What are the effects of a temporary decrease in aggregate demand if the Fed adopts a fixed-rule policy.
8. How do real GDP and the price level respond to a permanent decrease in aggregate demand when the Fed adopts:
    a. A fixed-rule monetary policy?
    b. A feedback-rule policy?
9. Explain the main problems in using fiscal policy for smoothing the business cycle.
10. Why do economists disagree with each other on the appropriateness of fixed-rule and feedback-rule policies?
11. What are the effects of a rise in the price of oil on real GDP and the price level if the Fed employs:
    a. A fixed-rule policy?
    b. A feedback-rule policy?
12. What is nominal GDP targeting and why might it reduce real GDP fluctuations and inflation?
13. How can the Fed avoid cost-push inflation? Does a fixed rule or a feedback rule do the better job?
14. Why is lowering inflation costly?
15. What must the Fed do to minimize the cost of lowering inflation?
16. Why does having a reputation as an inflation fighter help in fighting inflation?

1. A productivity growth slowdown has occurred. Explain its possible origins and describe a policy package that is designed to speed up growth again.
2. The economy shown in the figure is initially on aggregate demand curve $AD_0$ and short-run aggregate supply curve $SAS$. Then aggregate demand decreases, and the aggregate demand curve shifts leftward to $AD_1$.

a. What are the initial equilibrium real GDP and price level?
b. If the decrease in aggregate demand is temporary and the government follows a fixed-rule fiscal policy, what happens to real GDP and the price level? Trace the immediate effects and the adjustment as aggregate demand returns to its original level.
c. If the decrease in aggregate demand is temporary and the government follows a feedback-rule fiscal policy, what happens to real GDP and the price level? Trace the immediate effects and the adjustment as aggregate demand returns to its original level.
d. If the decrease in aggregate demand is permanent and the government follows a fixed-rule fiscal policy, what happens to real GDP and the price level?
e. If the decrease in aggregate demand is permanent and the government follows a feedback-rule fiscal policy, what happens to real GDP and the price level?

3. The economy shown in the figure is initially on aggregate demand curve *AD* and short-run aggregate supply curve $SAS_0$. Then short-run aggregate supply decreases, and the short-run aggregate supply curve shifts leftward to $SAS_1$.

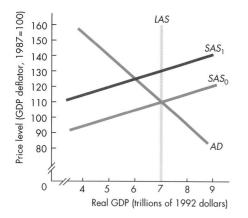

a. What are the initial equilibrium real GDP and price level?

b. What type of event could have caused the decrease in short-run aggregate supply?

c. If the government follows a fixed-rule monetary policy, what happens to real GDP and the price level? Trace the immediate effects and the adjustment as the short-run aggregate supply returns to its original level.

d. If the government follows a feedback-rule monetary policy, what happens to real GDP and the price level? Trace the immediate effects and the adjustment as aggregate demand and short-run aggregate supply respond to the policy action.

4. The economy is experiencing 10 percent inflation and 7 percent unemployment. Set out policies for the Fed and Congress to pursue that will lower both inflation and unemployment. Explain how and why your proposed policies will work.

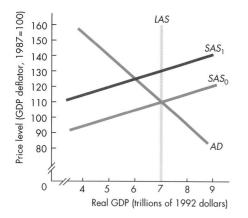
http://hepg.awl.com/parkin/econ100

# CRITICAL THINKING

1. Study *Reading Between the Lines* on pp. 414–415 and then:
   a. Describe the dilemma faced by the Fed and explain why the dilemma was particularly acute during 1997.
   b. What is the short-run relationship between inflation and unemployment?
   c. What signs do you look for to determine whether the economy is in the "danger zone"?
   d. What in your opinion does the Fed's dilemma of 1997 tell us about the relative merits of a fixed-rule monetary policy and a feedback-rule monetary policy?

2. The economy is booming and inflation is beginning to rise, but it is widely agreed that a massive recession is just around the corner. Weigh the advantages and disadvantages of the Congress pursuing a fixed-rule and a feedback-rule *fiscal* policy.

3. The economy is in a recession, and inflation is falling. It is widely agreed that a strong recovery is just around the corner. Weigh the advantages and disadvantages of the Fed pursuing a fixed-rule and a feedback-rule policy.

4. You have been hired to draw up an economic plan that will maximize the chance of the President being reelected.
   a. What are the macroeconomic stabilization policy elements in that plan?
   b. What do you have to make the economy do in an election year?
   c. What policy actions would help the President achieve reelection?
   (In dealing with this problem, be careful to take into account the effects of your proposed policy on expectations and the effects of those expectations on actual economic performance.)

5. Visit the World Wide Web site of the Economic Report of the President at http://www.stat-usa.gov/BEN/erp1/erp.html (or via the link at the Parkin Web site) and review Chapter 2 of the report, "Macroeconomic Policy and Performance." Write a summary and critique of this chapter.

# Part 7

# The Global Economy

## It's a Small Word

The scale of international trade, borrowing, and lending, both in absolute dollar terms and as a percentage of total world production expands every year. One country, Singapore, imports and exports goods and services in a volume that exceeds its Gross Domestic Product. The world's largest nation, China, returned to the international economic stage during the 1980s and is now a major producer of manufactured goods. ◆ International economic activity is large because today's economic world is small and because communication is so incredibly fast. But today's world is not a new world. From the beginning of recorded history, people have traded over large and steadily increasing distances. The great Western civilizations of Greece and Rome traded not only around the Mediterranean but also into the Gulf of Arabia. The great Eastern civilizations traded around the Indian Ocean. By the Middle Ages, the East and the West were trading routinely overland on routes pioneered by Venetian traders and explorers such as Marco Polo. When, in 1497, Vasco da Gama opened a sea route between the Atlantic and Indian Oceans around Africa, a new trade between East and West began, causing prices of Eastern goods to tumble in Western markets. ◆ The European discovery of America and the subsequent opening up of Atlantic trade continued the process of steady globalization. So, the developments of the 1990s, amazing though many of them are, represent a continuation of an ongoing expansion of human horizons. ◆ The chapters in this final part study the interaction of nations in today's global economy. ◆ Here, you will learn about international trade in goods and services. Here, you will come face to face with one of the biggest policy issues of all ages, free trade versus protection. You will learn how all nations can benefit from free international trade. And you will see how protection from competition brings big benefits to a few and small losses to the many. The total gains from protection are dwarfed by the losses, but because the losses are spread thinly and the gains thickly, protectionism always has its supporters and political backers. ◆ Chapter 18 does not explain international deficits and surpluses. You will meet this topic if you take a course in *macroeconomics*. In such a course, you will learn that our international deficit depends not on how efficient we are, but on how much we save. Nations with low saving rates, everything else being the same, have international deficits. ◆ Before we begin Chapter 18, let's spend some time with the economist who first explained the fundamental idea of comparative advantage, David Ricardo. And we'll talk with one of today's leading international economists, Stanley Fischer, formally a professor at MIT and now First Deputy Managing Director of the International Monetary Fund.

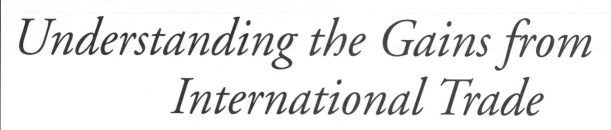

# Economic Legends *Past & Present*

# Understanding the Gains from International Trade

## The Economist: David Ricardo

**David Ricardo (1772–1832) was a highly successful 27-year-old stockbroker when he stumbled on a copy of Adam Smith's *The Wealth of Nations* (see p. 2) on a weekend visit to the country. He was immediately hooked and went on to become the most celebrated economist of his age and one of the all-time great economists. One of his many contributions was to develop the principle of comparative advantage, the foundation on which the modern theory of international trade is built. The example he used to illustrate this principle was the trade between England and Portugal in cloth and wine.**

**The General Agreement on Tariffs and Trade (GATT) was established as a reaction against the devastation wrought by beggar-my-neighbor tariffs imposed during the 1930s. But it is also a triumph for the logic first worked out by Smith and Ricardo.**

*"Under a system of perfectly free commerce, each country naturally devotes its capital and labor to such employments as are most beneficial to each."*

DAVID RICARDO

*THE PRINCIPLES OF POLITICAL ECONOMY AND TAXATION*

## The Issues and Ideas

Until the mid-eighteenth century, it was generally believed that the purpose of international trade was to keep exports greater than imports and to pile up gold. If gold were accumulated, it was believed, the nation would prosper; and if gold were lost through an international deficit, the nation would be drained of money and impoverished. These beliefs are called *mercantilism*, and the *mercantilists* were pamphleteers who advocated with missionary fervor the pursuit of an international surplus. If exports did not exceed imports, the mercantilists wanted imports restricted.

In the 1740s, David Hume explained that as the quantity of money (gold) changes, so also does the price level, and the nation's *real* wealth is unaffected. In the 1770s, Adam Smith argued that import restrictions would lower the gains from specialization and make a nation poorer, and 30 years later, David Ricardo proved the law of comparative advantage and demonstrated the superiority of free trade. Mercantilism was intellectually bankrupt but remained politically powerful.

Gradually, through the nineteenth century, the mercantilist influence waned and North America and Western Europe prospered in an environment of increasingly free international trade. But despite remarkable advances in economic understanding, mercantilism never quite died. It had a brief and devastating revival in the 1920s and 1930s when tariff hikes brought about the collapse of international trade and accentuated the Great Depression. It subsided again after World War II with the establishment of the General Agreement on Tariffs and Trade (GATT).

But mercantilism lingers on. The often expressed view that the United States should restrict Japanese imports and reduce its deficit with Japan and fears that the NAFTA will bring economic ruin to the United States are modern manifestations of mercantilism. It would be interesting to have David Hume, Adam Smith, and David Ricardo commenting on these views. But we know what they would say—the same things that they said to the eighteenth century mercantilists. And they would still be right today.

## THEN...

In the eighteenth century, when mercantilists and economists were debating the pros and cons of free international exchange, the available transportation technology limited the gains from international trade. Sailing ships with tiny cargo holds took close to a month to cross the Atlantic Ocean. But the potential gains were large, and so was the incentive to cut shipping costs. By the 1850s, the clipper ship had been developed, cutting the journey from Boston to Liverpool to only $12\frac{1}{4}$ days. Half a century later, 10,000-ton steamships were sailing between America and England in just 4 days. As sailing times and costs declined, so the gains from international trade increased and the volume of trade expanded.

## ...AND NOW

The container ship has revolutionized international trade and contributed to its continued expansion. Today, most goods cross the oceans in containers—metal boxes—packed into and piled on top of ships like the one above.

Container technology has cut the cost of ocean shipping by economizing on handling and by making cargoes harder to steal, lowering insurance costs. It is unlikely that there would be much international trade in goods such as television sets and VCRs without this technology. High-value and perishable cargoes such as flowers and fresh foods, as well as urgent courier packages, travel by air. Every day, dozens of cargo-laden 747s fly between every major U.S city and destinations across the Atlantic and Pacific oceans.

**As the world economy has become more integrated, new international institutions have evolved. One of these institutions is the International Monetary Fund, or IMF. Let's talk with Stanley Fischer, one of today's outstanding economists, who now plays a leading role at the IMF.**

**Stanley Fischer** has served as the First Deputy Managing Director of the International Monetary Fund since 1994. Born in Zambia in 1943, he received a B.S. and an M.S. from the London School of Economics in 1965 and 1966, respectively, and a Ph.D. from MIT in 1969. Professor Fischer has taught at the University of Chicago and MIT. He served as Vice President of Development Economics and Chief Economist at the World Bank from 1988 to 1992.

Michael Parkin talked with Professor Fischer about his work at the International Monetary Fund and World Bank, the goals of these two institutions, the importance of trade liberalization, and how the thinking of economists such as David Ricardo provide insights to address today's international trade challenges.

**Dr. Fischer, how did you get into economics?**

I was at high school in Zimbabwe (then Rhodesia) and went through the British educational system, and in the sixth grade I began to specialize in physics, chemistry, and math. Then I heard about economics, and switched one of my science courses to economics—and loved it.

This was the perfect field, one that provided an analytic way of understanding an important part of how societies work, and also one in which I could use my quantitative skills. I went to the London School of Economics for my Bachelor's and Master's degrees and then to MIT for my Ph.D. My first appointment was at the University of Chicago, at a time when Milton Friedman was still the dominant influence there.

**As someone who has worked both at the University of Chicago and at MIT, how would you characterize the two approaches to economics?**

When I was at Chicago in the early 1970s, MIT was more theoretical and Chicago was low-tech and more policy-oriented. Now they've switched: Chicago's macro is far more theoretical and less policy-oriented than that at MIT.

One of the things I learned at Chicago was to try to figure out whether a particular theoretical point was quantitatively important (though I should have learned that at MIT, from Bob Solow, who is famous for his back-of-the-envelope calculations). I remember Milton Friedman saying in one of the first Money Workshops I went to, "There's no reason to think the real interest rate should vary systematically with inflation." I replied, "Oh, but you know that in the Sidrauski (non-maximizing) model, changes in the inflation rate change capital intensity and so the real interest rate." And he said, "Well now, how does that work?" And then we went through the exercise of calculating the possible size of the various effects involved and concluded that the overall effect would have to be very small. Of course, as later empirical work shows, the real interest rate is negatively affected by inflation, just not mainly through that particular mechanism.

**What is the role of the IMF and what are the main problems that it seeks to address?**

The IMF has three main functions. The first is *surveillance*, which means that it is an institution in which countries discuss problems of the international economy, as well as each other's economies. Twice a year, the Fund staff presents its survey of the world economy, the *World Economic Outlook.*

In addition, Fund staff presents an annual report—the Article IV report—on the economy of each member country. The Article IV reports are based on the staff's analysis and discussions with the economic policy makers in each country.

The second function of the Fund is to *make loans to countries* that are in economic trouble. These loans typically provide balance of payments support to countries in crisis and countries to which the private capital markets are reluctant to lend. The biggest such loan ever made was to Mexico in 1995, after its December 1994 devaluation, when the private capital markets dried up and the country had to achieve a massive turnaround—8 percent of GDP—in its balance of payments within a year. These loans come with conditions on the country's policies that were designed to deal with the problems that caused the crisis.

The third IMF function is technical assistance and training. We provide technical assistance to

help improve the monetary and fiscal systems, for instance, to explain how to set up a system to undertake open market operations or how to institute a value-added tax. This is hands-on advice. We also provide technical assistance to improve statistical systems. We provided a lot of technical assistance to the transition economies of Eastern Europe and the former Soviet Union. Many of those countries now have well-functioning central banks after only 5 years of transition.

**You've also worked at the World Bank. What is the role of the World Bank and what are the main problems that it seeks to address?**

The World Bank was established at the end of World War II to lend to countries undergoing reconstruction and also to lend to developing countries. At that time, private capital flows were small and very little went to developing countries. Initially, the Bank lent to finance projects, such as ports or dams, and it still does project lending. Over time, it was realized that lending for projects didn't do a whole lot for development in the face of bad economic policies. In the late 1970s, and particularly the 1980s, the Bank began to undertake *lending for structural adjustment*—providing loans to governments on the condition they change their economic policies, for instance, and most important, by liberalizing trade.

**International trade is an important factor in the success of any country. How has trade liberalization featured in the success cases of countries such as Mexico?**

Mexico was a closed economy in the 1970s and even in the early 1980s. The World Bank, in collaboration with the Fund, encouraged the authorities to liberalize their

> *Every one of the successful East Asian countries has succeeded by integrating with the world economy.*

trade regime. The World Bank didn't pull its punches on these issues, and it was right. The success of the Mexican reforms is evident from the differences in the response of the economy to its debt crises in 1982 and 1995. In the 1980s, it took Mexico about 8 years to dig out from its crisis. In 1995, it took only 2 years to adjust and to resume growth at 5 percent a year, as well as to repay most of the loans made by the United States and the IMF. That contrast is a result of the reforms Mexico undertook during the 1980s and early 1990s. It is now a much more open, flexible, and private-sector-oriented economy.

**What are the gains and losses of the international trade liberalization process of the post–World War II years? Have the industrial countries or the developing countries gained most?**

I'm not sure there's a scientific way of making that appraisal. But if you were to look at what has happened in the postwar period to the industrialized countries, which, despite some slowing since the 1960s, have grown faster, more consistently, and with less disruption than in any period of similar length in history, you would have to say that the architecture of the postwar economy has been very successful. And then if you look at the developing countries, you will find that, on the average, they have grown faster yet. In the most populous part of the globe, namely, East Asia and China and, to some extent, India, we have had absolutely unprecedented growth. Every one of the successful East Asian countries has succeeded by integrating with the world economy, by promoting exports and increasing imports, especially of capital and intermediate goods. This process of opening up and using world markets for exports and imports has been absolutely critical. This outcome is what most economists from Adam Smith and David Ricardo on would have predicted.

The one part of the world where progress has, on the average, been most disappointing, is Africa. But there are countries in Africa that have done well and others that have not. The countries that have been serious about trying to trade in the global economy and about implementing market-friendly policies have done better on the whole. There are countries where the per capita income has grown substantially. We have seen significant growth in per capita income in Africa in the last few years. The prospects for South Africa look good, and that could be very important for a large part of the continent. In addition, there are countries such as Mozambique and Uganda, which have begun growing very fast after terrible civil wars, and there is Botswana, which has been one of the fastest-growing economies in the world for the past two decades.

**What do you foresee as the challenges facing the world economy?**
There are the continuing challenges of making sure that this present period of lower inflation and reasonable growth continues.

Second, to make sure that the global trading system keeps opening up—a task in which the newly created World Trade Organization (WTO) has a vital role to play. Third, to focus on the challenge of opening capital accounts—not one of the original functions of the IMF but becoming an increasingly important part of our activities. That's a challenge. Bringing the transition economies, particularly Russia, into the global system is a huge challenge. Bringing the countries that have been failing, many of them in Africa, into the global system is another major challenge. In addition, there is the challenge of maintaining momentum in a variety of countries where things are changing. For example, India used to be regarded as inherently a 3 percent a year growth country; in fact, it's been growing at 5 to 7 percent a year for the last few years. Maintaining that growth rate would make all the difference. In the Middle East, similarly, we're seeing signs of countries turning around. For the IMF, World Bank, and WTO the challenges facing the world economy are to keep the good things

*For the IMF, World Bank, and WTO, the challenges facing the world economy are to keep the good things going and take care of the countries that are falling behind.*

going and take care of the countries that are falling behind.

**What kinds of jobs do economics graduates get in international organizations such as the IMF and the World Bank? What should students be doing as undergraduates to prepare themselves to be in such positions?**
People who want to work in the Fund and the Bank should take courses in macroeconomics, international trade and finance, development, monetary economics, and public finance. From the viewpoint of the Bank, it would also be useful to study more micro-oriented policy issues. The Fund and the Bank have entry programs designed for people who may be destined for their professional ranks. The World Bank's is called Young Professionals, and the IMF's is called the Economist Program.

The IMF and the World Bank are terrific places to work. You get to use your analytic skills all the time, in the real world. You have to decide what really matters, you have to be sure that what you're recommending will improve the lives of people. And then if you work in the operational parts of the Fund or Bank, you have to persuade the countries with which you're working that you're right. If you are right, and if you succeed, you have the satisfaction of having done something useful.

In the process, you'll have had the benefit of learning some diplomacy. You are also likely to learn some humility—for you will realize that the really hard work of implementing policies is done by the politicians and officials of the countries that undertake them. Your job is to help them do their own jobs better, always bearing in mind that the benefits or costs are borne by their people.

# Chapter 18

# Trading with the World

Since ancient times, people have expanded their trading as far as technology allowed. Marco Polo opened up the silk route between Europe and China in the thirteenth century. Today, container ships laden with cars and machines and Boeing 747s stuffed with farm-fresh foods ply sea and air routes, carrying billions of dollars worth of goods. Why do people go to such great lengths to trade with those in other nations? ◆ Low-wage Mexico has entered into a free trade agreement with high-wage Canada and the United States—the North American Free Trade Agreement, or NAFTA. According to Texas billionaire Ross Perot, this agreement will cause a "giant sucking sound" as jobs are transferred from Michigan to Mexico. Is Ross Perot right? How can we compete with a country that pays its workers a fraction of U.S. wages? Are there any industries, besides perhaps the Hollywood movie industry, in which we have an advantage? ◆ In 1930, Congress passed the Smoot-Hawley Act, which imposed a 45 percent tariff (rising to 60 percent by 1933) on one third of U.S. imports. This move provoked widespread retaliation and a tariff war among the world's major trading countries. After World War II, a process of trade liberalization brought about a gradual reduction of tariffs. What are the effects of tariffs on international trade? Why don't we have completely unrestricted international trade? ◆ In this chapter, we're going to learn about international trade. We'll discover how all nations can gain by specializing in producing the goods and services in which they have a comparative advantage and trading with other countries. We'll discover that *all* countries can compete, no matter how high their wages. We'll also explain why countries restrict trade.

## Silk Routes and Sucking Sounds

**After studying this chapter, you will be able to:**

- Describe the patterns in international trade
- Explain comparative advantage and explain why all countries can gain from international trade
- Explain how economies of scale and diversity of taste lead to gains from trade
- Explain why trade restrictions reduce our imports, exports, and consumption possibilities
- Explain the arguments used to justify trade restrictions and show how they are flawed
- Explain why we have trade restrictions

## Patterns and Trends in International Trade

THE GOODS AND SERVICES THAT WE BUY FROM people in other countries are called **imports**. The goods and services that we sell to people in other countries are called **exports**. What are the most important things that we import and export? Most people would probably guess that a rich nation such as the United States imports raw materials and exports manufactured goods. Although that is one feature of U.S. international trade, it is not its most important feature. The vast bulk of our exports *and* imports is manufactured goods. We sell foreigners earth-moving equipment, airplanes, supercomputers, and scientific equipment, and we buy televisions, VCRs, blue jeans, and T-shirts from them. Also, we are a major exporter of agricultural products and raw materials. We also import and export a huge volume of services.

### Trade in Goods

Manufactured goods account for 50 percent of our exports and for 60 percent of our imports. Industrial materials (raw materials and semimanufactured items) account for 17 percent of our exports and for 20 percent of our imports, and agricultural products account for only 7 percent of our exports and 3 percent of our imports. Our largest individual export and import items are capital goods and autos.

But goods account for only 74 percent of our exports and 83 percent of our imports. The rest of our international trade is in services.

### Trade in Services

You may be wondering how a country can "export" and "import" services. Here are some examples.

If you take a vacation in France and travel there on an Air France flight from New York, you import transportation services from France. The money you spend in France on hotel bills and restaurant meals is also classified as the import of services. Similarly, the vacation taken by a French student in the United States counts as an U.S. export of services to France.

When we import TV sets from South Korea, the owner of the ship that transports them might be Greek and the company that insures them might be British. The payments that we make for the transportation

and insurance are imports of services. Similarly, when an American shipping company transports California wine to Tokyo, the transportation cost is an export of a service to Japan. Our international trade in these types of services is large and growing.

### Geographical Patterns

The United States has trading links with every part of the world, but Canada is our biggest single trading partner for both exports and imports. We buy 45 percent of our imports from Japan and other Asian countries such as China, Hong Kong, South Korea, and Taiwan, and we sell a similar percentage of our exports to Asia, Europe, Latin America, and Canada.

### Trends in the Volume of Trade

In 1960, we exported less than 5 percent of total output and imported 4 1/2 percent of the goods and services that we consumed ourselves. Over the years since then, these percentages have steadily increased, and today they are more than twice their 1960 levels.

On the export side, capital goods, automobiles, food, and raw materials have remained large items and held a roughly constant share of total exports, but the composition of imports has changed. Food and raw material imports have fallen steadily. Imports of fuel increased dramatically during the 1970s but fell during the 1980s. Imports of machinery have grown and today they approach 50 percent of total imports.

### Balance of Trade and International Borrowing

The value of exports minus the value of imports is called the **balance of trade.** In 1996, the U.S. balance of trade was a negative $95 billion. Our imports were $95 billion more than our exports. When we import more than we export, as we did in 1996, we borrow from foreigners or sell some of our assets. When we export more than we import, we make loans to foreigners or buy some of their assets.

We study the *balance* of trade in Chapter 19. In this chapter, our goal is to understand the factors that influence the *volume* and *directions* of international trade rather than its balance. And the keys to this understanding are the concepts of opportunity cost and comparative advantage.

# Opportunity Cost and Comparative Advantage

THE FUNDAMENTAL FORCE THAT GENERATES international trade is *comparative advantage*. And the basis of comparative advantage is divergent *opportunity costs*. You met these ideas in Chapter 3, when we learned about the gains from specialization and exchange between Tom and Nancy.

Tom and Nancy each specialize in producing just one good and then trade with each other. Most nations do not go to the extreme of specializing in a single good and importing everything else. Nonetheless, nations can increase the consumption of all goods if they redirect their scarce resources toward the production of those goods and services in which they have a comparative advantage.

To see how this outcome occurs, we'll apply the same basic ideas we learned in the case of Tom and Nancy to trade among nations. We'll begin by recalling how we can use the production possibility frontier to measure opportunity cost. Then we'll see how divergent opportunity costs bring comparative advantage and gains from trade for countries as well as for individuals even though no country completely specializes in the production of just one good.

## Opportunity Cost in Farmland

Farmland (a fictitious country) can produce grain and cars at any point inside or along its production possibility frontier, *PPF*, shown in Fig. 18.1. (We're holding constant the output of all the other goods that Farmland produces.) The Farmers (the people of Farmland) are consuming all the grain and cars that they produce, and they are operating at point *a* in the figure. That is, Farmland is producing and consuming 15 billion bushels of grain and 8 million cars each year. What is the opportunity cost of a car in Farmland?

We can answer that question by calculating the slope of the production possibility frontier at point *a*. The magnitude of the slope of the frontier measures the opportunity cost of one good in terms of the other. To measure the slope of the frontier at point *a*, place a straight line tangential to the frontier at point *a* and calculate the slope of that straight line. Recall that the formula for the slope of a line is the change in the value of the variable measured on the *y*-axis divided by the change in the value of the variable measured on the *x*-axis as we move along the line.

Here, the variable measured on the *y*-axis is billions of bushels of grain, and the variable measured on the *x*-axis is millions of cars. So the slope is the change in the number of bushels of grain divided by the change in the number of cars.

As you can see from the red triangle at point *a* in the figure, if the number of cars produced increases by 2 million, grain production decreases by 18 billion bushels. Therefore the magnitude of the slope is 18 billion divided by 2 million, which equals 9,000. To get one more car, the people of Farmland must give up 9,000 bushels of grain. Thus the opportunity cost of 1 car is 9,000 bushels of grain. Equivalently, 9,000 bushels of grain cost 1 car. For the people of Farmland, these opportunity costs are the prices they face. The price of a car is 9,000 bushels of grain, and the price of 9,000 bushels of grain is 1 car.

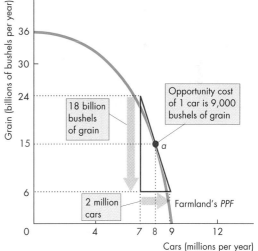

**FIGURE 18.1**

## Opportunity Cost in Farmland

Farmland produces and consumes 15 billion bushels of grain and 8 million cars a year. That is, it produces and consumes at point *a* on its production possibility frontier. Opportunity cost is equal to the magnitude of the slope of the production possibility frontier. The red triangle tells us that at point *a*, 18 billion bushels of grain must be forgone to get 2 million cars. That is, at point *a*, 2 million cars cost 18 billion bushels of grain. Equivalently, 1 car costs 9,000 bushels of grain or 9,000 bushels cost 1 car.

---

## Opportunity Cost in Mobilia

Figure 18.2 shows the production possibility frontier of Mobilia (another fictitious country). Like the Farmers, the Mobilians consume all the grain and cars that they produce. Mobilia consumes 18 billion bushels of grain a year and 4 million cars, at point $a'$.

Let's calculate the opportunity costs in Mobilia. At point $a'$, the opportunity cost of a car is equal to the magnitude of the slope of the red line tangential to the production possibility frontier, *PPF*. You can see from the red triangle that the magnitude of the slope of Mobilia's production possibility frontier is 6 billion bushels of grain divided by 6 million cars, which equals 1,000 bushels of grain per car. To get one more car, the Mobilians must give up 1,000 bushels of grain. Thus the opportunity cost of 1 car is 1,000 bushels of grain, or, equivalently, the opportunity cost of 1,000 bushels of grain is 1 car. These are the prices faced in Mobilia.

### FIGURE 18.2
## Opportunity Cost in Mobilia

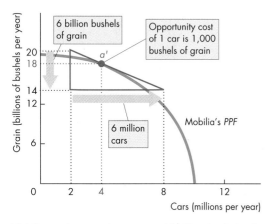

Mobilia produces and consumes 18 billion bushels of grain and 4 million cars a year. That is, it produces and consumes at point $a'$ on its production possibility frontier. Opportunity cost is equal to the magnitude of the slope of the production possibility frontier. The red triangle tells us that at point $a'$, 6 billion bushels of grain must be forgone to get 6 million cars. That is, at point $a'$, the opportunity cost of 6 million cars is 6 billion bushels of grain. Equivalently, 1 car costs 1,000 bushels of grain or 1,000 bushels of grain cost 1 car.

## Comparative Advantage

Cars are cheaper in Mobilia than in Farmland. One car costs 9,000 bushels of grain in Farmland but only 1,000 bushels of grain in Mobilia. But grain is cheaper in Farmland than in Mobilia—9,000 bushels of grain costs only 1 car in Farmland, while that same amount of grain costs 9 cars in Mobilia.

Mobilia has a comparative advantage in car production. Farmland has a comparative advantage in grain production. A country has a **comparative advantage** in producing a good if it can produce that good at a lower opportunity cost than any other country.

Let's see how opportunity cost differences and comparative advantage generate gains from international trade.

## Gains from Trade

IF MOBILIA BOUGHT GRAIN FOR WHAT IT COSTS Farmland to produce it, then Mobilia could buy 9,000 bushels of grain for 1 car. That is much lower than the cost of growing grain in Mobilia, for there it costs 9 cars to produce 9,000 bushels of grain. If the Mobilians can buy grain at the low Farmland price, they will reap some gains.

If the Farmers can buy cars for what it costs Mobilia to produce them, they will be able to obtain a car for 1,000 bushels of grain. Because it costs 9,000 bushels of grain to produce a car in Farmland, the Farmers would gain from such an opportunity.

In this situation, it makes sense for Mobilians to buy their grain from Farmers and for Farmers to buy their cars from Mobilians. Let's see how such profitable international trade comes about.

### Reaping the Gains from Trade

We've seen that the Farmers would like to buy their cars from the Mobilians and that the Mobilians would like to buy their grain from the Farmers. Let's see how the two groups do business with each other, by concentrating our attention on the international market for cars.

Figure 18.3 illustrates such a market. The quantity of cars *traded internationally* is measured on the *x*-axis. On the *y*-axis, we measure the price of a car. This price is expressed as the number of bushels of grain that a car costs—the opportunity cost of a car.

**FIGURE 18.3**

## International Trade in Cars

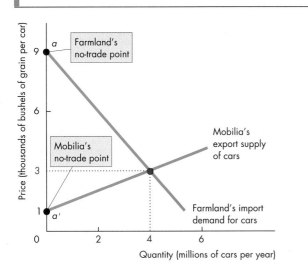

As the price of a car decreases, the quantity of imports demanded by Farmland increases—Farmland's import demand curve for cars is downward sloping. As the price of a car increases, the quantity of cars supplied by Mobilia for export increases—Mobilia's export supply curve of cars is upward sloping. Without international trade, the price of a car is 9,000 bushels of grain in Farmland (point *a*) and 1,000 bushels of grain in Mobilia (point *a'*).

With free international trade, the price of a car is determined where the export supply curve intersects the import demand curve—a price of 3,000 bushels of grain. At that price, 4 million cars a year are imported by Farmland and exported by Mobilia. The value of grain exported by Farmland and imported by Mobilia is 12 billion bushels a year, the quantity required to pay for the cars imported.

If no international trade takes place, the price of a car in Farmland is 9,000 bushels of grain, indicated by point *a* in the figure. Again, if no trade takes place, the price of a car in Mobilia is 1,000 bushels of grain, indicated by point *a'* in the figure. The no-trade points *a* and *a'* in Fig. 18.3 correspond to the points identified by those same letters in Figs. 18.1 and 18.2. The lower the price of a car (in terms of grain), the greater is the quantity of cars that the Farmers are willing to import from the Mobilians. This fact is illustrated by the downward-sloping curve, which shows Farmland's import demand for cars.

The Mobilians respond in the opposite direction. The higher the price of cars (in terms of bushels of grain), the greater is the quantity of cars that Mobilians are willing to export to Farmers. This fact is reflected in Mobilia's export supply of cars—the upward-sloping line in Fig. 18.3.

The international market in cars determines the equilibrium price and quantity traded. This equilibrium occurs where the import demand curve intersects the export supply curve. In this case, the equilibrium price of a car is 3,000 bushels of grain. Four million cars a year are exported by Mobilia and imported by Farmland. Notice that the price at which cars are traded is lower than the initial price in Farmland but higher than the initial price in Mobilia.

### Balanced Trade

The number of cars exported by Mobilia—4 million a year—is exactly equal to the number of cars imported by Farmland. How does Farmland pay for its cars? By exporting grain. How much grain does Farmland export? You can find the answer by noticing that for 1 car, Farmland has to pay 3,000 bushels of grain. Hence, for 4 million cars, they have to pay 12 billion bushels of grain. Thus Farmland's exports of grain are 12 billion bushels a year. Mobilia imports this same quantity of grain.

Mobilia is exchanging 4 million cars for 12 billion bushels of grain each year, and Farmland is doing the opposite, exchanging 12 billion bushels of grain for 4 million cars. Trade is balanced between these two countries. The value received from exports equals the value paid out for imports.

### Changes in Production and Consumption

We've seen that international trade makes it possible for Farmers to buy cars at a lower price than that at which they can produce them for themselves. Equivalently, Farmers can sell their grain for a higher price. International trade also enables Mobilians to sell their cars for a higher price. Equivalently, Mobilians can buy grain for a lower price. Thus everybody gains. How is it possible for *everyone* to gain? What are the changes in production and consumption that accompany these gains?

An economy that does not trade with other economies has identical production and consumption possibilities. Without trade, the economy can consume only what it produces. But with international trade, an economy can consume different quantities of goods from those that it produces. The production possibility frontier describes the limit of what a country can produce, but it does not describe the limits to what it can consume. Figure 18.4 will help you to see the distinction between production possibilities and consumption possibilities when a country trades with other countries.

First of all, notice that the figure has two parts, part (a) for Farmland and part (b) for Mobilia. The production possibility frontiers that you saw in Figs. 18.1 and 18.2 are reproduced here. The slopes of the two black lines in the figure represent the opportunity costs in the two countries when there is no international trade. Farmland produces and consumes at point *a*, and Mobilia produces and consumes at *a'*. Cars cost 9,000 bushels of grain in Farmland, and 1,000 bushels of grain in Mobilia.

**Consumption Possibilities**   The red line in each part of Fig. 18.4 shows the country's consumption possibilities with international trade. These two red lines have the same slope, and the magnitude of that slope is the opportunity cost of a car in terms of grain on the world market—3,000 bushels per car. The *slope* of the consumption possibilities line is common to both countries because its magnitude equals the *world* price. But the position of a country's consumption possibilities line depends on the country's production possibilities. A country cannot produce outside its production possibility curve, so its consumption possibility curve touches its production possibility curve. Thus Farmland could choose to consume at point *b* with no international trade or at any point on its red consumption possibilities line with international trade.

**Free Trade Equilibrium**   With international trade, the producers of cars in Mobilia can get a higher price for their output. As a result, they increase the quantity of car production. At the same time, grain producers in Mobilia get a lower price for their grain, and so they reduce production. Producers in Mobilia adjust their output by moving along their production possibility frontier until the opportunity cost in Mobilia equals the world price (the opportunity cost in the world market). This situation arises when Mobilia is producing at point *b'* in Fig. 18.4(b).

But the Mobilians do not consume at point *b'*. That is, they do not increase their consumption of

cars and decrease their consumption of grain. Instead, they sell some of their car production to Farmland in exchange for some of Farmland's grain. They trade internationally. But to see how that works out, we first need to check in with Farmland to see what's happening there.

In Farmland, producers of cars now get a lower price and producers of grain get a higher price. As a consequence, producers in Farmland decrease car production and increase grain production. They adjust their outputs by moving along the production possibility frontier until the opportunity cost of a car in terms of grain equals the world price (the opportunity cost on the world market). They move to point *b* in part (a). But the Farmers do not consume at point *b*. Instead, they trade some of their additional grain production for the now cheaper cars from Mobilia.

The figure shows us the quantities consumed in the two countries. We saw in Fig. 18.3 that Mobilia exports 4 million cars a year and Farmland imports those cars. We also saw that Farmland exports 12 billion bushels of grain a year and Mobilia imports that grain. Thus Farmland's consumption of grain is 12 billion bushels a year less than it produces, and its consumption of cars is 4 million a year more than it produces. Farmland consumes at point *c* in Fig. 18.4(a).

Similarly, we know that Mobilia consumes 12 billion bushels of grain more than it produces and 4 million cars fewer than it produces. Thus Mobilia consumes at *c'* in Fig. 18.4(b).

## Calculating the Gains from Trade

You can now literally see the gains from trade in Fig. 18.4. Without trade, Farmers produce and consume at point *a* (part a)—a point on Farmland's production possibility frontier. With international trade, Farmers consume at point *c* in part (a)—a point *outside* the production possibility frontier. At point *c*, Farmers are consuming 3 billion bushels of grain a year and 1 million cars a year more than before. These increases in consumption of both cars and grain, beyond the limits of the production possibility frontier, are the gains from international trade. Mobilians also gain. Without trade, they consume at point *a'* in part (b)—a point on Mobilia's production possibility frontier. With international trade, they consume at point *c'*—a point outside the

## FIGURE 18.4
## Expanding Consumption Possibilities

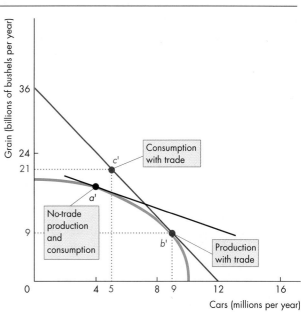

**(a) Farmland**

With no international trade, the Farmers produce and consume at point *a* and the opportunity cost of a car is 9,000 bushels of grain (the slope of the black line in part a). Also, with no international trade, the Mobilians produce and consume at point *a'* and the opportunity cost of 1,000 bushels of grain is 1 car (the slope of the black line in part b). Goods can be exchanged internationally at a price of 3,000 bushels of grain for 1 car along the red line in each part of the figure. In part (a), Farmland decreases its production of cars and

**(b) Mobilia**

increases its production of grain, moving from *a* to *b*. It exports grain and imports cars, and it consumes at point *c*. The Farmers have more of both cars and grain than they would if they produced all their own goods—at point *a*. In part (b), Mobilia increases car production and decreases grain production, moving from *a'* to *b'*. Mobilia exports cars and imports grain, and it consumes at point *c'*. The Mobilians have more of both cars and grain than they would if they produced all their own goods—at point *a'*.

production possibility frontier. With international trade, Mobilia consumes 3 billion bushels of grain a year and 1 million cars a year more than without trade. These are the gains from international trade for Mobilia.

### Gains for All

Trade between the Farmers and the Mobilians does not create winners and losers. Everyone wins. Sellers add the net demand of foreigners to their domestic demand, and so their market expands. Buyers are faced with domestic supply plus net foreign supply and so have a larger supply available to them.

### REVIEW

- When countries have divergent opportunity costs, they can gain from international trade.
- Each country can buy some goods and services from another country at a lower opportunity cost than that at which it can produce them for itself.
- Gains arise when each country increases its production of those goods and services in which it has a comparative advantage.
- All countries gain from international trade. There are no losers.

# Gains from Trade in Reality

THE GAINS FROM TRADE THAT WE HAVE JUST studied between Farmland and Mobilia in grain and cars occur in a model economy—in a world economy that we have imagined. But these same phenomena occur every day in the real global economy.

## Comparative Advantage in the Global Economy

We buy TVs and VCRs from Korea, machinery from Europe, and fashion goods from Hong Kong. In exchange, we sell machinery, grain and lumber, airplanes, computers and financial services. All this international trade is generated by comparative advantage, just like the international trade between Farmland and Mobilia in our model economy. All international trade arises from comparative advantage, even when trade is in similar goods such as tools and machines. At first thought, it seems puzzling that countries exchange manufactured goods. Why doesn't each developed country produce all the manufactured goods its citizens want to buy?

## Trade in Similar Goods

Why does the United States produce automobiles for export and at the same time import large quantities of them from Canada, Japan, Korea, and Western Europe? Wouldn't it make more sense to produce all the cars that we buy here in the United States? After all, we have access to the best technology available for producing cars. Autoworkers in the United States are surely as productive as their fellow workers in Canada, Western Europe, and Asian countries. So why does the United States have a comparative advantage in some types of cars and Japan and Europe in others?

## Diversity of Taste and Economies of Scale

The first part of the answer is that people have a tremendous diversity of taste. Let's stick with the example of cars. Some people prefer a sports car, some prefer a limousine, some prefer a regular, full-size car, and some prefer a minivan. In addition to size and type of car, there are many other dimensions in which cars vary. Some have low fuel consumption, some

have high performance, some are spacious and comfortable, some have a large trunk, some have four-wheel drive, some have front-wheel drive, some have a radiator grill that looks like a Greek temple, and others look like a wedge. People's preferences across these many dimensions vary. The tremendous diversity in tastes for cars means that people value variety and are willing to pay for it in the marketplace.

The second part of the answer to the puzzle is *economies of scale*—the tendency for the average cost to be lower, the larger the scale of production. In such situations, larger and larger production runs lead to ever lower average costs. Many goods, including cars, experience economies of scale. For example, if a car producer makes only a few hundred (or perhaps a few thousand) cars of a particular type and design, the producer must use production techniques that are much more labor-intensive and much less automated than those employed to make hundreds of thousands of cars in a particular model. With short production runs and labor-intensive production techniques, costs are high. With very large production runs and automated assembly lines, production costs are much lower. But to obtain lower costs, the automated assembly lines have to produce a large number of cars.

It is the combination of diversity of taste and economies of scale that determines opportunity cost, produces comparative advantages, and generates such a large amount of international trade in similar commodities. With international trade, each car manufacturer has the whole world market to serve. Each producer can specialize in a limited range of products and then sell its output to the entire world market. This arrangement enables large production runs on the most popular cars and feasible production runs even on the most customized cars demanded by only a handful of people in each country.

The situation in the market for cars is also present in many other industries, especially those producing specialized equipment and parts. For example, the United States exports computer central processor chips but imports memory chips, exports mainframe computers but imports PCs, exports specialized video equipment but imports VCRs. Thus international exchange of similar but slightly differentiated manufactured products is a highly profitable activity.

Let's next see what happens when governments restrict international trade. We'll see that free trade brings the greatest possible benefits. We'll also see why, in spite of the benefits of free trade, governments sometimes restrict trade.

# Trade Restrictions

GOVERNMENTS RESTRICT INTERNATIONAL TRADE to protect domestic industries from foreign competition by using two main tools:

1. Tariffs
2. Nontariff barriers

A **tariff** is a tax that is imposed by the importing country when an imported good crosses its international boundary. A **nontariff barrier** is any action other than a tariff that restricts international trade. Examples of nontariff barriers are quantitative restrictions and licensing regulations that limit imports. First, let's look at tariffs.

## The History of Tariffs

U.S. tariffs today are modest compared with their historical levels. Figure 18.5 shows the average tariff rate—total tariffs as a percentage of total imports.

You can see in this figure that this average reached a peak of 20 percent in 1933. In that year, three years after the passage of the Smoot-Hawley Act, one third of imports was subject to a tariff, and on those imports, the tariff rate was 60 percent. (The average tariff in Fig. 18.5 for 1933 is 60 percent multiplied by 0.33, which equals 20 percent.) Today, the average tariff rate is only 4 percent.

The reduction in tariffs since World War II followed the signing in 1947 of the **General Agreement on Tariffs and Trade** (GATT). Since its formation, the GATT has organized several rounds of negotiations that have resulted in tariff reductions. One of these, the Kennedy Round which began in the early 1960s, resulted in large tariff cuts starting in 1967. Another, the Tokyo Round, resulted in further tariff cuts in 1979. The most recent, the Uruguay Round, which started in 1986 and was completed in 1994, was the most ambitious and comprehensive of the rounds. The Uruguay Round also led to the creation of a new **World Trade Organization** (WTO). Membership of the WTO brings greater obligations on countries to observe the GATT rules.

---

**FIGURE 18.5**

## U.S. Tariffs: 1930–1996

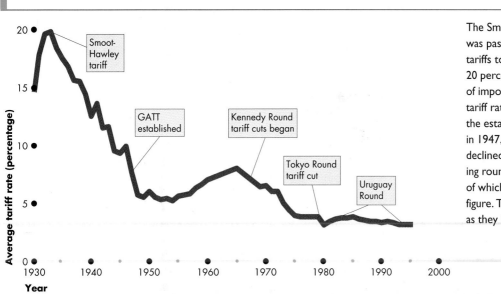

The Smoot-Hawley Act, which was passed in 1930, took U.S. tariffs to a peak average rate of 20 percent in 1933. (One third of imports was subject to a tariff rate of 60 percent.) Since the establishment of GATT in 1947, tariffs have steadily declined in a series of negotiating rounds, the most significant of which are identified in the figure. Tariffs are now as low as they have ever been.

*Sources:* U.S. Bureau of the Census, *Historical Statistics of the United States, Colonial Times to 1970*, Bicentennial Edition, Part 1 (Washington, D.C., 1975), Series U-212: *Statistical Abstract of the United States: 1986*, 106th edition (Washington, D.C., 1985); and *Statistical Abstract of the United States: 1996*, 116th edition (Washington, D.C., 1996).

In addition to the agreements under the GATT and the WTO, the United States is a party to the **North American Free Trade Agreement** (NAFTA), which became effective on January 1, 1994, and under which barriers to international trade between the United States, Canada, and Mexico will be virtually eliminated after a 15-year phasing-in period.

In other parts of the world, trade barriers have virtually been eliminated among the member countries of the European Union, which has created the largest unified tariff-free market in the world. In 1994, discussions among the Asia-Pacific Economic group (APEC) led to an agreement in principle to work toward a free-trade area that embraces China, all the economies of East Asia and the South Pacific, and the United States and Canada. These countries include the fastest-growing economies and hold the promise of heralding a global free-trade area.

The effort to achieve freer trade underlines the fact that trade in some goods is still subject to extremely high tariffs. The highest tariffs faced by U.S. buyers are those on textiles and footwear. A tariff of more than 10 percent (on the average) is imposed on almost all our imports of textiles and footwear. For example, when you buy a pair of blue jeans for $20, you pay about $5 more than you would if there were no tariffs on textiles. Other goods protected by tariffs are agricultural products, energy and chemicals, minerals, and metals. The meat, cheese, and sugar that you consume cost significantly more because of protection than they would with free international trade.

The temptation on governments to impose tariffs is a strong one. First, tariffs provide revenue to the government. Second, they enable the government to satisfy special interest groups in import-competing industries. But, as we'll see, free international trade brings enormous benefits that are reduced when tariffs are imposed. Let's see how.

## How Tariffs Work

To analyze how tariffs work, let's return to the example of trade between Farmland and Mobilia. Figure 18.6 shows the international market for cars in which these two countries are the only traders. The volume of trade and the price of a car are determined at the point of intersection of Mobilia's export supply curve of cars and Farmland's import demand curve for cars.

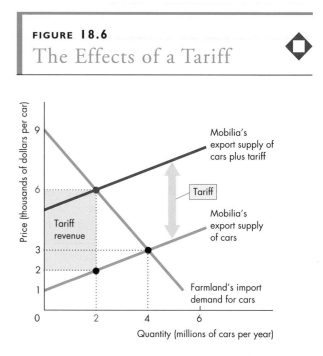

**FIGURE 18.6**

## The Effects of a Tariff

Farmland imposes a tariff on car imports from Mobilia. The tariff increases the price that Farmers have to pay for cars. It shifts the supply curve of cars in Farmland leftward. The vertical distance between the original supply curve and the new one is the amount of the tariff, $4,000 per car. The price of cars in Farmland increases, and the quantity of cars imported decreases. The government of Farmland collects a tariff revenue of $4,000 per car—a total of $8 billion on the 2 million cars imported. Farmland's exports of grain decrease because Mobilia now has a lower income from its exports of cars.

In Fig. 18.6, these two countries trade cars and grain in exactly the same way that we saw in Fig. 18.3. Mobilia exports cars, and Farmland exports grain. The volume of car imports into Farmland is 4 million a year, and the world market price of a car is 3,000 bushels of grain. Fig. 18.6 expresses prices in dollars rather than in units of grain and is based on a money price of grain of $1 a bushel. With grain costing $1 a bushel, the money price of a car is $3,000.

Now suppose that the government of Farmland, perhaps under pressure from car producers, decides to impose a tariff on imported cars. In particular, suppose that a tariff of $4,000 per car is imposed. (This is a huge tariff, but the car producers of Farmland are pretty fed up with competition from Mobilia.) What happens?

- The supply of cars in Farmland decreases.
- The price of a car in Farmland rises.
- The quantity of cars imported by Farmland decreases.
- The government of Farmland collects the tariff revenue.
- Resource use is inefficient.
- The *value* of exports changes by the same amount as the *value* of imports and trade remains balanced.

**Change in the Supply of Cars**   Farmland cannot buy cars at Mobilia's export supply price. It must pay that price plus the $4,000 tariff. So the supply curve in Farmland shifts leftward. The new supply curve is that labeled "Mobilia's export supply of cars plus tariff." The vertical distance between Mobilia's export supply curve and the new supply curve is the tariff of $4,000 a car.

**Rise in Price of Cars**   A new equilibrium occurs where the new supply curve intersects Farmland's import demand curve for cars. That equilibrium is at a price of $6,000 a car, up from $3,000 with free trade.

**Fall in Imports**   Car imports fall from 4 million to 2 million cars a year. At the higher price of $6,000 a car, Farmland's car producers increase their production. Grain production in Farmland decreases as resources are moved into the expanding car industry.

**Tariff Revenue**   Total expenditure on imported cars by the Farmers is $6,000 a car multiplied by the 2 million cars imported ($12 billion). But not all of that money goes to the Mobilians. They receive $2,000 a car, or $4 billion for the 2 million cars. The difference—$4,000 a car, or a total of $8 billion for the 2 million cars—is collected by the government of Farmland as tariff revenue.

**Inefficiency**   The people of Farmland are willing to pay $6,000 for the marginal car imported. But the opportunity cost of that car is $2,000. So there is a gain from trading an extra car. In fact, there are gains—willingness to pay exceeds opportunity cost—all the way up to 4 million cars a year. Only when 4 million cars are being traded is the maximum price that a Farmer is willing to pay equal to the minimum price that is acceptable to a Mobilian. Thus restricting trade reduces the gains from trade.

**Trade Remains Balanced**   With free trade, Farmland was paying $3,000 a car and buying 4 million cars a year from Mobilia. Thus the total amount paid to Mobilia for imports was $12 billion a year. With a tariff, Farmland's imports have been cut to 2 million cars a year and the price paid to Mobilia has also been cut to only $2,000 a car. Thus the total amount paid to Mobilia for imports has been cut to $4 billion a year. Doesn't this fact mean that Farmland now has a balance of trade surplus?

It does not. The price of cars in Mobilia has fallen. But the price of grain remains at $1 a bushel. So the relative price of cars has fallen, and the relative price of grain has increased. With free trade, the Mobilians could buy 3,000 bushels of grain for one car. Now they can buy only 2,000 bushels for a car. With a higher relative price of grain, the quantity demanded by the Mobilians decreases and Mobilia imports less grain. But because Mobilia imports less grain, Farmland exports less grain. In fact, Farmland's grain industry suffers from two sources. First, there is a decrease in the quantity of grain sold to Mobilia. Second, there is increased competition for inputs from the now expanded car industry. Thus the tariff leads to a contraction in the scale of the grain industry in Farmland.

It seems paradoxical at first that a country imposing a tariff on cars hurts its own export industry, decreasing its exports of grain. It may help to think of it this way: Mobilians buy grain with the money they make from exporting cars to Farmland. If they export fewer cars, they cannot afford to buy as much grain. In fact, in the absence of any international borrowing and lending, Mobilia must cut its imports of grain by exactly the same amount as the loss in revenue from its export of cars. Grain imports into Mobilia are cut back to a value of $4 billion, the amount that can be paid for by the new lower revenue from Mobilia's car exports. Thus trade is still balanced. The tariff cuts imports and exports by the same amount. The tariff has no effect on the *balance* of trade, but it reduces the *volume* of trade.

The result that we have just derived is perhaps one of the most misunderstood aspects of international economics. On countless occasions, politicians and others call for tariffs to remove a balance of trade deficit or argue that lowering tariffs would produce a balance of trade deficit. They reach this conclusion by failing to work out all the implications of a tariff.

Let's now turn our attention to the other tool for restricting trade: nontariff barriers.

## Nontariff Barriers

The two main forms of nontariff barriers are:

1. Quotas
2. Voluntary export restraints

A **quota** is a quantitative restriction on the import of a particular good, which specifies the maximum amount of the good that can be imported in a given period of time. A **voluntary export restraint** (VER) is an agreement between two governments in which the government of the exporting country agrees to restrain the volume of its own exports.

Quotas are especially prominent in textiles and agriculture. Voluntary export restraints are used to regulate trade between Japan and the United States.

## How Quotas and VERs Work

To see how a quota works, suppose that Farmland imposes a quota that restricts its car imports to 2 million cars a year. Figure 18.7 shows the effects of this action. The quota is shown by the vertical red line at 2 million cars a year. Because it is illegal to exceed the quota, car importers buy only that quantity from Mobilia, for which they pay $2,000 a car. But because the import supply of cars is restricted to 2 million cars a year, people in Farmland are willing to pay $6,000 per car. This is the price of a car in Farmland.

The value of imports falls to $4 billion, exactly the same as in the case of the tariff. So with lower incomes from car exports and with a higher relative price of grain, Mobilians cut back on their imports of grain in exactly the same way that they did under a tariff.

The key difference between a quota and a tariff lies in who collects the gap between the import supply price and the domestic price. In the case of a tariff, it is the government of the importing country. In the case of a quota, it goes to the person who has the right to import under the import quota regulations.

A voluntary export restraint is like a quota arrangement in which quotas are allocated to each exporting country. The effects of voluntary export restraints are similar to those of quotas but differ from them in that the gap between the price in the importing country and the export price is captured not by domestic importers but by the foreign exporter. The government of the exporting country has to establish procedures for allocating the restricted volume of exports among its producers.

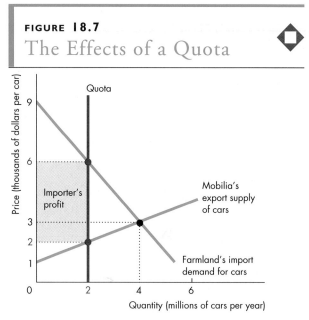

**FIGURE 18.7**

## The Effects of a Quota

Farmland imposes a quota of 2 million cars a year on car imports from Mobilia. That quantity appears as the vertical line labeled "Quota." Because the quantity of cars supplied by Mobilia is restricted to 2 million, the price at which those cars will be traded increases to $6,000. Importing cars is profitable because Mobilia is willing to supply cars at $2,000 each. There is competition for import quotas.

---

### R E V I E W

▪ When a country opens itself up to international trade and trades freely at world market prices, it expands its consumption possibilities.

▪ When trade is restricted, some of the gains from trade are lost.

▪ A country might be better off with restricted trade than with no trade but not as well off as it could be if it engaged in free trade.

▪ A tariff reduces the volume of imports, but it also reduces the volume of exports.

▪ Under both free trade and restricted trade (and without international borrowing and lending), the value of imports equals the value of exports. With restricted trade, both the total value of exports and the total value of imports are less than under free trade, but trade is still balanced.

Let's now look at some commonly heard arguments for restricting international trade.

# The Case Against Protection

FOR AS LONG AS NATIONS AND INTERNATIONAL trade have existed, people have debated whether a country is better off with free international trade or with protection from foreign competition. The debate continues, but for most economists, a verdict has been delivered and is the one you have just seen. Free trade promotes prosperity for all: protection is inefficient. We've seen the most powerful case for free trade in the example of how Farmland and Mobilia both benefit from their comparative advantage. But there is a broader range of issues in the free trade versus protection debate. Let's review these issues.

Three arguments for restricting international trade are:

■ The national security argument
■ The infant-industry argument
■ The dumping argument

Let's look at each in turn.

## The National Security Argument

The national security argument for protection is that a country must protect industries that produce defense equipment and armaments and those on which the defense industries rely for their raw materials and other intermediate inputs. This argument for protection does not withstand close scrutiny.

First, it is an argument for international isolation, for in a time of war, there is no industry that does not contribute to national defense. Second, if the case is made for boosting the output of a strategic industry, it is more efficient to achieve this outcome with a subsidy to the firms in the industry financed out of taxes. Such a subsidy would keep the industry operating at the scale judged appropriate, and free international trade would keep the prices faced by consumers at their world market levels.

## The Infant-Industry Argument

The so-called **infant-industry argument** for protection is that it is necessary to protect a new industry to enable it to grow into a mature industry that can compete in world markets. The argument is based on the idea of *dynamic comparative advantage*, which can arise from *learning-by-doing* (see Chapter 3).

Learning-by-doing is a powerful engine of productivity growth, and comparative advantage evolves and changes because of on-the-job experience. But these facts do not justify protection.

First, the infant-industry argument is valid only if the benefits of learning-by-doing *not only* accrue to the owners and workers of the firms in the infant industry but also *spill over* to other industries and parts of the economy. For example, there are huge productivity gains from learning-by-doing in the manufacture of aircraft. But almost all of these gains benefit the stockholders and workers of Boeing and other aircraft producers. Because the people making the decisions, bearing the risk, and doing the work are the ones who benefit, they take the dynamic gains into account when they decide on the scale of their activities. In this case, almost no benefits spill over to other parts of the economy, so there is no need for government assistance to achieve an efficient outcome.

Second, even if the case is made for protecting an infant industry, it is more efficient to do so by a subsidy to the firms in the industry, with the subsidy financed out of taxes.

## The Dumping Argument

**Dumping** occurs when a foreign firm sells its exports at a lower price than its cost of production. Dumping might be used by a firm that wants to gain a global monopoly. In this case, the foreign firm sells its output at a price below its cost to drive domestic firms out of business. When the domestic firms have gone, the foreign firm takes advantage of its monopoly position and charges a higher price for its product. Dumping is usually regarded as a justification for temporary countervailing tariffs.

But there are powerful reasons to resist the dumping argument for protection. First, it is virtually impossible to detect dumping because it is hard to determine a firm's costs. As a result, the test for dumping is whether a firm's export price is below its domestic price. But this test is a weak one because it can be rational for a firm to charge a low price in markets in which the quantity demanded is highly sensitive to price and a higher price in a market in which demand is less price-sensitive.

Second, it is hard to think of a good that is produced by a natural *global* monopoly. So even if all the domestic firms were driven out of business in some industry, it would always be possible to find several and usually many alternative foreign sources of supply and to buy at prices determined in competitive markets.

Third, if a good or service were a truly global natural monopoly, the best way of dealing with it would be by regulation—just as in the case of domestic monopolies. Such regulation would require international cooperation.

The three arguments for protection that we've just examined have an element of credibility. The counterarguments are in general stronger, so these arguments do not make the case for protection. But they are not the only arguments that you might encounter. The many other arguments that are commonly heard are quite simply wrong. They are fatally flawed. The most common of them are that protection:

- Saves jobs
- Allows us to compete with cheap foreign labor
- Brings diversity and stability
- Penalizes lax environmental standards
- Protects national culture
- Prevents rich countries from exploiting developing countries

## Saves Jobs

The argument is: When we buy shoes from Brazil or shirts from Taiwan, U.S. workers lose their jobs. With no earnings and poor prospects, these workers become a drain on welfare and spend less, causing a ripple effect of further job losses. The proposed solution to this problem is to ban imports of cheap foreign goods and protect U.S. jobs. The proposal is flawed for the following reasons.

First, free trade does cost some jobs, but it also creates other jobs. It brings about a global rationalization of labor and allocates labor resources to their highest-value activities. Because of international trade in textiles, tens of thousands of workers in the United States have lost jobs because textile mills and other factories have closed. But tens of thousands of workers in other countries have gotten jobs because textile mills have opened there. And tens of thousands of U.S. workers have gotten better-paying jobs than textile workers because other export industries have expanded and created more jobs than have been destroyed.

Second, imports create jobs. They create jobs for retailers that sell imported goods and firms that service those goods. They also create jobs by creating incomes in the rest of the world, some of which are spent on imports of U.S.-made goods and services.

Although protection does save particular jobs, it does so at inordinate cost. For example, textile jobs are protected in the United States by quotas imposed under an international agreement called the Multifiber Arrangement. It has been estimated by the U.S. International Trade Commission (ITC) that because of quotas, 72,000 jobs exist in textiles that would otherwise disappear and annual clothing expenditure in the United States is $15.9 billion, or $160 per family higher than it would be with free trade. Equivalently, the ITC estimates that each textile job saved costs $221,000 a year.

## Allows Us to Compete with Cheap Foreign Labor

With the removal of protective tariffs in U.S. trade with Mexico, Ross Perot said we would hear a "giant sucking sound" of jobs rushing to Mexico (one of which is shown in the cartoon). Let's see what's wrong with this view.

The labor cost of a unit of output equals the wage rate divided by labor productivity. For example, if a U.S. auto worker earns $30 an hour and produces 15

*"I don't know what the hell happened—one minute I'm at work in Flint, Michigan, then there's a giant sucking sound and suddenly here I am in Mexico."*

Drawing by M. Stevens; © 1993
The New Yorker Magazine, Inc.

units of output an hour, the average labor cost of a unit of output is $2. If a Mexican auto assembly worker earns $3 an hour and produces 1 unit of output an hour, the average labor cost of a unit of output is $3. Other things remaining the same, the higher a worker's productivity, the higher is the worker's wage rate. High-wage workers have high productivity. Low-wage workers have low productivity.

Although high-wage U.S. workers are more productive, on the average, than low-wage Mexican workers, there are differences across industries. U.S. labor is relatively more productive in some activities than in others. For example, the productivity of U.S. workers in producing movies, financial services, and customized computer chips is relatively higher than in the production of metals and some standardized machine parts. The activities in which U.S. workers are relatively more productive than their Mexican counterparts are those in which the United States has a *comparative advantage*. By engaging in free trade, increasing our production and exports of the goods and services in which we have a comparative advantage and decreasing our production and increasing our imports of the goods and services in which our trading partners have a comparative advantage, we can make ourselves and the citizens of other countries better off.

## Brings Diversity and Stability

A diversified investment portfolio is less risky than one that has all the eggs in one basket. The same is true for an economy's production. A diversified economy fluctuates less than an economy that produces only one or two goods.

But big, rich, diversified economies like those of the United States, Japan, and Europe do not have this type of stability problem. Even a country like Saudi Arabia that produces almost only one good (oil) can benefit from specializing in the activity at which it has a comparative advantage and then investing in a wide range of other countries to bring greater stability to its income and consumption.

## Penalizes Lax Environmental Standards

A new argument for protection is that many poorer countries, such as Mexico, do not have the same environment policies that we have and, because they are willing to pollute and we are not, we cannot compete with them without tariffs. So if they want free trade with the richer and "greener" countries, they must clean up their environments to our standards.

This argument for trade restrictions is weak. First, not all poorer countries have significantly lower environmental standards than the United States has. Many poor countries and the former Communist countries of Eastern Europe do have bad environment records. But some countries enforce strict laws. Second, a poor country cannot afford to be as concerned about its environment as a rich country can. The best hope for a better environment in Mexico and in other developing countries is rapid income growth through free trade. As their incomes grow, developing countries will have the *means* to match their desires to improve their environment. Third, poor countries have a comparative advantage at doing "dirty" work, which helps rich countries achieve higher environment standards than they otherwise could.

## Protects National Culture

The national culture argument for protection is not heard much in the United States, but it is a commonly heard argument in Canada and Europe.

The expressed fear is that free trade in books, magazines, movies, and television programs means U.S. domination and the end of local culture. So, the reasoning continues, it is necessary to protect domestic culture industries from free international trade to ensure the survival of a national cultural identity.

Protection of these industries is common and takes the form of nontariff barriers. For example, local content regulations on radio and television broadcasting and in magazines is often required.

The cultural identity argument for protection has no merit, and it is one more example of rent-seeking. Writers, publishers, and broadcasters want to limit foreign competition so that they can earn larger economic profits. There is no actual danger to national culture. In fact, many of the creators of so-called American cultural products are not Americans, but the talented citizens of other countries, ensuring the survival of their national cultural identities in Hollywood! Also, if national culture is in danger, there is no surer way of helping it on its way out than by impoverishing the nation whose culture it is. And protection is an effective way of doing just that.

## Prevents Rich Countries from Exploiting Developing Countries

Another new argument for protection is that international trade must be restricted to prevent the people of the rich industrial world from exploiting the poorer people of the developing countries, forcing them to work for slave wages.

Wage rates in some developing countries are indeed very low. But by trading with developing countries, we increase the demand for the goods that these countries produce, and, more significantly, we increase the demand for their labor. When the demand for labor in developing countries increases, the wage rate also increases. So, far from exploiting people in developing countries, trade improves their opportunities and increases their incomes.

We have reviewed the arguments that are commonly heard in favor of protection and the counter-arguments against them. There is one counter-argument to protection that is general and quite overwhelming. Protection invites retaliation and can trigger a trade war. The best example of a trade war occurred during the Great Depression of the 1930s when the Smoot-Hawley Tariff was introduced. Country after country retaliated with its own tariff, and in a short period, world trade had almost disappeared. The costs to all countries were large and led to a renewed international resolve to avoid such self-defeating moves in the future. They also led to the creation of GATT and are the impetus behind NAFTA, APEC, and the European Union.

## R E V I E W

■ Trade restrictions aimed at national security goals, stimulating the growth of new industries, and restraining foreign monopoly have little merit.

■ Trade restrictions to save jobs, compensate for low foreign wages, make the economy more diversified, compensate for costly environmental policies, protect national culture, and protect developing countries from being exploited are misguided.

■ The main arguments against trade restrictions are that subsidies and antitrust policies can achieve domestic goals more efficiently than protection and that protection can trigger a trade war in which all countries lose.

## Why Is International Trade Restricted?

WHY, DESPITE ALL THE ARGUMENTS AGAINST protection, is trade restricted? There are two key reasons:

■ Tariff revenue
■ Rent seeking

### Tariff Revenue

Government revenue is costly to collect. In the developed countries such as the United States, a well-organized tax-collection system is in place that can generate billions of dollars of income tax and sales tax revenues. This tax-collecting system is made possible by the fact that most economic transactions are done by firms that must keep properly audited financial records. Without such records, the revenue collection agencies (the Internal Revenue Service in the United States) would be severely hampered in the work. Even with audited financial accounts, some proportion of potential tax revenue is lost. Nonetheless, for the industrialized countries, the income tax and sales taxes are the major sources of revenue and the tariff plays a very small role.

But governments in developing countries have a difficult time collecting taxes from their citizens. Much economic activity takes place in an informal economy with few financial records. So only a small amount of revenue is collected from income taxes and sales taxes in these countries. The one area in which economic transactions are well recorded and audited is in international trade. So this activity is an attractive base for tax collection in these countries and is used much more extensively than in the developed countries.

### Rent Seeking

The major reason why international trade is restricted is because of rent seeking. Free trade increases consumption possibilities *on the average* but not everyone shares in the gain and some people even lose. Free trade brings benefits to some and imposes costs on others, with total benefits exceeding total costs. It is the uneven distribution of costs and benefits that is the principal source of impediment to achieving more liberal international trade.

Returning to our example of trade in cars and grain between Farmland and Mobilia, the benefits to Farmland from free trade accrue to all the producers of grain and those producers of cars who would not have to bear the costs of adjusting to a smaller car industry. These costs are transition costs, not permanent costs. The costs of moving to free trade are borne by those car producers and their employees who have to become grain producers. The number of people who gain will, in general, be enormous compared with the number who lose. The gain per person will therefore be rather small. The loss per person to those who bear the loss will be large. Because the loss that falls on those who bear it is large, it will pay those people to incur considerable expense to lobby against free trade. On the other hand, it will not pay those who gain to organize to achieve free trade. The gain from trade for any one individual is too small for that individual to spend much time or money on a political organization to achieve free trade. The loss from free trade will be seen as being so great by those bearing that loss that they *will* find it profitable to join a political organization to prevent free trade. Each group is optimizing—weighing benefits against costs and choosing the best action for themselves. The anti-free-trade group will, however, undertake a larger quantity of political lobbying than the pro-free-trade group.

## Compensating Losers

If, in total, the gains from free international trade exceed the losses, why don't those who gain compensate those who lose so that everyone is in favor of free trade? To some degree, such compensation does take place. When Congress approved the NAFTA deal with Canada and Mexico, it set up a $56 million fund to support and retrain workers who lost their jobs because of the new trade agreement. During the first six months of the operation of NAFTA, only 5,000 workers applied for benefits under this scheme.

The losers from freer international trade are also compensated indirectly through the normal unemployment compensation arrangements. But only limited attempts are made to compensate those who lose from free international trade. The main reason why full compensation is not attempted is that the costs of identifying all the losers and estimating the value of their losses would be enormous. Also, it would never

be clear whether a person who has fallen on hard times is suffering because of free trade or for other reasons, perhaps reasons that are largely under the control of the individual. Furthermore, some people who look like losers at one point in time may, in fact, wind up gaining. The young auto worker who loses his job in Michigan and becomes a computer assembly worker in Minneapolis resents the loss of work and the need to move. But a year or two later, looking back on events, he counts himself fortunate. He has made a move that has increased his income and given him greater job security.

It is because we do not, in general, compensate the losers from free international trade that protectionism is such a popular and permanent feature of our national economic and political life.

---

## R E V I E W

▪ International trade is restricted because tariffs raise revenue for governments and because tariffs create gains (economic rents) for some and losses for others.

▪ The revenue from tariffs is important for developing countries but not for developed countries such as the United States.

▪ Gains from trade are spread thinly, and gains from protection accrue to a few people. It pays the few to organize to ensure that their interests are protected.

---

◆ You've now seen how free international trade enables all nations to gain from specialization and trade. By producing goods in which we have a comparative advantage and trading some of our production for that of others, we expand our consumption possibilities. Placing impediments on that trade restricts the extent to which we can gain from specialization and trade. Opening our country up to free international trade expands the market for the things that we sell and raises their relative price. The market for the things that we buy also expands, and the relative price falls. *Reading Between the Lines* on pp. 442–443 looks at a recent example of the removal and reintroduction of a tariff in the small but politically sensitive market for brooms.

In the final chapter, we're going to examine the balance of international trade and the forces that influence the exchange rate.

# Policy
## WATCH

## NAFTA in Action

THE ORLANDO SENTINEL, JULY 30, 1996

# U.S. Broom Makers Swept Aside by NAFTA

THE ASSOCIATED PRESS

GREENUP, ILL.—In a long room filled with the smell of straw and the clatter of stitching machines, Ed Graves feeds fistfuls of broomcorn under a thin wire.

He works quickly, cutting the extra stalks away with a long knife as the spinning machine turns wood, wire and straw into the familiar shape of a household broom.

It's a good job, the top of the broom-making profession. He can earn up to $100 a day.

But it's a job Graves and fellow employees at the Quinn Broom Works fear could soon be gone, the victim of the North American Free Trade Agreement and cheaper labor at broom factories in Mexico.

The U.S. broom industry is a small one—only about 600 workers scattered in small plants in Illinois, Ohio, California, Texas and the Southeast. But small broom makers such as the Quinn Broom Works could be among the first manufacturers protected from Mexican competition under NAFTA.

On Friday, the U.S. International Trade Commission recommended restoring a 32 percent tariff on Mexican brooms. The ITC ruled that competition from Mexican factories poses a serious threat to the domestic broom industry. ...

Last year, the average Mexican broom cost $1.92, compared with $3 to $3.40 a broom for U.S.-made brooms ... .

"Our sales are down from the first of the year because of NAFTA by about 50 percent," said Alvin Wingler of Warren Manufacturing in Arcola, Ill. "We were closed down for three weeks, and for another few weeks we ran at 25 percent of our production capacity." ...

The Associated Press. Reprinted with permission.

- American broom makers fear that cheap Mexican labor and NAFTA will destroy their jobs.

- One manufacturer says that NAFTA has decreased broom sales by 50 percent.

- Broom makers could be one of the first to be protected from Mexican competition under NAFTA.

- The International Trade Commission is recommending the restoration of a 32 percent tariff on Mexican brooms.

- Mexican brooms sell at an average price of $1.92. American brooms sell in the $3.00 to $3.40 price range.

# Economic

## A N A L Y S I S

■ On January 1, 1994, the United States, Mexico, and Canada began a process of tariff reduction that by 2009 will have eliminated most restrictions on trade among the three countries.

■ One tariff eliminated was that on brooms. But protests from U.S. broom producers have brought the broom tariff back.

■ Brooms come in many types. The price of the simplest, least durable, and cheapest broom is less than $2. The most elaborate, durable, hand-made brooms cost as much as $50!

■ To study the economics of trade in brooms, we'll consider a standard broom that costs $2 to produce in Mexico.

■ Figure 1 shows the U.S. market for this standard broom, both with and without a tariff. The demand curve is $D$. The supply curve of Mexican brooms is $S_M$. The supply curve of U.S. brooms is $S_{US}$.

■ With no tariff, $QC_1$ brooms are bought in the United States. Of these, $QP_1$ are produced in the United States and the rest are imported, as shown by the arrow in Fig. 1.

■ To keep the numbers simple, suppose we put a 50 percent tariff on broom imports. The price of the Mexican broom is now $2 plus the $1 tariff, so the supply curve of brooms from Mexico shifts to become $S_M + tariff$.

■ With the tariff, $QC_0$ brooms are bought in the United States. Of these, $QP_0$ are produced in the United States and the rest are imported. U.S. consumption and imports decrease and U.S. production increases.

■ Figure 2 shows the winners and the losers in the United States.

■ U.S producers gain additional economic profit (the blue area) and the U.S. government collects additional revenue (the purple area).

■ The loser is the U.S. consumer. The consumers' loss equals the producers' gain plus the government's gain plus the deadweight loss, shown by the two gray areas.

■ The sum of the blue, purple, and gray areas is the loss of consumer surplus that results from the tariff.

Figure 1  Tariffs and imports

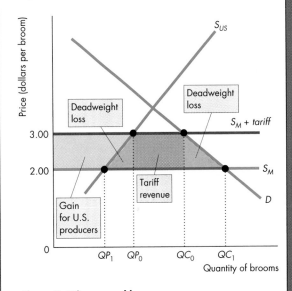

Figure 2  Winners and losers

## You're

### THE VOTER

■ Are you for or against the tariff on brooms?

■ What do you predict Mexico will do about the broom tariff?

■ Write a report to your Congress member explaining why you favor or oppose the removal of the broom tariff.

# SUMMARY

## Key Points

### Patterns and Trends in International Trade (p. 426)

- Large flows of trade take place between countries, most of which is in manufactured goods exchanged among rich industrialized countries.
- Since 1960, the volume of U.S. trade, as a percentage of total output, has more than doubled.

### Opportunity Cost and Comparative Advantage (pp. 427–428)

- When opportunity costs between countries diverge, comparative advantage enables countries to gain from international trade.

### Gains from Trade (pp. 428–431)

- By increasing its production of goods in which it has a comparative advantage and then trading some of the increased output, a country can consume at a point outside its production possibility frontier.
- In the absence of international borrowing and lending, trade is balanced as prices adjust to reflect the international supply of and demand for goods.
- The world price balances the production and consumption plans of the trading parties. At the equilibrium price, trade is balanced.

### Gains from Trade in Reality (p. 432)

- Comparative advantage explains the international trade that takes place in the world.
- But trade in similar goods arises from economies of scale in the face of diversified tastes.

### Trade Restrictions (pp. 433–436)

- Countries restrict international trade by imposing tariffs and quotas.
- Trade restrictions raise the domestic price of imported goods, lower the volume of imports, and reduce the total value of imports.

- Trade restrictions also reduce the total value of exports by the same amount as the reduction in the value of imports.

### The Case Against Protection (pp. 437–440)

- Arguments that protection is necessary for national security, to allow infant industries the chance to grow, and to prevent dumping are weak.
- Arguments that protection saves jobs, allows us to compete with cheap foreign labor, makes the economy diversified and stable, protects national culture, and is needed to offset the costs of environmental policies are fatally flawed.

### Why is International Trade Restricted? (pp. 440–441)

- Trade is restricted because tariffs raise government revenue and because protection brings a small loss to a large number of people and a large gain per person to a small number of people.

## Key Figures

## Key Terms

# QUESTIONS

1. What are the main exports and imports of the United States?
2. With which countries does the United States do most of its international trade?
3. What is comparative advantage?
4. Why does comparative advantage lead to gains from international trade?
5. Explain what the gains from trade are.
6. Explain why international trade brings gains to all countries.
7. Explain why all countries have a comparative advantage in something.
8. Explain why, when a country begins to trade, the price received for the good exported rises and the price paid for the good imported falls.
9. Explain why we import and export such large quantities of certain similar goods—such as cars.
10. What are the main ways in which we restrict international trade?
11. What are the GATT and the WTO? When was each established and what is its role?
12. What is NAFTA? When did it begin, and what have its effects to date been?
13. What are the effects of a tariff?
14. What are the effects of a quota?
15. What are the effects of a voluntary export restraint?
16. What is an infant industry? Explain why some people argue that an infant industry needs protection from international competition and also explain the main flaws in the argument.
17. What is dumping? Explain why dumping occurs.
18. Describe the main trends in tariffs.
19. What are the main arguments for trade restrictions? Explain the flaw in each argument.
20. Why do countries restrict international trade?
21. What is a voluntary export restraint and who gains from it?
22. Explain the effect of trade with low-wage countries on jobs in the United States.

# PROBLEMS

1. Figures 18.1 and 18.2 illustrate Farmland's and Mobilia's production possibilities.
   a. Calculate Farmland's opportunity cost of a car when it produces 2 million cars a year.
   b. Calculate Mobilia's opportunity cost of a car when it produces 8 million cars a year.
   c. With no trade, Farmland produces 2 million cars and Mobilia produces 8 million cars. Which country has a comparative advantage in the production of cars?
   d. If there is no trade between Farmland and Mobilia, how much grain is consumed and how many cars are bought in each country?
2. Suppose that the two countries in problem 1 trade freely.
   a. Which country exports grain?
   b. What is the change in the amount of each good produced by each country?
   c. What is the change in the amount of each good consumed by each country?
   d. What can you say about the price of a car under free trade?
3. Compare the total production of each good produced in problems 1 and 2.
4. Why does Mobilia export cars in the chapter (pp. 427–431) but import them in problem 2?
5. The following figure depicts the international market for soybeans.

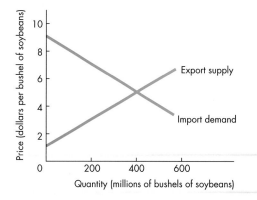

   a. If the two countries did not engage in international trade, what would be the prices of soybeans in the two countries?

b. What is the world price of soybeans if there is free trade between these countries?
c. What quantities of soybeans are traded?
d. What is the balance of trade?

6. If the country in problem 5 that imports soybeans imposes a tariff of $2 per bushel, what is the world price of soybeans and what quantity of soybeans gets traded internationally? What is the price of soybeans in the importing country? Calculate the tariff revenue.

7. The importing country in problem 5(b) imposes a quota of 300 million bushels on imports of soybeans.
a. What is the price of soybeans in the importing country?
b. What is the revenue from the quota?
c. Who gets this revenue?

8. The exporting country in problem 5(b) imposes a VER of 300 million bushels on its exports of soybeans.
a. What is the world price of soybeans now?
b. What is the revenue of soybean growers in the exporting country?
c. Which country gains from the VER?

9. Suppose that the exporting country in problem 5(b) subsidizes production by paying its farmers $1 a bushel for soybeans harvested.
a. What is the price of soybeans in the importing country?
b. What action might soybean growers in the importing country take? Why?

10. Countries Atlantis and Magic Kingdom produce only food and balloon rides. The figure shows their production possibility frontiers.
a. If Atlantis produces at point *a*, what is its opportunity cost of a balloon ride?
b. What are the consumption possibilities of Atlantis?
c. If Magic Kingdom produces at point *a'*, what is its opportunity cost of a balloon ride?
d. What are the consumption possibilities of Magic Kingdom?
e. Which country has a comparative advantage in producing food?

11. If Atlantis and Magic Kingdom in problem 10 enter into a free trade agreement:
a. How does the price of a balloon ride in each country change?

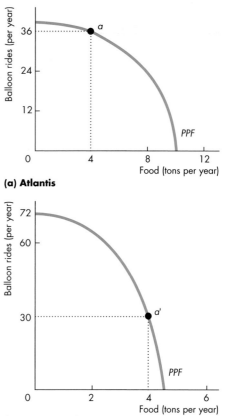

**(a) Atlantis**

**(b) Magic Kingdom**

b. How does the price of food in each country change?
c. Which country exports balloon rides?
d. Which country exports food?
e. What are the gains from trade for each country?
f. Are there any losers as a result of the free trade agreement?

# CRITICAL THINKING

1. Study *Reading Between the Lines* on pp. 442–443, and then answer the following questions.
a. Why did NAFTA give U.S broom producers a hard time?
b. What are the effects of the tariff on brooms?
c. Who are the winners and who are the losers from the tariff on brooms?
d. Why do you think the government reinstated the tariff on brooms?

# 19

# The Balance of Payments and the Dollar

In 1988, the United States owned $1.9 trillion in assets abroad and foreigners owned $1.9 trillion of assets in the United States. Before 1988, U.S. residents' ownership of foreign assets exceeded foreigners' ownership of assets in the United States; since 1988, the balance has tipped increasingly the other way. During these years, foreign entrepreneurs such as Australian-born Rupert Murdoch and Sony's Akio Mori roamed the United States with giant shopping carts and loaded them up with such items as Twentieth Century Fox, the Rockefeller Center, and MGM. Why have foreigners been buying more U.S. real

## A Climbing Debt and a Tumbling Dollar

estate and businesses than Americans have been buying abroad? ◆ In 1971, one U.S. dollar was enough to buy 360 Japanese yen. By mid-1995, that same dollar bought only 84 yen. But the slide from 360 to 84 yen was not a smooth one. At some times, the dollar held its own or even rose in value against the Japanese currency, as it did, for example, in

1982. But at other times, the dollar's slide was precipitous, as in the period between 1985 and 1988 and again in 1995. But since mid-1995, the dollar has increased against the yen, and by April 1997, it had climbed to more than 120 yen. The dollar has risen in recent years against the German mark, the French franc, the Swiss franc, and the Canadian dollar. But it has fallen slightly against the British pound. What makes our dollar fluctuate in value against other currencies? Why were the fluctuations particularly extreme during the 1980s? Is there anything we can do or should do to stabilize the value of the dollar? ◆ We're going to discover why the U.S. economy has become attractive for foreign investors, why the dollar fluctuates against the values of other currencies, and why interest rates vary from country to country.

## After studying this chapter, you will be able to:

■ Explain how international trade is financed

■ Describe a country's balance of payments accounts

■ Explain what determines the amount of international borrowing and lending

■ Explain why the United States changed from being a lender to being a borrower in the mid-1980s

■ Explain how the foreign exchange value of the dollar is determined

■ Explain why the foreign exchange value of the dollar fluctuates

## Financing International Trade

WHEN A SONY STORE IN THE UNITED STATES imports CD players from Japan, it does not pay for them with U.S. dollars—it uses Japanese yen. And when a French construction company buys an earth mover from Caterpillar, Inc., it uses U.S. dollars. Whenever we buy things from another country, we use the currency of that country to make the transaction. It doesn't make any difference what the item being traded is; it might be a consumption good or a capital good, a building, or even a firm.

We're going to study the markets in which money—different types of currency—is bought and sold. But first we're going to look at the scale of international trading and borrowing and lending and at the way in which we keep our records of these transactions. Such records are called the balance of payments accounts.

### Balance of Payments Accounts

A country's **balance of payments accounts** records its international trading, borrowing, and lending. There are in fact three balance of payments accounts:

1. Current account
2. Capital account
3. Official settlements account

The **current account** records payments for imports of goods and services from abroad, receipts from exports of goods and services sold abroad, net interest paid abroad, and net transfers (such as foreign aid payments). The *current account balance* equals exports minus imports, net interest, and net transfers. The **capital account** records foreign investment in the United States minus U.S. investment abroad. The **official settlements account** records the change in official U.S. reserves. **Official U.S. reserves** are the government's holdings of foreign currency. If U.S. official reserves increase, the *official settlements account balance* is negative. The reason is that holding foreign money is like investing abroad. U.S. investment abroad is a minus item in the capital account. By the same reasoning, if official reserves decrease, the *official settlements account balance* is positive.

The sum of the balances on the three accounts always equals zero. That is, to pay for our current account deficit, either we must borrow more from abroad than we lend abroad or use our official reserves to cover the shortfall.

Table 19.1 shows the U.S. balance of payments accounts in 1996. Items in the current account and capital account that provide foreign currency to the United States have a plus sign; items that cost the United States foreign currency have a minus sign. The table shows that in 1996, U.S. imports exceeded U.S. exports and the United States had a current account deficit of $160 billion. How do we pay for our current account deficit? We pay by borrowing from the rest of the world. The capital account tells us by how much. We borrowed $430 billion (foreign investment in the United States) but made loans of $240 billion (U.S. investment abroad). Thus our identified net foreign borrowing was $190 billion. There is a statistical discrepancy of $40 billion between our capital account and current account transactions such as unidentified borrowing from the rest of the world, illegal international trade—for example, the import of illegal drugs—and

**TABLE 19.1**

## U.S. Balance of Payments Accounts in 1996

| Current account | Billions of dollars |
|---|---|
| Imports of goods and services | −940 |
| Exports of goods and services | +830 |
| Net interest income | −10 |
| Net transfers | −40 |
| Current account balance | −160 |
| **Capital account** | |
| Foreign investment in the United States | +430 |
| U.S. investment abroad | −240 |
| Statistical discrepancy | −40 |
| Capital account balance | +150 |
| **Official settlements account** | |
| Increase in official U.S. reserves | −10 |

*Source: Survey of Current Business* (January 1997), vol. 77. Data for the full year of 1996 were not available when this book went to press. The data here cover January to September 1996 and have been scaled up by the author to an annual rate.

transactions that are not reported in order to illegally evade tariffs or other international trade protection measures.

Our net borrowing from abroad minus our current account deficit is the change in official U.S. reserves. In 1996 those reserves decreased by $10 billion. Net borrowing from foreigners was $150 billion, the current account deficit was $160 billion, and the difference, $10 billion, was the decrease in official U.S. reserves.

The numbers in Table 19.1 give a snapshot of the balance of payments accounts in 1996. Figure 19.1 puts that snapshot into perspective by showing the balance of payments between 1975 and 1996. Because the economy grows and the price level rises, changes in the dollar value of the balance of payments do not convey much information. To remove the influences of growth and inflation, Fig. 19.1 shows the balance of payments as a percentage of nominal GDP.

As you can see, the capital account balance is almost a mirror image of the current account balance. The official settlements balance is very small in comparison with the balances on these other two

accounts. A large current account deficit (and capital account surplus) emerged during the 1980s but declined from 1987 to 1991. Since then, it has increased again.

You will perhaps obtain a better understanding of the balance of payments accounts and the way in which they are linked together if you consider the income and expenditure, borrowing and lending, and bank account of an individual.

**Individual Analogy**    An individual's current account records the income from supplying the services of factors of production and the expenditure on goods and services. Consider, for example, Joanne. She worked in 1995 and earned an income of $25,000. Joanne has $10,000 worth of investments that earned her an interest income of $1,000. Joanne's current account shows an income of $26,000. Joanne spent $18,000 buying goods and services for consumption. She also bought a new house, which cost her $60,000. So Joanne's total expenditure was $78,000. The difference between her expenditure and income is $52,000 ($78,000 minus of $26,000). This amount is Joanne's current account deficit.

**FIGURE 19.1**

The Balance of Payments: 1975–1996

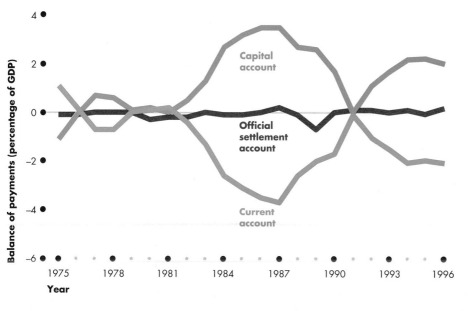

During the 1970s, fluctuations in the balance of payments were small, but during the 1980s, a large current account deficit arose. That deficit decreased in the late 1980s but increased again after 1991. The capital account balance mirrors the current account balance. When the current account balance is negative, the capital account balance is positive—we borrow from the rest of the world. Fluctuations in the official settlements balance are small in comparison with fluctuations in the current account balance and the capital account balance.

*Source: Economic Report of the President, 1997, and Survey of Current Business (January 1997), vol. 77.*

To pay for expenditure of $52,000 in excess of her income, Joanne has to use the money that she has in the bank or has to take out a loan. In fact, Joanne took a mortgage of $50,000 to help buy her house. This mortgage was the only borrowing that Joanne did, so her capital account surplus was $50,000. With a current account deficit of $52,000 and a capital account surplus of $50,000, Joanne is still $2,000 short. She got that $2,000 from her own bank account. Her cash holdings decreased by $2,000.

Joanne's income from her work is analogous to a country's income from its exports. Her income from her investments is analogous to a country's interest income from foreigners. Her purchases of goods and services, including her purchase of a house, are analogous to a country's imports. Joanne's mortgage—borrowing from someone else—is analogous to a country's borrowing from the rest of the world. The change in her own bank account is analogous to the change in the country's official reserves.

## Borrowers and Lenders, Debtors and Creditors

A country that is borrowing more from the rest of the world than it is lending to it is called a **net borrower**. Similarly, a **net lender** is a country that is lending more to the rest of the world than it is borrowing from it. A net borrower might be going deeper into debt or might simply be reducing its net assets held in the rest of the world. The total stock of foreign investment determines whether a country is a debtor or creditor. A **debtor nation** is a country that during its entire history has borrowed more from the rest of the world than it has lent to it. It has a stock of outstanding debt to the rest of the world that exceeds the stock of its own claims on the rest of the world. The United States became a debtor nation in 1989. A **creditor nation** is a country that has invested more in the rest of the world than other countries have invested in it. The largest creditor nation today is Japan.

At the heart of the distinction between a net borrower/net lender and a debtor/creditor nation is the distinction between flows and stocks, which you have encountered many times in your study of macroeconomics. Borrowing and lending are flows—amounts borrowed or lent per unit of time. Debts are stocks—amounts owed at a point in time. The flow of borrowing and lending changes the stock of debt. But the outstanding stock of debt depends mainly on past flows of borrowing and lending, not on the current period's flows. The current period's flows determine the *change* in the stock of debt outstanding.

When a nation has a string of current account deficits, it eventually becomes a net debtor nation.

The United States is a newcomer to the ranks of net borrower nations. Throughout the 1960s and most of the 1970s, the United States had a surplus on its current account and a deficit on its capital account. Thus the country was a net lender to the rest of the world. It was not until 1983 that the United States became a significant net borrower from the rest of the world. Between 1983 and 1987, its borrowing increased each year. It then decreased and was briefly zero in 1991, after when it started to increase again. The average net foreign borrowing by the United States between 1983 and 1995 was $91 billion a year.

Most countries are net borrowers like the United States. But a small number of countries, including Japan and oil-rich Saudi Arabia, are net lenders.

The United States is not only a net borrower nation. It is also a debtor nation. That is, its total stock of borrowing from the rest of the world exceeds its lending to the rest of the world. The largest debtor nations are the capital-hungry developing countries. The international debt of these countries grew from less than a third to more than a half of their gross domestic product during the 1980s and created what was called the "Third World debt crisis."

Should the United States be concerned about the switch from being a net lender to being a net borrower? The answer to this question depends mainly on what the net borrower is doing with the borrowed money. If borrowing is financing investment that in turn is generating economic growth and higher income, borrowing is not a problem. If the borrowed money is being used to finance consumption, then higher interest payments are being incurred, and as a consequence, consumption will eventually have to be reduced. In this case, the more the borrowing and the longer it goes on, the greater is the reduction in consumption that will eventually be necessary. We'll see below whether the United States is borrowing for investment or for consumption.

## Current Account Balance

What determines a country's current account balance and net foreign borrowing? You've seen that net exports (*NX*) is the main item in the current account.

We can define the current account balance (*CAB*) as

$$CAB = NX + \text{Net interest income} + \text{Net transfers.}$$

Fluctuations in net exports are the main source of fluctuations in the current account balance. The other two items are small and have trends but do not fluctuate much. So we can study the current account balance by looking at what determines net exports.

## Net Exports

Net exports are determined by the government budget and private saving and investment. To see how net exports are determined, we need to recall some of the things that we learned about the National Income and Product Accounts in Chapter 6. Table 19.2 will refresh your memory and summarize some calculations. Part (a) lists the national income variables that are needed, with their symbols. Part (b) defines three surpluses and deficits.

**Net exports** is exports of goods and services minus imports of goods and services.

The **government sector surplus or deficit** is equal to net taxes minus government purchases of goods and services. If that number is positive, a government sector surplus is lent to other sectors; if that number is negative, a government deficit must be financed by borrowing. The government sector deficit is the sum of the deficits of the federal, state, and local governments.

The **private sector surplus or deficit** is saving minus investment. If saving exceeds investment, a private sector surplus is lent to other sectors. If investment exceeds saving, a private sector deficit is financed by borrowing from other sectors.

Part (b) also shows the values of these deficits and surpluses for the United States in 1996. As you can see, net exports were –$99 billion, a deficit of $99 billion. The government sector's revenue from net taxes was $1,340 billion, and it purchased $1,407 billion worth of goods and services. The government sector deficit was $67 billion. The private sector saved $1,084 billion and invested $1,116 billion, so it had a deficit of $32 billion.

Part (c) shows the relationship among the three deficits. From the national income accounts, we know that real GDP (*Y*) is the sum of consumption expenditure (*C*), investment, government purchases, and net exports. Real GDP also equals the sum of consumption expenditure, saving, and taxes. Rearranging these equations tells us that net exports is the sum of the government sector deficit and the private

**TABLE 19.2**

## Net Exports, the Government Budget, Saving, and Investment

◆

| | Symbols and equations | United States in 1996* (billions of dollars) |
|---|---|---|
| **(a) Variables** | | |
| Exports | $X$ | 855 |
| Imports | $M$ | 954 |
| Government purchases | $G$ | 1,407 |
| Net taxes | $T$ | 1,340 |
| Investment | $I$ | 1,116 |
| Saving | $S$ | 1,084 |
| **(b) Surpluses and deficits** | | |
| Net exports | $X - M$ | $855 - 954 = -99$ |
| Government sector | $T - G$ | $1,340 - 1,407 = -67$ |
| Private sector | $S - I$ | $1,084 - 1,116 = -32$ |
| **(c) Relationship among surpluses and deficits** | | |
| National accounts | $Y = C + I + G + X - M$ | |
| | $= C + S + T$ | |
| Rearranging | $X - M = S - I + T - G$ | |
| Net exports | $X - M$ | $-99$ |
| equals: | | |
| Government sector | $T - G$ | $-67$ |
| plus | | |
| Private sector | $S - I$ | $-32$ |

*Source:* National Income and Product Accounts and *Survey of Current Business,* (January 1997), vol. 77.

*The National Income and Product Accounts measures of exports and imports are different from the Balance of Payments Accounts measures in Table 19.1 on p. 822.

sector deficit. In the United States in 1996, the government sector had a deficit of $67 billion and the private sector had a deficit of $32 billion. The government sector deficit plus the private sector deficit equals net exports of –$99 billion.

### The Twin Deficits

You've seen that net exports equal the sum of the government sector deficit and the private sector deficit. But how do these deficits fluctuate over time? Figure 19.2 answers this question. It shows the government sector deficit (the red line) and net exports *two years later* (the blue line).

You can see that there is a strong tendency for net exports to decrease (to become increasingly negative) when the government budget has gone into a deeper deficit (has become increasingly negative). Because of the tendency for the government sector

deficit and the net exports deficit to move in the same direction, they are sometimes called the **twin deficits**.

Why are the two deficits linked? It is because capital is highly mobile in today's world. If the U.S. government increases expenditure or lowers taxes, total spending in the United States rises. But with the economy at or near full employment, the extra goods and services demanded are sucked in from the rest of the world. Imports rise. Capital flows in to pay for those imports. Saving and investment don't change. In reality, these adjustments take time, which is why net exports lag behind the government sector deficit by about two years.

### Is U.S. Borrowing for Consumption or Investment?

In 1996, net exports were a negative $99 billion and this amount was borrowed from abroad. Did we borrow for consumption or to finance investment? The answer depends on how much of the government sector deficit arises from investment. The government buys structures such as highways and dams that exceed $200 billion a year. This expenditure adds to the nation's capital and increases productivity. Government also spends on education and health care services, which increase *human capital*. Our international borrowing is financing private and public investment, not consumption.

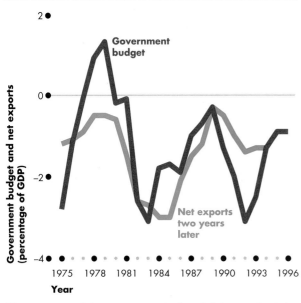

**FIGURE 19.2**

## The Twin Deficits

Net exports and the government budget deficit move in similar ways but with a time lag of two years. If the government sector deficit increases, as it did in 1980–1983 and again in 1990–1992, net exports two years later decrease.

*Source: Survey of Current Business, March 1997, Vol. 77.*

---

### R E V I E W

■ When we buy goods from or invest in the rest of the world, we use foreign currency; and when foreigners buy goods from or invest in the United States, they use U.S. currency.

■ We record international transactions in the balance of payments accounts—current account (exports and imports of goods and services), capital account (net foreign borrowing or lending), and official settlements account (change in holdings of a foreign currencies).

■ The net exports deficit is equal to the sum of the government sector deficit and the private sector deficit.

■ Changes in the government sector deficit can change both the private sector deficit and the net exports deficit.

# The Exchange Rate

WHEN WE BUY FOREIGN GOODS OR INVEST IN another country, we have to obtain some of that country's currency to make the transaction. When foreigners buy U.S.-produced goods or invest in the United States, they have to obtain some U.S. dollars. We get foreign currency, and foreigners get U.S. dollars in the foreign exchange market. The **foreign exchange market** is the market in which the currency of one country is exchanged for the currency of another. The foreign exchange market is not a place like a downtown flea market or produce market. The market is made up of thousands of people—importers and exporters, banks, and specialists in the buying and selling of foreign exchange, called foreign exchange brokers. The foreign exchange market opens on Monday morning in Hong Kong, which is still Sunday evening in New York. As the day advances, markets open in Singapore, Tokyo, Bahrain, Frankfurt, London, New York, Chicago, and San Francisco. As the West Coast markets close, Hong Kong is only an hour away from opening for the next day of business. The sun barely sets on the foreign exchange market. Dealers around the world are in continual contact by telephone, and on a typical day in 1996, $1.3 trillion changed hands.

The price at which one currency exchanges for another is called a **foreign exchange rate**. For example, in April 1997, one U.S. dollar bought 123 Japanese yen. The exchange rate was 123 yen per dollar. We've just expressed the exchange rate between the yen and the dollar as a number of yen per dollar.

The actions of the foreign exchange brokers make the foreign exchange market highly efficient. Exchange rates are almost identical around the world. If U.S. dollars were cheap in London and expensive in Tokyo, people would buy in London and sell in Tokyo. The London price would rise and the Tokyo price would fall until the prices were equal.

Figure 19.3 shows the exchange rate of the U.S. dollar in terms of the Japanese yen between 1975 and 1997. From 1975 to 1978 and again from 1982 to 1995, the value of the dollar fell against the yen—the dollar depreciated. **Currency depreciation** is the fall in the value of one currency in terms of another currency. For example, if the dollar falls from 100 yen to 80 yen, the dollar depreciates by 20 percent. From 1978 to 1982 and again during 1996 and 1997, the

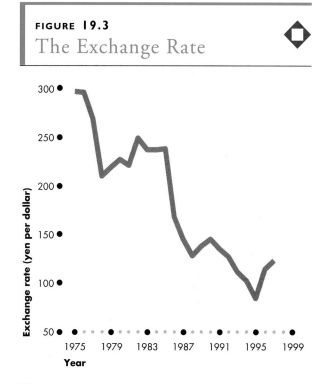

**FIGURE 19.3**

## The Exchange Rate

The exchange rate is the price at which two currencies can be traded. The yen-dollar exchange rate, expressed as yen per dollar, shows that the dollar has generally fallen in value—depreciated—against the yen. But since 1995, the dollar has risen against the yen.

*Source: Economic Report of the President, 1997.*

dollar rose in value against the yen—the dollar appreciated. **Currency appreciation** is the rise in the value of one currency in terms of another currency. For example, if the dollar rises from 100 yen to 120 yen, the dollar appreciates by 20 percent.

Why does the U.S. dollar sometimes depreciate and sometimes appreciate? What happened during 1996 and 1997 to make the dollar appreciate? To answer this question, we need to understand the forces that determine the exchange rate.

The exchange rate is a price—the price of one country's money in terms of another country's money. And like all prices, demand and supply determine the exchange rate. So to understand the forces that determine the exchange rate, we need to study demand and supply in the foreign exchange market. We'll begin by looking at the demand side of the market.

## Demand in the Foreign Exchange Market

The quantity of dollars demanded in the foreign exchange market is the amount that traders plan to buy during a given time period at a given exchange rate. This quantity depends on many factors. The main ones are:

- The exchange rate
- Interest rates in the United States and other countries
- The expected future exchange rate

Let's look first at the relationship between the quantity of dollars demanded in the foreign exchange market and the exchange rate.

## The Law of Demand for Foreign Exchange

People do not buy dollars because they enjoy them. The demand for dollars is a *derived demand*. People demand dollars so that they can buy U.S.-made goods and services (U.S. exports). They also demand dollars so that they can buy U.S. assets such as bank accounts, bonds, stocks, businesses, and real estate. Nevertheless, the law of demand applies to dollars just as it does to anything else that people value.

Other things remaining the same, the higher the exchange rate, the smaller is the quantity of dollars demanded in the foreign exchange market. For example, if the price of the U.S. dollar rises from 100 yen to 120 yen but nothing else changes, the quantity of U.S. dollars that people plan to buy in the foreign exchange market decreases. Why does the exchange rate influence the quantity of dollars demanded?

There are two separate reasons, and they are related to the two sources of the derived demand for dollars:

- Exports effect
- Expected profit effect

**Exports Effect**   The larger the value of U.S. exports, the larger is the quantity of dollars demanded in the foreign exchange market. But the value of U.S. exports depends on the exchange rate. The lower the exchange rate, with everything else the same, the cheaper are U.S.-produced goods and services and the greater is the value of U.S. exports and the greater is the quantity of U.S. dollars demanded on the foreign exchange market to pay for these exports.

**Expected Profit Effect**   The larger the expected profit from holding dollars, the greater is the quantity of dollars demanded in the foreign exchange market. But expected profit depends on the exchange rate. The lower the exchange rate, other things remaining the same, the larger is the expected profit from buying dollars and the greater is the quantity of dollars demanded on the foreign exchange market.

To understand this effect, suppose you think the dollar will be worth 120 yen by the end of the month. If today, a dollar costs 115 yen, you buy dollars. But a person who thinks that the dollar will be worth 115 yen at the end of the month does not buy dollars. Now suppose the exchange rate falls to 110 yen per dollar. More people think they can profit from buying dollars, so the quantity of dollars demanded increases.

For the two reasons we've just reviewed, other things remaining the same, when the foreign exchange rate rises, the quantity of dollars demanded decreases, and when the foreign exchange rate falls, the quantity of dollars demanded increases. Figure 19.4 shows the demand curve for U.S. dollars in the foreign exchange market. In this figure, when the foreign exchange rate rises, other things remaining the same, there is a decrease in the quantity of dollars demanded and a movement upward along the demand curve as shown by the arrow. When the exchange rate falls, other things remaining the same, there is an increase in the quantity of dollars demanded and a movement downward along the demand curve as shown by the arrow.

## Changes in the Demand for Dollars

A change in any other influence on the dollars that people plan to buy in the foreign exchange market brings a change in the demand for dollars and a shift in the demand curve for dollars. Demand either increases or decreases. These other influences are:

- Interest rates in the United States and other countries
- The expected future exchange rate

**Interest Rates in the United States and Other Countries**   People and businesses buy financial assets to make a return. The higher the interest rate that people can make on U.S. assets compared with foreign assets, the more U.S. assets they buy. What matters is not the level of U.S. interest rates, but the U.S. interest rate minus the foreign interest rate, a

## FIGURE 19.4
## The Demand for Dollars

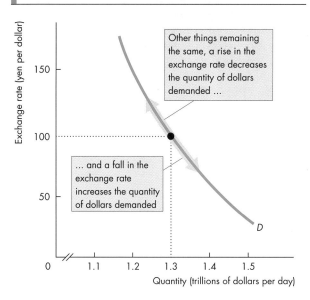

The quantity of dollars that people plan to buy depends on the exchange rate. Other things remaining the same, if the exchange rate rises, the quantity of dollars demanded decreases and there is a movement upward along the demand curve for dollars. If the exchange rate falls, the quantity of dollars demanded increases and there is a movement downward along the demand curve for dollars.

gap that is called the **U.S. interest rate differential**. If the U.S. interest rate rises and the foreign interest rate remains constant, the U.S. interest rate differential increases. The larger the U.S. interest rate differential, the greater is the demand for U.S. assets and the greater is the demand for dollars on the foreign exchange market.

**The Expected Future Exchange Rate**   Other things remaining the same, the higher the expected future exchange rate, the greater is the demand for dollars. To see why, suppose you are Toyota's finance manager. The exchange rate is 100 yen per dollar and you think that by the end of the month, it will be 120 yen per dollar. You spend 100,000 yen today and buy $1,000. At the end of the month, the dollar is 120 yen, as you predicted it would be, and you sell the $1,000. You get 120,000 yen. You've made a profit of 20,000 yen, or almost $167. The higher the

expected future exchange rate, other things remaining the same, the greater is the expected profit and the greater is the demand for dollars today.

Figure 19.5 summarizes the above discussion of the influences on the demand for dollars. A rise in the U.S. interest differential or a rise in the expected future exchange rate increases the demand for dollars and shifts the demand curve rightward from $D_0$ to $D_1$. A fall in the U.S. interest differential or a fall in the expected future exchange rate decreases the demand for dollars and shifts the demand curve leftward from $D_0$ to $D_2$.

## FIGURE 19.5
## Changes in the Demand for Dollars

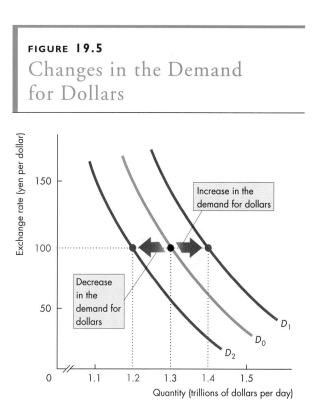

A change in any influence on the quantity of dollars that people plan to buy, other than the exchange rate, brings a change in the demand for dollars.

The demand for dollars:

| *Increases if:* | *Decreases if:* |
|---|---|
| ■ The U.S. interest rate differential increases | ■ The U.S. interest rate differential decreases |
| ■ The expected future exchange rate rises | ■ The expected future exchange rate falls |

## Supply in the Foreign Exchange Market

The quantity of U.S. dollars supplied in the foreign exchange market is the amount that traders plan to sell during a given time period at a given exchange rate. This quantity depends on many factors. The main ones are:

- The exchange rate
- Interest rates in the United States and other countries
- The expected future exchange rate

Let's look first at the relationship between the quantity of dollars supplied in the foreign exchange market and the exchange rate.

## The Law of Supply for Foreign Exchange

People supply dollars in the foreign exchange market when they buy other currencies. And they buy other currencies so that they can buy foreign-made goods and services (U.S. imports). They also supply dollars and buy foreign currencies so that they can buy foreign assets such as bank accounts, bonds, stocks, businesses, and real estate. The law of supply applies to dollars just as it does to anything else that people plan to sell.

Other things remaining the same, the higher the exchange rate, the greater is the quantity of dollars supplied in the foreign exchange market. For example, if the price of the U.S. dollar rises from 100 yen to 120 yen but nothing else changes, the quantity of yen that people plan to buy in the foreign exchange market increases and so the quantity of U.S. dollars supplied increases. Why does the exchange rate influence the quantity of dollars supplied?

There are two reasons and they parallel the two reasons on the demand side of the market:

- Imports effect
- Expected profit effect

**Imports Effect**   The larger the value of U.S. imports, the larger is the quantity of foreign currency demanded to pay for these imports. And when people buy foreign currency, they supply dollars. So the larger the value of U.S. imports, the greater is the quantity of

dollars supplied in the foreign exchange market. But the value of U.S. imports depends on the exchange rate. The higher the exchange rate, with everything else the same, the cheaper are foreign-produced good and services to Americans, the more the United States imports, and the greater is the quantity of U.S. dollars supplied on the foreign exchange market to pay for these imports.

**Expected Profit Effect**   The larger the expected profit from holding a foreign currency, the greater is the quantity of that currency demanded and the greater is the quantity of dollars supplied in the foreign exchange market. But the expected profit from holding a foreign currency depends on the exchange rate. The higher the exchange rate, other things remaining the same, the larger is the expected profit from selling dollars and the greater is the quantity of dollars supplied on the foreign exchange market.

### FIGURE 19.6

## The Supply of Dollars

The quantity of dollars that people plan to sell depends on the exchange rate. Other things remaining the same, if the exchange rate rises, the quantity of dollars supplied increases and there is a movement upward along the supply curve for dollars. If the exchange rate falls, the quantity of dollars supplied decreases and there is a movement downward along the supply curve for dollars.

For the two reasons we've just reviewed, other things remaining the same, when the foreign exchange rate rises, the quantity of dollars supplied increases, and when foreign exchange rate falls, the quantity of dollars supplied decreases. Figure 19.6 shows the supply curve for U.S. dollars in the foreign exchange market. In this figure, when the foreign exchange rate rises, other things remaining the same, there is an increase in the quantity of dollars supplied and a movement upward along the supply curve as shown by the arrow. When the exchange rate falls, other things remaining the same, there is a decrease in the quantity of dollars supplied and a movement downward along the supply curve as shown by the arrow.

### Changes in the Supply of Dollars

A change in any other influence on the dollars that people plan to sell in the foreign exchange market brings a change in the supply of dollars and a shift in the supply curve for dollars. Supply either increases or decreases. These other influences parallel the other influences on demand but have exactly the opposite effects. These influences are:

■ Interest rates in the United States and other countries
■ The expected future exchange rate

**Interest Rates in the United States and Other Countries** The larger the U.S. interest rate differential, the smaller is the demand for foreign assets and so the smaller is the supply of dollars in the foreign exchange market.

**The Expected Future Exchange Rate** Other things remaining the same, the higher the expected future exchange rate, the smaller is the supply of dollars. To see why, suppose the dollar is trading at 100 yen per dollar today and you think that by the end of the month, the dollar will be 120 yen per dollar. You were planning on selling dollars today, but you decide to hold off and wait until the end of the month. If you supply dollars today, you get only 100 yen per dollar. But at the end of the month, if the dollar is 120 yen per dollar as you predict, you'll get 120 yen for each dollar you supply. You'll make a profit of 20 percent. So, the higher the expected

future exchange rate, other things remaining the same, the smaller is the expected profit from selling U.S. dollars today and the smaller is the supply of dollars today.

Figure 19.7 summarizes the above discussion of the influences on the supply of dollars. A rise in the U.S. interest differential or a rise in the expected future exchange rate decreases the supply of dollars and shifts the demand curve leftward from $S_0$ to $S_1$. A fall in the U.S. interest differential or a fall in the expected future exchange rate increases the supply of dollars and shifts the supply curve rightward from $S_0$ to $S_2$.

**FIGURE 19.7**

## Changes in the Supply of Dollars

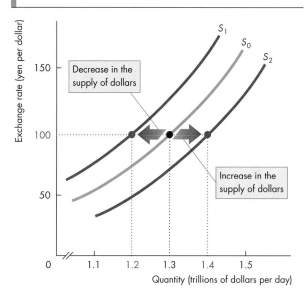

A change in any influence on the quantity of dollars that people plan to sell, other than the exchange rate, brings a change in the supply of dollars.

The supply of dollars:

| Increases if: | Decreases if: |
|---|---|
| ■ The U.S. interest rate differential decreases | ■ The U.S. interest rate differential increases |
| ■ The expected future exchange rate falls | ■ The expected future exchange rate rises |

## Market Equilibrium

Figure 19.8 shows how demand and supply in the foreign exchange market determine the exchange rate. The demand curve is *D*, and the supply curve is *S*. Just like all the other markets you've studied, the price (the exchange rate) acts as a regulator.

If the exchange rate is too high, there is a surplus of dollars—the quantity supplied exceeds the quantity demanded. In Fig. 19.8, if the exchange rate is 150 yen per dollar, there is a surplus of dollars. If the exchange rate is too low, there is a shortage of dollars—the quantity supplied is less than the quantity demanded. In Fig. 19.8, if the exchange rate is 50 yen per dollar, there is a shortage of dollars.

At the equilibrium exchange rate, there is neither a shortage nor a surplus. The quantity supplied equals the quantity demanded. In Fig. 19.8, the equilibrium exchange rate is 100 yen per dollar. At this exchange

rate, the quantity demanded equals the quantity supplied and $1.3 trillion a day is bought and sold.

The foreign exchange market is constantly pulled to its equilibrium by the forces of supply and demand. Foreign exchange dealers are constantly looking for the best price they can get. If they are selling, they want the highest price available. If they are buying, they want the lowest price available. Information flows from dealer to dealer through the worldwide computer network, and the price adjusts second by second to keep buying plans and selling plans in balance. That is, price adjusts second by second to keep the market at its equilibrium.

## Changes in the Exchange Rate

If the demand for dollars increases and the supply of dollars does not change, the exchange rate rises. If the demand for dollars decreases and the supply of dollars does not change, the exchange rate falls. Similarly, if the supply of dollars decreases and the demand for dollars does not change, the exchange rate rises. If the supply of dollars increases and the demand for dollars does not change, the exchange rate falls.

These predictions about the effects of changes in demand and supply are the same as for other markets.

**Why the Exchange Rate Is Volatile**   Sometimes the dollar depreciates and at other times it appreciates, but the quantity of dollars traded each day barely changes. Why? The main reason is that supply and demand are not independent of each other in the foreign exchange market.

When we studied the demand for dollars and the supply of dollars, we saw that unlike other markets, the demand side and the supply side of the market have some common influences. A change in the expected future exchange rate or a change in the U.S. interest rate differential changes both demand and supply—and in opposite directions. These common influences on both demand and supply explain why the exchange rate can be volatile at times, even though the quantity of dollars traded does not change.

Everyone in the foreign exchange market is potentially a demander and a supplier. Each has a price above which he or she will sell and below which he or she will buy. Let's see how these common supply and demand effects work by looking at two episodes: one in which the dollar appreciated and one in which it depreciated.

**FIGURE 19.8**

## Equilibrium Exchange Rate

The demand curve for dollars is *D*, and the supply curve is *S*. If the exchange rate is 150 yen per dollar, there is a surplus of dollars and the exchange rate falls. If the exchange rate is 50 yen per dollar, there is a shortage of dollars and the exchange rate rises. If the exchange rate is 100 yen per dollar, there is neither a shortage nor a surplus of dollars and the exchange rate remains constant. The market is in equilibrium.

**A Depreciating Dollar: 1994–1995**  Between 1994 and the summer of 1995, the dollar fell from 100 yen to a low of 84 yen per dollar. Figure 19.9(a) explains this fall. In 1994, the demand and supply curves were those labeled $D_{94}$ and $S_{94}$. The exchange rate was 100 yen per dollar. During 1994, traders expected the U.S. dollar to depreciate. They expected a lower exchange rate. As a result, the demand for dollars decreased and the supply of dollars increased. The demand curve shifted leftward to $D_{95}$, and the supply curve shifted rightward to $S_{95}$. The exchange rate fell to 84 yen per dollar.

**An Appreciating Dollar: 1995–1997**  Between 1995 and 1997, the dollar appreciated against the yen. It rose from 84 yen to 123 yen per dollar. Figure 19.9(b) explains why this happened. In 1995, the demand and supply curves were those labeled $D_{95}$ and $S_{95}$. The exchange rate was 84 yen per dollar— where the supply and demand curves intersect. During the next two years, Japan was in recession

and the U.S. economy was expanding. Interest rates in Japan fell, and the yen was expected to depreciate. The demand for yen decreased. As a result, the demand for dollars increased, and the supply of dollars decreased. The demand curve shifted from $D_{95}$ to $D_{97}$, and the supply curve shifted from $S_{95}$ to $S_{97}$. These two shifts reinforced each other, and the exchange rate increased to 123 yen per dollar.

### Exchange Rate Expectations

The changes in the exchange rate that we've just examined occurred in part because the exchange rate was *expected to change.* This explanation sounds a bit like a self-fulfilling forecast. But what makes expectations change? The answer is new information about the deeper forces that influence the value of money. Two such forces are:

- Purchasing power parity
- Interest rate parity

---

**FIGURE 19.9**

## Exchange Rate Fluctuations

**(a) 1994 to 1995**

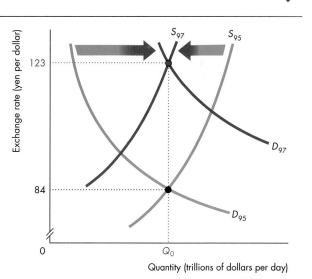

**(b) 1995 to 1997**

The exchange rate fluctuates because changes in demand and supply are not independent of each other. Everyone in the foreign exchange market is a potential buyer and seller. Between 1994 and 1995 (in part a), the dollar depreciated from 100 to 84 yen per dollar. The exchange rate was expected to depreciate, which decreased the demand for dollars and increased the supply. Between 1995 and 1997 (part b), the dollar appreciated from 84 to 123 yen per dollar. This appreciation occurred because a weak Japanese economy and low interest rates in Japan generated an expectation of a weak yen and a strong dollar. The supply of dollars decreased, the demand for dollars increased, and the dollar rose in value.

**Purchasing Power Parity**    Money is worth what it will buy. But two kinds of money, U.S. dollars and Canadian dollars for example, might buy different amounts of goods and services. Suppose a Big Mac costs $4 (Canadian) in Toronto and $3 (U.S.) in New York. If the Canadian dollar exchange rate is $1.33 Canadian per U.S. dollar, the two monies have the same value. You can buy a Big Mac in both Toronto and New York for either $4 Canadian or $3 U.S.

The situation we've just described is called **purchasing power parity**, which means *equal value of money*. If purchasing power parity does not prevail, some powerful forces go to work. To understand these forces, let's suppose that the price of a Big Mac in New York rises to $4 U.S., but in Toronto it remains at $4 Canadian. Suppose the exchange rate remains at $1.33 Canadian per U.S. dollar. In this case, a Big Mac in Toronto still costs $4 Canadian or $3 U.S. But in New York, it costs $4 U.S. or $5.33 Canadian. Money buys more in Canada than in the United States. Money is not of equal value in both countries.

If all (or most) prices have increased in the United States and not increased in Canada, then people will generally expect that the value of the U.S. dollar on the foreign exchange market must fall. In this situation, the exchange rate is expected to fall. The demand for U.S. dollars decreases and the supply of U.S. dollars increases. The exchange rate falls, as expected. If the exchange rate falls to $1.00 Canadian and there are no further price changes, purchasing power parity is restored. A Big Mac now costs $4 in either U.S. or Canadian dollars in both New York and Toronto.

If prices increase in Canada and other countries but remain constant in the United States, then people will generally expect that the value of the U.S. dollar on the foreign exchange market is too low and that it is going to rise. In this situation, the exchange rate is expected to rise. The demand for U.S. dollars increases and the supply of U.S. dollars decreases. The exchange rate rises, as expected.

Ultimately, the value of money is determined by the price level, which in turn is determined by aggregate supply and aggregate demand (see Chapter 7, pp. 150–151, and Chapter 15, pp. 341–345.) So the deeper forces that influence the exchange rate have tentacles that spread throughout the economy. If prices in the United States rise faster than those in other countries, the exchange rate falls. And if prices rise more slowly in the United States than in other countries, the exchange rate rises.

**Interest Rate Parity**    Money is worth what it can earn. Again, two kinds of money, Canadian dollars and U.S. dollars for example, might earn different amounts. Suppose a Canadian dollar bank deposit in Toronto earns 5 percent a year and a U.S. dollar bank deposit in New York earns 3 percent a year. In this situation, why does anyone deposit money in New York? Why doesn't all the money flow to Toronto? The answer is: Because of exchange rate expectations. Suppose people expect the Canadian dollar to depreciate by 2 percent a year. This 2 percent depreciation must be subtracted from the 5 percent interest to obtain the net return of 3 percent a year that an American expects to earn by depositing funds in a Toronto bank. The two returns are equal. This situation is one of **interest rate parity**, which means *equal interest rates*.

Adjusted for risk, interest rate parity always prevails. Funds move to get the highest return available. If for a few seconds a higher return is available in New York than in Toronto, the demand for U.S. dollars rises and the exchange rate rises until expected interest rates are equal.

### The Fed in the Foreign Exchange Market

Interest rates in the United States are determined by the demand for and supply of money (see Chapter 14, pp. 327–328). But the supply of money is influenced by the Fed, so ultimately, the exchange rate is influenced by monetary policy. When interest rates in the United States rise, relative to those in other countries, the demand for U.S. dollars increases, the supply decreases, and the exchange rate rises. (Similarly, when interest rates in the United States fall, relative to those in other countries, the demand for U.S. dollars decreases, the supply increases, and the exchange rate falls.)

But the Fed can intervene directly in the foreign exchange market. It can buy or sell dollars and try to smooth out fluctuations in the exchange rate. Let's look at the foreign exchange interventions that the Fed can make.

Suppose the Fed wants the exchange rate to be steady at 120 yen per dollar. If the exchange rate rises above 120 yen per dollar, the Fed sells dollars. If the exchange rate falls below 120 yen per dollar, the Fed buys dollars. By these actions, it changes supply or demand and keeps the exchange rate close to its target rate of 120 yen per dollar.

Figure 19.10 shows this Fed intervention in the foreign exchange market. The supply of dollars is $S$, and initially the demand for dollars is $D_0$. The equilibrium exchange rate is 120 yen per dollar. This exchange rate is the Fed's target rate, shown by the horizontal red line in the figure.

When the demand for dollars increases and the demand curve shifts rightward to $D_1$, the Fed sells $0.1 trillion. This action increases the supply of dollars by $0.1 trillion and prevents the exchange rate from rising. When the demand for dollars decreases and the demand curve shifts leftward to $D_2$, the Fed buys $0.1 trillion. This action decreases the supply of dollars by $0.1 trillion and prevents the exchange rate from falling.

If the demand for dollars fluctuates between $D_1$ and $D_2$ and on the average is $D_0$, the Fed can repeatedly intervene in the way we've just seen. Sometimes the Fed buys and sometimes it sells, but on the average, it neither buys nor sells.

But suppose the demand for dollars increases permanently from $D_0$ to $D_1$. The Fed cannot now maintain the exchange rate at 120 yen per dollar indefinitely. To do so, the Fed would have to sell dollars every day. When the Fed sells dollars in the foreign exchange market, it buys foreign currency. So the Fed would be piling up foreign currency.

Now suppose the demand for dollars decreases permanently from $D_0$ to $D_2$. Again the Fed cannot maintain the exchange rate at 120 yen per dollar indefinitely. In this situation, to hold the exchange rate at 120 yen per dollars, the Fed would have to buy dollars every day. When the Fed buys dollars in the foreign exchange market, it uses its holdings of foreign currency. So the Fed would be losing foreign currency. Eventually, it would run out of foreign currency and would then have to abandon its attempt to fix the exchange rate.

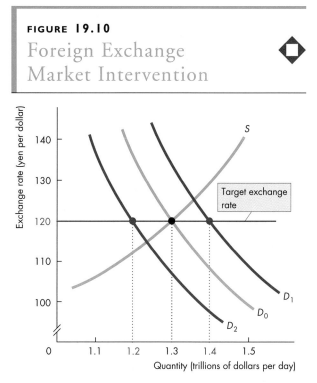

**FIGURE 19.10**

Foreign Exchange
Market Intervention

Initially, the demand for dollars is $D_0$, the supply of dollars is $S$, and the exchange rate is 120 yen per dollar. The Fed can intervene in the foreign exchange market to keep the exchange rate close to its target rate (120 yen in this example). If demand increases from $D_0$ to $D_1$, the Fed sells dollars to increase supply. If demand decreases from $D_0$ to $D_2$, the Fed buys dollars to decrease supply. Persistent intervention on one side of the market cannot be sustained.

## REVIEW

- The exchange rate is determined by demand and supply in the foreign exchange market.
- Changes in interest rates and in the expected future exchange rate change both demand and supply and bring changes in the exchange rate.
- Expectations are influenced by purchasing power parity and interest rate parity and by the wider influences on the price level and interest rates.
- The Fed can intervene in the foreign exchange market to try to smooth out fluctuations in the exchange rate but it cannot resist a permanent change in the equilibrium exchange rate.

◆ *Reading Between the Lines* on pages 462–463 looks at exchange rates in 1997 and the relative purchasing power of different currencies in terms of a Big Mac.

You have now reached the end of your economics course. Go back to the big ideas that define the way of economic thinking (on pp. 6–11) and see how much more they mean to you now than they did when you first read them. I hope that your instructor and I have helped to open your eyes and shown you a new way of seeing the world. If we have, you can now do your own "reading between the lines" every day. Keep your economics text handy. Use it to refresh you memory of the economic principles that help you make sense of your world.

# Policy
## WATCH

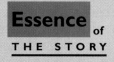

## Purchasing Power Parity

THE ECONOMIST, APRIL 12, 1997

# Big MacCurrencies

Is the world's exchange-rate system on the brink of collapse? Just like the old gold standard and the fixed rates of the Bretton Woods system, another international currency benchmark could be doomed: the hamburger standard. For more than a decade, *The Economist*'s Big Mac index has provided a delectable guide to whether currencies are at their "correct" level. But news in February that McDonald's was about to slash the American price of its Big Mac by 65% sent shivers through financial markets. Would this blatant competitive devaluation reduce the hamburger standard to ashes?

It certainly threatened to leave us in a pickle. The Big Mac index is based on the theory of purchasing-power parity (PPP)—the notion that a dollar should buy the same amount in all countries. In the long run, argue PPP fans, currencies should move towards the rate which equalises the prices of an identical basket of goods in each country. Our "basket" is a McDonald's Big Mac, which is now produced in over 100 countries. The Big Mac PPP is the exchange rate that would leave hamburgers costing the same in America as abroad. Comparing actual exchange rates with PPP provides one indication of whether a currency is under- or over-valued.

### The hamburger standard

| | Big Mac prices | | Local currency under(-)/over(+) valuation,[†]% |
|---|---|---|---|
| | In local currency | In dollars | |
| United States[‡] | $2.42 | 2.42 | — |
| Argentina | Peso2.50 | 2.50 | +3 |
| Australia | A$2.50 | 1.94 | −20 |
| Austria | Sch34.00 | 2.82 | +17 |
| Belgium | BFr109 | 3.09 | +28 |
| Brazil | Real2.97 | 2.81 | +16 |
| Britain | £ 1.81 | 2.95 | +22 |
| Canada | C$2.88 | 2.07 | −14 |
| Chile | Peso1,200 | 2.88 | +19 |
| China | Yuan9.70 | 1.16 | −52 |
| Czech Republic | CKr53.0 | 1.81 | −25 |
| Denmark | DKr25.75 | 3.95 | +63 |
| France | FFr17.5 | 3.04 | +26 |
| Germany | DM4.90 | 2.86 | +18 |
| Hong Kong | HK$9.90 | 1.28 | −47 |
| Hungary | Forint271 | 1.52 | −37 |
| Israel | Shekel11.5 | 3.40 | +40 |
| Italy | Lire4,600 | 2.73 | +13 |
| Japan | ¥294 | 2.34 | −3 |
| Malaysia | M$3.87 | 1.55 | −36 |
| Mexico | Peso14.9 | 1.89 | −22 |
| Netherlands | Fl5.45 | 2.83 | +17 |
| New Zealand | NZ$3.25 | 2.24 | −7 |
| Poland | Zloty4.30 | 1.39 | −43 |
| Russia | Rouble11,000 | 1.92 | −21 |
| Singapore | S$3.00 | 2.08 | −14 |
| South Africa | Rand7.80 | 1.76 | −27 |
| South Korea | Won2,300 | 2.57 | +6 |
| Spain | Pta375 | 2.60 | +7 |
| Sweden | SKr26.0 | 3.37 | +39 |
| Switzerland | SFr5.90 | 4.02 | +66 |
| Taiwan | NT$68.0 | 2.47 | +2 |
| Thailand | Baht46.7 | 1.79 | −26 |

[†]Against dollar  [‡]Average of New York, Chicago, San Francisco and Atlanta

Source: McDonald's

**Essence** of **THE STORY**

■ *The Economist* publishes a Big Mac index of world currencies.

■ The index is based on the price of a McDonald's Big Mac, which is now produced in over 100 countries.

■ The Big Mac purchasing-power parity (PPP) is the exchange rate that makes a Big Mac cost the same in all countries.

■ *The Economist* uses this index to judge whether currencies are at their "correct" PPP level.

■ In April 1997, the Big Mac cost an average of $2.42 (including tax) in the United States. It cost least in China, $1.16, and most in Switzerland, $4.02.

■ *The Economist* concludes that the Chinese yuan is the most undervalued currency (by 52%) and the Swiss franc the most overvalued (by 66%).

# Economic

## A N A L Y S I S

■ Although *The Economist* is having a bit of fun with its Big Mac index, it is also doing some misleading and potentially wrong economics.

■ The basic assumption is that a Big Mac is the same good the world over. Because it is the same good, it should have the same price. Any price differences are due to currencies being undervalued or overvalued.

■ The assumption is wrong. When McDonald's sells a Big Mac, it sells a *service*—a fast food service—as well as a good.

■ And the price of the service component of a Big Mac varies from place to place and depends on local demand and supply conditions.

■ The figure shows the range of prices *inside the United States*. The highest price is in New York City, where a Big Mac costs $3.13 with tax. The lowest price is in Jonesboro, Arkansas, where the price is $1.80.

■ Of the 32 countries in *The Economist's* table, 21 have prices that fall inside the range of those in the United States.

■ Four of *The Economist's* countries, Switzerland, Denmark, Israel, and Sweden have prices that exceed that in New York City.

■ Seven of *The Economist's* countries, Thailand, South Africa, Malaysia, Hungary, Poland, Hong Kong, and China, have prices below those in Jonesboro.

■ There are many reasons why the local price of a Big Mac varies—some demand-side and some supply-side.

■ A major supply-side influence is the cost of labor. An hour of labor in Switzerland costs 75 times that of an hour of labor in China!

■ To make PPP comparisons, we must use goods that are easily transported among countries and that have a small or no service component. The price of a floppy disk, a PC, or a computer chip would do a much better job of revealing PPP than the price of a Big Mac.

■ *The Economist* should replace its Big Mac standard with the Intel chip standard.

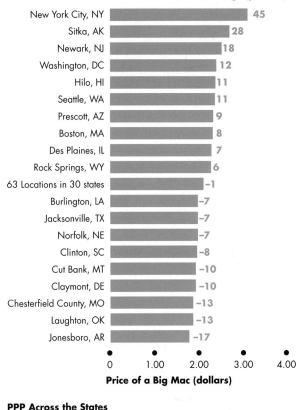

| Location | Deviation from U.S. average (percent) |
|---|---|
| New York City, NY | 45 |
| Sitka, AK | 28 |
| Newark, NJ | 18 |
| Washington, DC | 12 |
| Hilo, HI | 11 |
| Seattle, WA | 11 |
| Prescott, AZ | 9 |
| Boston, MA | 8 |
| Des Plaines, IL | 7 |
| Rock Springs, WY | 6 |
| 63 Locations in 30 states | –1 |
| Burlington, LA | –7 |
| Jacksonville, TX | –7 |
| Norfolk, NE | –7 |
| Clinton, SC | –8 |
| Cut Bank, MT | –10 |
| Claymont, DE | –10 |
| Chesterfield County, MO | –13 |
| Laughton, OK | –13 |
| Jonesboro, AR | –17 |

Price of a Big Mac (dollars): 0, 1.00, 2.00, 3.00, 4.00

**PPP Across the States**

## You're

### THE VOTER

■ Why does it matter if the dollar is undervalued or overvalued?

■ What can the Fed do if it believes the dollar is undervalued or overvalued?

■ Thinking only about your own economic well being, what is better for you, an undervalued or an overvalued dollar?

## SUMMARY

### Key Points

#### Financing International Trade (pp. 448–452)

- International trade, borrowing, and lending are financed by using foreign currency.
- A country's international transactions are recorded in its balance of payments accounts.
- Historically, the United States has been a net lender to the rest of the world, but in 1983 that situation changed and the United States became a net borrower. In 1989, the United States became a net debtor.
- The net exports deficit is equal to the government sector deficit plus the private sector deficit.

#### The Exchange Rate (pp. 453–461)

- Foreign currency is obtained in exchange for domestic currency in the foreign exchange market.
- The exchange rate is determined by demand and supply in the foreign exchange market.
- The lower the exchange rate, the greater is the quantity of dollars demanded. A change in the exchange rate brings a movement along the demand curve for dollars.
- Changes in the U.S. interest rate differential and the expected future exchange rate change the demand for dollars and shift the demand curve.
- The lower the exchange rate, the smaller is the quantity of dollars supplied. A change in the exchange rate brings a movement along the supply curve for dollars.
- Changes in the U.S. interest rate differential and the expected future exchange rate change the supply of dollars and shift the supply curve.
- Fluctuations in the exchange rate occur because fluctuations in the demand for and supply of dollars are not independent.
- The Fed can intervene in the foreign exchange market to smooth fluctuations in the dollar.

### Key Figures and Table

### Key Terms

# QUESTIONS

1  What are the three accounts that make up the balance of payments accounts?

2  What are the transactions that are recorded in the current account and the capital account?

3. What is the relationship between the balance on the current account, the capital account, and the official settlements account?

4. Distinguish between a country that is a net borrower and one that is a debtor nation. Are net borrowers always debtor nations? Are debtor nations always net borrowers?

5. What is the connection between a country's net exports and the government sector deficit and the private sector deficit?

6. Why do fluctuations in the government sector balance lead to fluctuations in net exports?

7. What is a currency appreciation? What is a currency depreciation?

8. Explain why the quantity of dollars demanded in the foreign exchange market depends on the exchange rate.

9. Explain why the quantity of dollars supplied in the foreign exchange market depends on the exchange rate.

10. Review the main influences on the demand for dollars in the foreign exchange market.

11. Review the main influences on the supply of dollars in the foreign exchange market.

12. Why does the foreign exchange value of the dollar fluctuate so much?

13. What is purchasing power parity? Give an example of purchasing power parity.

14. What is interest rate parity? Give an example of interest rate parity.

15. How can the Fed limit the fluctuations in the exchange rate?

# PROBLEMS

1. The citizens of Silecon, whose currency is the grain, conduct the following transactions in 1995:

| Item | Billions of grains |
| --- | --- |
| Imports of goods and services | 350 |
| Exports of goods and services | 500 |
| Borrowing from the rest of the world | 60 |
| Lending to the rest of the world | 200 |
| Increase in official reserves | 10 |

a.  Set out the three balance of payments accounts for Silecon.

2. The figure at the bottom of the next page shows the flows of income and expenditure in Dream Land in 1996. The amounts are in millions of dollars. GDP in Dream Land is $60 million.
a.  Calculate Dream Land's net exports.
b.  Calculate saving in Dream Land.
c.  Calculate the government sector deficit.
d.  Calculate the private sector deficit.
e.  Show the relationship between your answers to (a), (c), and (d).

3. You are told the following about Ecflex, whose currency is the band:

| Item | Billion bands |
| --- | --- |
| GDP | 100 |
| Consumption expenditure | 60 |
| Government purchases of goods and services | 24 |
| Investment | 22 |
| Exports of goods and services | 20 |
| Government budget deficit | 4 |

Calculate the following for Ecflex:
a.  Imports of goods and services
b.  Saving
c.  Net taxes
d.  Private sector deficit

4. The foreign exchange market is shown in the figure. The demand for dollars decreases from $D_0$ to $D_1$.

Quantity of dollars

a. Explain the influences on the market that might have caused this fall in the demand for dollars.
b. Explain what happens to the exchange rate when the demand for dollars decreases from $D_0$ to $D_1$.
c. What action would the Fed have to undertake to keep the exchange rate steady?
d. In part (c), describe the effects of the Fed's actions on official U.S. reserves.

http://hepg.awl.com/parkin/econ100

# CRITICAL THINKING

1. Study *Reading Between the Lines* on pp. 462–463 and then answer the following questions.
   a. Which currencies does *The Economist* claim are undervalued and which overvalued?
   b. What is PPP?
   c. What is the key assumption used by *The Economist* to make its PPP calculations?
   d. What is wrong with *The Economist's* assumptions?
   e. Use the Parkin Internet exchange to share information on the prices of floppy disks around the world and do a PPP comparison based on the floppy disk standard.

2. Visit *FRED*, the Federal Reserve Bank of St. Louis Economic database on the World Wide Web at http://www.stls.frb.org/fred/fred.html (or via the link at the Parkin Web site) and find data on the exchange rate and international trade.
   a. When did the United States last have a current account surplus?
   b. Does the United States have a surplus or a deficit in trade in goods?
   c. Does the United States have a surplus or a deficit in trade in services?
   d. How has foreign investment in the United States changed during the past 10 years?
   e. Do you think the U.S. balance of payments record is a matter for concern? Why or why not?

# Glossary

**Above full-employment equilibrium** A macroeconomic equilibrium in which real GDP exceeds potential GDP.

**Absolute advantage** A person has an absolute advantage in the production of two goods if by using the same quantities of inputs, that person can produce more of both goods than another person; a country has an absolute advantage if its output per unit of inputs of all goods is larger than that of another country.

**Aggregate demand** The relationship between the aggregate quantity of real GDP demanded and the price level.

**Aggregate hours** The total number of hours worked by all the people employed, both full time and part time, during a year.

**Aggregate planned expenditure** The expenditure that households, firms, governments, and foreigners plan to undertake in given circumstances. It is the sum of planned consumption expenditure, planned investment, planned government purchases of goods and services, and planned exports minus planned imports.

**Aggregate production function** The relationship between the quantity of real GDP supplied and the quantities of labor and capital and the state of technology.

**Automatic fiscal policy** A change in fiscal policy that is triggered by the state of the economy.

**Automatic stabilizers** Mechanisms that stabilize real GDP without explicit action by the government.

**Autonomous expenditure** The sum of those components of aggregate planned expenditure that are not influenced by real GDP.

**Balanced budget** A government budget in which tax revenues and expenditures are equal.

**Balanced budget amendment** A requirement that the federal government's budget be balanced.

**Balance of payments accounts** A country's record of international trading, borrowing, and lending.

**Balance of trade** The value of exports minus the value of imports.

**Barter** The direct exchange of one good or service for other goods and services.

**Below full-employment equilibrium** A macroeconomic equilibrium in which potential GDP exceeds real GDP.

**Budget deficit** A government's budget balance that is negative—expenditures exceed tax revenues.

**Budget surplus** A government's budget balance that is positive—tax revenues exceed expenditures.

**Business cycle** The periodic but irregular up-and-down movement in production.

**Capital** The plant, equipment, buildings, and inventories of raw materials and semifinished goods and services that are used to produce other goods and services.

**Capital account** A record of foreign investment in a country minus its investment abroad.

**Capital stock** The total quantity of plant, equipment, buildings, and inventories.

**Central bank** A bank's bank and a public authority charged with regulating and controlling a country's monetary policy and financial institutions and markets.

*Ceteris paribus* Other things being equal—all other relevant things remaining the same.

**Chain-weighted output index** An index that measures the growth rate of real GDP.

**Change in demand** A change in buyers' plans that occurs when some influence on those plans other than the price of the good changes. It is illustrated by a shift of the demand curve.

**Change in supply** A change in sellers' plans that occurs when some influence on those plans other than the price of the good changes. It is illustrated by a shift of the supply curve.

**Change in the quantity demanded** A change in buyers' plans that occurs when the price of a good changes but all other influences on buyers' plans remains unchanged. It is illustrated by a movement along the demand curve.

**Change in the quantity supplied** A change in sellers' plans that occurs when the price of a good changes but all other influences on sellers' plans remain unchanged. It is illustrated by a movement along the supply curve.

**Classical growth theory** A theory of economic growth based on the view that real GDP growth is temporary and that when real GDP per person increases above subsistence level, a population explosion brings real GDP back to subsistence level.

**Commercial bank** A firm, licensed either by the Comptroller of the Currency (in the U.S. Treasury) or by a state agency to receive deposits and make loans.

**Command system** A system in which some people give orders and other people obey them.

**Comparative advantage** A person or country has a comparative advantage in an activity if that person or country can perform the activity at a lower opportunity cost than anyone else or any other country.

**Complement** A good that is used in conjunction with another good.

**Consumer Price Index** An index that measures the average level of prices of the goods and services that a typical urban family buys.

**Consumption expenditure** The total amount spent on consumption goods and services.

**Consumption function** The relationship between consumption expenditure and disposable income, other things remaining the same.

**Contractionary fiscal policy** A decrease in government expenditures or an increase in tax revenues.

**Convertible paper money** A paper claim to a commodity (such as gold) that circulates as a means of payment.

**Cost-push inflation** An inflation that results from an initial increase in costs.

**Council of Economic Advisers** The President's council whose main work is to monitor the economy and keep the President and the public well informed about the current state of the economy and the best available forecasts of where it is heading.

**Credit union** A financial intermediary owned by its depositors, who are a social or economic group, that accepts savings deposits and makes mostly consumer loans.

**Creditor nation** A country that during its entire history has invested more in the rest of the world than other countries have invested in it.

**Cross-section graph** A graph that shows the values of an economic variable for different groups in a population at a point in time.

**Crowding-out effect** The tendency for a government budget deficit to decrease in investment.

**Currency** The bills and coins that we use today.

**Currency appreciation** The rise in the value of one currency in terms of another currency.

**Currency depreciation** The fall in the value of one currency in terms of another currency.

**Currency drain** An increase in currency held outside the banks.

**Current account** A record of receipts from the sale of goods and services to foreigners, the payments for goods and services bought from foreigners, the interest payments paid to and received from the rest of the world, and net transfers paid to foreigners.

**Cyclical unemployment** The fluctuations in unemployment over the business cycle,

**Cyclically adjusted deficit** The budget deficit that would occur if the economy were at full employment.

**Debtor nation** A country that during its entire history has borrowed more from the rest of the world than it has lent to it.

**Deflation** A process in which the price level falls—a negative inflation.

**Demand** The relationship between the quantity of a good that consumers plan to buy and the price of the good when all other influences on buyers' plans remain the same. It is described by a demand schedule and illustrated by a demand curve.

**Demand curve** A curve that shows the relationship between the quantity demanded of a good and its price when all other influences on consumers' planned purchases remain the same.

**Demand-pull inflation** An inflation that results from an initial increase in aggregate demand.

**Deposit multiplier** The amount by which an increase in bank reserves is multiplied to calculate the increase in bank deposits.

**Depreciation** The decrease in the capital stock resulting from wear and tear and the scrapping of existing capital.

**Direct relationship** A relationship between two variables that move in the same direction.

**Discount rate** The interest rate at which the Fed stands ready to lend reserves to commercial banks.

**Discouraged workers** People who are available and willing to work but who have given up the effort to find work.

**Discretionary fiscal policy** A policy action that is initiated by an act of Congress.

**Discretionary policy** A policy that responds to the state of the economy in a possibly unique way that uses all the information available, including perceived lessons from past "mistakes."

**Disposable income** Aggregate income minus taxes plus transfer payments.

**Dumping** The sale of a good or service to a foreign country at a price that is less than the cost of producing the good or service.

**Dynamic comparative advantage** A comparative advantage that a person or country possesses as a result of having specialized in a particular activity and then, as a result of learning-by-doing, having become the producer with the lowest opportunity cost.

**Economic growth** The expansion of production possibilities that results from capital accumulation and technological change.

**Economic model** A description of some aspect of the economic world that includes only those features of the world that are needed for the purpose at hand.

**Economic theory** A generalization that summarizes what we think we understand about the economic choices that people make and the performance of industries and entire economies.

**Economic welfare** A comprehensive measure of the general state of economic well-being.

**Economics** The science that explains the choices we make and how those choices change as we cope with scarcity.

**Efficiency wage** The wage rate that maximizes profit.

**Efficient** Resource use is efficient when we produce the goods and services that we value most highly.

**Employment Act of 1946** A landmark Congressional act that recognized a role for government actions to reduce unemployment, keep the economy expanding, and keep inflation in check.

**Employment-to-population ratio** The percentage of people of working age who have jobs.

**Entitlement spending** Spending on government programs that entitle suitably qualified individuals and businesses to receive benefits and that result in transfer payments that depend on the economic state of individual citizens and businesses.

**Entrants** People who enter the labor force.

**Entrepreneurship** The resource that organizes the other three factors of production—labor, land, and capital. Entrepreneurs come up with new ideas about what, how, when, and where to produce, make business decisions, and bear the risk that arise from their decisions.

**Equation of exchange** An equation that states that the quantity of money multiplied by the velocity of circulation equals GDP.

**Equilibrium expenditure** The level of aggregate expenditure that occurs when aggregate planned expenditure equals real GDP.

**Equilibrium price** The price at which the quantity demanded equals the quantity supplied.

**Equilibrium quantity** The quantity bought and sold at the equilibrium price.

**Excess reserves** A bank's actual reserves minus its required reserves.

**Expansion** A business cycle phase in which real GDP increases.

**Expansionary fiscal policy** An increase in government expenditure or a decrease in tax revenues.

**Exports** The goods and services that we sell to people in other countries.

**Factors of production** The economy's productive resources—land, labor, capital, and entrepreneurship. Also see productive resources.

**Federal budget** A statement of the federal government's financial plan, itemizing programs and their costs, tax revenues, and the proposed deficit or surplus.

**Federal Open Market Committee** The main policy-making organ of the Federal Reserve System.

**Federal Reserve System** The central bank of the United States.

**Feedback-rule policy** A rule that specifies how policy actions respond to changes in the state of the economy.

**Financial innovation** The development of new financial products—new ways of borrowing and lending.

**Financial intermediary** A firm that takes deposits from households and firms and makes loans to other households and firms.

**Fiscal policy** The government's attempt to influence the economy by setting and changing taxes, its purchases of goods and services, and transfer payments to achieve macroeconomic objectives such as full employment, sustained long-term economic growth, and low inflation.

**Fixed-rule policy** A rule that specifies an action to be pursued independently of the state of the economy.

**Flow** A quantity per unit of time.

**Foreign exchange market** The market in which the currency of one country is exchanged for the currency of another.

**Foreign exchange rate** The price at which one currency exchanges for another.

**Frictional unemployment** The unemployment that arises from normal labor turnover—people entering and leaving the labor force and from ongoing creation and destruction of jobs.

**Full employment** A situation in which the quantity of labor demanded equal the quantity supplied. At full employment, the unemployment rate equals the natural rate of unemployment and all unemployment is frictional and structural.

**GDP deflator** A price index that measures the average level of the prices of all goods and services that are included in GDP.

**General Agreement on Tariffs and Trade (GATT)** An international agreement designed to reduce tariffs on international trade.

**Goods and services** All the things that people are willing to pay for.

**Government budget deficit** The deficit that arises when federal government expenditure exceed the taxes collected.

**Government debt** The total amount of borrowing that the government has undertaken. It equals the sum of past budget deficits minus budget surpluses.

**Government purchases** Goods and services bought by the government.

**Government purchases multiplier** The magnification effect of a change in government purchases of goods and services on equilibrium expenditure and real GDP.

**Government sector surplus or deficit** An amount equal to net taxes minus government purchases of goods and services.

**Great Depression** A decade (1929–1939) of high unemployment and stagnant production throughout the world economy.

**Gross domestic product (GDP)** The value of aggregate production in a country in a year.

**Gross investment** The total amount spent on adding to the capital stock and on replacing depreciated capital.

**Growth accounting** A method of calculating how much real GDP growth has resulted from growth of labor and capital and how much is attributable to technological change.

**Human capital** The skill and knowledge of people, arising from their education and on-the-job training.

**Imports** The goods and services that we buy from people in other countries.

**Incentive** An inducement to take a particular action.

**Induced expenditure** The sum of the components of aggregate expenditure that varies with real GDP.

**Induced taxes** Taxes that vary as real GDP varies.

**Infant-industry argument** The proposition that protection is necessary to enable an infant industry to grow into a mature industry that can compete in world markets.

**Inferior good** A good for which demand decreases as income increases.

**Inflation** A process in which the price level is rising and money is losing value.

**Inflationary gap** The amount by which real GDP exceeds potential GDP.

**Insider-outsider theory** A theory of job rationing that says that to be productive, new workers—outsiders—must receive on-the-job training from existing workers—insiders.

**Interest rate parity** A situation in which the return on assets in different currencies are equal.

**Intermediate goods and services** Goods and services that firms buy from each other and use as inputs in the goods and services that they eventually sell to final users.

**Inverse relationship** A relationship between variables that move in opposite directions.

**Investment** The purchase of new plant, equipment, and buildings and additions to inventories.

**Investment demand** The relationship between investment and real interest rate, other influences on investment remaining the same.

**Job leavers** People who voluntarily quit their jobs.

**Job losers** People who are laid off, either permanently or temporarily, from their jobs.

**Job rationing** The practice of paying employed people a wage that creates an excess supply of labor and a shortage of jobs and increases the natural rate of unemployment.

**Job search** The activity of people looking for acceptable vacant jobs.

**Keynesian activist** An economist who believes that fluctuations in aggregate demand combined with sticky wages (and/or sticky prices) are the main source of economic fluctuations.

**Keynesian theory of the business cycle** A theory that regards volatile expectations as the main source of economic fluctuations.

**Labor** The time and effort that people allocate to producing goods and services.

**Labor demand curve** A curve that shows the quantity of labor that firms plan to hire at each possible real wage rate.

**Labor force** The sum of the people who are employed and who are unemployed.

**Labor force participation rate** The percentage of the working-age population who are members of the labor force.

**Labor supply curve** A curve that shows the quantity of labor that households plan to supply at each possible real wage rate.

**Land** All the gifts of nature that we use to produce goods and services.

**Law of diminishing returns** A law stating that as the quantity of one input increases with the quantities of all other inputs remaining the same, output increases but by ever smaller increments.

**Learning-by-doing** People become more productive in an activity (learn) just by repeatedly producing a particular good or service (doing).

**Linear relationship** A relationship between two variables that is illustrated by a straight line.

**Liquidity** The property of being instantly convertible into a means of payment with little loss in value.

**Long-run aggregate supply curve** The relationship between the real GDP supplied and the price level in the long run when real GDP equals potential GDP.

**Long-run macroeconomic equilibrium** A situation that occurs when real GDP equals potential GDP—the economy is on its long-run aggregate supply curve.

**Long-run Phillips curve** A curve that shows the relationship between inflation and unemployment when the actual inflation rate equals the expected inflation rate.

**Lump-sum tax multiplier** The magnification effect of a change in lump-sum taxes on equilibrium expenditure and real GDP.

**Lump-sum taxes** Taxes that do not vary with real GDP.

**M1** A measure of money that consists of currency and traveler's checks plus checking deposits owned by individuals and businesses.

**M2** A measure of money that consists of M1 plus savings deposits and time deposits.

**Macroeconomic long run** A time frame that is sufficiently long for real GDP to return to potential GDP.

**Macroeconomics** The study of the national economy and the global economy, the way that economic aggregates grow and fluctuate, and the effects of government actions on them.

**Macroeconomic short run** A period during real GDP has decreased below or increased above potential GDP.

**Marginal benefit** The benefit that a person receives from consuming one more unit of a good or service. It is measured as the maximum amount that a person is willing to pay for one more unit of the good or service.

**Marginal cost** The opportunity cost of producing one more unit of a good or service. It is the best alternative forgone. It is calculated as the increase in total cost divided by the increase in output.

**Marginal propensity to consume** The fraction of an increase in disposable income that is consumed.

**Marginal propensity to import** The fraction of an increase in real GDP that is spent on imports.

**Marginal propensity to save** The fraction of an increase in disposable income that is saved.

**Market** Any arrangement that enables buyers and sellers to get information and to do business with each other.

**Market failure** A state in which the market does not use resources efficiently

**Means of payment** A method of settling a debt.

**Microeconomics** The study of the decisions of people and businesses, the interactions of those decisions in markets, and the effects of government regulation and taxes on the prices and quantities of goods and services.

**Monetarist** An economist who believes that fluctuations in the money stock are the main source of economic fluctuations.

**Monetarist theory of the business cycle** A theory that regards fluctuations in the money stock as the main source of economic fluctuations.

**Monetary base** The sum of the Federal Reserve notes, coins, and banks' deposits at the Fed.

**Monetary policy** The Federal Reserve's attempt to keep inflation in check, maintain full employment, moderate the business cycle, and contribute towards achieving long-term

growth by adjusting the quantity of money in circulation and interest rates.

**Money** Any commodity or token that is generally acceptable as a means of payment.

**Money market mutual fund** A financial institution that obtains funds by selling shares and that uses these funds to buy highly liquid assets such as U.S. Treasury bills.

**Money multiplier** The amount by which a change in the monetary base is multiplied to determine the resulting change in the quantity of money.

**Multiplier** The amount by which a change in autonomous expenditure is magnified or multiplied to determine the change in equilibrium expenditure and real GDP.

**National saving** Saving by households and businesses plus government saving.

**Natural rate of unemployment** The unemployment rate when the economy is at full employment. There is no cyclical unemployment, all unemployment is frictional and structural.

**Negative relationship** A relationship between variables that move in opposite directions.

**Neoclassical growth theory** A theory of economic growth that proposes that real GDP grows because technological change induces saving and investment.

**Net borrower** A country that is borrowing more from the rest of the world than it is lending to it.

**Net exports** The exports of goods and services minus imports of goods and services.

**Net investment** Net increase in the capital stock—gross investment minus depreciation.

**Net lender** A country that is lending more to the rest of the world than it is borrowing from it.

**Net taxes** Taxes paid to governments minus transfer payments received from governments.

**New classical theory of the business cycle** A rational expectations theory of the business cycle that regards unanticipated fluctuations in aggregate demand as the main source of economic fluctuations.

**New growth theory** A theory of economic growth based on the idea that real GDP grows because of the choices that people make in the pursuit of ever greater profit and that growth can persist indefinitely.

**New Keynesian theory of the business cycle** A rational expectations theory of the business cycle that regards unanticipated fluctuations in aggregate demand as the main source of economic fluctuations but leaves room for anticipated demand fluctuations to play a role.

**Nominal GDP** GDP valued in current prices.

**Nominal GDP targeting** An attempt to keep the growth rate of nominal GDP steady.

**Nontariff barrier** An action other than a tariff that restricts international trade.

**Normal good** A good for which demand increases as income increases.

**North American Free Trade Agreement** An agreement signed in 1994 between the United States, Canada, and Mexico to virtually eliminate all barriers to international trade between them in 15 years.

**Official settlements account** A record of the change in a country's official reserves.

**Official U.S. reserves** The government's holdings of foreign currency.

**Open market operation** The purchase or sale of government securities by the Federal Reserve System in the open market.

**Opportunity cost** The opportunity cost of an action is the highest-valued alternative forgone.

**Phillips curve** A curve that shows a relationship between inflation and unemployment.

**Positive relationship** A relationship between two variables that move in the same direction.

**Potential GDP** The value of production when all the economy's resources (labor, land, capital, and entrepreneurship) are fully employed. Unemployment is at its natural rate and the economy is at full employment.

**Price level** The average level of prices as measured by a price index.

**Private sector surplus or deficit** An amount equal to saving minus investment.

**Producer efficiency** A situation in which firms cannot lower the cost of producing a given output by changing the resources they use.

**Production possibility frontier** The boundary between those combinations of goods and services that can be produced and those that cannot.

**Productive resources** The economy's resources—land, labor, capital, and entrepreneurship. Also called the economy's resources.

**Productivity function** A relationship that shows how real GDP per hour of labor changes as the amount of capital per hour of labor changes with a given state of technology.

**Productivity growth slowdown** A slowdown in the growth rate of output per person.

**Property rights** Social arrangements that govern the ownership, use, and disposal of resources, goods, and services.

**Quantity demanded** The amount of a good or service that consumers plan to buy during a given time period at a particular price.

**Quantity supplied** The amount of a good or service that producers plan to sell during a given time period at a particular price.

**Quantity theory of money** The proposition that in the long run, an increase in the quantity of money brings an equal percentage increase in the price level.

**Quota** A quantitative restriction on the import of a particular good, which specifies the maximum amount that can be imported in a given time period.

**Rational expectation** A forecast based on all available relevant information.

**Real business cycle theory** A theory that regards random fluctuations in productivity as the main source of economic fluctuations.

**Real Gross Domestic Product (real GDP)** The value of total production of all the nation's farms, factories, shops, and offices linked back to the prices of a single year. It is calculated as GDP in the base year scaled up by the growth rate of real GDP since the base year.

**Real interest rate** The nominal interest rate adjusted for inflation; the nominal interest rate minus the inflation rate.

**Real wage rate** The quantity of goods ands services that an hour's work can buy.

**Recession** A business cycle phase in which real GDP decreases for at least two successive quarters.

**Recessionary gap** The amount by which potential GDP exceeds real GDP.

**Reentrants** People who reenter the labor force.

**Relative price** The ratio of the price of one good or service to the price of another good or service. A relative price is an opportunity cost.

**Required reserve ratio** The ratio of reserves to deposits that banks are required, by regulation, to hold.

**Reserve ratio** The fraction of a bank's total deposits that are held in reserves.

**Reserves** Cash in a bank's vault plus the bank's deposits at Federal Reserve banks.

**Resources** The economy's resources are land, labor, capital, and entrepreneurship. Also called the productive resources or factors of production.

**Saving** The amount of income remaining after meeting consumption expenditures.

**Saving function** The relationship between saving and disposable income, other things remaining the same.

**Savings and loan association (S&L)** A financial intermediary that receives checking deposits and savings deposits and that makes personal, commercial, and home-purchase loans.

**Savings bank** A financial intermediary that is owned by its depositors and accepts deposits and makes loans, mostly home-purchase loans.

**Saving supply** The relationship between saving and the real interest rate, other things remaining the same.

**Scarcity** The state in which the resources available are insufficient to satisfy people's wants.

**Scatter diagram** A diagram that plots the value of one economic variable against the value of another.

**Short-run aggregate supply curve** A curve that shows the relationship between the quantity of real GDP supplied and the price level in the short run when the money wage rate, other resource prices, and potential GDP remain constant.

**Short-run macroeconomic equilibrium** A situation that occurs when the quantity of real GDP demanded equals quantity of real GDP supplied—at the point of intersection of the *AD* curve and the *SAS* curve.

**Short-run Phillips curve** A curve that shows the relationship between inflation and unemployment, when the expected inflation rate and the natural rate of unemployment remain the same.

**Slope** The change in the value of the variable measured on the *y*-axis divided by the change in the value of the variable measured on the *x*-axis.

**Stagflation** The combination of a rise in the price level and a decrease in real GDP.

**Stock** A quantity that exists at a point in time.

**Structural deficit** A budget that is in deficit when real GDP equals potential GDP; expenditures exceed tax revenues.

**Structural unemployment** The unemployment that arises when changes in technology or international competition change the skills needed to perform jobs or change the locations of jobs.

**Subsistence real wage rate** The minimum real wage rate needed to maintain life.

**Substitute** A good that can be used in place of another good.

**Supply** The relationship between the quantity of a good that producers plan to sell and the price of the good when all other influences on sellers' plans remaining the same. It is described by a supply schedule and illustrated by a supply curve.

**Supply curve** A curve that shows the relationship between the quantity supplied and the price of a good when all other influences on producers' planned sales remaining the same.

**Tariff** A tax that is imposed by the importing country when an imported good crosses its international boundary.

**Technological efficiency** A situation that occurs when it is not possible to increase output without increasing inputs.

**Time-series graph** A graph that measures time (for example, months or years) on the *x*-axis and the variable or variables in which we are interested on the *y*-axis.

**Tradeoff** A constraint that involves giving up one thing to get something else.

**Trend** The general direction (rising or falling) in which a variable is moving over the long term.

**Twin deficits** The tendency for the government sector deficit and the net exports deficit to move together.

**Unemployed** A person who does not have a job but is available for work, is willing to work, and has made some effort to find work within the previous four weeks.

**Unemployment** Resources that are available but are not being used.

**Unemployment rate** The percentage of the people in the labor force who are unemployed.

**U.S. interest rate differential** The interest rate on a U.S. dollar asset minus the interest rate on a foreign currency asset.

**Value added** The value of a firm's output minus the value of the intermediate goods that the firm buys from other firms.

**Velocity of circulation** The average number of times a dollar of money is used annually to buy the goods and services that make up GDP.

**Voluntary export restraint** A self-imposed restriction by an exporting country on the volume of its exports of a particular good. Voluntary export restraints are often called VERs.

**Wealth** The value of all the things that people own.

**Working-age population** The total number of people aged 16 years and over who are not in jail, hospital, or some other form of institutional care.

**World Trade Organization** An international organization that places obligations on its member countries to observe the GATT rules.

# Index

# The Addison-Wesley Series in Economics